NEW YORK

A Guide to the Metropolis

WALKING TOURS OF ARCHITECTURE AND HISTORY

Revised Edition

by GERARD R. WOLFE

McGRAW-HILL BOOK COMPANY

New York   St. Louis   San Francisco   Auckland   Bogotá   Guatemala
Hamburg   Johannesburg   Lisbon   London   Madrid   Mexico
Montreal   New Delhi   Panama   Paris   San Juan   São Paulo   Singapore
Sydney   Tokyo   Toronto

Designed by Philip Grushkin

Maps by Henry Siwek

Reprinted by arrangement with New York University Press

First McGraw-Hill paperback edition, 1983

1 2 3 4 5 6 7 8 9 D O C D O C 8 7 6 5 4 3

ISBN 0-07-071396-0

Library of Congress Catalog Card Number: 74-21706

Library of Congress Cataloging in Publication Data

Wolfe, Gerard R   1926–
        New York, a guide to the metropolis.

        Bibliography: p.
        1. New York (City)—Description—1951–   —Tours.
2. New York (City)—Buildings.   I. Title.
F128.18.W58   917.47′1′044   74-21706

ISBN 0-07-071396-0

To my students, colleagues, and friends,
whose keen enthusiasm for learning
about New York's fascinating cityscape
was the inspiration for this book.

Contents

Note: The following are the landmark symbols used in this Guide:

 Designated Landmark by the New York City Landmarks Preservation Commission

Listed in the National Register of Historic Places

Foreword

My goal in preparing this guide is to help you learn to look at buildings with a discerning and appreciative eye. New York City is a treasure house of architecture, with virtually every style—original or revival—represented in its varied repertory of public buildings, residences, and commercial structures.

With the passage of the Landmarks Preservation Law in 1967, the city succeeded in stemming the relentless destruction of its heritage, although not before the tragic loss of such gems as Pennsylvania Station, the Produce Exchange, the Singer Tower, and the Jerome Mansion. Enough does remain, however, to provide miles of exciting discoveries, not only of our rich past, but also of the new and innovative building designs that have broken with the dull tradition of the glass box and are now offering bright punctuation to the changing skyline.

In selecting the walking tours it was necessary to choose the most important areas, both architecturally and historically, and to keep the number to twenty—the maximum if the book were still to be portable. Unfortunately, some interesting neighborhoods had to be omitted, which perhaps in a forthcoming supplement can be included. The tours begin in lower Manhattan and are arranged to correspond with the northward growth of the city, ending uptown with the Upper East Side and Upper West Side. The five tours of Brooklyn follow the same chronological route, from Brooklyn Heights, the first suburb, to Fort Greene and Clinton Hill. The tour of Flushing, in Queens, includes several examples of surviving Dutch Colonial architecture, since not one building in Manhattan erected when the Dutch built New Amsterdam survived the Great Fire of 1835.

The tours vary in length from two to five hours, and some, such as Brooklyn Heights or Manhattan's Financial District, may be divided into two itineraries. The tours are all marked on accompanying maps, with travel directions included. Buildings or districts that have been designated as New York City landmarks by the Landmarks Preservation Commission are identified with a small black disk, those which are National Historic Landmarks, that is, listed on the National Register of Historic Places, are indicated with a star. Following the practice of the Landmarks Commission, no individual buildings within a historic district are identified separately, since technically all buildings within a designated district are landmarks. A glossary of common architectural terms will be found at the end of Chapter 7. In some tours whose points of interest are at some distance from each other, key numbers have been used in the text and on the corresponding map.

For the first-time visitor to New York, the New York Convention and Visitors Bureau (located at No. 2 Columbus Circle) can provide free literature on the city's major tourist attractions which are not within the purview of this book. The Landmarks Commission (20 Vesey Street) sells a pocket directory to all designated landmarks, and the Urban Center Bookstore of the Municipal Art Society (457 Madison Avenue) has the largest collection of current books on New York for sale at their landmark location.

This guide is designed not only for the out-of-towner, but for the usually blasé New Yorker as well, who rarely, if ever, looks at buildings above the first floor. I learned to my surprise that my students, who were so enthusiastic about my New York University course, "The Many Faces of Gotham," were mostly native Gothamites themselves who were perpetually astonished at the beauty of the buildings they had passed every day without so much as an upward glance. I therefore earnestly hope that you will be encouraged to explore New York on foot and derive pleasure and satisfaction from the discovery of our great architectural heritage . . . and at the same time become an outspoken and vigorous advocate of its preservation.

GERARD R. WOLFE
November 1982

Acknowledgments

In putting together a book of this scope, one must rely on the knowledge, advice, and suggestions of many people and organizations. By the time the first New York University Press edition was ready for the printer in 1975, I had amassed a list of individuals who had been particularly helpful, and I feel it only proper to include them again. In addition there are a number of others who made significant contributions to this revised, updated McGraw-Hill edition, and they are listed separately below.

For help in the preparation of the first edition, I owe a special debt of gratitude to the New York City Landmarks Preservation Commission, who in the interest of having the public better informed about the architectural and historic importance of New York buildings, granted me permission to make occasional quotes from their landmark designation reports. Among the members of the professional staff of the Commission who read the original manuscript and made many helpful suggestions, Dr. Ellen Kramer and Alan Burnham deserve special thanks.

Much valuable assistance came from the staffs of the Long Island Historical Society, the South Street Seaport Museum, the Queens Historical Society, the New-York Historical Society, the Museum of the City of New York, the Colonial Dames of America, the Brooklyn Heights Association, and the Friends of Cast-Iron Architecture.

Among the individuals who gave of themselves to provide background information, old newspaper clippings and letters, and personal reminiscences were Joseph Roberto, architect emeritus of New York University; Bob Gesslein, Long Island University; John Virgil, Wurlitzer Music Company; Dr. George Litch Knight, Lafayette Avenue Presbyterian Church; Rev. David L. Slater, Cadman Memorial Church; Capt. Joseph Zito, New York City Police Department (retired); Harry Kirschbaum, architect; Alex Parker, One Times Square; Judith Ann Yavarkovsky, Metropolitan Life Insurance Company; Gruzen & Partners; Barbara Bruer; and my father, Samuel Wolfe, whose recollections of life on the Lower East Side were priceless.

For the contribution of old photographs and prints, I am indebted to Ernest Pawel, New York Life Insurance Company; William H. Hand, Brooklyn Union Gas Company; Henry J. DiRocco, Office of the Borough President of Queens;

Susan C. Holahan, Consolidated Edison Company of New York; Eleanor C. Waters, Seamen's Bank for Savings; Dorothy C. Gates, Home Insurance Company; Margaret Knowles, Community Service Society of New York; David G. Oates, *Flushing Tribune;* The Library of the Metropolitan Life Insurance Company; the American Telephone & Telegraph Company; the South Street Seaport Museum; the Equitable Life Assurance Society of the United States; the Singer Company; the Fred F. French Investing Company; the Firefighting Museum of the Home Insurance Company; the Religious Society of Friends of Flushing; the Morgan Guaranty Trust Company; the Port Authority of New York & New Jersey; the United Nations Photo Service; and the late Margaret I. Carman, Bowne House Historical Society.

I acknowledge with thanks the permission of Warner Brothers Music, Hollywood, to reproduce Al Dubin's lyrics to "Forty-Second Street"; and to Fleet Press Corporation, New York, for a quote from Robert Baral's "Turn West on 23rd," copyright 1965.

Two friends who were especially helpful throughout, lending support, counsel, and encouragement, were Dr. Toby B. Bieber and the late Professor Mendor T. Brunetti, great teacher and close colleague.

For their invaluable contributions to the updated and revised edition, special recognition must go to Chris Gray, Office of Metropolitan History, and to Hugh A. Dunne, Electric Railroaders' Association, who voluntarily checked every entry in the book and made a number of extremely useful suggestions for any subsequent edition, which I am happy to incorporate in this printing.

Again, I must express my appreciation to the Landmarks Commission and to its chairman, Kent Barwick, for their support and for the information from their more recent landmark designation reports. Thanks are also due to the following members of the Landmarks staff: Edwin Friedman, Andrew S. Dolkart, and Louella Adams, who gave generously of their time to answer questions, provide information, and open doors for me.

Others who made important contributions to this edition were Isadore Ginsberg, former correspondent of the *East Side News;* Pratt Institute; Fox & Fowle, architects; Capt. Wolf Spille, Sirius Brokers, Inc.; and Leo Katz.

Finally, a note of appreciation to those who walked the tours and who took the trouble to write to me to express their pleasure at discovering a whole new city.

G. R. W.

NEW YORK

A Guide to the Metropolis

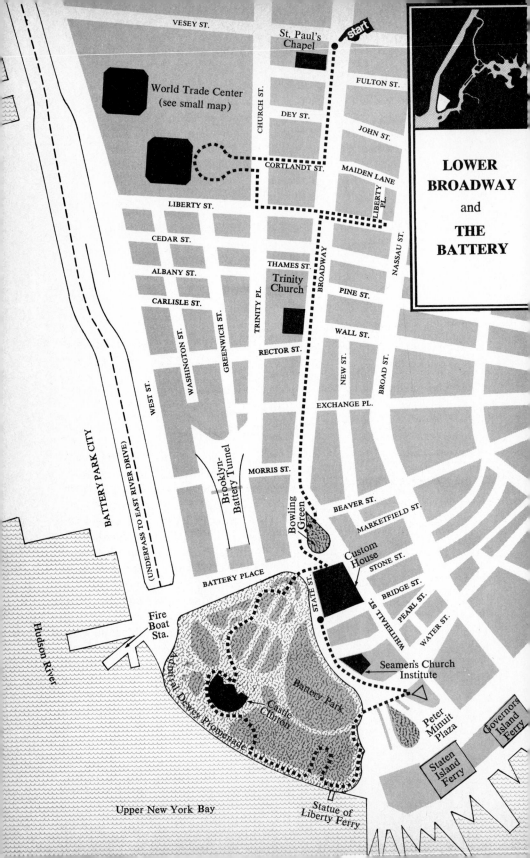

1. Lower Broadway and the Battery

[*IND A, E lines to Broadway-Nassau Street station; IRT Lexington Avenue and Broadway-Seventh Avenue lines to Fulton Street; BMT J, M lines to Fulton Street; Broadway (M-1 or M-6) bus to Fulton Street*]

The walking tour begins at Fulton Street and Broadway.

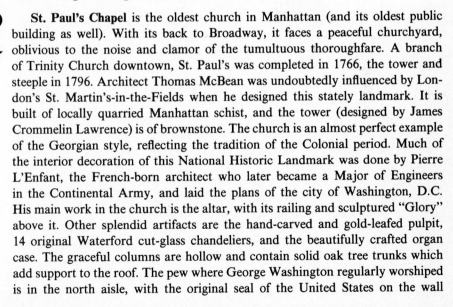

St. Paul's Chapel is the oldest church in Manhattan (and its oldest public building as well). With its back to Broadway, it faces a peaceful churchyard, oblivious to the noise and clamor of the tumultuous thoroughfare. A branch of Trinity Church downtown, St. Paul's was completed in 1766, the tower and steeple in 1796. Architect Thomas McBean was undoubtedly influenced by London's St. Martin's-in-the-Fields when he designed this stately landmark. It is built of locally quarried Manhattan schist, and the tower (designed by James Crommelin Lawrence) is of brownstone. The church is an almost perfect example of the Georgian style, reflecting the tradition of the Colonial period. Much of the interior decoration of this National Historic Landmark was done by Pierre L'Enfant, the French-born architect who later became a Major of Engineers in the Continental Army, and laid the plans of the city of Washington, D.C. His main work in the church is the altar, with its railing and sculptured "Glory" above it. Other splendid artifacts are the hand-carved and gold-leafed pulpit, 14 original Waterford cut-glass chandeliers, and the beautifully crafted organ case. The graceful columns are hollow and contain solid oak tree trunks which add support to the roof. The pew where George Washington regularly worshiped is in the north aisle, with the original seal of the United States on the wall

---

Note: Since most of the points of interest on this tour are situated quite close to each other, the customary system of numbering each stop in the text and on the map will not be used; rather, the description and location of each point of interest will be a separate entry, indicated in boldface type. As usual the route is shown on the map.

Broadway, 1850, at the foot of City Hall Park, looking south. Barnum's Museum, left, was destroyed by fire in 1865. The Astor House, the city's finest hotel at the time, is to the right, with the portico of St. Paul's Chapel adjoining. Trinity Church's spire dominates the thoroughfare. (The J. Clarence Davies Collection, Museum of the City of New York)

behind. It was originally the canopied pew of the royal governor of the Province of New York. The pew of first governor of the state, George Clinton, is in the south aisle. Among other distinguished worshipers were Prince William of Orange (later King William IV), Lords Cornwallis and Howe, Maj. John André, the Marquis de Lafayette, and presidents Grover Cleveland and Benjamin Harrison.

The quiet churchyard with its numerous 18th-century headstones of prominent early New York families is well worth a visit.

The American Telephone & Telegraph Building, just south of St. Paul's, was built in 1917 from plans by Welles Bosworth. No other building in the city can boast so many columns; in fact, in its eight Ionic tiers stacked on a Doric base, it has more columns than the Parthenon. A gilt statue that once graced the tower (*The Spirit of Communication,* by Evelyn Beatrice Longman), has been removed and will be installed in the lobby of AT&T's new corporate headquarters at 550 Madison Avenue. A weekday visit to the marble colonnaded lobby reveals a sculpture of Alexander Graham Bell, and two lovely brass floor medallions, as well as a large marble and bronze sculpture, *Service to the Nation,* by Chester Beach.

No. 192 Broadway, across the street, is an undistinguished survivor from the 1880s, somehow bypassed by the land developers. Interesting are the so-called Queen Anne cast-iron bay windows. A few feet around the corner was the **site of the John Street Theater,** from 1767 to 1798. During the British occupation of New York in the Revolutionary War, General Howe's army officers frequently would take part in the cast and production of plays. Later, Royall Tyler's play, *The Contrast,* opened as the first comedy work by a native author ever produced in America. George Washington was an often-seen theatergoer here.

No. 175 Broadway, the Germania Building, an even older survivor, is a typical commercial building, erected in 1865 in Italian Renaissance style. This was the style so often copied by the cast-iron architects and later recopied in stone. That this 1865 building remains at all is a minor miracle.

Cross Broadway to the northeast corner of Maiden Lane.

Set in the sidewalk is a large glass clock. Dating from 1925, it replaced an earlier model installed by the same firm of William Barthman in 1896. The timepiece is adjusted from the basement, and the protective glass—1½ inches thick—must be changed three times a year because of the constant scuffing from millions of pedestrians' shoes. In 1911 a runaway horse smashed into the store window, splintering the showcase and scattering a quarter-of-a-million dollars' in jewelry across Broadway. Yet the street clock below the pavement remained undamaged.

Busy Broadway in the mid-1880s, lined with horse-drawn traffic. All the buildings on the right side, to the corner of Cortlandt Street, are still standing; but only one, the narrow, white Germania Building, erected in 1865, has not undergone a "face-lifting." (American Telephone & Telegraph Company)

Turn right (west) at Cortlandt Street.

Until the arrival of the World Trade Center, Cortlandt Street was the center of the amateur radio hobbyist. Rows of stores selling electronic gadgets, used parts, and an endless variety of radio hardware lined both Cortlandt Street and neighboring Church Street.

The East River Savings Bank, at the northeast corner of Cortlandt and Church streets, is an almost perfect example of the Art Deco style of the 1930s. This was the approximate **site of a large windmill** built ca. 1686 that appears in many old prints of the early city. New York became an important flour-milling center, and two flour barrels and a pair of crossed windmill arms are a part of the city's Great Seal.

The World Trade Center, created by the Port Authority of New York and New Jersey, was planned as a center of world commerce, and took more than ten years to complete. Consisting of two 110-story towers rising 1,350 feet, three low-rise Plaza Buildings, and the Vista International Hotel, on a 16-acre site, it is the world's largest commercial complex. The design of the towers involved some revolutionary concepts in skyscraper technology. The conventional skyscraper is built as a skeleton of structural steel supports, with the outer walls as the "skin." In the World Trade Center Towers, the exterior walls bear the load and consist of closely spaced vertical columns, tied together by massive horizontal spandrel beams that girdle the tower at every floor. The only interior columns are in the core, which contains the elevators. Thus there is a maximum open, column-free floor space, but large "picture windows" had to be sacrificed. Because of their near-record height, the towers had to be erected from within. Four kangaroo cranes, nestled in the elevator shafts, lifted the tons of steel

The twin Hudson Terminal buildings were razed to make way for the 110-story World Trade Center. Underneath was the terminal of the Hudson & Manhattan "Tubes," now called the PATH, and presently located about 100 yards west, beneath the twin Trade Center towers. (Port Authority of New York & New Jersey)

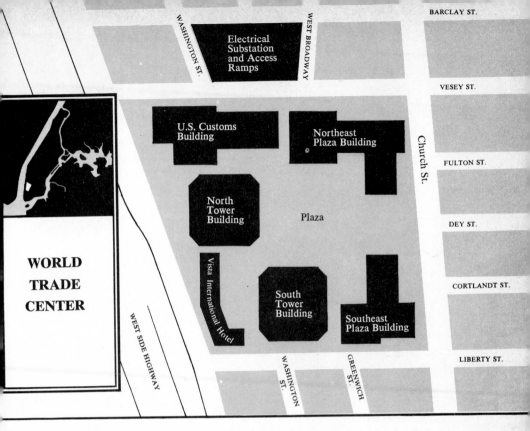

up the sides of the building; and when the walls rose to the height of the cranes, they were jacked up to a new position to begin again. When the top was finally reached, each crane was dismantled and lowered by a neighboring crane. The last one hoisted up a guy derrick that disassembled the remaining kangaroo crane, lowered its parts to the ground, and was in turn dismantled and brought down by freight elevator. A neat trick and a spectacular show for the thousands of lunchtime "sidewalk superintendents."

To provide efficient access to the upper floors of the towers, the elevator system is divided into three zones, each with its own lobby. Above the Concourse are "skylobbies" on the 44th and 78th floors. There are 23 express and 72 local elevators plus 4 large freight elevators in each tower.

The five-acre central plaza is dominated by an enormous bronze sculptured revolving globe by the German sculptor, Fritz Koenig, and set on a fountain. More than 1.2 million cubic yards of earth and rock were removed from the excavation to be used for landfill for the nearby Battery Park City project. The architects of this mammoth center were Minoru Yamasaki and Emery Roth & Sons.

Turn south on Church Street (now called Trinity Place) to Liberty Street and left (east) toward Broadway.

The United States Steel Building (1 Liberty Plaza), designed in 1974 by Skidmore, Owings & Merrill to emphasize the "steel I-beam look," occupies

New York's skyline lost one of its great landmarks when U.S. Steel demolished the Singer Tower in 1968 to erect its own building on the site. The Tower was the crowning achievement of architect Ernest Flagg, and was completed in 1908. For a brief time it was the world's tallest building.

the site of the late lamented Singer (Sewing Machine Company) Building as well as the ornate City Investing Building. When the Singer Tower was completed in 1908, it was the tallest building in the world, until eclipsed by the Metropolitan Life Tower 18 months later. Architect Ernest Flagg's liberal use of metal and glass, incorporated into a graceful shaft in Renaissance Eclectic style, produced one of the most beautiful buildings ever to grace the New York skyline. Its replacement, built in 1968, adds nothing exciting to the cityscape and only heightens the feeling of loss. (The *AIA Guide* calls the building "a gloomy, cadaverous hulk.") The plaza area was built in accordance with the new zoning regulations, which impose a ratio of open space to a building's verticality. Stop in during working hours at Merrill Lynch's exhibit "The Money Tree," on the main floor.

The Westinghouse Building (150 Broadway), on the northeast corner of Liberty Street, has an attractive plaque marking the site of the founding of the National Board of Underwriters in 1866.

Continue east on Liberty Street.

The New York Chamber of Commerce Building (65 Liberty Street) is an attractive example of the French Beaux Arts style. Designed in 1901 by James Barnes Baker, it was built for the State Chamber of Commerce, which was founded at Fraunces Tavern in 1768. The solid Ionic columns seem to frame empty spaces. Originally there were three large sculpture groups, which did not survive New York's air pollution (and pigeons) and suffered so much decay that they were removed some years ago. The impressive white marble edifice was dedicated by President Theodore Roosevelt in an elaborate ceremony witnessed by former President Grover Cleveland and several foreign ambassadors. In 1973, the Chamber of Commerce merged with the Commerce and Industry Association, and seven years later the organization moved to other quarters at 200 Madison Avenue. This created a problem for the future of the 300 portraits that have been hanging in the magnificent Great Hall of the building; and at this writing, it appears that the collection will have to be dispersed.

The **Liberty Tower** (55 Liberty Street) is a good example of the neo-Gothic style applied to commercial skyscrapers. It was designed by Henry Ives Cobb in 1909, but is now overwhelmed by its neighbor across the street. The building is now a cooperative apartment house. Step back a few yards down narrow Liberty Place, and observe the fantasy of Gothic reflections in the glassy façade of the Marine Midland Building.

Return to the plaza in front of 140 Broadway.

The **Marine Midland Building,** designed by Skidmore, Owings & Merrill in 1967, is one of the first New York skyscrapers to have its own plaza. The use of matte black spandrels between rows of glass gives an unexpected effect of sleekness, in sharp contrast to the ornamented façades of nearby buildings. The dark, smooth appearance is further offset by the orange, cube-shaped stabile in the plaza, by sculptor Isamu Noguchi. Before the Marine Midland Bank erected its tower, the site was occupied by the Guaranty Trust Company Building—a very impressive Classic structure designed by York & Sawyer in 1912 which received the American Institute of Architects Medal for Distinguished Architecture two years after its completion.

Continue south on Broadway.

The **U.S. Realty Building** (115 Broadway) and its neighbor to the south, **The Trinity Building** (111 Broadway), are a delightful pair of early 20th-century skyscrapers. Both were designed in the year 1906 by architect Francis H. Kimball, in a modified Gothic style. There is an intimate quality about these narrow twins lacking in most modern buildings. Despite their height, they seem almost like charming residences. Look up at the catwalk connecting the two like a prop for a silent thriller movie. Diminutive Thames Street was originally an 18th-century carriageway leading to the DeLancey stables. Stephen DeLancey's home would later become Fraunces Tavern.

The **Equitable Building** (120 Broadway), designed by Ernest R. Graham in 1915, replaced an earlier Equitable Life Building that was destroyed by fire in 1912. Using every square inch of space, this blockbuster of a building rises 41 stories without setback for a total of 1,200,000 square feet of floor space on a site slightly under an acre! The result is a floor area of about 30 times the plot's. Present zoning laws allow less than 12. Upon completion of the building there arose such a tremendous clamor against the enormous building density that in 1916 new zoning laws were introduced, establishing the setback requirements that have been progressively tightened through the years.

The Bank of Tokyo (100 Broadway) was formerly the American Surety Building, and was built in 1895 from plans by Bruce Price. The eight allegorical figures were sculpted by J. Massey Rhind.

Trinity Church, designed by Richard Upjohn in 1846, is the third church on the site. Its location at the head of Wall Street makes it one of the best-known landmark churches in the city. The original church was established in 1697 by Royal Charter of King William III of England, but it remained for Queen Anne to grant the land in 1705. The first church was destroyed by the Great Fire of 1776, and the second was demolished because of structural failure. With its six chapels, the Trinity Parish is one of the largest of the Episcopal Church. (St. Paul's, St. Christopher's, St. Luke's, etc., are *chapels* of Trinity Parish.) Artistically, the most striking feature of Trinity Church is the three sets of huge bronze doors, designed by Richard Morris Hunt. They were a gift of William Waldorf Astor, and are patterned after the famous Ghiberti bronze doors of the Baptistery in Florence. The sculpture work for the main entrance doors was executed by Karl Bitter, the south doors by Charles H. Niehaus, and the north doors by J. Massey Rhind. The splendid stained-glass chancel window was designed by Upjohn himself. The building exterior is of brownstone. The 280-foot spire was for years a prominent New York landmark

The classic Guaranty Trust Company Building, built in 1912, was awarded the AIA Medal for Distinguished Architecture. In its place at 140 Broadway stands the Marine Midland Building. (Morgan Guaranty Trust Company)

until it was dwarfed by the surrounding skyscrapers. The "ring" of ten bells in the steeple is played before services, and adds a quieting note to the commotion of the neighborhood. The side wall buttresses, while inserting a touch of Gothic glamor, are false, as the ceiling vaults are made of plaster and are hung for decoration only. The interior, however, is somber and majestic. To the left of the sanctuary is the lovely All Saints Chapel, built in 1913.

 Surrounding the church is the **burial ground,** shaded by trees of many species. In the north section is the ornate Gothic-style Martyrs' Monument, a memorial to Continental soldiers who, during the American Revolution, died while imprisoned in a sugar house on Liberty (then Crown) Street. The various monuments read like a page from American history: Alexander Hamilton, Robert Fulton (whose steamboat *Clermont* set sail from the foot of Cortlandt Street), Captain James Lawrence (who, as commander of the ship *Chesapeake* in the War of 1812, immortalized himself with his dying command, "Don't Give Up the Ship!"), Albert Gallatin (twice Secretary of the Treasury under Thomas Jefferson, and a founder of New York University), Francis Lewis (signer of the Declaration of Independence), and William Bradford (early champion of freedom of the press, and editor of New York's first newspaper, the *New York Gazette*). The churchyard is a favorite lunch-hour retreat in warm weather for office workers in the surrounding financial district; and the Church presents noontime concerts every Wednesday.

The Irving Trust Company Building (1 Wall Street) is a massive limestone pile of Art Deco. An interesting touch by architects Voorhees, Gmelin & Walker in this 1932 building are the fluted walls and chamfered corners. An addition to the building was built in 1965. The attractive lobby is decorated with a polychrome mosaic design that gives a startling flamelike appearance. When seen from the street at night it literally glows in patterns of bright red and orange.

Wall Street is named for the original palisade fence or wall, built in 1653 on orders from Dutch Governor Peter Stuyvesant. Although generally believed to have been erected as a defense against hostile Indians, it was intended as a bulwark against an invasion by British colonists from New England. The wall stood from river to river for about 50 years. [For a tour of the Wall Street area and neighboring streets, *see* Manhattan's Financial District walking tour.]

No. 71 Broadway, the Empire Building (Renwick, Aspinwall and Tucker, 1894) at the southwest corner of Rector Street, still houses offices of the United States Steel Corporation, in spite of a newer building at 165 Broadway.

The American Express Company Building (65 Broadway) is the New York headquarters of the worldwide firm that began as a one-man operation in 1839, when William F. Harnden made four trips by train to Boston every week to deliver parcels and make collections. In 1850 he merged with two other express companies, operating a fleet of delivery wagons. Under the leadership of president Henry Wells and secretary William G. Fargo, the American Express Company's new subsidiary, Wells Fargo, helped open the West. The novel "Traveler's Cheque" was introduced in 1891, but by 1918 express services were abandoned altogether. With its merger in 1981 with Shearson Loeb Rhoades, the company expanded its financial operations, which are now conducted at its new corporate headquarters at 125 Broad Street (American Express Plaza). Travel services, however, are still conducted here. The building also hosts the American Bureau of Shipping.

No. 55 Broadway, called **One Exchange Plaza,** at the corner of Exchange Alley, is in striking contrast to its neighbors. Designed in 1982 by Fox & Fowle, it is a 31-story office tower with buff-colored horizontal brick spandrels and clear glass bands, with radial corners. In the rear, facing Trinity Place, is a second-level shopping way, required by the City Planning Commission to provide appropriate pedestrian space and a continuous link with the street. Its neighbor down the street at No. 45, **The Broadway Atrium,** due for completion in late 1983, is another Fox & Fowle–designed building, of the same height and color scheme, but set back, and with serrated corners in a sawtooth pattern. It, too, will have a second-level shopping way on Trinity Place.

No. 50 Broadway marks the **site of New York's first skyscraper.** The Tower Building, designed by Bradford L. Gilbert, was an 11-story steel-skeleton building, completed in 1889. Gilbert had to occupy the topmost floor himself to dispel the fears of New Yorkers that the structure might collapse.

No. 39 Broadway has a plaque indicating the site of the Alexander McComb Mansion—George Washington's second presidential residence, occupied from February 23 to August 30, 1790.

No. 26 Broadway, the **former Standard Oil Building,** was the corporate headquarters of John D. Rockefeller's Standard Oil. Later, the company became SOCONY (*S*tandard *O*il *CO.* of *N.Y.*) when the government "trust busters" took action; then Socony-Mobil; and with a final simplification to Mobil Oil, the firm moved into its new headquarters on East 42nd Street [*see* 42nd Street, p. 304]. A statue of the founding father oversees the lobby. The curved façade conforms to the principle of the "street wall"—so vital in good urban planning. Architects Carrère & Hastings (who designed the New York Public Library at Fifth Avenue and 42nd Street, among other fine buildings) and the firm of Shreve, Lamb & Blake planned this imposing building in 1922 with the skyline in mind. Although the lower section of the building conforms to the path of Broadway, the upper tower coincides with the geometry of the Manhattan street grid. Atop the tower, an appropriately symbolic oil-burning lantern (actually the chimney) crowns the massive structure. The building is best viewed from a distance. Before the rash of post–World War II boxlike skyscrapers obscured it from view, the Standard Oil Building formed an integral part of the lovely New York skyline, and was clearly visible from the harbor.

Across Bowling Green, the immense **Cunard Building** (25 Broadway) is a harmonious counterpart to the Standard Oil Building. Constructed in 1921 from plans by Benjamin Wistar Morris, when a transatlantic crossing by luxurious ocean liner was "the only way to travel," it is one of the finest office buildings in the world. The Cunard Line arrived in New York with the maiden voyage of Samuel Cunard's *Britannia* on July 4, 1840, and remained in the forefront in ocean travel until fairly recently. Merging with the White Star Line in the 1920s, it became the largest passenger ship company in the world. (The names

of Cunard ships always ended in -*ia: Mauretania, Lusitania,* etc., White Star's
in -*ic: Britannic, Titanic,* etc. Later exceptions were the great "Queens" including
the *QE2.*) The building's ornate Renaissance façade is quite handsome with
its three arched entranceways and second-story colonnade, but the charm of
the impressive structure is in its vestibule and Great Hall—certainly one of
the most beautiful interior spaces anywhere. Passing through one of the central
bronze doors, the visitor enters the high vaulted vestibule whose ornament was
created by artist Ezra Winter. Beyond high wrought-iron gates (by Samuel
Yellin) is the *pièce de résistance,* the Great Hall. Now housing a post office
branch, the octagonally shaped chamber measures 185 feet long by 74 feet
wide, and the central section is surmounted by a dome 65 feet above the floor.
Study the magnificent murals and pendentives covered in fresco. The walls
and floor are covered with travertine with considerable detail, and the artistic
maps of the world were executed by Barry Faulkner. The aesthetic climax of
the great room is its groined, vaulted ceiling ornamented with arabesques and
a multitude of design motifs. Ezra Winter and most of the artists who combined
their talents here were winners of the Rome Prize. The four supporting pendentives created by Winter represent the ships of Christopher Columbus, John
Cabot, Sir Francis Drake, and Leif Ericson. In the heyday of steamship travel,
the rooms were called the Freight Distribution Hall and the Bill of Lading
Hall. Thomas Hastings (of the firm of Carrère & Hastings) was a consultant
to architect Morris, and is said to have suggested the plan of the Great Hall
based on Raphael's Villa Madama in Rome. The Cunard Building is unquestionably one of the finest examples of the American Renaissance, and, in the words
of Henry Hope Reed, author of *The Golden City* and curator of Central Park,
"Great art is to be found not in a glorified warehouse called a museum, but
in such buildings as 25 Broadway."

   Bowling Green was New York City's first park. It lay just beyond the original
fort, and was merely an open space leading into *De Heere Wegh* (The Main
Street, or Broadway). It served as a cattle market and also as a parade ground.
In 1733 it was rented privately for "one peppercorn per year for the recreation
and delight of the inhabitants of this city." An iron fence ornamented with
crowns was erected in 1771 to protect the little park and its newly erected
statue of King George III. A symbol of British tyranny, the gilt-lead statue
was pulled down by patriots after General Washington ordered the Declaration
of Independence read publicly on July 9, 1776. The crowns that topped the
fence posts also were destroyed. Curiously, parts of the original statue still
exist, and pieces later turned up near the town of Wilton, Connecticut, where
the pieces had been taken to be melted into musket balls. The **park** and **fence**
have been restored recently as part of a major renovation of Bowling Green,
which also included a pedestrian mall and a reconstructed IRT subway station
beneath.

   No. 11 Broadway, on the west side of Bowling Green, is an amusing hodgepodge of styles. Framing the entrances are "Egyptian" pylons, while above
the third story the building takes on the bold look of the Chicago School of
Architecture, with its glazed brick piers and articulated spandrels. It was de-

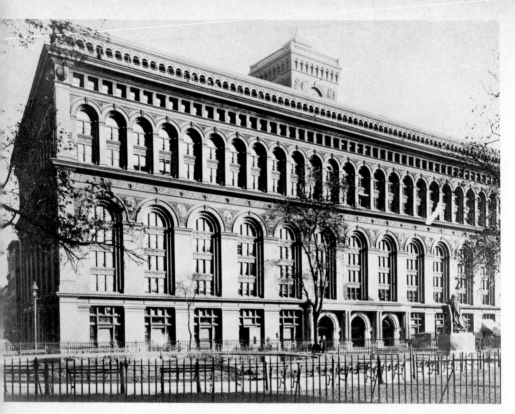

The Produce Exchange on Bowling Green was completed in 1884 and was replaced in 1957 by No. 2 Broadway. One of George B. Post's most notable works, the enormous red brick structure had a true iron skeleton and a main hall measuring 220 by 144 feet. At the right foreground is the statue of Abraham de Peyster which has been moved to Hanover Square. (Museum of the City of New York)

signed in 1898 by **W. G. Audsley.** Adjacent **No. 9 Broadway,** the Bowling Green Offices, is a continuation of the "west wall."

No. 1 Broadway, the United States Lines–Panama Pacific Lines Building, also hearkens to the days of sea power, when our country had at least some semblance of a respectable merchant marine. Built in 1921 from plans by Walter B. Chambers, the enormous structure is more famous for what used to be there. This was almost the southern tip of Manhattan Island and the site of the original Dutch fort that stood just a few yards to the south. During the late 18th century the Kennedy House was headquarters for Generals Washington and Lee. More recently, an ornate commercial structure named the Washington Building stood on the site until 1919.

No. 2 Broadway (to the left of the Custom House), built in 1959 by Emery Roth & Sons, marks the site of one of our most tragic building losses, the Produce Exchange. Designed in 1881 by noted architect George B. Post and completed three years later, it was a true iron skeleton building, faced with dark red brick, and several years ahead of its time. The façade was adorned with terra-cotta motifs of the various products traded within. The second-floor Main Hall was an astonishing 220 feet by 144 feet, with a huge latticework skylight 60 feet above the floor. As Nathan Silver sadly comments in *Lost New York,* "The Produce Exchange, one of the best buildings in New York, was replaced after 1957 by one of the worst."

The former United States Custom House is considered the finest example of the French Beaux Arts style in the city. Although the government has moved the operations of the Customs Service to the World Trade Center, this magnificent building, designed by Cass Gilbert and completed in 1907, is a designated landmark, but its future is uncertain. Contrasting with the dark gray granite of the building are four monumental white limestone sculpture groups by Daniel Chester French. Left to right, they represent the continents of Asia, America, Europe, and Africa. Above the cornice are statues symbolizing the 12 great mercantile nations of history: Greece, Rome, Phoenicia, Genoa, Venice, Spain, Holland, Portugal, Denmark, Germany, England, and France. The heroic cartouche atop the upper balustrade is by sculptor Karl Bitter. Ranged around the richly adorned Custom House are 44 Corinthian columns.

The **interior's** second-floor rotunda has a splendid display of Reginald Marsh murals depicting early events on the site and various seafaring themes. It is hoped that some appropriate use will be found for one of our most magnificent public buildings.

The original fortification called Fort Amsterdam was constructed in 1623 with the arrival of the first settlers. Then a more substantial fort was built in 1626, going through eight name changes, until as Fort George, it was demolished in 1787. Government House, intended as the presidential residence, replaced the fort three years later, but with the removal of the nation's capital to Philadelphia, it became the Governor's Mansion. It later became a boarding house, then the Custom House, and after a fire, was razed in 1815. Subsequently, town houses lined the site, but by midcentury they were taken over as shipping offices and known as "Steamship Row," as the area became devoted entirely to commerce. (Detailed and colorful dioramas of the early Dutch fort and surrounding settlement are displayed at the Museum of the City of New York.)

Enter Battery Park at the main entrance, directly to the right of the Custom House.

Battery Park is named for the battery of cannon that, between 1683 and 1688, were mounted along what is now the sidewalk opposite the Custom House, extending to just below the present Battery Place. From then until 1807 the area was fortified with additional batteries of artillery pieces. Most of the Park is built on landfill added periodically through the years.

The tall flagpole and sculptured pedestal is the **Netherlands Memorial Monument,** inscribed in both English and 17th-century Dutch, giving a brief history of the settlement of the Colony of New Netherland.

Bear to the right at the first path to the Statue of John Ericcson.

John Ericcson was the Swedish-born mechanical engineer who designed and built the first ironclad warship, the *Monitor*—the famous "cheesebox on a raft,"

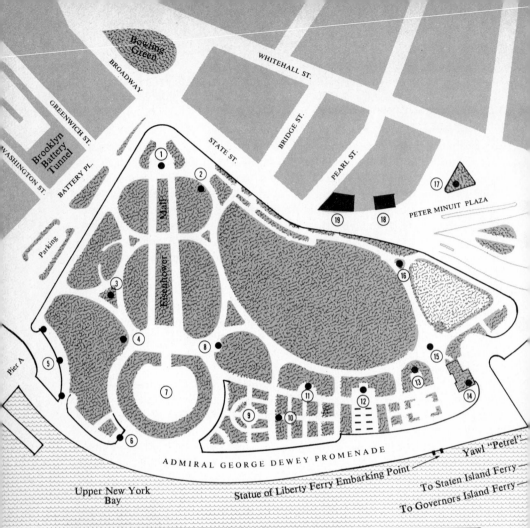

BOWLING GREEN
BROADWAY
WHITEHALL ST.
GREENWICH ST.
WASHINGTON ST.
Brooklyn Battery Tunnel
BATTERY PL.
STATE ST.
BRIDGE ST.
PEARL ST.
PETER MINUIT PLAZA
Parking
Eisenhower Mall
Pier A
ADMIRAL GEORGE DEWEY PROMENADE
Upper New York Bay
Statue of Liberty Ferry Embarking Point
Yawl "Petrel"
To Staten Island Ferry
To Governors Island Ferry

THE BATTERY

1 — Netherland Memorial
2 — Fort George Memorial
3 — John Ericsson Statue
4 — Walloon Settlers Memorial
5 — Breakwater Memorial Flagpoles
6 — Emma Lazarus Tablet
7 — Castle Clinton National Monument
8 — Salvation Army Memorial
9 — Verrazano Statue
10 — Peter Caesar Alberti Tablet
11 — Wireless Operators Memorial
12 — East Coast War Memorial
13 — Coast Guard Memorial
14 — John W. Ambrose Memorial
15 — Marine Flagpole
16 — Pre-Revolutionary War Cannon
17 — First Jewish Immigrants Monument
18 — Watson House — Shrine
19 — Seamen's Church Institute

which, on March 9, 1862, at Hampton Roads, Virginia, engaged the Confederate frigate *Merrimac* (renamed *Virginia*) and altered the course of naval history. The *Monitor*'s deck stood only 18 inches out of the water, while its revolving turret carried two 11-inch guns. Note the model in Ericcson's hand. The statue was executed by Jonathan Scott Hartley in 1893.

Turn left to the entrance gate of Castle Clinton.

Castle Clinton National Monument. In 1807 it appeared that another war with England was imminent, and several fortifications were hastily erected to protect the unguarded harbor. Among them was Castle Williams on nearby Governors Island, and the West Battery (now Castle Clinton) on a small rocky islet connected to the tip of Manhattan by a 200-foot causeway. (The intervening land was not filled in until the mid-19th century.) Constructed from plans by John McComb, Jr., in a circular shape with red sandstone walls over eight feet thick, the battery's 28 guns never fired a shot in anger. Renamed in 1815 in honor of DeWitt Clinton, former mayor and later governor, the fort remained in the hands of the military until 1821, when Commanding General Winfield Scott moved the garrison to Governors Island. Two years later Castle Clinton was ceded to the City of New York.

In June 1824 the city leased it as a place of public entertainment, and redecorated with a garden, shrubbery, a fountain, and a promenade above, it opened as **Castle Garden.** Among the variety of public events presented, including concerts, fireworks displays, and balloon ascensions, was Samuel F. B. Morse's demonstration in 1842 of his electric telegraph. Then, on September 11, 1850, P. T. Barnum, in the musical event of the century, presented Jenny Lind, the "Swedish Nightingale," in her American concert debut. At the close of the sellout performance at which more than 6,000 had paid the exorbitant fee of at least three dollars a seat, the audience broke into a "tempest of cheers."

In 1855 Castle Garden became the immigrant landing station, and for the next 34 years witnessed the arrival of over 8 million new Americans. With the closing of the Garden in 1890, the nearby Barge Office (now demolished) handled the growing tide of immigrants until the new immigration depot was opened two years later on Ellis Island.

The Garden was then remodeled by the architectural firm of McKim, Mead & White to serve as the **New York Aquarium,** opening on December 10, 1896, to a crowd of 30,000. In 1941 the Aquarium was closed, moving to new and spacious quarters at Coney Island, and the building was slated for demolition to make way for access roads to the new Brooklyn-Battery Tunnel. However, public hue and cry saved it, and in 1946 Congress authorized the establishment of Castle Clinton as a national monument under the administration of the National Park Service of the Department of the Interior. It has been carefully restored as a fort, and provides a dramatic, if somewhat fanciful, link with the past.

In the rear of Castle Clinton, facing the waterfront, is the **plaque to Emma Lazarus,** who in 1883 penned her immortal sonnet "The New Colossus" to

The Lusitania *arrived on her maiden voyage to New York on September 13, 1907. Crowds jammed the waterfront between the Aquarium (formerly Castle Garden) and Pier A as the liner steamed up the Hudson, eight years before her ill-fated rendezvous with a U-boat off the English coast. (New-York Historical Society)*

help raise money for the pedestal and ultimate erection of the Statue of Liberty. Her oft-quoted lines, "Give me your tired, your poor,/Your huddled masses yearning to breathe free . . ." are emblazoned on the base of the statue she helped secure.

Follow the path around Castle Clinton leading to the statue of Verrazano.

Giovanni da Verrazano was the first to sight these shores. Arriving in the small caravel *La Dauphine* in 1524, the Florentine merchant sailing for Francis I of France claimed the new land for the king, naming it *Terre d'Angoulême*. The French, however, did not follow up the claim, and Verrazano himself fell victim to cannibals on a voyage to the Caribbean four years later. The statue is the work of Ettore Ximenes, and was completed in 1909.

The same year, Esteban Gómez, a Portuguese mariner sailing under the Spanish flag, entered the harbor and named the mouth of the river Río San Antonio. It was not until 1609 however, that Henry Hudson, in his *Half-Moon*, actually sailed up the river that bears his name and brought back to Holland extensive reports on this "Great River of the Mountains." Four years later Adriaen Block, a Dutch trader, landed at the tip of Manhattan Island with a small group of men. When their ship *Tiger* caught fire and burned to the water, they were forced to spend the winter. The following spring they built a new ship which they called the *Onrust* (Restless), and returned to Holland. One can only admire these stalwart men who with their bare hands were able to fashion a seaworthy vessel from the trees of the forest and sail it thousands of miles safely across the rough Atlantic.

An almost deserted view of Broadway, looking north from Cortlandt Street in the mid-1880s. Midday crowds often gathered in front of the tall Western Union Building to watch a ball descend from the top of the pole precisely at noon. George B. Post's flamboyant Renaissance structure, built in 1873–75—and considered one of New York's first skyscrapers—was demolished when the City Investing Building was erected. After the Blizzard of 1888 the maze of telegraph wires was removed and buried beneath the street. (New-York Historical Society)

During the deep excavation for the World Trade Center, the two tubes of the PATH subway lines were exposed, and passers-by could hear the eerie roar of the trains in what at first glance seemed to be enormous sewer pipes. The eastbound tube is in the foreground, the westbound is just visible, passing to the right rear of the early framework of the WTC's North Tower. (Port Authority of New York & New Jersey)

The statue of stern-faced Abraham de Peyster, son of a leading Dutch burgher and mayor of New York from 1691 to 1695, was formerly situated in Bowling Green. After the renovation of the late 1970s, de Peyster was "banished" to Hanover Square. Except for the Bowling Green Offices at left, not one building survives from the time this photo was taken about 1900. (Museum of the City of New York)

A lithograph of Wall Street looking east from Trinity Church in 1834. In the distance is the cupola of the Merchants' Exchange, destroyed the following year in the Great Fire of 1835. (The J. Clarence Davies Collection. Museum of the City of New York)

Looking west on Fulton Street across Broadway in 1892, horsecars have been replaced by electric trolleys, but Dobbin still reigns. In the background are the Sixth and Ninth Avenue els. (American Telephone & Telegraph Company)

The former Equitable Building on Broadway, between Cedar and Pine streets. The Second Empire–style structure, built in 1872, was destroyed in a spectacular fire which burned for three days in January 1912. A replacement, completed in 1916, caused objections due to its sheer bulk, leading to a drastic revision in the building code. (King's Views of New York, 1909.)

Firefighters work in vain to save the Equitable Building. The conflagration had begun in the basement Café Savarin and quickly engulfed the entire structure. (Museum of the City of New York)

Equitable founder Henry B. Hyde seems to be contemplating the destruction of the lobby. Only slightly damaged, the statue by J. Q. A. Ward now graces the lobby of the Company's present headquarters at 1285 Avenue of the Americas. (Equitable Life Assurance Society of the United States)

Metropolitan Telephone and Telegraph Company,
16, 18 & 20 COURTLANDT ST., NEW YORK.
One large STORE ROOM on ground floor, and rooms in suits or singly for OFFICES to suit tenants

FOR RENT.

For Diagrams showing location and prices, apply to
THE METROPOLITAN TELEPHONE AND TELEGRAPH COMPANY,
144 GREENWICH STREET.

A mid-1880s advertisement for loft space in the headquarters of a predecessor of the New York Telephone Company (then located on the north side of Cortlandt Street between Broadway and Church Street). The Romanesque Revival–style building was one of several newly opened exchanges. (American Telephone & Telegraph Company)

Castle Garden in 1870 when it served as the State Emigrant Landing Depot. Millions of immigrants passed through its portals between 1855 and 1892, when a new center was opened on Ellis Island. (New-York Historical Society)

In this lithograph by Nathaniel Currier, "Swedish Nightingale" Jenny Lind makes her American debut on September 11, 1850, as P. T. Barnum inaugurates Castle Garden as the city's leading showplace. The structure has now been restored to its original appearance as Castle Clinton National Monument. (New-York Historical Society)

A Sunday promenade along the Battery in an 1830 engraving, depicting Castle Clinton to the right, and Castle Williams on Governors Island across the busy harbor to the left. (New-York Historical Society)

The City Hall area from atop the American Telephone & Telegraph Company Building, ca. 1917. In front of the lofty Woolworth Tower (the tallest skyscraper in the world at the time) is the Second Empire–style "Mullett" Post Office which virtually obscures City Hall from view. To the left rear are the "Tweed" Court House and twin wings of the Emigrant Industrial Savings Bank. To the right, the massive Municipal Building faces the diminutive Probate Court Building. Farther to the right are the twin cupolas of the Park Row Building, just beyond the narrow St. Paul Building in the right foreground. (American Telephone & Telegraph Company)

Nieuw Amsterdam as a permanent settlement was established in 1625, and one year later, Peter Minuit made his famous purchase from the Indians. In 1664 the Colony was captured by the English and named for the Duke of York. For a few months in 1673 the Dutch regained control, but they lost it again to Britain.

Facing the waterfront and looking to the right, one can see **Pier A,** the fire-boat station built in 1886. The clock on the 70-foot tower was donated in 1918 by Daniel Reid, a founder of the United States Steel Corporation, as a memorial to the 116,000 servicemen who died while serving in World War I. The clock peals the time on ships' bells.

A short distance to the east (and a bit difficult to find) is the **Wireless Operators Memorial Monument,** dedicated to those radiomen who went down with their ship. A bronze plaque is added with each tragedy, and some are quite recent. Note the plaque for the wireless operator of the *Titanic,* which struck an iceberg on her maiden voyage to America and sank on the night of April 14–15, 1912, with a loss of 1,517 out of 2,000 passengers.

Walk out on the **Admiral George Dewey Promenade,** at the water's edge. Considered the finest view in the city, the broad panorama includes (from left to right) Brooklyn Heights, Governors Island, distant Staten Island, the Statue of Liberty on Liberty Island, Ellis Island with its former immigration depot, and the New Jersey harborfront. And in the bay is the constant parade of ships of all types, which bring the harbor to life. Turning around, the view of the lower Manhattan skyline, now somewhat obscured by modern, and rather uninteresting additions, is awesome. The finest view, of course, is from the Staten Island Ferry or from the Statue of Liberty excursion boat.

Facing the Promenade is the **East Coast War Memorial,** which honors every seaman, soldier, and airman lost in the American coastal waters of the North Atlantic during World War II. All the names are carved into the eight granite pylons. In the center is an immense sculpture of an American Eagle by sculptor Albino Manca, unveiled in 1963 by President Kennedy.

Follow the Promenade eastward to the end, and walk north on the park side of State Street.

On the way, the **Battery Maritime Building (formerly the Municipal Ferry Piers)** can be seen to the right. These are the last remaining ferry terminals, which once served a number of routes. The huge Roman Classical green metal arched buildings were built in 1907–09 and served the ferries to Brooklyn. They were closed in 1938 and are now used by the Governors Island Ferry, the Staten Island Ferry having its own new terminal alongside.

At approximately the site of the Governors Island Ferry slip was the point of embarcation in Dutch Colonial times for ships sailing to the mother country or to other distant points. The little wharf was soon called **Schreijers Hoek** (Weepers' Point), since the perils of a long sea voyage threatened the safe return of loved ones. The name was taken from the *Schreijerstoren* (Weepers' Tower) on the Amstel River in Amsterdam, where relatives bade a tearful farewell to those departing on distant journeys.

Just inside the park fence is the **Oyster Pasty Mount Cannon,** a relic from English Colonial days which was uncovered during building excavations. The Oyster Pasty was a derisive name given to the battery mounted near a pile of oyster shells.

Cross Peter Minuit Plaza.

The flagpole in the mini-park is New York City's tribute to the first group of Jews to arrive at these shores in 1654—23 men, women, and children, refugees from the Inquisition in Brazil. Attempting to return to Holland, their ship was taken by a Spanish pirate who in turn was captured by a French privateer. Pledging their possessions to the French captain, they were brought to Nieuw Amsterdam, where Peter Stuyvesant gave them a less-than-cordial welcome, but permitted them to stay. The townspeople paid off the captain, allowing the refugees to discharge their debt and keep the clothes on their backs. Practicing their religion privately, the small group of Sephardic Jews was later able to rent a room for services in a windmill, and ultimately built the first synagogue in America in 1730 on Mill Street (now South William Street), about one-quarter mile north.

Peter Minuit Plaza is named for one of the first Dutch governors, who purchased the Island of "Manhattes" in 1626 from the Reckagawawanc Indians (who didn't really own it anyway, as the concept of private land ownership was foreign to them), for an amount of trinkets valued at 60 guilders, or about $24.

At 7 State Street the former **James Watson House** is now the **Shrine of the Blessed Elizabeth Ann Seton,** the first American-born saint. Mother Seton (1774–1821) was the founder of the American Sisters of Charity, the first order of nuns in the United States. She is also credited with the establishment of the American Catholic parochial school system. Mother Seton was elevated to sainthood in September 1975. The house is a lone survivor of a magnificent row of elegant Federal mansions that lined State Street. Note the freestanding slender Ionic columns and the Georgian details. The building is completely original, and was built in the early 1800s, probably by John McComb, the architect of City Hall. What a splendid sight the long colonnade must have presented to approaching ships. The church of Our Lady of the Rosary, adjoining the shrine, occupies the site of a former residence of Mother Seton.

The Seamen's Church Institute (15 State Street), supported by Trinity Parish, provides lodging and services for seamen, including educational programs, a library, school, chapel, and cafeteria. The attractive modern building, designed by Eggers & Higgins in 1969, in a nautical motif, replaces an earlier structure built in 1913 at 25 South Street, which occupied a conspicuous site overlooking the harbor. The Institute building is a veritable museum and is open to the public seven days a week (ground floor and second floor only). The cafeteria offers inexpensive meals, and visitors are welcome. After a look at the lobby with its nautical artifacts, visit the intimate chapel with its bright stained glass, capstan baptismal font, and ship models. Then walk up the winding staircase to the second floor, noting the collection of bronze plaques from the former Institute building. Along the walls of the second floor corridor are prints and photographs of old ships; and mounted on pedestals are ship's bells salvaged from stranded vessels. The most tragic is the bell from the *Atlantic,* which sank in a gale off Fisher's Island in Long Island Sound, on Thanksgiving Day, 1846. The tale is recounted on a wall plaque. Nearby is the bell from the *Norman-die.* (Tap them gently with a coin.) The Institute began in 1834 as a sort of houseboat seamen's mission, called the Floating Church of the Comforter, and was anchored at an East River pier at the foot of Pike Street. The site of the Institute was the birthplace of author Herman Melville, who in his youth served aboard a whaling ship. A commemorative plaque can be seen on the Pearl Street side of the building.

The little subway entrance building on the park side is one of the last remaining kiosks of the city's first subway system, and is known as the **Battery Park Control House.** The name derives from the original concept that once passengers had entered the building they were under the control of the transit company. The structure was built in 1904–05 in French Beaux Arts style from plans by Heins & LaFarge.

End of tour. Walk up State Street to the new Bowling Green station of the IRT Lexington Avenue subway. Take any northbound train two stops to Fulton Street for connections to other subways.

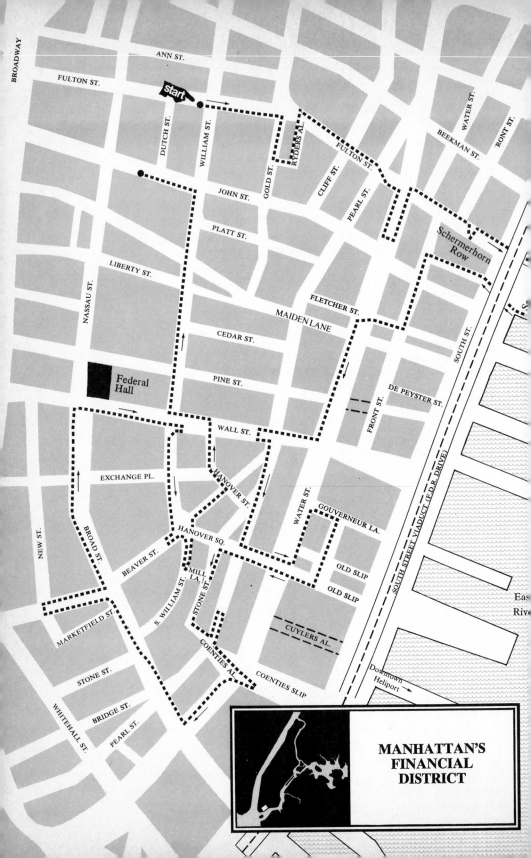

MANHATTAN'S
FINANCIAL
DISTRICT

2. Manhattan's Financial District

[*IRT Broadway-Seventh Avenue line to Fulton Street; IND A line to Broadway-Nassau Street; BMT M, J to Fulton Street; IRT Lexington Avenue line to Fulton Street; Second/First Avenue (M-15) bus to Fulton Street*]

The walking tour begins at the corner of Fulton and William streets.

William Street is known as **"Insurance Row,"** with its rows of tall buildings that house the offices of dozens of large insurance companies and brokerage firms. On the northwest corner is the massive Aetna Life & Casualty Company; on the northeast, the neo-Georgian-style building of the Royal Globe Insurance Company; and on the southeast, in a similar style, the Fidelity & Deposit Company of Maryland. On the southwest corner is the site of the birthplace in 1783 of Washington Irving (No. 131 William Street), who wrote *Knickerbocker's History of New York, The Legend of Sleepy Hollow* and many other works, and who coined the expression, "The Almighty Dollar."

Turn right on Gold Street.

A few yards down Gold Street, on the right side and almost hidden among its neighbors, is a surprising relic of the beginning of the mechanical age—the **Excelsior Power Company** building. Completed in 1888 from plans by William G. Grinnell, it was one of the city's first power houses. The coal-loading docks and wagon-wheel deflectors are still in place; but the whine of the huge dynamos has long since been silenced, and the sturdy Romanesque Revival Industrial–style building has been converted into a co-op. Excelsior Power built the plant just six years after Thomas Edison inaugurated the world's first central electrical generating station, a few blocks away at 225 Pearl Street.

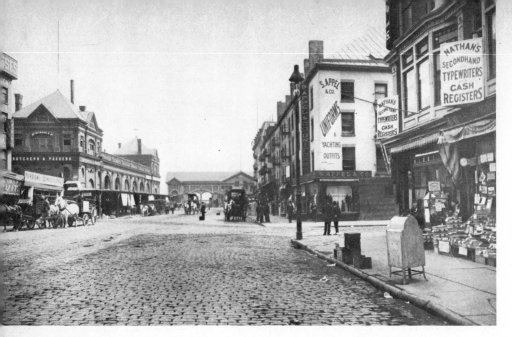

Looking east on Fulton Street toward the Fulton Ferry Terminal about 1900. The Fulton Fish Market building, to the left, is long since gone, but the gabled-roof block across the street, known as Schermerhorn Row, survives from the first decade of the 19th century, and is a designated landmark—the focus of the South Street Seaport Area. (South Street Seaport Museum)

Walk up the little cobblestoned lane, called **Ryder's Alley,** which makes an abrupt left turn, returning to Fulton Street. The street is named for Robert Ryder, an English surveyor during the Colonial Period.

The Southbridge Towers housing project was completed in 1972. The plans originally called for enormous high-rise apartment houses, but the city fathers felt that such height would overwhelm the adjacent South Street Seaport area. The modified plan by Gruzen & Partners is a pleasant blending with the surroundings, with considerable "breathing space."

At the corner of Water and Fulton streets is New York's "fun skyscraper," known only by its official address, **127 John Street.** Walk around the building and see for yourself. According to the owners, it is designed "to create an atmosphere of pleasure, humor, and excitement for people." See for yourself, as you relax for a moment on the north-side sun deck; then enter through the main entrance's neon-lit "vacuum cleaner pipe" and step into either a red or blue elevator. Set your watch by the world's largest digital clock mounted on the east wall. Note, too, the iron "bicycle rack" sculpture and *Telephone Booth* by Albert Wilson; and from a distance, the gaily painted adornments up to the roof's water tank. The clock was built as an extension of the wall to hide an old building whose owner would not sell to complete the land parcel. This imaginative building, which houses the New York Cocoa Exchange, was designed by Emery Roth & Sons in 1972; and the amusing and creative sidewalk and ground-floor adornments are the work of developer Mel Kaufman, who also planned the pedestrian areas of 77 Water Street (to be seen later). The site was occupied in the mid-19th century by the famous United States Hotel.

Cross Water Street to the South Street Seaport area.

The Titanic Memorial Lighthouse marks the entrance to the South Street Seaport. This memorial to the 1,517 victims of the *Titanic* who perished when the "unsinkable" liner struck an iceberg and sank on the night of April 14–15, 1912, was erected by public subscription in 1913 and stood atop the old Seamen's Church Institute Building on South Street until 1967. The time ball at the top of the lighthouse would drop down the pole to signal the hour of twelve noon to the ships in the harbor, its mechanism activated by a telegraph signal from the National Observatory in Washington, D.C.

The South Street Seaport Historic District is a 19th-century waterfront area that survives almost intact. The entire Seaport area is being developed by the Rouse Company, whose restorations of Boston's Quincy Market and Baltimore's Harbor Place have been highly acclaimed. Plans call for the reopening of many of the crafts and industries of the last century in the restored buildings. At present only a few are available for visit: the **Model Shop** at 207 Water Street and the **Seaport Gallery** at 213–215 (the South Street Seaport Museum's research library is located on the second floor).

Be sure to visit **Bowne and Company Stationers**, at 211, a re-creation of a 19th-century printing establishment and a working commercial enterprise. In addition to its modern equipment, there are old hand presses with original

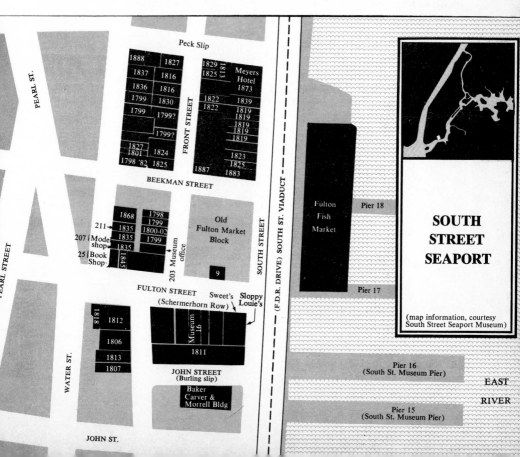

typefaces and a display of early printing machinery. Interestingly, the original tenant of this 1836 building was a printer. There is also a small maritime gift shop maintained by the museum.

Walk down Fulton Street under the South Street Viaduct to the **South Street Seaport Museum piers** to see the display of ships berthed at Piers 15 and 16. At the entrance is the main information center in the Tugboat Pilot House, rescued from old New York Central Railroad Tugboat No. 23. Although admission to the piers is free, there is a small charge to visit the ships. Among the attractions are the square-rigger *Wavertree,* the lightship *Ambrose,* the Gloucester schooner *Lettie G. Howard,* a retired city ferryboat, and a variety of other vessels. But the *pièce de résistance*—and not to be missed—is the spectacular 321-foot four-masted bark *Peking,* one of the largest sailing ships ever built and the pride of the South Street Seaport Museum.

Among the splendid views from the piers is that of the **Brooklyn Bridge** [*see* page 398]. Considered by many to be the most beautiful bridge ever built, it was designed by John A. Roebling in 1867 and took 16 years to complete. Before the work was finished, Roebling suffered a fatal injury and turned over the job to his son, Washington A. Roebling. It was the first bridge across the East River, and for many years the longest suspension bridge in the world. Its pink granite towers with Gothic-style arches are a familiar sight against the dramatic New York City skyline. Although the bridge was opened in 1883, it was not until 1924 that the Fulton Ferry, which connected Fulton Street in Manhattan with Fulton Street in Brooklyn, was retired from its two-century-old river crossing service. The site also marks the location of General George Washington's strategic withdrawal from Brooklyn after the defeat of the Continental Army at the Battle of Long Island, when on the night of August 29, 1776, under cover of darkness and fog, small boats rowed the 9,500-man army across the river to Manhattan.

Spend some time exploring the streets of the Seaport area. Begin by crossing back to Fulton Street to examine the block between South and Front streets, known as **Schermerhorn Row.** Built in 1811–12, this row of peaked-roof buildings is the only surviving block of Georgian-Federal–style and Greek Revival commercial structures in the city. When the area prospered in the Great Age of Sail, these structures housed a variety of industries serving the sea, with ships' chandleries, sail and rope lofts, and naval-store warehouses. The Row, originally developed by merchant Peter Schermerhorn, will be restored by the State of New York, with space to be shared by the South Street Seaport Museum and the Rouse Company for commercial development. In No. 2 is the oldest seafood restaurant in the city, **Sweet's,** which still retains much of its 19th-century atmosphere, including the sawdust on the floor. It was here that illegal slave traders, called "blackbirders," met during the last century to conduct their nefarious deals. Around the corner on South Street is a more modest, yet colorful, seafood establishment called Sloppie Louie's.

Walk north on Front Street to Peck Slip to see the *trompe l'oeil* mural of the Brooklyn Bridge, by artist Richard Haas, on Con Edison's Seaport Substation; then turn right to the corner of South Street to **Meyer's Hotel,** built in 1873 and now being renovated.

Walk south on South Street past the Fulton Fish Market and Fulton Street to the next corner, Burling Slip, and turn right to Water Street.

The extension of John Street is still called **Burling Slip.** The "slips" (the others are Peck, Old, Catherine, Beekman, Pike, and Coenties) are reminders of the early days when these were docking areas. At 170–176 John Street (Burling Slip) is the former **Baker, Carver & Morell Building (1840).** Once a ship's chandlery, it was a type of commercial structure introduced to New York from Boston in 1829 by Ithiel Town and Alexander Jackson Davis. The building is faced with granite from top to bottom, with massive piers separating the display windows. In 1982 it was converted into a condominium.

Walking south on Water Street, we pass a trio of new skyscrapers begun in the winter of 1981–82. **One Seaport Plaza,** according to its architects, Swanke Hayden Connell, is designed as a "contextual" 34-story office tower with two distinctly different façades "in context" with its surroundings. The Front Street side is planned to be "reminiscent of another architectural era, echoing the mood of the 19th-century seaport community," while the Water Street side, with its polished granite face and ribbon windows, "is designed to be totally

During the "Great Age of Sail" of the mid-to-late 19th century, South Street was lined with the tall masts of graceful sailing ships from all over the world. Here, near Burling Slip, are a four- and three-master, loading cargo for far-distant ports. (South Street Seaport Museum)

Young boys enjoying an illegal dip "in the raw" at the Fulton Fish Market pier at the foot of Beekman Street, ca. 1892, apparently oblivious to the photographer, the man dragging the basket of fish, and the law banning swimming in the East River. Among the myriad sailing ships' masts in the background are the twin pilot houses of a Fulton Ferryboat. (New-York Historical Society)

The bow and figurehead of a square-rigger cast a long shadow across two curious onlookers at South Street near Maiden Lane in the late 1880s. (South Street Seaport Museum)

Looking north on New Street the morning after the Great Blizzard of 1888. The storm wreaked such havoc with the overhead wires that the City thereafter required all utilities to run their wires underground. (Museum of the City of New York)

modern and compatible with its neighboring high-rise buildings in an urban environment."

No. 175 Water Street, a 30-story office building designed by Fox & Fowle, is the headquarters of the National Westminster Bank Group. During the excavation for the foundation, workers made a fascinating and important discovery. Buried in the mud only six feet below ground level they uncovered the complete hull of a mid-18th-century British merchant ship! The developer halted work and summoned archaeologists who, working under the supervision of the Landmarks Commission, rushed to learn as much as possible about the vessel. The 85-foot-long wooden hull belonged to a ship that had been scuttled some time between 1746 and 1755 to be used as part of a harbor landfill project extending Manhattan Island. The unexpected find attracted tens of thousands of visitors who waited in line for hours in the bitter cold for a view of the derelict ship, before it would disappear forever into the concrete foundations of the emerging skyscraper. The unusually shaped building is representative of the new postmodernistic approach to high-rise construction, a welcome relief from the ubiquitous "glass boxes" that dominated architectural thought beginning in the 1950s.

The Continental Tower, 180 Maiden Lane, between Front and South streets, designed by Swanke Hayden Connell in 1982, is an even more dramatic example of post-modernism. A 41-story hexagonally shaped building, its blue-green reflective skin contrasts sharply with its neighbors.

Look up Pine Street to the towering **former Cities Service Building,** one block west at Pearl Street. Until recently it had an annex at 60 Wall Street connected by a skywalk. The skyscraper, built in 1932 from plans by Clinton & Russell, boasted a Wall Street address until its annex on Wall Street was demolished; now it is merely 70 Pine Street.

At Fletcher Street, turn right to Water Street and turn south (left).

No. 160 Water Street, completed in 1971, is more interesting for its sidewalk geometrical designs than for its own architecture. Water Street was once the commercial hub of a thriving waterfront. The street was widened some years ago to provide a much needed traffic artery. In the process, however, many lovely old buildings were lost, and nothing now remains from the 19th century.

Maiden Lane, translated literally from the Dutch *Het Maagde Paatje,* was the site of a freshwater stream where young maidens in the 17th century did their laundry. Look up Maiden Lane to the fortresslike Federal Reserve Bank.

A refreshing change from the usual uninspired "glass box" is **No. 88 Pine Street,** a breezy, light tower of white-painted metal and large windows. Designed by James I. Freed of I. M. Pei Associates and completed in 1971, the building occupies a pleasant plaza, and with its see-through quality is ideally suited for a site close to the river. Look for the *Queen Elizabeth* plaque and two-piece mirrored sculpture by Yu Yu Yang.

On the southeast corner of Wall and Water streets was the **Merchants' Coffee House,** built in 1740. It was a popular gathering place for Revolutionary War plotters, and the area became known as Coffee House Slip.

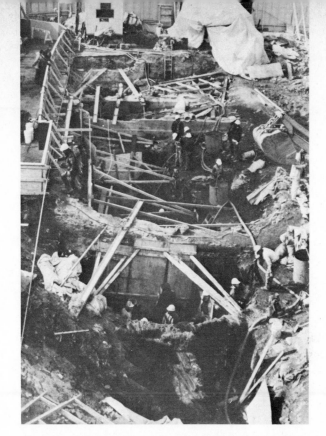

Archaeologists scramble over the hull of a derelict mid-18th-century British merchant ship, unearthed unexpectedly during the excavation for a new office tower at 175 Water Street, near the South Street Seaport. The ship had been scuttled and used for landfill, and remained undiscovered until the site was cleared in the late winter of 1982. (Fox & Fowle, Architects)

Charming Hanover Square was not enhanced by the Third Avenue El roaring overhead along Pearl Street. At the time this photo was taken in the early 1880s India House was then the Cotton Exchange, and the lower level was rented to commercial tenants. (Museum of the City of New York)

At the turn of the century the Consolidated Stock Exchange operated briefly as a rival to the "Big Board," dealing mostly in mining stocks. The huge Greek Revival–style building stood at the southeast corner of Broad and Wall streets. (King's Views of New York, 1909)

Looking west on Wall Street, ca. 1890, from South Street to Trinity Church, with the Third Avenue El passing overhead at Pearl Street. To the right of the church is the cupola of the Gillender Building, now the site of the Bankers Trust Company Building at the corner of Nassau Street. (Museum of the City of New York)

The northwest corner was the site of the **Tontine Coffee House,** erected in 1792. It was here that the Stock Exchange had its beginnings, with transactions taking place on the street under a buttonwood (sycamore) tree and later within the Coffee House, the present site of No. 70 Wall Street. The building at the northwest corner (No. 82 Wall Street) commemorates the site in its name, Tontine House.

Turn right on Wall Street to Pearl Street.

Pearl Street was originally the shore of the East River in Dutch Colonial times and is named for the mother-of-pearl oyster shells that were scattered along the beach. **No. 100 Wall Street** on the north side, and **No. 111** on the south were built on landfill added in 1801. The Third Avenue El once followed the winding course of narrow Pearl Street.

Wall Street is the site of the original protective wall, built by order of Governor Peter Stuyvesant in 1653, at the northern limits of the town of Nieuw Amsterdam. At the site of Wall and Pearl streets, a blockhouse commanded the eastern end of the wall, and a large water gate was built between the blockhouse and the wall itself. It was called *'t Water Poort* to distinguish it from *'t Landt Poort* at Broadway. The Dutch referred to the path along the wall as *de Cingel* (the Rampart). The wall was a fortified palisade fence, not, as is commonly believed, to keep out hostile Indians, but to prevent an invasion by the English from the New England colonies. The fortification gradually deteriorated (helped by colonists who "borrowed" planks for house repairs and firewood), and as the city grew northward, it was demolished around 1695. In 1709 the area became a slave market and later a grain market.

No. 74 Wall Street, at the northwest corner of Pearl Street, was built for the Seamen's Bank for Savings in 1926 from plans by Benjamin Wistar Morris, and is now occupied by a branch of the Williamsburgh Savings Bank. The handsome building has an attractive façade of multicolored seamed-face granite blocks, and upon completion was cited by the Downtown League as "the finest building of the year." The tall structure with its artistic setbacks cannot be categorized as belonging to any particular style, but the huge entrance arch is Romanesque in character, while the graceful upper buttresses are vaguely Gothic. Stretching a point, it might be called a very early example of Art Deco. Attractive are the low-relief blocks around the arch, representing nautical themes. The Seamen's Bank for Savings is the city's second oldest, chartered in 1829. Its original charter restricted banking activities to seamen only, in the belief that too many sailors were losing their hard-earned wages, accumulated during long sea voyages, in waterfront saloons as soon as their ships returned to port. When the building was dedicated, the directors decided to change the street address from 76 to 74 Wall Street, as some "old salts" who had been longtime depositors suggested that the combination of numbers totaling 13 "was a thing to make a good seaman wary."

A plaque on the building marks the site of the home of Edward Livingston, Secretary of State in 1831, who may hold the record in number of public offices held: senator, mayor, congressman, and minister to France.

Turn back (east) and take the first right to Pearl Street as far as Beaver Street.

Beaver Street honors the little furry rodent on which so much of early commerce depended. Beaver pelts were shipped in such large quantities, and figured so vitally in the early colony's business life, that the animal was incorporated into the seal of Nieuw Amsterdam and later into the seal of the City of New York. The building at **82–92 Beaver Street** was formerly the New York Cocoa Exchange until its move to 127 John Street.

Return to the intersection of Pearl Street and turn right (south) on Pearl Street.

Note how **No. 140 Pearl Street** conforms to the curve of the street, preserving the unity of the "street wall." The name of the original owner is emblazoned in the pediment of this ornate cast-iron structure.

Hanover Square is an attractive oasis among the towering canyons of lower Manhattan. The intersection where Hanover, Pearl, Stone, and William streets meet Old Slip was originally a public common as far back as 1637, surrounded by elegant residences and situated very close to the river. At the site of nearby No. 119 Pearl Street, Captain (William) Kidd maintained a home. Captain Kidd was really not the pirate he was reputed to be. Although he was tried and hanged in England in 1699 for piracy, recent studies seem to indicate that he was an honorable sea captain who was the scapegoat of an unfair trial. Hanover Square, named for the royal house of England, is one of the few public places whose name was not changed during the Revolution, perhaps because George I was not disliked as much as his descendant, two Georges later. As the district became commercial, Hanover Square was the first "Printing House Square" of the city [see City Hall, "Old Newspaper Row," Foley Square, and "Five Points" Nos. 2, 3, 4]. It was here that New York's first newspaper, the *New York Gazette,* was published by William Bradford in 1725.

Dominating Hanover Square is the landmark **India House.** It was built in 1851–54 by Richard Carman, a carpenter, for the Hanover Bank. From 1870 to 1885 it housed the New York Cotton Exchange, and later W. R. Grace & Company. India House was organized as a private businessmen's club in 1914, and is dedicated to the furtherance of foreign trade. It contains a large collection of maritime artifacts and paintings in the charmingly reconstructed Marine Room. The lower floor of India House is occupied by *Harry's,* a restaurant popular with bankers and brokers. The brownstone exterior in Italianate style is reminiscent of a Tuscan villa.

Hanover Square was recently remodeled and converted into a pedestrian mall, and **the statue of Abraham de Peyster** (George E. Bissell, 1896) was moved here from Bowling Green. The carved legend in the base records the list of public offices held by de Peyster during his long career as a civil servant. (For some reason, de Peyster turns his back on the square.)

No. 7 Hanover Square, a 26-story office tower (Emery Roth & Sons, and Norman Jaffe, 1982), stands on the site of the old W. R. Grace & Company Building. Unable to find a tenant for its Florentine-style *palazzo* when the firm moved its headquarters uptown to 42nd Street in 1974, they demolished it, and the lot then lay "fallow" until recent demand for office space brought a developer to the site. Had the need come a few years sooner, the lovely old predecessor might have had a new lease on life.

Walk east on Hanover Square to Water Street and turn left (north).

No. 77 Water Street, designed by Emery Roth & Sons in 1970, is another iconoclastic structure two years older than the same architect's 127 John Street building. Although the superstructure is not particularly engaging, the handling of the open lobby area and its "fantasies" is most pleasant, and is a credit to developer Mel Kaufman. Walk across the mini-stream's bridges, examine the metal sculptures, including *Rejected Skin,* by sculptor William Tarr (and indeed made from rejected parts of the building's aluminum siding), and visit Ye Olde Time Country Candy Store, with Virginia, the laughing soda dispenser. Then explore little Bennett Park to the north. It's all fun and a pleasant departure from the staid traditions of the Financial District.

Walk back around the building to Old Slip, between the old U.S. Assay Office and the Police Station.

The United States Assay Office, designed in 1930 by James A. Wetmore, fell victim to government budget-slashing in 1982, and has emptied its vaults of gold and silver, turned its electrolytic furnaces on "cold," and locked its doors, leaving New York City without an assay office for the first time since 1854. [*See* page 51.]

Across Old Slip from the Assay Office, where sailing ships once docked, is the **former First Precinct Police Station,** once called the "Old Slip Station." Built in the style of an Italian *palazzo,* it is a trim, solid Italian Renaissance–style structure of pleasing proportion, and was designed by Joseph Howland Hunt and Richard Howland Hunt in 1909.

Return to Hanover Square and turn left (south) just beyond India House into narrow Stone Street.

Stone Street's winding course parallels the old East River shoreline, and appears to be appropriately named. It was originally called *Brouwers Straet,* after Stephanus Van Cortlandt's brewery situated on the lane. Legend has it that his wife and her neighbors objected so strenuously to the dust raised by passing wagons on the unpaved street that the good burghers persuaded the city to pave the street with cobblestones; and the practical-minded Dutch colonists, who shared the cost, then changed the street's name accordingly. Stone Street is said to have been the colony's first paved thoroughfare—the cobblestones were laid in 1657—and the present paving stones are erroneously thought by many to be original. These are Belgian blocks, laid in the 19th century.

Continue to Coenties Alley and turn left to Pearl Street.

At the southwest corner of Pearl Street and Coenties Alley once stood the **Stadt Huys,** the first City Hall. Built originally as the *Stadt Herberg,* or City

The Stadt Huys, *the first New York City Hall, situated at the waterfront on Pearl Street and Coenties Slip, as seen in an 1869 print. (The J. Clarence Davies Collection, Museum of the City of New York)*

Tavern, by Governor William Kieft in 1641, it was an imposing five-story stone structure—the tallest in town—overlooking the harbor. When Nieuw Amsterdam was granted its municipal charter 12 years later, New York's first hotel was converted into the *Stadt Huys,* and remained the seat of city government until 1699. Two years later a new City Hall was built on Wall Street (on the site of the present Federal Hall). Not long ago, when the buildings which occupied the site of Nos. 71 and 73 Pearl Street were removed, the *Stadt Huys*'s foundations were discovered underneath. A team of archaeologists studied and mapped the site before the plot was resurfaced. In addition to the foundation walls, the dig unearthed Delft and English pottery, fragments of Indian wampum, as well as clay pipes and wine bottles from Lovelace Tavern, built by Francis Lovelace, the second English governor of New York. The commercial building of the early 19th century which stood on the site of No. 71 was carefully dismantled, declared a landmark, and placed in storage pending re-erection at the South Street Seaport. The old *Stadt Huys* served a number of functions, including a jail and debtors' prison, a courthouse, and a public warehouse. In front of the building, at the river's edge, stood the gallows, a pillory and stocks; and even a ducking stool, in which violators of the strict Dutch Reformed moral codes were tied and plunged repeatedly into the cold water of the East River.

Further north on Pearl Street, at the site of No. 81, William Bradford installed **New York's first printing press** in 1693. Note the commemorative plaque on the mid-19th-century building.

Return to Coenties Alley and turn left into Coenties Slip.

Coenties Slip was one of the early city's largest wharfs, with a diagonally-shaped breakwater projecting far out into the East River [*see* Great Fire map];

however, the inlet has been completely filled in, even out beyond the end of the old pier. Coenties Slip is named for Conraet Ten Eyck, who operated a tannery on nearby Broad Street. ("Coentje" is the Dutch diminutive for Conraet.) At this point the old Third Avenue El made a dizzying zigzag turn as it twisted sharply east from its southward path down Pearl Street, over Coenties Slip, then south again into Water Street—on the last lap of its tortuous route to South Ferry. Built in 1879, the El survived until 1950.

Across Water Street is diminutive **Jeanette Park,** a paved multilevel plaza made entirely of brick similar to adjacent No. 4 New York Plaza. Designed by landscape architect W. Paul Friedberg, it is terraced and equipped with an underground shopping mall, but is sterile in appearance, lacking much of the former park's shrubbery. The mini-park's name is a memorial to the sailing ship *Jeanette* which met disaster on the George Washington De Long Expedition to the North Pole in 1881. The ill-starred venture was sponsored jointly by the U.S. Navy and James Gordon Bennett, publisher of the *New York Herald.* It was the *Herald,* in its tradition of sensationalism, which sent Stanley to Africa to find Livingstone. For years, Jeanette Park was a favorite port of call for unemployed seamen, and boasted a popular oyster bar in the middle of a shady mall.

To the left of Jeanette Park is enormous **55 Water Street** (Emery Roth & Sons, 1972), a twin building connected by an exterior escalator bank. Take the escalator to the plaza level and enjoy the river views. To the south is **No.**

The famous S-curve of the Third Avenue El, about 1879, at Coenties Slip. The serpentine structure was finally scrapped in 1950, depriving straphangers of a spectacular ride through the "canyons" of lower Manhattan. (The New-York Historical Society)

4 New York Plaza (Carson, Lundin & Shaw, 1968), one of the first of the behemoths to line Water Street.

On the west side of Water Street, directly opposite No. 4 New York Plaza, is a **block of typical 19th-century commercial buildings** that survived because the street was widened on the east side only. It was later decided to save the entire block, which includes historic Fraunces Tavern, to re-create the atmosphere of the mid-19th-century commercial district. The group includes Federal, Greek Revival, and Victorian buildings, and has been designated the **Fraunces Tavern Block Historic District.** Unfortunately, the 19th-century atmosphere and scale is destroyed by the towering buildings that surround the block and overwhelm it.

Turn right at Broad Street to Pearl Street.

At the corner of Broad and Pearl streets is one of our most cherished landmarks, **Fraunces Tavern.** A handsome neo-Georgian building, it is a splendid re-creation of the Stephen DeLancey house, built in 1719. Except for some Dutch brick in the west wall, nothing remains of the original structure. Nonetheless, it is an excellent example of a formal English house of the 18th century. James DeLancey, a descendant of the wealthy merchant, lost all his family holdings by choosing the wrong side in the American Revolution, and suffered confiscation of his property. (Delancey Street on the Lower East Side is today the only physical reminder of the family name and the large estate he once owned in that part of Manhattan.) In 1757 the building became a warehouse, and five years later was purchased by Samuel Fraunces who converted it into the *Queen's Head Tavn.* Fraunces, a West Indian of black and French ancestry, operated the ta n successfully for a number of years and subsequently came into the employ of George Washington as his chief steward. What is now the New York State Chamber of Commerce was founded here in 1768, and just before the outbreak of the Revolutionary War, the Committees of Correspondence—soon to become the Continental Congress—held their first meetings at the tavern. On November 24, 1783, Governor Clinton gave a gala dinner here to celebrate the British evacuation of the city, and that December 4th, Washington bade his famous farewell to his officers in the Long Room on the second floor. During the 19th century, the tavern gradually deteriorated, suffered several fires, and fell victim to a number of unauthentic reconstructions. In 1904 the Sons of the Revolution of New York State purchased the building and spent three years restoring it to its present elegance. The Fraunces Tavern Museum is open Monday to Friday, 10 A.M. to 4 P.M., and conducts frequent programs for young and old (phone 425-1778). There is also a library and a charming ground-floor restaurant.

Take a moment for a brief lesson in Georgian-style architecture by crossing the street and admiring the details: the slate hipped roof crowned by a balustrade, the tall chimneys, shed-roof dormers, a cornice set over a row of modillions, red brick walls with stone trim, and an ornate doorway flanked by classic columns and crowned by a pediment. The style was inspired by the north-Italian Renaissance as applied by the architect Palladio to many of the great Venetian and Lombardian villas.

On January 24, 1975, a bomb was exploded in the adjacent Anglers' Club, causing several deaths and many injuries. Allegedly placed by a Puerto Rican extremist group, the blast virtually destroyed the club, but luckily caused only minor damage to Fraunces Tavern.

After walking north on Broad Street for about 100 yards, turn around and view the broad panorama of new "monoliths" that have sprung up along the downtown waterfront. From left to right (east to south): **55 Water Street;** Manufacturers Hanover's **No. 4 New York Plaza;** and behind it, American Express Plaza; Chase Manhattan's **No. 1 New York Plaza** with its recessed windows; **No. 1 State Street Plaza;** and **No. 1 Battery Park Plaza.** The erection of these massive buildings has virtually obliterated the traditional Lower Manhattan skyline.

Continue north on Broad Street.

Diagonally across from Fraunces Tavern, at **No. 104,** is one of the many New York Telephone Company buildings; and on the triangular plot of land bounded by Pearl and Bridge streets, the austere **New York Clearing House** (No. 100), built in 1962, which oversees the clearing of billions of dollars of member banks' checks daily.

Broad Street in Dutch Colonial days was a wide canal, called the *Heere Graft* (Great Canal) which extended inland from the East River as far as the present Exchange Place, with a small side canal up Beaver Street. (The broad dimensions of the old canal account for the disproportionately wide size of Broad Street today). By 1676, the canal became polluted and rather malodorous, and was filled in. In its place, *Brede Straet* survives in translation to the present. It is interesting to note that unlike other north-south streets, the numbers on Broad Street *decrease* in a northward direction.

No. 85 Broad Street (Skidmore, Owings & Merrill, 1982) rises 30 stories and occupies what was once several blocks of low-rise 19th-century commercial buildings. The rough-textured surface of the office tower is precast concrete exposed aggregate. In making way for this giant, it was necessary to close diminutive Stone Street at Coenties Alley, and some of the early street's history will be depicted in the lobby. As you reach South William Street, notice how the "street wall" of the 85 Broad Street building has been designed to conform to the curvature of the winding street.

No. 67 Broad Street, the **R.C.A. Global Communications Building,** once also housed the Commodities Exchange (now at the World Trade Center), where futures are traded in silver, gold, hides, soybeans, pork bellies, wheat, etc. Note the splendid entranceway with its colorful mosaic ceiling. Visible on the roof are R.C.A.'s radio antennas.

Directly across the street, a narrow plaza leads to the rear of multicolored No. 2 Broadway, where a plaque marks the **site of the first Huguenot church in New York.** Return to Broad Street and continue to Marketfield Street.

Another plaque at the entrance to tiny Marketfield Street marks the site of "the lost thoroughfare, Petticoat Lane." The diminutive street takes its name from the *Marcktveldt,* or Market Place, that once existed along the old canal. A market was held every Friday morning at the cattle bridge, one of several that crossed the *Heere Graft.*

Turn left on Beaver Street to New Street.

No. 18 Beaver Street is an ornate survivor of the "Elegant '80s"—probably a fancy restaurant of yesteryear, better known then as a dining saloon.

Nowhere else in the city can the expression **"The Canyons of New York"** be more dramatically visualized than from this point looking north on New Street. (Return to Broad Street.)

At the southwest corner of Beaver and Broad streets is the Renaissance Revival–style **American Bank Note Company Building.** Before the establishment of the government's Bureau of Engraving and Printing, many security printers such as the American Banknote Company printed our paper currency, bonds, and postage stamps. The company, which traces its origin to 1795, still produces paper currency for many foreign countries and is the largest printer of securities in the world.

Walking up Broad Street, observe the variety of early 20th-century office buildings: No. 50; No. 37; and No. 25, the **Broad-Exchange Building,** which when completed just after the turn of the century, was the largest office building in the world.

Exchange Place, named for a merchants' exchange located here during the Dutch Colonial period, is one of the city's narrowest streets. The surprising little hill leading to Broadway gives it the dubious distinction of being the steepest street in downtown Manhattan.

Across from the Broad-Exchange Building, on the northeast corner of Broad Street and Exchange Place, stood the **Old Ferry House** from which boats to Long Island shore points departed down the "Great Canal." Passengers were sometimes forced to spend the night here waiting for fair winds to make the trip. Looking up Exchange Place with its massed skyscrapers, it is hard to conceive that the area during the mid-17th century was a sheep pasture.

Approaching the end of Broad Street is one of the most famous panoramas of the financial center (left to right): **The New York Stock Exchange** (southwest corner), the **Bankers Trust Company** with its stepped pyramid atop the tower (northwest corner), **Federal Hall National Memorial** (northeast corner), and the **Morgan Guaranty Trust Company** (southeast corner).

The New York Stock Exchange (8 Broad Street), synonymous with Wall Street, is the largest securities exchange in the world. The "big board" lists more than 3,500 different stocks and bonds owned by about 30 million share- and bond-holders. Transactions are printed on a nationwide ticker network, and activity is centered on the trading floor, two-thirds the size of a football field, where member firms' telephoned orders to buy and sell are handled at 22 horseshoe-shaped trading posts on the main floor and in annexes. The often hectic scene, which seems almost incomprehensible to the casual visitor in the gallery, is explained on the daily tours given by the Exchange. The enormous Classic-style building was completed in 1903 by George B. Post, with a 22-story addition in 1923 by Trowbridge & Livingston. The sculpture in the pediment is by John Quincy Adams Ward and Paul W. Bartlett. The busy Stock Exchange is a far cry from the old Tontine Coffee House and buttonwood tree of 1792, when 24 brokers drew up the original trading agreement. A reminder of those days is the little buttonwood tree planted in front of the Exchange.

Until the opening of the American Stock Exchange on nearby Trinity Place, some stock transactions were conducted along the sidewalks of Broad Street, with brokers or their representatives waving frenetic hand signals signifying "buy" or "sell" orders to correspondents in adjacent buildings. This very active "Curb Exchange" is now housed in the much more modern "Amex."

Federal Hall National Memorial, built in 1842 as the U.S. Custom House, is considered the Parthenon of public buildings in the city and possibly its finest Greek Revival–style building. Its predecessor on the site was our second City Hall, which replaced the *Stadt Huys* in 1701. It was here that Peter Zenger, editor of the *New York Weekly Journal,* was tried in 1735 for "seditious libels" against the royal government, and particularly against Governor William Cosby. His acquittal for printing the truth was the first major victory in the battle for a free press. Thirty years later, the Stamp Act Congress met to draft a Declaration of Rights and Grievances in which the colonists strongly protested the imposition by England of the Stamp Act. After this first public protest by a colony against "taxation without representation" and a subsequent boycott of the hated stamps, the British government repealed the tax. On July 18, 1776, the Declaration of Independence was read here. During the Revolutionary War, the occupying British forces used the City Hall as their headquarters. After the war, The Second Continental Congress met here in 1785, and two years later passed the Northwest Ordinance (explained on the building plaque to the left). In 1789 the building was renovated under supervision of Maj. Pierre L'Enfant (who was responsible for the master plan of the City of Washington), and became the Capitol of the United States for just over a year. Congress met here for the first time on March 4, 1789, and as its first official act, counted the electoral ballots for President George Washington's unanimous election. On April 30, Washington was inaugurated on the steps of the renamed Federal Hall. **The statue of Washington,** sculpted by J. Q. A. Ward in 1883, stands at about the same place where Washington took his oath of office. Congress also adopted the Bill of Rights here on September 25, 1789, and sent it out to the states for adoption.

Unfortunately, the building later fell into disuse and was sold in 1812 for scrap for the sum of $425. In 1862, after 20 years as the Custom House, the present building became a branch of the Independent Treasury System under President Van Buren. Of the six subtreasuries established, New York's was the most important and, as the Subtreasury Building, served until 1920. One of the old thick-walled vaults may be seen inside. Federal Hall was designed by Ithiel Town and Alexander Jackson Davis, under surveillance of John Frazee

In 1826 this charming Greek Revival structure was built by the government as the New York branch of the Bank of the United States. Later, it became the Assay Office, and upon demolition in 1915 its dignified façade was carefully dismantled and later re-erected in the American Wing of the Metropolitan Museum of Art. A subsequent Assay Office occupied the site briefly, and the building was acquired by the Seamen's Bank for Savings. (The Seamen's Bank for Savings)

and Samuel Thomson, and is built of Westchester marble. The rather incongruously shaped **interior rotunda** (a circular space in a rectangular building) forms part of an extensive museum which should not be missed. [Federal Hall is open seven days a week, 9:00 A.M. to 4:30 P.M., enter on Pine Street.] It is one of seven national sites within the City of New York administered by the National Park Service of the Department of the Interior.*

The Morgan Guaranty Trust Company Building, across from Federal Hall, was formerly the offices of J. P. Morgan & Company, America's most powerful private bank. The austere building, completed in 1914 from plans by Trowbridge & Livingston, was the assumed target of an anarchist's bomb. At about noon

---

* **Castle Clinton National Monument,** in Battery Park; **The Statue of Liberty National Monument** and **Ellis Island; General Grant National Memorial,** in Riverside Park at 122nd Street; **Theodore Roosevelt Birthplace National Historic Site,** 28 East 20th Street; **Hamilton Grange National Memorial,** Convent Avenue between 141st and 142nd street; and **Federal Hall National Memorial,** Wall Street, corner of Nassau Street.

on September 16, 1920, a horse-drawn wagon parked in front of the bank exploded, killing 33 passers-by (and the horse), and injuring scores of others. The devastating blast occurred during the post–World War I period of antiradical hysteria, and was said by some to be an act of violence against "one of the strongest bastions of capitalism." Another theory is that the wagon belonged to an explosives manufacturing company, and had been traveling on a prohibited street when the dynamite accidentally ignited. Numerous scars from the explosion are plainly visible on the bank's façade—and for some reason, the bank has never made an effort to patch them up.

Continue east on Wall Street.

No. 30 Wall Street, now the **Seamen's Bank for Savings,** has an interesting architectural history. Its predecessor on the site, a lovely Greek Revival–style building designed by Martin E. Thompson, was built in 1826 as the New York branch of the Bank of the United States. After ten years the building was turned over to private banking interests, and in 1853 it was acquired by the Federal Government for the Assay Office. In 1915, the structure—by now the oldest federal edifice in the city—was demolished, but its charming Tuckahoe marble façade was carefully dismantled and stored away, to be re-erected in 1924 outside the American Wing of the Metropolitan Museum of Art. With the opening of the new American Wing in 1980, the lovely façade is now the centerpiece of the gallery. A new Assay Office was constructed on the 30 Wall Street site from plans by York & Sawyer, supervised by James A. Wetmore, and was completed in 1919, "designed to last a thousand years." However, it remained only until the most recent Assay Office was constructed at Old Slip, where Wetmore's experience was again called on for the design.

In 1955 the handsome building was purchased by the Seamen's Bank for Savings, which found the five underground floors of bullion vaults in excellent condition and preserved them for the bank's archives. The 1919 Assay Office building was considered one of the best examples of Renaissance-style architecture. Because of its quality and beauty and the architectural harmony with adjoining Federal Hall, it was decided to preserve this historic landmark and retain its limestone façade while an eight-story addition was erected above it. Architects Halsey, McCormack & Helmer incorporated the superstructure most successfully, proving that a good building need not be demolished when more space is required. In the lobby, to the right of the main banking rooms, are the original marble cornerstones of the 1826 and 1919 buildings. The Seamen's Bank for Savings maintains a collection of ship models, marine paintings, scrimshaw, antique coin banks, and sailing cards in a sixth-floor museum, and portions of the collection are part of the decor in all offices of the bank.

Across the street, at No. 37, is the Renaissance Eclectic–style building designed by Francis H. Kimball in 1907 for the Trust Company of America. At the time of its completion, it was the tallest on Wall Street.

Across from the Cotton Exchange is lofty **40 Wall Street,** built in 1929 for the Bank of the Manhattan Company. Designed by architects H. Craig

Severance and Yasuo Matsui, it was planned to be the tallest building in the world. At the same time, Severance's former partner, William Van Alen, was completing the Chrysler Building uptown—also touted to become the world's tallest. The developing rivalry led Severance to add two feet to his 40 Wall tower when it was announced that the Chrysler Building had reached its maximum height of 925 feet. To everyone's surprise (and Severance's chagrin), Van Alen's workmen secretly assembled a towering stainless-steel spire *inside* the building, and raised the Chrysler Building to a record height of 1,046 feet— the uncontested winner. Within nine months, however, Severance enjoyed the last laugh, as the newly completed Empire State Building rose almost 40 feet higher! The Bank of the Manhattan Company (since merged with the Chase National Bank to become the sprawling Chase Manhattan Bank) began its career as the city's first water supply company, a quasi-public utility known as **The Manhattan Company.** Founded by Aaron Burr in 1799, and chartered by the State Legislature, the company was the target of severe criticism from Alexander Hamilton, for the terms of the charter permitted it to engage in rather disparate financial pursuits, including banking. Hamilton saw this as an opportunity for Burr to gain banking privileges for his political party. This was one of the first confrontations between the two men that ultimately led to their tragic duel in 1804. The Manhattan Company did provide water to the growing city by means of pine-wood pipes bringing water from a reservoir on Chambers Street; however, banking became its primary interest. When the Croton Water System was opened in 1842, the Bank of the Manhattan Company became a financial institution exclusively, ultimately merging with the Chase National Bank to become today's Chase Manhattan Bank. Nevertheless, its assets are still "liquid." [*See* pages 58 and 59.]

The imposing Classic façade of the **Citibank Building** at No. 55 (the southeast corner of William Street) is a dominant landmark on Wall Street. The original ground floor was built in 1836–42, from plans by Isaiah Rogers, as the Merchants Exchange. An earlier Merchants Exchange was destroyed in the Great Fire of 1835. From 1862 to 1907 it served as the Custom House after moving from its former Federal Hall site. When the present Custom House at Bowling Green was opened, the vacant building was remodeled for the National City Bank by the firm of McKim, Mead & White [Stanford White was murdered the year before; *see* Madison Square, 11], and a second tier was added, doubling the size of the building. Note that the lower colonnade is Ionic, the upper, Corinthian. In designating the building a landmark, the New York City Landmarks Preservation Commission called it "a remarkable example of how a notable building can be sympathetically extended." The successor, the First National City Bank, now Citibank, chartered in 1812 and an outgrowth of the First Bank of the United States, still occupies the impressive structure.

Turn right into William Street, to the corner of Exchange Place.

Named for William Beekman, who came from Holland with Peter Stuyvesant (not for King William of England, as is commonly believed), **William Street** forms another of the deep, winding canyons that give the neighborhood so much atmosphere. Beekman's descendants settled farther uptown in the area now known as Beekman Place [*see* East River Panoramas, 6].

The 20 Exchange Place Building (also known as No. 22 William Street and No. 65 Beaver Street) is a striking 57-story limestone Art Deco shaft on an irregularly shaped base, designed by Cross & Cross and completed in 1931. Formerly the City Bank Farmers Trust Company and later the First National City Trust Company, it is now one of the major buildings of Citibank. The history of coinage is vividly displayed on plaques above the ground-floor windows (even our old Buffalo Nickel is there!). A "Bridge of Sighs" connects with the No. 55 Wall Street Citibank building. Although the street pattern is helter-skelter, the tower of the tall building conforms to the north-south city grid.

The west side of William Street, between Exchange Place and Beaver Street, is still in the late 19th century. **The Lords Court Building** (27 William Street and 40 Exchange Place) is a functional Renaissance-style structure of ca. 1895 with the usual ornamentation found on the first skyscrapers built with structural-steel skeletons. The tiny adjacent building, **No. 23,** somehow survived—no doubt because of its small, irregular plot—and was likely an early residence, and later a bank. Note the ornate hooded lintels over the windows and the classic cornice supported by four console brackets—a real anachronism among its lofty neighbors. **No. 15,** built in 1894 for the Farmers Loan & Trust Company, is similar in dimensions to the Lords Court Building, but has a far more ornate façade. The horizontal courses and "columns" of recessed windows break up the feeling of verticality created by the "arches" of windows. Once a commercial building, it is now a residential apartment house, converted under the J-51 program that provides for both property-tax abatements and the forgiveness of property taxes to encourage the renovation of run-down buildings.

The former Delmonico's Restaurant, at 56 Beaver Street, was founded in 1827 by Peter and John Delmonico, recent immigrants from Italy. In 1836 they built Beaver Street House for their establishment, which remained until the present building, designed by James Lord, replaced it in 1890. Another branch of the famous restaurant was operated on Madison Square, and later at Fifth Avenue and 44th Street. The establishment was always fashionable, and in Moses King's 1893 *Handbook of New York City,* it is described as "a familiar name among the epicures of two continents for nearly three-quarters of a century . . . where it will cost you from $3 upward for a good dinner" (a high price in those days!). The building was converted to residential apartments under the J-51 program soon after the demise of Delmonico's in 1980.

Across William Street (now called South William Street) was the investment banking house of **Lehman Brothers,** now at 55 Water Street. The building was erected in 1907 in a Renaissance Revival style from plans by Francis H. Kimball and Julian C. Levi, for the banking firm of J. & W. Seligman & Company (who are still in business at 65 Broadway). The cupola set above an indented corner can best be seen from a distance.

Continue down South William Street to Mill Lane.

South William Street was originally called Mill Street, and near this site in 1626, the Dutch West India Company had erected a large mill. Not only did it grind flour, but its large upper room served as a house of worship for the first settlers until their Reformed Church was completed within Fort Amsterdam (on the site of the present Custom House). The room later served the first Jewish immigrants, who had arrived in 1653 but were not permitted to hold services until several years later. Two millstones from the old mill are preserved in the Spanish & Portuguese Synagogue at 8 West 70th Street [*see* West of Central Park, 1]. It was here, too, that on August 29, 1664, the Dutch formally signed the document of surrender of Nieuw Amsterdam to the English.

The view down Mill Lane to Stone Street (visited earlier in the tour) is in sharp contrast to the surrounding tall buildings, and with a little squinting it is not difficult to imagine oneself back in the early 19th century.

Farther down South William Street, at No. 26, is the **site of the first synagogue in America,** built in 1730. An informative plaque with an early map of New York may be seen on the building just beyond the garage.

Return to Beaver Street, and proceed to Hanover Street and turn left.

Note again the coin motifs on the 65 Beaver Street entrance of the 20 Exchange Place Building, this time Biblical coins, as well as the transportation motifs of the 1920s on the bronze doors. The corner of the building at the

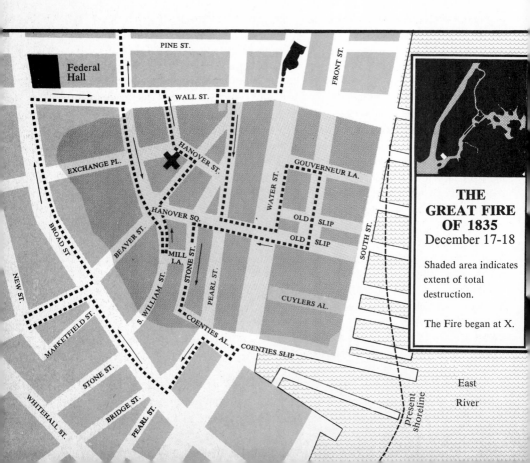

THE GREAT FIRE OF 1835
December 17-18

Shaded area indicates extent of total destruction.

The Fire began at X.

The Merchants' Exchange ablaze during the Great Fire of 1835, the worst conflagration in the city's history. A valiant attempt was made to rescue the statue of Alexander Hamilton (seen in this lithograph brightly lit by the flames) but the cupola, tilting dangerously, collapsed through the roof and shattered the sculpture. (New-York Historical Society)

juncture of Beaver and Hanover streets is the **site of the Great Fire of 1835** (*see* map).

At nine o'clock in the evening on December 17, fire broke out in the store of Comstock & Adams at 25 Merchant Street (the street has since been de-mapped). The temperature had dropped to a near record −17° and a howling gale was blowing. The fire, caused by a gas-pipe explosion, spread rapidly to adjoining buildings and within minutes the blaze raged out of control, fed by stores of dry goods and chemicals and driven by the wind. Fire companies fought desperately but ineffectively to stem the conflagration, hampered by frozen hydrants and hoses that became clogged almost instantly with ice. As the fire advanced in both east and west directions, whole blocks seemed to erupt sponta-neously into flames. By the early morning hours the blaze had engulfed almost every block to the East River from Wall Street to Coenties Slip, and west nearly to Broad Street. Help was summoned from as far away as Philadelphia, and pump wagons were hastily put aboard freight cars of the newly built railroad and transported to New York. It is said that the flame-reddened sky was visible as far away as Camden, New Jersey, and New Haven, Connecticut. By noon the following day, the fire had consumed all of Hanover Square, including the

The corner of Broad and Wall streets in 1882. In the center, the former New York Stock Exchange Building dominates Broad Street, and to the left are the banking offices of Drexel, Morgan & Company (now the site of the Morgan Guaranty Trust Co.). (The J. Clarence Davies Collection, Museum of the City of New York)

merchandise that had been saved from threatened buildings and stacked for protection in the square. Adding to the horror were mobs of looters who converged on the area and overwhelmed the small police force in their mad scramble to steal what had not been burned. A supply of gunpowder was obtained from the Navy Yard in Brooklyn and rowed across the East River to blast a firebreak and hopefully to contain the still-roaring inferno. Fortunately, the masonry walls of the line of buildings along Wall Street helped contain the flames, although the magnificent Merchants Exchange, one of the city's commercial and architectural showplaces, was itself completely destroyed. By late December 18, the fire burned itself out, leaving an area of 17 blocks—about 20 acres—a smoldering field of ashes, with the incredible loss of 674 buildings from the very heart of the financial district! The disaster was compounded by the total destruction of many fire insurance companies, which left their insureds with no chance of compensation. The 1835 fire was the worst in our young nation's history and completely obliterated every remaining Dutch Colonial building in the city. That is why there is not a single structure left in Manhattan from the 17th century. As if this were not enough, another fire ten years later destroyed 345 buildings in the same general area.

Wall Street in 1864, seen from the Subtreasury Building. In the rear is the Merchants' Exchange, rebuilt after the Great Fire of 1835, now sporting another story as the Citibank Building—and the only building in the view still standing. (Museum of the City of New York)

A classic view of Wall Street, Trinity Church and the Subtreasury Building (now Federal Hall), as seen in a magic lantern slide photo taken about 1875. (The Picture Decorator, Inc., N.Y.C.)

Continue on Hanover Street to Wall Street.

The building to the right, **No. 63 Wall Street,** is also decorated with coin plaques—drachmas of Ancient Greece on large plaques above the fourth floor.

Turn left on Wall Street to the northeast corner of William Street.

The view to Trinity Church down Wall Street is one of the best known scenes of New York. [Trinity Church is described in the tour of Lower Broadway and the Battery, *see* pages 10 and 11.]

The oldest commercial bank in the country is the **Bank of New York,** founded by Alexander Hamilton in 1784. Several plaques describe its history, including the story of its predecessor on the site, the United States Branch Bank. The original cornerstone of the Bank of New York has been reset several times for each new building in its history. A low-relief bronze plaque above the subway entrance, commemorating the famous Wall, includes an early map, and was placed there in 1909 during the Hudson-Fulton Celebration. The building, long a landmark in the lower Manhattan skyline, was designed in 1927 by Benjamin Wistar Morris. It is a graceful structure with a Georgian-style cupola and lantern, best seen at a distance.

Turn right (north) on William Street to Pine Street.

To the left soars the 800-foot aluminum and glass **Chase Manhattan Bank,** set on one of the largest plazas in the city. When completed in 1960 it was the trendsetter for the series of plazas to follow, conforming to the revised zoning regulations requiring more street-level space. The plaza is elevated at the William Street end due to the topography. Take a few minutes and climb the stairs to the plaza level. The sunken circular courtyard with its fountain is paved with granite blocks in an unusual undulating form. It was originally planned to have fish and even dolphins in the fountain, but the idea was quickly abandoned because of the dangers of pollution (by air and people). Sculptor Isamu Noguchi is responsible for the innovative design, and Skidmore, Owings & Merrill for the towering 800-foot aluminum and glass shaft. Stand beneath the edge of the lofty building and listen as the wind plays delicate tunes on the vertical metal strips. Dominating the plaza is Jean Dubuffet's enormous free-form white and black sculpture, *Group of Four Trees,* the subject of considerable comment since its installation in 1972. A weekday visit to the building's concourse reveals an atomic clock run by gamma rays from its cesium power supply; and to the left of the lobby a charming Japanese garden. The 60th-floor restaurant provides a spectacular view of the Financial District and its surrounding waterways. There are guided tours of the building (telephone for schedule), which include many antiques and works of art in the executive offices, as well as paintings from president David Rockefeller's private collection. The building also houses the world's largest bank vault, five levels below ground. The vaults are reputed to hold over $40 billion in securities, and just a few scant millions in cash. The bank is the successor to the Bank of the Manhattan Company and the Chase National Bank. The latter was named for Salmon P. Chase, Secretary of the Treasury in Lincoln's administration, and founder of our national currency system and the federal banking system. (There was no government-issued paper money prior to 1861.) Chase Manhattan occupies the first 35 of the 60 stories above ground.

Continue north on William Street to Liberty Street.

The Federal Reserve Bank of New York, occupying the entire block between Liberty Street and Maiden Lane, is *the* great bank for banks—one of 12 of our Federal Reserve System. A Florentine *palazzo* that would have warmed the heart of Lorenzo de' Medici, it is actually based on the design of the Strozzi Palace of the Italian Renaissance. Completed in 1924 from plans by York & Sawyer, the Federal Reserve Bank is a dramatic and imposing structure with its massive walls of rusticated Ohio sandstone and Indiana limestone, fortresslike machicolations, and extensive wrought-iron ornamentation. The lovely triple lanterns and the window grilles in the great arched windows were executed by Samuel Yellin. An enormous subterranean vault five stories below street level and protected by 90-ton doors contains gold bullion stored for many foreign governments; when trade balances are settled, gold is moved from one nation's room to another, rarely leaving the building. The tremendous volume of check handling and coin operations can be seen on visitors' tours, which begin in the impressive entrance lobby on Liberty Street (telephone 791-6130 for reservations). All paper currency issued by the Government through the New York branch of the Federal Reserve Bank bears the letter *B* on the face of each note. Bank notes issued by the Federal Reserve Bank in Boston have an *A,* Philadelphia, *C,* etc., through San Francisco, *L.* The Federal Reserve System, our nation's central banking establishment, was organized in 1913. All national banks must belong to a regional branch and keep a specific cash reserve on deposit. It is said that the vaults here house more gold than does Fort Knox.

Louise Nevelson Plaza, the triangular plot where Liberty Street joins Maiden Lane, and once the site of the Germania Life Insurance Building, has been remodeled into an outdoor gallery of the sculptor's work. *Shadows and Flags* dominates the little plaza.

The Home Insurance Company Building occupies a neat little plaza between Maiden Lane and John Street. Designed by the office of Alfred Easton Poor, the building was completed in 1966. Enter on a weekday and zip up to the 15th floor for a visit to the **Harold V. Smith Firefighting Museum,** maintained by the Home Insurance Company. On display is the world's finest and most extensive collection of firefighting memorabilia. A splendid gooseneck fire pumper of 1838, named *Hope* (which was designed three years too late for use in the Great Fire), competes with one that saw service in the Great Fire of London of 1666. The American *Hope* was considered elegant enough to participate in President Grover Cleveland's inaugural parade. The Museum also boasts a large collection of fire marks—decorative plaques that early fire-insur-

Intersection of William Street and Maiden Lane, looking west, ca. 1760. The site is now occupied by The Home Insurance Company Building. In this E. P. Chrystie drawing, a beer barrel is being lowered from the third floor of Rutgers' Brew House. During the British occupation of New York it was a storehouse. (The Home Insurance Company)

ance companies and volunteer brigades required homeowners to display prominently on their house fronts, or the fire would not be extinguished and compensation would not be paid. There is also a fine collection of Currier & Ives prints on "The Life of a Fireman," and many working models of old-time firefighting apparatus. The *pièce de résistance,* however, is the detailed re-creation of the firehouse of Eagle Engine Company No. 13, which in 1790 was located on Maiden Lane near Gold Street. A plaque in the triangular plaza marks the site of Thomas Jefferson's residence while he lived in New York City serving as the nation's first Secretary of State. New York was the seat of the federal government when Jefferson took office on March 21, 1790.

No. 100 William Street, on the northeast corner of Platt Street, is the city's first building to take advantage of the special 1970 zoning resolution that encouraged builders to create a covered pedestrian space as an alternative to the open plaza—outdoor space that was often uninspired and of minimal utilitarian design and, of course, subject to the vagaries of the weather. This 21-story building, sheathed in green slate, was completed in 1972 from plans by Davis, Brody & Associates with Emery Roth & Sons. Taking advantage of provisions of the new law, the architects have designed an impressive 80-foot *galleria,* cutting diagonally through the ground floor of the building, providing an attractive arcade between William and John streets. The arcade is lined with shops, lit in part by angular windows and light troughs. The building received the Award for Excellence in Design for 1973 from the New York Society of Architects. A central escalator leads to the office of Chubb & Sons, one of the city's largest insurance brokerage houses. Walk through the stainless-steel, black glass, and slate *galleria* (open weekdays only).

Continue to the corner of John Street.

About a hundred yards to the east, at the present corner of John and Gold streets, was a small hillock covered with bright yellow flowers, which the Dutch had called *De Gouwenberg,* or Golden Hill. On January 18, 1770, it was the site of the first bloodshed between the colonists and the British army. Tempers had been running high since the imposition of the hated tax on tea, and particularly over the event of the previous night when soldiers knocked down a Liberty Pole and deposited the remnants in front of a tavern that was the meeting place of the Sons of Liberty. That afternoon several thousand citizens massed in "The Fields" near Broadway to vow punishment to any soldiers caught armed in the streets. The British reacted with taunts and ridicule, and after a series of provocative acts on both sides, a running brawl broke out between the mob and 20 British soldiers. Both groups then retired to nearby Golden Hill where they were met by a detachment of regulars who opened fire on the civilians, killing one and wounding several. The encounter, known as the **Battle of Golden Hill,** occurred two months before the Boston Massacre and five years before the first major hostilities at Bunker Hill.

Turn left on John Street.

The John Street United Methodist Church, built in 1841, is the third on the site. The first Methodist church in America was built on this site in 1768, and traces its roots to John Wesley, the founder of Methodism. Under the leadership of Philip Embury and Barbara Heck, the congregation, which had been meeting in a rigging loft on Horse and Cart Street (now William Street), established the meeting house. Since that time the building has been rebuilt twice, in 1818 and 1841, and was restored in 1965. Spend a moment and enjoy the intimate quality of the Georgian-style interior, including the original Wesley Chapel. Built in late Georgian style, the church is somewhat austere, yet cozy and inviting. Many of the original artifacts from the 1768 chapel still remain, including candelabra, John Wesley's great clock, foot warmers, and Embury's hand-carved pulpit. Climb the narrow staircase to the gallery for a good perspective of the interior. The small brownstone church is a delightful and welcome surprise in the bustling financial district.

Knighthood is in flower again, in the shape of **33 Maiden Lane,** a striking example of post-modernism in skyscraper construction. The 26-story office tower, designed by Philip Johnson and John Burgee, offers one of the most unusual and eye-catching features of any of the new creatively conceived high-rise buildings, the crenellated towers. Nicknamed "A Landmark Among Landmarks," its plan is intended to be contextual with the adjacent fortresslike Federal Reserve Bank. The Johnson/Burgee partnership is also responsible for the iconoclastic headquarters building of the American Telephone and Telegraph Company at 550 Madison Avenue.

End of tour. Walk west to Broadway, and right one block to Fulton Street, for nearest subway stations.

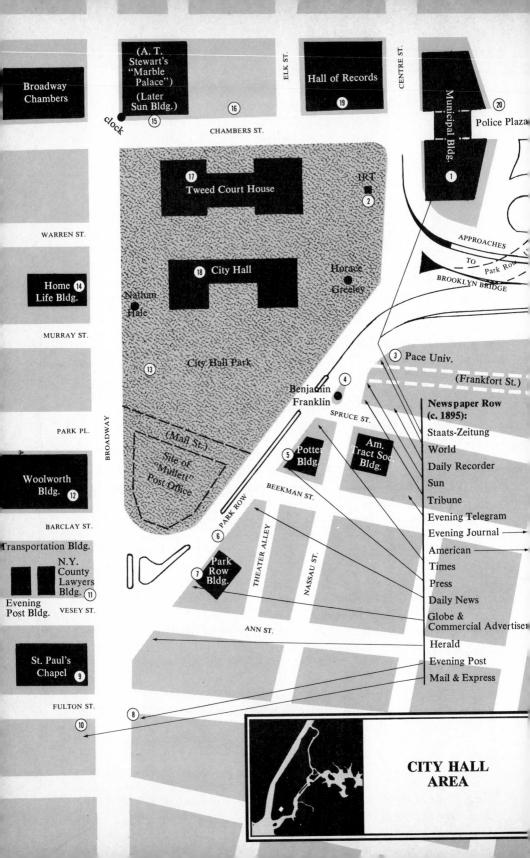

Broadway
Chambers

(A. T.
Stewart's
"Marble
Palace")
(Later
Sun Bldg.)
clock
(15)

(16)

ELK ST.

Hall of Records

(19)

CENTRE ST.

Municipal Bldg.

(1)

(20)

Police Plaza

CHAMBERS ST.

(17) Tweed Court House

IRT
(2)

WARREN ST.

Home
Life Bldg. (14)

(18) City Hall

Nathan
Hale

Horace
Greeley

APPROACHES

TO Park Row

BROOKLYN BRIDGE

MURRAY ST.

City Hall Park

(13)

(3) Pace Univ.

(Frankfort St.)

Benjamin
Franklin

(4)

SPRUCE ST.

Newspaper Row
(c. 1895):

PARK PL.

BROADWAY

(Mail St.)
Site of
"Mullett"
Post Office

Potter
Bldg.

(5)

Am.
Tract Soc.
Bldg.

BEEKMAN ST.

Staats-Zeitung

World

Daily Recorder

Sun

Woolworth
Bldg. (12)

Tribune

Evening Telegram

BARCLAY ST.

Transportation Bldg.

N.Y.
County
Lawyers
Bldg. (11)

Evening
Post Bldg.

(6)

PARK ROW

(7) Park
Row
Bldg.

THEATER ALLEY

NASSAU ST.

Evening Journal

American

Times

Press

Daily News

Globe &
Commercial Advertiser

VESEY ST.

ANN ST.

Herald

St. Paul's
Chapel

(9)

Evening Post

Mail & Express

FULTON ST.

(10)

(8)

CITY HALL
AREA

3. City Hall, Old "Newspaper Row," Foley Square, and "Five Points"

[*IRT Lexington Avenue Line to Brooklyn Bridge; BMT Nassau Street J Line to Chambers Street; M-101 or M-102 bus to City Hall*]

The tour begins at Centre and Chambers streets.

1. Classic in style and original in design, the imposing **Municipal Building** is our greatest civic skyscraper and the focus of the new Civic Center plan. In scale it is complementary to nearby City Hall as well as to the modern counterparts mushrooming about it. Built in 1914 from plans by McKim, Mead & White, it now houses only a fraction of the city offices which oversee the functioning of the metropolis. Particularly attractive is the row of freestanding columns, the extensive sculpture work, and the lofty colonnaded tower topped by Adolph A. Weinman's 25-foot high gilt statue of *Civic Fame.* Pause for a moment to examine the sculpture: on the north arch, *Progress;* on the north panel, *Civic Duty;* on the central arch, *Guidance* and *Executive Power;* on the south panel, *Civic Pride;* and on the south arch, *Prudence.* Between the windows on the second floor are symbols of the various city departments. Note the collection of plaques, among which is the "triple-X" emblem of the city of Amsterdam, Holland. A lavish subway entrance is incorporated into the south section, under a vaulted ceiling. Chambers Street, which originally passed through the building, is now closed to vehicular traffic and forms a part of a pedestrian mall leading to Police Plaza. (We will return later after a loop around City Hall Park.)

Cross Centre Street to City Hall Park.

2. Go down the IRT subway stairs directly in front of the Greeley statue. At the foot of the staircase, mounted on the right-hand wall, are three enormous bronze plaques honoring those responsible for the construction of **"The First Municipal Rapid Transit Railroad of the City of New York."** The subway, a brainchild of financier August Belmont, took four years (and three mayors) to build (1900–04). The first station, City Hall, is no longer in service, although local IRT trains still rumble past it on a loop underneath City Hall Park. The original line followed the present Lexington Avenue route to Grand Central, swung west under 42nd Street to Times Square, then north on Broadway to 145th Street.

The **statue of Horace Greeley** in the park was executed in 1890 by John Quincy Adams Ward, and was moved here from its former site in front of the Tribune Building in 1916. Ward was the first American sculptor not trained abroad. His sculpture is typical of post–Civil War realism and captures the relaxed attitude, moon face, and odd beard of the *Tribune*'s founder. The base is by Richard Morris Hunt.

Continue south about 100 yards.

3. Across Park Row (Centre Street joins it at this point), where modern Pace University is situated, was the beginning of the so-called **"Newspaper Row"** from the 1840s till after the turn of the century. In the year 1893, for example, there were 19 daily newspapers printed in the City of New York plus a score of foreign-language papers. In the year 1982, there were only three, yet the population of the city has grown from a million and a half in 1893 to almost five times that number!

Where the Municipal Building's south section is now was the site of the building of the *New-Yorker Staats-Zeitung,* the largest German-language newspaper in the country (and still publishing). To the right of the intertwining ramps of the Brooklyn Bridge stood the 26-story gold-domed *New York World,* the tallest building in the world when completed in 1890. Designed by George B. Post, the "World Tower" was a dominant feature of the lower Manhattan skyline. After Joseph Pulitzer purchased the *World* seven years earlier, the newspaper soon became one of the most literate and influential in the city.

Immediately to its right, across narrow Frankfort Street, stood the **Sun Building.** The *Sun* really "shone" after its acquisition by Charles Anderson Dana, becoming the city's first penny newspaper, with a broad popular appeal. The paper lived out its remaining years in a building which will be discussed shortly.

Adjacent to the *Sun* stood the exuberant Victorian Gothic–style **Tribune Building,** designed by famed architect Richard Morris Hunt and built in 1873. The *Tribune* was founded by Horace ("Go west, young man") Greeley in 1841, and soon was acknowledged as New York's most important newspaper. When Greeley departed from the *Tribune* to help found the Republican party, he

*City Hall and its panorama of newspaper office buildings around 1910. Left to right,
the domed* World, *the diminutive* Sun, *and Richard Morris Hunt's* Tribune Tower.
The Times *had moved uptown from the large building at the right. Between City Hall
and the* World *is the Park Row terminal of the Second Avenue El, connected to a large
iron train shed serving Brooklyn Bridge trains. Note the kiosk entrance to the now-
abandoned City Hall subway station (although trains still roll by its darkened platform
underneath). (New-York Historical Society)*

left the management to Whitelaw Reid, himself an active political leader (minister
to France and unsuccessful candidate for vice-president in 1892). Reid was
one of a line of distinguished journalists who began their careers on the *"Trib"*;
others were Carl Schurz, William Dean Howells, Charles A. Dana, Henry James,
Bayard Taylor, and Margaret Fuller, to name but a few. When the Tribune
Tower was demolished, the city lost a great architectural treasure.

4. A bit farther we see little **Printing House Square** with Ernst Plassman's
statue of Benjamin Franklin, presented in 1872. Behind Franklin, at the corner
of Spruce Street, is the former **American Tract Society Building.** Designed in
1896 by R. H. Robertson, it is a massive Romanesque Revival–style edifice
that no longer houses any religious publishing concern, and is known merely
by its address, No. 150 Nassau Street.

A block east of Printing House Square, on William Street, were William Randolph Hearst's *New York American* (an outgrowth of the earlier *Morning Journal*) and the *New York Evening Journal*. His *Journal* represented the archetype of "yellow journalism," as its rabble rousing and drum beating were held in great part responsible for our entry into the Spanish-American War.

To the right, at the corner of Park Row (No. 41), is the **former New York Times Building,** now an integral part of the Pace campus. Designed in 1889 by George B. Post, and later remodeled by Robert Maynicke (1895), it housed the *Times* until its move to Longacre Square (now Times Square) in 1904. Note the plaque commemorating "Newspaper Row."

5. Abutting the former New York Times Building is the dazzlingly ornate **Potter Building** (38 Park Row), constructed in 1883. It has two "firsts" to its name, as the earliest surviving edifice built with a structural steel framework, and the first to sport an ornamental terra-cotta façade in both cast and pressed forms. The fireproof quality of terra cotta was appropriately chosen, as the predecessor on the site, the old New York World Building, was destroyed a year before in one of the city's most spectacular blazes. For a time, the *Press* was published in the Potter Building.

To the right rear, at 5 Beekman Street, are the twin pyramidal towers of the curious **Temple Court Building.**

6. "Newspaper Row" continued with a line of five-story brick buildings that housed a number of popular dailies. The *New York Daily News,* at 26

The Park Theater ca. 1820 on Park Row, facing City Hall. One of the nation's first legitimate theaters, it was built at the time of the American Revolution. (Consolidated Edison Company of New York)

Park Row, was a relatively small evening paper at the turn of the century, and pro-Democratic at that. Adjoining was the *Morning Advertiser,* and two doors farther, the *Mail and Express.* Cyrus Field purchased the *Evening Mail* and the *Evening Express* in 1880 and 1882 respectively, and made them a financially successful enterprise. He later housed them in an interesting, rococo, T-shaped building near the corner of Fulton Street. The *Recorder* was at No. 21 and nearby, the *Evening Telegram.* Near Ann Street was the *Globe and Commercial Advertiser,* at the time the oldest newspaper in New York, dating from 1797.

7. When completed in 1899, the **Park Row Building,** at No. 15, was one of the tallest in the world. Its twin cupolas added interest and variety to the growing skyline. The skyscraper was designed by R. H. Robertson, and the four caryatids (including the 16 figures on the cupola) are attributed to J. Massey Rhind. The Park Row Building was also the birthplace of the Associated Press.

At the southeast corner of Park Row and Ann Street stood the white marble French Second Empire **Herald Building.** Founded in 1835 by James Gordon Bennett, it soon gained popularity for its frequent "scoops," as well as for printing news of the financial world. Although a penny newspaper, it made Bennett a fortune. His son, James Gordon Bennett, Jr., startled the "Fourth Estate" by moving the *Herald* uptown in 1894 to a magnificent McKim, Mead & White *palazzo* on what is now Herald Square. Although the Herald Building is now gone from the uptown square, the Bennett Clock still rings the hours while figures with hammers strike an enormous bell. The building on "Newspaper Row" was later replaced by the 25-story St. Paul Building, which in turn was razed for the present Western Electric Building.

8. Occupying the same relative position one block south was the **Evening Post Building.** Founded in 1801 by Alexander Hamilton, the *Evening Post* was possibly the most conservative of all New York dailies. Under the leadership of editor William Cullen Bryant, the paper spoke out for free trade. Bryant, by the way, staunchly opposed allowing women to enter the journalism field. Later, under Carl Schurz, the paper adopted a more liberal attitude, both politically and toward women. In 1906 it moved to new quarters on Vesey Street (to be seen shortly).

9. The oldest church in Manhattan (and the oldest building as well) is magnificent **St. Paul's Chapel.** Turning its back on Broadway, it faces a peaceful churchyard, oblivious to the noise and clamor of the crowded thoroughfare. St. Paul's, a chapel of Trinity Church downtown, was completed in 1766, the tower and steeple in 1796. Architect Thomas McBean undoubtedly was influenced by London's St. Martin's-in-the-Fields when he designed this majestic landmark. It is built of locally quarried Manhattan schist, and the tower (by James Crommelin Lawrence) is of brownstone. The church is an almost perfect example of Georgian style, reflecting the elegant tradition of the Colonial period. Much of the interior decoration of this National Historic Landmark was done by Pierre L'Enfant, the French-born architect who later became a Major of Engineers in the Continental Army and laid out the City of Washington, D.C. One can still see the pew where Washington regularly worshiped. Among the

list of distinguished worshipers were Prince William (later King William IV), Lords Cornwallis and Howe, Maj. John André, the Marquis de Lafayette, and Presidents Grover Cleveland and Benjamin Harrison. [*See* pages 3 and 4 for a description of the interior.]

The quiet churchyard is well worth a visit. Note the numerous 18th-century headstones with names of well-known families of early New York.

To the right of the churchyard on Vesey Street are two interesting landmark buildings. At No. 20 is the **Garrison Building,** formerly the home of the *Evening Post,* from 1907 to 1926. This is a rare example of Art Nouveau architecture. The bronze-finished cast-iron spandrels are decorated with the colophons of well-known 16th- and 17th-century printers, and the statues on the ninth floor represent "The Four Periods of Publicity," by Gutzon Borglum and Estelle Rumbold Kohn. The building, designed by Robert D. Kohn, was completed in 1906.

To its right, at No. 14, is the **New York County Lawyers Association Building**—"the Home of Law." Constructed in 1930 of Vermont marble and limestone, it was designed by Cass Gilbert in a neo-Federal style. Its auditorium is a reproduction of Independence Hall in Philadelphia. Vesey Street is named for William Vesey, first rector of Trinity Church.

10. Looking south from the churchyard, across Fulton Street, is the multi-columned **American Telephone & Telegraph Building,** built in 1917 from plans by Welles Bosworth. It was formerly crowned with a gilt statue, *The Spirit of Communication,* by Evelyn Beatrice Longman; but the statue was removed and will be placed in the lobby of AT&T's new headquarters at 550 Madison Avenue. A weekday visit to the spacious lobby reveals an interesting and educational display, including sculptor Chester Beach's marble and bronze statue, *Service to the Nation.* Interestingly, the American "Tel & Tel" Building, with its eight tiers of colonnades, has more columns than the Parthenon—or any other building, for that matter.

11. Turn north on Broadway to No. 225. The **Transportation Building,** designed by York & Sawyer in 1915, occupies the site of one of New York's most celebrated hostelries, the Astor House, which catered to affluent visitors from 1836 to 1913. Note the wall plaque with its low-relief representation of the Astor House in its heyday.

12. Possibly the most beautiful commercial building in the world is the dramatic Gothic Revival–style **Woolworth Building.** When dedicated in 1913, the Rev. S. Parkes Cadman, a famous New York clergyman, in a burst of enthusiastic rhetoric, referred to it as a "Cathedral of Commerce"—and the sobriquet still stands. Many believe it to be architect Cass Gilbert's greatest triumph. Rising 729 feet (plus 1 inch!), the Woolworth Tower eclipsed the Metropolitan Life Tower to become the tallest building in the world for 17 years. The opening ceremony was climaxed when President Wilson pressed a button in Washington, illuminating 80,000 bulbs on the 60-story structure. Two years later, at the Panama-Pacific Exposition, it received a gold medal as the "most beautiful building in all the world erected to commerce." The observation deck on the 55th floor, which unfortunately is no longer open to the public,

The Federal Building at the intersection of Broadway and Park Row became the city's main post office in 1875. An elaborate Second Empire pile designed by government architect A. B. Mullett, it obstructed the view of City Hall until its demolition just before World War II. (Museum of the City of New York)

provided a breathtaking view, as visitors were whisked to the top at dizzying speed in the newest in high-speed electric elevators.

Frank Woolworth, the founder of the ubiquitous five-and-ten-cent-store chain, paid the $15,500,000 cost of the building in cash! Note the typical Gothic elements: gargoyles, flying buttresses, arches, spires, traceries, trefoils, etc., all seen to good advantage after an extensive face-lifting of the entire building. The style is followed in the interior as well. The lobby presents one of the most striking interior spaces in the city, with its vaulted, mosaic ceiling that sparkles in a jewellike effect; the delicate bronzework; the walls of veined marble; an imposing grand staircase; lacy wrought-iron cornices covered with gold leaf; polished terrazzo floors; and the amusing little sculptured caricatures of Mr. Woolworth (counting his nickels and dimes), Cass Gilbert (holding a model of his pet project), Louis Horowitz, the builder, and others involved with the construction of the "Cathedral." The 25th-floor office of Frank Woolworth, who died in 1919, is preserved as a private museum. (Ask the guard for a free descriptive leaflet.)

13. Cross Broadway to **City Hall Park.** Called the Common in the 18th century, it was then at the northern edge of the city, a triangular plot formed by the confluence of the Bloomingdale Road (now Broadway) and the Boston Post Road (now Park Row and farther north, the Bowery). On the Common a prison was constructed, and nearby, a poor house, as well as a powder house and barracks as part of the city's defenses. Just to the north was the Negroes'

Burial Ground, and a short distance to the west, King's College (now Columbia University). As the city expanded northward, it became a popular public gathering place, and figured in a series of anti-British incidents for a ten-year period prior to the Revolution, in which patriots forcefully displayed their displeasure with the Crown by harassing the military post and erecting a series of Liberty Poles. After the Revolution, the city entered an era of prosperity and growth that required the construction of a new City Hall. In 1811 the present seat of town government was erected in what was the new City Hall Park. The park was enlarged to its present size in the late 1930s with the razing of the old Federal Building that occupied most of the southern corner of the triangle and housed a post office and court. The so-called "Mullett" (after the architect) Post Office was a massive granite pile of "wedding cake" built in 1878 in the French Second Empire style; its demolition provided light and space and a sweeping view of (and from) City Hall.

A bit farther north, beyond the private driveway leading to City Hall, is the splendid **statue of Nathan Hale,** by Frederick MacMonnies, erected in the Park in 1893. Hale, a young schoolteacher captured by the British for spying early in the Revolution, shows a disdainful look as he is about to be hanged. It is doubtful that he said, "I regret that I have but one life to lose for my country." Stanford White designed the pedestal. On the lawn beyond, the flagpole commemorates the raising of the five **Liberty Poles** by Colonial patriots. Those poles were anathema to the British, not only for their symbolism, but also because they were cut from the prohibited white pine, a tree reserved exclusively for the masts of His Majesty's navy. The name Sons of Liberty was first applied to those who demonstrated against the hated Stamp Act by freedom-sympathizer Lt. Col. Sir Isaac Barré, a Member of Parliament, who is remembered with a plaque on the far side of the lawn (beside City Hall) and also in the names of Barre, Vermont, and Wilkes-Barre, Pennsylvania. At the side of City Hall is a **"bishop's crook" lamppost.** Several more of these cast-iron relics have been rescued and placed around the building.

Located under Broadway, between Murray and Warren streets, was the **City's first subway.** In a short-lived experiment using compressed air for propulsion, Alfred Ely Beach constructed a 312-foot-long tube that was opened to the public in 1870. The subway was built in secret to prevent interference from corrupt "Boss" Tweed who had his own plans for mass transit. The passengers rode in a luxurious car, built to fit snugly against the tube's wall, and the "train" was propelled by air from a huge fan blowing through the tunnel. An elaborate waiting room was fully carpeted and furnished with paintings, a fountain, and even a grand piano. The entrance, waiting room, and ticket office were located at the southwest corner of Warren Street and Broadway. After his failure to secure adequate financial backing to extend the line, Beach abandoned the pneumatic underground railway a year later. In 1912, workmen excavating for the BMT subway came upon the old tube with its single car and lavish station.

14. No. 255 is the elegant former headquarters of the **Home Life Insurance Company.** Designed in Eclectic style by Napoleon LeBrun and completed in 1894, its pyramided gable atop the building is best seen from a distance.

The recently completed American Telephone & Telegraph Company Building dwarfs St. Paul's Chapel at Fulton Street and Broadway in this ca. 1919 view. Nestled in the T-shaped structure is the Victorian-style Evening Mail Building which was later demolished when AT&T extended its building to Fulton Street. To the extreme left is the St. Paul Building, now the site of the Western Electric Building. (The American Telephone & Telegraph Company)

The oldest German daily in the United States, the Staats Zeitung, began publishing in this Victorian pile on Park Row and Centre Street in the 1870s. Statues of Gutenberg and Franklin by Ernst Plassman adorn the third floor. To the right is the City Hall terminal of the Second Avenue El. The site is now occupied by the Municipal Building. (*Museum of the City of New York*)

The buildings at Centre and Chambers streets represent a variety of styles. Note the pedestrian crossings, slightly elevated so rain could run off and vehicles would slow down, and also much easier on the feet than cobblestones. (Museum of the City of New York)

The Rhinelander Building at Duane and Rose streets was demolished in 1971. The marble entrance columns as well as the barred "Old Sugar House" window are now preserved on Police Plaza. (New York City Landmarks Preservation Commission)

Mulberry Street with its infamous "bend" between Park and Bayard streets in the early 1880s was, and remains, heavily Italian. Mulberry Bend Park (later Columbus Park) replaced the buildings on the left side of the street. (New-York Historical Society)

One of the few surviving photos (left) of the Beach Pneumatic Subway shows the approach to the Warren Street station in 1870. Below, the remains of the subway car found in a 1912 excavation. (New-York Historical Society)

At the northwest corner of Chambers Street, No. 277, the **Broadway Chambers,** designed by Cass Gilbert and completed in 1900, is a good example of "tripartite" skyscraper construction, where the building façade is divided into three basic sections, similar to the components of a Classic column.

15. Continue north to Chambers Street, where on the northeast corner is the **former A. T. Stewart "Marble Palace"** [*see* Ladies' Mile, 1]. Designed by John B. Snook and Joseph Trench, with marble cutting by Ottavino Gori, it was completed in 1846, and promptly became a trendsetter in American architecture. As the first commercial Italianate building, its *palazzo* style was copied widely; and in this extravagant edifice, the tradition of the large retail emporium was firmly established. After Stewart moved his flourishing dry-goods business uptown in 1862, he retained the building as a warehouse. His later successor added two additional floors, and in 1884 the building was converted to commercial use. In 1917, the *Sun* moved in from across the Park, publishing here until its demise in 1952. The attractive **Sun Clock** on the corner of the building, bearing the motto "The Sun it Shines for All," has been preserved through the efforts of a local committee of businessmen and city employees who raised the funds to restore it, and it has become a kind of unofficial landmark. The *Sun*'s thermometer on the opposite corner, however, remains adamantly at 40°. In 1966, New York City acquired the Sun Building, and its future is uncertain. Hopefully our City Fathers will recognize its historic and artistic value, and will find an appropriate use for it.

16. To the east at 51 Chambers Street is the twin-sectioned **Emigrant Industrial Savings Bank Building.** No longer the bank's home office, its impressive

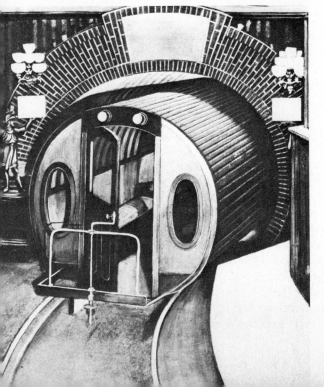

New York's first subway was the Beach Pneumatic Tube, built in 1869–70. It ran one block on Broadway from Warren Street to a point just south of Murray Street. In this rendering of the proposed car, the giant steam-operated fan which supplied the power through air pressure cannot be seen. (New-York Historical Society)

Faced with demolition as part of the projected Civic Center, the Criminal Courts Building on Chambers Street behind City Hall is a monument to civic corruption. Between $8 and $12 million of taxpayers' money went into "Boss" Tweed's pocket. The building now serves as additional office space for City Hall and houses the City Archives. (Photo by author)

double towers, topped by spread eagles and globes and built in 1908, must have inspired confidence in the strength and security of the bank. Slated for possible demolition along with the Sun Building, it is now used as municipal office space.

17. The Italianate "villa" back-to-back with City Hall is the famous (or infamous) Criminal Courts Building. Known familiarly as the **Tweed Courthouse,** it stands as a monument to graft and corruption. Completed in 1872, it took nine years to construct, and the city's treasury found itself between $8 million and $12.5 million poorer. Approximately three-quarters of that amount was diverted into the pockets of "Boss" William Marcy Tweed and his Ring. Nevertheless, the city did inherit an attractive architectural addition. Its future, however, is in question, as the Mayor's Civic Center Task Force reports that the much needed renovation would be "substantially more costly" than building a new City Hall Annex. But considerable opposition has arisen from within the administration and from the public at large, and any plans to destroy the historic Tweed Courthouse will doubtless meet with determined resistance. Visit the interior with its imposing central well, then walk to the rear to the *pièce de résistance* of the tour, City Hall.

18. The greatest architectural treasure in the city is palatial **City Hall,** built in 1811. The competition for its design was won by Frenchman Joseph F. Mangin, and Scotsman John McComb, Jr., who combined their talents to produce a French Renaissance–Georgian-style building of consummate beauty. McComb remained the guiding hand throughout the period of construction, but Mangin seems to have slipped into obscurity.

City Hall has always been the nerve center and civic hub of the metropolis, the site of many public celebrations, and the traditional place of welcome for heroes. Noteworthy were the receptions given in honor of Lafayette, the opening of the Erie Canal, the state visits of a parade of royalty, the welcoming of Lindbergh in 1927, and, in more recent times, of the hometown winners of the baseball World Series. The rotunda of City Hall was also the laying-in-state site of a number of famous citizens: Maj. Gen. William J. Worth [see Madison Square, 18], Horace Greeley, John Howard Payne, President U. S. Grant, and Mayors Gaynor and Mitchell. Nothing, however, could equal the homage paid to Abraham Lincoln after his assassination, when his remains lay in the rotunda on April 24 and 25, 1865. In the following funeral procession, 60,000 New Yorkers joined in the mournful parade up Broadway.

The structure has undergone many renovations and repairs throughout its history. The first addition was an illuminated public clock—the first in the city—installed in the cupola in 1831. In the same year an ugly fire tower was erected on the roof, remaining for 34 years until the volunteer fire department was replaced by a paid staff. In 1858 City Hall suffered extensive damage in a

City Hall, 1826, from a colored aquatint by W. G. Hall. Mangin and McComb's French Renaissance and Georgian-style building, completed in 1811, is considered one of New York's greatest architectural treasures. (The J. Clarence Davies Collection, Museum of the City of New York)

roaring blaze resulting from a fireworks display on the roof during the Atlantic Cable Celebration. Following the fire, City Hall began to deteriorate, neglected through the years by many corrupt city administrations. Someone referred to those days as the "tobacco juice period," as the building became more and more decrepit and dismal. It was even suggested that City Hall be demolished in favor of a new, "more modern" municipal building.

In 1895 the Board of Aldermen declared that ". . . the present appearance and condition of the City Hall is an offence to the sight of the community and a menace to the health of those whose business necessitates their presence in the building." A minor renovation followed. During the next 20 years, additional restoration was conducted with outside philanthropic assistance. In 1917, fire struck again, this time from a workman's charcoal burner in the cupola. Major reconstruction was begun under the direction of Grosvenor Atterbury, who restored the copper dome to its original appearance. Little was done, however, to save the decaying exterior until 1954, when the Board of Estimate voted the necessary funds for a complete restoration of the building. The eroded Massachusetts marble façade was carefully cut away and replaced with Alabama veined limestone, the base with Missouri red granite. The north façade, which was originally faced with brownstone ("Who would see it, since nobody of importance in those days lived north of City Hall"), was also refaced with limestone.

The **interior,** too, was completely restored to what was believed to be its original elegance. City Hall is open to the public, weekdays, 10 A.M. to 4 P.M. Among the most attractive features are the double curved staircase, the colonnaded rotunda, the Office of the President of the City Council, the City Council Chamber, the Board of Estimate Chamber, the Mayor's Reception Room, the Committee of the Whole Room (for Board of Estimate executive sessions), and the Governor's Room (now a museum) with its famous Trumbull portrait of Washington and the desk used by Washington at Federal Hall.

Return to Park Row, past the Horace Greeley statue, to the corner of Chambers Street.

19. Directly across Chambers Street is the city's second most splendid Beaux Arts–style building (after the old Custom House at Bowling Green), the **Surrogate's Court, originally the Hall of Records.** The sculpture groups at the entrance represent "New York in its Infancy" and "New York in Revolutionary Times," by Philip Martiny. The eight cornice figures are: David Pietersen de Vries, Caleb Heathcote, DeWitt Clinton, Abram S. Hewitt, Philip Hone, Peter Stuyvesant, Cadwallader D. Colden, and James Duane, all by the same sculptor. In the attic are ten allegorical figures by Henry Kirke Bush-Brown. The building dates from 1901 and was designed by architects John R. Thomas, and Horgan and Slattery. On a weekday, visit the colonnaded rotunda.

20. Cross Centre Street to the Municipal Building, and walk through to the pedestrian mall that was formerly Chambers Street into **Police Plaza.** As the first major accomplishment in the Civic Center plan, this enormous public space, together with its decorations and adjoining modern structures, is a tribute to the Office of Lower Manhattan Development, as well as to the architectural firm of Gruzen and Partners.

As you enter the Plaza, designed by landscape architect W. Paul Friedberg, turn right to the small **"prison window"** monument of the Rhinelander Sugar House, which commemorates the dismal Revolutionary War prison in which hundreds of American patriots died of starvation, neglect, and disease. When the Sugar House was demolished in 1892, a window from the prison was preserved and built into the Rhinelander Building, which occupied the site until it, too, was razed in 1968, to make way for the new Police Headquarters Building. The window was rescued again and mounted here in the Plaza.

In the center of the three-acre plaza—the city's largest public plaza—is the arresting **steel sculpture** by Bernard Rosenthal, *Five in One,* consisting of five 30-foot-high rolled steel discs which have weathered to a russet hue.

To the right are rows of newly planted honey-locust trees in front of the entrance to a five-tier **Municipal Parking Garage,** hidden beneath the Plaza. Just beyond is an 8-foot waterfall surmounted by fountains.

Looking ahead, the dominant feature of Police Plaza is the red-brick-and-concrete **Police Headquarters Building.** Designed by Gruzen & Partners in 1972, this $58 million center for "New York's Finest" is a restrained and tasteful addition to the city skyscape. Enter (ask permission at the desk), and enjoy the broad lobby with Josef Twirbutt's 20-foot-square brick sculpture, and the vista of the Municipal Building and the panorama of City Hall Park skyscrapers seen through the plate glass entrance windows.

Leaving Police Headquarters, turn left and walk down the staircase to the Madison Street entrance and the "Grecian Ruin." This **group of five Ionic marble columns** is a nostalgic artifact of the old Rhinelander Building, which stood on the site from 1892. To the east is **Murry Bergtraum High School for Business Careers,** named for a late president of the Board of Education; and behind it, a New York Telephone Company skyscraper, whose unusual height was achieved by "borrowing" the air rights from the adjacent high school.

Return to Police Plaza.

To the right is the spanking new **Federal Court House Annex** and the 12-story **Federal Metropolitan Correctional Center** (Gruzen & Partners, 1973), the lines of its gray split-faced concrete façade blending well with neighboring buildings. Note that the support columns are of the same height as those of adjoining St. Andrew's Church and the Municipal Building. A special type of tinted shatterproof glass with built-in alarm system has been installed in the prison section, replacing the traditional gloomy look of barred windows.

St. Andrew's Church was consecrated in 1939, replacing an earlier church, named Carroll Hall, built in 1842. Just before the Civil War when the City Hall area became the center of the printing and newspaper industry, the church received special dispensation to say a "Printer's Mass" at 2:30 A.M. for the night shift of newsmen and printers. It later became the first parish church to

Rhinelander's "Old Sugar House," at the corner of Rose and Duane streets, was erected in 1763 and during the Revolutionary War served as a prison during the British occupation of New York. It was demolished in 1892 to make way for an office building which kept the Rhinelander name. The building preserved a barred window of the "Old Sugar House" prison in its façade, and when the structure was razed in 1968 the window was removed and mounted on a special base adjacent to the Municipal Building, along with a commemorative plaque. (New-York Historical Society)

offer a noon mass for the growing number of businessmen in the area. The Latin phrase in the frieze means "Blessed are those who walk in the law of the Lord." The Plaza at this point, where Duane Street once penetrated, is now called St. Andrew's Plaza.

Walk through to Centre Street and Foley Square.

A STROLL AROUND FOLEY SQUARE

Follow the route of the broken line on the Foley Square Area map, beginning (and ending) at St. Andrew's Plaza:

   U.S. Court of International Trade, 1 Federal Plaza (Alfred Easton Poor, Kahn & Jacobs, Eggers & Higgins, 1966). The customs court is an attractive glassy box set above ground level. Walk under it and explore its broad passageways and ceramic tile murals. During hot summer days, the neighboring community finds it a place of respite.
   Jacob K. Javits Federal Building, 26 Federal Plaza (same architectural firms as above). Built in two sections, in 1967 and 1976, the whole appears to overwhelm the Foley Square complex. The eastern wing, built first, resembles a gargantuan checkerboard.

Department of Health of the City of New York Building (1933). Note the names of great men of medicine emblazoned around the frieze of this dignified but otherwise undistinguished civic building.

Old New York Life Insurance Company Building, 346 Broadway (1870; remodeled on the Broadway side in the 1890s by McKim, Mead & White). Architect Griffith Thomas created a very imposing but appropriately sober headquarters for the company. Note the two clock towers, minus their cupolas, on this Renaissance Revival–style early skyscraper. The tower facing Broadway once sported a huge iron globe surmounted by an eagle. The company moved its headquarters to Madison Square in 1928, and the building is now temporarily used for government offices and the Clocktower Art Gallery. Cast-iron ornamentation on the Broadway side shows the New York Life Insurance monogram.

Family Court and Office of Probation (Haines, Lundberg & Waehler, 1975). The newest addition to Foley Square, this polished black granite behemoth is overbearing and pretentious; and its angular façade is distracting rather than relieving.

Municipal and Civil Court Building (William Lescaze and Matthew Del

The original "Tombs" prison in an 1873 view. Built across Centre Street from the present "Tombs" site, this was the main city jail from 1838 to 1892. Compared to a pharaoh's tomb because of its columns, sun god motifs, and trapezoidal windows, this and the Croton Reservoir at Forty-Second Street were two examples of Egyptian-style architecture in the city. (Museum of the City of New York)

Gaudio, 1960). This undistinguished building houses the Small Claims Court and the spillover from the Criminal Courts' calendar, as well as the courts of civil claims.

Engine Company 31 (Napoleon LeBrun & Sons, 1895). This French Renaissance "château," no longer in use as a fire house, is a delightful gem of a building—a pleasant surprise in this neighborhood of towering monoliths. The building stands vacant, awaiting adaptive re-use.

New York City Criminal Courts Building and former Manhattan Detention Center for Men (1939). The dramatic zigguratlike towers represent the height of the 1930s "moderne" or Art Deco style. Known familiarly as the **"Tombs"** since it incorporates the Men's House of Detention, it was built opposite the site of the original "Tombs" prison (so called because of its Egyptian-style architecture) which stood across Centre Street. The Men's House of Detention was moved in 1974 to Riker's Island, but reopened a few years later to relieve crowding at the island prison. The "Tombs" was designed by Harvey Wiley Corbell.

In the area encompassed by Franklin, Worth, Centre, and Lafayette streets was a small pond known as the **Collect.** A source of fresh water during colonial

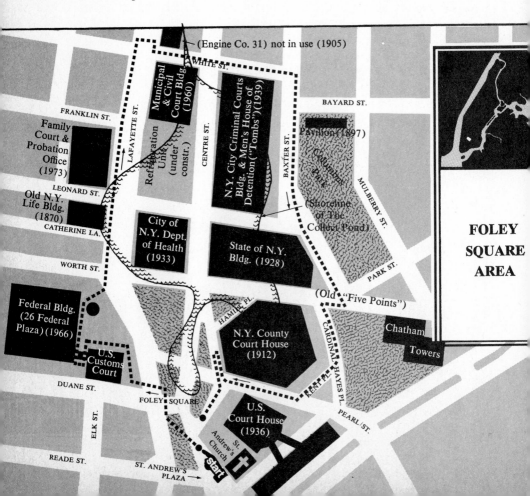

Dominating the lower Manhattan skyline at the turn of the century was the 26-story gold-domed "World Tower," the tallest building in the world when it was completed in 1890. Designed by George B. Post for Joseph Pulitzer's Evening World, it was demolished in the early 1950s to make way for new approaches to the Brooklyn Bridge. (New-York Historical Society)

The most notorious section of the city in the mid-19th century was the festering slum and den of criminals called Five Points. In this 1859 print from Valentine's Manual we see the crossing of three of the five streets: Baxter, Park, and Worth streets. (Museum of the City of New York)

days, it became polluted as the city grew around it, and was ultimately filled in at the beginning of the 19th century. John Fitch tested his prototype of a steamboat on the Collect in 1796. Aboard was Robert Fulton, who received all the accolades for the invention some years later.

Columbus Park, formerly Mulberry Bend Park, was created just before the turn of the century after the razing of many of the Five Points slums. Its name was changed in 1911.

State of New York Building (1928). Built on a wedge-shaped plot, this functional building is known by all as the location of the automobile License Bureau.

Five Points [*see* special map] was probably the worst festering slum in the history of this country. So named because of the intersection of three streets, it began as a district of cheap amusement at the beginning of the 19th century, but by 1840 it had become a foul, crime-ridden "rabbit warren" of the most depraved elements of the city. Centered about an old brewery, whose surrounding

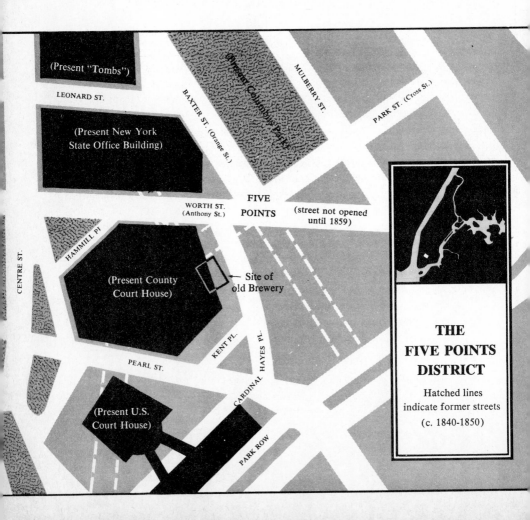

(Present "Tombs")

LEONARD ST.

(Present New York State Office Building)

BAXTER ST. (Orange St.)

Present Columbus Park

MULBERRY ST.

PARK ST. (Cross St.)

WORTH ST. (Anthony St.)

FIVE POINTS

(street not opened until 1859)

CENTRE ST.

HAMMILL PL

(Present County Court House)

← Site of old Brewery

KENT PL.

CARDINAL HAYES PL.

PEARL ST.

(Present U.S. Court House)

PARK ROW

THE FIVE POINTS DISTRICT

Hatched lines indicate former streets

(c. 1840-1850)

The Old Brewery at Five Points was the City's most infamous slum. Known locally as the "Den of Thieves," it is shown in this pen and ink sketch, just before its purchase and demolition by the Ladies' Home Missionary Society for the Construction of the Five Points Mission. (Museum of the City of New York)

lane was known as Murderers' Alley, it housed over a thousand men, women, and children in filth, squalor, and crime. More than a murder a day occurred in the former brewery and its surrounding slums; the area was so dangerous that even the police shunned it. It was the hangout of such notorious gangs as the "Plug Uglies," "Shirt Tails," and "Dead Rabbits." By mid-century the brewery was finally demolished and many of the ramshackle Five Points houses were razed. With the completion of the Foley Square courthouse complex, not a trace remains of that infamous district.

New York County Court House (1912). The New York State Supreme Court occupies this hexagon-shaped building with an enormous Corinthian portico. Architect Guy Lowell won the competition for the unique design of a building to occupy the irregularly shaped plot.

United States Court House (1936). Designed by Cass Gilbert and Cass Gilbert, Jr., its gold pyramid set on a skyscraper shaft above a neo-Classic base is a familiar site on the city skyline. A pedestrian walkway has been created between the Court House and its brand-new Annex. Note the two connecting bridges in the rear. The old powerhouse was preserved, and can be seen nestled in the new addition.

End of tour. Return to Foley Square, turn left (south) on Centre Street to the Municipal Building. Underneath and across the street are the IRT Lexington Avenue line and the BMT Nassau Street J line.

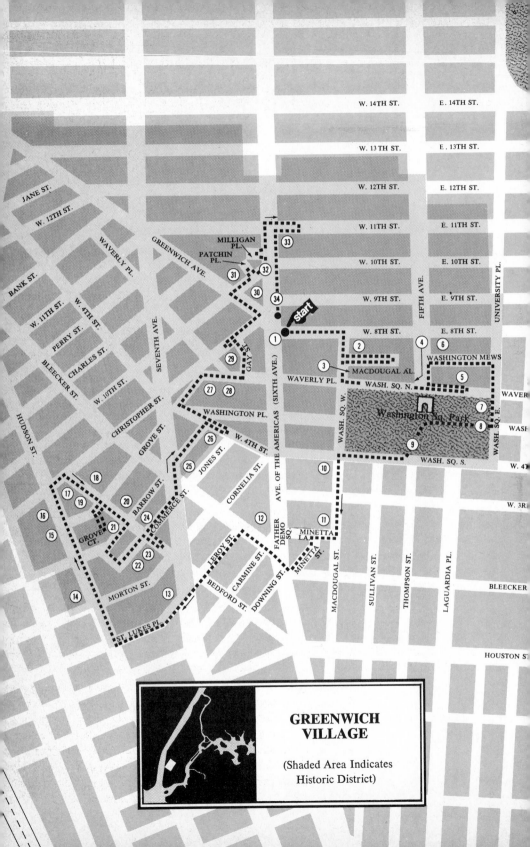

GREENWICH
VILLAGE

(Shaded Area Indicates
Historic District)

4. Greenwich Village

[*IND A, AA, CC, B, D, E, or F, lines to West 4th Street-Washington Square*]

Greenwich Village, a town within a city, has a unique character and personality of its own. Designated a **Historic District** of New York City, the Village dates back to an old Algonquin Indian settlement called Sapokanickan. When the Dutch arrived in 1626 they named it *Bossen Bouwerie* (Farm in the Woods) and developed it as a large tobacco plantation. After the British captured Nieuw Amsterdam in 1664, the plantation was purchased by naval squadron commander Sir Peter Warren, who then renamed it Greenwich. Gradually the settlement was transformed into a small town, and by the early 19th century, "Village" was added to the name. A series of smallpox and yellow fever epidemics in the lower city in the early 1800s drove thousands of city dwellers northward to the town of Greenwich, seeking the "healthful climate and quiet" of this distant suburb which somehow escaped these recurring plagues.

You may note that the streets of the Village do not conform to the orderly grid pattern of most of Manhattan, since the town of Greenwich had already been established with its own layout of streets before the city expanded northward. As the Village grew, its crazy-quilt pattern of streets spread from the banks of the Hudson River to what is now Broadway. Many of the winding streets were originally cow paths, or followed meandering brooks. One of these waterways, Minetta Brook, still causes problems far beneath today's busy streets, especially when foundations are dug for new buildings. The visitor may be flabbergasted to discover that West 4th Street, for example, runs west only briefly, then abruptly swings north to intersect West 10th, West 11th, and West 12th streets!

In the 19th century the Village began to attract writers and artists, and boasted such residents as O. Henry, Mark Twain, Edgar Allan Poe, Henry James, Stephen Crane, Winslow Homer, John La Farge, and Augustus St. Gau-

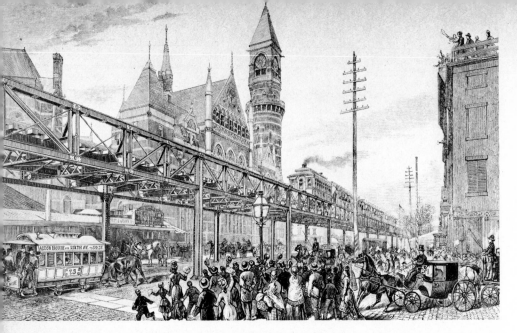

Engraving of the Jefferson Market Police Court on Sixth Avenue looking north from 9th Street, showing the first train of the Gilbert Elevated Railway (ultimately the Interborough Rapid Transit's Sixth Avenue El), on April 29, 1878. (Museum of the City of New York)

dens. Rents were low and the atmosphere was very attractive. After the turn of the century, Greenwich Village began to earn its reputation as the cradle of bohemia in America. The rents are much higher now, and many of the *literati* have departed, but the Village still retains much of its charm in its narrow, winding streets, the houses of many architectural styles, the variety of curious shops, and an assortment of colorful Village "types." There are many boutiques, exotic food stores, coffee shops, fine restaurants serving food from many nations, art schools, and drama workshops, as well as the world's largest private university.

1. The tour begins at the corner of **Avenue of the Americas and West 8th Street,** facing Village Square, the hub of the Village. Most Villagers refer to Avenue of the Americas by its former (and more logical) name, Sixth Avenue. The sidewalk along the Avenue just south of 8th Street is a gathering place during warm weather for exponents of a wide variety of political and religious views. On weekends particularly, throngs gather to listen—and often to heckle the speechmakers. Stroll along bustling, brassy 8th Street. It has become the main shopping thoroughfare of the Village in recent years. Turn right at the first corner (Macdougal Street), and walk the short distance to the gates of Macdougal Alley.

2. Macdougal Alley, with its picturesque and individually redesigned carriage houses, is a private dead-end street, of which there are several in the Village. (Tiptoe in!) The little houses were built as stables in the 1850s for the wealthy residents of 8th Street (then called Clinton Place) and Washington Square. Some residents claim that the two gas lamps are the last remaining in the city maintained free by the Consolidated Edison Company, but " 'taint so!"

At No. 1, now a restaurant, poet Edwin Arlington Robinson wrote his famous *Tristram,* winning himself his third Pulitzer Prize. Facing the alley across Macdougal Street is the massive brick façade of the Tenth Church of Christ Scientist, remodeled in 1967. Turn left on leaving the Alley and walk to the corner of Washington Square.

3. **Washington Square** was originally a marshland teeming with wildlife and a favorite hunting ground of the colonists. In 1797 it became a municipal Potter's Field. Recent excavations during the park's renovation revealed skeletons of some of the 10,000 early New Yorkers buried here. Equally grim was the field's popularity as a dueling ground and its use as a site of public executions. Directly across from you is the famous (or infamous) **Hanging Elm,** said to be the oldest tree in the city. It is one of 27 varieties in the park. The public hangings drew large crowds in a festive mood from the downtown districts. In 1824, on his triumphal return to America, the Marquis de Lafayette was the honored guest at the hanging of 20 highwaymen. Two years later, the park was officially designated as the Washington Military Parade Grounds, and at its dedication, two oxen, 200 hams, and a quarter-mile of barreled beer were consumed in the largest public picnic ever held here. In 1831, the grounds became the unofficial campus of the newly established University of the City of New York—now New York University, the largest private university in the country.

As you turn left and walk along Washington Square North, note the group of imposing town houses, Nos. 26–21. These elegant homes were built in the 1830s for the social elite, as were the houses farther down the street across Fifth Avenue. Known as **"The Row,"** they represent the finest group of Greek Revival–style houses in America. Henry James's novel *Washington Square,* written in 1881, had its setting at No. 18—his grandmother's house. Unfortunately, the building was demolished along with neighboring houses in 1950 to make way for the huge apartment house at the corner. The five-story annex in a pseudo-Georgian style is a sad replacement, but represents a compromise, as the builders of the huge apartment house originally intended to erect it directly on the square. Ask the doorman at the Fifth Avenue entrance to let you see the evidence of Minetta Brook, which bubbles under a glass dome in the lobby (when the pipes aren't clogged).

4. **The Washington Arch,** designed by famed architect Stanford White, is one of the world's finest triumphal arches. Built of marble in 1891–92, it commemorates the centenary of George Washington's inauguration as first President. This arch replaces an earlier model constructed of wood in 1889, which spanned Fifth Avenue near the corner. The arch had proved so popular that the permanent stone monument was erected afterward by public subscription. The civilian statue of Washington was sculpted by Alexander Stirling Calder, the military statue, by Hermon Atkins MacNeil. The carved relief work on the arch was done by Frederick William MacMonnies, whose statue of Nathan Hale can be seen in City Hall Park. At Christmastime, a tall fir tree is placed in front of the arch, illuminated with hundreds of colored bulbs. Neighbors gather to sing carols, often to the accompaniment of student musicians from N.Y.U., or

even guitars. At night, the floodlighting on the arch can be seen from as far north as 42nd Street.

There is an interior staircase in the right section leading to the top, which figured in an unseemly escapade back in 1916, known as John Sloan's Revolution. Sloan, considered the father of the "Ashcan School" of painting, forced open the door to the stairs and led a group of slightly tipsy art students and fellow bohemians to the top of the arch on a cold January night. They built a fire in a large beanpot, spread out food, and lit an array of colorful Japanese lanterns— all to the consternation and indignation of the very staid and proper residents of "The Row." The boisterous group read poems, fired cap pistols, and noisily declared the independence of the state of "New Bohemia." The arrival of a detachment of unsympathetic constabulary brought a quick end to the abortive "rebellion."

On weekends and during the warmer weather, the fountain and mall areas are a mecca for roller skaters, instrumentalists, frisbee "pros," speechmakers, and exhibitionists of all kinds, as well as a gathering place for crowds of sightseers who come to watch them "do their thing." In June and September, the adjacent streets are host to the semiannual Greenwich Village Outdoor Art Show, where professional and amateur painters have the opportunity to "show and sell."

Fifth Avenue just north of Washington Square in 1889, showing the temporary wooden arch built for the centennial of Washington's inauguration. A horse-drawn omnibus waits for passengers as a street vendor dispenses goodies to well-dressed youngsters on this once fashionable avenue. (New-York Historical Society)

Stereograph view of the Washington Arch, taken as it neared completion in 1892. The arch, larger than any in antiquity, is considered one of architect Stanford White's major achievements. (New-York Historical Society)

Celebrating the completion of the Washington Arch, community and civic leaders gather for their picture on the roof of the arch. William Rhinelander Stewart, one of the driving forces behind its construction, with ceremonial mallet and top hat, poses thoughtfully while architect Stanford White, to his right, looks down. In the rear is N.Y.U.'s neo-Gothic building. (New-York Historical Society)

Nos. 4, 6, and 8 Fifth Avenue, corner of 8th Street—stately town houses designed by Henry J. Hardenbergh (the Plaza Hotel, the Dakota, etc.). The photo was taken in 1936 by Berenice Abbott for the Federal Art Project "Changing New York." All three buildings were razed in the early 1950s for an enormous apartment house. (Museum of the City of New York)

Cross Fifth Avenue and walk down Washington Square North to the lions in front of No. 6.

5. This magnificent **row of Greek Revival houses,** like their counterparts which you saw before, were built around 1831 for wealthy New York merchants. In later years, "The Row" was the residence of writer John Dos Passos, artists Rockwell Kent and Edward Hopper, and Mayor Stephen Allen. Although the houses are similar (except for No. 3), each has its own minor architectural differences. The stately entranceways, graced by marble columns and carved wooden colonnettes, are evidence of the graceful style of living of the original owners. Observe the brickwork—an alternating long and short brick in each row. This arrangement is called Flemish Bond, and was used on the more expensive early houses. Nos. 7–13 are mere façade, as all were gutted in 1939 to make way for an apartment house, carefully hidden behind. Sacrificed was the elaborate cornice, which still remains on the houses to the right, to make way for a fifth floor. How different, and how much more aesthetic a treatment than the architectural vandalism committed on the previous block! The cast-iron fence, in a remarkable state of preservation, helps unify the row of houses. Note the honeysuckle adornments, called anthemions, the intervening obelisks, the fret design along the base, and the lyres at intervals. These are all Greek motifs so popular during the Greek Revival period. As for the bronze lions in front of No. 6, they were cast in 1883 by sculptor Samuel Kitson, and are said to be from the former William K. Vanderbilt Mansion on Fifth Avenue.

Return to Fifth Avenue, turn right, passing the arcaded entranceway to the apartment house masked by the Greek Revival façade on the square, and the little fake Greek Revival house of red brick, and enter Washington Mews.

6. Charming **Washington Mews,** like Macdougal Alley, was formerly a row of stables—in fact it was called Stable Alley until the 20th century. These converted carriage houses are vaguely reminiscent of London's Chelsea district, and were the residences of such celebrities as Gertrude Vanderbilt Whitney (founder of the Whitney Museum), diplomat and writer Walter Lippmann, and former Official City Greeter Grover Whalen. Walk through the cobblestoned mews to University Place. The last house on the right is the French House of New York University, remodeled in an authentic rural French architectural style. Across from it is the German House. Turn right to the northeast corner of Washington Square.

7. Diagonally across the street (southeast corner) is the **Main Building of New York University.** Built in 1894, it replaced a handsome Gothic Revival structure completed in 1837, six years after the founding of the University. Then called the University of the City of New York, it had as one of its founders

Stalled in the snow on University Place and 9th Street, the morning after the Great Blizzard of 1888, the horse car's "motive power" is nowhere to be seen, in spite of the rush hour crowd aboard. In the rear is the Hotel Martin, an elegant French establishment with a famous basement restaurant. (Museum of the City of New York)

Albert Gallatin, Secretary of the Treasury under Thomas Jefferson, and boasted many creative teachers. Among them was a member of the art faculty who in his spare time changed the course of history by inventing the telegraph—Samuel F. B. Morse. Professor John W. Draper made the first successful outdoor photographic portrait on the roof of his house adjoining the university building. Walt Whitman conducted classes in poetry, and Winslow Homer painted in a top-floor studio. Less academic perhaps was science professor Samuel Colt's invention of the "six-shooter." In later years, Thomas Wolfe gave courses in fiction writing.

The construction of the original building led to a riot which lasted for several days. It seems that some of the founding fathers thought they could save money by using inmates from the nearby state prison. This aroused the anger of guild laborers who demonstrated so forcefully that the local National Guard unit had to be summoned to quell the violence. The university gave in and peace was restored, and the incident became known as the Stone Cutters' Guild Riot, the first demonstration by organized labor in New York City.

Note the plaque honoring Manhattan's first schoolteachers; then walk south along the Main Building to Washington Place. Turn east to the northwest corner

The great neo-Gothic building of New York University completed in 1837, facing Washington Square. It was in this building that Samuel F. B. Morse perfected the electric telegraph, John W. Draper made the first successful outdoor photographic portrait, Walt Whitman conducted classes in poetry, Winslow Homer painted in a top floor studio, and Samuel Colt invented the six-shooter. N.Y.U. demolished it in 1894 to build its present Main Building. (New-York Historical Society)

of Washington Place and Greene Street. Novelist Henry James was born on Washington Place near the northeast corner in 1843.

8. This is the architecturally undistinguished Brown Building of N.Y.U. Built in 1900 for commercial use and known then as the Asch Building, it was advertised as a fireproof structure. Nevertheless, on March 25, 1911, fire *did* break out in piles of discarded cloth in the ninth-floor workroom of the **Triangle Shirtwaist Company.** Efforts to extinguish the blaze were unsuccessful, and within minutes the eighth, ninth, and tenth floors became a roaring inferno. Although the building was equipped with fire exits, the terrified workers discovered to their horror that the ninth-floor exit doors had been locked by supervisors. A single fire escape was wholly inadequate for the crush of panic-stricken employees from the three floors, and the firemen's hastily stretched nets proved useless in breaking the fall from the upper floors of the dozens of workers who leaped— often hand-in-hand, and with hair and clothing ablaze—to their death on the pavement below. In less than an hour it was over. One hundred forty-six young people, most of them recent immigrants living on the Lower East Side, had perished—and the city was in a state of shock! As a result of the tragedy, improved fire-safety regulations were quickly adopted by the City Council, and the newly organized International Ladies' Garment Workers Union succeeded in having labor laws enacted to improve working conditions for the tens of thousands still working in similar sweatshops. A plaque commemorates the sad event.

Return to Washington Square and enter the park. Walk past the imposing statue of Garibaldi, the Italian patriot who made Staten Island his home for a number of years. Sculpted by Giovanni Turini in 1888, it is said that Garibaldi will always draw his sword to protect a damsel in distress. Spend a few minutes walking around the mall and fountain area, and observe the variety of people (most of the more colorful types enjoy being looked at, anyway). You may be drawn into a folk-music session, a frisbee-tossing match, a political discussion, or a volleyball game; but be discreet!

Turn left and leave the park at Washington Square South, opposite the tall tower of the Judson Memorial Church.

9. Named for the first American Baptist missionary, Adinoram D. Judson, the **Judson Memorial Church and Tower** are fine examples of the Italian Renaissance style, designed by Stanford White and built in 1892 by his architectural firm of McKim, Mead & White. If the church is open, look inside at the splendid stained-glass work of artist John LaFarge, the painter who is credited with reviving the lost art of stained-glass making in this country. The tower now serves as a dormitory wing of the adjacent **Judson Residence Hall** of N.Y.U. Looking east (left) across Thompson Street is the Generoso Pope Catholic Center with modern stained-glass windows, and farther east is the N.Y.U. Loeb Student Center. The Student Center occupies the site of Mrs. Marie Branchard's Boarding House, demolished in 1948. Known as the "House of Genius," some of its famous boarders were Metropolitan Opera singer Adelina Patti; writers Theodore Dreiser, who penned his *American Tragedy* in a tiny garret room in 1915; Stephen Crane, who began *The Red Badge of Courage* in a neighboring room;

Firemen pouring tons of water into the Asch Building at the corner of Washington Place and Greene Street on March 25, 1911, as the Triangle Shirtwaist Company burns in one of the worst disasters in the city's history. One hundred forty-six young garment workers lost their lives in this tragic fire which engulfed the upper three stories of the structure. The building still exists as the Brown Building of New York University. (Brown Brothers)

Burned out sewing machines are the only recognizable artifact in the charred debris of the 9th floor, the morning after the dread Triangle Fire. (Brown Brothers)

O. Henry; Frank Norris; Gelett Burgess; Willa Cather; Eugene O'Neill; and Maxwell Bodenheim. Mrs. Branchard outlived most of her celebrated tenants and died just after her 81st birthday in 1937.

During the time when the Square was the site for public executions, the hangman's house was located where the Catholic Center is now. The shack later became a gathering place for early bohemians, and was known as Bruno's Garret, after the somewhat eccentric owner. Bruno invited the public to visit (for a fee) and observe at first hand how the ostentatious tenants lived.

In the annex of the Judson dormitory was the **studio of artist John Sloan.** Other painters of "The Eight" who rebelled against the sugary style of the National Academy of Art, and who had studios on Washington Square, were Maurice Prendergast, Everett Shinn, Ernest Lawson, and William Glackens. The artists' own show, staged at the 69th Regiment Armory in 1913 together with others, became known as the "Armory Show," and is considered the birth of modern American art. Their realistic work was derided by critics who called it the "ashcan school."

Walk west to Sullivan Street, and go around the corner to the entrance to the **Hagop Kevorkian Center for Near Eastern Studies** of N.Y.U. Designed by Philip Johnson and Richard Foster, the entrance hall contains a reconstruction of the interior of a 1797 house built in Damascus, Syria, for a merchant family, in whose possession it remained until the mid-1920s. The interior work was supervised by university architect Joseph Roberto.

Continue west along the square to N.Y.U.'s neo-Georgian style **Vanderbilt Hall** (Eggers & Higgins, 1951), modeled after an English Inn of Court. Previously on the site was a rather pathetic structure known as "Papa Strunsky's," a rooming house for artists, most of whom could rarely afford the rent and who were subsidized by the beneficent Strunsky who never pressed them for payment. Among the threadbare boarders was the young writer Lincoln Steffens. The lease of the property was held by Columbia University, which was less

A Fifth Avenue bus parked in Washington Square in 1936. These popular "double deckers" disappeared after World War II, and there is now some movement to bring them back. In the rear is the Washington Arch and No. 1 Fifth Avenue. (Photograph by Berenice Abbott for the Federal Art Project "Changing New York," Museum of the City of New York)

charitable than Strunsky, and by the late 1940s they foreclosed, knowing that N.Y.U. needed the space for its Law School. Columbia held out for a reported $1 million to close the deal so that Vanderbilt Hall could be erected.

Walk to the corner of Macdougal Street where a ca. 1890 apartment house has given itself No. 39½ to keep its identity with Washington Square.

10. Macdougal Street and its adjacent blocks south of Washington Square are considered the "real Village" by the mobs of young people who throng here evenings and weekends. The scene has begun to shift to 8th Street, but there's still plenty of "action" here. Before turning down Macdougal Street, make a short detour straight ahead along West 4th Street (the continuation of Washington Square South). John Barrymore, "The Great Profile," lived at No. 132; and at a former café at No. 148, Al Jolson and Grace Moore were discovered, while Norma Shearer worked as a hat-check girl. At No. 150, once "The Mad Hatter" Café, Hendrik Willem van Loon wrote his *Story of Mankind.*

As you stroll down Macdougal Street, note the Provincetown Playhouse, Eugene O'Neill's theater. Nos. 127–131 (best seen from across the street) are little Federal houses that were built for Aaron Burr in 1829 and are among the oldest in the city. Notice the typical dormer windows in the peaked roof, and the pineapples on the cast-iron newel posts—traditional symbols of hospitality. Around the corner at 106 West 3rd Street, Aaron Burr's ghost is reputedly still haunting the building. At 130 Macdougal Street, Louisa May Alcott wrote her classic *Little Women.* Take an optional side trip one block farther to Bleecker Street and turn left. Try some of the exotic foods from around the world at the "hand held" food shops that line the street: souvlaki, tacos, sweet and hot sausage, empanadas, tandoori chicken, knishes, shish kebab, and Turkish coffee (but not all at once!).

11. Turn down **Minetta Lane.** No. 1, at the corner of Macdougal Street, is the birthplace of the *Reader's Digest.* Founded in 1922, its first edition had a press run of only 5,000 copies. At narrow **Minetta Street** turn left. During the Prohibition Era, these narrow alleys were lined with speakeasies. Later these night spots became legitimate cabarets offering drink and amateur theatrical productions. Now, with stricter city licensing, few genuine cabarets remain, and the small theater groups have moved into their own "Off-Off" Broadway playhouses. Both streets follow the winding path of old Minetta Brook; and it is said that on a very quiet night, the gurgling waters can be heard below ground. However, there are very few quiet nights in this neighborhood. You will emerge at Sixth Avenue—rather, Avenue of the Americas—on Father Demo Square. Cross the avenue, turn half right, and you will be at the corner of Bleecker and Carmine streets.

12. The Roman Catholic **Church of Our Lady of Pompeii** (1926) is the parish church of the large Italian community in this part of the Village. Mother Francis Xavier Cabrini, the first American saint, often prayed here. Walk along Bleecker Street and savor the aroma of the many Italian food specialty shops, and buy a fresh-baked bread at Zito's at No. 259 Bleecker Street. Turn west on Leroy Street, and notice the variety of architectural styles, ranging from Federal-style houses to "Old Law" tenements. Cross Seventh Avenue (carefully!).

13. As you round the bend on Leroy Street, the atmosphere suddenly changes. You are now on **St. Luke's Place,** with its charming row of Italianate brownstone town houses of the 1850s. The gingko trees, which line both sides of the street, are particularly resistant to air pollution. The twin lanterns on the stairway of No. 6 mark the former residence of Mayor James J. Walker—the popular "Jimmy" Walker of Prohibition days. Rampant corruption in municipal government forced his resignation, but he remained a beloved and colorful figure till his death in 1946. Until Gracie Mansion was made the official residence of all New York City mayors, a pair of lanterns customarily adorned the entrance to "his honor's" home. Across the street in James J. Walker Park, there is an interesting monument near the entrance, which honors two firemen from the Eagle Fire Engine Company who lost their lives in a building collapse in 1834. The memorial is the lone surviving artifact from the former Trinity Parish cemetery which occupied this site before the park was built. Turn right at Hudson Street one block to Morton Street.

14. Had you stood on this spot 300 years ago, you would have been on the bank of the Hudson River. The land to the west was filled in gradually, until today the river is three blocks away. Looking down Morton Street, the S.S. *John W. Brown,* a Board of Education schoolship of Park West High School, is berthed at the Morton Street Pier. The ship, of World War II vintage, is quite seaworthy, but vital mechanical parts have been removed lest any adventurous students decide to make an unauthorized voyage. The Pier is open to the public and provides good river views and cool breezes.

To the northwest, on Washington Street, is the enormous red brick **former U.S. Federal Building.** Completed in 1899 as the Customs Appraisers' Warehouse, it took seven years to build, and its style is the fortresslike Romanesque Revival. It once housed records from the National Archives and had a branch of the U.S. Post Office. The architect of this massive masonry building with its great brick arches is unknown; however, the designer of the lower two floors was Willoughby J. Edbrooke. It is presently being recycled by a private developer for mixed residential and commercial use. Continue north on Hudson Street two blocks to St. Luke's Chapel.

15. "**St. Luke's-in-the-Fields,**" as it was called when the cornerstone was laid in 1821, stood at the river's edge and overlooked small farms, wandering streams, and shady country lanes. In those days most visitors came from the lower city by boat, as the trip by carriage was very arduous, and the canal that bisected most of Manhattan island (site of present Canal Street) could be crossed in only two places. The first warden of St. Luke's was Clement Clarke Moore, who immortalized himself not with his dedicated church duties, but with the poem *'Twas the Night Before Christmas.* The church, a branch of the downtown Trinity Parish, has always been dedicated to education, and today boasts an excellent elementary school, visible behind the church. A tragic fire in 1981 virtually destroyed the landmark church, and at this writing, support is being sought to help rebuild it.

16. Adjoining the church are **Nos. 487–491 Hudson Street.** Observe how these restored Federal houses form a harmonious unit with the brick church.

Built in 1825, they are the property of St. Luke's. Bret Harte, journalist, teacher, "gold rusher," and author of *Tales of Roaring Camp* and *The Outcasts of Poker Flat,* lived at No. 487 and maintained a steady feud with his contemporary Mark Twain, also a Villager.

Continue to Christopher Street, turn right, then right again into Bedford Street.

17. As you rounded the corner, you probably noticed the Lucille Lortel Theater on Christopher Street, one of the oldest off-Broadway playhouses, formerly called the Theater de Lys. Kurt Weill's *Three Penny Opera* had its New York premiere here and ran for nine years, with Weill's wife Lotte Lenya in a starring role.

You now are entering the most charming section of the so-called West Village. Homeowners take special pride in restoring and preserving their attractive houses. There are more original Federal-style houses in this neighborhood than anywhere else in the city. Note the **row of houses at Nos. 115–111** and **109– 107,** the latter only two bays wide. Stop just before the next corner, which is Grove Street, and stay on the right side of Bedford Street.

18. The wooden house on your left, **No. 100 Bedford Street,** was originally the workshop of sash maker William Hyde, who lived in the corner house. The sash maker's trade has now been assumed by the glazier and carpenter. In the early 19th century, window making was an important craft. The workshop is now a private residence. **No. 102,** which you just passed, is best seen from a distance. It is no accident that it resembles a fairy-tale house. Although the building dates from 1835, it was remodeled extensively in 1926 by Clifford Reed Daily and financed by Otto H. Kahn, who sought to convert the decaying house into "an inspiring home for creative artists." When the city's Building Department approved the radical plans, **"Twin Peaks"** was born.

At the corner, **No. 17 Grove Street,** which dates from 1822, is the most complete wooden frame house in Greenwich Village. Turn right on Grove Street to No. 4.

19. The row of **Nos. 4–10** (1825–34) presents one of the most authentic groups of classic Federal-style houses in America. Enter **Grove Court** (unobtrusively!) and peek at this secluded, shady mews. Now converted into triplexes, the row of old houses was built as laborers' quarters in 1854, and Grove Court was known by the not-so-charming name of Mixed Ale Alley. Return to Bedford Street and turn right, stopping opposite No. 86.

20. Can you guess what **No. 86 Bedford Street** is (or was)? There are no visible signs of identification, but to Village *cognoscenti* it is Chumley's Restaurant. It was a notorious speakeasy during the Prohibition days, and patrons had to identify themselves at the little glass window in the door before being admitted. It was also a favored hangout for writers, and faded dust jackets of long-forgotten titles line the walls inside. The restaurant's popularity is so widespread in the Village, that former owner Lee Chumley never felt the need for a sign. During Prohibition, when the premises were raided by the police, patrons could beat a hasty retreat out a back exit in the rear of the restaurant, opposite the bar. This passageway, which leads through the courtyard of the adjacent building to Barrow Street, is still there. See for yourself! Turn right on Barrow Street to No. 70.

21. No. 70 Barrow Street, when built in 1852, was Empire Hose Company No. 1. In those days each neighborhood had its own volunteer fire brigade. Look carefully and you will see where the old carriageway was bricked in.

Across the street is a rather large double house with mansard roofs, **Nos. 39 and 41 Commerce Street.** Both halves were built in 1831 for Peter Huyler, a milkman. "The Twins," as they are called, were built in Federal style with Second Empire roofs superimposed, and share a common garden. Walk ahead into Commerce Street, around the bend to the little theater.

22. A group of local playwrights seeking a stage for their own works converted an old brewery malt house into the **Cherry Lane Theater** (Commerce Street was then called Cherry Lane). Among some premieres were Samuel Beckett's *Waiting for Godot* and *Endgame,* as well as plays by Ionesco and Edward Albee.

23. At the corner of Bedford Street is the **Isaacs-Hendricks House,** built in 1799. Like the two wooden houses seen earlier, it is typical of the architecture of old Greenwich, and is the oldest surviving house in the Village. Its entrance is in the rear, behind the fence. Around the corner at **No. 75½ Bedford Street** is the narrowest house in the city, measuring only 9½ feet wide! The first

A row of pristine Federal town houses, Nos. 3 through 6 Sheridan Square, was lost forever when an apartment was erected on the site in the early 1950s. The photo by Wurts Bros. was taken in 1915. A saddle and harness shop is barely visible at right. (Consolidated Edison Company of New York)

floor was formerly a carriage entrance, with living quarters above. A cobbler had his shop here, and later it was a candy factory. Between 1923 and 1924, poet Edna St. Vincent Millay lived here. Like the Isaacs-Hendricks House, this diminutive structure had its entrance facing the rear. Spend a few moments looking at Nos. 66 and 64, noting the historical plaques. Turn right on Commerce Street to No. 17.

24. Two years before killing Alexander Hamilton in that fateful duel in 1802, Aaron Burr lived briefly at **the site of No. 17. Nos. 16–18** across the street were built in 1830, as was No. 17. At **No. 11,** the plaque informs us that Washington Irving was a resident, where he was supposed to have penned his *Legend of Sleepy Hollow.* Continue to Seventh Avenue, turn left one block, and cross to Barrow Street.

25. At the corner of Barrow Street and Seventh Avenue is **Greenwich House.** Originally a settlement house, it has expanded its services to the community with recreational facilities, arts and crafts studios, concerts, antique shows, and cultural programs for senior citizens. Proceed along Barrow Street. **No. 15** was once a stable. Note the horse heads indicating that it was a public livery stable.

26. At **Sheridan Square,** turn right briefly on West 4th Street to Numbers 175–185, charming houses dating from the 1830s. West 4th Street has many interesting little shops, and, except for the storefronts, most of the buildings remain unchanged. Return to Sheridan Square, bearing to the right, and make a sharp right turn into Grove Street, just before reaching Seventh Avenue.

27. Sheridan Square is shaped like a huge butterfly, with two distinct "wings." So many streets converge at this point that visitors often become confused (Villagers, too, for that matter). Because of heavy traffic at this intersection, the corner has been called "The Mousetrap." Pass through the second "wing" of the butterfly by walking along Grove Street, opposite the little park with the equestrian statue of Civil War Cavalry General Philip Henry Sheridan (Joseph Pollia, 1936). Actually, this half of Sheridan Square is called **Christopher Park,** but nobody ever calls it that. The Ellsworth Flagpole honors a 24-year-old colonel, the first of his rank to be killed in the Civil War. The square figures in another aspect of the Civil War—the Draft Riots. In 1863, mobs of bloodthirsty rioters, in the worst civil insurrection in the city's history, gathered in the square and attacked a number of freed slaves. They would certainly have hanged them from nearby lampposts, had not the residents of **No. 92 Grove Street** risked their lives to save them. The house has since been extensively remodeled, and is now called the Burges Chambers Studio. Its design won a prize from the American Institute of Architects.

28. Grove Street now becomes Waverly Place, and as you stand before **the Northern Dispensary,** you are at the corner of Waverly Place and Waverly Place! Since the street divides at this point to meet Grove Street and also to swing northward, it has given rise to the saying that the Dispensary "has two sides on one street, and one street on two sides." Built in 1831 in Greek Revival style by Henry Bayard, carpenter, and John C. Tucker, stonemason, and surprisingly unchanged in appearance, the Northern Dispensary still functions as a public clinic. According to its records, Edgar Allan Poe was treated here (free) for a head cold in 1837.

Continue in the same direction, and turn left into narrow Gay Street.

29. Gay Street was the center of a small black neighborhood in the latter half of the 19th century. In the 1920s the street was lined with speakeasies. **No. 14** was the site of Ruth McKenny's play *My Sister Eileen*. Later it was filmed here on location. Walk ahead to Christopher Street, and spend a few minutes window shopping in the curious shops to the left. Then turn right to Greenwich Avenue, and turn left and walk to the corner of West 10th Street.

30. The garden across the street marks the **site of the former New York City Women's House of Detention.** The massive orange brick Art Deco structure was demolished in 1973–74 after considerable community pressure, and the inmates were moved to Riker's Island. Cross Greenwich Avenue to the Peacock Caffé, 24 Greenwich Avenue, and enjoy a cup of capuccino and an Italian pastry. Turn east on West 10th Street to the entrance gates of Patchin Place. Lighting the entrance is **one of the few remaining cast-iron "bishop's crook" lampposts** in the city.

31. The houses on quaint **Patchin Place** were built in the mid-19th century to house workers of the then-posh Brevoort Hotel on Fifth Avenue. The narrow street later became the residence of such famous authors as poet laureate John Masefield, Theodore Dreiser, e. e. cummings (at No. 4), as well as Harry Kemp (the "Hobo Poet"), and William Brinckley, who wrote *Don't Go Near the Water*. Enjoy the peaceful atmosphere of this unusual cul-de-sac, away from the noise and clamor of nearby thoroughfares. Turn left, walk to Avenue of the Americas (we'll get to the "castle" across the street shortly), and turn left again. Watch carefully, or you'll miss the iron gates marking the entrance to Milligan Place.

32. Milligan Place is named for the original landowner, Samuel Milligan, who settled here in 1799. His daughter married the surveyor of his property, Aaron Patchin. Perhaps part of the dowry was the small street named for him. Many native Villagers are unaware of this tiny, secluded mews. Walk ahead to West 11th Street, turn right and cross the avenue. Fifty feet down the street is a small cemetery.

33. The Second Cemetery of the Spanish & Portuguese Synagogue was one of three burial grounds of this first Jewish congregation in New York. The first cemetery, near Chatham Square, and the third, on West 20th Street, kept pace with the northward growth of the Jewish community from the 17th through the 19th centuries. The peculiar triangular shape of the cemetery resulted from the opening of West 11th Street through to Sixth Avenue in the mid-19th century, cutting off a substantial piece of the graveyard. Return to Avenue of the Americas, turn left, and stop at the "castle."

34. The Jefferson Market Library, the Village's most magnificent Victorian Gothic structure, was built in 1874–77 as a courthouse, with an adjoining jail, firehouse, and market. Designed by architects Frederick Clarke Withers and Calvert Vaux, it was listed among the ten most beautiful buildings in America at the time. (Vaux, by the way, helped design Central Park.) Note the striking effect of the red brick and white stone, the Gothic motifs, stained-glass windows, and dramatic clock tower. The tower replaces an earlier wooden fire lookout, one of many throughout the city, long before the advent of the electric fire-alarm system. In 1967 the building was saved from the wrecker's ball at the eleventh hour by a dedicated committee of neighborhood residents, who not only saved it but convinced the city to restore it and make it a branch of the New York Public Library. Architect Giorgio Cavaglieri designed and supervised the restoration. The clock, known affectionately as "Old Jeff," was repaired and illumination for the dials installed. During the Christmas season the belfry is festooned with gaily colored lights. Read the plaques at the base of the tower and visit the library. Take the elevator to the third floor and walk down the intriguing spiral staircase to the dungeonlike basement, which houses the reference room. As you leave the building, cross the avenue and explore **Balducci's,** the Village's major gourmet landmark; then walk south one block to West 8th Street, where the tour began.

End of tour. The entrance to the IND subway is a half-block down Avenue of the Americas toward Waverly Place.

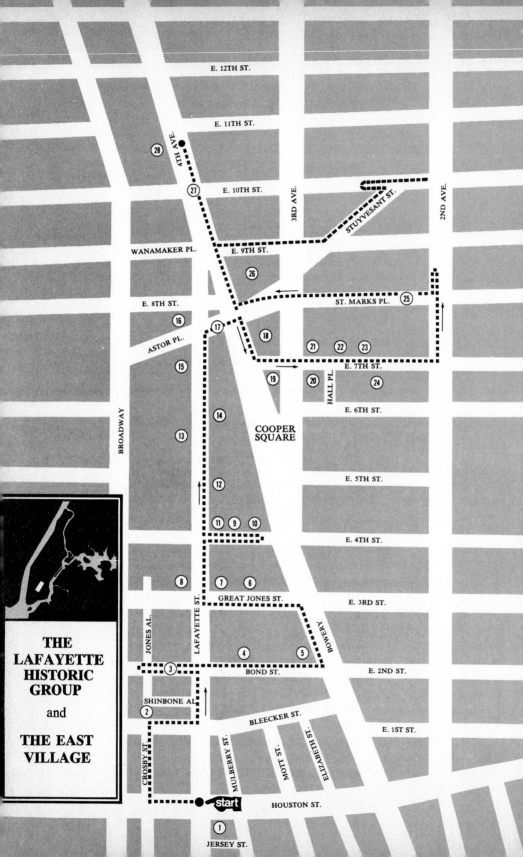

THE
LAFAYETTE
HISTORIC
GROUP

and

THE EAST
VILLAGE

5. The Lafayette Historic Group and the East Village

[*IRT Lexington Avenue line to Bleecker Street; IND B, D, F lines to Broadway-Lafayette station; Lexington Avenue–Third Avenue (M-101 or M-102) bus to Houston Street; Broadway (M-1 or M-6) bus or Fifth Avenue (M-5) bus to Houston Street*]

With the end of the American Revolution, New York City, which had stagnated under years of British occupation, came alive again, regaining its position as an important port and commercial center. A burgeoning population began to push the city's frontiers northward, swallowing up the once-remote and peaceful farms of mid-Manhattan and crisscrossing them with a latticework of newly opened streets.

In 1811, the City Commissioners drew up their famous plan, laying out a gridwork street pattern for the entire island, numbering all east-west streets and north-south avenues, commencing roughly at the point of departure of this tour. By the end of the 19th century the last farms disappeared from Manhattan, yielding to the ever increasing needs for *lebensraum*.

By the 1830s this neighborhood became the "gold coast" of the city, boasting the most lavish residences—including that of the nation's wealthiest citizen, John Jacob Astor. Within 20 years the area gave way to commerce and public entertainment, and by the 1880s and 1890s it became a center for the printing trades. Light industry followed with factories, loft buildings, and warehouses.

Surprisingly, so many vestiges remain from each period of development that within the half-square-mile area can be found such diverse "artifacts" as opulent Greek Revival residences, Italian Renaissance cultural institutions, Romanesque Revival industrial structures, cast-iron commercial "palaces," plus a number of historic and architecturally unique buildings—most in an excellent state of preservation.

The tour begins at Houston and Lafayette streets. [For background information on Houston Street, *see* SoHo Cast-Iron District, page 180.]

1. On the southwest corner stands the **Puck Building** (295–309 Lafayette Street). Built in 1885, with an addition in 1892, it is a fine example of the industrial Romanesque Revival style so popular in the last two decades of the 19th century. Architect Albert Wagner designed it for the publishers of the humor magazine *Puck,* whose Shakespearean character proclaimed "What Fools These Mortals Be!" across the magazine's cover. The publication lasted more than a "Midsummer's Night," entertaining New Yorkers for some 30 years, until it was absorbed by the now-defunct *New York Journal-American,* which kept only the old magazine's logo. Puck, however, lives on in two larger-than-life statues perched on a third-floor ledge at the northeast corner of the building and above the elegant marble-columned entranceway, which opens on Lafayette Street.

Walk west on Houston Street to Crosby Street. Turn north (right), and stop about three-quarters of the way to Bleecker Street.

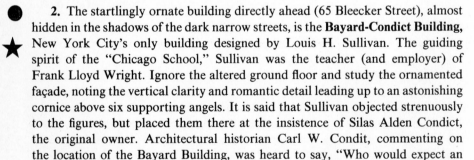

2. The startlingly ornate building directly ahead (65 Bleecker Street), almost hidden in the shadows of the dark narrow streets, is the **Bayard-Condict Building,** New York City's only building designed by Louis H. Sullivan. The guiding spirit of the "Chicago School," Sullivan was the teacher (and employer) of Frank Lloyd Wright. Ignore the altered ground floor and study the ornamented façade, noting the vertical clarity and romantic detail leading up to an astonishing cornice above six supporting angels. It is said that Sullivan objected strenuously to the figures, but placed them there at the insistence of Silas Alden Condict, the original owner. Architectural historian Carl W. Condit, commenting on the location of the Bayard Building, was heard to say, "Who would expect an aesthetic experience on Bleecker Street?" The building was erected 1879–99.

To the right, on the southeast corner, are the decaying remains of a once-proud Federal-style residence, with dormers in both the front and rear of its typical peaked roof.

Turn east (right) to Lafayette Street, past Jones Alley, turning left into Bond Street.

3. In the 1830s Bond Street was one of the city's most fashionable. Lined with Greek Revival–style houses, it was a secluded, peaceful street whose most

The last horse car in the City of New York on the Bleecker Street Line, on its farewell trip on Bleecker Street, between Mercer Street and Broadway, July 26, 1917. Horse car service began in 1832. Although electrification was begun before the turn of the century, New York held on tenaciously to a number of its "horse power" lines long after most other cities had electrified theirs. (Museum of the City of New York)

celebrated resident, Albert Gallatin, lived at No. 1. As Secretary of the Treasury under Thomas Jefferson and later minister to France, he helped reshape the financial structure of the country, and was a founder of the nearby University of the City of New York, later to be called N.Y.U. A few badly misshapen Federal-style houses survive on the north side of the street. Curiously, Shinbone Alley makes a right turn in the middle of the block, and emerges as Jones Alley for a brief block and a quarter.

On the site of Gallatin's residence is one of the best preserved cast-iron buildings in the city. Built in French Second Empire style, it was designed by Stephen D. Hatch in 1871 for the firm of **Robbins & Appleton,** watchmakers. Shortly thereafter, the publishing house of D. Appleton & Company (no relation) moved into No. 1-3-5 Bond Street. The six-story office building, with floor upon floor of large recessed plate glass windows separated by graceful columns and surmounted at each level by a simple cornice, is topped by an enormous mansard roof with three ornate pavilions. The light and airy interior must have provided a relatively pleasant place to work. Adjacent No. 7-9, also in cast iron, is far less interesting.

At the northeast corner of Bond Street and Broadway is the very handsome red brick **former Brooks Brothers Store** (670 Broadway). Best viewed from across Broadway, this engaging 1873 Victorian pile, planned by George E. Harney, clearly shows the influence of English designer Charles Eastlake in its many decorative motifs. Find the date of construction in the ornaments on

Broadway, looking north from the old Broadway Central Hotel toward Great Jones Street, ca. 1895. Elegantly clad ladies and gentlemen walk by hanson cabs waiting at the curb, while horse drawn traffic and Broadway cable cars clatter by. (Consolidated Edison Company of New York)

the four pilasters. This was Brooks Brothers' third location. An earlier site was at 466–468 Broadway [*see* pages 186 and 187].

Return to Lafayette Street again, and continue east on Bond Street.

4. No. 26 Bond Street is an unusually large late Federal-style house, and was probably the residence of an affluent family.

5. At the northwest corner of the Bowery, the **former Bond Street Savings Bank** is pure wedding cake in cast iron. Built in 1874 from plans by Henry Engelbert, it is another attractive example of the French Second Empire style. With the influx of many German immigrants into the neighborhood, it later became the German Exchange Bank; and with its subsequent failure in the early 20th century, it ended its banking career as a deteriorating loft building. But in 1963, with the growing popularity of off-Broadway theater, it gained a new lease on life as a playhouse. The newborn **Bouwerie Lane Theater,** home of the Jean Cocteau Repertory Company, won additional recognition when it was designated an official New York City Landmark. Note the lovely façade with its rows of paired Corinthian and Ionic columns flanking the windows, the ornate modillions under the cornices of the roof and surmounting pediment, and the stately entranceway guarded by paneled cast-iron newel posts. Diagonally across the Bowery is the Amato Opera, long a cultural landmark in the East Village.

Walk north one block on the Bowery.

Originally **"Bouwerie"** in Dutch, the street's name hearkens back to the days of Peter Stuyvesant, when he had it built as a road from the lower city past the "bouweries," or farms, to his own estate a half-mile north. Although the Bowery is now synonymous with the unfortunate flotsam of society who inhabit much of this now-dismal thoroughfare, it was for a time a lively center of entertainment. Music halls, theaters, and beer gardens were numerous in the late 19th century, and the street is recalled in the humorous lyrics of the Gay '90s song "The Bowery—I'll Never Go There Anymore!"

The building on the south side, across the Bowery (do not bother to cross the street!), is the **Men's Shelter,** administered by the City's Social Services Administration. It offers a free bed and meals to the indigent. Careful scrutiny of the near wall reveals an old sign indicating that this was once the Bowery Branch of the Y.M.C.A.

Turn left (west) on Great Jones Street.

There never was anyone named "Great Jones"! The land for the street was deeded to the city by Samuel Jones, a lawyer and New York's first comptroller. The agreement called for the street to be named for him; however, there was

The Broadway Central Hotel, built in 1871 in Second Empire style by Henry Engelbert, replaced an earlier hotel called the LaFarge House. A year after it opened, it witnessed the sensational shooting of Jim Fisk. The enormous hotel deteriorated badly in its last years and gave up the ghost in a spectacular cave-in of its north wing in 1973. The site is now occupied by an N.Y.U. Law School dormitory. (New York City Landmarks Preservation Commission)

already a Jones Street (in Greenwich Village), and it was named for his brother-in-law, Dr. Gardiner Jones. Neither would relinquish his prerogative, so for a time there were *two* Jones Streets. To resolve the dilemma, Samuel Jones suggested that *his* street be named Great Jones Street. (Logically, it should have been called East Third Street, which it really is, anyway!)

6. Midway down the block, at No. 44, is the home of **Engine Company 33 and Hook & Ladder 9.** Formerly the headquarters of the New York City Fire Department, it is a splendid example of the French Beaux Arts style and was designed by Ernest Flagg and W. B. Chambers in 1898. At the time of its construction, it was the headquarters of the chief of the Fire Department, so it is appropriately flamboyant in appearance. Imagine the excitement and thrill when the scarlet and gold horse-drawn engines, their steam boilers belching smoke, would dash out to answer the calls!

Across the street, at **Nos. 31 and 33,** are two mid-19th-century commercial buildings. A glance at the pediment reveals that they were once a pair of livery stables. Serving a similar purpose as today's public garage and rent-a-car establishment, Bienecke's boarded horses and also rented various types of rigs to those who were unable to maintain their own private stable.

7. Reaching the corner of Lafayette Street, look through the parking lot on the northeast corner, and seek out the apse of an old neo-Gothic church protruding from the rear of a nondescript commercial building. About a hundred years ago it was St. Bartholomew's Protestant Episcopal Church. With the industrialization of the neighborhood, the congregation departed, and the building was sold. Don't look for the front of the church on the East 4th Street side . . . it isn't there any more.

8. **No. 376–380 Lafayette Street** (on the northwest corner) is a solid and imposing Romanesque Revival–style loft building. It was built in 1888, from plans by Henry J. Hardenbergh, who designed, among others, the Plaza Hotel, the Dakota Apartments, and the Consolidated Edison Building. The ornamental detail is in brick and terra-cotta—a remarkably handsome structure for an industrial building.

Turn right (north) on Lafayette Street, then right into East 4th Street.

9. **The Old Merchant's House,** at 29 East 4th Street, is probably the only surviving Greek Revival–style house in the city—intact within as well as outside. Built in 1830–32 by Joseph Brewster from plans attributed to famed architect Minard Lafever, it was purchased in 1835 by Seabury Tredwell, a wealthy merchant. It remained in the Tredwell family until the last surviving member, Gertrude Tredwell, died in 1933. To save the house and its original furnishings from the auctioneer's block, the property was then purchased by George Chapman, a distant relative, whose sole interest was to maintain it as a unique example of a New York City family's house and style of living. Among the furnishings are the original furniture, mirrors, carpets, draperies, chinaware, and a collection of dresses, shawls, and bonnets. The interior architectural elements also preserved are the mantelpieces, wainscoting, moldings, columns, banisters, and the kitchen.

Lafayette Place (now Lafayette Street) was an elegant, tree-lined cul-de-sac around 1870. Not visible on the left of the street are the imposing façades of Colonnade Row, the houses of the wealthiest citizens in town. Note the raised pedestrian crosswalks and Greek Revival–style fence. The view is north from Great Jones Street. (New-York Historical Society)

There is even a secret passageway that leads under the house from an upstairs closet. Chapman organized the Historic Landmark Society to maintain the Old Merchant's House as a public museum.

Time and neglect, however, had begun to take their toll. To protect and preserve the landmark, which had suffered from the effects of weather and vandalism, a major renovation was undertaken in 1973–79 under the supervision of New York University architect Joseph Roberto; and now the Old Merchant's House, completely restored with all its furnishings, is open for all to enjoy. (Open Sundays, 1–4 P.M.)

10. At 37 East 4th Street, a few doors east, is the **Samuel Tredwell Skidmore House.** Built in 1844–45 for a cousin of Seabury Tredwell, it is a late Greek Revival–style house, and much less imposing than its nearby neighbor. At one time the entire block was lined with similar houses.

Return to Lafayette Street.

11. On the northeast corner, at No. 393–399 Lafayette Street, stands the massive **De Vinne Press Building.** One of the great printing "giants" of the late 19th and early 20th centuries, Theodore L. De Vinne was the founder of the Grolier Club and the publisher of such popular magazines as *Scribner's, Century,* and *St. Nicholas.* The De Vinne Press was famous for its innovative typefaces and high-quality books. The architects, Babb, Cook, & Willard, designed this "Romanesque Utilitarian" structure in 1885, in a style reminiscent of the aqueducts of Ancient Rome. Notice how thick the masonry bearing walls are, since it was built before the advent of steel skeletons. The name of the old establishment is still visible on the upper façade.

12. No. 409–411 Lafayette Street demonstrates how different building mediums can be employed together successfully (in this case, cast iron and brick) to produce a functional and aesthetic effect. Viewed from a distance, the ornate two-story-high cast-iron columns of the **Durst Building,** designed in 1891 by

Alfred Zucker, are an imposing base for this former men's clothing store and factory. The "squared" style of the larger columns adds a feeling of strength, while lightness results from the beaded bands on all the columns, the ornate design on the spandrel panels above the ground floor, and the round-arch windows on the second floor; while slender iron columns divide the paired windows above.

13. The superb Corinthian colonnade across the street (Nos. 428, 430, 432, and 434) is all that remains of one of the most magnificent rows of Greek Revival town houses in America. On the site of John Jacob Astor's Vauxhall Gardens Amusement Park, and completed in 1833 by developer Seth Geer from plans by Alexander Jackson Davis, **Colonnade Row** is an architectural treasure and an outstanding example of early urban design. Originally named LaGrange Terrace, after the Marquis de Lafayette's country estate in France, the group consisted of nine mansions on what was then Lafayette Place. (Lafayette Street was not opened till much later; Lafayette Place was a shady, cobblestoned cul-de-sac extending only to where Great Jones Street is now. *See photographs below and on page 113.*)

Constructed of Westchester marble and set back behind a 30-foot courtyard, the impressive row was separated from the street by an iron fence. The nine

Colonnade Row, on the west side of Lafayette Street, was a group of nine marble town houses built in 1833, which became the most fashionable addresses in the city. Today only four of these survive. (Museum of the City of New York)

houses were reduced to four when the John Wanamaker Department Store callously destroyed them early in this century to make way for a garage for their delivery trucks. (The John Wanamaker name appears on the ugly building to the left.) When he built the row, Geer was criticized for speculating "so far out in the country," but his plan was vindicated when possession was taken by such notables as John Jacob Astor, Cornelius Vanderbilt, Warren Delano (Franklin Delano Roosevelt's grandfather), and other wealthy citizens. Washington Irving stayed here for a time, as did two distinguished visitors from England, William Makepeace Thackeray and Charles Dickens. In 1844, then-President John Tyler secretly married the daughter of resident David Gardner. John Jacob Astor died here in 1848 at the age of 85, leaving a fortune of $20 million. An interesting reminder of John Jacob Astor's lucrative fur business can be seen in the colorful ceramic panels depicting beavers, imbedded in the tile walls of the IRT Astor Place subway station, one block north.

The houses, now subdivided into apartments and commercial properties, are in a rather depressing state. The original stoops have been removed, outrageous disfigurements have sprung up on the roof, and many of the ornate details are either damaged or missing (observe what is left of the lovely row of anthemions on the cornice). In addition, a patina of a hundred years of neglect covers the entire façade. Some attempt at preservation and restoration is being undertaken by a few of the owners, which may possibly return this landmark to a modicum of its former opulence.

14. Facing the beautiful row is the **former Astor Library,** now the **New York Shakespeare Festival Building.** Begun in 1849 as Astor's bequest to the City of New York, the Library was built in three stages (south wing, by Alexander Saeltzer, completed in 1853; center wing, by Griffith Thomas, in 1859; and north wing, by Thomas Stent, in 1881). It was the city's first major library accessible to the public, and was combined in 1895 with the Tilden Foundation and the Lenox Library to form the nucleus of the New York Public Library.

From 1921 to 1965 the building was the headquarters of the HIAS—the Hebrew Immigrant Aid & Sheltering Society—which since 1884 has been a worldwide migration agency responsible for the rescue of almost four million refugees and their settlement in lands of freedom. When the HIAS moved uptown to larger quarters, the survival of this lovely Italian Renaissance *palazzo* was seriously threatened. Virtually at the eleventh hour it was saved through the efforts of impresario Joseph Papp and a group of concerned citizens who ultimately convinced a skeptical City Council to recommend municipal purchase of the building as a permanent home for the New York Shakespeare Festival.

Renovation began in 1967 under the supervision of architect Giorgio Cavaglieri (who restored the Jefferson Market Courthouse; *see* Greenwich Village, 34), and was completed several years later. The Festival Building is an ideal example of adaptive reuse, proving that one can deal with old spaces and make them work. Contrary to the custom of gutting the interior and merely preserving the façade, Cavaglieri saved the elaborate interior, converting the two-tier skylit atrium of the former main reading room into the 300-seat Anspacher Theater. Two other large spaces were likewise made into theaters. The entrance and lobby remains a classic Corinthian colonnade. (Walk in, look around . . . and purchase a subscription to a performance series!)

15. No. **436–440** is a large cast-iron commercial building in virtually pristine condition. Although no architectural beauty, it is typical of this type of construction [*see* SoHo Cast-Iron District walking tour]. It was designed by Edward Kendall in 1870 for Alfred Benjamin & Company, which manufactured men's clothing. Note their initials on the six escutcheons mounted on the pilasters. Interesting are the ram's horn volutes on the capitals, and the full ram's horn on the shields.

Adjacent No. **442–450,** occupying the corner lot, is maintained in almost original appearance by appreciative owners. Built in 1875 from plans by Griffith Thomas, it was for many years the headquarters of book publisher J. J. Little & Company (now Little, Brown & Co.), and is another example of the pleasing wedding of cast iron and masonry.

16. The **District 65 Building,** formerly Clinton Hall, and before that the Mercantile Library Building (George E. Harney, 1890), has little to recommend it architecturally; however, it occupies the site of the old Astor Place Opera House, and "thereby hangs a tale. . . ."

A black page in New York City history was written on the evening of May 10, 1849, when a rampaging mob of thousands stormed the theater in one of the city's bloodiest outbursts of violence. **The Astor Place Riot,** as the event came to be called, stemmed from a bitter rivalry and ongoing feud between English tragedian William Macready and America's greatest actor, Edwin Forrest. Against a background of anti-British sentiment and a general antipathy toward foreigners as well as home-grown aristocrats, feelings had been running high for a number of weeks—spurred in great measure by rumormongers, know-nothings, and a sensationalist press.

That evening, when the curtain rose on the English actor's performance of *Macbeth,* a large and noisy crowd gathered in Astor Place, spilling over into the adjoining streets from Broadway to the Bowery. During the play, Macready was pelted with a steady stream of rotten eggs, copper pennies, and an assortment of vegetables. In the third scene a group of gangsters, led by small-time politician Isaiah Rynders, interrupted Macready's performance with screams and epithets, while a group of supporters of the English actor hurled back abuse with equal vigor. When the play was able to resume, the continuing commotion drowned out the stage. By the time the third act had begun, the mob outside started to assault the theater with bricks and stones. The police, although forewarned, were hopelessly outnumbered, and could do nothing to quell the screaming, cursing multitude that was now advancing on the theater's entrance. Estimates numbered the raging crowd at between 10,000 and 20,000.

In the meantime, the militia had been summoned from the nearby Tompkins Market Armory, but was restrained from action by nervous Mayor Caleb Woodhull, who feared the political consequences of any drastic action. Woodhull himself quietly fled the scene, leaving decisions to the unit's commanding officer. Finally, the order was given to fire, and after a warning volley over the heads of the rioters, the militiamen reluctantly fired volley after volley at point-blank range, killing 31 persons and leaving 150 wounded, putting an end to the worst theater riot in history.

17. At the time of the riot, Astor Place extended to where the "black cube" now rests, at the juncture with 8th Street (then called Clinton Place). Little St. Ann's Church occupied the site until Lafayette Street was pushed through to meet Fourth Avenue. Now occupying the traffic island is sculptor Bernard Rosenthal's stabile, **Alamo,** erected in 1967. Another of his works, an enormous five-disk steel sculpture, adorns Police Plaza, near the Municipal Building downtown. The sculpture can be rotated if you push hard enough.

18. Against the backdrop of a wide-open sky, the stunning **Cooper Union Foundation Building** stands as a most pleasing sight. Completed in 1859, this gift to the people by industrialist-engineer-philanthropist Peter Cooper played a significant role in the development of the city. The "Union" was established as the first free, private, nonsectarian, coeducational college. Dedicated to the fields of science and art, it occupies a special place of respect among American colleges and universities.

Peter Cooper (1791–1883), a self-educated "Renaissance Man," was responsible for the first successful American railway locomotive (the "Tom Thumb"); he worked with Cyrus W. Field in the laying of the Atlantic Cable, and, with Samuel F. B. Morse, developed the telegraph. Cooper also battled corrupt politi-

Watercolor drawing of the Astor Place Riot of May 10, 1849, as militia from the nearby Tompkins Market Armory were firing into the crowd. A rampaging mob of between 10,000 and 20,000 stormed the Astor Place Opera House as the culmination of bitter feelings against English actor William Macready. When order was finally restored, 31 lay dead and 150 were injured. (Museum of the City of New York)

cians and helped to improve the city's public school system. With the profits from his ironworks and a glue factory, he built Cooper Union. In 1876 he ran unsuccessfully for president on the Greenback ticket, although his son Edward was elected mayor of the city, as was his son-in-law, Abram S. Hewitt.

The building, designed in a kind of "Italian Renaissance cum Industrial" architectural style, is a unique achievement in itself, being the first to be constructed with wrought-iron beams as its framework. The exterior is of brownstone and rough-hewn sandstone, with cast-iron columns, pilasters, and arches. It was originally a five-story building, but the "factory-roof" art studios were subsequently superimposed. The street level was built with rows of small shops to provide a steady source of revenue for the institution. On the south end of

Diagonally across from Clinton Hall and the former Astor Place Opera House was Aberle's Theater, previously St. Ann's Roman Catholic Church. The theater opened in 1879, changed its name to the Germania in 1894, and was demolished in 1903. St. Ann's, a national Catholic shrine, is now located at 110 East 12th Street. (The J. Clarence Davies Collection, Museum of the City of New York)

The Astor Place Opera House at the intersection of Astor and Clinton places (later 8th Street) was rebuilt after the riot of 1849 and later became Clinton Hall and the Mercantile Library. In this photo taken ca. 1868, the building also houses auction rooms and the Sixpenny Savings Bank. The present building on the site, the District 65 Center, was also called Clinton Hall. (New-York Historical Society)

the roof, the cylindrical protuberance houses the shaft of the original circular elevator. Cooper anticipated a lift system and installed the shaft even before a practical elevator was available. The novel construction of the building, employing steel railroad rails produced in his Trenton foundry, demanded that the supported sections of the "Union" coincide in measurement with the standard length of these rails. The rails spanned the brick bearing walls and supported the brick floor arches. In a recent renovation, architecture students were fortunate in obtaining a first-hand view of the original rail placement, as the central section of the interior was literally jacked up several floors while the old masonry walls were replaced by more modern steel and reinforced concrete. Note the historical plaques on the north side.

The showpiece of the interior is the **Great Hall,** a magnificent auditorium, crisscrossed by arcades of supporting columns topped by granite arches. It was in the Great Hall that the Institution's inaugural lecture was given by Mark Twain in 1859. A year later Abraham Lincoln delivered his momentous "Might makes Right" speech, establishing a Cooper Union lecture tradition followed by every president up to Woodrow Wilson.

The reconstruction, adhering essentially to the original plans of architect

Frederick A. Peterson, was carried out by Cooper Union graduate architects under the direction of architecture department head John Hejduk.

Walk south along the Cooper Union Building to the small park on Cooper Square.

19. The **statue of Peter Cooper** was executed in 1897 by one of the country's foremost sculptors, Augustus Saint-Gaudens. Among his best known works are the equestrian statue of General Sherman near the Plaza Hotel, the statue of David G. Farragut in Madison Square Park, the marble altar relief in the nearby Church of the Ascension, as well as the design of one of our former 20-dollar gold pieces. The base and canopy of the monument are by Stanford White.

Notice the attractive, and very visible, Cooper Union clock with its seven-foot frosted glass face. Once driven by an enormous weight and pendulum, it is now powered by a tiny electric motor.

The Bowery, which becomes Third Avenue at this point, was once darkened by the **Third Avenue El,** which rumbled by overhead from 1879 to 1950, on its way from South Ferry and Chatham Square to several points in the Bronx. Old-timers still look back with relish at the speedy, open-air ride provided by the old El. Although the Bowery and Third Avenue were never thoroughfares

An engraving of Cooper Union, with the Tompkins Market (right) and Bible House (left), enlivened by prancing horses and richly clad citizens as seen in Valentine's Manual of 1861, looking north from Fourth Avenue and 6th Street. (Museum of the City of New York)

of scenic beauty, the exciting cityscape panoramas provided by these elevated trains cannot be duplicated by the much slower-moving ground-level buses.

20. The **Abram S. Hewitt Memorial Hall** of Cooper Union (Clinton & Russell, 1905), named for Peter Cooper's partner and son-in-law, occupies the site of the Tompkins Market Armory. Before it burned down, the old barnlike structure was a public market on the ground floor and an armory above. It was from here that the 27th Regiment of the New York National Guard was summoned to quell the Stone Cutters' Riot at the Washington Parade Ground [now Washington Square; *see* Greenwich Village, 7]; some years later, the Astor Place Riot; and in 1863, the Draft Riots (although in the latter disturbance, the militia had to be hastily called back from the just ended Battle of Gettysburg). The unit later became the 7th Regiment and is now based in the landmark Seventh Regiment Armory, at Park Avenue and 67th Street.

Cross the Bowery to the northeast corner of East 7th Street.

The area east of the Bowery, roughly between Houston Street and East 14th Street, and extending almost to the East River, is the **"East Village,"** formerly considered part of the Lower East Side.

From the early 19th century, successive waves of immigrants occupied the crowded tenements, leaving their individual ethnic stamp on the neighborhood. First came the Irish, followed by Germans, Jews, Poles, Ukrainians, and after World War II, the Spanish-speaking, mainly from Puerto Rico. In the 1950s and '60s the low rents attracted artists, writers, "beatniks," "hippies," and many who just liked the ethnic mix.

In the several-square-block area just east of the Bowery, centered on East 7th Street, there remains an active, tight-knit **Ukrainian enclave.**

21. The former Metropolitan Savings Bank, now the **First Ukrainian Assembly of God,** is an ornate pile of marble, very similar in style to the cast-iron buildings for which it served as a model. Attributed to architect Carl Pfeiffer and built in 1868, its stately French Second Empire façade must have presented a convincing appearance of strength to its depositors, and it was one of the city's first fireproof buildings. (The old name is still barely visible above the first floor.)

22. At 11 East 7th Street is **Surma's Ukrainian Shop**—a fascinating emporium offering Ukrainian books, music, and records, colorful "peasant" clothing, painted (real) eggs, jewelry, and owner-cultivated honey.

23. **McSorley's Old Ale House** (No. 15) antedates the Ukrainian influx by many years, and claims to be the oldest saloon in the city (1854). Formerly a man's domain, it now permits women to share the authentic old-time atmosphere. In the dimly lit tavern, dozens of aging photographs and yellowing newspaper clippings hang on the grimy sheet-tin walls.

24. **St. George's Ukrainian Catholic Church** (Appolinare Ocsada, 1977) replaced an earlier church which was situated on an adjacent lot. St. George's, with its large school, is the religious and cultural center of the Ukrainian Catholic community.

Continue toward Second Avenue.

At No. 31, across the street, is the Hebrew Actors' Union and Actor's Club, which hearkens back to the golden age of the Yiddish theater at the turn of the century.

At the height of the Jewish immigration, Second Avenue from Houston Street to 14th Street was known as the **Yiddish Rialto.** Little now remains of the once lively Yiddish theater except for an occasional on-Broadway production. The old playhouses that once lined Second Avenue were either demolished or stand vacant. One of a small handful of surviving buildings is the ornate little **Orpheum Theater,** around the corner at 126 Second Avenue. It still hangs in as a legitimate theater, but no longer as a Yiddish playhouse.

Continue north on Second Avenue to just beyond St. Mark's Place.

Side by side, at Nos. 135 and 137 Second Avenue, are the **Ottendorfer Branch of the New York Public Library** and the **Stuyvesant Polyclinic.** Both were donated by Ann and Oswald Ottendorfer, German-American philanthropists who were deeply concerned with the cultural and physical welfare of the large German community of the Lower East Side. Both buildings were designed by the same architect, William Schickel, and were erected in 1883–84. The library and clinic, formerly the *Freie Bibliothek und Lesehall* and the German Dispensary, respectively, are a unified pair, the former in Victorian style, with some elements of neo-Italian Renaissance and Queen Anne; and the latter in an exuberant version of neo-Italian Renaissance style, with innovative and decorative use of terra cotta.

Walk west on St. Mark's Place.

25. St. Mark's Place is the "main drag" of the East Village and it was the center of New York City's "counterculture." It is difficult to conceive that this was a most fashionable residential block in the early 19th century, with rows of elegant Federal and Greek Revival–style town houses. Vestiges still survive here and there along the block, covered by coats of garish paint and hidden by all manner of "improvements."

No. 20 was once the **Daniel LeRoy House** (1832). The last holdout of the row of town houses on the south side of the street, it shows many late Federal-style features. (Note the historical plaque.)

Sprawling **Nos. 21–25,** a group of old Federal houses joined together to form a single large hall, were until the 1960s the *Dom,* or Polish National Home, a social and cultural center for the Polish community of the Lower East Side. It later went commercial and housed the Electric Circus, a major rock 'n' roll establishment.

No. 12 was built for the **German American Shooting Society** in 1885. Like the *Dom,* it was also a social club. (The beer drinking was done here, the shooting elsewhere.)

A plaque on the next-to-last building on the south side claims that James Fenimore Cooper once lived in a house on the site. **No. 4** is another survivor of the early town-house row.

26. Diagonally across St. Mark's Place, between 8th and 9th streets, is the modern **Cooper Union Engineering Building** (Voorhees, Smith, Smith, and Haines, 1961). It occupies the site of the old "Bible House," headquarters of the American Bible Society from 1852 to 1956, when it moved uptown to the Lincoln Center area—probably the last publishing house to move from the district.

Continue east to Fourth Avenue and turn right to 9th Street.

27. With the large number of local institutions dedicated to books and book production (Astor Library, Mercantile Library, Cooper Union, Scribner's, Bible House, the many publishing houses, as well as nearby New York University), it was no surprise that Fourth Avenue north to 14th Street became the second-hand book center of the city. The five blocks that once comprised **"Booksellers' Row"** boasted no fewer than two dozen book dealers. Sidewalk stands in front of the shops were always piled high with cheap books of every description, but the *cognoscenti* would seek out the real "finds" on the dusty shelves of the dark, labyrinthine interiors. Only a scant few of the booksellers remain: Abbey, No. 61; Biblo & Tannen, No. 63; Fourth Avenue Bookstore, No. 138; and Strand, at 828 Broadway. As in the past, browsers are always welcome.

28. On the west side of Fourth Avenue, between 10th and 11th streets, is the charming Gothic Revival–style **Grace Church Houses and School.** Enriching the appearance of the street, it was built in harmony with the landmark Grace Church, around the corner on Broadway. [For a description of Grace Church, *see* Ladies' Mile, 2.] The attractive neo-Gothic-style group of buildings were erected in sections over a 35-year period: **The Clergy House,** No. 92 (Heins & LaFarge, 1892); **Grace Memorial House** (Huntington House), No. 94–96 (James Renwick, Jr., 1882–83); **Neighborhood House,** No. 98 (Renwick, Aspinwall & Tucker, 1906–07). In 1974–75 the church sought to demolish Nos. 92 and 94–96 to enlarge its school, and became engaged in a bitter struggle with preservationists. The matter was resolved by gutting the interior but preserving the façades.

End of tour.

Although the tour ends here, an optional side trip may be made to the nearby **St. Marks Historic District:**

Return to 9th Street and turn left, passing Third Avenue, and enter Stuyvesant Street. This diagonally running street was once the driveway from the Bouwerie Road to Peter Stuyvesant's estate. No. 21, the Stuyvesant-Fish House, is a rare early Federal residence (1803–04), and was built by the great-grandson of the governor as a wedding gift for his daughter Elizabeth, when she married Nicholas Fish.

The houses Nos. 21–35 and 42–46, plus 106–128 and 109–129 East 10th Street, are a unified group of Anglo-Italianate row houses which form part of the **"Renwick Triangle."** These handsome brick houses were erected in 1861 by Mathias Banta, a well-known speculative builder, who had purchased the property, once the site of Elizabeth Fish's garden, from her son, Hamilton Fish. The restoration of the buildings, which had begun to deteriorate badly after years of rooming-house occupancy, began in the mid-1960s. Stanford White lived for a time at No. 118 East 10th Street.

Georgian-style **St. Mark's-in-the-Bowery Church** at Second Avenue and 10th Street was built in 1799 on Governor Peter Stuyvesant's *Bouwerie* (farm). The Greek Revival belfry, clock tower, and steeple were added by Ithiel Town in 1828, and the Italianate porch in 1854, contributing harmoniously to the appearance of the church. The governor himself is buried in a vault adjacent to the east wall, and it is said that his private chapel was located at this precise spot; and his manor house was across what is now the intersection of Second Avenue and East 10th Street. A disastrous fire in July 1978, which heavily damaged the interior and caused the roof to collapse, virtually wiped out the landmark, but the dedicated and activist minister and congregation vigorously sought funds through a series of promotional campaigns, and the church has been almost completely restored. Walk through the churchyard and note the various monuments and plaques, including those of American statesman Daniel D. Tompkins and Queen Wilhelmina of the Netherlands.

The IRT Lexington Avenue subway is at Astor Place and Fourth Avenue.

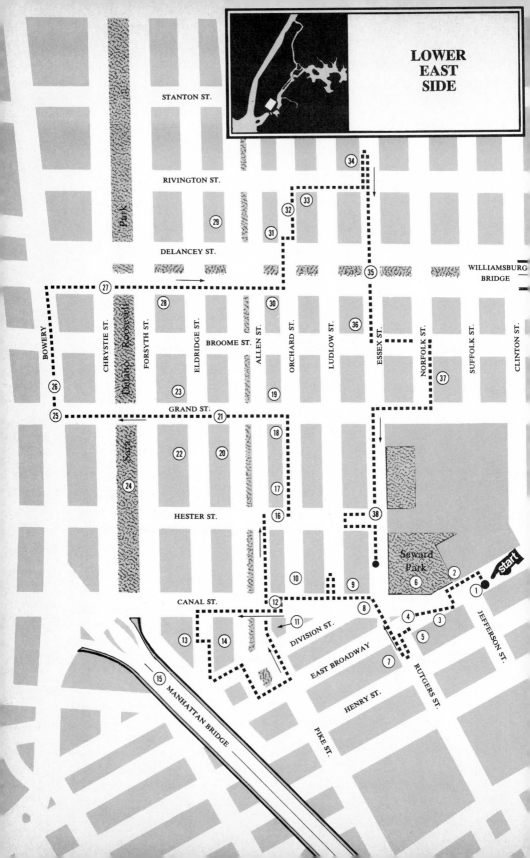

6. The Lower East Side

[*IND F line to East Broadway, walk one block east on East Broadway to Jefferson Street*]

The first tides of mass immigration to this country began sweeping across our shores just before the mid-19th century, with millions of refugees, mostly from Europe, seeking a haven from famines, wars, economic and political repression, and religious persecution. In successive waves they came—Irish, English, Germans, Swedes, Jews, Italians, Slavs—from northern Europe to the eastern Mediterranean, enduring the hardships of a long steerage voyage in crowded, foul ships. Mostly poor and strange to our ways, they would frequently gather together in the larger cities, creating with their fellow countrymen sprawling ghettos that were to become a kind of staging area in the gradual process of assimilation into the new culture.

Among the largest of the immigrant groups were the Jews from eastern Europe, who after 1870 began arriving in ever increasing numbers, fleeing the widespread pogroms and economic restrictions that had become commonplace throughout Poland, Hungary, Bohemia, Russia, and the Balkans. Settling largely on the Lower East Side—a four-square-mile corner of Manhattan bounded roughly by 14th Street on the north, Catherine Street on the south, the Bowery on the west, and the East River on the east—they moved into the squalid, hastily constructed tenements that filled every block in the area. As new arrivals continuously swelled the teeming ghetto, it became the most densely populated district in the world. By 1894, the population reached an astonishing 986 people per acre—one-and-a-half times that of Bombay, India! The immigrant Jews, seeking to maintain their Old World ties, also tended to band together by country of origin, thus creating within the Lower East Side enclaves of Russians, Poles, Rumanians, Lithuanians, Hungarians, and Levantines. In common, however, they shared their religious beliefs and rituals, their miserable living conditions, and their hopes for a better life. Many of the immigrants were drawn to the needle trades, and eked out a meager existence working in the unregulated sweatshops, or laboring in their tiny, crowded cold-water flats in what soon became a cottage garment industry centered about the family sewing machine. Others were employed in the numerous small retail shops and factories that proliferated on the street floors of the tenements, while many chose "private enterprise" as pushcart vendors, hawking an endless variety of wares from these peripatetic two-wheeled establishments that lined the main thoroughfares of the Lower East Side.

In spite of their grinding poverty, the struggle for survival, and the drudgery of daily life, Jewish institutions flourished. More than 500 synagogues and *talmud torahs* (religious schools) were constructed; a Yiddish theater was founded; Hebrew and Yiddish book publishers flourished; and more than a dozen Yiddish newspapers appeared on the newsstands. Rapid naturalization was the immediate goal of all immigrants, and evening classes in English and Americanization at the neighborhood public schools were always jammed to overflowing. Every newcomer dreamed of the day when, no longer a greenhorn, he could climb the economic ladder, become a "real American," and make a better life for himself and his children.

With the passage in the 1920s of restrictive laws, the great flood of immigration was finally halted and the growth of the ghetto stemmed. As families moved to better neighborhoods in the city, the "old neighborhood" began to decline, and the Jewish ghetto is now largely gone. The depressing tenements are being replaced by high-rise apartments; the small family-run shops are giving way to supermarkets and large retail stores; the hundreds of synagogues—many of them awesome architectural masterpieces—are reduced to a scant, crumbling handful; and the *lingua franca,* once exclusively Yiddish, is yielding to a babel of Spanish, Chinese, and Hindi.

The walking tour of the Lower East Side is largely an imaginative glimpse of the past through a number of the vestiges and surviving artifacts of that era of Jewish immigration—a sort of last look at the remnants of the old neighborhood, which in a few short years will be no more. It was a wonderfully rich and fruitful period of American history in which millions of Jews came to the United States through the port of New York and spread across the entire country making their contributions to the total fabric of American life.

Begin the Lower East Side tour at the corner of East Broadway and Jefferson Street (on the park side), one block east of the IND East Broadway subway station. (The tour is best made on a Sunday.)

1. The Educational Alliance (197 East Broadway), known as the Hebrew Institute when the building was erected in 1891, was organized by a group of "uptown Jews" as an educational, cultural, intellectual, and social service center for the residents of the Lower East Side. It provided training in Americanization for the newly arrived immigrants, and is credited with helping speed up the immigrants' process of assimilation with its day and evening classes in English and citizenship. It housed a free library at a time when no public libraries existed in the city, and its classes were later used as models for the New York City Board of Education's citizenship program for the foreign-born. The Alliance also distributed clothing and food to the needy. Classes for children were also offered in Jewish religion and history, and the Alliance conducted free Sabbath and High Holy Day services for those too poor to be members of a synagogue congregation. It was also a pioneer in the concept of summer camp for children.

Through the years the Alliance has expanded its educational work, offering free courses in a wide spectrum of disciplines: art, music, philosophy, drama, science, and vocational skills. Although its original constituency is largely gone, it holds classes in English and citizenship for new Spanish- and Chinese-speaking immigrants. It is also very active in community social service projects, and conducts many programs for senior citizens.

The Lower East Side's population is now approximately 50 percent Puerto Rican (and other Spanish-speaking groups), 15 percent Chinese, 10 percent black, 5 percent others (Indian, Ukrainian, Polish, Albanian, and Italian), and only 20 percent Jewish. The original East Broadway building of the Alliance was modernized in 1970–71 and renamed the David Sarnoff Building. Adjoining the Educational Alliance on Jefferson Street is the David L. Podell Residence for Senior Citizens. This new annex contains subsidized efficiency apartments for the elderly, and has a direct connection into the Alliance building.

2. To the left (in the park) is the **Seward Park Branch of the New York Public Library.** Built in 1910, it was one of the first branches of the newly established free municipal library system. The public library was founded by Andrew Carnegie, who was instrumental in merging the Astor, Tilden, and Lenox libraries—the three largest private collections in the city.

So great was this free library's popularity with the immigrants when it opened that it was not uncommon to see long lines of adults and youngsters patiently awaiting their turn to enter the crowded building. Until recently this branch had the largest Yiddish collection in the city. Next to the library, at the turn of the century, stood the office of *Der Groisser Kundess* (The Big Stick), a popular Yiddish weekly that published humorous stories and cartoons, and offered a bit of comic relief from the grim realities of immigrant life.

3. Across the street, at 175 East Broadway, towers the ten-story **Jewish Daily Forward Building** (George A. Boehn, 1911). The building is no longer occupied by the *Forward,* as the newspaper has moved its offices uptown, where it continues to publish, with an annual deficit made up by contributions from loyal supporters. Founded in 1897 by Abraham Cahan, the *Forward* became the most influential newspaper in the Jewish community, and was read with a dedication second only to that given to the religious books. As an ardent campaigner for the improvement of the human condition, Abe Cahan and the *Forward* supported the labor movement, fought dishonest politicians, and led in the battle to eliminate the sweatshops, at the same time helping the immigrants adapt to the New World and encouraging them to become informed, loyal citizens. The *Forward* always lent a sympathetic ear to the problems of its readers, and until 1982 conducted a daily column called the *Bintel Brief* (Bundle of Letters), in which problems of readers were printed and answered by the editor. (The column has yielded to one on Social Security.) The paper has always provided a forum for the greatest Yiddish writers (Isaac Bashevis Singer is still a regular contributor), and as the last surviving Yiddish daily in North America, it maintains a small staff of foreign correspondents who provide material not available from the usual wire services. Its present circulation is barely a fifth of the 1924 peak of 200,000, but there is still sufficient interest in Yiddish and support from charitable contributions to keep it alive.

The building, which housed not only the *Forward* but also an active Yiddish theater and the offices of many Jewish labor organizations, is now in the hands of a Chinese church, which is converting it to use by the fast-growing Chinese community of the Lower East Side. To the east of the Forward Building, at No. 189, in a structure which now houses a Chinese noodle factory, was the home of the large-circulation *Morning Journal–Day,* once two Yiddish dailies that merged in the late 1920s. Its closing in 1972 was mourned by many faithful readers.

4. Triangular **Nathan Straus Square** is named for the Jewish philanthropist who in 1919 sponsored a program of free sterilized-milk stations for children throughout the country. Nathan Straus, a partner in the R. H. Macy enterprise with his brother, Isadore, was active for many years in charitable causes. (Isadore and his wife went down on the *Titanic* in 1912.)

The circular marble column was erected in tribute to the servicemen of the Lower East Side who gave their lives in both World Wars.

5. The **Garden Cafeteria,** at the corner of Rutgers Street and East Broadway, is very much a Lower East Side landmark, albeit unofficial. For years, the "Garden" has been a favored meeting place of writers, actors, and other local "intelligentsia," as well as for a colorful assortment of East Side characters. It offers such typical Jewish gastronomical dairy delights as blintzes, borscht, matzoh ball soup (of course!), herring, carp, pirogen, kashe varnishkes, and a tempting variety of vegetarian steaks and roasts, as well as sinfully luscious desserts. This kosher establishment has a cafeteria in front and a restaurant in the rear. The waiters in the restaurant section add a special touch with their zealous dedication to stuffing patrons "just like mother did," frowning in undisguised disapproval if a recommended specialty is rejected or if food is left afterward on the plate. Don't miss the mural on the wall of the cafeteria depicting the former artisans' market of Hester Park (now Seward Park). In former times, if one needed a plumber, carpenter, or electrician, he went to the artisans' market, bargained for the man's services, and brought him to the apartment for the job.

6. **Seward Park,** carved out of a former slum district, provides a pleasant retreat for the inhabitants of the surrounding crowded and shadeless streets. A small but busy "thieves market" near the Essex Street entrance should be avoided.

7. **St. Teresa's Roman Catholic Church,** at the corner of Rutgers and Henry streets, was founded in 1863 to serve the growing Irish immigrant community that at the time occupied much of the Lower East Side. Built in 1841 as the

Hester Street was the main shopping thoroughfare of the Lower East Side, with pushcarts, shops, and stalls lining both sides of the street. This view, looking east from Essex Street to Norfolk Street, was taken in 1899, at the height of Jewish immigration. (Museum of the City of New York)

First Presbyterian Church of New York, it was purchased through the efforts of then-Archbishop Corrigan, and now serves new immigrant groups. It is possibly the only trilingual Catholic church in the city, offering masses in English, Spanish, and Chinese. (Only one other Catholic church offers services in Chinese, the Church of the Transfiguration, on Mott Street in Chinatown.) Its adjacent parking lot was once the site of the Hebrew National *wurstfabrik.*

Rutgers Street is named for the Henry Rutgers family, whose farm occupied much of the land from this point to the East River during the Colonial period. Their property bordered the James DeLancey farm, and the boundary, once a country lane, is now appropriately called **Division Street.** Division Street beyond the Manhattan Bridge was famous early in the century for its millinery district and its very aggressive "pulleresses"—women employees who stood outside the store and pulled in the unwary to get "bargains." From the 1920s until the early 1970s it was a well-known center for women's outerwear.

8. The nameless square (or triangle) formed by the confluence of Canal and Division streets is particularly colorful during the Jewish festival of Succoth, or Feast of Tabernacles, which according to the lunar calendar can fall anywhere from late September to mid-October. The sidewalks are lined with vendors, many in Hasidic garb, selling myrtle leaves, palm fronds, and citrons imported from the Holy Land. These are bought by religious Jews to decorate their *Succah,* or outdoor lattice hut, where meals are taken during the holiday in celebration of the harvest.

9. Walk one block west on Canal Street, noting the number of Hebrew and Yiddish bookstores as well as some new East Indian retail establishments. A faint aroma of curry emanates from several Indian restaurants on the south side of Division Street.

Turn right on Ludlow Street. On the right is the massive structure of the now-defunct **Canal Theater.** When you return to Canal Street, see if you can discover the somewhat altered but still ornate former entrance to this defunct silent-film movie house. It is now occupied by a discount electrical appliance store, and the dark recesses of the theater are used as a warehouse.

At No. 5 Ludlow Street is the equally defunct **Independent Kletzker Brotherly Aid Society** building (1910), whose name and founding date may be read in the pediment. It was customary for newly arrived immigrant groups to maintain association with those from the same *shtetl,* or small town. If the group was large or wealthy enough, they might build a synagogue and a *talmud torah,* purchase a cemetery lot, and sometimes establish a benevolent or mutual-aid society, called a *landsmanshaft,* for their members. This is the only such surviving building in the neighborhood, and was constructed for an immigrant group from the Polish village of Kletsk. The L-shaped building was sold early in this century to Max Kobre's Bank, a private Jewish bank which failed after World War I. (Note the beehives on the second-floor ledge.) In recent times it was the Zion Funeral Chapel; however, changing population patterns forced Zion to move and sell out to two other morticians, one Italian and the other Chinese, and the main floor was then divided in half. The upper stories, which once housed the *landsmanshaft*'s synagogue, have been converted into co-op apartments.

Return to Canal Street and continue west to Orchard Street.

10. Orchard Street for the seven blocks north of Canal Street has been the principal commercial thoroughfare for many years. For those living outside the neighborhood, Orchard Street, originally the location of the DeLancey estate's orchards, is now synonymous with the Lower East Side. Hectic, bustling, and noisy, it is the closest thing to a "native market." Before the pushcarts were ruled off the streets by city ordinance, it was even busier. Here on Sundays come thousands of bargain hunters from all over the New York metropolitan area, taking advantage of the discounts—real and fanciful—offered by the endless row of small retail shops. It is said that the Lower East Side is the only complete mercantile district in the city, where virtually anything can be purchased, and at a lower price than anywhere else. (A stroll along Orchard Street comes later in the tour.)

11. On the southwest corner of Canal and Orchard streets looms the tallest structure on the Lower East Side—**Jarmulovsky's Bank** building. Only a few old-timers remember that active financial institution, founded in 1873 (the building dates from about 1895), which served as the local Baron Rothschild for more than 40 years, ultimately bringing grief to thousands of unlucky depositors when it collapsed during World War I. Federal banking regulations were quite lax in those days, and private banks flourished throughout the country. Sender Jarmulovsky was a shrewd financier whose success was climaxed in the construction of this imposing building at the height of the immigration period. However, the Panic of 1907 and Jarmulovsky's subsequent passing left the bank in shaky condition. A few years later it closed its doors, insolvent, owing its creditors millions and ruining thousands of trusting immigrants.

At the corner of Allen Street, look back at the tall west wall of Jarmulovsky's Bank building, and notice the fading advertisements for the long-gone Perlman Piano Company, a Jewish-owned piano manufacturer whose factory occupied an upper loft, and whose showroom was on Grand Street; and the ad for "House-dresses and Hooverettes" (the latter a woman's apronlike garment), also made in a loft sweatshop.

12. Allen Street, one block west, was once a dark and dingy thoroughfare, echoing with the rattle of the former Second Avenue Elevated, and boasting one of the largest red-light districts in town. With the El gone and the street widened in 1930 (note the absence of building fronts on the east side), it is a main north-south artery of the city, and now has a rather extensive antiques center. Dealing mostly in old (and not-so-old) brass and copper, these shops offer hours of interesting browsing, and good buys can occasionally be had in old candelabra, chandeliers, lamps, and fixtures. But don't try to outsmart the dealers—they've been in business for a long time.

At Eldridge Street turn south (left).

13. The Old Law tenement at **Number 19** is purported to be the birthplace of actor Eddie Cantor. Old Law tenements prevail throughout most of the Lower East Side. Prior to the passage of the "Old Law" in 1879, there was little regulation of the construction of multiple dwellings. Houses were often built of wood, without fire escapes, toilets, or water supply; and there was no provision for the ventilation of interior rooms, as only the front and rear rooms had windows. The 1879 law corrected many of these evils, and included among its requirements that an airshaft be built between adjacent tenement houses to provide (some) light and air for inside rooms, that hallways and stairways be wider and constructed of fireproof materials, that water be piped into each apartment, and that there be a toilet for each two apartments. Thus backyard privies and curbside water pumps became a thing of the past, and the tenements became a bit safer, and possibly a trifle more comfortable. Another prohibition was the construction of the so-called "backyard houses"—multiple dwellings that were built behind other houses, without direct access to the street. The addition of the airshaft to the tenement changed the overhead shape of the building from a simple rectangle to that of an exercise dumbbell—and the name "dumbbell tenement" is still applied to those built under the Old Law. In 1901 the "New Law" was passed, further modifying the building code, widening the airshaft and including a provision that houses higher than five stories must be equipped with an elevator. Seven-story walk-ups were not uncommon in the old days!

Compare this row of Old Law tenements with the row of red brick buildings further south (with curved lintels over the windows), built in the 1870s. These are without airshafts and have narrow hallways with sheet-tin walls and ceilings, and wooden floors and staircases. Fire escapes were added as mandated by the 1879 Law, otherwise these nonfireproof buildings would be frightening fire traps. Scores of pre–Old Law tenements still exist throughout the Lower East Side.

14. The imposing synagogue, **Congregation Khal Adath Jeshurun and Anshe Lubz,** at 12–14 Eldridge Street, was once the largest Jewish house of worship in the neighborhood. Built in 1886 from plans by the renowned architectural firm of Herter Brothers, it is built mainly in Moorish Revival style with some Gothic elements. Except for missing finials on the cornice, the façade is in an excellent state of preservation. The stained-glass windows, however, have suffered from vandalism and neglect. The interior is exceptional, with a hand-carved ark of Italian walnut, sculptured wooden balcony, enormous brass Victorian chandeliers and candelabra, high-quality stained glass, brightly painted wall murals, and a lofty, barrel-vaulted ceiling. Since the building has suffered years of neglect, the effects of weather and vandalism have taken a dreadful toll. A leaking roof and smashed windows have allowed rain and snow to wreak havoc, with the result that the stairways and balcony are threatened with imminent collapse. As the Jewish population of the neighborhood declined through the years, the congregation dwindled to the point where fewer than 20 active members remained to support this great house of worship. The magnificent sanctuary was abandoned in the mid-1930s, and services are held in the basement whenever a *minyan,* or quorum of ten adult males, can be assembled.

Until recently, the future of the synagogue was very much in doubt; however, a group of interested citizens (including the author) organized a preservation committee, and together with newly elected officers, are working to obtain funds to restore the building to its original elegance. As a first step, the synagogue was successfully nominated for landmark status, and simultaneously achieved listing on the National Register of Historic Places. To visit the sanctuary, come on a Saturday or Sunday morning, and if services are being held, ask the volunteer sexton to show it to you . . . and "you don't have to be Jewish." Occasional tours of the building are conducted by the 92nd Street YM–YWHA (telephone 427-6000, ext. 179). A small donation would be received with gratitude, and will be used for the building's preservation.

Continue south on Eldridge Street, turning left on Division Street to Pike Street.

15. The **Manhattan Bridge** overhead was begun in 1905 and completed four years later. It is the last-built of a trio of downtown bridges connecting Manhattan with Brooklyn. (The first, the Brooklyn Bridge, was completed in 1883, and was referred to in Yiddish as the *Alte Brick,* or Old Bridge. The Williamsburg Bridge, opened in 1903, was the *Naiye Brick,* or New Bridge.) A three-cent fare was charged on the creaky trolley that shuttled back and

The Police Court on Essex Street at the corner of Broome was replaced by Seward Park High School. In this view, taken in 1892, the high wall visible in the background was the Ludlow Street Jail, where corrupt "Boss" Tweed had died 14 years before. (New-York Historical Society)

The opening of the Manhattan Bridge in 1909 improved transportation to Brooklyn, and to an extent encouraged further emigration from the Lower East Side. The Manhattan Bridge Three Cents Trolley provided a cheap trip across the East River. (Long Island Historical Society)

(Left) This photograph of a poor Jew with his chalah, *preparing for the Sabbath in a coal cellar, is touching evidence of the struggle for human dignity under conditions of abject poverty. The sign at left indicates that the man may have been a shoemaker by trade. (Photograph by Jacob A. Riis. The Jacob A. Riis Collection. Museum of the City of New York)*

(Left, below) The squalor of tenement life is dramatically apparent in this picture by an unknown photographer, taken, according to the wall calendar, some time in June 1916. The rear room, without window or ventilation, indicates that this is a pre–Old Law tenement, built before 1879. (Community Service Society of New York)

(Below) Sociologist-photographer Jacob Riis visited the old Essex Market School and recorded this crowded little classroom with its coal stoves and gas illumination. The closely-shaven-headed youngsters seem unusually well behaved, doubtless after strong admonition by the usually very strict teachers. (The Jacob A. Riis Collection. Museum of the City of New York)

For youngsters growing up in the crowded, unsanitary Lower East Side tenements, the daily life of grinding poverty left little time to enjoy the pleasures of childhood. They were expected to work in the sweatshops and shoulder their share of the family's struggle for survival.

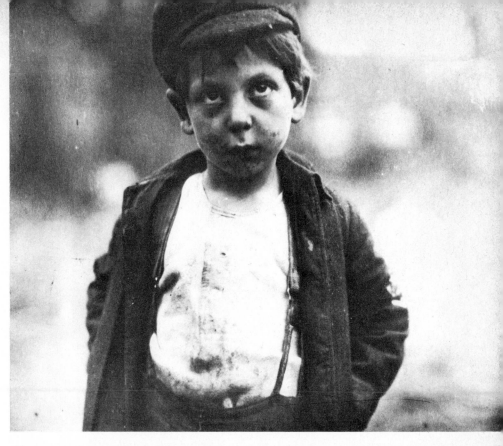

(*Community Service Society of New York*)

(*Photograph by Jessie Tarbox Beals, Community Service Society of New York*)

Sweatshops took many forms. Here a family of Bohemian cigar-makers work busily at their trade. (Photograph by Jacob A. Riis, The Jacob A. Riis Collection. Museum of the City of New York)

Tightly parked rows of pushcarts virtually block access to the sidewalk in this Lower East Side street scene taken in the 1890s. Youngsters generally sought the freedom of the streets to escape the overcrowded condition of their squalid tenement homes. (Community Service Society)

A group of three women buying eggs just before the Sabbath, on Hester Street, 1895. (Photograph by Alice Austen, Staten Island Historical Society)

Photographer Jessie Tarbox Beals posed this Italian immigrant family in the kitchen of their East Side flat. Few apartments consisted of more than a kitchen, small in-between room, and a parlor, or "front room." Communal toilets in the Old Law tenements were located in the halls, adjacent to the cold water faucet. Note the tiny bedroom whose only window opens into the kitchen. The gas stove was considered a "modern improvement," and the kerosene lamp on the stove was the room's only source of illumination. (Museum of the City of New York)

The intersection of Delancey and Clinton streets at the entrance to the Williamsburg Bridge was the busiest on the Lower East Side when this photo was taken in 1919. Motor vehicles and horse-drawn wagons shared the bridge with trolleys and the BMT subway. Then, many more pedestrians than now used the wide bridge walkway, saving themselves the 2¢ carfare. The ornate square buildings in the foreground were entrance kiosks to the underground bridge trolley station. Most of the Old Law tenements along the north side of Delancey Street are still lived in. (*The Edward B. Watson Collection*)

A smoky elevated train has just passed the Chatham Square junction of the 2nd and 3rd Avenue Els in the mid-1880s. The station was later rebuilt with an upper level to eliminate the dangerous rail crossovers. The train is headed for South Ferry, while the tracks on the left lead to City Hall. Below the elevated structure are Park Row (*left*), East Broadway (*right*), and the Bowery (*rear*). The 2nd Avenue line swings around the left side of Congress Hall up Division Street. (*Museum of the City of New York*)

forth when the Manhattan Bridge was opened. In addition to four lanes of motor-vehicle traffic, it also carries several subway lines.

At the corner of Allen Street (called Pike Street as it curves toward the East River) is the **former power house of the Second Avenue El.** Note the old metal letters on the wall of the original Manhattan Elevated Railway building, as well as the row of holes for the power cables. Since the El made a sharp curve at this point to swing into Division Street, the corner of the power house was flattened. It is now a Chinese-owned warehouse.

Diagonally across the street at 15 Pike Street is another threatened synagogue, the **Congregation Sons of Israel Kalwarie,** built in 1903. This Classic Revival–style building also suffered from a dwindling congregation, and at present is abandoned.

Continue north on Pike Street (which becomes Allen Street as it passes Canal Street), to Hester Street.

16. By the 1880s **Hester Street** had become the busiest market in the Lower East Side. With both sides of the street lined with pushcarts and the wares of all the shops piled high on the sidewalks, the crowded street took on the atmosphere of an Oriental bazaar. Especially on Thursday evenings, the congestion and clamor reached its weekly peak, as Jewish housewives shopped for the Sabbath. Anything could be bought on Hester Street—dry goods, food, housewares, books, jewelry, furniture—and haggling was always the rule. On hot summer days the lack of refrigeration was very much in evidence, as fish peddlers pressed to sell out before nature took its course. Everywhere was the smell of decay as the gutters and sidewalks accumulated "mountain ranges" of fruit peels, paper, fish scales, nutshells, rotting vegetables, and rubbish of all sorts. The horses that pulled the many wagons added an immense contribution, too.

Turn right on Hester Street and left on Orchard Street.

17. Note the **seven-story walk-up** on the west side of Orchard Street (No. 45), a short distance from the corner. One can only speculate on the number of unfortunate souls whose hearts were surely overtaxed by the wearying daily ascents to the upper floors. Jewish stars in terra cotta appear on the adjacent building to the right and on the façades of a number of tenements—no doubt a ruse by the builders to attract religious, but naïve, tenants.

18. At the southwest corner of Orchard and Grand streets is the **former E. S. Ridley Department Store.** Its imposing rounded corner and ornate cast-iron façade are all that remains of one of the most fashionable stores in the city during the Gay '90s. Together with competitor Lord & Taylor's, four blocks west on Grand Street, they presented an almost incongruous element of elegance to a neighborhood that could ill afford their wares.

Ridley's, established in the early 1870s, gave up the ghost in 1901, and a year later, Lord & Taylor's moved all of its retail operations to its main store at Broadway and 20th Street [*see* Ladies' Mile, 27]. A bizarre epilogue to the

The Yiddish Theater was an important aspect of Lower East Side cultural life. The Grand Theater, which stood on the southeast corner of Grand and Chrystie streets until the blocks between Chrystie and Forsyth streets were leveled for the construction of Sara Delano Roosevelt Park, boasted many famous actors. In this 1908 photo, Jacob Adler stars in the Yiddish version of King Lear. (*Museum of the City of New York*)

Ridley story took place in 1964, when the proprietor of the store occupying the old Ridley building was handed an envelope by the letter carrier who inquired if it was addressed to him. On examining the letter they were astonished to see that it was a Ridley business-reply envelope, recently postmarked, and addressed to the mail order department. On opening it they found a yellow slip of paper on which a message was scrawled from a man in Florida inquiring why Ridley's had not sent their catalog "for some time"—63 years after the firm went out of business!

Turn west (left) on Grand Street.

   19. Across the street at the corner of Allen Street, the large Romanesque Revival building was formerly a very popular **sports arena** when it opened in the mid-1880s. Indoor sports at that time were mainly confined to boxing.
   20. Look across Allen Street, about 100 yards to the left of Grand Street. The tall building now housing a public garage was **formerly the wagon house and stables of Ridley's Department Store.** A closer look will reveal the old bumpers designed to prevent the wagon wheels from striking the wall, and

many of the Romanesque Revival details so popular with architects in the mid-1880s.

21. Continue west on **Grand Street,** which for many years was one of the city's major east-west thoroughfares. Its double horsecar line connected the New Jersey ferries on Manhattan's West Side with the East River ferries to Long Island. On the north side of Grand Street, between Allen, Eldridge, and Forsyth streets, are four diminutive **Federal-style houses** of the 1820s. No longer residences, these old houses with peaked roofs and twin dormers somehow managed to survive.

22. At the corner of Eldridge Street, look left at No. 87, formerly a syna-

The Third Avenue El looking north from the Grand Street station in 1895. Before the Els were electrified, the little steam locomotives created problems for those below, spewing hot cinders and oil, and littering the streets with ashes. In this photo, made from a magic lantern slide, the buildings on the left are still standing today, from the Bowery Savings Bank (extreme left), the early nineteenth-century houses with dormers, the long defunct Germania Bank (tall white structure), to distant Cooper Union. (The Picture Decorator, Inc., N.Y.C.)

gogue, and in the late 1970s, a black church. It is now an apartment house. Jewish symbols still remain in the façade.

23. Across Grand Street, at 107 Eldridge Street (now a fabric store), is the **former Eldridge Street Police Station.** The building is in surprisingly good condition, and except for first-floor modifications, looks very much as it did when built as the local station house in the late 1870s.

24. Seven blocks of tenements were demolished between Forsyth and Chrystie streets in the late 1930s to make way for **Sara Delano Roosevelt Park,** named for the mother of F.D.R. The Lord & Taylor store stood at the southwest corner of Grand and Chrystie streets from 1853 until 1902.

25. One block farther west on Grand Street, at the Bowery, the theatrical district of New York in the mid-19th century, is **"Bank Corner."** The landmark **Bowery Savings Bank,** occupying the L-shaped plot on the northwest corner, was built in 1894 by the famed architectural firm of McKim, Mead & White, and represented the newly popular Classical Revival style. On the same corner, surrounded on two sides by the Bowery's "temple of savings," is the former **Bowery Bank** (note the old insignia in wrought iron), now a branch of Citibank. Across the street on the southwest corner, in a building now occupied by the Manufacturer's Hanover Trust Company, was another victim of the Depression, the **Chatham & Phenix Bank.** Disgruntled depositors sometimes referred to it as the "Cheat 'em & Fix 'em" Bank.

26. Turn north on the Bowery, observing the number of Federal-style houses remaining, particularly **Nos. 133, 134, 136,** and **140.** For years this block has been the "interior lighting center" of the city. Formerly specializing in gas lighting equipment, the dozen or so brilliantly lit stores now offer just about every possible type of electric lighting fixture.

27. Turn right into **Delancey Street.** Once a rather fashionable retail center, it is now shabby and forlorn, serving mainly as an approach route to the Williamsburg Bridge, a half-mile to the east. In its heyday, the city fathers renamed it Schiff Parkway in honor of philanthropist Jacob Schiff; but the name didn't stick, and so it again honors James DeLancey, the original 18th-century landowner. DeLancey chose the wrong side in the American Revolution, and at the conclusion of the war, his property was confiscated and he left for England. Delancey Street is the sole public reminder of his name.

28. On the southeast corner of Forsyth and Delancey streets is the **former Forsyth Street Synagogue,** Congregation Anshe Ileya (J. Cleveland Cady, 1890), now occupied by a Dominican Seventh-Day Adventist Church. The old synagogue was once one of the wealthiest and most exclusive *shuls* on the Lower East Side. The designers of the building shrewdly planned for future financial security by having a row of stores built into the Delancey Street side. Continue east on Delancey Street.

29. At Allen Street take a short detour north to the **Municipal Bathhouse.** Built in 1905, it is the only remaining free public bathhouse in a city that had 15 such facilities at the beginning of the century. There are 54 men's showers and 34 women's showers in the white brick and limestone building. Few residents of this or any poor neighborhood had the luxury of bathing facilities in their

Looking west on Hester Street at the turn of the century. The excavation at left is for Seward Park, which was to become a welcome oasis in the maze of crowded, depressing tenements. In the background, a horsecar passes on Essex Street while in the distance, the Second Avenue El structure can be seen on Allen Street. (*New-York Historical Society*)

dismal apartments, so the city built a series of public baths in the more densely populated districts. To this day, occupants of most of the tenements still do not have adequate bathrooms. Some have a bathtub in the kitchen, but must share a common toilet in the hall. Central heating and landlord-supplied hot water are the exception.

30. The tall building with templelike columns at the southeast corner of Delancey and Allen streets was once the home of the **Hebrew Publishing Company.** Founded before the turn of the century to cater to the immigrants' thirst for Yiddish and Hebrew reading material, it is still the world's largest publisher of prayer books, language texts, and literary works in both languages, although no longer in the retail business. Stand directly in front of the building, near the curb, and examine the wide concrete panel above the first floor. With a little squinting one can discern the old sign, *Bank of the United States.* This was originally the Lower East Side branch of a largely Jewish-owned bank. Doing business with branches throughout the city, it prospered for many years. It is said that part of its success was due to immigrants' belief that because of its name, the Bank of the United States was actually a government institution, hence safe beyond a doubt. Its failure in 1932 was caused by the collusion of several big city banks that refused to grant it short-term credit. It was customary

for banks to help each other when one was momentarily short of working capital, but in this case it was felt that anti-Semitism was the reason. Depositors ultimately received most of their money, but the bank's collapse was a sensation for a number of years.

31. Across the street, the crumbling **Delancey Theater** is the last of the neighborhood's old silent-film playhouses. Note the aging advertisements on the walls of the building behind the theater, some dating from the turn of the century.

32. Turning north on **Orchard Street,** the atmosphere suddenly changes. Formerly identical in character to the blocks to the south, it has in recent years become a largely Hispanic neighborhood. The sights, sounds, and smells are reminiscent of a typical "south of the border" public market. There is a gaiety and liveliness absent until now, with Latin rhythms blaring from record shops, storekeepers aggressively peddling their merchandise on the sidewalk, and the aroma of an assortment of savory, exotic delicacies being cooked by street vendors. So busy is this street that vehicular traffic is banned on Sundays. Walk north to Rivington Street and turn right.

Busy Grand Street at the turn of the century was the major east-west artery of Manhattan, as its street cars connected with both New Jersey and Long Island ferries. In this view looking west, a trolley is turning north into Forsyth Street. Directly behind it is the Grand Theater, and in the distance, the Third Avenue El. In the foreground, a policeman keeps a stern eye on a group of schoolboys. (Community Service Society of New York)

33. **The First Roumanian Congregation in America,** *Shaari Shamoyim* (89 Rivington Street), was organized in 1885. Only the name is Rumanian now, as the synagogue serves a different constituency. The building, in Romanesque Revival style, was built as the Allen Street Methodist Church in 1888, four years before its purchase by the Hebrew congregation. The sanctuary is very spacious, with a particularly beautiful pulpit set against an array of brightly colored stained-glass windows.

Rivington Street is named for James Rivington, a well-known printer and newspaper publisher during the late 18th century. Thought to have been a Tory during the American Revolution, recent historical discoveries show that he was a very successful spy for General Washington, and is credited with breaking the British naval code.

34. At the corner of Essex and Rivington streets is a gastronomical landmark, the **Economy Food Shop.** The counters, both inside and on the sidewalk, are stacked high with such goodies as dried fruit, nuts, gelatin candies, and halvah.

A short detour north is **Bernstein-on-Essex Street,** a Jewish delicatessen and also a genuine kosher Chinese restaurant! Peek inside at the Chinese waiters wearing *yarmulkes.*

Farther down Rivington Street (across Essex Street) are two other food landmarks: **Shapiro's Wine Company,** at the corner of Norfolk Street; and **Streit's Matzoth Company,** one block farther at Suffolk Street. The winery and matzoth bakery are the only ones left in Manhattan. Shapiro's gives free tours and wine-tastings every Sunday. Try not to miss the underground walk past countless enormous vats and casks extending far beneath the buildings on the block, accompanied by an explanation of the kosher winemaking process. But go easy on the generous samples if you intend to continue the walking tour with some degree of sobriety! Return to Essex Street and turn left (south).

Along the east side of Essex Street, extending for several blocks, is the **Essex Street Market,** built by the city just before pushcarts were banned from the streets.

35. Continue south on Essex Street to **Delancey Street.** This busy intersection, with its approach to the Williamsburg Bridge, was once even busier! When the bridge was opened in 1903, Delancey Street became a major artery, not only for the horse-drawn vehicles and early motorcar traffic, but for horsecars and the new electric trolleys as well. A few years later, the newly built Brooklyn & Manhattan Transit extended its subway line over the bridge, and beneath the intersection a new station was constructed for the train and bridge trolleys. The bridge trolleys have long since disappeared, their elaborate subway entrance kiosks have been demolished, and the large underground station lies dark and abandoned. [*See* photo, page 142, top.]

To the left, the **former Loew's Delancey** was one of the grandiose movie and vaudeville palaces of the early 1920s, its façade still showing traces of the then-popular Moorish Revival style. Adjacent is **Ratner's** (138 Delancey Street), a well-known Jewish dairy restaurant, the last of many famous dining places that were once located here.

Virtually every tenement had its share of "sweatshops," operating in crowded apartments from dawn to late night, six days a week. In this view taken around 1905 in a Ludlow Street tenement, renowned photographer Jacob Riis captured the activity and working conditions of a group of cloth cutters. (The Jacob A. Riis Collection, Museum of the City of New York)

Continue south on Essex Street to Broome Street.

36. The building on the northwest corner (with the "Bell Yarn" sign) was formerly the **Eastern Dispensary** (ca. 1895), later the Good Samaritan Dispensary, and was one of four large privately endowed clinics that provided free medical care for the needy. Only the Northern Dispensary now remains [*see* Greenwich Village, 28].

Seward Park High School occupies the entire block between Ludlow, Essex, Broome and Grand streets. The school was built on the site of the Essex Market Court House and the Ludlow Street Jail (which stood on the western half of the block). Infamous politician William Marcy "Boss" Tweed died there as a convicted felon in 1878 [*see* City Hall, 17].

37. Walk east on Broome Street to Norfolk Street, and turn right to the **Beth Hamedrash Hagodol** (*Greater House of Study*) **Synagogue** (60 Norfolk Street). This austere Gothic Revival building was built in 1850 as the Norfolk Street Baptist Church and was sold to this congregation in 1885. Priding itself on having been the largest Russian synagogue in the country for many years, its membership is now quite small. Open for daily prayer, the sanctuary is magnificent and should be visited. Most attractive are the ornate ark and pulpit, the center *bimah* (reader's platform) with etched glass lamps, cantilevered balconies, Gothic vaulted ceiling, and colorful wall paintings. When the converted gas fixtures are illuminated at twilight, the atmosphere is awesome!

Walk south on Norfolk Street to Grand Street and turn right to Essex Street. Delicious bagels, bialys and other exotic breadstuffs can be purchased at **Kossar's Bialystoker Bakery** (367 Grand Street).

38. In the two blocks of Essex Street between Grand and Canal streets are a variety of small retail establishments catering to the Orthodox Jewish community. Working in ground-floor tenement shops, much as they did almost

The synagogue was the center of spiritual and cultural life of most Jewish immigrants in the Lower East Side. At times, the need for new houses of worship could not keep up with the influx of new worshipers. Typically, a new congregation would purchase and recondition an old church. The Sineerer Shul, *which stood at Madison and Montgomery streets until destroyed by fire in 1972, was formerly the Madison Street Presbyterian Church. (New York City Landmarks Preservation Commission)*

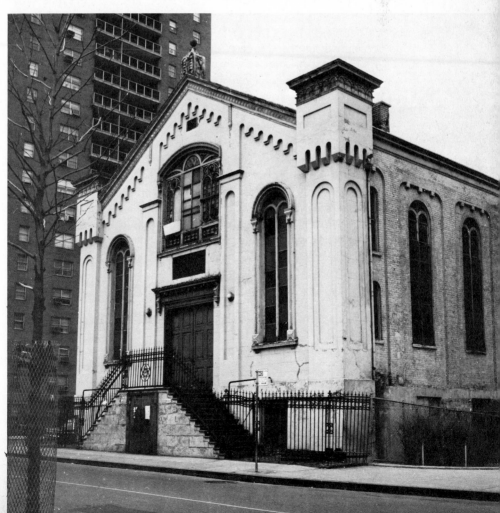

a hundred years ago, are the *yarmulke* (skull-cap) makers, torah scribes, *talith* (prayer-shawl) manufacturers, *tefillin* (prayer-phylacteries) repairers, and vendors of religious articles and books. There are also *glat* (strictly) kosher groceries and restaurants. The proprietors, many belonging to the Hasidic sect and wearing their traditional garb, will often stop business operations, close their doors, and with the shop filled with patrons, pause to conduct afternoon prayers. Miller's Kosher Cheese Agency, at 13 Essex Street, is known throughout the city, and before the Passover holiday, long lines of customers are a usual sight.

Adjoining Miller's, at No. 13½, is the small workshop of a *sofer,* or torah scribe. The craftsmen can be seen repairing Torah scrolls or phylacteries, or even writing delicately on a piece of parchment with the traditional quill pen made from a turkey feather.

A few steps before the corner of Hester Street is **Guss' Pickle Works** (follow your nose!), one of two fiercely competitive pickle vendors; the other is Hollander's on the same Essex Street block. Both claim to sell "the best pickles in the world!" Dozens of varieties of tasty pickles are dispensed from large casks on the sidewalk. Around the corner on Hester Street are two more food shops to tempt the palate of those wishing to explore further the world of Jewish appetizers. Continue to the corner of Ludlow Street.

This corner had another function during the sweatshop era. It was here that the garment industry contractors would gather every morning to hire their daily contract laborers. The noise and commotion was so great that the intersection and its surroundings earned the rather paradoxical name, **Khazzer Mark,** or Pig Market.

Return to Essex Street, and continue to Canal Street, to the IND East Broadway station.

Two additional short tours can be made to other Lower East Side points of interest. Supplementary Tour "A" is a visit to the old Chatham Square Cemetery and a few other landmarks. Tour "B" visits the Henry Street Settlement, the remaining great synagogues, and some additional points of interest.

SUPPLEMENTARY TOUR "A"
TO THE HISTORIC CHATHAM SQUARE CEMETERY

From the original starting point, follow East Broadway about a half-mile west to Chatham Square. At 145 East Broadway is the **Mesivtha Tifereth Jerusalem,** one of the oldest and most prestigious Orthodox rabbinical schools in America.

Some old-timers still recall the lumbering battery-operated "Green Cars," which rolled along East Broadway at an exasperating eight miles per hour, and which in the winter trailed smoke from the chimney of a pot-belly stove inside the car. In the distance is a striking panorama of new and old New York, with the Municipal and Telephone buildings set against the twin towers of the World Trade Center; while almost hidden below is the dark spire of St. Paul's Chapel.

At Chatham Square, with its Chinese-American War Memorial, turn left into St. James Place. Just beyond Oliver Street is the Chatham Square Cemetery, called officially the **First Shearith Israel Cemetery.** Built in 1682, this National Historic and New York City Landmark is the burial ground of the first Jewish congregation in the United States, which arrived in 1654 [*see* page 28]. It also has the distinction of being the oldest surviving man-made artifact on Manhattan Island! An earlier cemetery was consecrated in 1656 farther downtown, but no trace of it exists today, and its exact location is uncertain.

The historic burial ground is still maintained by the descendants of the original Sephardic congregation, *Shearith Israel,* the Spanish & Portuguese Synagogue, at 8 West 70th Street. The cemetery contains the graves of many of the early founders, including Gershon Mendes Seixas (1745–1816), the first American-born Jewish minister. Seixas served as a trustee of Columbia College and represented the Jewish community at Washington's inauguration. His brother Benjamin, also buried here, was a lieutenant in the New York militia and a founder of the New York Stock Exchange. The graves of 18 Jewish soldiers who fought for our independence have been marked by the Daughters of the American Revolution. The tombstone of Benjamin Bueno de Mezquita (1683) is the city's oldest. The site also played a role in the defense of the city during the early days of the Revolutionary War, when General Charles Lee mounted two batteries of cannon in the burial ground in an attempt to thwart the British invasion. The cemetery was closed in 1831, and two subsequent burial grounds were opened [*see* Greenwich Village, 33; and Ladies' Mile, 16].

Return to Oliver Street, and turn right to the **Mariners' Temple.** Now a Chinese Baptist Church, this brownstone Greek Revival–style church was designed in 1844 by architect Isaac Lucas for the Oliver Street Baptist Church. The attractive building replaces three earlier churches that were destroyed by fires, and in 1863 it was acquired by the Mariners' Temple. Note the enormous ship's bell to the right of the portico, hearkening back to the days when this was primarily a seamen's house of worship.

Turn left at Henry Street. This block was known as **"Doctors' Row"** in the 1840s. Don't miss "Dr. Naughton's Office" carved into the wall of No. 46. At the site of 97 Henry Street, Beth Israel Hospital was founded by Jews in 1889–92, in a simple four-story building with a stoop in front. **St. Christopher's Chapel** (No. 48), now the Chinese Church of Our Saviour, was once an elegant Federal-style residence.

At the corner of Market Street is the landmark **Sea and Land Church.** Another "mariners' temple," it was built in 1817 of local Manhattan schist in Georgian style for the First Dutch Reformed Church, but with some elements that anticipated the later Gothic Revival period. In 1869 it became the Sea and Land Church, but now is the **First Chinese Presbyterian Church.**

At **51 Market Street** is the former William Clark House. Built in 1824–25, it is a late Federal-style house of rather large proportions, retaining much of the original architectural detail, including a fine doorway.

Follow Henry Street, past Mechanics Alley (nothing remains to explain its name), under the Manhattan Bridge to Pike Street; turn left one block to East Broadway, then right to where the tour began.

SUPPLEMENTARY TOUR "B"
TO OTHER LOWER EAST SIDE LANDMARKS

From the original starting point, turn east on East Broadway (the opposite direction of Chatham Square), past the Educational Alliance building. In the block between Jefferson and Clinton streets are over a dozen small synagogues incorporated into the row of apartment houses that line the street. Some belong to small ultra-Orthodox groups; and it was in such a house of worship that the Young Israel movement was founded in 1913. The organization was established for Orthodox young people as a bulwark against the growing liberalization of the religion as exemplified by Reform Judaism, and is still very strong to this day. Many of these storefront synagogues, or *shtiebls,* however, belong to Hasidic groups, of which there are two major communities, the Lubavitcher and the Satmar sects. The *Hasidim* are a very special ultra-Orthodox group (*hasid* means "pious one") who dress distinctively and stay apart from other Jewish groups, mingling with the outside world only when necessary. Modern Hasidism was founded in 18th-century Poland by Israel ben Eliezer, called *Baal Shem Tov* ("Master of the Good Name") by his followers. The movement began as a reaction to the overly academic attitudes of Jewish religious leaders at the time. The essence of the Hasidic spirit is in their intense concentration

A cigarette factory sweatshop, ca. 1910. The worker in shirtsleeves at the extreme left is the author's grandfather. (Photograph, courtesy Samuel Wolfe)

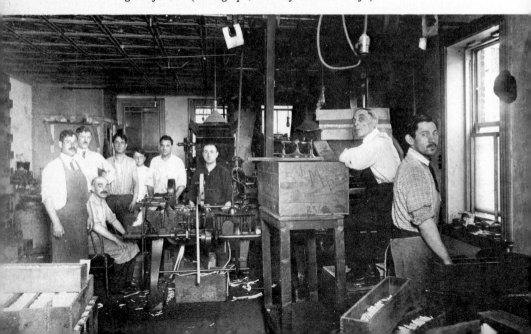

while performing religious acts and their unbounded joy in devotion—believing that to be truly religious, one must enjoy his relationship with God. The Hasidim frequently sing, sway, and dance during prayers. Although considered extremists by fellow Jews who do not accept their fundamentalist philosophies, dress, and attitudes toward worldliness and women, the Hasidic movement has nevertheless been growing in popularity since the arrival in this country of so many Hasidim after World War II. The Lubavitchers came mostly from Poland, while the Satmar Hasidim are Hungarians who fled their country after the 1956 Russian invasion.

While there are variations, the traditional Hasidic attire is adapted from the costume of the Polish nobleman of the 18th century, with a long black coat (*kapote*) and a broad-brimmed beaver or sable hat. Hasidim wear the traditional side locks and do not shave their beards. Married women shave their heads and wear a wig, and never expose bare arms or legs.

No. 235 East Broadway was until the mid-1970s the home of the *East Side News,* the Lower East Side's only newspaper. Today the building is occupied by the United Jewish Council of the East Side, a charitable organization which helps the aged sick and poor of the neighborhood. Across the street is the Bialystoker Home for the Aged.

At Clinton Street, turn right one block to Henry Street. The trio of houses, Nos. 263, 265, and 267, is the **Henry Street Settlement House.** Built in 1827 as residences when the neighborhood was just beginning to be settled, these Federal-style houses are a designated New York City Landmark as well as a National Historic Landmark. In 1893 the Settlement was organized through the efforts of social reformer Lillian Wald with the financial backing of Jacob H. Schiff. It was the pioneer social agency on the Lower East Side, and a model for later neighborhood settlement houses throughout the country. It is still carrying on its original purpose of helping to improve living conditions and providing a health and social center for the neighborhood. Among its cultural activities is a highly successful drama and creative arts program.

Return to East Broadway and turn right two blocks to the intersection of Grand Street.

The Classic Revival building at the intersection of East Broadway and Grand Street (311–13 East Broadway), formerly the Young Men's Benevolent Association (1904), is now a **ritualarium,** or *mikveh.* Among Orthodox Jews it is customary for the bride-to-be to take a ritual bath prior to the wedding ceremony, and for all women to go to the *mikveh* at least once a month. In former times, many synagogues had their own ritual bath chamber, although there were many nonaffiliated *mikvehs* such as this.

Turn west on Grand Street to Willett Street, then right (Marinus Willett was a patriot in the Revolutionary War and mayor of New York City in 1807–08). Standing alone in the middle of the block is the **Bialystoker Synagogue** (7 Willett Street). Built in 1826 in Federal style, its fieldstone construction gives it a simple but rugged appearance. Originally the Willett Street Methodist Episcopal Church, it was sold in 1905 to an immigrant Jewish congregation from Bialystok, Poland, which had arrived in the late 1870s. Still serving an active constituency mostly from the adjacent Sidney Hillman Houses, the East River Houses, and the Seward Park Houses, the synagogue is well maintained and has an impressive interior. A three-story-high carved wooden ark dominates the simple sanctuary. Colorful ceiling and wall paintings represent the signs of the zodiac and views of the Holy Land, while sparkling rays of blue and red stream down from a huge, arched stained-glass window. Contrary to the custom of facing east, the Bialystoker Synagogue must, because of its original design, face west.

Returning to Grand Street and continuing west, we pass the **Arts for Living Center and Neighborhood Playhouse of the Henry Street Settlement** (Prentice & Chan, Olhausen, 1975), and turning down Pitt Street toward the Williamsburg Bridge we see the **Police Station and Fire House,** completed in 1974. The new 7th Precinct building replaces the former Clinton Street station house, which for over 70 years stood at the southeast corner of Delancey and Clinton streets, near the end of the Williamsburg Bridge.

Walk under the bridge, turn left on Delancey Street to Attorney Street, then right to the small synagogue in the middle of the block.

This diminutive Greek Revival building was erected about 1845 as the First Protestant Methodist Church. Some years later it was acquired by a black congregation, which renamed it the Emanuel African Methodist Episcopal Church. The adjacent house, which now stands abandoned, served as the former church's rectory. With the influx of Jewish immigrants in the 1880s the church was sold and converted to a synagogue. **Congregation Beth Haknesseth Mogen Avraham** ("Synagogue of the Shield of Abraham") (87 Attorney Street) is little changed, however. Only a *bimah* (reader's platform) was added in the sanctuary, and the stained-glass windows modified with Stars of David; the tall windows and brightly painted walls give the interior a cheerful and cozy atmosphere. The downstairs *beth medrash* ("house of study"), reached by a narrow wooden staircase, is used for weekly services. On Sabbath eve, when the handful of elderly worshipers gather together in the small, dimly lit room, the somber scene is reminiscent of a Rembrandt canvas. The building, never really modernized, is probably the only synagogue still to have outside plumbing.

Walk north on Attorney Street to Rivington Street, then turn left one block to Clinton Street, and turn right.

At the beginning of the century, **Clinton Street** was a busy commercial street and the center for religious-goods merchants. Store after store offered such articles as prayer books, prayer shawls, *yarmulkes, mezzuzahs,* phylacteries, torahs, candelabra, and ceremonial wine goblets. The street is now almost entirely Spanish-speaking. Walk north one and one-half blocks to the **Chasam Sopher Synagogue** (8 Clinton Street). Built in 1853 for the German congregation Rodeph Shalom, it is the second oldest surviving synagogue building in New York. Its design, rather unique for a synagogue, is of the Round-Arch Romanesque Revival style. In 1886, Rodeph Shalom moved uptown and sold the building to a Hungarian immigrant congregation which renamed the *shul* in honor of a 19th-century religious leader. The exterior has suffered many alterations through the years, losing an ornate iron balustrade and the street-level doors that gave access to the women's galleries. The sanctuary, however, is virtually unchanged—spacious, bright, and unpretentious, its quiet atmosphere a relief from the tumult of busy Clinton Street. The design of the hand-carved ark is a model of the synagogue's front façade, with most of the architectural details faithfully reproduced in miniature. The synagogue is named for Moshe Schreiber (1762–1839), a highly respected rabbi and talmudic scholar who traveled widely through eastern Europe founding religious institutions, and who left over 100 manuscript volumes of his writings. The future of Chasam Sopher is uncertain. The small group of devoted members can no longer support a rabbi and must rely on a volunteer "reader."

Return to the corner of Stanton Street, turn right, walk two blocks west to Norfolk Street and turn right again.

Halfway down the block, almost hidden by its taller neighbors, is the abandoned **Congregation Anshe Chesed** synagogue. Little evidence remains of the former glory of this, the oldest synagogue in New York, and one of the oldest in the country! The smashed windows and doors, peeling stucco, broken fence, and overall state of deterioration are a melancholy end for such a historic building. Designed by architect Alexander Saeltzer in 1849 for the first Reform Congregation in America, Anshe Chesed, it was for a time the largest synagogue in the city. Gone now are the polygonal pyramids that once graced the twin towers of this Gothic Revival–style building, as well as the elaborate windows, traceries, and other medieval details of the façade. It is said that the architect was influenced by Germany's Cologne Cathedral, which had just celebrated its 600th anniversary the year before. In any case, the decade of the 1840s *was* the period of the Gothic Revival. Saeltzer's reputation as an architect was assured two years later when he designed the famous Astor Library on Lafayette Street, later the Hebrew Immigrant Aid Society building, now the New York City Shakespeare Festival Theater [*see* Lafayette Historic Group and East Village, 14]. As with neighboring Rodeph Shalom, the German Anshe Chesed congregation also moved uptown, and the building eventually passed to a Hungarian immigrant group, Ohab Zedek. Changing names several times as different congregations took over the building, it ultimately became Anshe Slonim in 1922, taking its name from a tiny village in Poland. The membership has long since departed, and the neighborhood, now in transition, is slated for urban renewal. What lies ahead for this venerable building is anyone's guess. Lack of maintenance and the inability to cope with constant vandalism took a terrible toll and the few remaining congregants abandoned the venerable but decaying synagogue in 1974. The city thereupon had the entrance and windows sealed, and issued a demolition order. Regrettably there seems little that can be done to save this historic landmark.

Walk back on Norfolk Street, past Stanton Street, to Rivington Street. Turn right one block to Essex Street. The IND Delancey Street station is one block south.

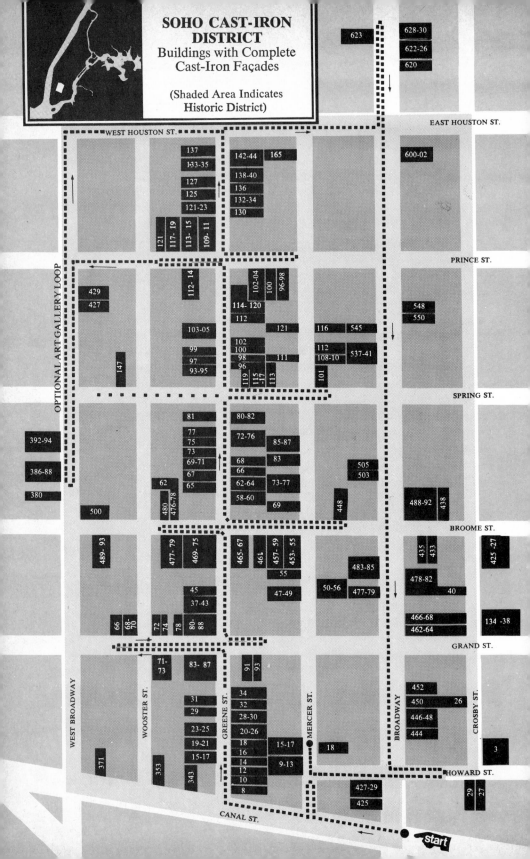

SOHO CAST-IRON DISTRICT
Buildings with Complete Cast-Iron Façades

(Shaded Area Indicates Historic District)

7. SoHo Cast-Iron District

[*BMT Broadway line or IRT Lexington Avenue line to Canal Street; Broadway (M-1 or M-6) bus to Canal Street*]

Cast iron as a building material had its origins in England in the mid-18th century. It was discovered that pig iron could easily be heated to the melting point by the use of coke, later coal, thus freeing it of impurities while maintaining the proper carbon content needed for strength. The molten mass could then be cast into sand molds of the desired size and shape. In 1779 a cast-iron bridge was completed over the River Severn, and in the last decade of the century a number of iron-framed buildings, mostly textile mills, demonstrated the feasibility of this type of construction. Subsequently, the use of cast iron to support large glass greenhouses became very popular, and in 1851 the world was treated to the awesome spectacle of architect Joseph Paxton's London Crystal Palace Exhibition Building. Two years later New York City was witness to another Crystal Palace Exhibition, which was built on the present site of Bryant Park on 42nd Street. The style lent itself successfully to the construction of the dome of the U.S. Capitol, completed in 1865, and to numerous railway train sheds around the world. Some of those expansive iron and glass stations are still in use today.

Cast iron, however, achieved its greatest popularity here in the United States during the period 1860–90, when more commercial buildings with iron fronts were built in New York City than anywhere else in the world! A surprising number of these structures still stand, and can be found within the one-half-square-mile area shown on the map.

Recognizing the importance of cast-iron architecture to the growth and development of the city, as well as its aesthetic and historic importance, the New York City Landmarks Preservation Commission in 1973 designated this 26-block area as the **SoHo Cast-Iron Historic District**—the first such commercial district to be so named. "SoHo" is an acronym for the area *So*uth of *Ho*uston Street. Although still a commercial neighborhood, it has become in recent years a popular center for artists and sculptors who find the high-ceilinged loft buildings ideal for studios and workshops. The influx of these artists has given the area a new dimension, demonstrating that with imaginative zoning, industry and art can coexist successfully.

Until the end of the 18th century the area was largely rural, difficult to reach by road from the lower city because of extensive marshland. With the filling in of the Collect Pond, the draining of Lispenard's Meadow, and the subsequent paving of Broadway to Astor Place in 1809, the character of the area soon changed to middle-class residential. By 1825 it had grown to be the most populous ward in the city, with a large freed-slave population. Large, fashionable retail emporiums established themselves along Broadway with such familiar names as Arnold Constable, Lord & Taylor, and Tiffany's; while elegant hotels were erected alongside. For years to come, such hotels as the St. Nicholas, the Metropolitan, and the Prescott House would be synonymous with extravagance and luxury. An array of theaters and music halls soon followed, and by 1850, the Bowery was displaced by Broadway as the entertainment center of the city. And around it grew one of the biggest red-light districts in town.

But the glitter and gaiety lasted only ten years. Keeping pace with the northward growth of the city, the entertainment district moved up to 14th Street, and what was left of the former residential section gradually disappeared. In its place came large textile and other mercantile establishments which commissioned the construction of new buildings, selecting for the most part the new cast-iron front designs. For the next 30 years some of the largest and most prestigious textile firms in the country were housed side-by-side in those cast-iron "palaces" whose surviving Renaissance façades are reminiscent of Venice's Grand Canal. By the early 20th century, the industrial pattern changed again, as the district became New York's millinery manufacturing center. And with the felt hatmakers came the fur and feather processors to add the essential details to milady's headgear. Until recently the area was devoted exclusively to diverse light manufacturing and to warehousing; but with the rapidly growing colony of artists, it has achieved a new and charming atmosphere not seen in any of the city's other commercial districts. Many claim that SoHo has now replaced Greenwich Village as the center of artistic creativity. However, with the enormous popularity of SoHo as a place to live and work, there followed the usual skyrocketing rents which began to drive out young artists and craftsmen. In their place came the "chic" bars, noisy discos, expensive restaurants, pretentious boutiques, so-called antique shops, and the usual health-food and fast-food establishments. The resulting "gentrification" of the artist community and the remaining manufacturing industry poses a serious threat to the future of SoHo as a center of artistic inspiration. And while the area now houses the largest concentration of art galleries in the city, the talent that supplies the galleries is gradually moving to less expensive and more distant neighborhoods.

CHARACTERISTICS OF CAST-IRON CONSTRUCTION. In a masonry building, the weight (load) is borne by the exterior and interior walls, which must be

The aesthetics of cast-iron architecture are shown to advantage in the Dittenhoffer Warehouse, 427–429 Broadway, erected in 1870. (Photo by author)

built of a thickness corresponding to the height of the building. On the other hand, in pure iron construction, the load is borne by a skeleton of vertical and horizontal rolled-iron beams, with the exterior brick walls attached to the framework, serving only as a "skin." The cast-iron parts making up the façade are then attached to the street wall. Cast iron, in effect, anticipated the principle of modern skyscraper construction, where similar "curtain walls" surround a structural steel framework.

Cast iron was employed not only functionally, but decoratively as well. Each iron foundry employed its own architect who designed the building details. At first architects imitated the style of stone buildings, copying in cast iron the ornate French and Italian Renaissance motifs which were so fashionable in the mid-19th century. Some went so far as to add sand to the beige-colored paint to give the finished product the look of rough stone. It is interesting to note that after cast iron achieved widespread popularity, many builders copied the Palladian cast-iron fronts in masonry! It is therefore difficult at times to visually determine whether a façade is of iron or stone . . . unless, of course, one has a magnet handy.

Later architects developed their own particular style, which will be examined on the tour. Most of the iron-front buildings erected from the 1850s through the mid-1870s were essentially Renaissance in style, followed by the influence of the French Second Empire. The French neo-Grec style, characterized by

Representation of the first cast-iron building erected in 1848–49 at the corner of Centre and Duane streets by James Bogardus for his Eccentric Grinding Mill. (Museum of the City of New York)

incised floral and geometric designs, using slender columns and mostly Ionic capitals, became popular in the 1880s. By the '90s, cast iron began to fall out of fashion, and only an occasional example can be found. When structural steel was developed, the skyscraper soon followed.

There are many advantages to the novel cast-iron medium. In 1835 New York suffered a disastrous fire that literally burned off most of the southern tip of Manhattan. Again in 1845 another conflagration, this one consuming 300 buildings! Less combustible building materials were sought (masonry was expensive), and cast iron seemed to offer the solution. It could be melted only in a blast furnace. It was also lightning-proof—the iron framework, acting as a "Faraday's Cage," conducted the electricity safely to the ground. Cast iron was lighter and cheaper than stone, and much cheaper to erect. It could be mass-produced from standardized molds—the iron parts being interchangeable and easily replaced from the foundry's catalog. Cast iron, once painted, was weatherproof and required little maintenance. The building's appearance could be "renewed" with a different color paint. Iron's coefficient of expansion and contraction was similar to that of the brickwork to which it was attached, obviating the danger of separation under extremes of weather. In addition, an iron framework had greater structural integrity than other building materials, and could withstand stresses that would collapse wood or stone structures. A particular advantage was the space gained by the elimination of massive bearing walls. With a cast-iron façade, large windows were now possible for the first

time, affording light and ventilation hitherto impossible. Finally, the simplicity
of erection was such that an iron front could be raised almost overnight, with
no more tools than a wrench, much like a child's Erector Set, since all parts
were fastened together with nuts and bolts.

There were, however, some disadvantages. Although the builders described
cast-iron structures as fireproof, in reality they were not. Flooring, beams, joists,
and staircases were frequently made of wood; and while a fire would not damage
the cast-iron front, it would gut the interior. Cast iron, although highly compres-
sible, was brittle, lacking the tensile strength of modern steel. The iron panels,
which could withstand the heat of a building fire, would often crack under
the shock of cold water from the firemen's hoses.

The success of cast iron as a structural and architectural medium is credited
to two contemporary engineers, Daniel D. Badger and James Bogardus. Badger's
foundry mass-produced the first complete iron-front building. Bogardus, who
invented the I-beam, designed the longest surviving cast-iron building in New
York, the famous Edgar Laing Store, which stood on the corner of Washington
and Murray streets from 1848 to 1971, about a mile from the Historic District.
The store was carefully dismantled when the neighborhood was urban-renewed,
to be re-erected later on the new campus of the Borough of Manhattan Community College. Measured drawings were made by students in a restoration and
preservation of historic architecture program of Columbia University, and the

*The former Edgar Laing Store, until recently the oldest surviving cast-iron building in
New York. Built in 1848 at the corner of Murray and Washington streets, it was dismantled
in 1971 for future re-erection. Thieves subsequently made off with most of the iron sections.
(Photo by author)*

pieces were inventoried, all under the supervision of the Landmarks Commission. Unfortunately the remains fell victim to thieves, and most of the parts were stolen—sold as scrap iron! Hopefully, molds will be made from the drawings so that replacement parts can be recast and the landmark Bogardus building erected again. Bogardus's original warehouse still stands at 85 Leonard Street, a few blocks south of Canal Street.

Badger and his Architectural Iron Works left us with possibly the finest example of commercial cast-iron architecture in America, the Venetian Renaissance–style Haughwout Building, to be seen later on the tour. Completed in 1857, it is the city's oldest surviving iron-front building.

Within a few years at least three dozen iron foundries were busily producing façades and decorations for the hundreds of new buildings going up in the area. The names of these iron works can be seen embossed in the base blocks of many of these structures: *Aetna, Architectural, Atlantic, Cornell, Excelsior, Jackson,* etc. With the lone exception of the Cornell Iron Works, which now casts other kinds of iron products, all the original building foundries are now gone. The advent of the "iron age" also brought immortality to such architects as Isaac F. Duckworth, Henry Fernbach, Robert Mook, Jarvis Morgan Slade, John B. Snook, Griffith Thomas, and Samuel Warner.

The walking tour map indicates *every* building with a complete cast-iron front; however, there are at least as many masonry buildings whose ground floors are full cast iron. Some stone buildings have only cast-iron ornamentation, such as columns, cornices or simply designs. Notice the iron loading docks, light platforms, and sidewalk vault covers. Watch also for old Bishop's Crook lampposts, built of cast iron and once prevalent throughout the city.

Note: A glossary of architectural terms appears on pages 191–193.

BROADWAY TO GREENE STREET (along Canal Street)

The tour begins at Canal Street and Broadway. Named for the drainage ditch that was built in the late 18th century to connect the old Collect Pond with the Hudson River, Canal Street was paved in 1820, and has grown to become one of the city's busiest crosstown thoroughfares. In recent years, Canal Street between Broadway and West Broadway has become one of the city's lively markets, specializing in such unusual used and surplus items as machinery, electrical supplies, hardware, and plastics of every description. The frenetic street scene reaches a fever pitch on weekends when the sidewalks are jammed with displays of merchandise and throngs of bargain hunters and sightseers.

Walk west on Canal Street to **No. 307–311.** Built in 1856–65 for the Arnold Constable "Marble House" [*see* Ladies' Mile, 29] this stone building is in a good state of preservation. It has an Italianate marble façade on Canal Street, and brick on the Mercer and Howard street sides. Note the second-story round-arched windows with decorative keystones, flanked by pilasters with Corinthian capitals. The windows on the third through fifth floors are topped by segmental

The Arnold Constable Store, called the "Marble House," was erected in 1856 when the firm moved to Canal and Mercer streets, to open one of the city's most elegant dry goods emporiums. Constructed of brick and stone, the Italianate building survives today in a surprisingly good state of preservation. (The Edward W. C. Arnold Collection, lent by the Metropolitan Museum of Art. Museum of the City of New York)

arches. Above the fifth-floor windows, paired volutes rise toward the center, forming a modified pediment. The building is capped by a simple cast-iron cornice. Walk around this old department-store building and compare the three façades; then continue west on Canal Street to Greene Street and turn right (north), past one of the city's busiest weekend flea markets.

CANAL STREET TO WEST HOUSTON STREET (along Greene Street)

Greene Street, named after Revolutionary War hero General Nathanael Greene, was opened just after the turn of the 19th century. It is still cobblestoned (they are actually called Belgian blocks), and boasts the largest aggregation of cast-iron buildings in the world! The view up the street is virtually unchanged in a hundred years. On a Sunday, when few automobiles are to be seen, only the modern lampposts and the buildings' fire escapes give any hint that we are not walking up the street in the year 1876.

The row of ten buildings on the east side of the street, from No. 8 through No. 32–34, is **the longest continuous row of such iron-front buildings anywhere. No. 8** dates from 1883, and **Nos. 10–14** from 1869—all four designed by architect John B. Snook. **Nos. 16** and **18,** built in 1882, and **No. 20–26,** built in 1880, were designed by Samuel Warner. In front of No. 10–12 is the original iron stoop and light platform, which was converted into a loading platform. Note the glass circle lights on the risers. These glass disks also permitted sunlight to illuminate the basement. The system was invented by Thaddeus Hyatt in

1845 for installation in sidewalk vaults, and is still to be seen throughout the city. Note the founder's mark, S. B. Althause & Co., on the vault covers.

Warner also designed **No. 15–17,** across the street, in 1894. A rather late cast-iron building, its "flattened" façade shows the simpler style that supplanted the earlier ornate Renaissance motifs. There is a Cornell Iron Works trademark at the base. Adjacent **No. 19–21** is by Henry Fernbach, and was built as a warehouse in 1872.

No. 23–25, designed in a French Renaissance style by Isaac F. Duckworth (1873), is particularly impressive with its triangular pediment with delicate finials set over two central bays, its iron moldings, partially fluted columns, and stylized Corinthian capitals topped by a symmetrical cornice line. There are rosette designs in the frieze panel and two flanking vertical rows of quoins that extend from the base of the building to the cornice.

The block, however, is dominated by **No. 28–30** on the east side of the street, designed in 1873 by Duckworth (who had a strong predilection for the French Second Empire style) for Picaut, Simon & Capel Company. Note the immense mansard roof with central pavilion, dormers, half-round attached columns, bell-shaped capitals, keystoned and segmental arches over wide windows, and projecting central bays which give a dramatic three-dimensional effect—to say nothing of the effect of the bright blue coat of paint! Notice, too, the light disks in the iron vault covers surrounded by six metal studs. The risers have circle lights with hexagonal frames. What was formerly the stoop now serves as a loading platform. Except for the removal of the acanthus leaves from the columns' capitals, this imposing building is in as pristine condition as the day it was built!

No. 32, with a small bonnet cornice, is another Duckworth building (1873). Its neighbor, **No. 34,** by Charles Wright, and built the same year, continues the cornice line.

No. 31, across the street (George W. DaCunha, 1876), is interesting because of its neo-Grec details. Note the three square-topped windows on each floor, the freestanding Corinthian columns, flanking pilasters with neo-Grec designs on the terminal blocks at each floor's cornice level, and the repeating rosettes and concave brackets on the entablature. The building, unfortunately, is in a sad state of decay and its future is uncertain. There is another identical building by the same architect at 74 Grand Street (to be viewed soon).

Turn east briefly on Grand Street.

Grand Street got its name from its unusual width, as it was a major east-west thoroughfare when first laid out early in the 19th century.

Nos. 91 and **93** (John B. Snook, 1869) are quite unusual in that their façades are not copied from the Renaissance or French Second Empire styles but cast in the appearance of ashlars (large masonry panels). At first glance one would take these for stone buildings. A dead giveaway is the tiny "J. L. Jackson & Bro. Iron Works" label at the base, to the left.

The remains of the once opulent St. Nicholas Hotel, this pair of stone buildings at 521 and 523 Broadway. Completed in 1854, the million-dollar hotel was second in luxury only to the Astor House downtown. [See p. 183] (Photo by author)

Looking north on Greene Street near Broome Street in the heart of the Soho Cast-Iron District where an almost unbroken panorama of cast-iron buildings presents itself. (Photo by author)

James Bogardus's only surviving iron-front building, his former warehouse at 85 Leonard Street, erected in 1862. (Photo by David Bishop)

The old New York Life Insurance Company building at 346 Broadway at Leonard Street, built in 1870 from plans by Griffith Thomas, still stands but is hardly recognizable from this early engraving. A turn-of-the-century addition by McKim, Mead & White added nine floors, a clock tower, and winged globe (now removed). The company moved to Madison Square in 1928. (New York Life Insurance Company)

An 1870s steel engraving showing the lavish interior of the New York Life Insurance Company building at 346 Broadway. (New York Life Insurance Company)

The Greene Street side of this neo-Grec-style cast-iron building at 112–114 Prince Street is an enormous trompe l'oeil *painting, by artist Richard Haas, simulating rows of windows—a pleasant solution to a blank brick wall.* [See p. 178] (*Photo by author*)

An 1865 advertising poster for Daniel D. Badger's Architectural Iron Works, located between 13th and 14th streets, Avenues B and C. (*Museum of the City of New York*)

Return to the corner of Grand and Greene streets.

No. 83–87 Grand Street (on the southwest corner) is a rather large structure in a modified neo-Grec style, designed in 1872 by William Hume. The date appears conspicuously over the central bays. The iron for this former silk warehouse was cast by the firm of Lindsay, Graff & Megquier (see label on base).

Across the street, **No. 80–88** Grand Street (B. W. Warner, 1873) was built for a large importing and commission merchant. **No. 78,** alongside, was designed in 1882 by Robert Mook.

No. 72 and **74** (1885), as well as **No. 68–70** (1887) on the northwest corner of Wooster Street, are by George DaCunha, who favored the neo-Grec style. In the latter building, a high cornice is set on paired concave brackets above three wide pilasters.

No. 71–73, on the southeast corner (Mortimer C. Merritt, 1879, corner section 1888), demonstrates how a cast-iron front permits the use of large plate-glass windows. Set between fluted Corinthian columns on paneled bases, the ground floor presents a light and expansive appearance. Each floor has its own cornice, partitioned by ornamental blocks. The bays are framed by smooth pilasters topped by stylized neo-Grec capitals with incised floral designs. The relief panels above the fourth floor serve as a transition to the splendid upper cornice with its paired elongated brackets above each column and similarly elongated modillions. Merritt was the architect of the great Hugh O'Neill Department Store, which still stands on Avenue of the Americas between 20th and 21st streets [*see* Ladies' Mile, 15].

Return to Greene Street and turn left (north).

No. 37–43 (Richard Berger, 1884) is undistinguished and has lost its cornice.

No. 45 (J. Morgan Slade, 1882) is another typical neo-Grec–style iron-front building. The pilasters and columns are topped by Ionic capitals. Note the egg-and-dart molding above the windows, the deep columnar base blocks and connecting panels, and the architrave above the ground floor in the form of a scrolled grillwork strip. The economy of cast-iron construction can be seen in the similarity of sections on each floor—all cast from the same mold.

Although **No. 49** is a stone building, its street number is a lovely cast iron plaque set into a fluted iron column. Look for D. D. Badger's "Architectural Iron Works" label on the plinth, to the left of the entrance.

Across the street, **Nos. 42–44** and **46–50** are both masonry buildings that have attractive ornamental ironwork details. The former has an iron store front with fluted columns and pilasters. Its neighbor to the north is far more ornate. Observe the twin iron pilasters on the ground floor with bolted-on scrollwork and medallions, and the small stone pediment on the second floor. With all the surviving details on the lower façade, one can only speculate on the appearance of the now-missing cornice.

Turn left (west) on Broome Street.

Broome Street is named for John Broome, the city's first alderman after the Revolution and lieutenant governor of New York State in 1804. He is also credited with initiating the lucrative China tea trade when he imported the first 2 million pounds of tea.

One of the best-preserved cast-iron "palaces" in the city is the imposing Gunther Building, on the southwest corner, **No. 469–475** Broome Street. A Griffith Thomas masterpiece, it was built by the Aetna Iron Works in 1871–72 as a warehouse for William H. Gunther, a leading furrier. (The building that housed his old showroom still stands on the west side of Broadway just south of 23rd Street, near Madison Square.) Among its outstanding features are the impressive curved corner with unusual curved windowpanes flanked by columns of quoins, the bold cornice at each floor level, the rows of flat-arched windows, and a simple but firm roof cornice supported by heavy brackets over symmetrical rows of pilasters. The protruding pedestal blocks on both sides of the "Gunther Building" plaque once supported life-size statues (draped in furs?). A balustrade, similar to the one on the second floor, once graced the roof cornice. A significant architectural feature—handed down by the ancient Greeks—is the foreshortening of each successive story. By progressively diminishing the height of each floor, an illusion of greater height is achieved. The Aetna Iron Works was located in former times at 104 Goerck Street, near the corner of Grand Street, on the Lower East Side. Goerck Street has long since disappeared, demapped for a large housing project.

The adjacent building to the west, **No. 477–479,** was erected in 1872–73 by the Excelsior Iron Works from plans by Elisha Sniffen. A very classical building in the French manner, it was built for the Cheney Brothers Silk Mills. While the neighboring Gunther Building has a uniform treatment of the windows, this building shows great variety. Some bays are flanked by engaged columns with Corinthian capitals, others are capped by keystones, and still others are decorated with balustrades. Twin pediments surmount a bracketed cornice, giving the structure an appearance of great width. No. 477 has a four-step iron entrance stoop while 479 has five steps. Note the circle lights surrounded by six raised metal studs, and the name of the iron works.

Across the street, **No. 470** is a typical Griffith Thomas building in stone, completed in 1867. The ground-floor columns and the entablature, however, are of cast iron.

No. 472–474 was built by Thomas two years later, and was probably one of his last stone buildings, for from late 1869 on, he devoted himself exclusively to cast iron.

No. 476–478 is still another Griffith Thomas building (1872), now representing his cast-iron period. L-shaped, it wraps itself around No. 480 to become No. 62 Wooster Street, around the corner. Typical Thomas touches are a cornice line at each floor, flattened window arches, flanking three-quarter round Corinthian columns in the center section with connecting balustrades, and flat pilasters at the sides of the façade.

No. 480 was designed by Richard Berger in 1884.

Return to Greene Street and continue east on Broome Street.

Broome Street in former times was a major east-west artery, and is somewhat wider than its parallel neighbors. It is still a fairly busy thoroughfare, providing an alternate route to the nearby Holland Tunnel.

Situated in one of the finest cast-iron blocks in the district, **No. 465–467** Broome Street is another product of the Aetna Iron Works and was designed by Isaac F. Duckworth in 1872. The beauty of the building is severely diminished by the ground floor "modernization."

The stone building at the northwest corner of Broome and Greene streets, **No. 464–468,** designed in 1860 (architect unknown), was built for Aaron Arnold of the Arnold Constable emporium. Nine bays wide on Broome Street, it is divided into three sections of three windows each. The two-story-high columns flanking the windows are in the "sperm candle" style, for they resemble candles made from sperm whale oil. (More buildings, in both iron and stone, employing the "sperm candle" feature will be seen later on Broadway.) The graceful fluted iron columns on the ground floor were cast by the nearby Nichol & Billerwell Foundry on West Houston Street. The building is extremely handsome, and was a prototype for many later cast-iron copies.

No. 461 (1871) is another Griffith Thomas "iron-fronter."

Still in "Griffith Thomas Territory," **No. 457–459** (1871) is somewhat simpler than the adjacent corner building. Quoined pilasters are set at each end of this six-story, six-bay edifice. The windows are separated by modified Doric columns with egg-and-dart and floral-motif moldings above. Note the balustrade at the bases of the second-story windows. Above the cornice is a rather large pediment.

No. 453–455 (Griffith Thomas again, 1872–73) was built for the Welcome G. Hitchcock silk and veilings store. Two of Hitchcock's early partners were Aaron Arnold and James Constable. Five stories of foreshortened Corinthian columns, wide flat-arched windows, a cornice line at each floor, and quoined pilasters flanking the end bays give a bold look to this well-preserved cast-iron building. Lightness and charm result from the delicate Corinthian capitals, the second-story balustrade, the floral motifs, and the intricate modillions and brackets under the ground-floor and roof cornices. Above the fifth floor is a classic attic that once sported finial-tipped cast-iron urns.

No. 448, on the north side of Broome Street, just beyond Mercer Street, is an outstanding cast-iron creation. Designed in 1871 by the firm of Vaux & Withers, it has a style of ornamentation not seen elsewhere in the city. Capped by delicately ornate friezes and outlined by pellet moldings, the windows with their flanking triple groups of colonnettes are the most unusual feature of the building. The fifth-floor windows are subdivided into round-arched groups of two, separated by colonnettes. The intervening spandrels repeat the floral motifs. Observe the striking entablature with its rosettes set in panels in a concave architrave and the upper frieze; while "sprouting" from the fifth-floor colonnettes are elaborate brackets. One cannot but condemn the first-floor alterations. Calvert

The "Queen" and "King" of Greene Street cast-iron architecture; (left) No. 28–30, in Second Empire style; (right) No. 72–76 in Renaissance style, both designed by Isaac F. Duckworth in 1873. (Left, photo by author; right, New York City Landmarks Preservation Commission)

Vaux and Frederick Clarke Withers designed the landmark Jefferson Market Courthouse (now Library) in Greenwich Village [*see* Greenwich Village, 34]. Vaux also teamed up with Frederick Law Olmsted to give us Central Park and Prospect Park.

Returning to Greene Street, note **No. 458,** a three-bay stone building between Mercer and Greene streets. Built in 1867 by David and John Jardine, who shortly thereafter were "converted" to the cast-iron medium, the structure has interesting molded drop-lintels over the windows whose keystones incorporate an incised fleur-de-lis. The ground-floor stone entablature, and its row of columns beneath, divides the building into two distinct sections. The decorative main entablature is of cast-iron capped by a raised, curved pediment. It appears that this former store and warehouse is a kind of structural parasite as it has no side bearing walls of its own, and relies on its two stalwart neighbors for support. D. and J. Jardine ten years later designed the palatial B. Altman store that still occupies the northwest corner of Avenue of the Americas and West 18th Street [*see* Ladies' Mile, 10].

Turn right (north) on Greene Street.

The block from Broome to Spring Street has no fewer than 13 full iron-front buildings, representing the height of cast-iron architectural development.

No. 58–60 (1871) is one of nine buildings in the block designed by architect Henry Fernbach.

No. 62–64, erected one year later, is also by Fernbach. Observe how the first-floor columns are fluted on the lower section and topped by Ionic capitals. Each floor has its own entablature with Tuscan columns separating the four central bays. The ornamental double brackets in the roof entablature are a very dominant feature. The restrained curved pediment above the cornice shows the date of construction.

In front of No. 62–64 is one of the few remaining **"bishop's crook" lampposts.** The lamppost weighs 835 pounds, almost twice that of today's modern aluminum tubular posts. The base shows the ornate fluting, acanthus-leaf motif, rosettes, and egg-and-dart elements. In the "crook" above is the traditional curlicue known as a *feuille rinceau,* French for curling leaf. The next time you pass an older fire-alarm box, note the cast-iron flambeau above and the palmetto-leaf design on the shaft.

No. 66 (John B. Snook, 1873) was built as a store for the Lorillard (tobacco) Company. **No. 68,** identical in appearance, is also by Snook, and was built later in the same year.

Across the street, **No. 65** and **67** (1872) are another look-alike pair, although the former is by John B. Snook and the latter by Henry Fernbach. It appears that both buildings were ordered from the same catalog.

Looking to the east side again, we are confronted by the most regal cast-iron building in the block, **No. 72–76,** known as the "King of Greene Street." Considered to be the finest example of French Renaissance style in the district, this masterpiece was designed by Isaac F. Duckworth and completed in 1873 for the Gardner Colby Company, whose initials can be seen at the entrance. From its pedimented portico to its pedimented cornice, this stately "commercial palace" must have been considered the last word in cast-iron elegance. This ten-bay structure gives an imposing three-dimensional effect with its ranks of free-standing Corinthian columns—each group supporting its own cornice, with projecting centrally paired bays, as well as side bays that are set off on rusticated piers separated by Ionic pilasters. The broken pediments over the entrance and on the roof with their ornate iron urns further accent the central projection. In the roof pediment are decorative birdlike ornaments topped by a fleur-de-lis motif.

No. 69–71 on the west side (Henry Fernbach, 1876) is identical to **No. 73,** its next-door neighbor. Both were erected at the same time, designed by the same architect, are from the same Cornell Iron Works foundry . . . and were built for the same owner! **No. 75** is another member of the family, with only minor differences in the façade. **No. 77** is a "younger brother," completed in 1878 as the office for the Jennings Lace Works, the firm that introduced Chantilly, Point d'Alençon, and Breton lace to this country. And **No. 81** is the fifth member of the Fernbach family, built in 1877.

No. 80–82, on the east side, was built as a store and warehouse (Griffith Thomas, 1872).

No. 84–86 (122–124 Spring Street) is a Henry Fernbach building in stone

(1883), with brickwork trimmed with cast-iron ornamentation. It has an interesting, restrained façade with such features as wide stone window lintels and sills, segmentally arched lintels with keystones on the sixth floor, with alternating soldier courses of brick under each window.

(For a glimpse of two surviving Federal-style residences that somehow remained relatively undisturbed since they were built in 1819, turn left (west) on Spring Street to Nos. 156 and 146. Both still retain their peaked roofs, dormer windows, and original doorways.)

Turn right (east) on Spring Street.

Spring Street is named for a fresh-water spring that flowed nearby.

On the north side of the street are a trio of late-1870s iron buildings. **No. 119** (1878) is by Robert Mook, **Nos. 115–117** and **113** (1878) are by Henry Fernbach. Typical of the Fernbach touch are the separate cornices on each floor ending in a heavy terminal block supported by double brackets, windows flanked by columns with egg-and-dart molding, plus paneled pilasters delineating the buildings. Note the Excelsior Iron Works plaque on No. 111.

At the northwest corner of Mercer Street stands the **oldest house in the neighborhood, No. 107,** built *before* 1808! Its brickwork has been covered by stucco, but it shows its splayed lintels and keystones over the windows.

Across Mercer Street, on the northeast corner, is lovely **No. 101** (Nicholas Whyte, 1870). See how the expanses of plate glass, framed by slender columns, give it a light and airy look. Unusual decorative motifs appear in the clustered corner columns, which rest on piers with a unique rectangular design. Bizarre motifs also appear in the corners of the upper windows, while the ground-floor columns have ball-shaped capitals. The whole is an outstanding example of the success of cast iron as a functional and decorative medium. The building is now occupied by a sculptor.

Adjacent **No. 99** (D. and J. Jardine, 1871), a brick structure with an iron storefront, was built as a hotel. It has several architectural features worthy of note: all the windows have cast-iron drop lintels with a spiral molding and foliate design; above the storefront windows, two panels of stained glass still survive; and the roof displays an intricate iron cornice.

Return to Greene Street and continue west on Spring Street.

Wander down Spring Street to West Broadway and back to see the variety of new establishments that have taken root. Stop in at No. 137, Urban Archaeology, a firm that deals in artifacts rescued from demolished or reconverted buildings—anything from a stone gargoyle, bronze gate, stained-glass window, marble fireplace, to a cast-iron column. And drop a coin in their nickelodeon to create some turn-of-the-century atmosphere while you browse. Return to Greene Street and turn left (north).

Just up the street to the left, on the south wall of No. 93 Greene Street, is a blackened **"ghost" of an old Federal House** which once occupied the adjoining site. Clearly visible are the outlines of its walls, chimney, and peaked roof.

On the west side, **Nos. 93–95, 97, 99** are all neo-Grec–style buildings designed in 1881 by Henry Fernbach. At the base of the second-story windows is a row of vertically incised panels with a neo-Grec motif that, from a distance, simulates a balcony.

Across the street, **No. 96** is by Henry Fernbach (1879), while **Nos. 98** and **100** are by Charles Mettam (1880). The latter two are identical although built for different clients. The pair are flanked by two designed by Fernbach. Both Mettam and Fernbach were contemporaries, and quite similar in taste, but Mettam's work is lighter and somewhat more imaginative.

No. 103–105 (Fernbach again, 1879), occupying a double lot, was formerly one-third larger. **No. 101,** originally an iron-front building, was destroyed in a 1957 fire. The three central bays are framed by Corinthian columns, and each floor has a simple molded cornice. In spite of its present asymmetry it is a pleasing Fernbach building.

No. 112 across the street (1883) is another in the Fernbach line, but its neighbor, **No. 114–120** is a superlative example of his work. Occupying four lots, it is six stories high and ten bays wide. It was built in 1881 as a branch of the Brooklyn-based Frederick Loeser Department Store (which went out of business shortly after World War II). This is an appropriately elaborate building with a typical Fernbach cornice and entablature. The ground-floor piers are quite ornate, as is the treatment of the broad square windows, which are separated by fluted Ionic columns. Note the different arrangement of the top floor, with segmentally arched lintels separated by columns with egg-and-dart motifs. Imitation fanlights appear between the cornice brackets. Dominating the cornice are stylized acanthus-leaf antefixes located above the pilasters in the middle and at the ends.

(For refreshment, there are a number of restaurants on Spring and Prince streets, and soon on West Broadway, running the gamut from prosaic diners to ethnic and organic food establishments.)

Turn right (east) on Prince Street.

The origin of Prince Street's name is unknown. It may possibly be a reference to Prince William, who later became King William III of England (with Queen Mary II) in 1689.

No. 102–104 (Henry Fernbach, 1881) was also built for Frederick Loeser & Company, and was connected to No. 114–120 Greene Street in the rear. **Nos. 100** and **96–98** were also designed by Fernbach and completed in 1882.

Cross to the northeast corner of Prince and Greene streets.

By now you must have noticed the astonishing *trompe l'oeil* painting covering the entire east wall of No. 112–114. The details are so accurate, and the visual effect so realistic, that passers-by often fail to realize that an entire wall of

Iron foundries took pride in their prefabricated cast-iron buildings and frequently mounted a distinctive builder's plaque at the base. (*Photos by author*)

windows has been painted, complete with all the traditional cast-iron details, where none exists. The painstaking work even includes a window air conditioner and a cat! The painting was done by artist Richard Haas with the assistance of City Walls, Inc. Much of the building is occupied by the SoHo Center for Visual Artists. This is a rather late cast-iron building in neo-Grec style (Richard Berger, 1889), and the only full cast-iron building on the south side of the block. Among its graceful elements are the banded pilasters at each end of the building, fluted colonnettes with neo-Grec capitals flanking the windows, lintels with acanthus-leaf designs, an entablature dividing each story, and each cornice surrounded by incised terminal blocks and elaborate brackets. Above, the raised pediment encloses a fanlight motif. Continue west on Prince Street.

The corner building, **No. 109–111** Prince Street, is discussed later as No. 119 Greene Street. **Nos. 113–115, 117–119,** and **121** share a common façade. The three were designed by Cleverdon & Putzel for the Frank Seitz Warehouse in 1890. The whole is replete with French Renaissance designs in its frieze motifs, medallions and leaf ornaments. Note how the design changes at each successive story. Only No. 113–115 retains its original entablature; nonetheless, the unity of the group is striking.

Stop in at Dean & Deluca at No. 119 Prince Street, SoHo's major gourmet landmark, and rival to Zabar's uptown and Balducci's in Greenwich Village. Another local landmark is the Prince Street Bar at the corner of Wooster Street.

(If you have had enough cast iron for a while and would like to spend more time exploring the **"art scene" of SoHo,** continue another block farther to West Broadway, and make a small loop by walking south almost to Broome Street, then back on the other side of West Broadway, past Prince Street to Houston Street. Then turn right and rejoin the itinerary by either visiting that one block of Greene Street that was bypassed, or skip it and continue eastward on Houston Street.)

There are more art galleries in the immediate West Broadway area than in any other part of SoHo. Most are open to the public (some closed Sunday), and you are welcome to wander in and out. While it is not within the purview of this book to recommend specific galleries, for obvious reasons, there is one long-time establishment whose exhibits are of such historic and artistic value that one exception can be made. The **Jordan Volpe Gallery,** 457 West Broadway, specializes in the American Arts and Crafts Movement, and shows the "Mission Style" furniture of Gustav Stickel, made in 1900–15; Rookwood (and other) American Art Pottery of the period 1880–1930; plus authentic Louis C. Tiffany lamps.

Return to Greene Street and turn left (north).

No. 119 Greene Street (Jarvis Morgan Slade, 1882) is beautifully adapted to its corner site. The diagonal bay was once the grand entrance. Slade used French Renaissance motifs very effectively. Note how the projecting cornices separate each floor, and how all architectural features are simply realized. The main cornice is plain, as are the pilasters and window groupings. A circular design appears in the paneled frieze in the entablature.

No. 121–123 (Henry Fernbach, 1882) is doubtless the most ornate structure in the block. With its fluted pilasters with acanthus-leaf design, its columns with ornamented capitals, an elaborate "Fernbachesque" cornice topping the whole, we have a wedding of the architect's skill with the founder's technique.

No. 125 and **127** are twins. The former was one of Fernbach's last works, completed in 1883. The latter is credited, however, to William Baker, and was not completed till the following year. Possibly Baker was an associate of Fernbach, carrying out the design after his death. Again we have the typical Fernbach style: pilaster moldings with egg-and-dart; fluting; acanthus-leaf and pellet details separating the two buildings; and the cornice above also ornamented with egg-and-dart, as is the upper frieze with rosettes.

Across the street, **No. 130** (Richard Berger, 1888) is an almost perfect example of the neo-Grec style. The designs on the pilasters and pier capitals are clear and precise. The colonnettes are delicate and topped by huge Ionic capitals with egg-and-dart motifs. They are attached to the building wall by means of a screenlike element, pierced with a stylized flower-and-leaf design. Each story is separated by a simple cornice, and even the upper cornice is simply detailed, supported by curved brackets above the colonnettes and pilasters with a row of dentils under its molding. The slender colonnettes emphasize the verticality of the building and demonstrate the decorative possibilities of cast iron.

Nos. **132–134, 136,** and **140–142** share a common façade. All are by Alfred Zucker (1885).

No. **142–144** (1871) is another by Henry Fernbach.

No. **146** is a stone building, but still retains its cast-iron vault covers. Note the "S. B. Althause & Co." foundry name on the edge of the covers, and the "Galls & Mark" trademark on the edge of the light platform. The light platform has the typical circle lights surrounded by six metal studs.

Back across the street, Nos. **133–135** and **137** are others by Henry Fernbach (1882).

No. **143,** a brick, stone, and iron building, was designed by the architectural firm of DeLemos & Cordes in 1887. Nine years later they drew the plans for the famous Siegel-Cooper Department Store, the world's largest store at the time. Their professional skill can still be admired on the northeast corner of Avenue of the Americas and West 18th Street [*see* Ladies' Mile, 11].

GREENE STREET TO BROADWAY

Turn right and walk two blocks to Broadway.

Houston Street was named for William Houstoun by Nicholas Bayard III (who has a street named for him also, near Foley Square). His daughter, Mary, married Houstoun in 1788 after he served three terms as Georgia delegate to the Continental Congress. The current spelling is an error. Out-of-towners frequently associate the name with the Texas hero, Sam Houston, who was not even born when the Houstoun-Bayard wedding took place. And, the street is pronounced HOUSE-ton! The buildings along the south side of the street were razed in 1963 when the thoroughfare was widened.

The enormous building at the northwest corner of Broadway is McKim, Mead & White's **Cable Building,** 611 Broadway. Designed in 1894 by Stanford White, it was the headquarters of the Broadway Cable Traction Company, whose initials in wrought iron can be seen over the entrance. Above the entrance are two relief sculptures, and topping the main cornice is a row of antefixes in the typical Greek anthemion design.

Across the street, **No. 620** (John B. Snook, 1858) may be the second-oldest cast-iron building in New York. A gem of the Italian Renaissance *palazzo* style, this delightful former gaslight-fixture factory building has somehow survived intact, except for some ground-floor modifications. The façade, in imitation of rusticated blocks, gives a three-dimensional effect behind the rows of paired, free-standing Corinthian columns. Each pair of fluted columns supports its own entablature and is joined to its neighbor by ornate semicircular arches rich in design. The structure is a tribute to Daniel D. Badger's Architectural Iron

Works. A larger version of this delightful structure is the Cary Building, located at 105 Chambers Street, downtown. By curious coincidence, the present tenant also sells lighting fixtures.

A quick glance over your shoulder is all that **No. 623** Broadway requires. It is almost hidden by its larger neighbors, perhaps justly, as little remains of it that is worthy of mention.

No. 622–626 (1882) occupies the site of the former Laura Keene's Varieties Theater, later the Olympic Theater, a popular entertainment spot from 1856 to 1880, when it was destroyed by fire. Having suffered the ravages of "modernization," little remains except for the five floors of columns, and a rather attractive upper story. Curved-arch windows with keystones and an intricate cornice give some idea of its original ornamentation. Oddly, the building is unevenly divided into two sections of two and six bays, possibly because it was first planned as two separate entities.

No. 628–630 (1882) was designed by Philadelphia architect Henry Schwarzmann, the supervising architect of the 1876 Centennial Exposition. Built for Henry Newman's New York Mercantile Exchange, it has a rather flat but pleasing façade, with bamboolike colonnettes and extensive floral designs. The firm name emblazoned across the front adds to the overall effect. The decorative cornice is made of galvanized iron, and the wrought-iron cresting has disappeared.

Return to Houston Street and continue south on Broadway.

HOUSTON STREET TO CANAL STREET (along Broadway)

Broadway, in the six long blocks south to Canal Street, offers as diverse an array of commercial architecture as can be found anywhere. Virtually every style is represented, in both cast iron and masonry, dating from the period of the late 1850s to the early 20th century. Although the tour is concerned primarily with cast-iron architecture, one should not overlook the great variety of brick and stone buildings—some of which were the forerunners in style of the early cast-iron edifices, as well as those later steel-framework behemoths whose over-ornateness often approaches decadence. As if searching for an architectural style of their own, the enormous commercial loft buildings of the 1890s through the 1900s cling tenaciously to all the old classic motifs, draping themselves in reckless abandon with a profusion of carved stone and terra-cotta adornments, apparently unwilling to face the stylistic demands imposed by the new "skyscraper" technology.

With the widening of Houston Street, **No. 600–602** Broadway is now the corner building. Built in 1882 from plans by Samuel Warner, each floor is built successively shorter to give the impression of greater height.

Across the street, **No. 597**, a marble building (John Kellum, 1867), looks so much like a typical early cast-iron building that one is tempted to test it with a magnet. **No. 593** and **591** are also an interesting pair. The former is an attractive Classical-style building dating from 1860. No. 591, extensively altered about 1890, still has a great deal of charm. The iron arched doorways and ground-floor window seem to be original, and the window treatment is light and cheerful. Look up to the sixth floor with its attractive entablature and surmounting pediment.

No. 569–575, a brick and stone building (Thomas Stent, 1881), has a cast-iron storefront on the Prince Street side by the Heuvelman Iron Works (see label at the base).

No. 568–578 (the corner building across the street) is a typical 12-story stone, terra-cotta and brick structure of the mid-1890s, not unlike many in this four-block length of Broadway. It was designed in Renaissance Eclectic style by noted architect George B. Post, who produced buildings of much greater interest: the New York Stock Exchange, City College north campus, the Long Island Historical Society, the Williamsburgh Savings Bank, etc. On the northeast corner, from the mid- to late-19th century, stood the large and fashionable **Metropolitan Hotel,** one of the city's largest. Behind the hotel, extending to Crosby Street, was **Niblo's Theater,** a popular entertainment spot, whose entrance was through the basement of the Metropolitan Hotel.

(Look east on Prince Street to the diminutive red brick Federal-style house at the southeast corner of Crosby Street, a remnant of the former residential district of the early 19th century.)

One of the outstanding architectural achievements of the early 20th century is **No. 561–563,** occupying an L-shaped plot on the southwest corner of Prince Street. Known as the **"Little Singer Building,"** it was designed in 1903 by architect Ernest Flagg as an office and loft building for the Singer (sewing machine) Manufacturing Company. Flagg was also responsible for their famous tower—once the tallest skyscraper in the world—which was located at the corner of Broadway and Liberty Street until its unfortunate demolition in 1967. One of the most avant-garde uses of iron, the "Little Singer" presents an innovative 12-story façade of cast iron, decorative terra-cotta panels, and broad expanses of plate glass. Delicate balconies and balustrades with wrought-iron traceries, supported by fragile cast-iron colonnettes, are surmounted by a graceful, lacy arch; while above, curved wrought-iron brackets support the 11th-story cornice. The Prince Street side has a narrower but similar façade.

No. 560–566 (Thomas Stent, 1883), a six-story brick and stone building, occupies the entire Prince Street side to Crosby Street. Heavy brick piers flank both the end and center bays; and at the first, second, fourth, and sixth floors, the piers are decorated with floral capitals. Foliated iron pilasters separate the windows, which have curved lintels, and the entablature between each floor has its own foliated frieze.

On the west side of Broadway, **No. 549–555,** in gray granite with cast-iron colonnettes and spandrels, is the massive **Rouss Building.** Designed in 1889 by Alfred Zucker for Charles Rouss, it stands as a symbol of success of the self-made millionaire who arrived penniless in New York from Maryland shortly after the Civil War. Making his fortune as a wholesale merchant, Rouss attributed his success not only to hard work, but to the opportunities afforded him by Broadway, and in gratitude, he took "Broadway" as his middle name, emblazoning it for all to see in the scrolled pediment above. When an identical section was built in 1900, the roof was altered and the triangular mansardlike attic dormers added. The windows of the façade are divided into groups of three by heavy quoined pilasters, each window grouping having a pair of intervening slender colonnettes. Cast-iron spandrels separate each pair of stories. Although the much-altered ground floor spoils the unity of the building, it is, nonetheless, a bold and impressive structure.

Nos. 552–554, across the street, are among the oldest on Broadway (John B. Snook, 1855). Both are of stone and have two-story iron fronts, joined together later in 1897. Note the wide central window on the second floor, the four large console brackets that support the second-floor cornice, the rounded window lintels with incised keystones, and the elaborate upper cornice with its modillions and decorated brackets.

No. 550, alongside, completed in 1854, was **formerly the Tiffany & Company store.** However, little can be seen of the original façade as it was refaced with cast iron in 1901, probably one of the last such fronts to be erected.

On the west side of Broadway, much altered **No. 545** (1885) is by Samuel A. Warner.

In front of No. 542 is another "bishop's crook" lamppost.

Nos. 537–541 are a pleasing trio in cast iron (Charles Mettam, 1868). If one ignores the remodeled ground floor, the beauty can be seen in the harmonious treatment of the eight-bay façade set off by three-quarter round columns with Corinthianesque capitals and the flat arches with rope moldings. In the spandrels are rosettes above each column. The roof line, however, dominates the building. Above a paneled frieze are three pediments—two curved, and one triangular—supported by scrolled brackets and modillions. Ornate urns further highlight the intricate cornice.

Back across the street, **No. 542–544,** built of marble in 1864, has undergone several modifications; nevertheless the arrangement of the upper floors is quite eye-catching. The bays are separated by Corinthian columns, but on the very top floor they are separated by caryatidlike figures. The cornice, topped by two urns above the outer figures, is supported by large scrolled brackets.

No. 540 (D. & J. Jardine, 1867), built of marble, was once a store and warehouse. It has a most unusual two-dimensional effect created by the flatness of the pilasters, "capitals," window arches, lintels, and keystones—all with carved fleur-de-lis designs. Above the cornice, set in a small semicircular pediment, is the date of construction. Again, one can only speculate on how the motif was handled on the original ground floor.

The northwest corner of Broadway and Spring Street is the site of the luxurious Prescott House, built in 1852.

No. 521–523 is all that remains of the once opulent **St. Nicholas Hotel.** Completed in 1854 at a cost of over $1 million, it was one of the most elegant hotels in the city, competing in luxury only with the Astor House on lower Broadway. There is some controversy over who the architect was. Whether it was Griffith Thomas or John B. Snook, no one knows for sure. The 1,000-bed establishment occupied 11 lots from 507 through 527 Broadway, extending to the corner of Prince Street, opposite the Prescott House which was built two years earlier. During the Civil War, the St. Nicholas was taken over by the War Department as a headquarters, becoming one of the nerve centers of the Union Army. The life of the hotel, however, was relatively short. With the uptown move of the entertainment district, the plush hotels soon followed, and by the mid-1870s it closed its doors. This remaining section of the old hotel is faced with stone, showing only a trace of its former appearance. No. 521 still retains its ornamented moldings, and above each window there is a cornice ledge beneath which some carved designwork is evident. The old cast-iron Corinthian storefront has long since been removed, but the original stone entablature over both halves of the building is still in place. Virtually nothing remains of No. 523's original façade.

No. 513–519, designed by Samuel A. Warner in 1884 (on the site of part of the old St. Nicholas Hotel), is a 13-bay-wide commercial building in the then-popular Queen Anne style. It incorporates newly adopted terra-cotta elements into the building's multicolor façade. Heavy brick pilasters adorned with terra-cotta plaques and topped with ornate capitals divide the bays into three groups between the first, second, and fifth floors. The windows in the outer bays are separated by delicate cast-iron Ionic pilasters, while the center bay sections have iron columns with very ornate capitals. Scrolled brackets supporting the iron cornice alternate with terra-cotta plaques in the frieze. A half-story mansard roof is offset by three pediments—the center one enclosing an elaborate design. The dark red brick throughout is also typical of the Queen Anne style and became very popular in the contemporary Romanesque Revival style of the 1880s.

A "bishop's crook" lamppost stands in front of No. 515.

Nos. 503–505, 507–509, and **511** were all designed in cast iron by John B. Snook in 1878 to form a harmonious grouping, after the demise of the St. Nicholas Hotel. So many alterations have taken place that only the ornate entablature is really worthy of note. A row of vertical pseudo-brackets stretch across the broad concave frieze below the narrow cornice, with larger brackets topped by neo-Grec terminal blocks above the pilasters supporting the cornice. Note how the capitals have been stripped of their acanthus leaves, with only rusting bolt holes remaining. (Rusting bolts often cause cast-iron ornaments to break off and fall to the street, presenting a serious hazard to passers-by.)

Across the street, **No. 502–504,** designed by Kellum & Son in 1860, presents a striking façade with its "sperm candle" style. Named after the shape of old whale-oil candles, the motif is credited to Daniel D. Badger, whose Architectural Iron Works constructed the original storefront, and who used the design in full cast iron on a building erected in 1861 at 55–57 White Street (two blocks below Canal Street). The smooth white marble columns separate each window grouping into two-story units, forming a giant "double arcade." Under the cornice is a row of "inverse crenelation," and rising above the molded end brackets are small urns. Architecture buffs have long been arguing whether the "sperm candle" style originated in stone or cast iron.

Cross to the southwest corner of Broadway and Broome Street for the best view of the most beautiful commercial cast-iron building in the country, the **Haughwout Building,** at **No. 488–492** Broadway. Referred to as the "Parthenon of Cast-Iron Architecture in America," this impressive building was one of the first designated New York City Landmarks. Architectural writer Ada Louise Huxtable said of it: "The Haughwout Store's iron elegance contained all the seeds of the future; its metal façade was to lead in turn to the metal frame; the elevator, combined with the metal frame, was to produce the skyscraper; and its repetitive Palladian rhythms were to become the basis of today's aesthetic of pre-fabricated, mass-produced structural units." In 1856 Eder V. Haughwout engaged architect John P. Gaynor to design an appropriate store and showroom for his china and glassware business. The result a year later was this superb Venetian Renaissance *palazzo*. The finely detailed iron façade was cast by Daniel D. Badger's Architectural Iron Works, and later appeared in his illustrated iron works catalog [*see* Recommended Reading]. Haughwout's chinaware was so highly esteemed that it was used in the White House and was displayed at New York's Crystal Palace Exhibition. He also commissioned Elisha Graves Otis to install a steam-driven passenger elevator—the first of its kind anywhere— which years later was to make skyscrapers feasible, at the same time launching the industrial empire of the Otis Company. The basic design motif, repeated

Considered to be the "Parthenon of Cast-Iron Architecture" is the landmark Haughwout Building at Broadway and Broome Street. This superb Venetian palazzo was cast by Daniel D. Badger's Architectural Iron Works in 1856, and was equipped with the first commercial steam elevator by Elisha Graves Otis. It is probably the oldest extant cast-iron building in the city, and certainly the best preserved. (Photo by author)

on each level, is a keystoned round arch set on fluted Corinthian columns, flanked by taller columns supporting a full entablature, with an underlying balustrade in each bay. A delicate cornice rises above several bands of elaborate friezework; and in the center bay of the second floor hangs a large iron clock, now minus its hands. The building is in virtually pristine condition (although a restored clock would help); the ground floor, so often altered, is completely intact. Because of its architectural and historic significance, the Haughwout Building has been listed in the National Register of Historic Places.

On the west side of Broadway, **No. 483–485** is a five-story cast-iron building, very simply styled in the classic manner. Designed by Robert Mook in 1869, its cornice line with urns above the pilasters gives it a curious appearance, while the capitals of the columns have a "fake" Doric look, given by the egg-and-dart moldings. The ground-floor modernization is a disaster.

The adjoining **No. 477–479** (H. W. Smith & Sons, 1869) contrasts strongly with its neighbor. A center molded pilaster divides the bays into two distinct groupings. The bays themselves are separated by columns with hexagonal bases and stylized Corinthian capitals. The windows have rounded lintels, and abstract geometric detail decorates the spandrels. Simple cornices separate the upper stories. Note the fine leaf-pattern design on the brackets of the upper cornice. And the storefronts survive intact.

The **Roosevelt Building** across Broadway, at **No. 478–482,** is the only surviving Richard Morris Hunt commercial building in New York. The Paris-trained architect also designed the Metropolitan Museum of Art, the base of the Statue of Liberty, the bronze doors of Trinity Church, and the lovely old New York Tribune Building, which dominated Park Row, downtown. This unusual building, owned by Roosevelt Hospital, was built as a store for income-producing purposes in 1873. The visual impact of this original statement in cast iron is often lost on the thousands of riders and pedestrians who pass it daily, as *few New Yorkers are in the custom of looking any higher at buildings than ground-floor level.* Built to utilize the advantages of iron architecture to the utmost, it resembles no masonry predecessor nor any other cast-iron building either. The enormous front is divided into three main sections by four fluted pilasters at the tall ground-floor level and continued by bold Ionic columns for the next three levels. Slender colonnettes separate the triple windows, disappearing behind a curved screenlike tracery arch set over each group. The top floor, which repeats the three-window pattern, is shaded by a broad projecting cornice, now minus much of its former decoration. On each incised pilaster is mounted a large circular escutcheon with the street address in bold numerals. A single section of the building extends back to Crosby Street (No. 40), where its one-third-smaller front is graced with a proportionately scaled version of the Broadway façade.

Nos. 466–468 and **462–464** at the northeast corner of Grand Street combine to form a striking pair. Built from plans by John Correja in 1879, the pair was leased by the large textile importing firm of Mills & Gibb, specializing in linens and laces. An earlier tenant on the site was the **Brooks Brothers Store,** which during the Civil War had established its reputation by supplying uniforms

Now a vacant lot on the northwest corner of Broadway and Grand Street, the Lord & Taylor store occupied the site from 1860 until fire destroyed it a hundred years later. The firm sold the building shortly after the turn of the century when the retail district moved uptown to "Ladies' Mile." (The Edward W. C. Arnold Collection, lent by the Metropolitan Museum of Art. Museum of the City of New York)

for the Union Army. An interesting variation on the decorative theme is the sawtooth motif that embellishes the window lintels, and the rows of incised banding on the second- and fourth-story entablatures. On the third, fifth, and sixth floors, the pilasters have unique scallop-and-bandwork capitals, with a medallion motif halfway up the shaft. The cornice is rather heavy and is supported by brackets, while a row of modillions lines the architrave.

The parking lot across the street is the **site of an early Lord & Taylor department store** (1860–1872). The original Griffith Thomas–designed building suffered a disastrous fire in 1967 and had to be demolished. During the Draft Riots of 1863, Lord & Taylor armed its employees for protection against the raging mobs that were surging down Broadway (the rioters were finally dispersed by Union Army artillery about a mile north, at what is now 3rd Street). In 1865, when President Lincoln's funeral cortege moved slowly up Broadway, the store was draped in mourning, with merchandise removed from the windows and seats installed for the viewing of the procession.

Midway down the east side of the next block are **Nos. 452, 450, 446–448, and 444**—an interesting quartet in cast iron. The two outer buildings (Nos. 452 and 444) are identical (by Schweitzer & Gruwé); while the inner pair (Nos. 450 and 446–448) share a common façade (John B. Snook). All were completed in the same year, 1877. The flanking outer buildings immediately bring to mind Hunt's Roosevelt Building (at 478–482 Broadway), with their pierced stylized arches and wide spandrel panels, together with the slim colonnettes separating the windows. Crowning the front is a bold projecting cornice decorated with anthemions alternating with raised circular motifs, with neo-Grec console brackets at the ends. Look for the foundry label, which unexpectedly gives the names of the architects along with the Long Island Iron Works. The inner group of buildings is distinguished by quoined pilasters at each end, Corinthian columns defining the window bays and ground floor openings; while above, the entablature is flanked by large console brackets topped by neo-Grec terminal blocks, a common cornice stretches above a paneled frieze, and additional concave brackets with their own incised terminal blocks alternate with the frieze panels. The cast-iron fronts were supplied by the J. B. & J. W. Cornell Iron Works (see label).

A "bishop's crook" lamppost stands in front of No. 446–448.

Across the street, **No. 447** (architect unknown, 1860) has an iron storefront listed in D. D. Badger's Architectural Iron Works catalog of 1865.

No. 443–445 (Griffith Thomas, 1860) gives a very aesthetic appearance. Rows of pleasing round-arch windows are topped by individual projecting cornice slabs supported by brackets. A projecting balustrade runs along the second floor, with decorative urns at each end. Ornate scrolled brackets support the main cornice, above which a pediment adds the final touch.

Except for No. 441, built in 1876, the entire west side of the block dates from the 1860s.

"The Bank in the Park" at the northwest corner of Howard Street (Eggers & Higgins, 1967) offers an unexpected oasis of restful greenery. In spite of its fake Georgian style, the effect of the diminutive European-American Bank building and its landscaped plot is quite successful.

Howard Street is named for Harry Howard, a volunteer "fire laddie" of the early 19th century. It was called Hester Street until 1825, which, incidentally, is still the street's name after it makes a small zigzag at Centre Street on its way toward the Lower East Side.

Turn left (east) on Howard Street for a brief glance at **No. 27** and **29.** The former, a modified neo-Grec-style building, was designed by Samuel Warner in 1888. No. 29, 20 years its senior, is by the firm of Renwick & Sands. One must look beyond the added fire escape and the dingy atmosphere, abetted by the narrow and dark street, to enjoy the profusion of decorative elements. The rolling iron shutter in the center window was a novelty introduced in the "iron age." Amazingly, both buildings' ground floors remain completely intact. In front of No. 30, on the north side, is a large cast-iron light vault (Excelsior Iron Works), to admit sunlight into the basement.

Return to the northeast corner of Howard Street and Broadway.

Diagonally across the street is the exquisite **Dittenhoffer Warehouse, No. 427–429,** built (as advertised in the ornate triangular pediment) in 1870. The successive shortening of each story clearly creates a feeling of much greater height than would be expected from a five-story building. Architect Thomas

Jackson used both Venetian and French motifs to highlight this palatial edifice. Particularly noteworthy is the beautifully ornate façade, as exemplified by the spandrels between the window arches, the decorated column shafts, the Corinthian capitals, the keystoned arches over the windows, and the frieze below the bracket-supported cornice, which repeats the florid details of the spandrels. Except for one remaining show window on the Howard Street side, most of the ground floor has been altered beyond recognition. The foundry label carries the trademark of the Excelsior Iron Works. The corner was the site of the City Hotel from 1852 to 1869.

Adjacent **No. 425,** erected in 1869, is one of architect Griffith Thomas's first full iron-front buildings (Aetna Iron Works). How different from its neighbor are the square-headed windows with curved corners, the unadorned entablatures, the almost bare columns, and the curved broken pediments. It was built for the LeBoutillier brothers, who later moved their store uptown, opening one of the most fashionable women's wear emporiums during the gaslit era. [_See_ Ladies' Mile, 20].

Continue west on Howard Street.

No. 48, a stone building with a cast-iron storefront, was built in 1860 as an annex to the Arnold Constable "Marble House" across the street. The façade with its rows of round-arched windows, pilasters, heavy entablature, and elaborate cornice is a typical example of the masonry prototypes of early cast-iron buildings.

No. 50–52 was built in 1860 as a store for a gun dealer. Also a stone building with a cast-iron storefront, it is more imposing than No. 48. The ground level has lovely fluted Corinthian columns, above which are rows of French-style segmental-arch windows in a kind of "recessed" style that creates a flat, two-dimensional effect. The overall restrained appearance ends at the cornice, which is disproportionately ostentatious. During the Civil War, the building became the New York State Soldiers' Depot, a rest home and hospital for troops on leave.

Howard Street ends at Mercer Street (named for General Hugh Mercer, killed in the Battle of Princeton in 1777). Across the street at No. 11 Mercer Street is the **Museum of Holography,** where our tour ends. This unique museum is dedicated to exhibitions of how holography works. A hologram (from the Greek _holos,_ whole, and _gramma,_ message) is the recording of patterns of laser light waves reflected from an object onto the emulsion of light-sensitive film, resulting in a three-dimensional image focused in space. The hologram was invented in 1948 by Dr. Denis Gabor. (Open Wednesday to Sunday, 12–6 P.M., admission charge)

End of tour. Canal Street, the starting point of the tour, is one block south and one block east.

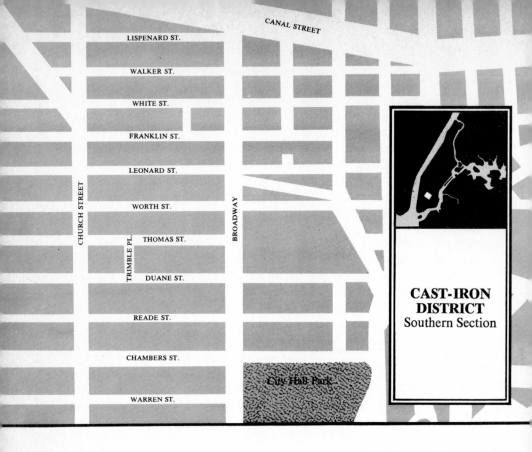

SUPPLEMENTARY TOUR BELOW CANAL STREET

A short walk through the neighborhood from Canal Street to Chambers Street, using Broadway as an axis, reveals a number of additional cast-iron buildings of more than casual interest. A few are listed below. *Except where indicated, all cast-iron buildings are located in the one block west of Broadway.* [*See* street map.]

CANAL STREET: **No. 268** (one block east) and **No. 351–353** (two blocks east).

LISPENARD STREET: **Nos. 48–40.** See also cast-iron decoration on **No. 39–41** Clark Building.

WALKER STREET: **Nos. 57, 49–43, 42.**

BROADWAY: **No. 385** Grosvenor Building.

WHITE STREET: **Nos. 57–55, 60, 41, 37–35,** and the avant-garde Civic Center Synagogue. Not cast iron, but astonishing!

FRANKLIN STREET: **Nos. 83–85, 86–88** (both east of Broadway).

BROADWAY:	No. 361 James S. White Building.
LEONARD STREET:	No. 85 James Bogardus's former warehouse.
BROADWAY:	No. 346 (east side). Not cast iron, this was the former New York Life Insurance Company Building.
BROADWAY:	No. 319 (corner of Thomas Street). No. 287 (corner of Reade Street).
READE STREET:	No. 96–100. Walk one block farther to Church Street to admire the Cary Building at No. 89–91. No. 93.
CHAMBERS STREET:	No. 105–107 (the rear façade of the Cary Building). No. 120 (just a bit farther west). The building has an identical façade in the rear at 50 Warren Street.

If you are still interested in cast iron . . .

There is a small but active organization, Friends of Cast-Iron Architecture, which conducts walking tours, sponsors lectures, and fights determinedly for the preservation and restoration of our cast-iron buildings. It is primarily to this group of dedicated cast-iron buffs that credit is due for the designation by the Landmarks Commission of the SoHo Cast-Iron Historic District. (For more information, write to the Friends at 235 East 87th Street, New York, N.Y. 10028.)

GLOSSARY OF TECHNICAL TERMS USED IN THE SOHO CAST-IRON DISTRICT WALKING TOUR

ANTEFIX, an ornament projecting above a roof cornice, frequently incorporating an anthemion motif

ANTHEMION, a conventionalized leaf motif based on a honeysuckle or palmette form, originating in Greek ornamental forms

ARCHITRAVE [*see* ENTABLATURE]

BALUSTRADE, a row of baluster columns topped by a railing, forming a parapet, usually set on a cornice or in front of a window

BAY, the general term for the window section

BEARING WALL, a wall upon which the structural load of a building rests

BRACKET, a projecting L- or S-shaped support used frequently below a cornice, balcony, or projecting sill

CONSOLE BRACKET, an elongated ornamental bracket, frequently in the form of an S-curve

CARYATID, a decorative column in the form of a female figure

CLASSICAL ORDERS. In discussing the buildings dating from the second half of the 19th century within the Historic District, references to the classical orders must be interpreted loosely. The architects of these buildings took great liberties in adapting Greek and Roman forms to commercial buildings.

Reference to a specific order refers only to the capital (the design element at the top of the column shaft).

TUSCAN CAPITAL, a very simple unadorned capital, resembling the Doric, but frequently of heavier proportions

DORIC CAPITAL, a relatively simple capital with a flat topmost member

IONIC CAPITAL, a capital with spiral volutes beneath its topmost member

CORINTHIAN CAPITAL, a capital embellished with carved acanthus leaves

CORINTHIANESQUE CAPITAL, a capital incorporating stylized leaf forms

COMPOSITE CAPITAL, a capital combining volutes and acanthus leaves (a composite of the Ionic and Corinthian orders)

CONSOLE BRACKET [*see* BRACKET]

CORNICE [*see* ENTABLATURE]

CORNICE SLAB, a cornicelike projection placed above a window

CURTAIN WALL, an exterior wall, separate from the structural framework, that supports only its own weight

DROP LINTEL [*see* LINTEL]

EGG-AND-DART MOLDING, a classical molding consisting of alternating egg-and-dart-shaped forms

ENTABLATURE, the group of horizontal members directly above column capitals. It consists of:

ARCHITRAVE, the lowest member, resting upon the column capitals. An architrave is also occasionally extended to enframe the sides of a door or window opening that is topped by an entablature.

FRIEZE, the middle member of an entablature, which in 19th-century architectural styles is frequently embellished by panels or medallions, and interrupted by large cornice brackets; 19th-century adaptations of classical orders often combine a frieze and cornice without an architrave

CORNICE, the horizontally projecting topmost member of an entablature. It is frequently found by itself as the crowning motif of a façade.

FANLIGHT, a semicircular window placed over a door, with bars radiating from its center like spokes of a fan

FINIAL, an ornamental form at the top of a pediment, spire, pinnacle, etc.

FRIEZE [*see* ENTABLATURE]

IRON VAULT COVERS, a number of iron plates with lights (*see below*) that lie over the vaults, and are on the same level as the sidewalk

KEYSTONE, the central voussoir (block) of an arch

LIGHT, generally, a pane of glass, but in this district it refers to pieces of hardened glass of various shapes, sizes, and colors that are inserted in iron plates

LIGHT PLATFORM, a flat, raised area in front of the façade of a building that is made up of a number of iron plates with lights, and which stands on the vault

LINTEL, a horizontal member placed over a window or door to support the superstructure

MODILLION, a small ornamental bracket used in a closely spaced, regular series below a projecting cornice

PALAZZO, an Italian "palace," usually associated with those from the Renaissance. When referring to 19th-century architectural styles, however, a *palazzo* can be any large, impressive building whose style was derived from the Italian Renaissance.

PEDIMENT, a low, usually triangular gable constructed in a classical style that is often filled by sculpture and usually framed by a cornice. It is used decoratively to crown central bays, porticoes, and important windows of a façade, and is sometimes segmental in shape or broken away in the center.

PIER, in masonry architecture, an upright supporting member carrying a structural load. When interpreted in cast iron, an exterior pier is, in most instances, merely a solid part of the curtain wall placed between the windows and/ or on either side of a façade.

PILASTER, a shallow, flat engaged (attached) column, normally serving only a decorative function

QUOIN, in masonry architecture, large stones used to reinforce a corner or salient angle of a building. When interpreted in cast iron, rusticated quoins were used decoratively to emphasize the flanking piers.

RISER, the vertical member between the treads of a stair

RUSTICATION, in masonry architecture, an emphasis of individual (usually large) stones by recessing their connecting parts

SEGMENTAL ARCH, an arch in which the curvature is a segment of a circle, but less than a semicircle

SOLDIER COURSE, a course (row) of bricks set on their ends

SPANDREL, the space between the outer curve of an arch and its rectangular enframement, or between two adjacent arches and a horizontal member above them

SPANDREL PANEL, in skeleton-frame construction, the wall panel between the head of one window and the sill of a window directly above it

TERMINAL BLOCK, a decorative block placed at the extreme ends of a cornice between floor levels, thus interrupting the quoin lines or flanking piers of a façade

TREAD, the horizontal surface of a step

VAULT, a cellar room used for storage, often extending under the sidewalk

VOLUTE, a spiral or scroll-like form, as with the Ionic capital

VOUSSOIR, a wedge-shaped stone forming part of a masonry arch

LADIES'
MILE
and
FASHION
ROW

c. 1900

8. Ladies' Mile and Fashion Row

[*BMT RR Broadway line to 8th Street; IRT Lexington Avenue line No. 6 train to Astor Place, walk west one block on 8th Street; Broadway (M-1 or M-6) bus to 8th Street*]

The department store as we know it today had its genesis in the small wholesale and retail dry-goods shops that began to proliferate along the busier thoroughfares of lower Manhattan during the 1820s. With the upsurge of immigration in the following decades, and the rapid growth of commerce and industry, many keen merchants seized the opportunity to expand and diversify, making fortunes by catering to the changing tastes and increased demands of the burgeoning city. By the 1870s and 1880s, the main shopping center of the city had moved uptown, following the northward growth of the city, to an area between 8th and 23rd streets along Broadway, and also on Fifth and Sixth avenues. With women shoppers always in the majority, it did not take long before this bustling row of large retail stores was known as Ladies' Mile.

Today not one of those fine old establishments can be found on the Mile. The stores either relocated farther uptown to keep abreast with the inexorable northward tide, or, unable to update their merchandising techniques, closed their doors forever. Astonishingly, most of the buildings that housed those elegant department stores still remain intact, although now occupied by other tenants.

Our itinerary takes us on a "shopping tour" of those glamorous "ghosts" of a bygone era, and using a little imagination, we can return to the bustling streets of those gaslit days. Listen carefully for the rhythmic clop-clop from the profusion of horse-drawn vehicles and the clatter of their iron-clad wheels on the cobblestoned street, the persistent bell-clanging of horsecars caught in the tangled traffic—their impatient conductors exchanging abuse with draymen and carriage drivers—and the shrill cries of "Extra! Extra!" from little boys hawking their penny papers at the street corners. When we reach Sixth Avenue, our walk will take us under the gloomy structure of the old El, whose wooden trains roar by overhead in an endless, ear-splitting clatter, their smoky locomotives spewing hot cinders and oil on the unwary below. Standing stiffly at the entrance portals to the fancy "magazines" that line the Avenue, liveried doormen await the arrival of the "carriage trade," and as a coach draws up, rush forward to escort the affluent patrons to the door. And clustered about the elaborate show windows, we glimpse elegantly clad women in trailing dresses, billowy hats, and frilly parasols, pressing to catch the latest fashions in furbelows, veils, shirtwaists, millinery, and high-button shoes.

1. The tour begins at 8th Street and Broadway, the southerly end of Ladies' Mile. The huge building at the northeast corner was formerly the **Wanamaker Department Store,** now known simply as 770 Broadway. Construction of this 16-story giant began in 1902 and took five years to complete. Designed by Daniel H. Burnham, architect of the Flatiron Building [*see* Madison Square, 24], the structure was planned as a modern extension to the older "Cast-Iron Palace" that occupied the block directly north. John Wanamaker came to New York in 1896 to open a branch of his Philadelphia store, and purchased the old cast-iron building from the successors of the faltering A. T. Stewart Company. Alexander Turney Stewart, who had been considered a merchandising genius, in 1846 opened New York City's first large department store, at Broadway and Chambers Street. Called "The Marble Dry-Goods Palace," the building still stands today [*see* City Hall, 15]. In 1862 he leased a portion of the old Randall Farm in Greenwich Village, and while maintaining his Marble Dry-Goods Palace as a warehouse, built the first large store in what was to become Ladies' Mile. His new emporium, employing the novel architectural medium of cast iron, occupied the entire block from 9th to 10th streets. Each of the six stories was supported by iron beams, the roof area enclosed by an enormous glass dome over a central court. Rows of cast-iron columns lined the façade, permitting sunlight to stream in through the wide intervening arched windows. A grand staircase and six steam-driven elevators provided easy access to all shopping floors. The exterior, painted a mottled white and sparkling like an architectural gem of the Italian Renaissance, was an immediate success.

When Stewart died in 1876, he was the second richest man in America, although his wealth had come mostly from real estate investments. His fashionable emporium, so successful during his lifetime, was now under the management of a former business associate, and the store was renamed Hilton, Hughes & Company. Later it was taken over by a firm called Dennings, and the once-great Stewart store began to founder. It would have gone under altogether were it not for an eleventh-hour reprieve from John Wanamaker who purchased it in 1896. The establishment was completely reorganized, a new building erected alongside (connected to the "Cast-Iron Palace" by a double-decker "Bridge of Progress" and three subterranean passageways, as well as a direct entrance from the newly built IRT subway station at Astor Place). Business began to boom again, and for nearly half a century the name Wanamaker's was synonymous with the ultimate in department store merchandising.

By 1952, the center of retail trade had moved uptown, and patronage fell

The great Palladian cast-iron palace which had been the A. T. Stewart Store on Broadway at 9th Street was under the operation of Hilton, Hughes & Co. when this photo was made in 1889. In the distance is Grace Church, the Gothic-style landmark which still stands at Broadway's bend at 10th Street. (New-York Historical Society)

off rapidly. Although the southbound end of the Fifth Avenue Bus line was still called the Wanamaker Terminal, few customers were to be seen getting off. The older store building was vacated and all operations shifted to the newer facility next door. Time was running out for the once-popular Wanamaker Store. Two years later the end came, and all retail business was transferred to a small downtown shop and to their suburban stores. In a rather dramatic exit, the old cast-iron building, which occupied the entire block between 9th and 10th streets, fell victim on July 15, 1956 to one of New York's most spectacular conflagrations, blazing out of control for two days in a fiery farewell to the old merchant prince. The apartment building that now occupies the site of the "Cast-Iron Palace" is named Stewart House.

2. **Grace Church,** at the northeast corner of Broadway and 10th Street, is an outstanding example of the Gothic Revival style. This lovely church, built on land formerly owned by Henry Brevoort, was designed in 1843 by James Renwick, Jr., when only 23 years of age. Renwick was also the architect of St. Patrick's Cathedral and the Smithsonian Institution, but many consider Grace Church to be his crowning work. Renwick himself was a parishioner and later vestryman. Particularly beautiful are the 46 medieval stained-glass windows and the intimate Chantry. The garden beside the Chantry is the site of the former Fleischmann's Vienna Model Bakery, a popular continental café in the days of Ladies' Mile. Bought by Grace Church and named Huntington Close, after a former rector, the plot adds much charm to the setting. The steeple is illuminated at night and can be seen for miles down Broadway. Among the scores of architecturally notable structures of the city built before 1930, the Municipal Art Society places Grace Church in its first category of seven buildings "of national importance to be preserved at all costs."

Fleischmann's Vienna Model Bakery, at the northeast corner of Broadway and 10th Street, photographed in 1898 by Percy C. Byron. Conveniently located between Grace Church and the former A. T. Stewart Store, it was a European-style café which produced its own baked goods and was one of the most popular places of refreshment along Ladies' Mile. (The Byron Collection. Museum of the City of New York)

The view of Grace Church is a debt to early settler Henry Brevoort, whose family owned the lands where Grace Church now stands. He was so intent on preserving a much loved apple orchard that stood in the way of Broadway's northward march that he succeeded in forcing the city fathers to divert the street to the west, and blocked 11th Street from penetrating to Fourth Avenue.

3. On the southwest corner of 11th Street and Broadway stands a rather nondescript 19th-century building, whose extensively altered façade masks its former identity. **The Hotel St. Denis,** built in 1848 and renovated in 1875, was one of the more fashionable hostelries in the city. *King's Handbook of New York,* 1893 edition, praises the attractiveness of this 250-room hotel and adds, "The equipments of the house, as to steam heating, electric lighting, ventilating, and hydraulic elevators, are supplemented by a perfect corps of polite and well-disciplined attendants." In its heyday, it hosted Presidents Lincoln, Grant, and Arthur, as well as Sarah Bernhardt, P. T. Barnum, and Col. William "Buffalo Bill" Cody. Probably the most significant date in the hotel's history was May 11, 1877, when Alexander Graham Bell gave a preview demonstration of his telephone to a spellbound audience of prominent guests in the second-floor parlor room. The wire was strung from the hotel across the Brooklyn

Bridge. The St. Denis closed in 1917, and shortly thereafter was converted to commercial use. At that time all the adornments were stripped from the façade. Enter at the 11th Street door, walk almost to the bank of elevators, turn right and admire the original cast-iron staircase, as well as a few surviving stained-glass windows.

4. Across 11th Street is the Palladian cast-iron establishment of the former **James McCreery & Co. Store.** Arriving in this country as a 20-year-old immigrant from Ireland in 1845, McCreery started in business opening a small shop selling Irish lace. Gradually expanding to larger quarters, and following the uptown tide, he commissioned architect John Kellum to build this large dry-goods store in 1868. He was reputed to be a kindly, tolerant man, whose flowing white beard and long shock of hair, together with a thick Irish burr, made him a very striking figure. He always showed great concern for the welfare of his employees in an era when social conscience in business was relatively un-

The St. Denis Hotel and Taylor's Saloon at the southwest corner of Broadway and 11th Street, ca. 1875. It was in the corner parlor room on the second floor that Alexander Graham Bell demonstrated his "speaking telephone" to a group of prominent New York citizens May 11, 1877. The hotel closed in 1917, but the building, much altered, still stands. (Museum of the City of New York)

known. McCreery, self-educated, became a patron of the arts and dedicated much of his later fortune to philanthropic and artistic causes, including helping to found the Metropolitan Museum of Art.

In 1895 he moved to an even larger building at the northern end of Ladies' Mile, at Sixth Avenue and 23rd Street. The present building miraculously survived years of occupancy by a variety of users, but a few years ago suffered a disastrous fire, which all but sealed its fate. Demolition seemed the only alternative until a developer, sensing the value of such a rare example of cast-iron elegance, converted it into an apartment house. The interior was gutted, but the beautiful façade was restored to its original appearance. Except for the ugly two-story addition on the roof, it looks much the same today as when it was first built. Since the interior vertical iron beams had to be retained, a curious result is that many tenants have an ornate Corinthian supporting column adorning the middle of their living room! This creditable restoration is an excellent example of adaptive (and profitable) reuse.

5. The building with the smooth mansard roof at the northeast corner of Broadway and 13th Street marks the location of the famous partnership of Charles B. Peet and Marvin N. Rogers. Although both gentlemen died before the firm moved into this building, **Rogers Peet Company** had been in business manufacturing men's clothing and army uniforms since 1874 at two previous lower Broadway addresses. A relative latecomer (1902) to Ladies' Mile, the company was the last to leave (1970), moving its executive offices to one of its Fifth Avenue stores uptown.

From 1861 to 1881, the site was occupied by famed **Wallack's Theater.** John Lester Wallack, who managed the playhouse, was also a leading actor, performing in many of the old comedies and contemporary English dramas which were so popular in the late 19th century. When Wallack's moved to the new Rialto district on 30th Street, the house was renamed the Star Theater (1893) and continued to offer dramatic productions until its razing for the Rogers Peet building.

6. Turn west on 14th Street and pause briefly at **Union Square.** Called "Union Place" in the Commissioners' Plan of 1811, its present attractive layout was not achieved until 1831, a credit to Samuel B. Ruggles who planned nearby Gramercy Park [*see* Gramercy Park, 8]. The name "Union" derives not from Civil War days, nor from any association with the labor unions whose activities were later identified with the square, but merely from the fact that this was the "place of union" of the Bowery Road with the northern extension of Broadway. Until the early 1860s it had been a beautiful residential district; then business took over the area. The statuary in the park is particularly worth seeing (return another time, however, for a closer view of the greatest equestrian statue in America and for other great works of sculpture). Gone from the west side of the square are the well known establishments of Tiffany & Company and Brentano's, as well as the array of piano manufacturers that lined the north side of 14th Street on both sides of Union Square, from Irving Place to beyond Sixth Avenue.

For the Broadway horsecars and omnibuses, making the detour around Union

The equestrian statue of Washington, by Henry Kirke Brown and John Quincy Adams Ward, executed in 1856 and considered one of the finest in America, is seen here at the intersection of Fourth Avenue (now Park Avenue South) and 14th Street. With the advent of the motor age, it was moved into adjacent Union Square. (Museum of the City of New York)

Square presented no problem; but when the later cable cars were installed, a major traffic hazard was created. The forward progress of the Broadway Cable Traction Company's cars was controlled by continuous sections of underground cable laid in a slot between the rails. To negotiate the sharp curve, the operator of the car, called the grip-man, had to get up speed, release his hold on the 14th Street cable section, stamp furiously on his warning bell as the car swung wildly around the bend, then catch the next underground cable section on Broadway. This repeated act of derring-do always attracted crowds of onlookers, and resulted in numerous accidents—some fatal. The spot soon earned the grim appellation, **"Dead Man's Curve."**

7. Continue west on 14th Street, passing the former **Baumann Brothers & Co.** store, at 22 East 14th Street, a large cast-iron edifice whose "modernized" ground floor belies its Classic-style upper façade. Baumann Brothers was a furniture dealer in the Gay '90s and for a time in the 20th century.

8. Midway between Fifth and Sixth avenues, on the south side of 14th Street (Nos. 34–40), a small vestige remains of what was once a prosperous and dynamic enterprise, **James A. Hearn & Son.** Arriving on 14th Street in 1879 after a brief association downtown with his uncle Aaron Arnold (later of Arnold, Constable & Company), James A. Hearn built up a large dry-goods business, and soon became an aggressive rival of R. H. Macy, then at the corner of Sixth Avenue. The two merchants often indulged in cutthroat competition, to their mutual detriment and the customers' delight. It is said that Japanese silk, a favorite with the ladies of the day, was offered by Macy at 41¢ per yard, whereupon Hearn immediately dropped the price by a few cents; and Macy followed suit. Again and again the price was slashed, until at the next day's closing, the fabric was being "sold" at 11 yards for 1¢!

Son George, who inherited the business on his father's retirement in 1886, followed the same merchandising path. He, like neighbor James McCreery, was very philanthropic and also became a benefactor of the Metropolitan Museum of Art.

The original building, with an immense cast-iron façade, was many times the size of the present relic. An apartment house to its left now occupies much of the old site, but still remains "tied" to Hearn's by a series of exposed reinforcing girders. For three-quarters of a century Hearn's remained a family "bargain" store. Older New Yorkers still recall the annual mini-riot at the Washington's Birthday Sale, when thousands of bargain-hungry shoppers pushed their way into the store, smashing plate-glass windows and doors, in their stampede to purchase a television set or major appliance for one cent! The store closed in 1955, although it did operate a liquor store for a brief period. Its name is still preserved in a store in the Bronx at East 149th Street and Third Avenue, now run by a department store chain.

The perils of Dead Man's Curve at Broadway and 14th Street are depicted in this woodcut from Harper's Weekly *of March 27, 1897.* (New-York Historical Society)

A rare old photograph of Lord & Taylor's dry goods store at 47–49 Catherine Street on the Lower East Side, just before the move to Grand and Chrystie streets. At this address Samuel Lord founded the oldest retail store in New York in 1826, taking on partner George Washington Taylor in 1838. Judging from the "selling off" signs, the picture by an unknown photographer was probably taken in 1853. [See p. 218] (The Consolidated Edison Company of New York)

Simpson Crawford Company occupied the west side of Sixth Avenue from 18th to 19th streets and opened a new building in 1900. In this 1905 view of their unusually large show window, photographer Percy C. Byron captured the latest fashions of the day. The building is still there, although the company closed in 1915. (The Byron Collection. Museum of the City of New York)

The James W. McCreery store on the southeast corner of Sixth Avenue and 23rd Street, erected in 1884, replaced the Edwin Booth Theater. The company moved uptown in 1907, and in 1975 its old building was razed. [See p. 214] (Photo by author)

Fourteenth Street decked out in patriotic bunting for the presidential election of 1892. The north side of the street, just west of Union Square, displays the signs for at least six different piano manufacturers as this was the music center of the city in the Gay '90s. Steinway Hall and the Academy of Music were just a few blocks east. (New-York Historical Society)

9. At 56 West 14th Street, look up above the first floor, and with a little squinting, the faded name of the original occupant, emblazoned on a wide stone panel, can be vaguely distinguished: MACY'S. This narrow Beaux Arts–style building is all that remains of a cluster of buildings that marked the early days of what is now the world's largest department store.

After a brief career as a whaler, Rowland Hussey Macy tried and failed three times to establish himself in the dry-goods business. His fourth attempt in 1858 with a small shop around the corner on Sixth Avenue, "buying and selling for cash," met with more success; and within a few years he acquired several adjacent buildings, connecting them with passageways, and offering a wide selection of merchandise. The store prospered, and by 1877 when Macy died, it had grown to a row of 11 buildings, with an annual sales volume of well over a million dollars. The store's well-known emblem, a large red star, was adopted by Macy from his arm tattoo, a reminder of his whaling days. The whale motif is still used to promote big sales.

Looking north from the 18th Street station of the Sixth Avenue El are Simpson, Crawford & Simpson (extreme left), the domes of Hugh O'Neill, and to the right, Cammeyer's, all bedecked with flags. The El, which gave so much impetus to the growth of Fashion Row, had its origin in the Gilbert Elevated Railway, later the Metropolitan Elevated Railway, then the Manhattan Railway Company, and finally as part of the Interborough Rapid Transit. The photo, taken in 1899, shows a train approaching with its locomotive running backward. (New-York Historical Society)

After several changes in management, direction of the store was assumed by brothers Isador and Nathan Straus who earlier had obtained from Macy a concession to operate a china and glassware department. Under their leadership, business boomed, and R. H. Macy & Company became the city's largest department store. Its more than 500 red-and-black delivery wagons could be seen all over town. Using novel sales and advertising techniques, manufacturing many products under its own name, and offering a wide selection of merchandise sold at highly competitive prices, Macy's set the trend for the future retail industry. Its stock ranged in variety from five-cent ice-cream sodas, straw hats, fabrics of all kinds, furniture, men's and women's clothing, to the newly popular bicycle. Bicycles, by the way, were demonstrated by professional riders on a specially designed track where customers could give their own new "wheels" a trial spin. Another innovation, soon copied by other stores, was the annual Christmas toy display—an event that attracted thousands of visitors.

By the turn of the century it became evident that newer and larger quarters were essential. Fourteenth Street's popularity as a shopping center had begun to wane, and in 1901 a site was chosen for a new building. Purchasing Oscar Hammerstein's Manhattan Opera House, located on the north side of 34th Street west of Sixth Avenue, Macy's demolished the theater and erected the first of its present buildings, opening its doors three years later.

Turn right on Sixth Avenue (Avenue of the Americas) to the northwest corner of 15th Street, and look back at the old Macy's store. On the west wall of the building one can still discern part of a 100-year-old advertisement, proudly proclaiming in letters several stories high, "Macy's—World's Largest Store."

Proceed north to the northeast corner of Sixth Avenue and 18th Street.

The old Sixth Avenue El, which cast its dark shadows from 1878 to 1938, is now just a memory. Its demolition, however, opened a vista not possible in the gaslit era. Lining both sides of the street in a five-block silent array from 18th to 23rd streets, stand "The Ghosts of Sixth Avenue." Huge, overbearing, and pretentious edifices—in stone, brick, or iron—they evoke the spirit of another day.

10. Across the street (northwest corner of 18th Street), the dark gray, shabby-looking cast-iron building was once **B. Altman & Company**—"The Palace of Trade," erected from plans by D. & J. Jardine in 1876. Until 1906, Altman's was the trend-setter of women's fashions, specializing in the finest silks, satins, and velvets. Ceramics and sculpture, too, graced the show windows and shelves, for Benjamin Altman was not only a keen entrepreneur, but a lover of objets d'art. A collector himself, he presented his accumulation of art works, worth over $15 million, to the Metropolitan Museum of Art shortly before his death in 1913.

As the age of the sewing machine had just arrived, women flocked to his block-long emporium in quest of the high quality dress goods that made Altman's famous. Benjamin Altman, a solitary man who remained a bachelor all his life, devoted himself exclusively to his enterprise. He took particular pride in appearances. His home-delivery wagons, seen in the more affluent precincts of the city, were rubber-tired, painted a shiny maroon, decorated with brass carriage lamps, and pulled by a matched team of horses driven by a pair of nattily uniformed men. Altman was a considerate employer who shortened the generally accepted 64-hour work week and installed restrooms and a subsidized cafeteria for his workers. In 1906 the store moved uptown to Fifth Avenue and 34th Street, and is still there today—continuing Ben Altman's tradition of selling only quality merchandise and maintaining good employee relationships. Across Sixth Avenue stood one of Altman's biggest competitors, Siegel-Cooper & Company.

11. New York was never the same after Henry Siegel arrived from Chicago! Fresh from successful participation in the 1893 Columbian Exposition, he joined with partner Frank H. Cooper to found a profitable department store in the windy city, and now sought to build the greatest one of them all in New York City—which he did in five short months! Six stories high and capped by a tall tower, the block-wide store extended almost to Fifth Avenue. Designed by architects DeLemos & Cordes in a grandiose style reminiscent of the Exposition, the new store was unprecedented in proportions. With great fanfare and a record-breaking crowd of 150,000, **Siegel-Cooper & Company** opened its doors on Saturday evening, September 12, 1896.

Its motto "The Big Store—A City in Itself" was no exaggeration. Henry Siegel soon earned the reputation as "the father of merchants," for he was

When the great Siegel-Cooper & Company opened its doors in 1896, it seemed that all New York flocked to the event. In this Byron photo, overflow crowds jam Sixth Avenue between 19th and 18th streets, as El trains bring even more sightseers. (The Byron Collection. Museum of the City of New York)

shrewd, innovative, and bold. Never before had such a variety of merchandise been seen under one roof. The central feature of the main floor, however, was the fountain. A circular marble terrace surrounded an enormous white marble and brass statue of *The Republic,* a replica of Daniel Chester French's towering sculpture at the Chicago Fair. Jets of water, illuminated by myriad colored lights, played around the granite pedestal; and from the open "well hole" in the second floor, protected by a mahogany balustrade, customers looked down in awe. The fountain was not only the prime attraction, but the major rendezvous place for shoppers, businessmen, lovers, and tourists. For Gothamites, "Meet Me at the Fountain" became an institution for years to come. To this day, old-timers will quote the slogan without hesitation when asked if they remember Siegel-Cooper.

Siegel showed great understanding of human nature when he introduced the "free sample," especially in his novel food department. After a round of taste-tempting goodies, people *did* buy. He also began the very effective demonstrator system, illustrating the possibilities of such disparate items as kitchen gadgets, wing collars, and sheet music. Among other revolutionary ideas, he installed an air-cooling system, which really brought in the masses on stifling

The latest styles are worn by mother and children entering the Siegel-Cooper store. Elaborate bronze columns and lanterns flank the Sixth Avenue entrance. (Photograph by Byron. The Byron Collection. Museum of the City of New York)

Siegel-Cooper advertisement in Pearson's Magazine *for September 1908 advertises the latest styles at prices which today seem unbelievable. Note the shirtwaists for only $1.00. (Author's collection)*

The business office of the Siegel-Cooper Department Store in a photograph taken ca. 1899 by Byron. (The Byron Collection. Museum of the City of New York)

The sales staff of Siegel-Cooper's sheet music counter poses for photographer Percy C. Byron with the latest tunes of 1899. (The Byron Collection. Museum of the City of New York)

An 1861 lithograph of Wallack's Theater, at the northeast corner of Broadway and 13th Street. The site is now occupied by the former Rogers Peet Building. (*Museum of the City of New York*)

The Eden Musée, an amusement hall and wax museum, stood in the middle of the north side of 23rd Street between Fifth and Sixth avenues. It was so popular in the gaslight era that all street cars made a special stop at the door. The Eden Musée was opened in 1884 and survived until 1916. Robert J. Horner's Furniture Store is at left, and is still there. (*The J. Clarence Davies Collection. Museum of the City of New York*)

summer days; he hired women in many of the sales departments; and he advertised widely in the daily newspapers and on billboards all over town.

But by the first decade of the 20th century the inevitable uptown exodus of the shopping trade had begun again. Henry Siegel, however, had resolute faith in his magnificent palace of retailing. Surely the fountain would always remain the favorite meeting spot in town. Alas, time proved otherwise, for the crowds were now meeting at Macy's and Altman's, and the great empire was beginning to crumble. A reorganization with the backing of financier Joseph B. Greenhut failed to pump new life into the faltering enterprise, and by World War I, Siegel-Cooper was no more.

The best view of the Big Store is from across Sixth Avenue. Note the intricately designed terra-cotta plaques with the firm's monogram, the huge bronze columns set in dramatic archways, and the overall effect of grandeur.

On the north side of West 17th Street, between Seventh and Eighth avenues, Siegel-Cooper's enormous wagon house and stable can still be seen. It, too, is heavily ornamented with distinctive terra-cotta S-C emblems and the company name in large letters on the parapet. During World War I, the store served for a time as a military hospital. Incidentally, the famous statue that graced the fountain now rests in Forest Lawn Memorial Park ("The Happy Cemetery"), in Glendale, California.

12. The large, somewhat restrained granite and limestone building occupying the whole block on the west side of Sixth Avenue between 19th and 20th streets reflects the type of establishment it was; for **Simpson Crawford & Simpson** catered exclusively to the "carriage trade." Partners Thomas and James Simpson and William Crawford opened their first retail store on the site in 1879, aiming for the patronage of the conservative moneyed classes, and dealing mostly in high-priced merchandise. A new building, designed by architects William H. Hume & Son, was opened in 1900—the first on the avenue with the newfangled Otis Escalators. It still shows evidence of the very large show windows, and even a trace of the mosaic floor (at the entrance). Price tags on merchandise and in advertisements were considered superfluous, as their elite clientele would never think of asking anyway. This led to Henry Siegel's sarcastic remark that this was indeed a "priceless" store. Tailor-made dresses were a specialty of the house, with men tailors working overtime to make up the orders for delivery in 24 hours! After James Simpson died, the name was shortened to Simpson Crawford Company, and in the ensuing reorganization, Henry Siegel became president. After the demise in 1914 of the great Siegel-Cooper Store across the street, Simpson Crawford limped on for another year, then expired.

13. The red brick and limestone Italianate building occupying most of the block across the avenue was built in 1893 for the largest shoe "department" store in town, **Cammeyer's.** The stately, well maintained *palazzo* remains as a tribute to the imagination and industriousness of Alfred J. Cammeyer and later partner Louis M. Hart. Together they raised the standard of the retail shoe business from the early custom of stringing up pairs of shoes on storefront poles to a distinguished and reputable enterprise on a scale comparable to their department-store neighbors. The store prided itself in its "standard of merit" slogan, which became synonymous with quality footwear. When the uptown exodus put an end to Ladies' Mile, Cammeyer's, still in the forefront of retail merchandising, moved to 34th Street in 1917, and four years later opened an elegant branch on Fifth Avenue. The pitfalls of specialization, however, ultimately doomed the firm, which disappeared after the Depression.

14. The former Church of the Holy Communion, on the northeast corner of 20th Street, dates from 1846, when the busy shopping center was a quiet and somewhat remote residential district. Architect Richard Upjohn, who designed the church—one of his lesser works—was one of the best-known advocates of the popular Gothic Revival style of the 1840s. The church was closed in the mid-1970s, and has seen a variety of uses, the most recent as a theater.

15. When the **Hugh O'Neill store,** designed by Mortimer C. Merritt, opened in 1876, it must have been a dazzling site to its first visitors. With flamboyant round towers topped by huge bulbous domes, an imposing pediment rising high above five stories of Corinthian columns and pilasters, and a building almost unrivaled in size, O'Neill's began a tradition that was to cause amazement and surprise to patrons and competitors alike for years to come. Hugh O'Neill was no ordinary merchant, but an aggressive, extravagant, and colorful salesman. Hardly a week went by without a dramatic sale accompanied by much hoopla and publicity, for his appeal was not to the staid, conservative clientele of his neighbors, but to the working classes. With the advent of Elias Howe's great invention, the motto of O'Neill became "Put a Sewing Machine in Every Home!" He offered the machines as loss-leaders and was thus able to move his tremendous stock of piece goods at a healthy profit. His tactics of undercutting and doing battle with his competitors earned him the name, "The Fighting Irishman of Sixth Avenue." Although a bit crusty and brusque, he was a deeply religious man who commanded the love and respect of his employees. He always insisted that they observe their religious holidays, no matter what their faith, and would give them time off with full pay; nor was he ever above discussing their personal problems with them. A special source of pride to Hugh O'Neill was his shiny fleet of delivery wagons; he frequently would be seen making an early morning inspection round, like a general reviewing his troops, as the teams lined up for the day's deliveries. After he died, there was no one to carry on in the same spirit. To save the store, a merger was arranged with its neighbor to the north, the Adams Dry-Goods Company, resulting in a most unlikely partnership that was destined to last only for a few years. Adams had a different retailing style and an even more dissimilar clientele, so the O'Neill-Adams alliance disintegrated and collapsed completely in 1915.

16. Around the corner on 21st Street, seemingly hidden and protected by the L-shape of the Hugh O'Neill Store, is the diminutive **Third Cemetery of the Spanish & Portuguese Synagogue.** This shady burial plot is the northernmost of three early cemeteries of this first Jewish congregation in America, and was in use between 1829 and 1851. [*See* Lower East Side *Supplementary Tour A;* Greenwich Village, 33.]

17. The ornate Beaux-Arts **Adams Dry-Goods Store,** designed by DeLemos & Cordes, the architects of the Siegel-Cooper store, reflects the architectural style that came into vogue around the turn of the century. A relative latecomer to the avenue, A.D.G. tried to capture the fancy (and patronage) of the "carriage trade" through conservative merchandising and a high-priced inventory. One of its novel offerings was men's ready-to-wear and made-to-measure clothing. Its founder, Samuel Adams, started in business much earlier, but did not erect this building until 1900 (note the date, set near the cornice). Since most department stores were family enterprises, Adams had no one to carry on the name. His only daughter, Eileen, showed no inclination for the retail trade, and married the son of march-king John Philip Sousa. When he sold out to Hugh O'Neill, the newly formed O'Neill-Adams Company made a desperate attempt to create a new image. The two firms now were connected not only by a hyphen, but also by an underground tunnel beneath 21st Street; and considerable sums were spent in promoting the new venture—but all in vain. They apparently could not keep abreast of the new, more scientific merchandising techniques, and in 1915, joined the roster of "ghosts."

18. Ehrich Brothers, the last of the old-timers in the Sixth Avenue row, was erected in 1889 from plans by Alfred Zucker, and stands dark and dingy, straddling the southwest corner of 23rd Street. The small corner plot, occupied by a cream-colored cast-iron building that juts into the old department store, was always a thorn in the Ehrich Brothers' side—they were unable to acquire the property and had to build around it (much the same as the problem that later faced Macy's when they purchased the 34th Street and Sixth Avenue site in 1904). This corner building, recently restored almost to its original appearance after a destructive fire, shows what cast-iron structures looked like when new. It was formerly a branch of the **Riker's Drug Company,** later absorbed into the Liggett chain.

Ehrich Brothers (Julius S. and Samuel W.) was known as a "bargain store," perhaps even more so than Hugh O'Neill. The store was famous for its sales of manufacturers' closeouts and for its "omnibus advertising" (many categories of merchandise grouped into a single large advertisement). Saturdays were "Children's Days" at Ehrich's, when mothers could leave their young ones to enjoy specially provided entertainment and be free to shop at leisure. One of Ehrich Brothers' young trainees learned the retail trade quite well, and after the store ultimately closed, went into business for himself, establishing the name of Nathan Ohrbach as one of the city's successful retail merchants.

In 1911 Ehrich's ceased operations for much the same reason as its neighbors. The brothers tried their hand briefly in a "horseless carriage" dealership, but that, too, proved a failure. On the 23rd Street side, one can still see the faded name "Ehrich Brothers" on a rusty panel above the ground floor.

19. On the southeast corner of 23rd Street and Avenue of the Americas from 1869 to 1883 stood the **Edwin Booth Theater,** designed by Renwick & Sands, with Booth himself as manager and frequent star performer. When **James W. McCreery,** known as the "Dean of the Retail Trade," acquired the site, he demolished the theater and erected his second department store. In 1907 he joined his competitors in the great move uptown, building his newest emporium on 34th Street at Fifth Avenue. McCreery's went out of business unexpectedly in 1954 and the store was purchased by Ohrbach's. The 23rd Street structure survived until 1975 as a loft building. When McCreery opened the store in 1884 he installed a marble bust of Shakespeare into the façade—a memento from the Booth Theater, together with a bronze commemorative plaque honoring the theater. Both the bust and plaque were rescued when the building came down and were donated by the former owner to New York University. It is said that Booth, dressed as Shakespeare, posed for the sculpture.

20. About 200 feet farther east on 23rd Street stood the twin buildings of **Best & Company,** which came to 23rd Street in 1881. Specializing in children's wear, it was known by its more popular name, "The Lilliputian Bazaar." The store departed in 1910, moving to Fifth Avenue and 35th Street (the impressive building still occupies the southwest corner); and later to 51st Street, where to the dismay of many New York shoppers, it closed its doors forever in 1970. The new Olympic Tower now stands in its place.

Alongside was the famed partnership of **Paul J. Bonwit and Edmund D. Teller.** "Bonwit's" began at Sixth Avenue and 18th Street in 1895, selling fine-quality apparel for women. It opened its 23rd Street store three years later, then in 1908 Teller sold out to Bonwit, and three years later the store moved uptown to Fifth Avenue and 30th Street. In 1930 it moved again, into a large building at the corner of 56th Street. In the late 1970s, the firm almost disappeared, as its building had to be demolished; but phoenixlike, it arose again, in its present location around the corner on 57th Street, next to Tiffany's.

The third member of the departed triumvirate was fashionable **LeBoutillier Brothers** (pronounced by all "Le-boo-ti-LEER"—even by founder Philip LeBoutillier himself). Arriving in 1898, the store soon became a mecca for the latest in women's styles. By 1913, hard times struck again, and Philip LeBoutillier, the only brother left in the business, closed his shop and joined Best's, ultimately rising to the rank of president of the company.

Across 23rd Street, No. 61–65 is another venerable cast-iron-front building, looking not much different from when it opened in 1877 as Robert J. Horner's Furniture Store. Designed by the noted architect of cast-iron buildings John B. Snook, it later merged with the Flint Furniture Company to become the well known **Flint & Horner Furniture Company.** Occupying the building until 1912, the firm then joined the great uptown procession to 34th Street. Like Wanamaker's, Stern's, and Arnold Constable, the company abandoned the city and moved its operations to a suburban location, in this case, Manhasset. Cast iron was ideally suited to the retail trades, as the showrooms could be well illuminated by the large areas of window glass that an iron front permitted. Note the building's feeling of height created by the successive diminishing of each story—an illusive device credited to the architects of ancient Greece.

21. In the middle of the block is the gargantuan white cast-iron building of the former **Stern Brothers Department Store** (best viewed from the parking lot across the street). From humble beginnings when they arrived from Buffalo in 1867, the children of poor immigrants, Stern brothers Isaac, Louis, and Bernard, plus three sisters, opened a small dry-goods shop around the corner on 22nd Street. Business prospered, and in 1878 they engaged architect Henry

Fernbach to design this imposing seven-story edifice—200 feet wide, extending through to 22nd Street, engulfing their old one-room store. Until the opening of the Siegel-Cooper Store 18 years later, it was New York's largest. A far cry from the little family shop was this luxury store, in front of which were posted blue-liveried doormen with top hats, giving the establishment a touch of class that it was to retain for years to come.

Although priding itself in its appeal to the carriage trade, Stern Brothers did not overlook the working classes, for their merchandise was priced for both extremes of the economic spectrum. Isaac, the guiding spirit of the firm, was frequently to be seen greeting customers by name; and it is said that on occasion he would make an urgent home delivery in his own carriage. A fourth brother, Benjamin, joined the partnership after Bernard's passing in 1884. A number of men working in the department stores of the gaslit era achieved later fame as merchandisers in their own right. One of them, a 13-year-old youngster starting as a stock boy, worked his way up in Stern's, eventually opening a store on 34th Street in 1902 bearing his own name, Franklin Simon.

By 1913, seeing the handwriting on the wall, Stern Brothers built a new

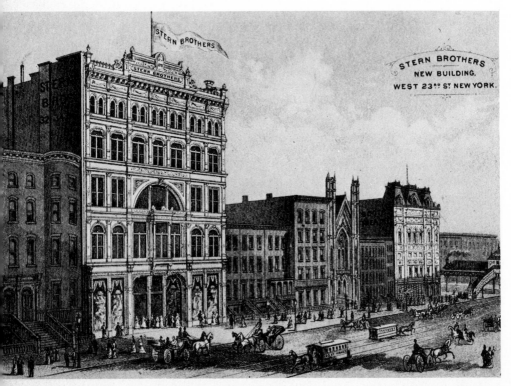

Stern Brothers' original store, in an 1878 print, shares the south side of 23rd Street with residences, a church, and the Edwin Booth Theater, as well as the recently completed Sixth Avenue El. (Museum of the City of New York)

West 23rd Street looking east from Sixth Avenue, ca. 1905, shows the northern limit of Fashion Row. Right to left are the stores of Best & Company, Bonwit Teller, LeBoutillier Brothers, and the enormous white cast-iron front of Stern Brothers. The newly completed Flatiron Building appears in the distance. The Stern Brothers building still remains in a good state of preservation. (Museum of the City of New York)

store on 42nd Street and Sixth Avenue and joined the "uptown club." To the regret of many, the store ceased operations in 1970, leaving only its suburban branches to carry on the name.

Note the company monogram and the ornate design motifs in the well-preserved façade. It is apparent that the present owners of the building take pride in the historic and aesthetic value of this beautiful cast-iron front.

22. At 14 West 23rd Street is a small iron-front building, now rather woebegone in appearance, which was once **James McCutcheon & Company.** Known as "The Linen Store," it arrived in Ladies' Mile in 1886 after progressive moves uptown, having started 31 years before at Broadway and Astor Place. Dealing exclusively in fine linens, its tablecloths, napkins, doilies, sheets, pillowcases, and such were in great demand from the moneyed classes. In 1907 the store moved to more fashionable quarters on Fifth Avenue. Ultimately it merged with Plummer & Company, becoming Plummer-McCutcheon. More recently it was taken over by Hammacher Schlemmer on 57th Street, and now functions as one of its departments. The building, incidentally, was the **birthplace in 1862 of novelist Edith Wharton.** The building, then a brownstone, was converted in 1882 to a retail store by architect Henry J. Hardenbergh (the Dakota, Plaza Hotel, etc.). The cast-iron front was installed ten years later by another architect, George H. Billings, for the new occupant, James McCutcheon's Linen Store.

23. Just before reaching Fifth Avenue, pause briefly at the red brick Queen Anne–style building also designed by Henry Hardenbergh that **The Western Union Company** built in 1883 as its uptown office. A terra-cotta plaque above the second floor bears the company name. Across the street is the unique **Flatiron Building,** erected in 1902 [*see* Madison Square, 24].

24. Turn south on Fifth Avenue to No. 170. The interesting cupola atop this narrow building built in 1897, which can be seen from quite a distance, marks the location of the former offices and showroom of **Sohmer Piano Company.**

Across Fifth Avenue is an Italianate brownstone building marked *Albert* in vertical gold letters. Although now a commercial building, it was originally the **Hotel Glenham,** built in 1861. Relatively unchanged in appearance, it gives a good idea of the style and scale of neighborhood buildings of the time.

At No. 153 was the **Charles Scribner's Sons** store, built in 1894 from plans by Ernest Flagg. Look for the "S" on the fourth-floor balcony. Not only was the firm a well-known book dealer (as it is today), but the publisher of one of the most popular periodicals of the time, *Scribner's Magazine.* The building was purchased in 1973 by the United Synagogue of America, a conservative Jewish organization.

At the southeast corner of 21st Street (No. 147 Fifth Avenue) is the imposing **Merchants Central Building** (Robert Maynicke, 1897), a highly ornate Renaissance Eclectic structure, with an enormous cupola.

25. At **150 Fifth Avenue** (southwest corner of 20th Street) is a particularly handsome building in a mixture of Queen Anne and Romanesque Revival styles of architecture. Emblazoned at the top are the letters M.B.C., announcing the home office of one of the largest religious book publishers of the "Mauve Decade," the Methodist Book Concern, as well as the headquarters of the Methodist Church in New York. There were, in fact, so many publishers of religious books along the street that the district was known as **"Pater Noster Row."** Except for the dreadful modernization of the entrance, the building, erected in 1889, is in an excellent state of preservation. By contrast, note the splendid original "grand entrance" to **No. 156,** on the northwest corner, built in a Romanesque Revival style.

Walk east to the northeast corner of Broadway and 20th Street.

26. The yellow brick and terra-cotta Renaissance-style building on the northwest corner, **No. 903 Broadway,** is a fine example of the genre. Diagonally across Broadway, No. 900, is the **Goelet Building** (1886), an example of McKim, Mead & White's design for a speculative commercial building. Its elaborate cornice is long gone and four stories have been added, yet the polychrome arches and rounded corner preserve the feeling of solidity and strength desired by the architects.

27. One of the most enduring partnerships in the retail trade was that of Messrs. **Lord and Taylor.** The spectacular structure on the southwest corner of 20th Street is a tribute to the courage and resourcefulness of these two English immigrants who together built one of the most respected fashion establishments in the trade. Opening a little shop on Catherine Street in 1826, Samuel Lord joined the growing number of dry-goods merchants; 12 years later he took on as a partner his wife's cousin, George Washington Taylor, and soon the firm of Lord & Taylor had the reputation for honest business practices and quality merchandise. A year after Taylor retired in 1852, the much expanded firm opened its first "department store" on the corner of Grand and Chrystie streets, a large gray stone building capped by an imposing glass dome, which was a Lower East Side landmark for almost 50 years. Grand Street at the time was one of the busiest shopping streets and a major east-west thoroughfare whose crosstown horsecars connected with the New Jersey and Long Island ferries.

Rapid development of business encouraged the firm to open another branch farther west on Grand Street, at the corner of Broadway; however, it lasted only 12 years. During the 1863 Draft Riots, some 100 employees rushed to secure arms and ammunition from an uptown armory, barricaded the building, and successfully discouraged any attempt by the unruly mobs to sack the store.

In 1872 this extraordinary five-story iron-front building, designed by James Giles in what was described as Bohemian Renaissance style, was opened to the public. Equipped with a steam elevator and other "modern" conveniences, it was an instant success. Surviving the following year's Panic of 1873, Lord & Taylor continued to be one of the most fashionable women's stores on the newly developing Ladies' Mile. When the store at Grand and Chrystie streets closed in 1902, the present building was greatly enlarged. Much of the elaborate emporium, however, has disappeared. An open lot on the 20th Street side now separates the main building from a segment that once extended to Fifth Avenue. (That amputated vestige is now a garishly painted cooperative apartment house which, after conversion, has taken for itself a Fifth Avenue address.) Particularly attractive is the mansard roof on the corner pavilion, complete with dormers, and all in cast iron.

The year 1914, when so many of these great establishments either failed or departed, saw Lord & Taylor move to its present location at Fifth Avenue and 38th Street.

28. The building at the northwest corner of 19th Street, whose irregular and picturesque roof is reminiscent of an English Victorian castle, was the sales office of the **Gorham Manufacturing Company.** The name survives today and is still synonymous with fine silver. The structure, designed by architect Edward H. Kendall in 1883 in Queen Anne style, housed the company whose specialty was custom-designed silverware and a wide variety of ecclesiastical metalwork. The firm subsequently moved its operations uptown, erecting an appropriately impressive building on the southwest corner of Fifth Avenue and 37th Street.

29. A year after Lord & Taylor opened its magnificent store on 20th Street, its die-hard competitor **Arnold Constable** followed suit one block south. The saga of Arnold Constable, New York's oldest department store, began with Aaron Arnold, a young English immigrant, opening a small dry-goods shop on Pine Street in what is now the financial district. With business flourishing, he moved to progressively larger sites; and taking in two nephews, George and James Hearn—the partnership became Arnold, Hearn & Co. [*see* 8.] A recently hired friend of the Arnold family, James Mansell Constable—in typical Horatio Alger fashion—fell in love with the boss's daughter, married her, and was taken into the partnership. Apparently disgruntled by the sudden rise of Constable, the Hearn brothers left Arnold and went into business for themselves. After another change in location, the firm built a large establishment at the corner of Canal, Mercer, and Howard streets, with an impressive white marble façade which Arnold referred to as his "Marble House." It was here that he renamed his firm Arnold, Constable & Company, and made his reputation selling luxury merchandise, soon becoming the darling of the carriage trade—with a customer list reading like the social register. The building, stripped of its fancy trappings, still stands. [*See* pages 164–165.]

In 1869 Arnold retired, leaving the reins of the company in the hands of James Constable. The same year marked the move to the 19th Street site. In a series of land acquisitions, the store, which was designed by Griffith Thomas, grew in size until 1877 when it covered the whole block to Fifth Avenue. The five-story brick and limestone structure, topped by an enormous French Second Empire mansard roof, was a sensation. Devoting itself exclusively to the sale of fabrics, carpets, and upholstery materials, it remained a prestige store for years to come. The vast selection of its dry goods, ranging from children's wear to mourning apparel, led to the comment that "Arnold Constable provides elegant clothing, from cradleside to graveside." The *New York Daily Graphic,* in its January 8, 1877 edition, described the store as "a new Emporium of Trade—a dominant and ornamental addition to the street architecture of New York."

In 1914, that famous "uptown moving year," the company abandoned its pretentious building and moved to its final location at Fifth Avenue and 40th Street. It is interesting to note that from 1860 to 1975, the two fierce competitors, Arnold Constable and Lord & Taylor, had never been more than two blocks apart! With the demise of Arnold Constable after 150 years, its rival survives as the oldest retail store in the city. Arnold Constable's last building is now the New York Public Library's Mid-Manhattan branch.

30. "The house of **W. & J. Sloane** stands indisputably at the head of the carpet and rug industry of this country," wrote Moses King in his *Handbook of New York* for 1893. Unlike the other department stores that had their origin in the dry-goods business, Sloane's dealt almost exclusively in rugs and floor coverings.

Arriving on a sailing ship in 1834, William Sloane, a young weaver from Scotland, found work in a Connecticut mill, learning American weaving techniques. Nine years later he established a small "Carpeting and Floor Cloth Shop" on lower Broadway, using the slogan "Dependable Merchandise at an Honest Figure." In 1852, brother John, the "J" of W. & J. Sloane, was taken into the business, but stayed with William for only nine years. At the closing of the 1876 Centennial Exposition in Philadelphia, William Sloane purchased a superb collection of Oriental rugs that had been a major display at the Fair, offering them to his growing list of wealthy clients. This marked the first time

Oriental rugs were sold by a retail house. In the meantime, he had moved up Broadway twice, keeping abreast of the familiar northward push, and a few years later accomplished another "first," contracting with a weaving firm in India to become the only American rug store with its own Oriental source of supply.

William Sloane achieved fame of another sort a few years earlier, when the criminal jury of which he was foreman convicted "Boss" Tweed. While on the jury he learned that merchant-prince A. T. Stewart was about to foreclose a mortgage on the Alexander Smith Carpet Company in Yonkers, N.Y. Sloane raised the money, saved the Smith Company, and in return received an interest and became its exclusive agent for many years. On his death in 1879, the firm's direction was taken over by his eldest son, John II. It was under John Sloane that the company achieved its greatest growth, inaugurating in 1881 the large store across the street from Arnold Constable and an equally spacious outlet in San Francisco. W. & J. Sloane achieved national fame with a contract to carpet some of the swankiest hotels in the city, including the newly opened Waldorf-Astoria on 34th Street; and the company won international fame with the commission to supply all the carpeting for the coronation of Czar Nicholas II. At the same time, the store expanded its operations into home decorating, selling antiques, and manufacturing "registered reproductions" of antique furniture.

As the gaslit era waned, Sloane's moved in 1912 to Fifth Avenue and 47th Street, where they remained until 1962. In a subsequent move down the avenue to 38th Street, they sold their building to E. J. Korvette, acquiring the store formerly occupied by Franklin Simon; and in a late 1982 move Sloane's abandoned their Fifth Avenue address for an adjacent smaller location farther west on 38th Street. Interestingly, the current occupant of the original Broadway store, coincidentally a rug and carpet retailer, has restored the exterior and interior to re-create the aura of elegance of the 1880s.

Find the "S" monogram on a small cast-iron shield set high on the building, as well as the date of construction in terra-cotta Roman numerals.

End of tour. The IRT and BMT subways are directly ahead at the south end of Union Square.

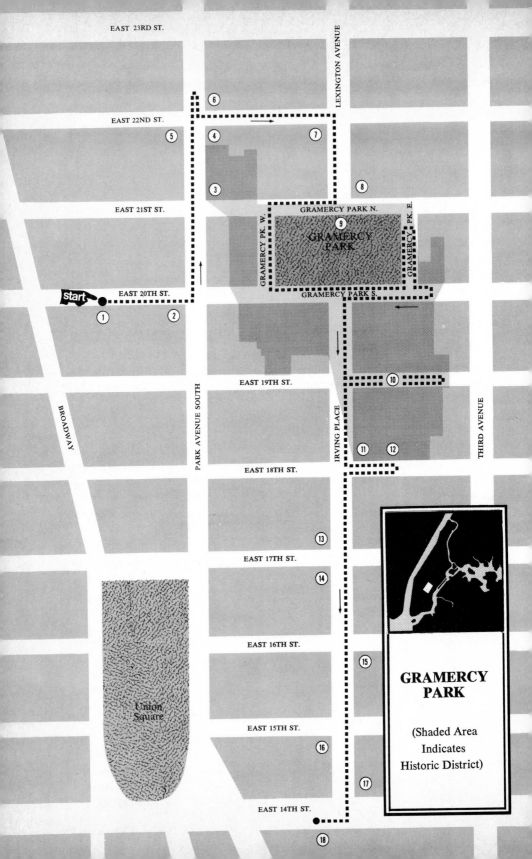

9. Gramercy Park

[*IRT Lexington Avenue line to 23rd Street; BMT RR Broadway line to 23rd Street; Broadway (M-1, M-6, or M-7) bus to 20th Street*]

In Dutch Colonial days the locality was known as *Crommessie Fly* (crooked stream), an area of woods and marshes situated just above the country estate of Governor Peter Stuyvesant. It later became the property of James Duane, mayor of New York City from 1784 to 1789, who named it Gramercy Seat. In 1831 land developer Samuel B. Ruggles purchased a substantial parcel from the Duane Farm and laid out the residential lots and park. Ruggles also laid out lower Lexington Avenue, naming it after the Revolutionary Battle of Lexington, and Irving Place, which he named for his friend Washington Irving. In spite of the growth of the surroundings and the encroachment of high-rise buildings, Gramercy Park has managed to remain one of the most charming residential districts of the city.

1. The tour begins at 28 East 20th Street, just east of Broadway, at the **birthplace of one of Gramercy Park's most illustrious residents, Theodore Roosevelt.** The original brownstone house in which he was born in 1858 was demolished in 1916 and replaced by a commercial building. After T.R.'s death in 1919, however, prominent citizens decided to purchase the site, raze the structure, and create a memorial by reconstructing Roosevelt's boyhood home as it appeared during the years 1865–72. The adjoining lot, No. 26, where T.R.'s uncle Robert had his residence, was also acquired and made into a museum. The birthplace was opened to the public in 1923, and in 1963 both sites were donated by the Theodore Roosevelt Association to the National Park Service. The rooms have been restored to the period of "Teedie's" boyhood. The parlor is furnished with crystal chandeliers, magnificent mirrors, and blue satin hangings, characteristic of the elegance of the day. The master bedroom in which he was born contains the original furniture and a portrait of his mother, Martha Bulloch Roosevelt. Next to it is the nursery and, beyond, the open porch that was used as a gymnasium. In addition to his widely known political accomplishments, Theodore Roosevelt was also an effective, reform-minded Police Commissioner

of New York City. (*The birthplace is open Wed.–Sun., 9 A.M.–5 P.M., 50¢.*)
Proceed east to Park Avenue South, known formerly by its more prosaic name,
Fourth Avenue.

2. 250 Park Avenue South (Rouse & Goldstone, 1912) is a large industrial
building in a neo-Gothic style. Built early in the century when decoration served
as a more important element of architecture than it does today, it is typical
of many such commercial structures in the city built in the first two decades
of the century.

3. Across the avenue, one block north, is **Calvary Church.** Designed in
1846 by James Renwick, Jr., architect of Grace Church and St. Patrick's Cathedral, it is in the tradition of the Gothic Revival so popular in the 1840s. The
stone towers, which replaced earlier wooden steeples, were removed in 1925.
Novelist Edith Wharton, born at nearby 14 West 23rd Street, was baptized
here in 1862.

4. No. 281 is the **Church Missions' House.** Built in a flamboyant Romanesque
Revival style in 1894 by R. W. Gibson and E. J. N. Stent, this imposing edifice,
best seen from a distance, houses the headquarters of the domestic and foreign
missionary service of the Protestant Episcopal Church, which was founded in
1821.

5. Across the street, at the southwest corner of 22nd Street, in a much
altered Classical style is the **former New York Bank for Savings Building—**
the "Beehive Bank." Chartered in Greenwich Village in 1819 as the Bleecker
Street Savings Bank, this oldest savings institution in the city moved into this
building, designed by C. L. W. Eidlitz, in 1894. With the opening of the bank's
uptown office, the building was abandoned and at this writing is slated for
demolition—its many tasteless renovations rendering it unsuitable for landmark
designation.

6. The former United Charities Building, at 105 East 22nd Street, was erected
in 1891–93 from plans by R. H. Robertson and Rowe & Baker in a modified
Romanesque Revival style, for the New York Association for Improving the
Condition of the Poor, now the Community Service Society, ". . . to improve
the condition of the working classes, and to elevate their physical state." It
also houses, among other charitable institutions, the Children's Aid Society.
Turn east on 22nd Street to Lexington Avenue.

7. The lavish Renaissance-style *palazzo* on the southwest corner, the Gramercy Towers, was designed for the **Russell Sage Foundation** in 1914 by Grosvenor Atterbury. Sage, a financier and philanthropist, died in 1906, leaving an
enormous fortune to charity. Among the legatees was Russell Sage College, in
upstate Troy, N.Y. He was known to be strongly opinioned, and it is said
that upon being approached by August Belmont to share in the financial backing
of the newly begun subway, he turned to the president of the Rapid Transit
Construction Company and commented scornfully that "New Yorkers would
never go into a hole to ride it." In recent years the building was occupied by
Catholic Charities, then in 1975 it was purchased by a developer who converted
it into an apartment house. A part of the ground floor has been converted
into a mini antiques mall.

The Hewitt Cooper House, built by Peter Cooper in 1848 at 9 Lexington Avenue, was later occupied by his son-in-law Ambram S. Hewitt, Mayor of New York, 1887–88. The house was demolished in 1939. (Museum of the City of New York)

Across 22nd Street is the **Mabel Dean Bacon Vocational High School,** formerly the Manhattan Trade School for Girls. It was built in 1917 from plans by C. B. J. Snyder, whose Collegiate Gothic style for school buildings was very popular early in the century.

Walk south one block to 21st Street. The northeast corner is the **site of the Cyrus W. Field Residence.** Field, with help from Peter Cooper (who lived just a few doors north, at 9 Lexington Avenue), promoted the Atlantic Cable, which after some initial failures was laid successfully in 1866. He was also responsible for the building of most of the elevated railroads in the city during the late 1870s, only to lose them a few years later to railroad tycoon Jay Gould.

8. Gramercy Park, whose name probably derives from the original Dutch *Crommessie Fly* (crooked stream), is a tribute to Samuel B. Ruggles's foresight, and is an excellent example of urban planning. By taking the 42 lots that comprise the 1½-acre park and deeding the parcel to the 60 surrounding lot owners, he established, in 1831, the only surviving private park in the city. (An earlier private plot, St. John's Park, owned by Trinity Parish, was destroyed by the takeover of adjacent land by the Hudson River Railroad, and ultimately obliterated by the entrance ramps to the Holland Tunnel.) The cast-iron fence was erected in 1832, with extensive planting undertaken thereafter. Although formerly restricted to adjacent property owners, this private park is now accessible to all who live close by and who pay the annual fee. The Park and surrounding lots, including Calvary Church and a stretch of property on 18th and 19th streets, were designated in 1966 by the Landmarks Preservation Commission as the **Gramercy Park Historic District.**

Turning west at the Gramercy Park Hotel, we pass **the site of Stanford White's residence** (the site of No. 82) from 1901 until his untimely death in 1906. White is acknowledged not only as an exemplary architect, but as one who established the American tradition of art collecting. His private collection of paintings and sculpture is now distributed among several museums.

At what was **formerly No. 70** stood the home of diarist George Templeton Strong, the peripatetic chronicler of mid-19th century life and events, who acquired the property by marrying Ruggles's daughter. To the east of his house lived Robert "Bob" Ingersoll, orator and lawyer, who, because of his highly publicized lectures on religion, was dubbed "The Great Agnostic."

Rounding the corner, **Nos. 1 and 2 Gramercy Park West** date from 1849–50. Dr. Valentine Mott, probably the most renowned surgeon in the days just before the Civil War, lived in No. 1. He was responsible for the founding of the New York University Medical College and Bellevue Hospital.

Charming Nos. 3 and 4 Gramercy Park West still remain, adding to the pleasant atmosphere of the neighborhood. This pair of houses, built in 1846, are attributed to architect Alexander Jackson Davis. Twin lanterns in front of No. 4 denote the residence of former Mayor James Harper. (Photograph by Berenice Abbott. Federal Art Project "Changing New York." Museum of the City of New York)

Lovely **Nos. 3 and 4,** with their lacy ironwork porches, were built in 1846 and are attributed to famed architect Alexander Jackson Davis. The pair of lanterns in front of No. 4 indicate that it was once a mayor's residence. James Harper, founder of the J. & J. Harper publishing house, was elected to the city's highest office in 1844 after a scurrilous anti-Irish, anti-"Popism" campaign, although he himself was a reformer, fought corruption, and organized the Police Department.

Turning east at the corner, we see the large double brownstone mansion of the **National Arts Club** at 15 Gramercy Park South. Built in 1845, the two single houses were remodeled from about 1881 to 1884 by Calvert Vaux for Samuel J. Tilden (Vaux, with Frederick Law Olmsted, designed Central and Prospect parks). Although the façade is not surviving well against air pollution and pigeons, it is nonetheless an engaging example of Ruskinian Gothic, inspired by the Medieval Revival style made famous by the 19th-century English author and artist John Ruskin. Tilden, an eminent lawyer and reformer, was governor of New York in 1875–76, but resigned the office to run as Democratic presidential contender against Rutherford B. Hayes. History records that he won the popular majority by a quarter of a million votes but lost the election—defeated by a group of Southern Republican electors. The National Arts Club purchased the landmark building in 1906.

Adjacent is **The Players,** 16 Gramercy Park South, built for a banker in 1845. It was later purchased by actor Edwin Booth, who in 1888 commissioned Stanford White to remodel it as a private club for the theatrical profession. The huge Tuscan stone porch and elaborate ironwork, including the two graceful lanterns, are some of White's additions. Not all the great "Players" were actors, however. The membership included such notables as Walter Damrosch, Thomas Nast, Mark Twain, Booth Tarkington, and even General William Tecumseh Sherman. But they were all *men,* as the Players' Club was, and still is, "no-woman's-land."

"No-man's-land," on the other hand, is just next door at **No. 17,** the **Salvation Army's Parkside Evangeline Residence Hall.**

Before crossing Irving Place, look through the park gates at the **statue of Edwin Booth** as Hamlet, sculpted by Edmond T. Quinn in 1916.

No. 19 Gramercy Park South is the **Stuyvesant Fish House.** Built for a Horace Brooks in 1845, it was acquired in 1887 by Stuyvesant Fish, wealthy socialite and president of the Illinois Central Railroad. The line had so many of the "400" on its board of directors that it was called the "Society Railroad." His wife, Mary "Mamie" Fish, succeeded Mrs. William Astor as the head of New York society. It is said that Mamie Fish curtailed the traditional dinner hour from a several-hour affair to a mere 50 minutes; she was also responsible for a new informality among members of society, by encouraging the use of guests' first names. The Victorian mansard roof with ornate iron cresting is a later addition to this beautifully maintained house.

No. 21, next door, built in 1853–54, was the residence of John Bigelow, author and diplomat. Bigelow was co-owner with William Cullen Bryant of the *New York Evening Post* from 1848 to 1861, when he gave up his newspaper business to become minister to France during the Civil War. He is credited with depriving the Confederacy of recognition by the French Government, and with stopping the construction of rebel warships.

Ignoring several nondescript remodelings, we come to the former **Friends' Meeting House,** 144 East 20th Street. Built by King & Kellum in 1859, it is a fine example of the dignified Italianate style so popular in the 1850s. For a time the fate of the Meeting House was uncertain, as the Friends had merged their meetings with the Stuyvesant Square congregation, selling the house to the United Federation of Teachers. There was even talk of demolition and the erection of a high-rise apartment house, in spite of its designation as a New York City Landmark. But early in 1975, the **Brotherhood Synagogue,** which had been sharing quarters with the Village Presbyterian Church on West 13th Street, purchased the building from the U.F.T. for conversion to a synagogue. Only minor interior changes were made, and the lovely building's future is now assured.

At the northeast corner of 20th Street is the venerable red brick Victorian apartment house, **The Gramercy.** Now a co-op, the well-preserved and dignified building is thought to be the oldest apartment dwelling in the city, and was erected in 1883 from plans by George da Cunha. Peek into its luxurious lobby! Alongside is a neo-Tudor Gothic apartment house with white terra-cotta bay windows, built in 1905. Guarding the entrance to the "castle" are a pair of knights in armor.

Return to Irving Place, walk south one block to 19th Street, and turn east.

9. The tree-lined and serene block between Irving Place and Third Avenue is known as the **"Block Beautiful."** Frederick Sterner was the prime mover in the rehabilitation of many of the old houses. Although none are particularly outstanding by themselves, they form a unity of "harmonious differences." Note the three "Gothic" conversions at **Nos. 127** (1854), **129** (1861), and **135** (1845). **No. 139** (1842–43), in a Tuscan style, earned Sterner his initial popularity. **No. 141** (1843), with its jockey hitching posts, belonged to the late sportscaster Ted Husing. **No. 132** (1910) was the residence of silent film ingenue Theda Bara, and of Mrs. Patrick Campbell, who in 1912 created the role of Eliza Doolittle in Shaw's *Pygmalion.* It was also the home of "muckraker" Ida M. Tarbell, who wrote the highly critical two-volume *History of the Standard Oil Company.* George Bellows, a founder of the Ashcan School of American painting, lived at **No. 140** (1852–53). The ceramic reliefs over the entrances of **Nos. 147–149** (1861) are the work of resident artist Robert Winthrop Chanler. Note also **Nos. 144** and **146.**

Return to Irving Place and continue south to 18th Street.

10. Pete's Tavern, at 66 Irving Place, dating from 1864 when it was called "Healy's," boasts to be the oldest saloon in New York City. The assertion, however, is strongly disputed by McSorley's Old Ale House, on East 7th Street,

The Academy of Music, built in 1854 at the corner of Irving Place and 14th Street, was New York's most popular and fashionable opera house until the advent of the Metropolitan Opera House in 1883. In 1910 it was razed to make way for Con Ed's new office building. Note the ad for Drake's Plantation Bitters painted on the curb. (The Consolidated Edison Company of New York)

which opened ten years earlier. Pete's also claims to have been a favorite haunt of O. Henry; but, knowing his proclivities, almost any saloon could have earned that distinction! Legend (and a few faded newspaper clippings) maintains that he wrote *The Gift of the Magi* in the second booth on the right (this is also disputed by a restaurant down the street at No. 55—in fact, they have a plaque on the building to "prove" it). Be that as it may, the Tavern has been a popular local landmark for many years. Two old carriage houses in the rear have been absorbed into the expanded establishment, and much of the flavor of the gaslit era remains.

11. Around the corner, **Nos. 135–143 East 18th Street** are a row of pre–Civil War houses (1855), each only two bays wide. When neighbors get together in a common effort to restore their properties, the result can be very gratifying. **Nos. 145–151** date from the same period (1853–54).

12. No. 55 Irving Place is the site of William Sidney Porter's (O. Henry's) residence. Now an apartment house, little remains of the original building or the old Blue Bell Tavern at the corner (another purported "favorite" of the author). The plaque at the entrance to the restaurant claims *this* to be the location of the writing of *The Gift of the Magi*.

13. The charming little red brick house on the southwest corner of 17th Street, **No. 40 Irving Place,** claims (on its bronze plaque) to have been the residence of Washington Irving. The house was actually built (ca. 1845) for his nephew, John T. Irving, but Washington Irving *was* a frequent visitor. (His home for a time was at 11 Commerce Street, in Greenwich Village.) From 1894 to 1911 the house was occupied by two remarkable women, Elsie de Wolfe and Elizabeth Marbury. Miss de Wolfe was considered "the best-dressed woman in town," and later shocked the interior design profession by becoming the first "lady decorator." Her friend Miss Marbury was a noted literary agent. Their Sunday afternoon socials for the literary world were the talk of the town.

14. In front of Washington Irving High School, built in 1912, is an enormous bust of the school's namesake, executed by Friedrich Baer in 1885 and originally placed in Bryant Park. One wonders what the sculptor (or Irving himself) would think if he could see the shade of paint that is supposed to protect the bust from the effects of pigeons, air pollution, and students' graffiti.

15. At the southwest corner of Irving Place and 15th Street is a mournful-looking pile whose woebegone appearance belies its history as the **Amberg Theater.** It opened in 1888 with the American premier of several Ibsen plays. Nearby 14th Street was still in its heyday as an entertainment district. When the theater

Tammany Hall, on the north side of 14th Street between Irving Place and Third Avenue in a ca.1870 photograph. Chief Tamanend, above, presides over the Society which was founded in 1789 as an outgrowth of the Sons of Liberty. Tammany became a political power through the efforts of Aaron Burr. (New-York Historical Society)

district moved uptown, the Amberg became the Irving Place Theater, offering silent films and vaudeville. For a time the hall even echoed the lines of the best-known actors of the Yiddish theater, but by the early 1930s it went back to films. It did achieve brief popularity again when Gypsy Rose Lee gave her burlesque performances, but the staid city fathers put a quick end to that lively theater art. Reverting once more to its movie-house status, it became a center for Russian film festivals, but after World War II it gave up the ghost.

16. Occupying the entire block to Third Avenue, between 15th and 14th streets, is **the headquarters of "Con Ed."** The main building was designed by Henry J. Hardenbergh (architect of the Plaza Hotel and the Dakota Apartments). Begun in 1911, the structure and its extensions developed in stages, and took 18 years to complete. The unique clock tower, a pleasing contribution to the cityscape, was planned by Warren & Wetmore (architects of Grand Central Station) and completed in 1926. The company's predecessor, the Manhattan Gas Light Company, was located near the corner of 14th Street from 1885 to 1910; and at the corner was the **Academy of Music,** built in 1854. Farther east in the block was Tammany Hall, and at the Third Avenue corner, the popular entertainment spot, Tony Pastor's Music Hall. The Academy of Music hosted such greats as Jenny Lind, Adelina Patti, Helena Modjeska, E. H. Sothern, Edwin Booth, and Julia Marlowe. When the Metropolitan Opera House opened at Broadway and West 39th Street in 1893, the Academy of Music soon declined, and for a number of years presented only vaudeville and silents. In 1926 it finally surrendered to the wrecker's ball, making way for the Consolidated Edison Company's main building extension. A description of the interior of the Academy of Music appears on the opening page of Edith Wharton's Pulitzer Prize–winning novel, *The Age of Innocence,* where she observes that "the world of fashion was still content to reassemble every winter in the shabby red and gold boxes of the sociable old Academy."

Walk a few steps left to 145 East 14th Street, the **Con Edison Energy Museum** (open Tuesday through Saturday, 10 A.M. to 4 P.M.). In a series of exhibits and dioramas, the age of electricity comes alive. On display with recorded narrations are a working model of Thomas Edison's 1882 generating station on Pearl Street in lower Manhattan, factories and offices of the 1890s and 1920s, antique kitchen appliances, and a cutaway view of a typical New York City street. (Admission free.)

17. Walking back east, stop in front of 110 East 14th Street. Until June 1982 this was the site of the famous **Lüchow's** restaurant. The Victorian-style building dates from 1840 when the neighborhood was still residential, but on May 1, 1882, when 14th Street had become the heart of the entertainment district, August Lüchow purchased the ground-floor beer hall from owner Baron von Mehlbach, and expanded it into what was to become the most popular German restaurant in the city. Concertgoers from the nearby Academy of Music and Steinway Hall (across the street) packed the mirrored and wood-paneled rooms, the oompah bands played night after night, and the beer flowed like the Rhine. Lüchow's soon became a mecca for the big names in the music world. Distinguished habitués were Paderewski, Caruso, and Fritz Kreisler;

and in later years, Cole Porter, Sigmund Romberg, Richard Rodgers, and Leonard Bernstein. Frequently seen at the turn of the century were Lillian Russell, William Steinway, and even Theodore Roosevelt, who preferred venison and champagne to the traditional fare. It was here that Victor Herbert founded the American Society of Composers, Authors & Publishers (ASCAP); and songwriter Gus Kahn penned "Yes Sir, That's My Baby" on a Lüchow tablecloth. But 14th Street no longer drew the crowds, so the present owners felt that the establishment should be closer to the theater district that had departed 80 years before, and Lüchow's was moved uptown opposite the Winter Garden, on Broadway.

End of tour. The IRT Lexington Avenue line and BMT RR line are one block west.

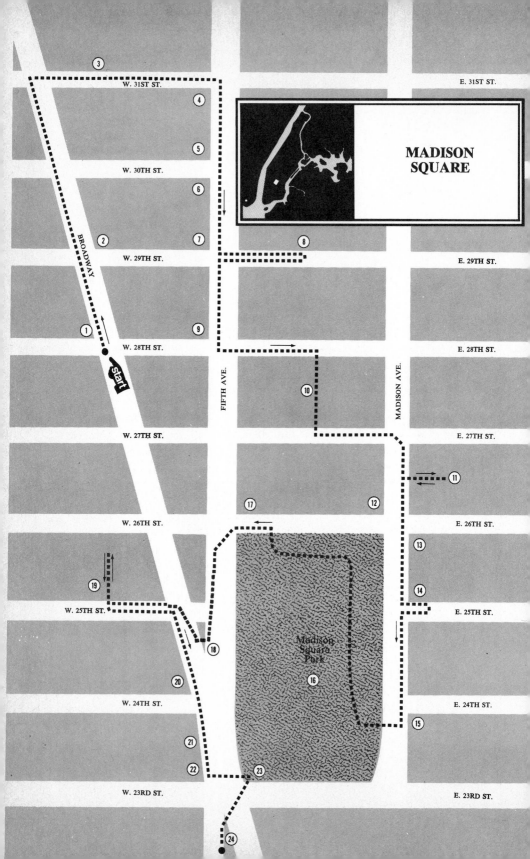

10. Madison Square

[*BMT RR Broadway line to 28th Street; Fifth Avenue (M-2, M-3, or M-5) bus, Broadway (M-6 or M-7) bus*]

Along Broadway from 23rd to 42nd streets, during the 1880s and 1890s, was the Rialto of New York—the celebrated Great White Way. Keeping pace with the northward drive of the city, the theater district, in a series of moves up Broadway, now reached to Longacre Square (called Times Square after 1904). Our uniquely American theater idiom, the musical comedy, was coming into its own, and the heyday of songwriting had begun. Along 28th Street, music publishers and tunesmiths by the score worked around the clock in a cacophony of musical sounds, to give birth to the appropriately named Tin Pan Alley. Facing nearby Madison Square arose Stanford White's monumental "Garden" to present a variety of entertainment on a scale hitherto unheard of by American audiences. Competing with the live entertainment of Broadway came the infant motion-picture industry, grinding out its silent films in hastily constructed studios in the West 20s.

Gone now are the legitimate theaters and music halls, the budding film industry, and the opulent hotels, restaurants, and cafés that lined Fifth Avenue and Broadway. Gone, too, is the din, glitter, and excitement that drew the throngs of nightly visitors. Even lavish Madison Square Garden bade farewell to its namesake site in 1925 and moved (twice) to other locations.

Broadway and adjacent Madison Square have quite a different flavor now. The 20th century witnessed the development of a bustling business district, bringing with it some of the most imposing commercial structures in the city. Shady Madison Square Park, however, still retains its quiet elegance—a refuge from the congestion and clamor of surrounding streets. And here and there, dwarfed by modern, multistoried neighbors, some architectural vestiges of the past still survive—mute reminders of that vibrant, exciting era of 80 years ago.

1. The tour begins at **West 28th Street and Broadway,** the former heart of "Tin Pan Alley."

On the 28th Street side of No. 1174 Broadway is a plaque recalling the time when Tin Pan Alley flourished during the early 20th century. Notice the typical early 20th-century skyscrapers, Nos. 1170 and 1181 Broadway, in which architects still displayed that *horror vacui,* or abhorrence of leaving any part of the building undecorated; hence the façades were usually divided into three distinct sections, similar to a Classic column: the "base," usually the first three or four stories; the "shaft," the tall, relatively unadorned center section; and the "capital," the top group of stories, frequently very ornate and topped with a projecting cornice. This "Tripartite" style of commercial building architecture remained popular until about 1910.

2. On the northeast corner of West 29th Street and Broadway is the splendid **Gilsey House** (Stephen D. Hatch, 1869). Built of marble and cast iron, it is a splendid example of the French Second Empire style. It was the favorite hotel of Oscar Wilde during his American lecture tours, and was also a frequent haunt of James Buchanan "Diamond Jim" Brady, the financier and *bon vivant* of the Gay '90s. The Gilsey House was the first hotel in the city to boast a telephone. The sympathetic and precise restoration of this magnificent pile is a credit to the developer, who purchased a deteriorating commercial building and converted it into a profitable and desirable co-op. Just up Broadway one block, its dark mansard roof almost hidden, is **the former Grand Hotel.** Built about the same time as the Gilsey House, it was considered one of the great hostelries of New York. In its present state as the Clark Apartments, it is but a ghost of its former appearance. Turn east on West 31st Street to the Hotel Clinton.

3. This rather seedy establishment, the Hotel Clinton, is **the former home of Life Magazine.** Before its purchase by the Time-Life Corporation in 1936, *Life* was a rather sophisticated humor weekly. Visible on the upper stone balcony is its name, as are groupings of L's on the ornate cast-iron balconies, together with the inscriptions of "wit" and "humor." The future is uncertain for this Classical-style building, designed in 1894 by the noted architectural firm of Carrère & Hastings.

4. **The Wolcott Hotel,** at 4–10 West 31st Street, is a fine example of Renaissance Eclectic–style hotel architecture so popular at the turn of the century. Turn south on Fifth Avenue to the southwest corner of West 27th Street. (Incidentally, Fifth Avenue is the east-west dividing line of all numbered streets, from 8th Street north.)

5. The dark red apartment house across the street (284 Fifth Avenue, entrance on West 30th Street) is the **Wilbraham Apartments.** Built in the mid-1880s, it was one of the first "French Flats," or residential apartments for the wealthy. Actress Lillian Russell occupied the top floor during the heyday of her career. Peek in the lobby at the wainscoting and wallpaper!

6. The building at 276 Fifth Avenue was **formerly the Holland House** (Harding & Gooch, 1891). Named for a similar hotel in the Kensington section of London, it was a gathering place for intellectuals and gourmets. The staircase of Siena marble and bronze and its famous restaurant made it a showplace until its closing in 1920. In its 1903 edition, *King's Views of New York* called it "the peer of any hotel in America . . . where the most fastidious people are its 'instant guests.' "

7. At the northwest corner of 29th Street is the well-known **Marble Collegiate Reformed Church,** where Dr. Norman Vincent Peale's Sunday sermons originate to reach a nationwide radio audience. Built in 1854 from plans by architect Samuel A. Warner, the church is a fine example of early Romanesque Revival style applied to what is essentially a Gothic Revival–style building. The congregation dates back to the founding of the Dutch Reformed Church in America in 1628. Note the huge bronze bell on the lawn. Cast in Holland, it summoned the faithful while it hung in the old North Church downtown on William Street in the 18th and 19th centuries.

8. Turn east on 29th Street to the landmark Episcopal Church of the Transfiguration. Known as the **"Little Church around the Corner,"** it dates from 1849–1856, and is New York City's unique example of the Cottage Gothic style of the 14th century. It earned its nickname from an incident that occurred in 1870. When actor George Holland died and was refused burial rites at a nearby church, a friend, Joseph Jefferson, was informed that there was a *little church around the corner* that would perform the rites—and the name stuck. The church has been closely connected with the acting profession since that time. The lich-gate at the entrance recalls the custom of conducting a preliminary burial service outside the church (*lic* is the Anglo-Saxon word for "body"). The interior is unusually beautiful, with a quiet, intimate atmosphere. Look for the stained-glass window (in the south transept) of actor Edwin Booth as Hamlet, done by John LaFarge. The reredos of the *Last Supper,* as well as the lich-gate, were designed by architect Frederick Clarke Withers. Note also the Chantry with its Brides' Altar, the carved wooden screens at the entrance to the nave, the Joseph Jefferson Memorial Window, the Mortuary Chapel with stained-glass copy of Raphael's *Transfiguration,* and the little chapel dedicated to actor José María Muñoz. The church takes pride in its history of helping the less fortunate. During the Draft Riots of 1863, it sheltered runaway slaves, and in the depressions of 1907 and the mid-1930s, it operated bread lines. It is still very active in community service, and also supports a small professional theater company, appropriately called "The Joseph Jefferson Players."

Return to Fifth Avenue.

9. 250 Fifth Avenue (McKim, Mead & White, 1907) was built for the Second National Bank of the City of New York, and is not one of the firm's best designs. For more excitement, look at the busy terra-cotta façade of nearby No. 256.

Turn east on 28th Street.

10. The Prince George Hotel, designed in typical turn-of-the-century Classic Eclectic style by Greenley & Murchison, opened its doors in 1904. The first hotel in the city with a private bath in every room, it catered to a wealthy and flamboyant clientele. In recent times the hotel has managed to keep up appearances and preserve some of the former elegant atmosphere. Perhaps you

The first Madison Square Garden building was originally the Union Depot of the New York & Harlem Railroad at 28th Street and Madison Avenue. It served for a time as P. T. Barnum's Hippodrome, then in 1879 it became the "Garden." It lasted only until 1890, when Stanford White's great masterpiece replaced it. (New York Life Insurance Company)

can persuade the manager to show you the splendid ballroom which looks much the same as it did when "Diamond Jim" Brady and Lillian Russell were frequent celebrants. In the center of the lobby is the rare *Martinique Clock,* the "granddaddy" of all long-case clocks. Made in England in the 17th century, with an intricately carved mahogany cabinet, it strikes the hours with incongruously delicate chimes. Walk through the lobby past the coffee shop to the 27th Street entrance, and turn left to Madison Avenue.

 11. The New York Life Insurance Company Building, designed by Cass Gilbert and built in 1926–28, is a most imposing structure. Although of no particular architectural style, the *AIA Guide to New York* refers to it as "Limestone Renaissance at the bottom, Birthday Cake at the top." The gilt pyramid that caps this mammoth structure is similar to the one Gilbert later designed for the top of the U.S. Court House on Foley Square. The lobby of the New York Life Building is particularly attractive. Its coffered ceiling, enormous hanging lamps, and ornate doors and paneling—all of bronze—make it one of the great interiors of the city. The "grand staircase" leading to the IRT subway station belies what is below. Compare this lavish lobby with Cass Gilbert's treatment of his Woolworth Building, built 13 years before.

This is the **site of the first two Madison Square Gardens.** Originally, the Union Depot of the New York & Harlem Railroad was built here after it had been moved uptown from its earlier location near City Hall. (The city fathers objected strenuously to the noise and air pollution of the old steam locomotives.) In 1871 the railroad terminal was shifted to the present site of Grand Central Terminal, and the Depot was sold to P. T. Barnum, who converted it into his popular Hippodrome. Nine years later it became the first Madison Square Garden.

In 1890, Stanford White designed the second Madison Square Garden, an imposing Spanish Renaissance–style structure, which occupied the entire block. Its central tower, modeled after the *Giralda* in Seville and topped by Augustus St. Gaudens's statue of Diana, would be a dominant feature of the city skyline for 35 years. Complete with the largest amphitheater in the country, Garden Theater, Roof Garden, concert hall, café, and even an immense swimming pool, it was an immediate sensation. Among some of the events staged in the Garden were operatic concerts, prize fights (Jack Dempsey knocked out Bill Brennan), Wild West Shows, aquatic exhibitions, the first American automobile show, six-day walks, six-day bike races, and Barnum & Bailey's circus. Diana now resides in the Philadelphia Museum of Art.

Architect White had an eye not only for beautiful buildings, but for beautiful women as well. His two homes nearby were the scenes of frequent and wild

Planned at first to be the site for annual horse shows, Stanford White designed Madison Square Garden to include a theater, concert hall, roof-garden, and restaurant, graced with a dramatic tower—the second highest in the city—and surmounted by a gilt statue of Diana. (New York Life Insurance Company)

all-night parties. Rumor had it that White installed a high red-velvet swing on the top floor of his West 24th Street love nest, on which girl friends were offered all manner of inducements to oscillate "in the altogether." One of these steady "swingers" was young Evelyn Nesbit, a former *Floradora* show girl who later married eccentric millionaire Harry K. Thaw. On the evening of June 25, 1906, Stanford White entered the Roof Garden Theater and was observed by Thaw and his recent bride, who were dining at a nearby table. Evelyn whispered something about White to her husband that infuriated him; whereupon he leaped up from the table, stalked across the floor, drew a revolver, and fired three fatal shots at the architect. After nine years and three prolonged trials, Thaw was acquitted.

After its demolition in 1925, the Garden was rebuilt at West 50th Street and 8th Avenue, where it remained until 1968. Ironically, its present location at Eighth Avenue between 31st and 33rd streets is on the site of McKim, Mead & White's greatest architectural achievement—Pennsylvania Station—which fell victim to the wrecker's ball and civic short-sightedness!

The elegant Leonard Jerome Mansion, built in 1859, later the Manhattan Club, graced the southeast corner of 26th Street and Madison Avenue. Daughter Jennie Jerome later became Lady Randolph Churchill, mother of Sir Winston. The Landmark Law came too late to save the beautiful house, and in its place is the enormously out-of-scale Merchandise Mart Building. (New York Life Insurance Company)

"Dr. Parkhurst's Church," as the Madison Avenue Presbyterian Church was called, was built in 1853 when the neighborhood was entirely residential. On this peaceful site of the late 1880s— the corner of 23rd Street and Madison Avenue—now stands the Metropolitan Life Tower. *(Metropolitan Life Insurance Company)*

Madison Square has managed to escape most alterations made in the name of progress. The drinking fountains and pavilion are gone, but the trees remain, sporting the foliage of more than three-quarters of a century of growth since this 1901 photo was taken by Byron. *(The Byron Collection. Museum of the City of New York)*

The young boy drinking from the common cup was a participant in a Madison Square clean-up campaign sponsored by the Metropolitan Life Insurance Company in 1913. (Metropolitan Life Insurance Company)

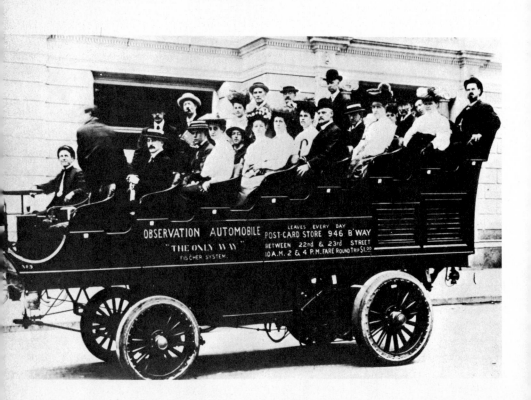

An early 1900s sightseeing bus in front of No. 1 Madison Avenue. (Metropolitan Life Insurance Company)

The triangular site of the Flatiron Building, the intersection of Broadway and Fifth Avenue at 23rd Street, as seen from the Fifth Avenue Hotel in 1884. Note the white Broadway omnibus at left. (New-York Historical Society)

The expression "Twenty-Three Ski-doo!" is said to have come from the efforts by Officer Kane, stationed at Fifth Avenue and 23rd Street, to "shoo" away the young men who gathered at the breezy corner to catch a glimpse of a lady's ankle. (Metropolitan Life Insurance Company)

The 28th and 29th Street crosstown car was one of the last to exchange horsepower for electric. In this undated photo, a two-horse team passes in front of 45 East 29th Street on its way to the New Jersey ferries. (Metropolitan Life Insurance Company)

Prim young ladies serving tempting desserts in Maillard's elegant confectionery shop, on the ground floor of the posh Fifth Avenue Hotel. (Photograph by Byron. The Byron Collection. Museum of the City of New York)

12. No. 50 Madison Avenue was built in 1896 by Renwick, Aspinwall & Owens for the American Society for the Prevention of Cruelty to Animals (ASPCA).

13. The glistening **Merchandise Mart Building** (Emery Roth & Sons, 1974), on the southeast corner of 26th Street, is a shocking example of utter disregard for scale. It would appear that the designers cared not at all about the height, shape, and style of adjacent buildings when they planned this one. By acquiring the air rights from the Court House to the south, they were able to raise this enormous dark shaft to an eye-boggling height, thus overwhelming its neighbors, destroying a pleasing skyline, and casting a visual pall over the park below. To make the picture even more dismal, the former occupant of the site was the Leonard Jerome House (Jerome's daughter, Jennie, became Lady Randolph Churchill—Winston Churchill's mother). The attractive mansion, built in 1859, later became the Manhattan Club where, it is said, the Manhattan cocktail was invented. Demolition took place with indecent haste, just before the passage of the Landmarks Preservation Law, and New York suffered another irretrievable loss.

14. The Appellate Division, New York State Supreme Court resembles a stately Greek temple and is a tribute to its architect, James Brown Lord. Built in 1896–1900, this magnificent building miraculously escaped the fate of its ex-neighbor, the Jerome House, when public outcry prevented the Court's consolidation into the Foley Square complex. An examination of the exterior sculpture is a must:

Madison Square side:

Balustrade (left to right): *Confucius* (Philip Martiny), *Peace* group (Karl Bitter), *Moses* (William Couper)

Four caryatids: *The Four Seasons* (Thomas Shields Clarke)

25th Street side:

Entrance: *Force* and *Wisdom* (Frederick Ruckstull)

Above portico windows: *Morning* and *Night, Noon* and *Evening* (Maximilian M. Schwartzott)

Pediment: *Triumph of Law* (Charles H. Niehaus)

Surmounting pediment: *Justice* flanked by *Power* and *Study* (Daniel Chester French)

Balustrade (left to right): *Zoroaster* (Edward C. Potter), *Alfred the Great* (Jonathan Scott Hartley), *Lycurgus* (George E. Bissell), *Solon* (Herbert Adams), *Louis IX* (John Donoghue), *Manu* (Augustus Lukeman), *Justinian* (Henry Kirke Bush-Brown), *vacant* (formerly *Mohammed,* Charles Albert Lopez; removed at the request of the Moslem community of New York City)

A visit to the interior is most rewarding (open weekdays only). The furniture was designed by the architectural and interior design firm of Herter Brothers, the cabinetry by George C. Flint Company, the sculpture of Charles O'Connor by James W. A. MacDonald, and the stained-glass windows by the Maitland Armstrong Company. Nothing was spared in making the Appellate Court House an aesthetic, architectural masterpiece.

15. The Metropolitan Life Insurance Company buildings complete the panorama of the west side of Madison Square. The original main building, at the corner of 23rd Street, was built in 1893. Its crowning glory, however, came in 1909 with the 700-foot tower addition, making it the tallest building in the world at the time, and the identifying symbol of the company—"the Light that Never Fails." Designed by the firm of Napoleon LeBrun & Sons, the tower is based on the *Campanile* of St. Mark's Square in Venice. Four years after its completion, its height record was surpassed by the 60-story Woolworth Building, downtown. In the mid-1950s, the original main building was demolished and the present 12-story structure erected in its place. The tower was given a "facelifting" as part of the overall modernization project, with most of the ornamentation stripped off the façade. Only the four three-story-high clocks and the surmounting gilded lantern escaped the butchery. Yet the tower glitters like a jewel in its new nighttime illumination.

An interesting event in the history of the 50-story tower occurred on election night 1908, one year before its completion. The *New York Herald* installed a giant searchlight among the still-exposed girders near the top of the spire to signal the election results far and wide. A northward-swinging beam would indicate a majority for the Republican presidential candidate William Howard Taft, and a southward beam for Democrat William Jennings Bryan. As the first returns showed a plurality for Taft, the beacon moved slowly up and down in a northward direction. By a little after 8 P.M., as the telegraphed vote count gave a clear majority to the Republican, the searchlight's rays were held steadily northward. Thus New Yorkers and suburbanites for miles around were the first to get the election results transmitted from the tall tower's beacon.

The **North Building,** occupying the block between 24th and 25th streets, was designed by Wald, Corbett, & Angilly, and built in three stages from 1932 to 1950. A striking example of the Art Deco style, the massive Alabama limestone exterior was planned to conform to the city's building regulations requiring extensive setbacks on tall buildings. Their "stepped" arrangement, along with the interesting angular upper walls and chamfered corners, can best be appreciated from across the square. Arched loggias at the four corners provide entrance arcades that lead to central elevator halls, and the huge building is connected to the Home Office Building by a skywalk and a tunnel. The lobby walls are faced with handsome Italian cremo marble. Just before the outbreak of World War II the company stockpiled huge blocks of this marble for fear that a war might destroy the northern Italian quarries and prevent a uniform completion of the building's interior. The North Building holds the distinction of being the first commercial structure in New York City to have central air conditioning.

On the site of the adjacent Metropolitan Life Tower stood the brownstone Gothic Revival–style Madison Square Presbyterian Church, built in 1853. Its outspoken minister, the Reverend Charles H. Parkhurst, led a vociferous campaign in 1893–94 against citywide crime and police corruption. Accused by angry Tammany politicians of being self-serving, Dr. Parkhurst documented his charges by personally visiting the dens of iniquity that City Hall denied existed and proving complicity and brutality by the police. After these revelations from Parkhurst's pulpit, the State Legislature convened the Lexow Committee, whose subsequent investigation corroborated Dr. Parkhurst's accusations and led to the defeat of Tammany Mayor Hugh Grant, a major shakeup in the Police Department, and the appointment of Theodore Roosevelt to the Board of Commissioners. The Metropolitan Life Insurance Company acquired the church property for needed building expansion, and in exchange for the corner plot, agreed to build a new house of worship across the street for Dr. Parkhurst's congregation. Stanford White was commissioned to design the new church, which was completed in 1906 in Italian Renaissance style. The bright, white granite New Madison Square Presbyterian Church was White's last public building and is considered by many authorities to be the most beautiful building he ever designed. In 1919, the ever-expanding company purchased the property and demolished the lovely church. (The parishioners had, for the most part, moved to more fashionable precincts uptown anyway, as the neighborhood by that time was almost exclusively commercial.) A "new" annex to the Home Office was erected, but it, too, was razed when the new North Building was designed.

16. Madison Square Park became the pleasant oasis it is now in 1870. At the time of the Revolution it was a swampy grassland traversed by a meandering

For a brief period in 1906 there were two Madison Square Presbyterian Churches standing side-by-side. Needing additional land to erect its famous tower, the Metropolitan Life Insurance Company bought and razed the older Gothic Revival–style church and built another for Dr. Charles H. Parkhurst's congregation. The neoclassic "temple," Stanford White's last commission, survived only until 1919 when the Insurance Company again acquired the property to build its North Building. (Metropolitan Life Insurance Company)

stream, abounding with game. Later it became a paupers' burial ground. By the first decade of the 19th century, a military outpost was established as part of the defenses of the lower city at the junction of the Eastern Post Road and the Middle Road—now Broadway—near the present intersection of Fifth Avenue. In 1811, the famous New York City Commissioners' Report officially designated the street pattern of much of Manhattan Island, and a "Parade" was laid out between 23rd and 34th streets and Third and Seventh avenues. A few years later it was greatly reduced in size and named in honor of the then fourth president, James Madison. In 1844 the Square was again reduced, to its present size. In its concept the plan was a forerunner of the one that subsequently gave us spacious Central Park.

Enter the Park at the Statue of Roscoe Conkling, near 23rd Street.

Elected as a Republican to the U.S. Senate in 1867, Conkling served the Empire State for 14 years. He resigned in 1881 after a dispute with President Garfield and retired to law practice. During the Great Blizzard of March 12, 1888, he was caught without transportation home from his downtown office, and set out on foot against the mounting drifts and sub-zero cold. He became lost in Madison Square, but was rescued and carried to his nearby home. The effects of the exposure, however, were fatal, and he died six weeks later. This bronze memorial statue, by sculptor John Quincy Adams Ward, was erected in 1893 through contributions by friends, and stands on the precise site where he was felled by the blizzard.

Walking north along the park path, we pass *Skagerrak* on the left (Antoni Milkowsky, 1972), a "minimal" sculpture of weathering steel cubic rectangles. Continue to the north end under the broad elms and horse chestnuts, to the imposing **statue of Admiral David Glasgow Farragut,** dedicated in 1881. In a dramatic posture as a rugged sailor facing the wind, Farragut is memorialized as the great naval hero of the Civil War. His victories at New Orleans and

Hansom cabs line the west side of Madison Square, across from the fashionable Fifth Avenue Hotel, as two young ladies stroll toward the camera of Percy C. Byron, 1905. (The Byron Collection. Museum of the City of New York)

Three types of horse-drawn carriages wait outside Delmonico's, at Fifth Avenue and 26th Street, in 1888, then the most fashionable dining place in town. A number of years later, the restaurant moved up Fifth Avenue to 44th Street where it finally closed in 1923. The restaurant on the site of Delmonico's first establishment, at Beaver and South William streets, tried to preserve the name and tradition, but it too gave up, and closed forever in 1981. (New-York Historical Society)

Mobile Bay finally closed all Gulf ports to the Confederacy. One can almost hear him shout that celebrated order, "Damn the torpedoes, full speed ahead!" He is represented in one of the great 19th-century statues by famed sculptor Augustus St. Gaudens, with Stanford White as the designer of the beautifully rendered pedestal bench.

A short distance to the west is the **statue of Chester A. Arthur,** 21st president, who assumed the office after the assassination of James Garfield in 1881. The monument, by George E. Bissell, was unveiled in 1899 and was a gift of Catherine Lorillard Wolfe, who lived in a brownstone on the site of the Metropolitan Life Tower.

17. Directly north of Madison Square, at the northeast corner of Fifth Avenue, is the attractive **225 Fifth Avenue** building. Built of red brick and limestone in a Renaissance Revival style, this commercial building's excellent state of preservation is a tribute to the artistic sensibilities of its present owners. It was formerly called the Brunswick Building, after a posh hotel that once occupied the site. Notice the elaborate iron balconies and the ornate copper cornices. On the northwest corner was Delmonico's in the late 19th century.

18. One block south is the **General William J. Worth Monument.** Designed by James C. Batterson and erected in 1857, this obelisk marks the only burial site of a public figure under a Manhattan thoroughfare. Worth fought in the Seminole and Mexican wars, and the names of some of his famous battles are carved on the granite shaft. Although a downtown street is named for him, he is perhaps more of a hero in the state of Texas, where the city of Fort Worth honors his memory. Interesting is the cast-iron fence with repeating sword motifs, now in a sad state of disrepair. The mysterious marble-faced structure behind the monument is a city water-metering station. The Catskill Water Supply tunnel passes just below.

Along Fifth Avenue and adjacent Broadway stood many famous hotels of the gaslit era. On the southwest corner of Broadway and 26th Street stood the St. James Hotel, whose name is borne today by the neo-Gothic skyscraper on the site. Occupying the west side of Broadway between 24th and 25th streets was the Hoffman House, an elegant hostelry of the time, whose bar was also a noted art gallery. Remembered particularly is Adolphe Bouguereau's huge, somewhat risqué painting, *Nymphs and Satyr,* which created quite a sensation in those Victorian days. The painting can be seen today, no longer causing a stir, at the Clark Art Institute, in Williamstown, Massachusetts.

● **19.** Make a brief detour along West 25th Street to the **Serbian Orthodox Cathedral of St. Sava.** Designed in 1855 by Richard Upjohn, it was built in

Looking north on Fifth Avenue at Madison Square Park. In 1876 the arm of the Statue of Liberty was brought from Philadelphia's Centennial Exposition to New York as a means of raising money for the base and the costs of assembling France's gift to America. The statue was finally erected ten years later. (New-York Historical Society)

Gothic Revival style as the Trinity Protestant Episcopal Chapel, and was the site of Edith Wharton's wedding in 1885. Alongside is the 1860 **Parish House,** in Victorian Gothic style, by J. Wrey Mould. The buildings were purchased by the Serbian Church in 1943.

Walk through the alleyway between the buildings and return to Broadway, turning south to the corner of 24th Street.

20. The building occupying the entire block to 24th Street, as well as its neighbor to the south, is linked together not only by a skywalk, but by the same street number: **200 Fifth Avenue.** This pair of commercial buildings is the Toy Center, home for most of the city's wholesale toy manufacturers and distributors.

A few yards down 24th Street stood the Madison Square Theater, famous at the turn of the century for its hydraulically operated double stage.

Across the street, at the edge of the park, is the **Eternal Light Monument.** Erected in 1924 from plans by Thomas Hastings (of the architectural firm of Carrère & Hastings) and Paul W. Bartlett, its star-topped light honors the fallen of World War I. At a point just to the left, the arm of the Statue of Liberty was displayed from 1876 to 1884 while funds were being raised to pay for the base. The arm and torch were first sent by France to the Philadelphia Centennial Exposition, then brought to Madison Square Park. The arm was later returned to France for attachment to the statue which was finally erected in 1886.

21. The tall **sidewalk clock** in the next block is one of the last remaining on the streets of New York, a vestige of the days when wristwatches were unknown and pocket watches were for the affluent. They were usually placed in front of a commercial establishment as an advertising gimmick. This cast-iron street clock, which still runs perfectly, was built by the Hecla Iron Works in the 1880s with a movement by Seth Thomas—the oldest surviving American clockmaker.

22. The plaque on the massive Italian Renaissance **Toy Center Building** (Maynicke & Franke, 1909), at the corner of 23rd Street, details the long and varied history of the site. The **Fifth Avenue Hotel** was the most luxurious in the city when it was completed in 1859. Earlier in the 19th century, there was a post tavern used for changing horses, and later a road house, known as Corporal Thompson's Madison Cottage. The *New York Herald* of May 9, 1847, carried the following notice about the inn:

> MADISON COTTAGE—*This beautiful place of resort opposite Madison Square, corner of Twenty-Third Street and Broadway, is open for the season, and Palmer's omnibuses drive to the door. It is one of the most agreeable spots for an afternoon's lounge in the suburbs of our city. Go and see!*

In 1853, Franconi's Hippodrome replaced the Cottage, offering a variety of public entertainment in an open-air arena, which included chariot races and circus performances.

The elegant dining salon of the subsequent Fifth Avenue Hotel was a favorite gathering place for the financial and political bigwigs of the day. A nightly spectacle at the main entrance was the steady procession of flashy carriages with matched teams of horses, bringing such giants as "Jay" Gould, "Jim" Fisk, "Larry" Jerome, Commodore Vanderbilt, and "Boss" Tweed. The powerful politico "Tom" Platt—credited with Theodore Roosevelt's presidential victory in 1898—held court before a coterie of adulating yes-men near the bar, in his so-called "Amen Corner." O. Henry, in his *Voice of the City,* vividly described the life and spirit of the times. The Hotel was also frequented by Mark Twain, Edwin Booth, William Cullen Bryant, and Stanford White.

Cross Fifth Avenue to the park.

23. The Statue of William H. Seward, by Randolph Rogers, was unveiled in 1876. As U.S. Senator from New York before the Civil War, and later as Lincoln's Secretary of State, Seward so distinguished himself as a statesman that President Andrew Johnson retained him in his own cabinet. A wise choice indeed, as Seward foresaw the importance of Alaska and was responsible for

Madison Square ca. 1916 is no longer dominated by the "Garden" but by the Metropolitan Life Insurance Company buildings rising on the east side. Horse-drawn vehicles are still plentiful, but the age of the motorcar has already begun. (Metropolitan Life Insurance Company)

its purchase. However, the statue was not well received. One critic proclaimed that "Mr. Seward was a man 'all head and no legs,' whereas the statue represents the statesman with unusual length and prominence,"—an observation that lends credence to the legend that the statue originally was not Seward, but *Abraham Lincoln Signing the Emancipation Proclamation!* (Note that one hand holds a scroll and the other a pen.) It is generally believed that Rogers, lacking the necessary funds to complete a Lincoln statue, switched heads at the last minute.

24. Directly across 23rd Street, in the triangle formed by the confluence of Fifth Avenue and Broadway, stands the striking **Flatiron Building.** Newly arrived from Chicago and his successful participation in the planning of the Columbian Exposition of 1893, Daniel H. Burnham designed this innovative and daring commercial structure in the Italian Renaissance style. With a towering steel framework and rusticated limestone walls in the shape of an enormous flatiron, it startled even blasé New Yorkers when it was completed in 1902. Visitors at first shunned the rooftop observation deck, predicting that strong winds would soon topple "Burnham's Folly." With fears allayed by the passage of time, the panoramic view attracted crowds of sightseers. On a clear day, the New Jersey palisades and Coney Island's beaches were easily visible. Although originally designated the Fuller Building, popular insistence on calling it by what it resembled forced the owners to yield and make the building's nickname official. It is now a designated landmark. Note the ornate yet restrained façade, whose undulating walls and sharp corners, topped by a classic cornice, result in a dramatic perspective. The protuberance on the ground floor extending toward 23rd Street was added a few years later, and was dubbed "the cow-catcher."

The busy intersection in front of the Flatiron Building has always been a particularly windy spot, and in the era when skirts trailed on the ground, it was a favorite vantage point for girl watchers hoping for a glimpse of a trim ankle. It is said that nearby traffic policemen would turn from their task of untangling the confusion of horsecars, omnibuses, wagons, and carriages, to shoo away these young voyeurs—hence the expression, "Twenty-Three Skidoo!"

End of tour. The BMT RR line 23rd Street station is at the corner. The IRT Lexington Avenue line is two blocks east on 23rd Street and Park Avenue South.

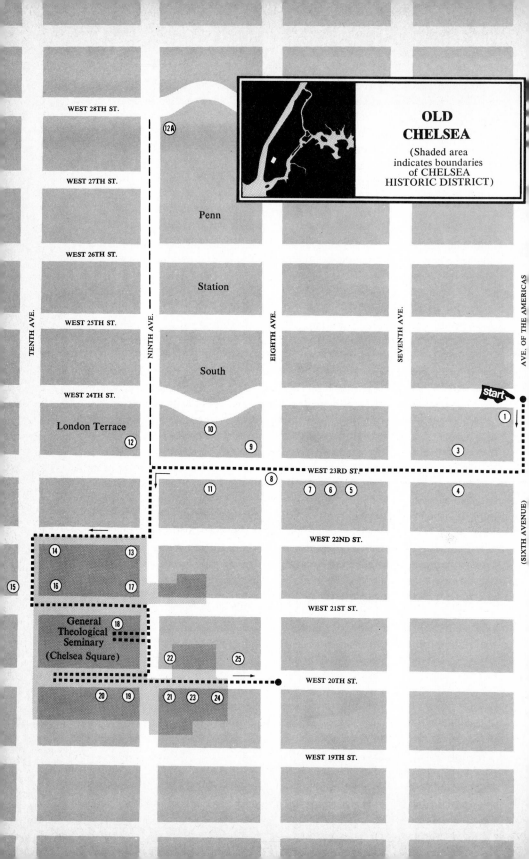

11. Old Chelsea

[*IRT Broadway-Seventh Avenue line, IND Sixth Avenue B or F line, BMT Broadway line, PATH Line to 23rd Street; Broadway, Fifth, Sixth, Seventh Avenue buses to 23rd Street*]

The neighborhood now encompassed by 14th to 30th streets and Avenue of the Americas to the Hudson River was rural farmland in 1750 when Captain Thomas Clarke bought a tract of land there and named it after the Chelsea Royal Hospital, an old soldiers' home built by Sir Christopher Wren in the Chelsea borough of London.

It was Clarke's grandson, however, who was to bring fame to Chelsea and immortality to himself. A professor of classics and biblical literature at General Theological Seminary, **Clement Clarke Moore** is remembered less for his scholarly *Compendious Lexicon of the Hebrew Language* than for his inspired poem, "A Visit from St. Nicholas," composed in 1822 while he was driving in a sleigh from the lower city, bringing goodies for the Christmas dinner. In addition to popularizing Santa Claus, Moore did much to influence the development and character of the neighborhood through foresight and wise urban planning. He served as vestryman at St. Luke's Church in Greenwich (Village), and was a founder of St. Peter's Church in Chelsea. He also donated the land for the General Theological Seminary and established guidelines for local residential zoning that in great measure contributed to the charming atmosphere of much of Chelsea today.

Moore is buried in uptown Trinity Church Cemetery (155th Street and Riverside Drive), where, every Christmas Eve, a candlelight procession of children carolers lays a wreath on the grave of the author of " 'Twas the night before Christmas. . . ."

By the mid-19th century Chelsea had grown into a peaceful residential area. Only the chugging of the locomotives of the Hudson River Rail Road on Eleventh Avenue, and the rattling Eighth Avenue horsecar—Chelsea's first "rapid" transit—disturbed the quiet of the streets. But the tranquility of the neighborhood was shattered some 20 years later with the arrival of the city's liveliest entertainment district. Once-sedate 23rd Street now echoed to the sounds of music halls and late-night revelers. The Ninth Avenue El, the city's first overhead railway, pushed through the Chelsea district in 1871, and the noisy steam-driven trains competed with the furor of iron-tire dray wagons, horse-drawn omnibuses and clanging bells of a proliferating network of horsecar lines. Along Sixth Avenue, a new and enormous shopping center was developing, as huge, palatial department stores opened their doors in what was to be the most popular retail district in the city. A year later the Sixth Avenue El added its roar to the growing clamor, and in the shadow of the El, at 30th Street, the "Haymarket" enjoyed the reputation of being the most-raided den of vice in the city's history.

As the century drew to a close, a new dimension was added to Chelsea with the birth of the motion-picture industry, as studios ground out silents in enormous, barnlike buildings east of Sixth Avenue.

Chelsea has become relatively quiet again. The music halls are all gone, the theaters have moved uptown, the great department stores either folded or relocated elsewhere, the film industry discovered Hollywood, and the Els were sent as scrap iron to Japan. And with the departure of commerce, the neighborhood began to decline. The lovely row houses deteriorated, and the area took on an air of neglect and decay. Then, at the last minute, Chelsea received a reprieve. With the shortage of housing and skyrocketing real-estate values, a new population entered the scene. Writers, actors, advertising executives, teachers, and other professionals discovered Chelsea and began buying up the aging town houses, restoring them with loving care. Overnight a "restoration revolution" began and the neighborhood has once again become an eminently desirable place to live—and just minutes from the heart of town. The designation by the Landmarks Commission of a part of Chelsea as a Historic District has added even greater impetus to maintaining the appearance and traditions of this charming quarter.

Many vestiges of the past are still to be seen: the old department store buildings, bits and pieces of the old theater district, several lovely churches, the delightful campus of the General Theological Seminary, and the row upon row of splendid town houses. But the special quality of Chelsea—still very much in evidence on almost every block—is the charming 19th-century atmosphere, all within the shadow of midtown Manhattan.

The tour begins at the corner of Avenue of the Americas (formerly Sixth Avenue) and West 24th Street.

1. The small red brick building on the southwest corner (best seen from across the street) is all that remains of one of the most popular entertainment spots of the gaslit era, Koster & Bial's Concert Hall. The hall itself used to face 23rd Street, and is long since gone, but this structure, once the beer-garden annex, was known as **The Corner.** Its name still survives in the upper cornice, and is the sole reminder of a once frenetic entertainment career.

Koster & Bial's opened in 1879, and was probably the liveliest vaudeville house in town. Here Victor Herbert conducted his 40-piece orchestra, and between the music, the free-flowing liquor, and imported talent, the Concert Hall became *the* place during the "Naughty '90s." Seeking a larger theater and anticipating another uptown move by the entertainment district, Koster & Bial closed their popular establishment and entered into a short-lived partnership with impresario-composer Oscar Hammerstein at his 34th Street Manhattan Opera House (on the present site of Macy's). The relationship was tempestuous at best, and ended in a court battle that saw the exit from "show biz" of Koster & Bial, while Hammerstein's star continued to rise.

2. On the southeast corner of 23rd Street and Avenue of the Americas from 1869 to 1883 stood the **Edwin Booth Theater,** with Booth himself as manager and frequent star performer. In spite of brother John Wilkes Booth's assassination of President Lincoln, Edwin remained one of the country's most popular actors. When James W. McCreery, known as the "Dean of the Retail Trade," acquired the site, he demolished the theater and erected his second department store. (The first still stands at Broadway and 11th Street, a cast-iron building converted into an apartment house.) In 1907 the firm moved uptown again, but his building remained until 1975. [For a detailed description of the department stores of the gaslit era, *see* Ladies' Mile.]

Across the avenue, on the southwest corner, is a small cast-iron building that once housed **Riker's Drug Company** and was later absorbed into the Liggett Drug chain. The Riker's name can still be distinguished on the Avenue of the Americas side, underneath a coat of paint on a panel below the second story.

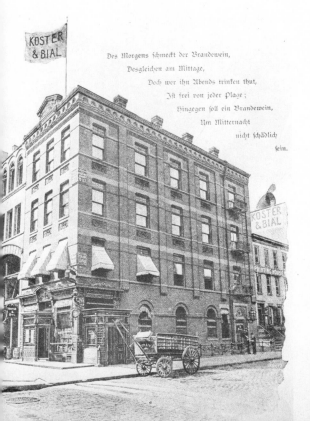

Des Morgens schmeckt der Brandewein,
Desgleichen am Mittage,
Doch wer ihn Abends trinken thut,
Ist frei von jeder Plage;
Hingegen soll ein Brandewein,
Um Mitternacht
nicht schädlich
sein.

*Koster & Bial's "The Corner,"
a beer-hall annex to the famous
23rd Street Music Hall, still
stands at the southwest corner of
Sixth Avenue and 24th Street.
This photo was taken in 1904.
(Museum of the City of New
York)*

Similarly, the name of **Ehrich Brothers,** another of the great emporiums, can barely be made out on a rusting iron panel on the adjoining building on 23rd Street. The huge store which faced both 23rd Street and Sixth Avenue, surrounding Riker's corner, gave up the ghost in 1911.

Cross to the north side of 23rd Street and walk west.

3. At what is now No. 141 West was **Proctor's Twenty-Third Street Music Hall.** Another of the great vaudeville showplaces, Proctor's opened in 1888, in a large Flemish-style building, packing them in with such top-flight stars as "Jersey Lily" Langtry, the inimitable Lillian Russell, Scotland's idol Harry Lauder, female impersonator Julian Eltinge, Eva Tanguay, the "I Don't Care" girl, and sparkling Lottie Collins, who never failed to stop the show cold with her rendition of "Ta Ra Ra BOOM De Ay!" E. F. Proctor later opened other theaters throughout the city as well as out of town, and when he died, his chain was sold to R.K.O. for a reported $16 million.

4. Continue west on 23rd Street, noting **No. 148–156,** a large Gothic Revival–style commercial building on the south side of the street. Again on the north

Proctor's became the most famous music hall in the city when it opened in 1888, and featured only topflight entertainers. In this Byron photograph, taken ca. 1910, Lillian Russell is the starred performer. (The J. Clarence Davies Collection. Museum of the City of New York)

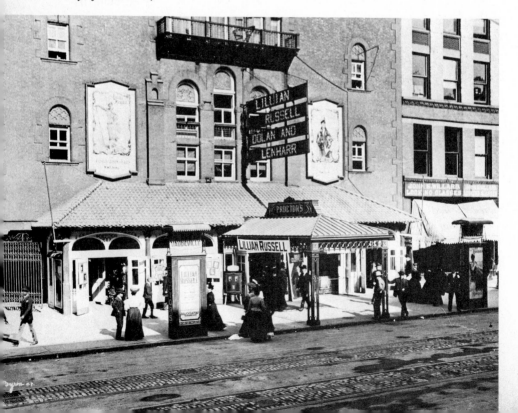

side, fanciful **Nos. 167** and **169,** a curious pair which resemble the backdrop for a comic opera, were originally residences. Their date of construction is uncertain, but in 1898 they received a dramatic face-lifting. To a full cast-iron façade was added a sheet-metal cornice, and atop No. 167, a Disneylike tower. Farther down the street at No. 209 is the **Muhlenberg Branch of the New York Public Library,** named for the pastor of the nearby Church of the Holy Communion (Avenue of the Americas and West 20th Street). Two doors beyond is the busy **McBurney Branch of the Y.M.C.A.,** built in 1904.

5. On the south side of the street, midway between Seventh and Eighth avenues, is a proud survivor of the quarter's Golden Age—the striking **Hotel Chelsea.** When opened in 1883 as a cooperative apartment house, it was a most luxurious address for those well-to-do artists who sought a quiet and elegant atmosphere to inspire creativity. In 1905 it became a hotel, and its guest register through the years reads like an artistic and literary *Who's Who.* Notice the bronze plaques honoring such greats as Mark Twain, Thomas Wolfe, Dylan Thomas, and Brendan Behan. Other notables who have graced the Hotel Chelsea are O. Henry, Sarah Bernhardt, Lillian Russell, Edgar Lee Masters,* John Sloan, Larry Rivers, James T. Farrell, Arthur Miller, Tennessee Williams, Virgil Thomson, Jackson Pollock, and Yevgeny Yevtushenko.

Designed by Hubert, Pirsson & Company in a style that has been described as Queen Anne or Victorian Gothic, its outstanding architectural features are its exuberant roofline with dormer and tall chimneys, and its richly ornamented iron balconies and interior grand staircase. The labels at the base show that the iron was cast by the J. B. & J. M. Cornell Iron Works. When built, its 11 stories made it one of the tallest structures in the city. Studios were added on the roof, making it the first such building to have duplexes. It also boasted the first penthouse in town. The lobby has been altered considerably and now doubles as a contemporary art gallery, presided over by owner-manager Stanley Bard, himself a patron of the arts. The broad iron staircase, which used to open with a broad sweep into the lobby, has been closed off at the ground-floor level because of fire laws. Its ten-story spiral ascent to the roof can, however, be admired from the second floor. Time has been kind to the old dowager. Its Edwardian charm still remains, just as faithfully as its devoted clientele.

6. The synagogue **Congregation Emunath Israel,** at No. 236–238, occupies the former house of worship of the Third Reformed Presbyterian Church.

7. No. 256 was the **site of Cavanagh's Restaurant,** which opened in 1876. A favorite dining spot for the elite in the heyday of Chelsea's entertainment era, it hosted such personalities as Lillian Russell, "Diamond Jim" Brady, and John L. Sullivan. It was also the hangout of powerful turn-of-the-century Tam-

---

* Edgar Lee Masters, known mainly for his *Spoon River Anthology* (1915), also wrote a short poem entitled "The Hotel Chelsea":

> Today will pass as currents of the air that veer and die.
> Tell me how souls can be
> Such flames of suffering and of ecstasy.
> Then fare as the winds fare?

The Grand Opera-House, on the northwest corner of 23rd Street and Eighth Avenue, was not only a theater, but the headquarters of Jim Fisk's Erie Railway. After Fisk was shot by Edward S. Stokes over a lover's quarrel and lawsuit in 1872, the Opera House was taken over by Jay Gould. The Grand Opera House later featured silent films and degenerated into a second-rate movie house, falling under the wrecker's ball in 1960. (The J. Clarence Davies Collection. Museum of the City of New York)

many Hall politicians. The exclusive establishment fell on hard times and had to close its gaslit-era dining room in 1970.

8. The intersection of Eighth Avenue and West 23rd Street marks the approximate **site of the original Thomas Clarke house.** The farm, named "Chelsea," was situated between the Fitzroy Road (which ran parallel to and just west of Eighth Avenue) and the Hudson River, from 19th to 24th streets. The Fitzroy Road was the principal north-south thoroughfare and began about two blocks south, at Love Lane, between the present 21st and 22nd streets. Love Lane ran east to the Albany Post Road (later Bloomingdale Road; now Broadway), the only route to the lower city. When the Clarke house burned down in 1777, his widow had it rebuilt farther west, on a bluff overlooking the Hudson, between the present Ninth and Tenth avenues. Two years later, a grandson, Clement Clarke Moore, was born there.

9. When Pike's Opera House opened on the northwest corner in 1868 with a performance of Verdi's *Il Trovatore,* it was an instant success . . . so successful that financiers Jay Gould and Jim Fisk bought it within the year. They changed its name to **The Grand Opera-House** and enlarged its repertoire to include all kinds of theatrical entertainment. Some of the productions were tailor-made for the talents of Josie Mansfield, Fisk's mistress. Josie lived in an adjacent mansion, connected to the Opera-House by an underground tunnel. The two partners even moved the offices of their Erie Railway into the theater. Next year, when Fisk and Gould attempted to corner the gold market, causing the "Black Friday" panic, it is said that Fisk, himself in a panic, hid in the vault of the Opera-House to avoid the wrath of the surging crowds. In the meantime, Josie, tiring of "Jubilee" Jim, began taking up with a former partner of his, Edward S. Stokes. This led to a series of lovers' quarrels and a sensational lawsuit, all paraded across the front pages of New York's dailies. A chance meeting on January 6, 1872, between Fisk and Stokes on a stairway of the old Grand Central Hotel resulted in Stokes drawing a revolver and shooting Fisk to death. Jay Gould continued to operate the theater for a number of years. During the first decade of the 20th century, the Opera-House inaugurated the "Subway Circuit," offering first-run productions shortly after their initial Broadway openings. By World War I, the theater, like so many of its contemporaries, switched to silent films with vaudeville, and continued as a movie house until 1960, when it was demolished to make way for the sprawling Penn Station South housing development.

10. Penn Station South (Eighth to Ninth avenues, 23rd to 29th streets) was built in 1962 from plans by Herman Jessor by the ILGWU (International Ladies' Garment Workers Union) as a middle-income housing co-op. Appropriately close to the Garment District, this mammoth urban-renewal project occupies 12 square blocks of former tenements, injecting new life into the Chelsea area.

11. The solid-looking Classic-style building across 23rd Street, at **No. 322–324,** was until recently the office of the T. E. Conklin Brass & Copper Company. The building was built for the American Jersey Cattle Club.

The **James N. Wells Real Estate Company,** at No. 340, is the oldest of its kind in Chelsea and dates back to 1845 when Wells, the manager of Clement Clarke Moore's estate, helped Dr. Moore with his plans for the residential development of Chelsea. He was also a skillful builder and was responsible for the construction of St. Luke's Church in Greenwich Village (where Moore served as vestryman). (More about James N. Wells later.)

12. Before the construction of the present **London Terrace Apartments** (occupying the entire block, Ninth to Tenth avenues, 23rd to 24th streets) in 1930, an earlier "London Terrace" stood on the site. Designed by famed architect Alexander Jackson Davis in 1845, the original row of Greek Revival buildings was set back from the street behind a shady garden and protected by an iron fence. A three-story high colonnade ran the entire length of the row, giving the town houses an air of stately elegance. With the wealth of its prominent tenants, London Terrace was soon known as "Millionaires' Row." On the 24th Street side was a similar row of town houses, but only two stories high, called the Chelsea Cottages.

The new complex, built by Farrar & Watmaugh, is in reality two separate rows of interconnecting apartment buildings surrounding a central garden. In addition to the 1,670 units, there is a swimming pool, solarium, a number of stores, a bank, and a post office. When the new London Terrace first opened, the doormen were uniformed as London "bobbies"—a touch of charming snobbery. After all, Chelsea was a London suburb, and this was thought to add upliftment to the area.

The Clement Clarke Moore residence stood alone in the block to the south until 1854 when land development forced the demolition of the large three-story house. Dr. Moore spent his summers at Chelsea, his winters on Charlton Street in Greenwich Village, and occasionally stayed at a third home in the village of Newtown (now Elmhurst) in what is now the Borough of Queens.

12A. An optional side trip may be made to the landmark **Church of the Holy Apostles,** at Ninth Avenue and 28th Street. The church, designed by noted architect Minard Lafever in 1848–49, is quite handsome but fits into no particular architectural style; although some say it was a forerunner of the Italianate style. Dominating the structure is the greatly oversized bronze and slate steeple, yet it is not incongruous among the towering apartment houses that surround it. Most attractive are the splendid stained-glass windows by William Jay Bolton, America's greatest stained-glass artisan of the time. The square glass panels with delicately painted circular medallions present a dazzling

The original London Terrace, designed by architect Alexander Jackson Davis in 1845 and known as "Millionaires' Row." A year after this photo was taken in 1929 the new 1,670-unit London Terrace apartments were erected. (The Consolidated Edison Company of New York)

*The house of Clement Clarke Moore, author of " 'Twas the Night before Christmas . . . ,"
which stood alone on high ground between Ninth and Tenth avenues, 22nd to 23rd Street,
until 1854, in a lithograph from* Valentine's Manual *of the same year. (Museum of the
City of New York)*

spectacle when brightened by the rays of a late afternoon sun. The transepts
were added in 1858, and were designed by another well-known architect, Richard
Upjohn (& Sons). The Ninth Avenue El once clattered overhead and darkened
the avenue, from the late 1870s to 1940.

**Return to 23rd Street and continue south. Turn west (right) on 22nd Street.
The tour route now enters the Chelsea Historic District.**

13. Nos. 400–412, built in 1856 in the Italianate style, are known as the
James N. Wells Row. These narrow houses were each designed with an English
basement and small entranceways, and form a harmonious unit with their original
roof cornice. All but one still retain their dormer windows. No. 408 is probably
the best in the row, except for its modified windows and lintels (which are
original in No. 406); however, only No. 404 has its original doors.

No. 419–421, on the north side, were also built in 1856.

No. 414 (1835) dates from the decade of the Greek Revival, and was the
residence of James N. Wells. An elegant mansion in its heyday, it is the last
surviving Greek Revival house with five bays (windows) in Manhattan. It was
remodeled 1864–66 in Italianate style, and in 1875 it was sold to the Samaritan
Home for the Aged. In the 1930s the Salvation Army acquired it for a women's
shelter. It is now a multiple-dwelling house.

No. 436 was the **residence of actor Edwin Forrest** [*see* East Village, 16] for more about Edwin Forrest and the Astor Place Riot]. Built in 1835 in Greek Revival style, it was bought by Forrest in 1839 together with the adjoining properties, Nos. 430–434. It was rumored that Forrest wanted the house as a sanctuary from his numerous in-laws who had moved in with him and his new bride when he lived downtown. Some years later the house was acquired by Christian Herter of the famous interior decorating firm of Herter Brothers. Sadly, the house has suffered too many "modernizations" through the years and is now barely a shadow of its former self.

No. 444 (1835–36) is a well-restored Greek Revival–style house, and was the property of Clement Clarke Moore. Note particularly the charming attic windows set in a wooden frieze (fascia) board below the cornice.

Nos. 446 and 448, the Berrian-Walker Houses, were built in 1854 in the popular Italianate style of the middle decade of the 19th century. No. 448 unfortunately suffered a major renovation when its front wall was reconstructed with the addition of two bays per floor, instead of one, as with No. 446.

No. 453, across the street, is from the mid-1850s and has interesting ornate hooded lintels over the windows.

The L. Monette apartment building, **No. 454,** was built in 1897 in a neo-

Actor Edwin Forrest purchased this stately town house (No. 436 West 22nd Street) four years after it was built in 1835, allegedly as a sanctuary from bothersome in-laws. In more recent times it was the home of former Secretary of State Christian Herter. Unfortunately, a series of mindless "modernizations" have all but obscured its original appearance. (Museum of the City of New York)

The interior of No. 436 West 22nd Street after Edwin Forrest's death, when it was owned by I. W. Drummond at the turn of the century. (Museum of the City of New York)

Renaissance style, and although a multifamily tenement house, is not an unpleasant addition to the street.

14. Clement Clarke Moore Park, on the southeast corner of Tenth Avenue, was designed by landscape architect Paul M. Friedberg as a multilevel play park, and was opened in 1968.

Turn left (south) on Tenth Avenue.

Before the successive landfill projects of the 19th century, the Hudson River shoreline extended to where the east side of Tenth Avenue is now. As the streets and avenues were pushed through, the hills were leveled, and the earth was used to reclaim the land to the west.

15. The Guardian Angel Roman Catholic Church (John Van Pelt, 1930), known familiarly as the Shrine Church of the Sea, was built in a fanciful Italian Romanesque Revival style when the port of New York was much busier than it is now, when much of the church's constituency came from the ships from far-flung parts of the world. It still serves a sea-oriented community.

On the east side of the avenue, **No. 188–192** (Andrew Spence, 1891) is a well-kept small tenement built in the Queen Anne style, still preserving its original storefronts. Note the oversize spandrels running the full height of the building, which may have covered chimney flues.

Turn east (left) on West 21st Street.

A pleasant feature of the north side of the street is the set-back arrangement of the houses, with a lush front yard complementing the dignified "halls of ivy" of the General Theological Seminary, across the street.

16. Nos. 473–465 are a well-preserved row of Greek Revival–style houses, built in the year 1853. **No. 471** is the best in the group, closest to the original design. Note the following architectural features of the houses: the bracketed entablature over the doorways, bracketed roof cornices, double-hung windows, the window lintels and window guards, cruciform paneled doors, and low stoops with cast-iron railings.

No. 463 was the first to be built on the block (1836) and dates from the Greek Revival period. Its brickwork is laid in Flemish bond (alternating short and long bricks, called "headers" and "stretchers"). Pedimented lintels cap the windows, and the attic windows are set in a wooden fascia board.

Nos. 461–459, now joined together as one house, were built separately in 1854. The pair is called the William Cummings House after a descendant of the original owner of No. 461, Thomas Cummings, and both are typical brownstones in the Italianate style. Compare them with adjacent **457 and 455.** The latter two, built in the same year, are of a somewhat different style. Note the difference in height of the stoops. Thoughtless renovations over the years have destroyed the symmetry of the row of houses.

No. 453 (1857) still preserves its splendid entranceway. Crowning the stoop with its cast-iron railings is an arched doorway, above which a huge cornice slab rests on stuccoed consoles.

No. 445 (1898) is another neo-Renaissance–style apartment house. Built of Roman brick and stone, it is typical of the so-called Eclectic Period of the late 1890s.

The brownstone doorway of **No. 407** (1852) is well preserved, although little else on the façade is. Note the carved head in the keystone of the arch and the doorway pediment supported by a pair of ornate consoles.

A better example of the Italianate style is **No. 405,** the last in the row of set-back houses, built the same year as No. 407. The Landmarks Commission, in its designation report for the Historic District, calls it "one of the purest examples of this style in Chelsea." All the original elements remain intact, with the single exception of the entrance doors.

17. Delightful No. 401, listed officially as **No. 183 Ninth Avenue,** was built in 1831–32, and is the second oldest house in the Historic District. It still preserves much of its original Federal-style appearance, and can best be viewed from across the street. The four-sided pitched roof, dormer windows, simple cornice above an equally simple fascia board, and side entrance are typical elements of the Federal style. The brickwork is in Flemish bond, the more expensive way of laying bricks, evidence of a wealthy original owner. Look up at the painted sign on adjacent No. 191 Ninth Avenue, advertising the James N. Wells & Son Real Estate firm. Wells lived here for a time (1833–34) and maintained his office on the second floor, where his descendants carried on for many years. The sign itself is probably over 80 years old. The ground-floor store was incorporated into the building very early in 1835. Note, too, the Historic District plaque on the 21st Street side.

The three small wooden houses to the right, **Nos. 185, 187, and 189** were all built for Wells, No. 185 in 1856, the other pair in 1868. Wooden houses are now a rarity in Manhattan, and these three, while not as old as they appear, add considerable charm.

18. The General Theological Seminary, No. 175 Ninth Avenue, occupies the entire block from Ninth to Tenth avenues, and 21st to 20th streets. The plot, known as **Chelsea Square,** was donated to the seminary by Dr. Clement Clarke Moore, himself a professor of Biblical Learning at the institution. The lovely campus with its shady lawns and small-town college atmosphere is a veritable oasis in the city; it is open to the public on Sundays (and at other times by appointment).

The modern building facing Ninth Avenue houses the administrative offices and the excellent St. Mark's Library; but one must first pass through the large entranceway into the inner quadrangle to appreciate the old-world quality of the campus.

Construction of the Episcopal Seminary began in 1825 with a Gothic-style East Building (now demolished), and was followed in 1836 by a counterpart on the west side, which still remains as a fine academic building. Early seminarians had an unobstructed view of the Hudson, as the riverbank reached the western edge of Chelsea Square. The completion of most of the seminary complex was accomplished during the brief period 1883–1902, when Eugene Augustus Hoffman, the third dean of the school, revolutionized the physical setting by engaging architect Charles Coolidge Haight to create a master plan for a campus

The Gothic-style General Theological Seminary on Chelsea Square in an 1841 lithograph, as seen from Ninth Avenue between 20th and 21st streets. (New-York Historical Society)

equal to that of most American colleges of the day. Through Hoffman's own financial contributions and his ability to interest wealthy laymen, an endowment was established for professorships and the groundwork laid for the development of a great theological library.

The St. Mark's Library, which was completed in 1969, replaces Haight's original building and contains 170,000 volumes available to the public for reference. It is the nation's outstanding ecclesiastical collection and has the largest collection of Latin Bibles in the world! Among the Rare Book Room's treasures are a collection of medieval manuscripts, prayer books and psalters, and an original Gutenberg Bible—one of six in the nation, a gift of Dean Hoffman.

Haight's plan called for an arrangement of buildings roughly in the shape of a letter "E" with the spine along West 21st Street. The style of construction was one that he himself pioneered, the English Collegiate Gothic. Centrally placed is the **Chapel of the Good Shepherd,** dominated by a 161-foot-high square **Bell Tower.** Interestingly, the interior of the chapel is devoted mainly to choir stalls, since most of the communicants are postulants for Holy Orders. The spectacular bronze doors, by J. Massey Rhind, were executed in 1899, in memory of Dean Hoffman's son.

Sherred Hall, a three-story classroom building flanked by dormitories, was the first to be erected, and expresses beautifully the simple quality and uniform character sought by the architect. Its arched main entrance is especially noteworthy.

The culmination of the building plan came with the opening of handsome **Hoffman Hall,** the refectory-gymnasium building. The enormous dining hall, like a medieval knights' council chamber, re-creates an atmosphere of the Middle Ages. The huge fireplaces at each end, a musicians' gallery, a coffered barrel-vaulted ceiling, and a stained-glass bay window, combine to make it one of New York City's most beautiful interior spaces.

On leaving the Seminary grounds, turn right, and right again into West 20th Street.

19. No. 402, a Renaissance-style apartment house, was designed in 1897 by C. P. H. Gilbert, the architect of the Warburg Mansion (now the Jewish Museum), the former National Democratic Club, the Convent of the Sacred Heart, and a host of other fine buildings. The name "DONAC" is an acronym for the original land owner, Don Alonzo Cushman. Tenants have a pleasant view down West 20th Street through their large concave bay windows.

No. 404 is the oldest house in the Historic District. Built in 1829–30, it still retains one clapboard side wall. A Federal-style house, it later received a Greek Revival doorway, had its roof raised one story, and in the 1850s was modified with Italianate parlor-floor windows.

20. Nos. 406–418, built for Don Alonzo Cushman in 1839–40, ranks among the most beautiful Greek Revival rows of town houses in the country. Equal in many respects to "The Row" on Washington Square North [*see* Greenwich Village, 3, 5], this group of seven pristine houses, called **"Cushman Row,"** displays a wealth of architectural detail. The ten-foot front yards are a most agreeable complement to the greenery of the Seminary across the street. Nos. 408 and

An 1854 engraving of Gothic Revival row houses which once lined 20th Street at the corner of Sixth Avenue before the arrival of the parade of Fashion Row department stores. (Museum of the City of New York)

414 are unchanged since the day they were built, except for the cast-iron newel posts. Notice the pineapples, a traditional symbol of welcome, atop the newels in front of Nos. 416 and 418. Exceptional are the charming attic windows encircled by cast-iron wreaths. Note, too, the well proportioned entablatures over the doorways, set on Doric pilasters; the molded window lintels and the six-over-six windows, typical elements of the Greek Revival style.

Don Alonzo Cushman (1792–1875) was a successful dry-goods merchant ("Don" *was* his first name, not a title) who became associated with Clement Clarke Moore and James N. Wells. He was a founder of the Greenwich Savings Bank—one of the oldest savings institutions in the city. With his later involvement in real estate, he helped influence the development and shape the character of the Chelsea neighborhood.

Return to Ninth Avenue.

21. The large Greek Revival–style house on the southeast corner, **No. 162 Ninth Avenue,** was the long-time residence of James N. Wells (he lived briefly at No. 414–416 West 22nd Street, and his offices were seen earlier at No. 183

Ninth Avenue). Built in 1834, it was one of the most imposing residences in Chelsea. Although somewhat modified, it still retains its original wide doorway, fluted Doric columns topped by a large entablature, and pedimented window lintels. The rambling, former *one*-family mansion is now occupied by 14!

Cross Ninth Avenue and continue east on West 20th Street.

22. The group of four Italianate buildings on the north side of West 20th Street **(Nos. 361–355)** were built for Don Alonzo Cushman. No. 361 was built in 1860, the other three in 1858. Although somewhat altered, they present a fine row of houses. The late 19th-century ironwork on the stoops is very attractive, as are the rope moldings on the inner doorways. No. 353 still preserves its original ornate cast-iron railings. Note the dormers, too.

23. On the south side, another Italianate row **(Nos. 348–358)** was built in 1853–54 for the six children of James N. Wells. Each house is only two bays wide and set behind a small front yard. The Landmarks Commission describes it as "one of the longest and most charming of the rows of English basement houses to be found in Chelsea." It is unfortunate that each house has suffered some alteration; however, Nos. 348 and 352 are probably closest to the original design. Note the "ear panels" on the doors of No. 358. The entire row of buildings is unified by its original cornice line, which has survived unscathed.

24. The **St. Peter's Church group,** consisting of rectory, church, and parish hall, was, like its nearby neighbor the General Theological Seminary, built on land donated to the institution by Dr. Clement Clarke Moore. The cornerstone for the original chapel, which is now the **Rectory Building,** was laid in 1832, making it the oldest church building in Chelsea and one of the oldest Greek Revival–style buildings in the city. It once had full-height Doric columns, but these were removed and replaced with unusual brick pilasters.

The **church building** was completed in 1838 in Gothic Revival style, and is considered a fine model of the English parish Gothic church—the first of its style in this country. Dr. Moore served as vestryman and organist for a number of years, and it is said that he was responsible for the selection of the church's design. Among the names on the cornerstone are those of Dr. Moore, James N. Wells, and architect-builder James W. Smith, himself a resident of Chelsea. The church building is virtually unchanged except for the loss of its beautiful Gothic wooden porches, which had to be removed because of rotting. The marks left by the old porches can still be seen on the church walls. Unlike the usual Gothic church built in cruciform shape, St. Peter's is built on the plan of a Greek temple. The pulpit, chancel rail, and lectern were presented as a memorial to Don Alonzo Cushman by members of his family.

The **Parish Hall,** called St. Peter's Hall, completes the group. It was designed in 1871 in the so-called Victorian Gothic style. The ornamental **wrought-iron fence** that embraces the three buildings is from St. Paul's Chapel downtown and was a gift in 1837 from the mother church, Trinity Church.

25. No. 331, on the north side of the street, is a rather late Greek Revival house, built in 1846. The side door opens on a passageway leading to a rear building. Although it is the only one in the Historic District with such a feature, nearby Nos. 311 to 305 have similar passageways, the first two open to view. Occasionally called "horsewalks," they also served as access-ways to rear stables.

End of tour. The IND Eighth Avenue A, AA, and E lines are three blocks north at 23rd Street. The IRT Broadway-Seventh Avenue line is at 23rd Street and Seventh Avenue. The IND F and B lines are at 23rd Street and Avenue of the Americas (Sixth Avenue).

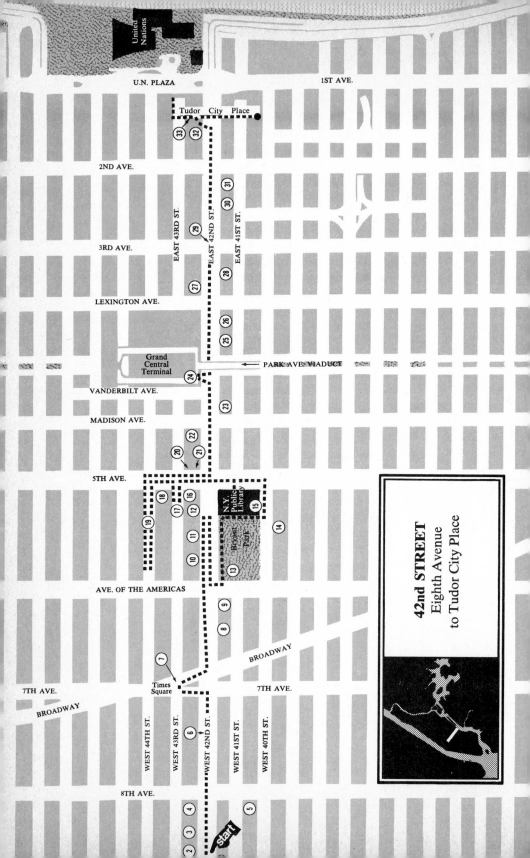

12. Forty-Second Street

Come and meet those dancing feet,
On the Avenue I'm taking you to,
Forty-Second Street.
Hear the beat of dancing feet,
It's the song I love the melody of,
Forty-Second Street.

Little "nifties" from the Fifties, innocent and sweet,
Sexy ladies from the Eighties, who are indiscreet.
They're side by side,
They're glorified.
Where the underworld can meet the elite,
Naughty, bawdy, gawdy, sporty,
Forty-Second Street.*

[Words by Al Dubin, Music by Harry Warren]

[IND A, AA, E lines to 42nd Street; BMT Broadway line, IRT Broadway-Seventh
Avenue line, or IRT #7 Flushing line, to Times Square; 42nd Street crosstown
(M-106) bus to Eighth Avenue]

Few thoroughfares in the world are as well known or as widely diversified
as 42nd Street—New York's major crosstown artery for almost three-quarters
of a century. Considered by New Yorkers as the center of the city and, at its
intersection with Broadway, the center of the world, it slices the middle of

Construction of the Ninth Avenue El (the New York Elevated Railroad) station at 42nd Street, 1875–76. (Museum of the City of New York)

Manhattan horizontally from the Hudson to the East River. Although the street was opened officially in 1836 with the removal of squatters' shanties and the filling in of the *Grote Kil* (Big Stream), the real history of 42nd Street begins late in the 19th century, and will be discussed block by block on the tour.

Before beginning the tour, you might want to take a quick stroll west on 42nd Street between Ninth and Tenth avenues. On the north side, the twin 45-story **Manhattan Plaza** towers (David Todd & Associates, 1977) provide federally subsidized rents to performing artists. Directly across the street is the new off-Broadway **Theater Row,** a group of six playhouses carved out of former warehouses, sleazy tenements, and a few disreputable "entertainment" establishments. The project was created by the nonprofit 42nd Street Development Corporation, and includes a central booking office just west of Ninth Avenue. The theaters are a bold experiment and a major phase in the revitalization of a once badly deteriorating neighborhood. Thus, with performing artists living in close proximity to a new and lively extension of the theater district, the contagion of this development can only spread, for the betterment of the entire area.

The tour begins in front of the old McGraw-Hill Building, 330 West 42nd Street, west of Eighth Avenue.

1. New York's "green skyscraper," the **former McGraw-Hill Building,** was completed in 1931 from plans by architect Raymond M. Hood, in collaboration with Fouilhoux & Godley, in a unique variation of the Art Deco theme. The building's shape, with its series of setbacks, was dictated by the Zoning Resolution of 1916, and architect Hood exploited these requirements boldly and effectively. Unusual are the metallic bands of green, silver, and gold that encircle the ground floor and continue into the lobby; while on the façade above, row upon row of bluish-green terra-cotta bands continue the motif. Two other examples of Hood's ingenuity will be seen later. When the McGraw-Hill Publishing Company opened its new office skyscraper at 1221 Avenue of the Americas, fear was expressed for the future of the lovely green tower. However, in late 1974, Group Health Incorporated (GHI) took possession of it for its own corporate headquarters.

2. The Holy Cross Roman Catholic Church (Lawrence J. O'Connor, 1870) hearkens back to the time when the neighborhood was predominantly Irish, and known as "Hell's Kitchen." An area of small factories and blocks of festering slums, it was one of the most notorious sections of the city, where even the police walked in fear and only in broad daylight. The church now ministers to a somewhat smaller, if more peaceful community. The simple exterior, in a transitional Byzantine style, belies the ornateness of the spacious interior. In a mixture of styles, primarily Italian Baroque, the architect has created an impressive nave and sanctuary. Observe the high barrel-vaulted ceiling, the wooden balcony, the fine paintings of Peter, Paul, and Jesus in the apse, and the Tiffany windows in the clerestory as well as the circular windows in the transept. The cupola was also decorated by Tiffany. This was famous Father Duffy's Church for many years—Francis P. Duffy, who worked so hard to uplift the old "Hell's Kitchen" neighborhood and break up the tough gangs that gave it such an unsavory reputation. It was Father Duffy who was closely associated with many theater personalities, and who served as chaplain of the "Fighting 69th" Division (actually the 165th Infantry Regiment) in the trenches of France during World War I. He served until his death in 1932, and an appreciative Broadway community erected a statue of him in Times Square.

3. A surviving row of tenement houses (ca. 1875) ends at No. 319 West, which is painted in "patriotic" colors to advertise the **Kaufman Surplus Company.** A local landmark for years, its pair of World War I French Hotchkiss cannons guarding the door are about the only war surplus items not for sale.

4. At the northwest corner of Eighth Avenue is the new home of the **Franklin Savings Bank,** completed in 1974 after its earlier building on the southeast corner was demolished. Although not eye-catching from without, except for the upper wall design which focuses on the building below, the interior presents an unexpected sight. Rising from the center of the hall to the tall ceiling is a massive column, from the top of which, like a gigantic open umbrella, radiate 16 "ribs" of bare pre-cast concrete reaching across to the far walls. The innovative architects were Poor, Swanke, Hayden & Connell.

5. The **Port Authority Bus Terminal,** the largest in the world, was opened in 1950, with the striking addition between 41st and 42nd streets completed in 1981 from plans by the architects and engineers of the Port Authority of New York & New Jersey Terminal Department. It has twin levels of bus ramps serving tens of thousands of daily commuters from New Jersey as well as long-distance bus riders. The upper levels are dominated by the dark brown steel trusses which project over sidewalk arcades. Step inside to see sculptor George Segal's grouping of three white-painted bronze *Commuters* waiting for their bus. (Segal, himself, is a bus commuter.)

6. The block between Eighth and Seventh avenues is commonly referred to as New York's **"Sin Street."** More seedy than sinful, it boasts no fewer than 15 movie houses (count 'em!)—possibly a world record. The theaters offer a wide range of films, including first-runs, foreign films, "oldies," and X-rated. Crowded cheek by jowl among the "flicks" are a dismal aggregation of penny arcades, "bargain" clothing shops, "porno" book dealers, and "going-out-of-business" stores. The block has grown to be a popular promenade with the more earthy elements of New York society and is regularly the target of (unsuccessful) clean-up campaigns by City Hall. Many of the older movie houses were once legitimate theaters and still show architectural traces of their more glamorous past behind garish new marquees. Plans are underway to refurbish a number of theaters in this block and return some of them to "legitimacy," as is imminent with the New Apollo and the New Amsterdam; or to convert a number to restaurants or retail space, or even to nonprofit use. Already, plans are well along to rebuild the east side of Eighth Avenue, north and south of 42nd Street, to a wholesale trade center, and the New York Mart will rebuild the area between 40th and 42nd streets; another developer will work on the blocks to the north.

Walking east we pass the following theaters (those nominated for landmark

The north side of 42nd Street just west of Times Square, ca. 1910, showing the Lyric and Belasco theaters. Oscar Hammerstein's Victoria faces Times Square at right. (Photograph by Byron. The Byron Collection. Museum of the City of New York)

The picturesque Casino Theater was built in 1882 on the southeast corner of Broadway and 39th Street as a concert hall, but played mostly comic operas. In this Byron photograph taken around 1900, shortly before it was acquired by the Shuberts, the Arabesque-style building is covered with advertisements for a long-forgotten musical. The Casino Theater survived until 1930. (The Byron Collection. Museum of the City of New York)

Posing for an unknown photographer in front of the Casino Theater entrance in 1924 is stage-door tender William Reilly. The gas lamp once stood in front of the Hoffman House Cafe, at Broadway and 26th Street; and was placed at the theater to recognize the 72-year-old Reilly's former career as a member of the city's once vast army of lamplighters. (The Consolidated Edison Company of New York)

Looking west on 42nd Street from in front of the original Grand Central Terminal in the early 1890s. Just beyond is the newly opened Hotel Manhattan, at the corner of Madison Avenue, now the site of the Sperry & Hutchinson Building. (Museum of the City of New York)

designation are indicated with an asterisk): the ***Empire** (formerly the Eltinge),
No. 236 (1912); the ***Liberty,** No. 234 (1904); the ***Harris** (formerly the Chan-
dler, the Cohan & Harris, and the Sam H. Harris), No. 226 (1914); the ***Selwyn,**
No. 229 (1918); the ***Times Square,** No. 219 (1920); and at the same address,
but with its façade facing West 43rd Street, the ***New Apollo** (1920); the ***Lyric,**
No. 213 (1903); and the ***Victory** (formerly the Belasco—not to be confused
with the present *Belasco Theater on West 44th Street), No. 207 (1900).

Perhaps the finest in the block is the landmark **New Amsterdam,** No. 214
(Herts & Tallant, 1903), with both exterior and interior designated. It might
just be worth the price of admission to visit the splendid interior with its highly
ornate auditorium, vestibules, and men's smoking room. The roof once housed
a second theater, the Ariel, which is now a rehearsal stage.

Just to the right of the Selwyn Theater, look north to the fancifully ornate
building which rises above 43rd Street with a black peaked roof perforated
with little dormer windows, and surmounted by a lantern. Built in 1913 for
the **New York Times** when it shifted operations from its Tower on Times Square,
it is a handsome structure in German Renaissance style, virtually hidden by
newer neighbors.

Of some architectural interest is the way-out-of-scale **Candler Building** (No.
220 West), rising high above its sleazy surroundings, and best viewed from
across the street. Designed by Willauer, Shape & Bready and completed in
1916, it represents no particular architectural style (some might call it Eclectic)
but it does have a pleasing, if somewhat grimy, façade flanked by its slanted
parapet "shoulder" buildings. The building is named for the owner of the Coca
Cola Company, Asa G. Candler, who in 1912 acquired the property and had
the structure built for his offices. The ground floor was occupied by a branch
of the Exchange Buffet, New York's pioneer chain of "honor system" cafeterias,
now long since defunct, in which patrons merely informed the cashier on leaving
what they had eaten, and were charged accordingly. (Spotters were stationed
inconspicuously to verify diners' purchases.)

**Cross Seventh Avenue, turn left and cross 42nd Street, walk past the former
Times Tower to Times Square, and proceed north.**

7. Known universally as "The Crossroads of the World," **Times Square** is
the heart of the entertainment district, and has been for almost a century. In
the 1880s and 1890s, the two vertical triangles forming the "square" were lined
with carriage dealers and called Longacre Square, after a London district (the
name lives on in the nearby *Longacre Theater* and in the *Longacre telephone
exchange*). Then the Rialto arrived! The Metropolitan Opera House opened
just to the south, at 39th Street and Broadway, in 1893; Charles Frohman
built his large Empire Theater across the street in 1894; Oscar Hammerstein
(*père*) moved up from his 34th Street Manhattan Opera House site to open
the dazzling Olympia Music Hall in 1895. The Olympia, looking for all the
world like a Renaissance palace, occupied the entire Broadway block front
from 44th to 45th streets, had a roof garden, café, concert hall, and theater,
and was the talk of the town. Hammerstein also built the lavish Victoria Theater

Times Square in 1900—then called Longacre Square—looking south from 45th Street, with the New York and Criterion theaters at left, and Rector's famous restaurant and the Hotel Cadillac in the next block. (Photograph by Byron. The Byron Collection. Museum of the City of New York)

on the northwest corner of 42nd Street, where the Rialto Theater is now. Others soon followed, one more grandiose than the other, offering not only legitimate theater, but vaudeville, cabaret, and music-hall entertainment. Many even had roof gardens with luxurious restaurants. And to further satisfy the appetites of the new theater crowds came such establishments as Shanley's, Rector's, Churchill's, and the Café de l'Opéra. Broadway is still synonymous with the stage, but only about three dozen legitimate theaters survive in the Times Square area; and very few new theaters have been built in the past 25 years. Most are clustered in the one block west of Broadway, between 44th and 52nd streets. Little Shubert Alley, connecting 44th and 45th streets, still evokes the glamor of "show biz," surrounded as it is by a number of theaters with brightly illuminated marquees.

With the rise of the film industry in the 1920s, enormous and opulent movie palaces opened along Broadway, displacing the "legit" theaters to the west. Who can forget such names as the Palace, Strand, Capitol, Paramount, Rialto, Rivoli, Warner (where in 1927 New Yorkers were treated to the first sound film, Al Jolson in *The Jazz Singer*), and the most lavish of them all, the Roxy? Some still remain, but mostly in name only. The Paramount Film Corporation (now swallowed up by the Gulf + Western conglomerate) erected the massive theater and office building on the west side of the square, between 43rd and

44th streets, a unique addition to the cityscape. The incredible shape of the
New York Paramount Building (Rapp & Rapp, 1927), with nine ascending
setbacks on each side, gives it the appearance of a symmetrical pile of gargantuan
children's building blocks assembled by some young Gulliver. The setback style
resulted from the Zoning Resolution of 1916. The tower clocks and black glass
globe top off this Art Deco edifice.

With the arrival of New York's first subway line in 1904, *New York Times*
publisher Adolph Ochs astonished his contemporaries by moving out of "Newspaper Row" downtown and erecting his famous wedge-shaped **Times Tower**
(Eidlitz & Mackenzie) at the intersection of 42nd Street, Broadway, and Seventh
Avenue. Ochs persuaded the city fathers to name the new subway station after
the *Times,* and with that, the name of the square soon followed. Built of pink
granite in Italian Renaissance style, and decorated with glazed terra cotta, the
Times Tower became the dominant landmark on the Square. When the *Times*
moved in on New Year's Eve of 1904, its fireworks display was to start a
tradition with New Yorkers. Each December 31 since 1908, enormous throngs
of revelers gather before the Tower awaiting the descent of the famous illuminated

*The Pabst Hotel, on 42nd Street, facing away from Longacre Square. The hotel and
adjoining four-story buildings were demolished in 1903 to make way for the Times Tower.
(Photograph by Byron. The Byron Collection. Museum of the City of New York)*

sphere announcing the arrival of the New Year. Even after the newspaper moved all of its operations into its former annex on West 43rd Street, and the Times Tower was reconstructed as the Allied Chemical Tower, the old custom was preserved. Another hallmark of the former building is the electric news "ribbon" with its 12,408 bulbs that flashes headlines around the building (not functioning at present). When Allied Chemical vacated the old Times Tower in 1975, the building was purchased by real estate developer Alex Parker and renamed **No. One Times Square.** Renovation plans called for sheathing the east and west walls with 5-by-7-foot mirrors, but the scheme was never carried out. The building is now just an office tower. On the east side of the building is a newsstand selling papers from major cities throughout the country.

Hotels also were built in the new theater district. For some 60 years the *grande dame* of them all, the **Hotel Astor,** was a familiar site on Times Square. Commissioned by Col. John Jacob Astor, it was built in a florid Beaux Arts

The changing faces of the Times Tower: (left) as it appeared when built for the New York Times in 1904; (center) as the Allied Chemical Building in 1964; (right) as it was planned to appear in 1976, sheathed in mirrors as One Times Square. The grandiose project was never carried out, and the building still looks much as portrayed in the middle photo (minus the Allied Chemical sign). (Alex Parker)

style with a huge mansard roof, opening its doors in 1904 on the block between 44th and 45th streets. In 1969, it was replaced by a 50-story office tower, designed by Kahn & Jacobs for the now defunct W. T. Grant Company. By changing its 1515 Broadway address to **One Astor Plaza,** it keeps the old hotel's name alive. From a distance the odd concrete "wings" atop the structure add a gaudy and bizarre (and not wholly inappropriate) touch to the Times Square scene. The building houses one of the few new Broadway theaters, the Minskoff, as well as a Theater Museum in the ground-floor arcade; and it has the distinction of being the first structure to take advantage of the new zoning laws which permit greater height in exchange for space set aside for a theater (it has a movie theater as well).

Dominating the east side of Times Square at 45th Street is the 16-story **Loew's State Theater Building** (Thomas W. Lamb, 1920), once the headquarters in New York of the Loew's Corporation. Its imposing Classic façade is a testament to the founder of the chain of movie houses, Marcus Loew, who is memorialized in a bronze low-relief sculptured plaque in the lobby.

●   Detour briefly east on 45th Street to the **Lyceum Theater.** Built by Herts & Tallant in 1903 in a florid and strong Beaux Arts style, it is the oldest house in the city still serving the legitimate stage, and possibly the most beautiful; and narrowly missed the wreckers' ball not long ago.

At the northeast corner of 46th Street is the I. Miller Building, once the showplace of the well-known women's shoe manufacturer. On the south façade (at second floor level) are a **row of sculptures by A. Stirling Calder,** depicting Ethel Barrymore as *Ophelia,* Marilyn Miller as *Sunny,* Mary Pickford as *Little Lord Fauntleroy,* and Rosa Ponselle as *Norma.* (Are there other figures hidden behind the enormous, ugly sign facing the Square?)

The traffic pattern in Times Square is much saner since the one-way routing was established. Before World War II, the scene was always one of bedlam, or at least total chaos. Adding to the confusion created by the number of intersecting streets were the trolley lines that crisscrossed Times Square on both Broadway and Seventh Avenue. The 42nd Street crosstown car, which either went west to the 42nd Street ferry or turned north on Broadway, contributed further to the disorder.

The upper "V" of Times Square is known as **Father Duffy Square.** His statue (Charles Keck, 1937) in front of a Celtic cross stands close by that of **George M. Cohan** (Georg Lober, 1959), "giving his regards to Broadway." The adjacent **TKTS booth,** established in 1973, sells half-price tickets to Broadway shows to those who line up on the day of the performance. It is a highly popular addition to the square, adding much-needed cultural upliftment to the rather sordid street scene. The attractive canvas and tubular-steel structure was designed by Mayers & Schiff.

The first major hotel to be built on Times Square in more than 75 years is the new **Portman,** occupying the block between West 45th and West 46th streets. Its conception created a storm of protest which continued for several years, as plans called for the demolition of three legitimate theaters, among them the Helen Hayes and the Morosco, playhouses that were revered by theatergoers and actors alike. Tumultuous demonstrations and repeated court challenges preceded the bulldozers which finally leveled the site (including part of the Helen Hayes Theater's façade that was supposed to have been saved) in the spring of 1982. As a result of this tragic loss, and to prevent similar destruction of other legitimate theaters, the Landmarks Commission has proposed the landmark designation of the exteriors and/or interiors of 45 playhouses in the midtown area. The Portman is to be named the Times Square Hotel.

Turn west on 45th Street to Shubert Alley. Walk down the Alley and turn left on 44th Street to Times Square again.

In this short loop of part of the theater district, one can see no fewer than 13 playhouses! **The *Booth** (Henry B. Herts, 1913) recalls the name of actor Edwin Booth, America's favorite in the late 19th century. (He built his own theater at Sixth Avenue and 23rd Street, which he ran and acted in, from 1869 to 1883; [*see* pages 214–215 and 257].) **The *Sam S. Shubert** (same architect and date as the Booth) honors the great impresario whose name is synonymous with show business.

Cross Times Square at 43rd Street to the east side. Look south across 42nd Street to No. 2 Times Square (slated for demolition in 1983), and gasp at the astonishing **trompe l'oeil mural,** one of several in the city by artist Richard Haas, that covers the entire building! It is a reproduction of the original Times Tower (across the street), as it looked when erected in 1904.

At the southwest corner of 42nd Street and Seventh Avenue is the **former Knickerbocker Hotel** (Marvin & Davis and Bruce Price, 1902), commissioned by Col. John Jacob Astor. Built two years before his Hotel Astor, it is the sole survivor of many Times Square hostelries built at the turn of the century, and was one of the most fashionable. Its King Cole Bar with Maxfield Parrish mural attracted many luminaries from the entertainment world, and George M. Cohan and Enrico Caruso both lived here for a time. The Classic Eclectic–style building has a prominent mansard roof, now virtually the only vestige of its former elegance. In a later incarnation it became the Newsweek Building, and now is known merely as 142 West 42nd Street. The Parrish mural was rescued and graces a bar with the same King Cole name at the St. Regis–Sheraton Hotel, uptown.

Continue east on 42nd Street.

8. Midway down the block, on the south side, stands the cathedrallike **former Bush Terminal Building** (No. 130 West). Although the structure was built in 1918, architects Helmle & Corbett seemed to have had a more recent tenant in mind—the Wurlitzer Music Company, formerly a next-door neighbor until No. 120 was demolished. The neo-Gothic–style building looks very appropriate to a company that sells organs—actually, it is the largest keyboard manufacturing company in the country, making pianos as well. Soon after Rudolph Wurlitzer founded the firm in 1856, he was called upon to produce musical instruments for the Union Army bands. Later the company specialized in keyboard instruments exclusively, producing in the early 1930s the largest organ in the city, the "Mighty Wurlitzer" for the Radio City Music Hall. For a time they made juke boxes too. Wurlitzer has been on 42nd Street for over 50 years and has resisted all temptation to move to a more "posh" location uptown, claiming that the company is unalterably rooted in this famous street.

Notice the *trompe l'oeil* effect on the side walls of the building, where vertical bands of tan and brown bricks are paired to give an illusion of depth. The sheer verticality of the structure is emphasized by its 480-foot height on a plot of ground only 50 feet wide.

9. The gleaming white marble and black glass **New York Telephone Company Building,** at the southwest corner of Avenue of the Americas, is one of a number of skyscraper office towers erected by "Ma Bell" for local corporate headquarters. Completed in 1974 from plans by Kahn & Jacobs, it serves as the "anchor"

Looking north from the top of the just-completed Times Tower, 1905. To the left is the then brand-new Hotel Astor with its fashionable roof garden. (Museum of the City of New York)

for a growing line of new "glass boxes" springing up along the avenue north of 42nd Street. The narrow plaza to the west of the building with its mini-waterfalls and tree plantings is a pleasant oasis between the tall towers—a concession to the zoning laws that require open space in proportion to building height. Above the new subway entrance in the west lobby is an attractive and colorful mosaic mural by Richard Kirk (but why hidden away from the main entrance?).

Avenue of the Americas, formerly called Sixth Avenue, was renamed by former Mayor Fiorello H. LaGuardia. In spite of the decorative coats of arms of the Latin American nations mounted on the Avenue's lampposts, most New Yorkers rejected the mayor's flamboyant gesture, and still refer to the thoroughfare by its original name.

From 1878 until 1938 the Sixth Avenue El rattled overhead, keeping the busy avenue in perpetual twilight. The broad vistas from the old wooden platform cars, however, were superb.

10. One of the newest additions to the city's ever growing skyline is the slope-fronted **W. R. Grace & Company Building** (No. 43 West), completed in 1974. The revolutionary profile derives from the architects' (Skidmore, Owings & Merrill) interpretation of the zoning regulations, which stipulate the ratio of a building's verticality to the amount of horizontal setback. The façade is covered with travertine, and although the shape is controversial, it is a relief from the endless rows of unimaginative "glass boxes" erected during the last 30 years. What is objectionable to many is the resultant destruction of the 42nd Street "street wall," considered an essential element in urban design. Also unsuccessful is the rear plaza, designed like an enormous checkerboard. The addition of trees (in boxes) has not helped much. To enter from the 43rd Street side, one is forced to cross the full length of the plaza. The two-story private reception area on the 47th and 48th floors (unfortunately not open to the public) is impressive, with a spiral staircase set against broad expanses of city panorama. A similar building (by the same architectural firm) was built simultaneously at 9 West 57th Street.

The Grace Building occupies the **site of the Stern Brothers Department Store,** which stood on the L-shaped plot from 1913 to 1970. (Interestingly, Stern's first store, an immense cast-iron building still in pristine condition, stands on the south side of West 23rd Street, between Fifth and Sixth avenues [*see* Ladies' Mile, 21].)

11. Adjacent No. 33 West, formerly a commercial office building, is now the **Graduate Center of the City University of New York.** The most striking feature is the renovation of the ground floor by architect Carl J. Petrilli, with its concrete cantilevered "canopy" and the open passageway to 43rd Street.

The Avenue of the Americas today is a far cry from the dark and dingy Sixth Avenue (as it was then called) of 75 years ago. Looking north from 42nd Street, the Manhattan Elevated Railroad seems to cast a pall of gloom over the avenue. (New-York Historical Society)

The split-faced concrete walls of the passage are in sharp contrast to the exterior—one can almost forget that the building was erected in 1912. Access is by a glassed-in bank of elevators in the passageway. Pleasant and convenient for pedestrians, the mall is used for exhibitions and has been tastefully planted with shrubbery (although one wonders how they can survive in the cavernous darkness). In the 1920s the building was famous for its third-floor concert hall, Aeolian Hall (note the lyres on the façade), and witnessed the premiere of George Gershwin's *Rhapsody in Blue.* The Graduate Center was dedicated in 1970 after a three-year renovation, and has been the recipient of many awards for excellence in design. The Municipal Art Society awarded it a special prize "for improvement of the aesthetic quality of life in New York City," and *New York Times* architecture critic Ada Louise Huxtable described the Center as "one of New York's most successfully recycled buildings."

12. No. 11 West, the **Salmon Tower** (York & Sawyer, 1927), is distinguished only in its elaborate entrance and luxurious lobby. Around the ornate arched entrance on both 42nd and 43rd streets are bas-relief sculptures of the months plus a row of classical figures above, representing the professions, and in the vaulted passage are marble walls and decorative bronze fixtures. Even the two mailboxes are adorned with low-relief bronze sculptures. The building also houses the Midtown Center of New York University. The "tower" section actually faces Fifth Avenue, as **No. 500 Fifth,** the two buildings being connected by a second-floor passageway. No. 500, completed in 1931 from plans by Shreve, Lamb & Harmon, is the second tallest building on the avenue, eclipsed only by the Empire State Building at 34th Street (built the same year by the same architectural firm). Known also as the Transportation Building, it formerly housed the New York offices of virtually every important railroad in the country. In their stead today are numerous foreign airlines.

Cross 42nd Street and return to Avenue of the Americas; turn left at the corner, and enter Bryant Park.

13. The entrance to **Bryant Park** is marked by a small square accommodating the memorial to José Bonifacio de Andrada e Silva, a Brazilian scientist and patriot. The statue, by José Lima, was executed in 1889 and presented by the United States of Brazil in 1954. To the right, dominating the western end of the landscaped park, is the Josephine Shaw Lowell Memorial Fountain. The pink Stoney Creek granite fountain honoring the pioneer social worker and philanthropist was designed by Charles A. Platt and presented to the city in 1912.

Bryant Park occupies the **site of the Crystal Palace Exhibition of 1853–54,** America's first World's Fair. Modeled after London's famous exhibition of two years earlier, it was an enormous domed iron-and-glass pavilion, designed to display fine arts and industrial products from around the world. Like a gargantuan greenhouse built with Victorian elegance, its pinnacles rose 76 feet above what was then called Reservoir Square. Although it was one of the most spectacular attractions ever to be presented in New York, it was a financial

The burning of the Crystal Palace, October 5, 1858. The Exposition, which was held in 1853–54, is now the site of Bryant Park. (New-York Historical Society)

failure, and in 1858 it was destroyed by a tragic fire. Although no one was injured, many priceless works of art were lost. Across 42nd Street, near the northeast corner, stood the tall, conical **Latting Observatory.** Built of timbers reinforced with iron girders, and equipped with steam elevators to the second landing, the tower provided excellent views of the Crystal Palace, the adjacent reservoir, and the growing city farther downtown. In 1856 it, too, was consumed by fire. During the Civil War, the park site was used as a drill field by Union troops.

Bryant Park was named for William Cullen Bryant in 1884, and finally built in 1934 after the successful entry in a competition for its design was won by Lusby Simpson, an unemployed architect from Queens. Walk down the flagstone path shaded by London plane trees to the east end, where the beautiful New York Public Library serves as an appropriate backdrop. To the left is the statue of William Earl Dodge by John Quincy Adams Ward. Dodge (1805–83) was a merchant and philanthropist, and a founder of the Y.M.C.A. In the center of the north-south axis, protected by a Roman-style arch, is the **statue of William Cullen Bryant** (1794–1878), poet, journalist, and orator. The sculpture was executed by Herbert Adams in 1911, and dominates the eastern end of the park. To the right is a bust of Johann Wolfgang von Goethe by Karl Fischer, presented to the city by the Goethe Society in 1932. (Stay out of the park after dark!)

14. The skyscraper panorama surrounding Bryant Park is striking. Look particularly to the West 40th Street side where, left to right, the following interesting buildings can be seen to good advantage:

The **Republic National Bank Building,** formerly the **Knox Building** (at the corner of Fifth Avenue). This ornate Classical showpiece with an imposing mansard roof was designed in 1902 by John H. Duncan for the Knox Hat Company. It suffered some modifications in 1965, but still retains much of its charm. Wrapped around the Knox Building on an L-shaped lot is the 27-story **Republic Tower,** world headquarters of the Republic National Bank (Eli Attia, 1982). Israeli-born architect Attia designed the glass-wall structure to serve as a backdrop for the landmark Knox Building, while at the same time preserving its own special geometric richness of form.

Freedom House (No. 20 West), a memorial to Wendell Willkie, is dedicated to gathering information on the status of human freedom throughout the world. A mixture of Classic and Flemish Renaissance styles, it was built ca. 1885 from plans by Henry J. Hardenberg for the New York Club.

The Engineers Club (No. 32 West) is a Classic-style building of satisfying proportions.

The American Standard Building (formerly American Radiator Building), designed in a bold, cubic massing of forms by architect Raymond M. Hood in 1923, is the undisputed beauty of the block. With its unique black-and-gold color scheme, it is most impressive. It has been said that its striking color combination, illuminated at night, gives it the appearance of an enormous glowing coal—ideal for the corporate offices of the American Radiator Company. In 1926 Talbot Hamlin, the noted architectural historian, described it as "the most daring experiment in color in modern buildings yet made in America." Note how the tower's setbacks terminate in gold-colored cubistic masses—forms often associated with the Art Deco style. The arched and pinnacled form at the top of the tower is a delightful crown to this artistic skyscraper.

No. 50 West 40th Street, now used by Daytop Village, is interesting for its massive segmented column shafts.

Note, too, the Beaux Arts–style former comfort stations at each end of the path, in complement to the style of the library. Bryant Park, because of the high quality of its landscape architecture, its historical and aesthetic interest, and its splendid urban location, has been designated an official Scenic Landmark by the New York City Landmarks Preservation Commission.

On exiting from the park at West 40th Street, note the bronze plaque to Wendell Willkie, mounted on the retaining wall.

Walk left to Fifth Avenue, then left to the main entrance to the library.

15. The New York Public Library building is considered the finest example of the Beaux Arts style in America. A majestic, delicate, and supremely aesthetic structure, its location at Fifth Avenue and 42nd Street is ideal. The site in the early 19th century was a potter's field, but with the opening of the Croton Aqueduct and water supply system for the city in 1842, a distributing reservoir was erected—a huge Egyptian-style enclosure with walls 50 feet high and 25 feet thick, surmounted by a promenade. With the construction of the Croton Dam, the reservoir was no longer needed, and was demolished in 1899 to make way for the new library.

In a competition to select the architect, winning plans were submitted by the firm of Carrère & Hastings, and the building was inaugurated in 1911. Attending the ceremonies were the President of the United States, the governor, and the mayor. Completed at a cost of $9 million, it is one of the truly great libraries of the world. The New York Public Library was the result of the merger in 1895 of the three largest private libraries in the city: the Astor, Tilden, and Lenox libraries, with endowments from each of the trusts, plus a building grant from Andrew Carnegie of $5.2 million. The New York Free Circulating Library joined the consolidation in 1901.

The exterior is built of Vermont marble, and the building, in the traditional Louis XVI Renaissance form, presents an ingratiating rather than imposing appearance. It is built around two inner courts with an immense central reading room occupying a half-acre of floor space. Dominating the grand entrance are the two famous lions designed by Edward C. Potter. The style of the majestic lions is from standard architectural forms, but they have been the source of humorous criticism since their installation, even to the unspeakable pun of "reading between the lions." The 95-foot tapered steel flagpoles are set on exquisite bronze bases designed by Thomas Hastings, and were installed in 1941 as a memorial to former reform Mayor John Purroy Mitchell. The sculptured figures on either side of the main entrance are by Frederick MacMonnies: The man seated on a sphinx on the northern side represents *Truth;* the woman seated on Pegasus on the south side represents *Beauty.* The six figures on the attic wall over the main entrance are by Paul Bartlett and are executed in Georgia marble for contrast. They depict, from left to right, *Philosophy, Romance, Religion, Poetry, Drama,* and *History.* The two groups in the pediment by George Gray Bernard represent *Art* and *History.* Look for the lions in the keystones above the first-floor windows.

The main lobby is reached by a flight of stairs to a triple-arched portico. The entire monumental space is of stone with barrel-vaulted arches, flanked by twin grand staircases supported on flying arches leading to the upper floors. Statues of John Merven Carrère and Thomas Hastings are set in niches on the first landing. The walls of the third-floor Central Hall are of dark wood, above which are plaster-paneled barrel vaults. Notice how the ceiling extends over the cornice line at each end to permit light to enter from segmental arch windows. An illusionistic painting above creates the impression of an open sky. The fine murals were painted by Edward Laning, under the auspices of the Artists Program of the WPA, and were completed in 1940. The four arched murals represent the four stages in the development of the recorded word: *Moses with the Tablets of the Law, The Medieval Scribe, Gutenberg Showing a Proof to the Elector of Mainz,* and *The Linotype—Mergenthaler and Whitelaw Reid.* The murals in the lunettes above the square-headed doors are *Learning to Read* (west side), and *The Student* (east side). The aerial mural on the ceiling, with its *trompe l'oeil* effect, tells the story of *Prometheus Bringing Fire to Men.*

Continue north on Fifth Avenue to the corner of 43rd Street.

16. The Manufacturers Hanover Trust Company Building (No. 510), on the southwest corner, was designed in 1954 by Skidmore, Owings & Merrill,

The ruins of the Crystal Palace as depicted in Harper's Weekly, *October 16, 1858. (New-York Historical Society)*

The transept of the cast-iron-and-glass Crystal Palace Exhibition Hall as seen from the gallery. Many nations were represented in this first American world's fair of science, industry, and art. (New-York Historical Society)

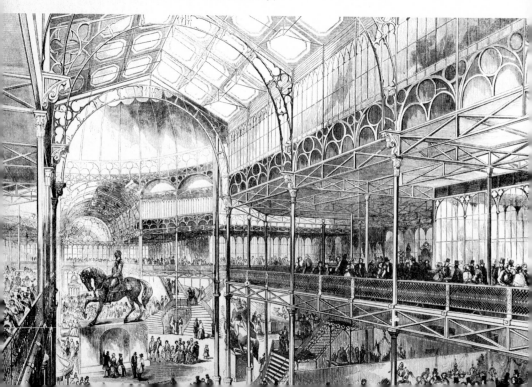

The height of satiety was reached in 1903 when C. K. G. Billings gave his famous Dinner on Horseback at Sherry's for a group of friends from his riding club. Diners were served on trays fastened to the horses' pommels by waiters in footman's livery. (Photograph by Byron. The Byron Collection. Museum of the City of New York)

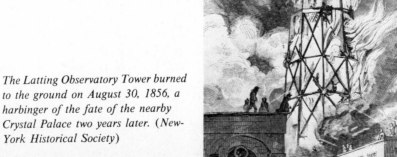

The Latting Observatory Tower burned to the ground on August 30, 1856, a harbinger of the fate of the nearby Crystal Palace two years later. (New-York Historical Society)

and is an example of the early use of the "glass cage" as a building style. Look through the broad glass pane at the exposed bank vault door.

Turn left (west) on West 43rd Street.

17. The former Columbia University Club (No. 4 West) is an example of Italian Renaissance style, but a much finer representation can be seen across the street in **the Century Association** (No. 7 West). Since two partners of the firm of McKim, Mead & White, which planned the club, were members (Stanford White and Charles Follen McKim), one could have safely expected a certain extra touch—an assumption clearly vindicated in the design of this grand old Veronese *palazzo*. The Century was the first of the firm's many Renaissance-style clubs, and was begun in 1889 from plans by McKM&W architect William Kendall, and took two years to complete. Typical Renaissance features are the monumental arched doorway and Palladian window above (once an open loggia), the rusticated base, and the wreathed round windows above the third-floor windows, which are skilfully joined to those below. Topping the building is a balustrade and ornate cornice. The Association dates from 1847 and was established "to promote the advancement of art and literature." The name "Century" refers to the original 100 members, among whom was William Cullen Bryant.

Return to Fifth Avenue, turn left, stopping in front of the Morgan Guaranty Trust Company.

18. The 20-foot-high **Seth Thomas street clock** is probably the oldest artifact on the block. Built of cast iron, these sturdy timepieces were prevalent throughout the country from the 1880s until World War I, when the popularity of the wristwatch eliminated the need of a public clock. Most served as advertising gimmicks for the shops in front of which they were erected. Seth Thomas is still in business—the last survivor of dozens of 19th-century American clockmakers.

The southwest corner of 44th Street was the site of famed **Sherry's,** one of the most lavish and fashionable establishments at the turn of the century. A combination restaurant and residential apartments, it catered to New York's most affluent clientele for 21 years. The building, erected for owner Louis Sherry, was subsequently remodeled by McKim, Mead & White for the Guaranty Trust Company, and remained until the early 1950s when it was demolished to make way for the present successor bank.

No less extravagant was **Delmonico's,** Sherry's arch rival, which, just six months before, moved up from its Madison Square location into an ornate Beaux Arts building designed by James Brown Lord on the northeast corner. The restaurant with its ballrooms and bachelor residences was closed in 1923, four years after the demise of Sherry's. [*See* front cover.]

Turn left (west) on West 44th Street (walk on the south side of the street).

19. [The points of interest can best be viewed from across the street.] **The Harvard Club** (No. 27 West) is a modest neo-Georgian-style building, designed by Charles Follen McKim, and completed in 1894. The red Harvard brick is laid in Flemish bond and the trim is in Indiana limestone. The club was extended through to West 45th Street in 1905 from plans by McKim, Mead & White, and was again enlarged in 1915. The interior Harvard Hall is an immense three-story Florentine-inspired "knights' chamber" with two great fireplaces.

The New York Yacht Club (No. 37 West) is one of the city's most romantic buildings. The sculptured design of three 17th-century sailing ships' sterns, complete with waves and dolphins built into the bay windows, is both innovative and aesthetic. The Beaux Arts Eclectic building was designed by Warren & Wetmore (who helped create Grand Central Terminal) in 1901. Founded in 1844, the New York Yacht Club is the patriarch of all American sailing clubs, and sponsors the internationally famous "America's Cup Race" held every four years. It was first won by the schooner *America* in 1851, and the coveted trophy has never been lost. The next race is scheduled for 1986. This is the sixth home of the club—a much earlier clubhouse built as a private mansion in 1846 still stands in Rosebank, Staten Island, overlooking the bay.

The Hotel Iroquois (No. 49 West) as well as the just passed **Hotel Mansfield** and **Hotel Royalton** are typical of the turn-of-the-century Classic Eclectic–style hotels that sprung up in the midtown area.

The **Hotel Algonquin** (Goldwyn Starrett, 1902) belongs to the same Classic Eclectic school, and has managed to maintain its *fin de siècle* elegance. The Algonquin has always been a favorite haunt of stage and literary personalities, though, alas, less so now. Enter and settle into one of the soft chairs in the oak-paneled lobby, order a drink, and imagine yourself a witness to the famous "Round Table" of the 1920s, when such figures as Alexander Woolcott, Robert Benchley, George S. Kaufman, Heywood Broun, Franklin P. Adams, Edna Ferber, Dorothy Parker, and others would gather and try to outdo each other in witty chatter, while pretending to act as the arbiters of the American cultural scene. Look, too, for Hamlet, the hotel's live-in cat and most famous guest.

Return to Fifth Avenue on the north side of the street.

The Association of the Bar (No. 42 West, adjacent to the Hotel Royalton) is a majestic structure, appropriate to its distinguished function. Two magnificent fluted Doric columns guard the portico of this Classic Eclectic limestone building, above which rise four pairs of Corinthian pilasters to an ornate cornice supported by finely detailed brackets. The Bar Association was founded in 1870 "for the purpose of maintaining the honor and dignity of the profession of the Law, of cultivating social relations among its members and increasing its usefulness in promoting the due administration of justice." The building was designed by Cyrus L. W. Eidlitz, and completed in 1895, and contains one of the largest law libraries in the country.

The General Society of Mechanics and Tradesmen of the City of New York (No. 20 West) was founded in 1785. It began as a technical institute offering free courses in the mechanical trades. The present building, formerly the Berkeley Preparatory School, was erected in 1891 from plans by Lamb & Rich. Note the equestrian frieze above the row of Ionic columns, and the very decorative wrought-iron balconies at each end of this restrained Classic-style building. The library is open to the public.

Cross Fifth Avenue and turn right to the southeast corner of 43rd Street.

20. The Israel Discount Bank (511 Fifth Avenue) remodeled the ground-floor space, preserving the remarkable character of the Renaissance façade and interior. Observe the splendid coffered ceiling. The building was originally the Postal Life Insurance Company, erected in 1917 from plans by York & Sawyer. The renovation in 1962 was designed by Luss, Kaplan & Associates.

Across 43rd Street on the northeast corner, from 1868 to 1927, stood **Temple Emanu-El,** the largest synagogue in the world. Its twin "Moorish" towers were conspicuous landmarks on Fifth Avenue for over half a century, until rising land values and the northward push of the business district forced relocation to the present site, 22 blocks north. It is still the world's largest.

21. The diminutive gray Italianate building at the northeast corner of Fifth Avenue and 42nd Street is a surprising anachronism on such a location. It was built ca. 1870 for Levi P. Morton, who in 1889 was elected vice-president

Temple Emanu-El, at the northeast corner of Fifth Avenue and 43rd Street, with its twin Moorish towers, was the largest synagogue in the world when it occupied the corner from 1868 to 1927. It still maintains the distinction at its present site at 65th Street. (New-York Historical Society)

on the ticket with Benjamin Harrison. The house was sold and converted to a residential hotel called the Hamilton Apartments, and in this century it became a nondescript commercial building. Its survival to the present can be attributed to its narrow width, making the erection of a high-rise building impractical.

Turn left (east) on 42nd Street.

The system of designating streets east and west of Fifth Avenue was inaugurated in 1838.

22. The Sperry & Hutchinson Building, on the northwest corner of Madison Avenue, is the home of (S & H) Green Stamps. The company was the first to introduce trading stamps as another way for merchants to encourage customer loyalty by giving them a little something extra. The company has been in business since 1896. The present building, which S. & H. leases, was built in 1964 from plans by Kahn & Jacobs. On the site previously was the Hotel Manhattan, and later the National City Bank.

23. The Lincoln Building (No. 60 East) towers 53 stories above 42nd Street, and was built in 1929–30 from plans by the architectural firm of J. E. R. Carpenter. A product of the skyscraper building boom of the late 1920s, it was designed according to the setback requirements of the zoning law. In the 1929 prospectus it claimed that "No other office structure has ever been created where clear fresh air is more abundant or where radiant sunlight is more plentiful. . . . Other buildings are far enough away to give unimpeded ventilation to all floors." On the walls of the vestibule are quotes from speeches by Abraham Lincoln, and in the center of the lobby a miniature bronze sculpture fashioned from Daniel Chester French's original model for the seated Lincoln at Washington's Lincoln Memorial.

The adjacent 26-story **Philip Morris Building,** begun in 1981, blends harmoniously with the 42nd Street "street wall," since architects Ulrich Franzen and Associates chose to have their rough-textured precast gray granite-paneled building face Park Avenue (No. 120), thus linking it to the axis of new skyscrapers that reach down Park Avenue to 32nd Street. The engaging three-story colonnade provides a covered pedestrian space, with access to street-level shops and a branch of the Whitney Museum. The site was formerly occupied by the noted Art Deco–style Airline Building, built in the late 1930s to serve as the in-town terminal for the newly opened LaGuardia Field. The previous tenant on the corner was the Hotel Belmont, built at the turn of the century by the financier and father of the New York subways, August Belmont. The magnate had a spur of the IRT subway built into the hotel, where his private car *Mineola* was always kept in readiness for a trip to his racetrack, Belmont Park.

24. Grand Central Terminal, a magnificent Beaux Arts Eclectic structure of mammoth proportions, has provided a dramatic gateway into New York City since its completion in 1913. Designed by Whitney Warren and James A. Wetmore together with engineers Reed and Stem, the master plan combined function, accessibility, and aesthetics, which resulted in a monumentally successful architectural achievement.

Looking across the intersection of Fifth Avenue and 42nd Street, ca. 1875, at the Croton Reservoir. (New-York Historical Society)

As late as 1902, Fifth Avenue and 44th Street still looked almost rural, with Henry H. Tyson's Fifth Avenue Market and Ye Olde Willow Cottage tavern. Temple Emanu-El is barely visible to the right. The photo was taken from in front of Sherry's. (New-York Historical Society)

The broad south façade, with its triple arches, provides great expanses of glass to illuminate the interior. Crowning the center arch is the imposing sculpture group by Jules Coutan, representing *Mercury, Hercules,* and *Minerva,* set above a 13-foot-high clock. Below is a statue of the founder of the original railroad empire, Cornelius "Commodore" Vanderbilt (the statue, by Albert De Groot, is visible from the south side of 42nd Street). The terminal covers the three blocks to 45th Street, but below ground are 33.7 miles of track on two levels—66 tracks on the upper, and 57 on the lower level—a practical plan devised by railroad engineer William J. Wilgus. Reed and Stem's ingenious series of ramps connect the two levels with streets, subways, adjacent office buildings, and hotels, separating pedestrian from vehicular traffic. The main concourse, one of the most awe-inspiring interior spaces in the country, is covered with a vaulted ceiling supported by 125-foot-high piers and hung from steel trusses. On the ceiling are illuminated constellations of the zodiac (the ecliptic line, through a designer's error, runs the wrong way). Sunlight entering through the 75-foot-high windows casts long rays across the marble floor, augmenting the feeling of height and grandeur. The upper level was formerly used primarily for long-distance trains and the lower for the hundreds of commuter trains, but with the decrease in passenger business, the lower level is restricted to weekday rush-hour service only. Particularly attractive are the Guastavino hollow tile vaultings in the lower level.

(*Photo, left*) *The same intersection forty years later shows a new type of Fifth Avenue omnibus. The "double decker" open-top models ended service in 1946, the closed-top models in 1953. The building on the northeast corner still stands. (Photograph by Alice Austen. Staten Island Historical Society)*

Commodore Vanderbilt's Grand Central Station gave New York its first direct rail link. The sprawling Second Empire building, built in 1871, hid an enormous ground-level train shed. The station was enlarged in 1899 and replaced by the present multi-level terminal in 1913. (Museum of the City of New York)

Who can forget the names of such great trains as the "Empire State Express," the "North Shore Limited," or the "Commodore Vanderbilt"? Or the rolling out of the red carpet for the daily departure to Chicago of the "Twentieth-Century Limited"? The terminal is still heavily used, however, with over 40 million passengers a year and about 120,000 daily commuters. Many physical changes over the years have not enhanced the appearance of the interior. The proliferation of small shops in the open spaces, the exhibition galleries, and the gaudy displays have spoiled it, despite a recent face-lift. Unused ticket windows are now used for off-track betting.

The New York & Harlem Railroad, which began chugging down Fourth Avenue in 1832, used a depot at 26th Street [the site of the first Madison Square Garden; *see* Madison Square, 11]. It then used horses to pull the coaches the rest of the way to the end of the line near City Hall. In 1854 the Common Council banned steam locomotives below 42nd Street because of the air and noise pollution, and in 1871 Commodore Vanderbilt had a huge cast-iron and glass terminal built at the present site. The former route down Fourth Avenue (now Park Avenue) cut through Murray Hill to 32nd Street. This "cut" was taken over by the Metropolitan Street Railway for use by its horsecars and later trolleys, and was covered over and converted into a tunnel. Today it is used by automobiles only and connects with an elevated viaduct that encircles the station on its way to upper Park Avenue. The viaduct also bypasses the huge Pan Am Building and passes through the former New York Central Office Building, which was later renamed the New York General Building, and in recent times, the Helmsley Building. A short spur of the Third Avenue El that connected with Grand Central Terminal was demolished when the viaduct was built in 1919.

The old station was enlarged in 1899, but with the 1902 regulation banning steam trains altogether from the city, the company—now the New York Central—had the choice of either relocating outside the city limits, or doing what it so wisely did, electrifying its lines. The railroad then acquired the subsurface land rights for an underground terminal and yards, and began building the huge station. With the new land and air rights, the Central was able to build itself an attractive office building and two hotels, the Commodore (now the Grand Hyatt) and the Biltmore (rebuilt as the headquarters of the Bank of America). The new terminal also served the former New York, New Haven & Hartford Railroad, allowing trains from New England direct access into the heart of the city.

Cross the main concourse and take the escalator for a brief visit to the lobby of the **Pan Am Building.** Built in 1963 and designed by Walter Gropius, Emery Roth & Sons, and Pietro Belluschi, it did much to destroy the scale of Grand Central Terminal. The enormous office building provided more floor space than any other in the world until the construction of the World Trade Center, adding additional traffic and congestion to an already overcrowded area. Its precast curtain-wall construction made it one of the first of its kind in the

The enormous cast-iron-and-glass train shed of Grand Central Station, ca. 1872. Electrification did not come until 1902. (Museum of the City of New York)

city. It also created an outpouring of discontent, not diminished by the helicopter landing pad on the roof (since discontinued). Former Landmarks Commissioner Harmon H. Goldstone referred to the Pan Am Building's interruption of the broad view of Grand Central Terminal from Park Avenue as "a monstrous bland blanket."

Several years ago the Penn Central Transportation Company (a result of the merger of the New York Central, New Haven, and Pennsylvania railroads) sought to obtain permission to construct a 55-story tower *above* Grand Central Terminal. In denying the application, the Commission felt that such a tall tower would in effect destroy the landmark, reducing it to the status of a "curiosity." The Penn Central then had the temerity to suggest that the front of the terminal should be demolished altogether! The Commission, of course, did not agree that this was an appropriate means of preserving the landmark. A major public outcry, supported by the Municipal Art Society and such public figures as Jacqueline Onassis, helped convince the courts that the destruction of Grand Central Terminal was really not in the best interest of the city or its citizens. However, the ultimate solution came with the transfer of the terminal's air rights. Exit from the terminal and cross 42nd Street to the east side of Park Avenue to study the recently restored south façade.

25. Although the name **Pershing Square** appears on the **Park Avenue Viaduct,** the square really no longer exists. A rectangular piece of land on the southeast corner of Park Avenue and East 42nd Street was cleared in 1914 after the demolition of the imposing Grand Union Hotel. Named for the Commander-in-Chief of the American Expeditionary Forces in World War I, the plot was acquired by the city for an open plaza. In 1920, it was sold to a developer who three years later erected No. 100 East 42nd Street, naming it the Pershing Square Building. A large plaque in the lobby relates the history of the site.

The main office of **The Bowery Savings Bank** (No. 110 East) was built in 1923 from plans by York & Sawyer. Designed in a Romanesque basilica style, the imposing arch leads into the huge banking room, 160 feet long and 65 feet high, with a beamed and coffered ceiling. The walls are of variegated limestone, interspersed with blocks of Ohio sandstone. On each side wall are six columns of different-colored marble, carrying five stone arches. Between the columns are panels of unpolished marble mosaic from quarries in France and Italy. The mosaic marble floors add to the artistic effect. The former massive bronze doors are hung for ornamentation on the east and west walls. Another dramatic interior space, it was cited for architectural merit by the Municipal Art Society and the Society of Architectural Historians. The Bowery Savings Bank, founded in 1834, is one of the city's oldest and boasts a magnificent Classic-style McKim, Mead & White landmark building in its 130 Bowery office downtown [*see* Lower East Side, 25]. The rich architectural detail has many lovely motifs, including the bull and bear of Wall Street, a rooster representing punctuality, a squirrel for thrift, and a lion for power. The sculpture is by Ricci & Zari. Many consider this the finest work of York & Sawyer.

26. The 56-story Art Deco **Chanin Building** is a delightful addition to the

city's panorama. Built in 1929 from designs by Sloan & Robertson, it came at
a period when decoration was still considered an essential element of the architectural whole. Note the wide ornate bronze band on the third floor, with motifs
of birds and fish running the full length of the façade, and the base of terra-
cotta plant forms. The lobby is a gem of Art Deco styling. Bronze is used
tastefully and artistically in the amazing convector grills, the low reliefs on
the elevator doors and mailboxes, the "jeweled" clocks, and even in the "waves"
on the floor at the 42nd Street entrance. One cannot help but rejoice at the
excellent building maintenance and the lack of "modernization" which has
helped keep the Chanin Building in pristine condition. Unfortunately, the top
floor observation deck is now closed. A theater on the 50th floor is also closed,
as is the former basement bus station of the Baltimore & Ohio Railroad train
connection.

Facing, or rather reflecting, the Chanin Building is the glistening **Grand
Hyatt Hotel** (Gruzen & Partners, with Der Scutt, 1981). This dazzling new
member of the Hyatt chain in New York City is, alas, disturbingly out of
context with its neighbor, Grand Central Terminal. The bronze-tone glass sheathing now covers the entire façade of what was once the Hotel Commodore,
designed by architects Warren & Wetmore as part of the original terminal
project. As a hotel, the Hyatt is a vast improvement over its predecessor, which
had declined badly in its later years. The striking Sun Garden cocktail lounge
is cantilevered over 42nd Street, and although intrusive on the street wall, it
provides a pleasant view with a tropical atmosphere. The plant-filled lobby,
with its metal geometric sculptures and comfortable seating, is reached from
the street entrance by an escalator gliding past a bubbling waterfall.

27. Perhaps the most unusually shaped building, and certainly one of the
most beautiful, is the 1,048-foot-high **Chrysler Building,** on the northeast corner
of Lexington Avenue. Its graceful vertical shaft tapering into a fine stainless-
steel point gives it a distinctive and artistic position in New York's skyline.
Designed by William Van Alen in 1929, it became, upon completion a year
later, the tallest building in the world, only to be relegated to second place a
few months later by the Empire State Building. Close examination of the lovely
Art Deco façade readily indicates that this was planned as the automotive tower
of the city. At each setback are stylized "motor" designs. The building flares
out sharply at the fourth setback into what appears to be shiny radiator caps—
for a 1929 Chrysler! At other levels are basket-weave designs and a band of
abstract automobiles. The Chrysler building was one of the first to have exposed
metal as an essential part of the design. An interesting event in the history of
its construction was the deception of a rival architect by Van Alen as the building
neared completion. When they reached a height of 925 feet, everyone assumed
that was the maximum; and when the downtown "40 Wall Tower" (40 Wall
Street) also reached that height, architects H. Craig Severance and Yasuo Matsui
added another two feet to make their building "the tallest in the world." To
the consternation of all, the stainless-steel spire of the Chrysler Building was
secretly assembled, raised through the dome, and bolted into place, adding a
victorious 123 feet. The elegant lobby is faced with African marble, and the

ceiling is covered with what is considered the world's largest mural, 97 by 100 feet, depicting transportation themes. Artist Edward Trumbell used as models some of the men who had actually worked on the construction of the building. In its early years, the lobby served as a showroom for Chrysler Motors products. The lavish observation deck has been closed and now houses electronic equipment; however, the installation of the spectacular illumination in the tower in the winter of 1981 (according to architect Van Alen's original plans, but with modern high-intensity light tubes) has added a brilliant touch to the nighttime city skyline. The successive rows of brightly lit inverted V's have been likened to some ethereal necklace suspended from the clouds. On the ground floor, Con Edison maintains a "Conservation Center," an exhibit open to the public which graphically illustrates ways to save energy.

Around the corner on 42nd Street (best viewed from the south side of the street), it will be noted that the east wall of the Chrysler Building's lower setback is not parallel to the north-south avenues. This is because the property line follows the route of the former East Post Road, which in the 18th century ran approximately between Lexington and Third avenues, wending its way up Manhattan Island.

28. The massive **Mobil Building** occupies the entire block to Third Avenue. Unusual are the embossed stainless-steel panels that cover the entire building. Originally the Socony-Mobil Building, it was built in 1955 from plans by Harrison & Abramovitz.

29. Third Avenue has changed drastically since World War II. For over 70 years the avenue was darkened by the rattling Third Avenue El and, like so many of the El-covered thoroughfares, was lined with dingy tenements, saloons, and cheap little shops. When the El came down in 1955—the last survivor of Manhattan's once-extensive overhead railway network—Third Avenue underwent a complete transformation. From 38th Street to 57th Street, modern office buildings were erected; and typical of the 1950s and early '60s, most were boxlike carbon copies of each other. There is little relief in the homogeneous and monotonous streetscape. **Second Avenue** was also relieved of its overhead El and enjoyed a similar renaissance, albeit somewhat later.

30. At the southeast corner of Third Avenue and 42nd Street is the last surviving **Automat.** Built by the Horn & Hardart Company in 1958, it re-creates the original Art Deco style of the once ubiquitous chain of self-service restaurants that had its genesis in Philadelphia in 1889, but did not become "Automatic" until 1908. New York's first Automat opened in 1911. A good place for a "pit stop" on the tour, the popular glass-enclosed coin-operated dispensers offer a variety of dishes, and the coffee, which once cost five cents a cup, still pours from brass lions' mouths at the crank of a handle. With the diminishing purchasing power of the nickel, tokens to unlock the goodies must be purchased from the marble-counter change booth.

The adjacent **Harley Hotel** (Emery Roth & Sons) opened its doors in 1981, replacing the former Central Commercial High School, which had occupied the site since 1906. The lofty structure blends well with its modern neighbors, although it adds little architectural excitement to the streetscape. The porte-cochère, a novelty on 42nd Street, helps relieve some of the traffic congestion (unlike its rival, the Hyatt); and its two-story-high, dark-toned, mirrored-glass overhang, while breaking the "street wall," shifts attention from the monotonous verticality of the row of buildings. The Harley, newest of seven New York City Helmsley hotels, derives its name from the first two letters of the first names of Harry Helmsley, chairman of the board, and his wife, Leona, president.

Step back across 42nd Street and notice the diminutive five-story Romanesque Revival–style structure (No. 202) tucked between the Harley and the corner building. Built in the mid-1880s, it became one of a number of "holdouts" in the city—buildings whose owners either refused to sell to site developers, or who held out for prohibitive sums, forcing architects and builders to work around them. An odd anachronism, this brick and masonry house gives some idea of the scale and type of building that lined the thoroughfare a hundred years ago.

31. The New York Daily News Building (No. 220 East) was completed in 1930, a year before architect Raymond M. Hood's opposite outpost, the McGraw-Hill Building. Differing sharply from it and from his American Radiator Building of seven years earlier, the News Building uses other means to stress its verticality. In cooperation with John Mead Howells, Hood resorted to rows of brown brick spandrels and windows to create an up-and-down stripe effect. In 1958, an addition was added by Harrison & Abramovitz, wisely following the original style. Not to be missed is the attractive lobby, designed as an educational exhibition. In the center is the world's largest interior globe, illuminated from within and rotating slowly on a recessed platform. An excellent geography lesson, the globe's details are constantly kept up to date. On the lobby floor are bronze lines pointing to cities around the world and to the relative positions of the planets. The back wall has various meteorological instruments. The *News*, which is printed in this building and in an annex to the south, has the largest circulation of any newspaper in the country. The attractive building was cited by the Municipal Art Society and the Society of Architectural Historians for "originality in design and influence on later work."

32. The Ford Foundation Building, midway down the north side of 42nd Street, stands as a significant contribution to the quality of life in the city. The L-shaped building arranged around a 130-foot-high "greenhouse" was designed by Kevin Roche, John Dinkeloo and Associates, and was completed in 1967. The architects' plan was "to provide a proper environment for the building's staff—a space that would allow them to enjoy the view, but at the same time, allow them to be aware of the existence of other members of the Foundation, people who share their common aims and purposes." They also felt that their building should contribute something to the city, maintaining a low profile and observing "the lines and planes created by other buildings which form the surrounding street." The result was eminently successful. The 12-story glassed-in area is anchored by granite piers and side walls, and shelters a one-third-acre lush garden. The shrubbery is frequently changed and is centered about a terraced garden with 17 full-grown trees, thousands of ground-cover plants, and aquatic plants in a still pool. Each season brings its own bloomings,

In the late 1920s, many rows of brownstones at the east end of 42nd Street were leveled to make way for Tudor City. This group of houses stood on the south side of 42nd Street near the present Tudor City Place before the thoroughfare was widened. (Fred F. French Investing Company)

and the entire area is floodlit, adding to the natural effect of filtered sunlight. The "greenhouse" also serves the additional purpose of a waste air chamber and thermal buffer. Ada Louise Huxtable, architecture critic of the *New York Times,* in praising its successful design, called the Ford Foundation Building "a splendid, shimmering Crystal Palace . . . one of the Foundation's more valid contributions to the arts." (The garden may be visited on weekdays.)

Across 42nd Street are the Church of the Covenant, the Hotel Tudor, and the broad Tudor City complex. Not officially part of Tudor City, the **Church of the Covenant** (J. Cleveland Cady, 1871) fits harmoniously into the architectural style of the complex. Cady was a member of the congregation, and the church was one of his first commissions. Built as the Covenant Memorial Chapel to serve as a mission for the working-class neighborhood, it became a regular church in 1893. The interior has great charm, with antique glass, bright stained-glass windows, and delicately carved wood traceries. When 42nd Street was depressed for the construction of Tudor City, the church ended up a full story above street level, requiring the construction of a staircase for access to the entrance.

Climb the stairway on the north side of 42nd Street to Tudor City Place, which spans the street.

33. Tudor City was developed in 1925–28 by the Fred F. French Company as a "self-contained city within walking distance of the city itself." There are 12 apartment houses with a total of 3,000 apartments, a 600-room hotel, shops, restaurant, post office, and private parks—all designed in a Tudor Gothic, or English Cottage, style. From the north end of Tudor City Place there is a superb view of the United Nations.

The site has had a checkered history, beginning with the rural Winthrop Mansion, "Dutch Hill," in the 18th century. The house was later converted into a tavern and rest stop for the stagecoaches of the old East Post Road. By mid-19th century the area deteriorated badly and became the hangout for gangs of criminals. In the early 20th century, the rocky crags were taken over by the notorious "Rag Gang," led by archfelon Paddy Corcoran. The neighborhood surrounding "Corcoran's Roost" became industrialized with breweries, slaughterhouses, glue factories and a gas works (this explains why there are few windows in the east side of the Tudor City apartment houses to provide unattractive views or admit unsavory odors). Tudor City remained a staid and tranquil enclave, enhanced by the arrival of the U.N. in the early 1950s. This pleasant oasis has been the subject of an ongoing threat by Tudor City owner Harry Helmsley, who for almost ten years has been planning to erect highrise apartment houses on the site of the shady little private parks. Vigorous and sustained opposition from residents, who see their precious patch of green as vital to the quality of life of the neighborhood, has stalled the offending project. Only time will tell whose values will prevail.

[The United Nations is described in the East River Panoramas tour.]

End of tour. The 42nd Street crosstown bus stops at the foot of the stairs leading down from Tudor City Place.

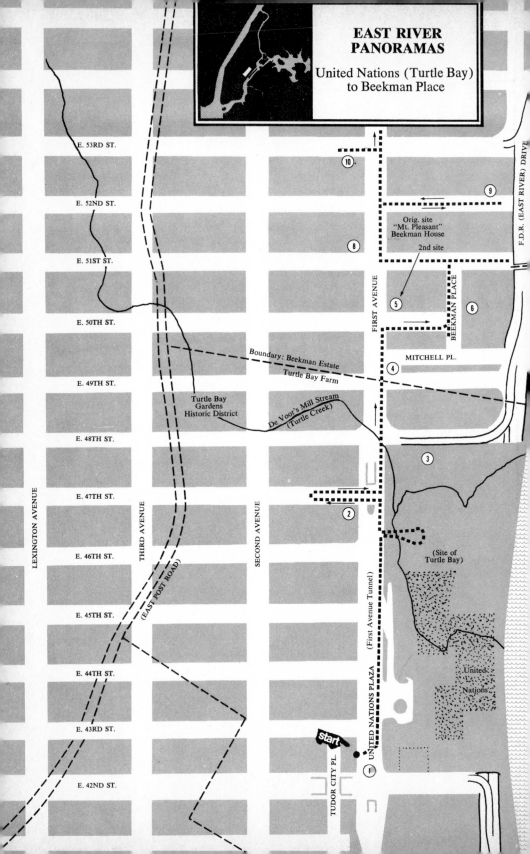

13. East River Panoramas

[*First/Second Avenue (M-15) bus to East 42nd Street; 42nd Street crosstown (M-104 or M-106) bus to First Avenue. Nearest subway: IRT Lexington Avenue line or 42nd Street Shuttle to Grand Central*]

The walking tour begins at United Nations Plaza, opposite the U.N. Secretariat Building, in Ralph J. Bunche Park, just north of 42nd Street, and follows the East River shoreline (with some detours) to Gracie Mansion, ending at the Henderson Place Historic District at East 86th Street.

1. Ralph J. Bunche Park honors the peace efforts of the United States' first black U.N. official, who served as secretary to the Palestine Peace Commission in 1947 and was awarded the Nobel Peace Prize three years later. He was subsequently appointed Under-Secretary General for Political Affairs, a post he held until his death. The aluminum sculpture, *Peace Form One,* is by the Los Angeles–born black artist, Daniel LaRue Johnson.

The backdrop for the little park is the **Isaiah Wall,** contributed by the City of New York to the United Nations, and it bears the oft-repeated quote from the Book of Isaiah, "They Shall Beat Their Swords into Plowshares, and Their Spears into Pruning Hooks . . ."

Climb the stairs for an excellent vantage point. Read the following text on the U.N., then cross United Nations Plaza and walk north toward the Visitors' Gate:

The United Nations. After several years in temporary quarters on Long Island, at the City of New York Building in the Flushing Meadow Park World's Fair Grounds, and at the Sperry Gyroscope Plant at Lake Success, the U.N. moved into its permanent headquarters on this Manhattan East River shorefront site in 1952. Technically outside the territorial jurisdiction of the United States, the U.N. complex consists of three main buildings: the 544-foot-high Secretariat, completed in 1950, the General Assembly Building (1952), and the Dag Hammarskjöld Library (1963).

*View of the United Nations site taken from Tudor City, looking north, December 1946.
In the distance, the graceful Queensboro Bridge leaps across Welfare (now Roosevelt)
Island. (Official United Nations Photo)*

The site that now appears so ideal for the location of the world body was
formerly a depressing aggregation of slums, coal docks, factories, slaughterhouses, and breweries. The original plan called for a site north of the city in
Westchester County, but a grant of $8.5 million from John D. Rockefeller
made it possible to purchase a parcel of land that had already been accumulated
by William Zeckendorf for private development. In the earlier Zeckendorf plan,
all buildings east of Third Avenue between 46th and 49th streets were to be
razed. The revised proposal proved more practical and saved many beautiful
houses from demolition, including the historic Turtle Bay Gardens.

The new plan was approved by Congress in record time and the city rushed
through all the enabling legislation, which included the waterfront rights and
tax-exempt status. An international team of renowned architects, led by America's Wallace K. Harrison, drew up the designs. Among the planners were Le
Corbusier (France), Sven Markelius (Sweden), Oscar Niemeyer (Brazil), plus
representatives from ten other countries. The library was designed by Harrison,
Abramovitz & Harris. The pool was a gift from American schoolchildren, its
freestanding stone sculpture by England's Barbara Hepworth, and the Council
Chambers a gift from Norway, Sweden, and Denmark. The buildings and
grounds display many beautiful art objects, with such items as a Peace Bell
and Shrine from Japan, mosaics from Tunisia, and even a model of Sputnik

from the Soviet Union. At the same time, New York City diverted busy First Avenue into a five-block-long tunnel and widened East 47th Street into Dag Hammarskjöld Plaza. The flags of the approximately 150 member nations line the east side of what was formerly First Avenue, now renamed United Nations Plaza.

2. The west side of **United Nations Plaza** has its own panorama of modern architecture. Among the more interesting buildings are:

No. 771, the Herbert Hoover Building, headquarters of the **Boys Clubs of America** (1960).

No. 777, the **Church Center for the United Nations** (William Lascaze, 1962). The impressive stained glass in the sanctuary of this Methodist church represents *Man's Struggle for Peace and Brotherhood,* by Henry L. Willet.

The United Nations Plaza Hotel (Kevin Roche, John Dinkeloo and Associates, 1976) is one of the most striking additions to the city skyline. This irregularly shaped aluminum and blue-green reflective-glass curtain-wall structure is a dramatic counterpart to the smooth, straight shaft of the U.N. Secretariat Building, and its gridiron skin looks for all the world like a sheet of misfolded graph paper, as it looms skyward from a street-level "skirt" to a sliced-off corner and 45-degree setbacks on the north side. It is a dizzying and exciting visual experience, and a welcome change from the traditional glass boxes of recent times. Visit the Ambassador Grill, whose mirrored skylights create the illusion of a night sky overhead. The 288-room hotel shares space with office tenants, and is managed by the Hyatt International Corporation.

No. 799, the **United States Permanent Mission to the United Nations** (Kelly & Gruzen and Kahn & Jacobs, 1959). It is an attractive, eye-catching building, and appropriate to the U.N.'s host country. The electric wires inside the precast concrete "honeycombs" were installed to shock pigeons into roosting on some other nation's edifice.

No. 809, the **Institute of International Education** (Harrison, Abramovitz & Harris, 1964). Architect Alvar Aalto designed the Edgar J. Kaufmann Conference Room in the penthouse.

No. 823 (345 East 46th Street), the **Carnegie Endowment International Center** (Harrison, Abramovitz & Harris, 1953).

Enter the United Nations at the Visitors' Gate, and spend some time exploring the General Assembly Building lobby and lower concourse; then take one of the free guided tours (daily 9 A.M. to 4:45 P.M., except on Christmas and New Year's, and when special security measures are in effect). The entrance to the attractive garden is farther up the street at the corner of East 48th Street.

On the north side of Dag Hammarskjöld Plaza:

No. 345 East 47th Street, the **United Engineering Center** (Shreve, Lamb & Harmon, 1961).

No. 333 East 47th Street, the **Japan Society Building** (Junzo Yoshimuro and Gruzen & Partners, 1971). Funded by John D. Rockefeller III to the tune of $4.3 million, this striking example of modern Japanese architecture was inaugurated by Prince and Princess Hitachi and is the U.S. headquarters of the society.

The "Old Store House at Turtle Bay, N.Y., 1852" in a lithograph from Valentine's Manual, *1857. The house was the site of a Liberty Boys' raid led by Marinus Willett, on the King's stores, just before the American Revolution. (Museum of the City of New York)*

The Holy Family Roman Catholic Church (rebuilt in 1964 by George J. Sole) is dominated by its gray granite and aluminum bell tower. The church was built on the site of a brewery stable.

Return to United Nations Plaza, and turn north to East 48th Street.

In the mid-17th century, the area along the river below the present East 49th Street was the **site of the Turtle Bay Farm.** The origin of "Turtle" is uncertain. Some claim it to come from the many turtles that were once common along the shore of Turtle Bay (where the U.N. is now); others attribute it to the early Dutch word *deutal,* a farm implement, which was later corrupted into "turtle." The original farm dated from 1639. Just before the Revolutionary War, the neighborhood figured in a bold act by a group of "Liberty Boys," under Marinus Willett, who sailed down from Greenwich, Connecticut, in a small sloop, seized a cache of arms from a British storehouse in the lower city, then attacked a small stone fort that stood at the foot of East 45th Street, surprising the guards and making off to Boston with a boatload of supplies for the new Continental Army.

Flowing deep below East 48th Street is **De Voor's Mill Stream,** later called Turtle Creek, which once emptied into Turtle Bay. Because of a cholera epidemic in 1854, the city fathers blocked the now polluted creek and channeled it into a culvert, which still empties into the East River under the present United Nations site.

Make a 100-foot detour left on the south side of West 48th Street. Across the street on the side wall of No. 339 is a clearly visible advertisement dating from before the turn of the century: *Wagon Manufacturer, Carriages Repaired and Painted.*

3. The twin monoliths of **Nos. 860 and 870 United Nations Plaza** (Harrison, Abramovitz & Harris, 1966) are luxury cooperative apartment houses. Originally they were planned to be the IBM World Trade Center, but now only the lower floors are used for commercial purposes.

4. The Beekman Tower (John Mead Howells, 1928) was built as the Panhellenic Hotel, a national meeting place for Greek-letter sororities, and is now a residential hotel. It is a bold Art Deco shaft whose 26-story-high deep window recesses emphasize the feeling of verticality. The Top of the Tower lounge offers a spectacular view.

5. Beekman Hill. The high ground that dominated the area between 50th and 51st streets was the site of the James Beekman mansion, *Mount Pleasant.* Built in 1766, the beautiful Colonial mansion stood near East 51st Street, but was later moved one block south when First Avenue was opened.

The Abigail Adams Smith House, a museum maintained by the Colonial Dames of America, was built originally in 1799 as a stable for Col. William Stephens Smith. The site has been much improved with the removal in the 1930s of the gas tanks. [See p. 318] (*Museum of the City of New York*)

Turn right on East 50th Street to Beekman Place.

6. The Beekman Place District. The two blocks, East 50th Street to Beekman Place, and Beekman Place between 50th and 51st streets, were formerly cobblestoned, and consist mainly of town houses, remodeled in the 1920s. This delightful group of luxury residences has a unique atmosphere of charm and tranquility, in striking contrast to the surrounding neighborhood. Although not startling architecturally, each house has a character of its own, reflecting the individual taste of the original owner and the imagination of its builder.

The town houses were favored particularly by great theater personalities. Alfred Lunt and Lynn Fontanne lived in the house on the northeast corner of East 50th Street and Beekman Place. Among others who enjoyed Beekman Place addresses were Ethel Barrymore, Katharine Cornell, and Irving Berlin. It was also home for members of the Rockefeller family and for former Secretary of the Navy and Defense James Forrestal.

Some of the more interesting remodeled town houses on East 50th Street: **Nos. 405, 416–420, 417,** and **419.** On Beekman Place: **Nos. 19–21, 23** (look up at the modern superimposition!), **33** (note its storybook roof and dormers, and the ropelike twisted bronze rainspout), **32–34,** and **35.** Notice the old **bishop's crook lamppost** on the southeast corner of Beekman Place and East 51st Street.

Turn right (east) on East 51st Street, pass through the little Peter Detmold Park, and down onto the footbridge over the East River Drive.

7. An excellent vantage point for a rear view of the Beekman Place District, the bridge is also a perfect site from which to view Cannon Point just to the north, where the Drive disappears under Sutton Place. Just to the south was a pleasant beach, where swimming was frequently enjoyed in the "altogether," and where Edgar Allan Poe came in 1846 to live with his young, sick wife, the former Virginia Clemm. Horace Greeley, the illustrious editor of the *Tribune,* came here to seek solace from the tragic loss of several children. Author Thomas Wolfe lived for a time on nearby First Avenue, and Yiddish novelist Sholem Asch described the neighborhood of the East 40s very vividly in his *East River,* published in 1946.

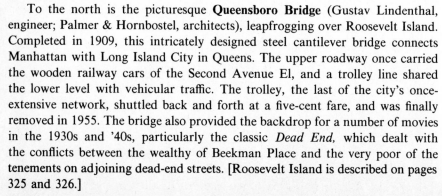

To the north is the picturesque **Queensboro Bridge** (Gustav Lindenthal, engineer; Palmer & Hornbostel, architects), leapfrogging over Roosevelt Island. Completed in 1909, this intricately designed steel cantilever bridge connects Manhattan with Long Island City in Queens. The upper roadway once carried the wooden railway cars of the Second Avenue El, and a trolley line shared the lower level with vehicular traffic. The trolley, the last of the city's once-extensive network, shuttled back and forth at a five-cent fare, and was finally removed in 1955. The bridge also provided the backdrop for a number of movies in the 1930s and '40s, particularly the classic *Dead End,* which dealt with the conflicts between the wealthy of Beekman Place and the very poor of the tenements on adjoining dead-end streets. [Roosevelt Island is described on pages 325 and 326.]

The **East River** or **Franklin D. Roosevelt Drive,** begun in the late 1930s during the administration of New York's colorful mayor Fiorello H. LaGuardia, was planned as a link in a projected "Circumferential Belt Parkway." It is built on landfill provided by the rubble of buildings destroyed during the World War II blitz on London and Bristol. Convoys of cargo ships returning from England during the war carried the broken masonry in their holds as ballast.

Return to East 51st Street and First Avenue.

8. On what is now the northwest corner of East 51st Street and First Avenue stood **James Beekman's mansion,** *Mount Pleasant,* from 1763 to 1874. During the American Revolution the house was used by the British for their military headquarters. Patriot Nathan Hale, captured on September 21, 1776, at the Dove Tavern (at the present site of Third Avenue and East 66th Street) was brought to the Beekman House, tried, and returned to the tavern where he was hanged as a spy. [*See* statue of Nathan Hale, page 70]. And it was here four years later that Major John André received his instructions to meet General Benedict Arnold and obtain the plans to the fort at West Point. Intercepted by patriots in Tarrytown, André, too, was hanged for the same offense. With the signing of the Treaty of Paris in 1783, the British Commandant, Sir Guy Carlton, was permitted to rent the mansion to carry out the plans for the British evacuation of the port of New York. A frequent visitor in the following years was newly elected President George Washington. The Beekman family continued to occupy the house until the cholera epidemic of 1854, and it was demolished 20 years later. Fortunately, a number of furnishings were saved and the reconstructed parlor, a bedroom, and three mantelpieces can be seen at the New-York Historical Society (Central Park West at West 77th Street).

The present building was erected in 1892 as **Primary School 35.** This yellow brick and brownstone structure, in a mostly Romanesque Revival style, once served as the United Nations International School, for the children of U.N. delegates. It now houses a nursery school and the Turtle Bay community center. An attempt to have the building designated a landmark failed, and its future in this real-estate-hungry area is in doubt. Go in and look at the original decorative sheet-tin ceilings and cast-iron support columns.

Across First Avenue, at No. 940, is **Pisacone Mid-Town Sea Food,** an old-style fish market which replaced a similar establishment that had been on the site since the building was built, ca. 1860. Look around inside; little has changed.

Near the corner of East 52nd Street is an equally old neighborhood store, **A. Fitz & Sons,** a butcher shop that has been there since 1867.

You have probably noticed that the east side of First Avenue, between 51st and 53rd streets, is virtually unchanged since the area was developed. The houses with straight window lintels were built in the 1860s, while those with the segmental-arc (curved) lintels date from the 1870s.

Turn east on East 52nd Street.

9. River House (Bottomly, Wagner & White, 1931), 435 East 52nd Street, enjoys one of the best panoramic views of the East River. A luxury cooperative apartment house, its facilities include tennis courts, a squash court, swimming pool, and ballroom, and at one time included a private dock for the convenience of visiting millionaires' yachts.

Return to First Avenue, go north one block, then west (left) on East 53rd Street.

● **10. Nos. 314 and 312 East 53rd Street** are surprising survivors from the days when the neighborhood was still semirural in character. The pair of wooden houses with their round-topped dormer windows and corbeled entrance hoods were built in 1866 and reflect the influence of the French Second Empire style, which became popular in this country after the Civil War. Only No. 312 has been designated a landmark. (No. 314's "wooden" slats are aluminum imitations.)

Return to First Avenue, turn left (north).

Cross First Avenue and take a short detour east on East 54th Street to **River Tower,** No. 420 (Schuman, Lichtenstein, Claman & Efron, 1981), on the right side. A 38-story "blockbuster" of an apartment house, it is set on an angle to the street, with an odd geometry, beginning with conventional horizontal bands of tan brick and glass and culminating in rows of pointed bay windows on the upper seven stories. And at street level, a Jean Dubuffet sculpture greets visitors at the entrance. In stark contrast is the **St. James's Tower,** No. 415 (Emery Roth & Sons, 1982), across the street. A solid vertical cube of dark purple brick with radial corners and flush windows, this condominium building emanates strength, if not innovation, and unlike its ostentatious neighbor, hides its massiveness behind the line of the street wall.

Return to First Avenue, and turn right (north) to East 55th Street.

On the northwest corner of East 55th Street is the Catholic Center Building (1973), which houses, among other offices of the archdiocese, Catholic Charities. While the building is not especially distinguished, the **Church of St. John the Evangelist** is worth a visit. The entrance façade has interesting low-relief sculpture work, and the sanctuary, which has seating on three sides, is dominated by a large carved mahogany reredos. The organ, to the left, is free standing. This is the church's fifth building and the second on the site, replacing an earlier structure of 1881. Its first location was on Fifth Avenue, and it was demolished to make way for St. Patrick's Cathedral in 1841.

Turn right (east) on East 57th Street to Sutton Place.

11. Sutton Place, named for late-19th-century land developer Effingham B. Sutton, was formerly called Avenue A (which now exists only between Houston and 14th streets). Lined with luxury apartment houses and elegant town

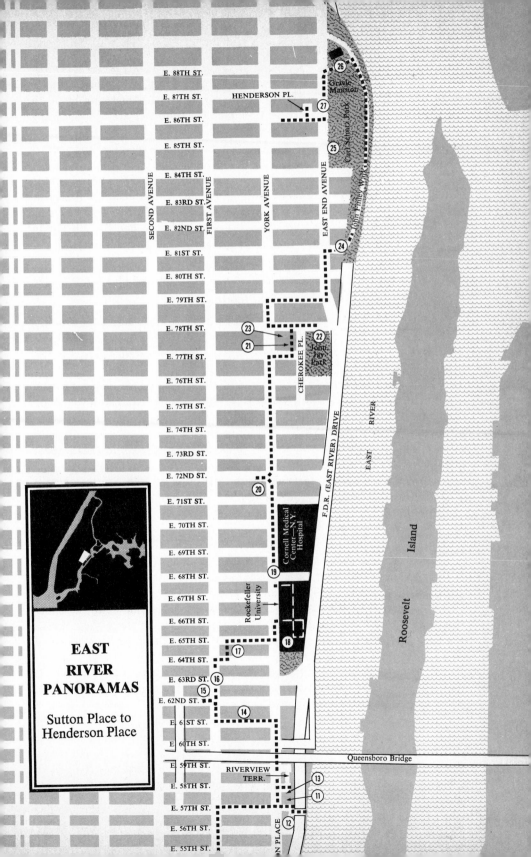

EAST RIVER PANORAMAS

Sutton Place to Henderson Place

houses, the street is another riverside bastion of the "upper crust," and continues north under the Queensboro Bridge approach, where it changes its name to York Avenue. Reminiscent of the Beekman Place district are the charming town houses along the short dead-ends on East 57th and 58th streets. No. 1 Sutton Place North is the residence of the Secretary General of the United Nations.

12. Walk ahead into little **East River Park** with its endearing bronze statue of the friendly wild boar and its tiny animal friends. The original, from ancient Greece, is in the Uffizi Gallery in Florence, Italy. Sculptor Pietro Tacca made two other copies—one stands in Florence's Straw Market, and the other is in Kansas City's Country Club Plaza. Years of children's caressing fingers have brightened the protruding parts.

Return to Sutton Place and turn right (north).

13. The row of town houses on the east side of Sutton Place is particularly charming, each with its own engaging features. **No. 19** has a carved Medusa's head in the keystone, while in a niche on the second floor of **No. 21**, St. Francis holds a little bird in his hands.

At the end of the delightful East 58th Street cul-de-sac called "Sutton Square," with its cozy minipark below, is another of New York City's seemingly endless source of surprises—secluded **Riverview Terrace,** one of the city's few remaining private streets. With its protective fence and entrance gate with "amputated" goats, and fronted by a lush sunken garden, the six fortunate town houses are quite removed from the bustle of city life. The shady little lane paved with Belgian blocks extends north only to East 59th Street, where a stockade fence keeps out the "injuns."

Continue north on Sutton Place (now York Avenue), and turn west (left) on East 61st Street.

Immediately to the right, on the north side, is **425 East 61st Street** (Liebman, Liebman & Associates, 1975), an office tower of unusual design. This block-through structure is "framed" between greenish-gray side walls, with the upper two floors successively cantilevered out (and commanding the highest rents). The side walls conceal the ventilation shafts for the floors and underground garage.

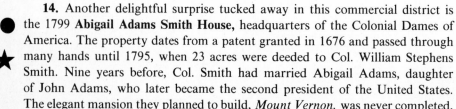

14. Another delightful surprise tucked away in this commercial district is the 1799 **Abigail Adams Smith House,** headquarters of the Colonial Dames of America. The property dates from a patent granted in 1676 and passed through many hands until 1795, when 23 acres were deeded to Col. William Stephens Smith. Nine years before, Col. Smith had married Abigail Adams, daughter of John Adams, who later became the second president of the United States. The elegant mansion they planned to build, *Mount Vernon,* was never completed, and they lived instead in the present stone building, which was then a stable and carriage house.

After remaining only a few short years the Smiths departed, and the Federal-style house was sold to William T. Robinson, who enlarged it and completed the structure in 1799 (the date can be seen in the gable on the south façade). Passing into new ownership, it was converted into a hotel, which boasted having "excellent facilities for fishing, shooting, and salt water bathing" (the East River was then only about 50 feet from the door). According to an advertisement of the time, the hotel offered "every day in season soup made from the fine green turtles fattening in a crawl made for that purpose in the East River."

In 1823 the building became "an academy for young ladies and gentlemen," but three years later suffered a disastrous fire. Rebuilt as the Mount Vernon Hotel, and named for the former Col. Smith's ill-starred mansion, it served a distinguished clientele for a number of years. The house subsequently came into the hands of the Jeremiah Towle family, who retained it until 1905, when the property was sold to the Standard Gas Light Company.

The lovely old house now began to suffer from the encroachment of urban blight as the once-fashionable rural neighborhood declined into a dismal commercial backwater. Three enormous, ugly gas tanks were erected on the property, blocking the formerly uninterrupted view of the river. And the proud house, now subdivided into cheap apartments, suffered the additional indignity during World War I of becoming a Salvation Army soup kitchen. But in 1919 the house was rescued by Miss Jane Teller, president of the Society of American Antiquarians, who rented it from the Gas Company and painstakingly restored it, furnishing it with her collection of early American furniture. In 1924, the Colonial Dames of America, the nation's first patriotic women's organization, purchased the Abigail Adams Smith House for their headquarters and made it a museum.

Although the beautiful and extensive collection of antiques in the restored rooms is not original with the house, it is quite authentic to the periods of its occupancy, and represents virtually every style from the late 18th through the mid-19th centuries. Time should be allowed for a leisurely visit to the historic house and charming garden. (Open weekdays, except legal holidays, from 10 A.M. to 4 P.M. Admission $2.00, $1.00 for students and senior citizens.)

The adjoining building, No. 417 East 61st Street, has been remodeled in a matching Federal style and serves as the office, with an auditorium and exhibit rooms, and facilities for group orientation lectures.

Continue west to First Avenue; turn north to East 62nd Street, then west about 50 feet.

15. On the north side of East 62nd Street, just west of First Avenue, is **No. 367.** Although extensively remodeled through the years, it does give some idea of the typical type of residence that lined the local streets in the 1870s. Built originally as a one-family house, it was later converted to multifamily use.

16. First Avenue in the East 60s and 70s, once quietly residential and later a decaying commercial thoroughfare, has since the early 1960s enjoyed a renaissance as New York's "swingles" district. With upbeat bars and restaurants attracting the young (and not-so-young) "unattached" from all over town, the avenue "swings" every night, reaching a crescendo by Saturday evening, as lines form in front of the more popular spots. The rebirth of First Avenue has also encouraged an influx of expensive restaurants, boutiques, antique shops, plant stores, and exotic food emporiums. Among the more flamboyant gathering places are Friday's, on the northeast corner of East 63rd Street, and Maxwell's Plum, on the northwest corner of 64th Street.

17. Between East 64th and 65th streets, on the east side of First Avenue, are the **City & Suburban Homes,** designed by architect Ernest Flagg in 1915 as a low-cost multiple-dwelling complex. One of two mammoth (for the time) housing developments on the Upper East Side, these multifamily units were planned to have as much light and air as possible in the days before air conditioning. Walk through the alley between the buildings to East 65th Street, noting how the architect used the areaways both economically and practically for the comfort of the tenants and the services for the buildings.

Turn right on East 65th Street to York Avenue.

The ornate Third Avenue Railway car barn between 65th and 66th streets was erected some time before 1873, then rebuilt in 1896 in Victorian style from plans by architect Henry J. Hardenbergh. Today no trace remains of the elaborate structure, its trolleys, nor the Third Avenue El. (Photograph by Berenice Abbott for Federal Art Project "Changing New York." Museum of the City of New York)

18. Rockefeller University, a research center for medical and related sciences, was founded by John D. Rockefeller in 1901 on the site of the former Schermerhorn estate. The shady campus is dominated by the Classic-style **Founders' Hall,** opened as a laboratory in 1903. Formerly known as the Rockefeller Institute for Medical Research, the name was changed in 1965, and in 1974 the institution was designated a National Historic Landmark by the National Park Service.

Ask permission of the guard at the 66th Street main entrance, and walk up the tree-lined hill. To the left, the incongruous hemisphere is the **Caspary Auditorium,** built in 1957 by the firm of Harrison & Abramovitz. Flanking Founders' Hall is the Hospital Building and Flexner Hall. Turn right and walk to the ramp overlooking the peaceful **Theodore H. Berlin Memorial Garden.** Descend the spiral staircase to the garden and walk north along the beautifully landscaped path, past the main entrance walk, exiting at the gate just beyond 67th Street.

Continue north on York Avenue.

19. York Avenue from Rockefeller University to East 72nd Street is devoted mainly to medical institutions:

Facing the University between East 66th and 67th streets is the "glassy" **Nurses' Residence of New York Hospital–Cornell Medical Center** (Harrison & Abramovitz, 1965).

Between East 67th and 68th streets is the **James Ewing Memorial Building of the Memorial Sloan-Kettering Cancer Center** (Skidmore, Owings & Merrill, 1950); and around the corner at 444 East 68th Street, the main building of the **Memorial Sloan-Kettering Center** (James Gamble Rogers, Inc., 1935).

For the next two blocks, the cityscape is overwhelmed by the massive complex of **New York Hospital–Cornell Medical Center,** designed in 1933 by the firm of Coolidge, Shepley, Bulfinch & Abbott, of Boston. This powerful group of buildings displays a neo-Gothic motif in its pointed-arch windows that rise to the full height of the walls. The medical center also shelters the **city's oldest hospital.** In 1769, Dr. Samuel Bard of King's College (now Columbia University) pleaded to King George III for "an hospital for the sick poor of the Colony which would also serve as a medical training school." Two years later the monarch granted its charter.

Between East 69th and East 70th streets, walk into the arcade and see the **carved lions' heads** brought from the former Medical College buildings at 477 First Avenue, and attached to the wall in 1969.

At the northwest corner of East 70th Street stands the towering **Lawrence G. Payson House** (Frederick G. Frost, Jr. & Associates, 1966), a residence of the Medical Center; and at 515 East 71st Street, around the corner, **the Institute for Muscle Disease** (Skidmore, Owings & Merrill, 1961).

Between 71st and 72nd streets on the east side is **Sotheby's** new auction gallery. Once the Eastman Kodak warehouse, the building was given an $8 million face-lift in 1980, and it now replaces the gallery's former Madison Avenue facility.

20. On the south side of East 72nd Street, just west of York Avenue, is the bold, multicolumned **former Murry and Leonie Guggenheim Children's Dental Clinic,** built in 1930. The Clinic served school children until 1967; one year later it was donated to the Society of the New York Hospital and is now used as a kidney dialysis center. Above, on the capitals, are carved animals, and below, griffins; the lantern on the entrance gate is supported by a bronze sculpture group of animal figures. The dramatic façade can best be appreciated from the north side of the street.

Look east across York Avenue for a reminder of the commercial past of the neighborhood in the **former Purepac Pharmaceuticals Company complex,** a rambling hodgepodge of castellated Romanesque Revival–style buildings on the north side of East 72nd Street. The firm, whose name is clearly visible on the buildings, moved its operations long ago to Elizabeth, New Jersey.

Just north of East 72nd Street on the east side of York Avenue are a pair of five-story ca. 1870 buildings with **"Alfredos Casinos"** emblazoned in the cornices of Nos. 1364–66. They were probably joined at street level as a dining saloon, or perhaps as a less-elegant tavern.

Continue north on York Avenue to East 77th Street, and turn right one block to Cherokee Place.

21. The Cherokee Apartments is an enormous multifamily project designed by Henry Atterbury Smith, and is particularly interesting. Walk into one of the Guastavino tile vaulted tunnels leading to a central courtyard. Notice the separate entranceways grouped around the court, each with a semienclosed stairway leading six flights to the top. A central alley for building service splits the complex in half; side deliveryways slope down to the basement, with deep grooves in the pavement to keep horses from slipping. The exterior wrought-iron French balconies add a touch of elegance, as do the Spanish-style overhanging cornices and bronze lamp standards. The large windows are all triple-hung, making each apartment light and cheerful. The entire design is living-oriented— an incredible concept for the year 1900!

22. John Jay Park, named for the nation's first chief justice, is the most popular recreational spot in the neighborhood. The swimming pool, picnic area, and athletic facilities on a site overlooking the river make this one of the most heavily used parks in the city.

Return to York Avenue on East 78th Street.

23. Observe the old carved stone street sign on the wall of Public School 158, hearkening back to the days when this was still **Avenue A.** Note, too, the boot-scrapers on the 78th Street entrance. This is a special school for the language and hearing impaired.

Across York Avenue, at No. 1465, is the **Webster Branch of the New York Public Library.** Built in 1905, it resembles a modest Italian Renaissance villa. The library until recently boasted an enormous Czech collection, as the neighborhood between East 71st and East 75th streets, east of Second Avenue, was known as **"Little Bohemia."** A dwindling number of Czechs and Slovaks still live in the area, and their restaurants are popular tourist attractions.

Look across the avenue at the three houses on the northwest corner of East 78th Street (Nos. 1477–81 York Avenue), and notice the **sunburst designs** in the cornice pediments. This typical Victorian motif also appears on the adjoining houses around the corner on 78th Street.

Crossing York Avenue, and continuing a few steps farther west on East 78th Street, one is astonished by a pair of beautifully preserved survivors— two aging wooden buildings, numbered **450a and 450b.** Once part of a row of five similar houses, they date from the 1850s when the area was completely rural. According to local legend, they were occupied by workers from an adjacent duck farm, and were not converted into stores until after the turn of the century.

On the north side of East 78th Street, No. 425, **The Multi-Level Apartments** (William Gleckman, 1972) is a reconversion to end them all! Formerly a remodeled tenement, it was gutted and rebuilt with broad balconies (that double as fire escapes), an interesting lobby and entranceway, and apartments that are either true duplexes or "multi-level" with raised bedrooms or lowered living rooms. The whole building has been stuccoed over, giving it a warm, Mediterranean look. A precursor of many such dramatic reconversions throughout the city, it received the 1975 annual award for "excellence in modernization of a residential building" from the Building Owners & Managers Association.

Return to York Avenue and walk north to East 79th Street. Turn right to East End Avenue.

Earlier in the tour we passed the housing complex designed by architect Ernest Flagg in 1915 for City & Suburban Homes Company, between 64th and 65th streets. This block of "model tenements" (78th to 79th streets) was also designed by Flagg for the same **City & Suburban Homes,** but 15 years earlier, in 1900. Not nearly as attractive as Henry Atterbury Smith's Cherokee Apartments, the group does represent a historically significant housing development. The stone plaque on No. 542 East 79th Street recognizes the contribution of one of the founders of the company, William Bayard Cutting. The little street on the east side, now an FDR Drive service road, was formerly named Madame Curie Avenue.

East End Avenue developed as an apartment-house row for the affluent at about the same time as Sutton Place, and looks rather similar. Before the street became fashionable in the 1920s, it was named simply Avenue B.

No. 2 East End Avenue, a former electrical underwriters' factory building, was converted in 1979 to apartments under the provisions of the J-51 program, which provides for both property-tax abatements and the forgiveness of property taxes to encourage the renovation of run-down buildings.

At East 81st Street, turn right and enter the promenade, called John Finley Walk.

A Currier & Ives lithograph, 1862, showing Blackwell's (now Roosevelt) Island and the East River from 86th Street. (Museum of the City of New York)

The 18th-century Blackwell farmhouse on Roosevelt Island before its restoration by architect Giorgio Cavaglieri as part of the new development project for the island. (New York City Landmarks Preservation Commission)

24. This splendid promenade built over the East River Drive is one of the great pedestrian walkways of the city. It is named most appropriately for **John Huston Finley** (1863–1940), past president of the City College of New York, state commissioner of education, and editor-in-chief of the *New York Times.* He was, in addition, a *great pedestrian,* who believed that "a good walk clears the mind and stimulates thinking." Finley walked to work daily until past the age of 70, and frequently hiked the 32 miles around Manhattan Island, declaring that he enjoyed the sights of the crowded city as much as the scenery of the open country.

Roosevelt Island, directly opposite, was for many years called Welfare Island. Prior to that, it was Blackwell's Island, and in Dutch Colonial times, Varcken Eylandt (Hog Island). Two miles in length by no more than 750 feet wide, it was first acquired by Dutch Governor Van Twiller and used for pasturage for hogs. Some years later it was purchased by Captain John Manning, a British officer who surrendered New York back to the Dutch in 1673. It is said that he retired here in disgrace after having had his sword broken over his head for not resisting the invasion with more enthusiasm. Robert Blackwell took title to the island in 1686 after marrying Manning's stepdaughter, and lived

Among the many municipal institutions on Blackwell's Island was the Hospital for Comsumptives. Doctors, nurses, and patients pose for Percy C. Byron's camera on a summer afternoon in 1903. (The Byron Collection. Museum of the City of New York)

The ferry Welfare *making its regular three-minute crossing between East 78th Street and Welfare Island, 1948. The elimination of this convenient service shortly thereafter virtually isolated the island for many years.* (*Gibbs Marine Photos*)

there until his death in 1717. The old Blackwell House has been restored as part of the Roosevelt Island Development. In the 19th and early 20th centuries, as Blackwell's Island, it was a city property used for a hospital, penitentiary, lunatic asylum, and "poor house." The notoriety of these institutions was so widespread that an investigation was conducted in 1921, with the result that the prison was moved to Riker's Island and the name changed to Welfare Island. Two city hospitals (Goldwater and Bird S. Coler) are still in service, and seven landmark structures, the octagonal Victorian tower of the old lunatic asylum, the Blackwell House, City Hospital, the Strecker Laboratory, the Chapel of the Good Shepherd, the Lighthouse, and the Smallpox Hospital, are preserved.

The new Roosevelt Island Development is a city within a city, combining low-, middle-, and high-income housing in a dense massing of multistory apartment buildings, with 5,000 families living on the island. Connection to the city proper is by an aerial tramway which carries commuters in small cabins suspended from an overhead cable—much like a ski lift—to a terminal at Second Avenue and East 60th Street, and by a vehicular lift bridge from Ravenswood in Queens. Cars are not permitted to drive on the island and must be parked in a central garage near the bridge, where mini-buses pick up passengers and make frequent trips on a fixed route around Roosevelt Island. A subway station near the Queensboro Bridge will provide access to Manhattan and Queens when the new 63rd Street tunnel is put into operation.

Follow Finley Walk to Carl Schurz Park.

25. Carl Schurz Park, dramatically situated on rocky bluffs overlooking a bend in the East River, offers unsurpassed views of the Triborough and Hell Gate bridges, Ward's and Randall's islands, Astoria in Queens, plus an exciting parade of ships sailing close by in the river's deep-water channel. Just off 96th Street is treacherous Mill Rock.

The site during the Dutch Colonial period was known as Hoek van Hoorn ("Hoorn's Hook"), named for the Hanseatic town on the Zuyder Zee. Just before the American Revolution, Jacob Walton built himself a house on the promontory, but his tenancy was short-lived, as the Continental army set up a battery of nine guns and took over the house as part of the fortifications. Known as Thompson's Battery, it was knocked out of action by a cannonade from British men-of-war seeking to isolate the island of Manhattan as the war began in earnest in 1776. The Americans fled and the site became a British Army outpost. In more peaceful times it became East End Park, and was renamed in honor of Schurz in 1911.

The park has a wide range of recreational facilities distributed about the wooded and hilly terrain, and provides a verdant backdrop to New York City's most famous residence, Gracie Mansion.

Carl Schurz (1829–1906) is considered the most notable German immigrant of the 19th century. Fleeing the unsuccessful Revolution of 1848, he came to America, learned the language in an astonishingly brief time, and involved himself in politics. Winning the confidence and respect of President Abraham Lincoln, he was appointed minister to Spain and, soon thereafter, a major general in the Union Army. He was also responsible for helping to shape the new liberal Republican party. After the war he was elected senator from Missouri, and in 1877 was named secretary of the interior in the Hayes administration. Returning to New York he assumed the editorship of the *New York Evening Post* and *Harper's Weekly.* Schurz settled in the nearby German community of Yorkville, where he remained until his death.

Continue following the promenade, and pause for a few moments at the flagpole marking **the site of Hoorn's Hook.** The East River is usually rather turbulent at this point, as tidal currents flowing up from New York Bay meet those from Long Island Sound, causing eddies and rifts that are hazardous to small boats. The river makes an S-turn as it passes under the **Triborough** (suspension) Bridge (O. H. Ammann and Aymar Embury II, 1936) and the lovely arch of the **Hell Gate Bridge** (Gustav Lindenthal, engineer, and Henry Hornbostel, architect, 1917). Both bridges connect Queens with Ward's Island and the Bronx. Hell Gate, once a graveyard of ships, has been cleared of most of its rock outcroppings by the Army Corps of Engineers. It is the supposed site of a sunken British treasure ship that was wrecked just before the Revolutionary War, and is still the object of occasional diving expeditions.

Hell Gate was also the site of the **General Slocum Disaster,** the second worst inland water catastrophe in American history. On June 15, 1904, the paddlewheel steamer *General Slocum* was sailing up the East River on a charter trip with over 1,300 passengers—mostly women and children—on a Sunday School picnic sponsored by the St. Mark's Evangelical Lutheran Church on East 6th Street. Just as it was passing opposite this point, fire broke out. Realizing that the fire was out of control, and seeing no favorable spot to beach the ship in the Hell Gate passage, the captain ordered full speed ahead with the hope of beaching his burning vessel on the Bronx shore. Lifesaving equipment proved inadequate, and the wind-fanned flames spread rapidly through the ship. In the ensuing panic, hundreds fell or jumped overboard to their deaths. By the time the *General Slocum* finally beached on North Brother Island, just off the Bronx, 1,021 lives were lost. A memorial service for the victims is conducted every year at the Trinity Lutheran Church of Middle Village, Queens, and a wreath-laying ceremony is held at the Slocum Monument in nearby Lutheran Cemetery. The Lower East Side German community was so stricken by the calamity that many moved out, settling uptown in the adjoining Yorkville neighborhood.

Follow the promenade to its end at the FDR Drive, and on the right is the **Fireboat House Environmental Center.** Until recently it was one of 22 fireboat stations that used to guard the harbor; now there are only four. The building and pier have been converted to a solar energy demonstration and education center, although not without considerable difficulty. A tug with barges in tow crashed into the pier, almost destroying it, and later a fire consumed most of the house. The former fireboat house is equipped with passive and active solar collectors, and classes are held in solar energy use; there is also a demonstration tank of harbor marine life. The facility is used by elementary-school science classes, as well as by the sponsoring Neighborhood Committee for the Asphalt Green Project, which conducts classes and seminars in solar energy, seamanship, fishing, the lore of the sea, and art. It also sponsors a Sea Scout group.

Across the FDR Drive, and accessible later in the tour, is the **Asphalt Green Sports and Arts Center,** formerly the **Municipal Asphalt Plant of the City of New York** (erected 1941–44). Architects Kahn & Jacobs, influenced by LeCorbusier, were the first in the country to make successful use of the parabolic arch form in reinforced concrete. An amazing example of form following function (that of concealing the asphalt-mixing machinery), the arresting structure was in use until 1968 for making of asphalt to pave the city's streets. In 1981 it was taken over by the Asphalt Green Project to be recycled as a community sports and arts center, with both indoor and outdoor recreational facilities.

Go back about 100 feet on the promenade and climb the stairs to the right; follow the path to Gracie Mansion.

26. Gracie Mansion. Built as a country manor house in 1799 by wealthy merchant Archibald Gracie, it is one of the best preserved and most striking examples of the Federal style, and is a place of gracious living. The Gracies entertained many famous guests, including Louis Philippe, later King of France; President John Quincy Adams; the Marquis de Lafayette; Alexander Hamilton; James Fenimore Cooper; Washington Irving; and John Jacob Astor.

In 1887 Gracie Mansion was purchased by the city. It was restored by the Parks Department in 1927 with early 19th-century antiques. Four years earlier, it had become the Museum of the City of New York, under the directorship of New York historian Henry Collins Brown. When the museum's new building was opened on Fifth Avenue and 103rd Street in 1932, the mansion lay dormant for a few years until selected by Mayor Fiorello H. LaGuardia to be the official mayor's residence. It now holds the distinction of being the only original county seat in Manhattan still occupied as a home. A ballroom and reception wing were added in 1966 in perfect harmony with the architectural style.

Unfortunately it is not possible to enjoy the broad river views from the colonnaded front porch, nor is the public permitted to study the exquisite entrance door with its fanlight and leaded-glass sidelights, so characteristic of the Federal style, nor wander about the private garden—unless, that is, one receives a special invitation from "hizzoner" the Mayor.

Exit from the park at East 87th Street.

(If you wish to visit the Asphalt Green Sports and Arts Center, turn right [north] on East End Avenue to 90th Street.)

27. Occupying less than a half acre between East 87th and 86th streets is the charming **Henderson Place Historic District,** a group of 24 homogeneously designed town houses. Begun in 1881 from plans by Hugo Lamb and Charles A. Rich, the quaint little houses are built in what is described as the Queen Anne style.

Originally farmland, the property was acquired at the turn of the 18th century by Archibald Gracie and John Jacob Astor (who also had an estate nearby). After some years it passed into the hands of John C. Henderson, a fur importer and hat manufacturer, who decided to expand into the real-estate business and build homes for "persons of moderate means."

Until the 1830s, the section had been part of the remote hamlet of **Yorkville,** surrounded by large country estates. With the arrival in 1834 of the New York

East 86th Street Park (now Carl Schurz Park) ca. 1890. Barren of trees, Gracie Mansion stands out prominently at the far end. (Photograph by Jacob A. Riis. The Jacob A. Riis Collection. Museum of the City of New York)

& Harlem Railroad, and a stagecoach line a year later, rapid development took place. Since the 1790s the neighborhood has been predominantly German, and has been swelled by periodic waves of immigration—the largest group moving up just after 1900 from the Tompkins Square area downtown. It has also been popular with immigrants from Austria, Hungary, and Czechoslovakia, and much evidence still survives throughout Yorkville of this intermingling of nationalities.

A walk around the Historic District takes but a few minutes.

Observe how the design of the individual houses combines to create a uniform effect. A turret marks the corner of each block; roof gables, pediments, parapets, chimneys, and dormer windows are arranged symmetrically; doorways, stoops, and basement entrances are paired under broad arches. The building walls are of smooth red brick, joined by black mortar, rising to meet sloping gray slate roofs. Note, too, the typical bay windows and the double-hung sash, in which the lower is a solid pane, while the upper is divided into small squares. In its *Designation Report* for the Henderson Place Historic District, the Landmarks Commission describes the dwellings as having been "designed with the characteristics of the Elizabethan manor house combined with Flemish classic detail in a style developed in England between the years 1870 and 1910, principally by

A view of Gracie Mansion seen only by invited guests. The north side porch of this 1799 manor house, now the mayor's residence, enjoys a splendid East River panorama. (*Museum of the City of New York*)

Richard Norman Shaw." Although having little to do with Queen Anne who reigned from 1702 to 1714, Shaw developed the design to create a "comfortable and romantic domestic style." The so-called Queen Anne style achieved its greatest popularity here in the 1880s and '90s. Walk around the corner of 86th Street to lovely **Henderson Place.**

Unfortunately, the scale of little Henderson Place is severely damaged by the towering apartment house on the west side, for whose construction eight of these picturesque townhouses were sacrificed. As a final indignity, the apartment house took the Henderson name for itself.

End of tour.

A walk west along 86th Street, the *Hauptstrasse* of Yorkville, is quite interesting. The 86th Street crosstown bus (M-18), at the northwest corner of York Avenue, one block west, connects with the IRT Lexington Avenue subway at Lexington Avenue, with the IND subway at Central Park West, and at Broadway with the IRT Broadway-Seventh Avenue subway.

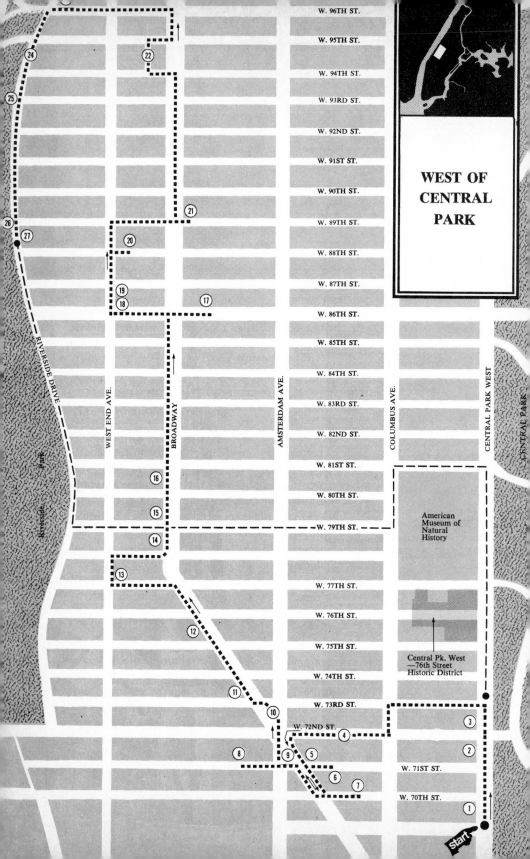

14. West of Central Park

[*IND AA Line to 72nd Street; IRT Broadway-Seventh Avenue line to 72nd Street; 72nd Street crosstown (M-30) bus to West 72nd Street and Central Park West*]

The tour begins at Central Park West and West 70th Street.

Central Park, 59th Street to 110thStreet, Fifth Avenue to Central Park West, is a tribute to the foresight of our early city fathers, and particularly to poet William Cullen Bryant, who pleaded the cause of a public park and recreation area close to the inner city. The land was acquired by the city in 1856, and a contest announced for the best plan of development. The winning entry, entitled "Greensward," was submitted by landscape architects Frederick Law Olmsted and Calvert Vaux, who spent the next 20 years supervising the creation of one of the most successful landscaped areas anywhere.

This charming piece of picturesque "country" includes several lakes, forest land, rocky hills, open meadows, secluded glens, a bird sanctuary, footpaths, bridle paths, extensive recreational facilities, an excellent zoo, and an array of artistic public sculpture.* Central Park is listed in the National Register of Historic Places and has been designated a Scenic Landmark by the New York City Landmarks Preservation Commission.

1. The Spanish & Portuguese Synagogue, Congregation Shearith Israel at the southwest corner of West 70th Street, is the oldest Jewish congregation in the United States. Its first house of worship was erected in 1730 by the descendants of a group of 23 men, women, and children who arrived in Nieuw Amsterdam in 1654—refugees from the Inquisition in Brazil. After three successive moves uptown, this Classic Revival building was built in 1897 from plans by

---

* Since Central Park is not included in this tour, detailed information, including a map and list of park activities, can be obtained from two organizations that are dedicated to preserving and protecting it: The Central Park Conservancy, 850 Fifth Ave., New York, N.Y. 10021, and The Greensward Foundation, Lenox Hill, P.O. Box 610, New York, N.Y. 10021.

Central Park West (then called Eighth Avenue) in 1895, looking north toward the Hotel Majestic on 71st Street and the Hotel San Remo two blocks farther. The hotels have long since been replaced by luxury apartment houses which retain the old names. (Museum of the City of New York)

Brunner & Tryon. The interior is very impressive, and can be visited Sunday mornings or during services on Friday evenings or Saturday mornings. The auditorium is arranged according to Sephardic tradition with the benches facing the centrally placed reading desk. The Little Synagogue, a small room in the rear of the building, is an accurate reconstruction of the Mill Street temple of 1730, with many of the original artifacts as well as some from subsequent buildings. Two huge millstones in the hall are from the old Dutch mill, which stood at the corner of Mill Lane and Mill Street (now South William Street), where services were conducted before the construction of the first synagogue. The congregation maintains the three Spanish & Portuguese cemeteries described on other tours [see Lower East Side, Supplementary Tour A; Greenwich Village, 33; and Ladies' Mile, 16]. The Synagogue still follows the Sephardic tradition handed down from the Jews of Spain and Portugal, and the ritual and Hebrew pronunciation differ somewhat from that of the Ashkenazic Jews, although Sephardic Hebrew is now the official language of Israel.

2. **The Majestic Apartments,** 115 Central Park West, was built in 1930 from plans by Jacques Delamarre of the architectural firm of Irwin S. Chanin, and is a fine example of the Art Deco style that became the rage in the late 1920s and '30s. The avant-garde brickwork is particularly attractive, as are the pair of roof towers. One of four twin-tower apartment houses that enliven

the cityscape of Central Park West, the Majestic is named for a French Renaissance–style hotel that once occupied the site. (One of the towers hides unsightly water tanks.) The Majestic was originally planned as a 53-story apartment hotel, but the newly enacted multiple-dwelling law, with its severe height restrictions, limited the number of stories to three times the width.

3. The Dakota, on the northwest corner of West 72nd Street, is the West Side's most prestigious address, and has been since it was completed in 1884. Designed by famed architect Henry Janeway Hardenbergh (Plaza Hotel, Con Edison Building, Hotel Martinique, Art Students' League Building, etc.) in a German Renaissance style, its picturesque setting facing Central Park has been the subject of many prints and photographs. The Dakota was the city's first luxury apartment house. Built of yellow brick with brownstone and terra-cotta trim, this massive eight-story edifice is considered one of the most notable buildings of its kind in the country. True to the architect's conception of a château, it is surrounded by a "moat," with access to the interior through a dramatic two-story segmental arch guarded by a sentry box. The entranceways to the building are in the four corners of the spacious courtyard, formerly a carriageway. On the south façade of the building are two end pavilions with semicircular oriel windows that extend from the ground floor to the roof. The fanciful roof,

The Dakota forms a backdrop for the throngs of skaters on Central Park Lake, ca. 1890. (New-York Historical Society)

with huge gables at each corner and in the center, is perforated with symmetrical dormer windows. The Dakota is indeed a fortress, as the load-bearing walls are several feet thick and each floor is separated by layers of thick concrete. When completed, it had extensive facilities for an army of servants and boasted a private restaurant for the exclusive tenants. The eight hydraulic elevators, although modernized, are still in use and are operated from a huge pump room in the basement. The cast-iron fence that surrounds the building was made by the Hecla Iron works in Brooklyn, in 1884.

The Dakota was built by Edward S. Clark, heir to the vast Singer Sewing Machine empire and manufacturer of "Clark's O. N. T. Thread." Clark's friends ridiculed the idea of his constructing a luxury house so far uptown and remarked that "it might just as well be in Dakota," which was then Indian territory. The name stuck, but "Clark's Folly" proved to be a sound investment. The Dakota, with its atmosphere of brooding hauteur, was the setting for the film *Rosemary's Baby,* and for the historical science-fiction novel *Time and Again,* by Jack Finney. It was also the site of the tragic murder of former Beatle John Lennon, on December 8, 1980.

Clark's Dakota added great impetus to the growth of the neighborhood. Coinciding with its completion, the city changed the name of Eighth Avenue

In splendid isolation, the Dakota rises above Central Park West and 72nd Street, ca. 1890. Completed in 1884 from plans by Henry J. Hardenbergh, the huge apartment building was the subject of jibes for being "so far out of town . . . it might just as well be in the Dakotas!" (And the name stuck!) (Museum of the City of New York)

above 59th Street to Central Park West. Until that time the Eighth Avenue horsecar line and a stagecoach on the Bloomingdale Road (now Broadway) provided the only "rapid" transit, but in 1879 the Ninth Avenue El was pushed north on what is now Columbus Avenue, as far as 81st Street, affording quick access from downtown. However, it was not until the late 1880s that the great building boom began on the West Side.

Walk back to Central Park West, turn left to West 73rd Street, and turn left again.

Clark and Hardenbergh combined their talents in another project, the development of rental row houses on West 73rd Street. The street, the south edge of the **Central Park West–West 73rd–74th Street Historic District,** is enlivened by these lovely polychrome beauties which are such a change from the unremitting rows of brownstones that lined the city's streets in the 1870s and '80s. Note **Nos. 15A–19** and **41–65** (1882–85). Alas, the symmetry is broken by the intrusion of a hotel in midblock. At the northwest corner of Columbus Avenue, **Nos. 101** and **103** (apartment houses) are also the work of Hardenbergh (1879).

Turn south to 72nd Street, then west.

4. Until the late 1940s **West 72nd Street** was one of the better addresses on the West Side. Some vestiges of former elegance can be seen in the building that was formerly the Hotel Margrave (**No. 112**), built in the typical Classic Revival style of architecture so favored during the so-called Eclectic Period at the turn of the century. **Nos. 129, 137, 139,** and **141** were elegant town houses, and **No. 166,** with its ornate projecting cornice, was once an opulent apartment house. No. 174 was also a stately residence until the remodelers arrived.

Turn south on Broadway to West 71st Street.

5. No. 171 West 71st Street, **the Dorilton,** still maintains some pretense of luxury. Built in 1900 from designs by Janes & Leo, it is a grandiose French Beaux Arts–style structure. The original copper sheathing that adorned the roof has been replaced by shingles. Note the pair of sculptured figures on the Broadway façade, the handsome iron gateway on the 71st Street side, the high supporting arch, as well as the very ornate lobby.

6. Farther down West 71st Street is the neo-Gothic-style **Church of the Blessed Sacrament** (Gustave Steinback, 1917). It is more noteworthy for its interior than for its somewhat disproportionately styled exterior. Note how the cleverly designed vaulted ceilings give the nave an impression of great height.

Return to Broadway and turn south to West 70th Street.

7. The **former Knights of Pythias Temple,** 135 West 70th Street, recently a branch of the Borough of Manhattan Community College and now reconverted

The Boulevard, now Broadway, looking north from 70th Street toward Sherman Square in 1907, showing some of the modes of transportation in use at the time. Somewhat blurred in the background is the newly completed Ansonia Hotel. To the right, the arched entrance of the Dorilton is clearly visible. (Photograph by Byron. The Byron Collection. Museum of the City of New York)

and appropriately named Alexandria Condominium, was erected in 1926. Unfortunately, the developer stripped away most of the Egyptian-style adornments. Architect Thomas W. Lamb drew on ancient Egyptian motifs for the styling of this fraternal organization's Grand Lodge. The polychrome designs, seated Pharaohs, ornate columns, and upper "temple" are straight out of Karnak! An Egyptian Revival style in architecture achieved brief popularity after the discovery in 1922 of the tomb of King Tutankhamen in Thebes.

Returning to Broadway, note the luxury apartment house at the southeast corner, No. 154. It began its life in elegance, ca. 1900, deteriorated through the years, and has now come full circle reflecting the changes that have taken place in the area.

Cross to the west side of Broadway and turn west (left) into West 71st Street.

8. Christ Church, designed in Romanesque Revival style by Charles C. Haight, was completed in 1890. Built of orange brick with terra-cotta trim, the Episcopal church is laid out in the form of a Greek cross parallel to the street, rather than perpendicular to it, since there was no obstructing corner building on Broadway when the church was erected. Architect Haight is best known for his building plans for the General Theological Seminary [*see* Old Chelsea, 18].

The trio of adjacent town houses (**Nos. 215–219**) were built in 1891 in the

Italianate style. Note how these brownstones are deceivingly painted to resemble marble.

9. At the intersection of Broadway and West 72nd Street, the **IRT Subway Entrance** on the center "island" (Heins & LaFarge, 1904) is one of the last of such structures remaining in the city. Technically called "control houses," because subway riders were under the control of the transit system once they entered, they date from the original subway line built in 1904, when many touches of elegance were included in our first underground railroad. The line's route began at City Hall, ran north to 42nd Street, crosstown to Times Square, then north on Broadway to 145th Street.

The intersection is divided into **Sherman Square** to the south of West 72nd Street, and **Verdi Square** to the north.

At the beginning of the 19th century this busy confluence of major thoroughfares was the sleepy **hamlet of Harsenville,** named for farmer Jacob Harsen, whose house stood approximately at the present intersection. When the Bloomingdale Road was opened in 1816 from the lower city to the Harlem River, the area began to lose its bucolic flavor. Toward the end of the century, the Bloomingdale Road north of 59th Street was renamed the Boulevard. Moses

Backyard of the Jacob Harsen homestead at the corner of Tenth Avenue (now Amsterdam Avenue) and 70th Street, ca. 1888. The present intersection of Broadway and 72nd Street was the site of the hamlet of Harsenville during the 18th century. The house was built in 1701 for the Dyckman family, and survived until 1893. (New-York Historical Society)

King, in his *Handbook of New York City,* 1893 edition, described the Boulevard as "two capital roadways, separated by a central strip of lawns, trees, and flowers. When finished it will be one of the most beautiful driveways in the world, traversing as it does, the remarkably picturesque region between Central Park and the Hudson River, much of the way over high ground, commanding beautiful views." The Boulevard was joined officially to Broadway early in this century, making it Manhattan's longest traffic artery.

10. Verdi Square, named for the great Italian composer, provides a small patch of green along busy Broadway. The benches are usually filled with older adults from the neighborhood who meet to gossip, reminisce, or take in the sun in warmer weather. The **Statue of Giuseppe Verdi,** commissioned by New York's Italian community in 1906 and executed in marble by Pasquale Civiletti, stands on a granite pedestal over four life-size figures representing characters from Verdi's operas *Otello, Aida, Falstaff,* and *La Forza del Destino.* The square is an officially designated New York City Scenic Landmark.

Dominating the north side of Verdi Square is the massive **former Central Savings Bank Building** (now the Harlem Savings Bank). Its limestone façade, designed in the style of an enormous Italian Renaissance palace by York & Sawyer in 1928, creates an atmosphere of solid financial security—no doubt the intention of the builders. The wrought-iron window grilles and the large lanterns (by Samuel Yellin) add an artistic touch, while a handsome clock flanked by two lions decorates the 73rd Street entrance. The bank, built on a trapezoidal plot (although the interior is rectangular), is a well designed and dignified structure—a fitting backdrop to Verdi Square.

11. One of the city's truly magnificent buildings is the French Beaux Arts–style **Ansonia Hotel** (Graves & DuBoy) on the northwest corner of Broadway and 73rd Street. Begun in 1899 and completed five years later, it is the dominant landmark of the West Side. When the Ansonia opened, it was one of the most opulent hostelries in town. The builder, William Earl Dodge Stokes, a wealthy land developer and inheritor of the Phelps Dodge Company fortune, brought architect-sculptor Paul E. M. DuBoy from France to carry out his grandiose plans for a sumptuous hotel in the style of the elegant palaces along the Parisian *grands boulevards.* Although its 17 stories would have made it second only to the Eiffel Tower in Paris, its dramatic setting here on Broadway is quite appropriate.

The corner round towers, surmounted by cupolas and railings in harmony with the convex mansard roof, are the most striking feature of the building. Rows of delicately ornate balconies break up the overwhelming verticality caused by tier upon tier of windows, while a series of recessed courts on the Broadway and West 73rd Street sides gives a feeling of depth and also provides a maximum of light and air.

Stokes, who owned the construction company, supervised every step in the building of the hotel. Thick masonry walls made it completely fireproof. The building also featured a roof garden, shops in the basement, and *two* swimming pools. The Ansonia is named indirectly for Stokes's maternal grandfather, Anson Greene Phelps, who founded the Ansonia Brass & Copper Company in his namesake town of Ansonia, Connecticut. In 1879, a subsidiary of the firm, the famous Ansonia Clock Company, moved its operations from the Connecticut town to Brooklyn, bringing the Ansonia name to the city 20 years ahead of the hotel. Stokes's most illustrious relative, however, was I. N. (Isaac Newton) Phelps Stokes, the architect-historian who wrote the definitive six-volume *Iconography of Manhattan Island.*

The fine reputation of the Ansonia through the years was due to its world-renowned clientele. Much the same way that the downtown Hotel Chelsea was the favorite of the *literati,* the Ansonia was the bastion of the musical world. The thick walls provided soundproofing that proved a most attractive feature. Among the "greats" who have stayed at the hotel were Enrico Caruso, Leopold Auer, Feodor Chaliapin, Mischa Elman, Geraldine Farrar, Lauritz Melchior, Ezio Pinza, Lily Pons, Yehudi Menuhin, Tito Schipa, Igor Stravinsky, and Arturo Toscanini. It was for a time the favorite of Sol Hurok, Billie Burke, Florenz Ziegfeld, and Theodore Dreiser.

Much of the early splendor of the hotel has now vanished. Several of the crowning cupolas and lanterns are missing, a number of the decorative railings and balconies have been removed, the immense ground-floor archways have been either blocked up or converted into small stores, the spacious lobby has

John C. van den Heuvel's country estate, ca. 1819, occupied the entire block now bounded by Broadway, West End Avenue, 78th and 79th streets. (The J. Clarence Davies Collection. Museum of the City of New York)

Pushed by a diminutive steam dummy (which was a locomotive encased in a boxlike structure to shield the machinery from public view for "cosmetic" reasons), a train of the newly-opened New York Elevated Railroad (later the Ninth Avenue El) enters the 59th Street station. The name of "Ninth Avenue" above 59th Street was later changed to Columbus Avenue. (Museum of the City of New York)

been partitioned into unrecognizability, and the whole exudes an atmosphere of commercialism. A restoration is now in progress, with results yet to be seen. But from a distance, the Hotel Ansonia is still a great lady!

Continue north on Broadway.

On the east side of Broadway near West 75th Street is the **Beacon Theater** (Walter Ahlschlager, 1928). Its front, lost in the façade of the àdjoining hotel, should be seen on its 75th Street side. Then, no matter what's playing, go in and view the magnificent interior (a designated landmark)! Across from the rear of the theater, the **Berkeley Garage,** 201 West 75th Street (C. Abbott French & Co., 1890), is a striking example of the Romanesque Revival style made popular by architect Henry Hobson Richardson in the 1880s and '90s. Once the stables of the New York Cab Company, the three huge half-round arches provided a grand entrance for the horses and carriages. The heavy stone base conflicts somewhat with the elaborate cornice, but it is nevertheless a worthy survivor. Skip the "modernized" Amsterdam Avenue side, and return to Broadway.

12. The Astor Apartments (Clinton & Russell, 1905), between 75th and

76th streets, once a luxurious apartment house, was built by real-estate magnate, William Waldorf Astor, who owned and developed much of the land in the neighborhood.

Continue north on Broadway to West 76th Street.

Walk a few steps west on West 76th Street to **No. 252,** whose recently well-restored Classic Eclectic façade is an upliftment for the block.

At the southwest corner of Broadway and West 77th Street is the **Hotel Belleclaire** (Emery Roth, 1903). Its ornate Classic Eclectic façade, particularly on the 77th Street side, offers an endless variety of dormers, bay windows, balconies with wrought iron railings, and unusual covered chimneys.

Walk west to West End Avenue.

13. West End Avenue was a "millionaires' row" of town houses until the early 20th century. When the New York Central Rail Road freight line, one block to the west, was covered over and Riverside Drive opened, the affluent residents were lured away to the new street with its unrivaled vistas of the Hudson River. An apartment-house building boom on West End Avenue after World War I and through the 1930s again attracted the wealthy (and near-wealthy); and the street, which declined somewhat after World War II, is again a choice location.

Look down the **west side of West End Avenue, between West 77th and West 76th streets**—a complete blockfront of lively, exuberant town houses (Lamb & Rich, 1891), that gives some sense of the first phase of development of the avenue. An engaging variety of gables, dormers, arches, and bay windows on a row of houses which fortunately escaped the second phase.

The West End Collegiate Church and Collegiate School incorporate both Dutch and Flemish features. Architect Robert W. Gibson created a charming "Netherlandisch" grouping with typical step-gables, pinnacles, and ornate dormer windows, modeling it after the *Vleeschhuis*—the 17th-century public meat market of Haarlem, Holland. This "Collegiate" church, built in 1891–92, is a descendant of the original Dutch Reformed Church, organized in 1628—the oldest Protestant congregation in America; and the Collegiate School is the country's oldest independent secondary school.

14. The entire block, West End Avenue to Broadway and West 78th to West 79th streets, is occupied by the **Apthorp Apartments.** A dignified luxury apartment house, it still preserves its original old-world elegance, despite the encroaching decrepitude of some of its neighboring streets. Built for William Waldorf Astor in 1906–08 from plans by Clinton & Russell, the enormous limestone structure is set around a broad central courtyard with fountain, access to which is through high vaulted passageways. The Broadway entrance is the grandest—a former carriageway whose bronze gates are reminiscent of the portcullis of some medieval castle. At each entrance, set in the spandrels of the façade, are two winged figures, and around the building runs a lovely ornate frieze. A cast-iron portico marks the entrance to each of the four separate units. Except for the addition of ground-floor shops on the Broadway side, the building remains virtually unchanged.

The apartment house is named for Charles Ward Apthorpe (*with an "e"*), who purchased the land in 1763. The property was passed to Apthorpe's son-in-law, Baron John C. van den Heuvel in 1792, and ultimately came into the Astor family in 1879.

Turn east on West 78th Street to Broadway, and north to West 79th Street.

15. The First Baptist Church, on the northwest corner of West 79th Street, was built in 1891 mainly in Romanesque Revival style from plans by George Keister. The asymmetry of its twin towers is puzzling, as is the incompleteness of the right member. Contrary to expectation, the auditorium is semicircular in shape, with a quality of intimacy contrasting strongly with the austerity of the exterior.

16. Zabar's, at 2245 Broadway, is a *gourmet* landmark. Known throughout the West Side (and by *cognoscenti* in all boroughs), it is a unique emporium whose mind-boggling variety of gustatory temptations defies cataloguing.

West 84th Street between Broadway and Riverside Drive is also named

The original building (1877) of the American Museum of Natural History at 77th Street and Central Park West. This photo, taken ten years later, shows a broad wasteland which was soon to be covered by many new wings of the Museum. [See p. 349] (Museum of the City of New York)

Edgar Allan Poe Street, in recognition of his residency at Broadway and 84th Street during the summers of 1843 and 1844. His favorite spot was a rock outcropping overlooking the Hudson, called Mount Tom, which will be seen later.

Continue north on Broadway. At West 86th Street, cross to the east side.

Broadway and West 86th Street marks the **site of the village of Bloomingdale,** the largest settlement on the west side of Manhattan Island in the late 18th century. Its counterpart on the east side was the village of Haarlem (which subsequently dropped an "a" from the spelling).

17. Another massive luxury residence is the **Belnord Apartments,** located between Broadway and Amsterdam Avenue, from West 86th to West 87th streets, in a setting quite similar to that of its "cousin," the Apthorp. Completed in 1908, architect H. Hobart Weekes designed it for gracious living. Its porte-cochere, formal central garden, cast-iron lampposts, and ornate separate entranceways are reminders of the affluent life-style of its former tenants.

Cross Broadway again and walk west on West 86th Street to West End Avenue.

18. On the northeast corner of West 86th Street and West End Avenue is the **Church of St. Paul and St. Andrew** (R. H. Robertson, 1895–97). In its designation report, the Landmarks Preservation Commission called the church ". . . a brilliant exemplar of the eclecticism that spread through American architecture in the late 19th century." Designed in an unusual combination of Early Christian, German Romanesque, and early Italian Renaissance architectural styles, this striking edifice of yellow brick with buff-colored terra-cotta trim is one of the outstanding church buildings of the city. Built originally for St. Paul's Methodist Episcopal Church, the congregation merged in 1937 with nearby St. Andrew's M. E. Church, which since 1890 has been located on West 75th Street, between Amsterdam and Columbus avenues. (St. Andrew's old building, designed by J. Cleveland Cady, still stands, and is now a synagogue.)

The major features of the church are its bold octagonal campanile; the broad entrance porch with triple round-arched doorways, surmounted by ornate ocular windows flanked by terra-cotta reliefs of angels, and topped by a balustrade; a smaller tower with open belfry, set at a 45-degree angle to the façade; the tall clerestory on the 86th Street side with its odd round-arched flying buttresses; and a Spanish tile roof.

When erected, St. Paul's was a significant visual landmark in the area, until the advent of the tall apartment houses that supplanted the rows of town houses. The impact, however, is still quite apparent, and the landmark church is considered a key work in the career of the architect, Robert Henderson Robertson.

Turn north (right) on West End Avenue.

19. Adjacent **St. Ignatius Episcopal Church** (1902), in Gothic Revival style, is another house of worship designed by architect Charles C. Haight, but not

one of his better works. This "ecclesiastical block" provides a pleasant break in the monotony of the seemingly endless rows of apartment houses along West End Avenue. Across West End Avenue from St. Ignatius's is the Tudor Gothic Revival–style **Cathedral Preparatory Seminary** in attractive red brick and limestone. The building was built for St. Agatha's School (Boring & Tilton, 1907), and later became a branch of Cathedral College.

Diagonally across West 87th Street, on the northwest corner, is an Art Deco–style apartment house, **565 West End Avenue** (Herman I. Feldman, 1937). Particularly attractive is the bright orange brick, with a course of black bricks in the base and a stainless-steel cornice over the entrance.

Turn east (right) on West 88th Street.

20. Dominating the middle of the block is **Congregation B'nai Jeshurun,** designed by Henry B. Herts and Walter Schneider in 1918. A broad Moorish façade of orange granite and a highly ornate carved limestone portal in Romanesque Revival style give this synagogue a stately and imposing appearance. The richly polychromed interior is well worth a visit. B'nai Jeshurun is the oldest Ashkenazic congregation in the city. It was founded in 1825 by a group of German and English Jews who split with the Spanish & Portuguese Synagogue and adopted the German ritual and language as opposed to the Sephardic Spanish-Portuguese.

Occupying the block on the west side of Broadway between 87th and 88th streets in one of the "mold-breakers" among recently designed apartment houses. In a welcome departure from the traditional (since the 1950s) glass box or white brick "wedding cake," architects Gruzen & Partners, in 1982, have created a twin-tower limestone-trimmed brick building which is reminiscent of the fine old apartments that line Central Park West (the Majestic, San Remo, Eldorado, and Beresford). While maintaining a respectful adherance to the "street wall," the first thirteen stories of the structure step back at the roof line of neighboring buildings, then leap skyward in two symmetrical towers for another thirteen stories.

Return to West End Avenue, turn north to West 89th Street, and east to Broadway.

21. Another of the immense luxury multiple dwellings is the **Astor Court Apartments** (89th to 90th streets, west side of Broadway), designed by Charles A. Platt in 1916. The interior garden courtyard and ornate balconies add grace and charm, but its crowning glory is the superb copper-clad cornice.

Continue north on Broadway to West 94th Street and turn west (left). About 50 yards down the north side of the block is the entrance to Pomander Walk.

22. New York City presents an almost inexhaustible supply of architectural surprises, and delightful **Pomander Walk** is no exception. Constructed in 1921, this diminutive double row of charming town houses was designed to imitate a small street in "Merrie England." The idea originated with the stage setting for the English play *Pomander Walk,* which opened in New York in 1911. In the play, the Walk was a small mews in the London suburb of Chiswick.

Although posted signs discourage visitors, walk in anyway, passing through to the West 95th Street exit. (Be sure to close the iron gate securely to avoid the wrath of the residents!)

Proceed to Broadway and West 96th Street, and turn west (left) to Riverside Drive. Walk under the viaduct, turn right and climb up to the Drive.

23. For the past hundred years or so, New Yorkers have been called "cliff dwellers" for reasons that are obvious. The architect of this otherwise undistinguished apartment house (Herman Lee Meader, 1914) displayed a keen sense of humor in the frieze that depicts motifs from the lives of the early Arizona Cliff Dwellers, with masks, buffalo skulls, mountain lions, and rattlesnakes. The interesting designs are more than symbolic to our contemporary "cliff dwellers."

Walk south on Riverside Drive along the west sidewalk.

24. Tree-lined Riverside Drive is one of the city's loveliest streets. Much of the dignity and elegance of yesteryear are gone, but the broad panoramic vistas are still unspoiled. As mentioned previously, the Drive began to flourish with the covering-over of the railroad that parallels the river. It was not long before Riverside Drive challenged Fifth Avenue as one of the most fashionable street addresses in town. Adding further to its beauty was the expansion in 1937 of **Riverside Park,** and the subsequent diversion of vehicular traffic to the new Henry Hudson Parkway, close to the riverbank. Riverside Park was designed by Frederick Law Olmsted, the landscape architect who revolutionized our ideas on park planning, and who gave us Central and Prospect parks, among many others. Riverside Drive was pushed north to West 129th Street by 1885, but the 96th Street viaduct was not built until 1902. Along the Drive can be seen the former opulent town houses and the newer luxury apartment houses that sprung up with the completion of the Park and Drive.

25. At West 93rd Street, on a slight crest overlooking Riverside Park, is the heroic **Joan of Arc Memorial Statue,** executed in 1915 by famed American sculptor Anna Vaughn Hyatt Huntington. The statue was commissioned by the Joan of Arc Statue Committee to commemorate the 500th anniversary of the birth of the Maid of Orleans, presumed to be in 1412. Her armor is historically accurate, having been researched by the Metropolitan Museum of Art's curator of armor. Sculptor Huntington has succeeded in capturing Joan of Arc's expression of intense fervor and sense of mission as she rode forth to lead the French troops in battle against the English and Burgundians. The bronze statue was cast by the well-known Gorham Company (which is still in business, but no longer casting huge statues). The Gothic-style pedestal of the monument was designed by architect John V. Van Pelt, and contains fragments from France's Rheims Cathedral (where in 1429 Joan of Arc reached the pinnacle of her career with the coronation of Charles VII) and stones from the Tower at Rouen (where she was burned at the stake two years later).

26. At the corner of West 89th Street stands one of the West Side's most significant public sculptures, **The Soldiers' and Sailors' Monument.** Sculptor Paul E. M. DuBoy and architects Charles W. and Arthur A. Stoughton completed the marble Civil War memorial in 1902 (just after DuBoy put the final touches to his work on the Ansonia Hotel), patterning it after the Choragic Monument of Lysicrates in Athens.

27. The imposing mansion on the southeast corner of the Drive and West 89th Street is the **former Isaac L. Rice Residence** (Herts & Tallant, 1901), now the Yeshiva Chofetz Chaim, a seminary. Rice, a lawyer, publicist, publisher, acclaimed chess player, and renowned pioneer in electric storage battery technology, named the house Villa Julia for his wife (who was the founder of an organization that would be much appreciated today, The Society for the Suppression of Unnecessary Noise). After his death, Julia Rice presented the city with a number of sports facilities, one of which survives in the Bronx, Rice Memorial Stadium. The mansion was acquired in 1908 by Samuel Schinasi, a partner in the Schinasi Brothers cigarette manufacturing firm. A year later, his brother, Morris, commissioned his own residence, which was erected about a mile north on the Drive, at West 107th Street. Coincidentally, these are the only two surviving free-standing mansions from the great number that once graced Riverside Drive. Although some alterations were made between 1906 and 1948, the maroon-colored brick, wildly eclectic house is a sheer delight! Note how the porte-cochere is partly recessed into the structure, and how the positioning of the house on its corner plot adds stature to the whole. Landmark status did not come easily, as the owners vigorously opposed designation, fearing that the restrictions would hamper growth of the institution by prohibiting what they felt were needed alterations.

Continue south to West 85th Street and turn east.

No. 350 West 85th Street, **The Red House** (Harde & Short, 1904), is a romantic gem! Built in the style of an Elizabethan manor house, this six-story apartment building provides a grand climax to the walking tour. The effect is pure *Merrie England,* from its Gothic detailing right up to the dragon and crown cartouche set high in the brickwork.

Return to Riverside Drive and turn south to West 84th Street.

In the park, directly opposite and partly veiled by the trees, is a prominent rock outcropping of Manhattan schist called **Mount Tom,** which Edgar Allan Poe found to be an attractive summer spot for contemplation of the river. The site was also the original choice for the location of the Soldiers' & Sailors' Monument.

Although this is the end of the walking tour, a pleasant stroll back to the starting point can be made as follows:

Continue south on Riverside Drive [*see* map] to West 79th Street; east to Columbus Avenue; north to West 81st Street; east to Central Park West; then south to West 72nd Street. (Or, alternatively, walk down Broadway to the Lincoln Center for the Performing Arts, West 66th to West 62nd streets.)

Following the first itinerary given above, the block between Columbus Avenue and Central Park West is quite attractive and faces the **Hayden Planetarium** (Trowbridge & Livingston, 1935). Along Central Park West to West 77th Street is the outstanding **American Museum of Natural History,** which houses one of the world's greatest scientific collections and is one of the most frequently visited places in town. The equestrian statue of Theodore Roosevelt flanked by an Indian chief and a Bantu was sculpted in 1939 by J. E. Frazer. The museum consists of a group of buildings occupying a four-block area formerly called Manhattan Square, whose construction began in 1873 with the original Jacob Wrey Mould and Calvert Vaux building (visible only from the Columbus Avenue side). Adjacent to it in the rear is the power house and a wing by Charles Volz (1908). The Central Park West side is dominated by the rather pretentious Beaux Arts–style Theodore Roosevelt Memorial Wing (John Russell Pope, 1935), now the main entrance, with side wings by Trowbridge & Livingston (1924–33). The **West 77th Street side of the museum,** however, includes the

An artist's conception of the completed American Museum of Natural History was not too far amiss when drawn for Moses King's Views of New York in 1908. *The central tower, however, was never built. (Author's collection)*

original entrance and is one of the city's great examples of Romanesque Revival–style architecture. The massive structure of pink Vermont granite, with carriage entrance, arcaded porch, grand staircase, turrets, and corner towers, was erected between 1892 and 1899 under the supervision of J. Cleveland Cady, and later by his firm of Cady, Berg & See. Many feel that this should have remained the main entrance to this great institution.

●   **The New-York Historical Society,** on the southwest corner of West 77th Street (York & Sawyer, 1908; with wings added in 1937–38 by Walker & Gillette), was built in classic style. The Society, founded in 1804, possesses a superb collection of books, prints, manuscripts, paintings, portraits, and other historical memorabilia, including the original Audubon *Birds of America* and the McKim, Mead & White files. There are also many interesting exhibitions and displays.

●   The two blocks between West 77th and West 75th streets mark the eastern
★   edge of the **Central Park West–76th Street Historic District,** a grouping of 40 town houses of unified scale and general design, plus the New-York Historical Society Building; the neo-Gothic **Universalist Church of New York** (formerly called Church of the Divine Paternity, built in 1897 from plans by William A. Potter); and the Beaux Arts–style **Kenilworth Apartments** (Townsend, Steinle & Haskell, 1908). The church presents a varied and interesting façade with its pointed arch windows, buttresses, finials, and gables, plus two magnificent stained-glass windows. Take a brief detour along quiet, tree-lined **West 76th Street,** and notice the variety of architectural styles with their handsome details—so typical of the late 19th-century period of eclecticism.

Continuing south, the two succeeding blocks are occupied respectively by the mammoth **San Remo Apartments** (Emery Roth, 1930) and the stately **Langham** (Clinton & Russell, 1905).

The IND AA line is at 72nd Street and Central Park West. Transfer at 59th Street-Columbus Circle for the IRT Broadway-Seventh Avenue line.

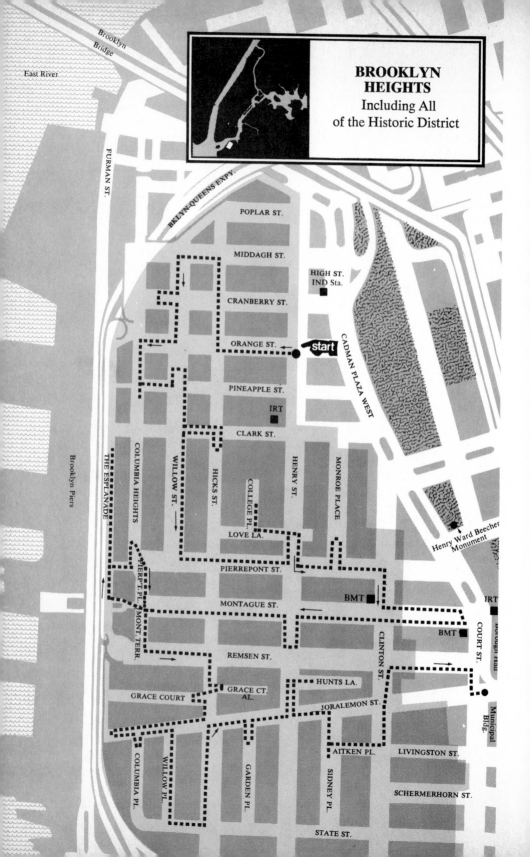

15. Brooklyn Heights and the Fulton Ferry Historic District

[*IND A line to High Street–Brooklyn Bridge (use the rear exit, and walk through Whitman Close town houses to Henry Street, turn left one block); IRT Broadway-Seventh Avenue line to Clark Street–Brooklyn Heights. On exiting from St. George Hotel, turn left to Henry Street, and left again two blocks to Orange Street*]

The section of Brooklyn known as Brooklyn Heights was New York City's first suburb. Situated on bluffs that rise steeply above New York Bay, the "Heights" was for over 250 years a relatively remote and rural area, undisturbed by the growth of the burgeoning port city across the East River. Before the arrival of the Dutch in 1626, the western portion of Long Island was inhabited by several tribes of the Algonkian Nation, particularly the Canarsees, who lived in long houses—some actually several blocks in length—on the high promontory facing Manhattan Island. When the first Dutch settlements were built, the Indians abandoned their village of Ihpetonga ("High Sandy Banks"), and in 1646 the village of Breuckelen (named for a town in the Dutch province of Utrecht) was established by Dutch settlers from Manhattan. When the British captured New York, they changed the name to Brooklyn. The beginning of the Revolutionary War saw the crucial Battle of Long Island lost by the patriots on August 27, 1776, as Washington's meager forces were overwhelmed by a superior British and Hessian army under Lord Howe. After their defeat at the Flatbush Pass (in the present Prospect Park) and the threat of total annihilation through a

The Plymouth Church in a Civil War–era engraving, showing crowds gathering to hear the fiery oratory of abolitionist minister Henry Ward Beecher. Except for a later Tuscan-style porch, the barnlike building is unchanged. (Long Island Historical Society)

flanking maneuver, a small regiment of Maryland Continentals fought a desperate delaying action at nearby Gowanus, as Washington successfully withdrew the army to Manhattan under cover of a heavy night fog.

Since Dutch colonial days, a small sail ferry operated to the foot of the Old Ferry Road (now Fulton Street) from Peck Slip, in Manhattan. A bell hung at each landing so that prospective "commuters" could summon the boat. However, the opening in 1814 of Robert Fulton's steam ferry *Nassau* signaled the beginning of the area's development as a residential community. Brooklyn Heights by 1820 was thickly settled, with much the same street layout as today. In 1834 the State Legislature granted a charter to the *City* of Brooklyn, and with its rapid growth and subsequent annexation of several other independent villages, by the mid-19th century it became the third largest city in the nation, with a population exceeding 85,000. Brooklyn has always been known as a city of churches and homes. It also has the distinction of having the most cemetery area in proportion to its size, which author Thomas Wolfe was keenly aware of when he said sardonically, "Only the dead know Brooklyn."

Laid out at right angles to the waterfront, the shady streets of Brooklyn Heights provided easy access to the river, and as late as the 20th century, there were no fewer than three ferries operating to lower Manhattan (Wall Street to Montague Street, South Ferry to Atlantic Avenue, and the Fulton Ferry connecting both Brooklyn's and Manhattan's Fulton streets). With the rapid development of the City of Brooklyn (which did not merge with the

City of New York until 1898) the "Heights" was bypassed and left undisturbed as land speculators and builders moved south and east. Thus, Brooklyn Heights today remains strikingly similar to its early appearance of more than 150 years ago. Of the approximately 1,100 houses in the neighborhood, more than 600 were built before 1860! The only major physical change was made in 1950 when the City of New York built the Brooklyn-Queens Expressway along the Brooklyn Heights waterfront, removing a number of old houses but substituting the magnificent Esplanade over the roadway, which provided residents with one of the most scenic views of New York Harbor. However, with the abandonment of the ferries and the construction of the new highway, the Heights is now permanently separated from the water. Its ties to Manhattan were greatly increased with the opening in 1883 of the Brooklyn Bridge; and by 1908 the first of several subway tunnels reached the Heights, although elevated trains had already been using the bridge for more than a decade. The arrival of the subway caused many of the patrician inhabitants to flee, and a number of their stately mansions were divided into small apartments. The neighborhood is still characterized by rows of lovely brick and brownstone houses—most with a uniform 50-foot height, representing virtually every architectural style of the 19th century. The Heights is also noted for several of its landmark churches designed by famous architects; but it is mainly regarded as one of the most charming and desirable residential sections of the city. In recognition of its aesthetic and historic value, Brooklyn Heights was designated in 1965 as **the city's first Historic District.**

Note: Brooklyn Heights is a rather extensive area with a great number of interesting and important sites. The chapter has therefore been divided into four sections, a **First Tour,** a **Second Tour,** and a **Brief Look at Brooklyn's Civic Center** followed by **a tour of the Fulton Ferry Historic District.**

FIRST TOUR

The first tour begins at the corner of Henry and Orange streets (one block west of Cadman Plaza).

Orange Street, and its two adjacent neighbors, Cranberry and Pineapple streets, were named by developers John and Jacob Middagh Hicks; or as a story goes, by one of their relatives, a Miss Middagh. Irked by wealthy neighbors who named the streets after themselves, she ripped down the immodest signs and replaced them with ones with botanical names. The city fathers promptly removed them, but after a protracted battle, the Board of Aldermen gave in and allowed her choices to remain. She is also credited with naming Poplar and Willow streets.

No. 69 Orange Street is one of the oldest houses in Brooklyn Heights. Built ca. 1829, it is typical of the wooden clapboard residences erected during the early development of the neighborhood. The mansard roof was added after 1870. Note the ornate brackets and consoles.

Alongside to the west is the famous **Plymouth Church of the Pilgrims.** Founded in 1847 by the fiery Henry Ward Beecher, its first minister, it was designed by architect Joseph C. Wells in an Italianate style and completed two years later. An austere, barnlike structure, it became one of the most influential churches in the nation. Beecher, an outspoken abolitionist, preached for many years and invited many noted public figures to share his pulpit. Among the antislavery agitators who shared his pulpit in passionate oratory were William Lloyd Garrison, Charles Sumner, and John Greenleaf Whittier. Abraham Lincoln worshiped here, and his pew, No. 89, is marked with a silver plaque. In 1867 Charles Dickens delivered an address on the occasion of his second visit to America; and through the years such greats as Horace Greeley, Mark Twain, and Booker T. Washington attended services here. In dramatic outpourings of rhetoric, Henry Ward Beecher fought with uncompromising vigor against slavery, and with equal grandiloquence campaigned for women's suffrage, temperance, and general reform. With typical dramatic flair, he once auctioned off a mulatto slave girl named Pinkie before an aghast congregation, using the money to purchase her freedom and arouse the attention of the entire country. Pinkie, actually Mrs. James Hunt, subsequently returned in 1927 to address the congregation from the very same platform where she had been "sold" almost 70 years before. Local Union Army units on their way to southern battlefronts would stop for services at the Plymouth Church, and at the height of the Civil War, Beecher made a trip to England to win sympathy away from the Confederate cause. President Lincoln later honored Beecher by having him deliver a speech at the symbolic raising of the flag at Fort Sumter. (Incidentally, Beecher's sister, novelist Harriet Beecher Stowe, will always be remembered for her very influential but overimaginative *Uncle Tom's Cabin.*) Beecher, who in a few short years had become a national hero, was later involved in a sensational "page-one scandal," accused of having committed adultery with the wife of a former associate. Although the minister was subsequently acquitted by the jury, that was the Victorian era, and his reputation and career suffered irreparable damage.

The exterior of the church is virtually without ornamentation, in the tradition of the New England Congregational Church—even lacking the usual steeple. Inside, the auditorium is simple, with white walls and woodwork. A balcony supported by cast-iron columns surrounds the hall, connecting with the organ in front. There are 19 stained-glass windows designed by Frederick Stymetz Lamb representing the "History of Puritanism and Its Influence Upon the Institutions and People of the Republic," with the broader theme of political, intellectual, and religious liberty. The pulpit furniture is made from an olive tree brought from the Mount of Olives in 1868 by members of a trip to the Holy Land, the occasion made famous by Mark Twain in his *Innocents Abroad.* Adjoining the sanctuary is **Hillis Hall,** a social center, named for a turn-of-the-century pastor. Its middle stained-glass window on the north side is a magnificent representation from the life of Christ, one of five from the Tiffany Studios. Hillis Hall was a gift of coffee merchant John Arbuckle, and was built in 1913 in Classic Eclectic style from plans by Woodruff Leeming. In the connecting arcade is a fragment of the Plymouth Rock brought from Massachusetts in 1840, and

68 Hicks Street, at the southwest corner of Cranberry Street, in 1920. Built 100 years before, most changes seem to have occurred in recent years. (Long Island Historical Society)

paintings of Abraham Lincoln, Beecher with Pinkie, and Harriet Beecher Stowe. In the lovely arcade garden is a statue of Beecher by sculptor Gutzon Borglum. The church was seriously damaged by fire in 1850, and in the early 20th century a Tuscan porch was added; otherwise the structure is in original condition. The Plymouth Church was merged in 1934 with the Congregational Church of the Pilgrims (whose former building still stands on the corner of Henry and Remsen streets, but is now Our Lady of Lebanon Maronite Cathedral).

Turn right (north) on Hicks Street.

Hicks Street is named for the family of the brothers John and Jacob Middagh Hicks, early residents and developers of the area.

No. 68 Hicks Street, at the southwest corner of Cranberry Street, is a two-and-a-half-story frame house topped by a gambrel rool, built ca. 1820. It was originally a grocery store and tavern. The clapboard walls have since been replaced with imitations. Note the Ionic colonnettes at the entranceway.

Brooklyn Heights was intimately involved in the life of poet **Walt Whitman.** In his childhood he lived on Cranberry Street almost directly behind the Plymouth Church, and some 30 years later his *Leaves of Grass* was printed in a shop just down the street at the corner of Fulton (the approximate site of the IND subway exit). "The Good Gray Poet" also served for a time as editor of the Brooklyn *Daily Eagle,* whose offices were located a few steps farther north, close to the Fulton Ferry.

No. 59, diagonally across the intersection, another frame house of ca. 1820, was the residence and shop of a cooper (barrel maker). The building has also suffered the ravages of modernization, with a stucco front and replacement entrance door. Adjacent **No. 57,** built about five years later, was the home of a merchant. The mansard roof was added during the period of the popular French Second Empire style in the 1870s. Actually, the mansard roof fits rather harmoniously with a number of the revival styles, and, as will be seen later, lent itself quite well to the Italianate brownstone row house also.

No. 51, with arched dormer windows, belonged to a sea captain, and was built ca. 1831. The low front stoop was removed and the entrance door installed on the basement level. The original door lintel is still visible.

Across the street, **Nos. 60** and **56** have been altered considerably. No. 60, a two-and-a-half-story frame house with a gambrel roof, has dormer windows similar to No. 51. The arch of a former fanlight doorway is still visible. No. 56, a three-story frame building, was probably a boardinghouse when built, and has subsequently had an additional floor added. Both houses were constructed before 1829.

Turn left (west) into Middagh Street.

Middagh Street was probably named after early resident John Middagh, either by himself or by relatives John and Jacob Middagh Hicks. One speculates on what the cantankerous Miss Middagh would have said after her successful campaign for botanical street names, only to see a street named after *her* family.

Typical residences of middle-class merchants and artisans of the early 19th century are **Nos. 33–25** Middagh Street. **No. 33–31** is a dual house, erected before 1847. The latter was a hairdressing salon; the former, a paint store. Doubtless, the rear and upper floors served as living quarters. **No. 29,** built ca. 1830, was the home of an engineer; the profession of **No. 27's** occupant is unknown, but the house dates from 1829; and the much-remodeled **No. 25,** a laborer's house, and smaller than the others, was built in 1824. It has suffered so many physical changes as to be almost unrecognizable (stuccoed front, lowered entrance, etc.).

Across Middagh Street, **No. 30,** a three-story frame house, was built in 1824, and has a street-level entranceway in Greek Revival style. Alas, the front wall has been defaced with asphalt shingles. Adjoining **No. 28** was erected ca. 1829 for a sea captain. Another unfortunate modernization has rendered this old house an aesthetic nonentity.

As if to make up for the architectural desecrations committed on its neighbors, **No. 24 Middagh Street** is a delightful gem of a house! An amazingly well preserved example of the Federal style, the **former Eugene Boisselet House,** built around 1829, is referred to by the *AIA Guide to New York City* as "The Queen of Brooklyn Heights," and is said to be the oldest house in the neighborhood. The brickwork basement is laid in typical Flemish bond (alternating rows of long bricks, called "stretchers," and short bricks, called "headers"), while the walls are built of clapboard. Two stories plus an attic with dormers is very characteristic of the Federal style, although the roof of this house, rather than peaked, is gambrel. The doorway is artistically carved and flanked by

Ionic colonnettes, with leaded-glass side lights (small windows), and surmounted by a transom and sculptured panel. On the attic level, twin quarter-round windows enframe an arched window, and twin chimneys strike a harmonious balance. A board fence connects the house with a small rear-garden cottage, probably a former carriage house. The missing back porch would likely complete the beautifully proportioned building.

Turn left (south) on Willow Street.

Nos. 20 through 26 Willow Street form a pleasing row of simple Greek Revival–style houses, built 1846–48. **No. 22** was the residence of Henry Ward Beecher. The entranceways are quite handsome, approached by stone stairs with ornate wrought-iron railings that terminate in a vertical swirl. Note the "Greek ears" on the door enframements, which are topped by a low-pitched pediment, and the recessed doors flanked by pilasters and side lights and surmounted by a transom. At the rear (not visible from Willow Street) are two-story open galleries facing the harbor, a typical and delightful addition to Brooklyn Heights houses facing the river.

Nos. 28 and **30** are a pair of Italianate brownstones, four stories high with a common cornice supported by brackets, and arched entranceways. No. 28 was built in 1858, its neighbor a year later.

At the corner of Cranberry and Willow streets stands one of the earliest apartment houses in the city, **"The Willows"** (No. 37). Elements of the Queen Anne style are evident in the high bay window with its classical swags and small broken pediment. This early multiple dwelling house was designed by architect A. F. Norris and erected in 1886.

Turn right (west) into Cranberry Street.

Nos. 13, 15, and **17** Cranberry Street show most of their original Federal-style details. No. 17 (sometimes numbered No. 19), at the corner of Willow Street, was built in 1833, and still retains its paneled window lintels and fanlight doorway as well as part of the original fence (with Greek Revival anthemion motifs) on the Willow Street side. The cast-iron balustrade on the stoop and the romantic mansard roof were added later. The entrance to No. 13, flanked by paneled blocks, probably supported ornate cast-iron basket newels. The fanlight doorway is enframed by a lovely archway with matching panel blocks; and the cornice, typical of the Federal style, is supported by rows of consoles above a bead-and-reel board. The house dates from about 1829.

Return to Willow Street and turn right (south).

Nos. 55 and **57** Willow Street, two-and-a-half-story Federal-style houses, were built ca. 1832 and 1825, respectively. Both have Flemish bond brickwork, indicative of more expensive construction. No. 57, at the northeast corner of Orange Street, is known as the Robert White House, after the merchant who first occupied it. Note the handsome dormer windows, which luckily escaped the improvements that destroyed the entrance, railings, and windows. The original size of the windows can be seen in the "blind windows" on the ivy-covered Orange Street side. A lovely frieze with Greek key motif, tooled stone lintels above the windows and doors, and tall twin chimneys add to the charm.

Turn right (west) on Orange Street to the corner of Columbia Heights.

The fenced-in grassy lot marks the **site of the Hotel Margaret,** which was destroyed in a raging fire while under renovation in 1980. The old landmark hotel, designed by Brooklyn architect Frank Freeman in 1889, was a familiar and appreciated building, and had been the residence during the 1920s of etcher Joseph Pennell and novelists Sigrid Undset (Norwegian-born winner of the 1928 Nobel Prize) and Betty Smith, who wrote *A Tree Grows in Brooklyn.* The conflagration was compared to the one which consumed Underhill's Colonnade at almost the same location in 1853 [*see* engraving on the following page].

Turn left (south) on Columbia Heights.

On the left side of Columbia Heights, at No. 107, is the **Brooklyn Heights Residence of the Watchtower Bible and Tract Society,** commonly called Jehovah's Witnesses (Frederick G. Frost & Associates, 1959). The Witnesses have established their headquarters in Brooklyn Heights, and the residence, as well as the apartment house across the street, are some of their ever-increasing number of facilities. Erected before the passage of the Landmarks Law which limited the height of new buildings in this historic district, it overwhelms neighboring buildings. The garden and fountain do provide some relief.

Walk south on Columbia Heights to Pineapple Street, and turn left (east).

Halfway down the block on the north side is a peaceful country-style house, charming **No. 13 Pineapple Street.** Built around 1830, it is a large residence with an interior central transverse stair hall, whose rooms are arranged on either side. A third floor was added to the building in the mid-19th century, requiring a new, bracketed cornice; and the front windows were then also enlarged. The stoop, too, is relatively new, as is the reproduction fanlight over the entrance. Nonetheless, it is a pleasant reminder of the past, enhanced by a spacious plot that breaks the monotony of the row houses.

Return to Columbia Heights and turn left (south).

On the southeast corner is the **World Headquarters Building of the Watchtower Bible and Tract Society.** Erected in 1970, the building's design won the approval of the Landmarks Commission only after several previous submissions had been rejected. The successful plans for the present structure, by Ulrich Franzen Associates, were accepted only because the Commission found them compatible with the style of the surroundings. (One of the rejected designs called for a 12-story tower, which the Landmarks Commission felt would have been totally out of scale with neighboring buildings.) An appealing aspect of the plan is the adaptation of the house fronts of the three adjacent brick houses to the south into the overall design, and the repetition of their bay-window motif in the theme of the office building's façade.

Across the street, **No. 138 Columbia Heights** is a lovely town house built ca. 1860 and a textbook example of the Italianate style. In pristine condition are its delicate cornice consoles, the segmental arch windows, the frieze and cornice over the window and door enframements, and the curved pediment set on consoles over the doorway.

Columbia Heights is named for the estate of early landowner Hezekiah Beers Pierrepont, whose mansion "Four Chimneys" and extensive property overlooked the harbor in the early 19th century. Pierrepont owned the Anchor Gin Distillery at the foot of Joralemon Street, which was operated by a large windmill and was conveniently close to the ferry. The wealthy merchant was also Robert Fulton's chief financial backer, helping him establish the first steam

Underhill's Colonnade on the Heights, overlooking the harbor in the late 1830s. The engraving is from the letterhead of a fire insurance company, showing a house on fire (fanciful or otherwise), which was doubtless intended to serve as a graphic warning to those not insured. The Colonnade itself was consumed by fire in 1853. (Long Island Historical Society)

ferry in the world. By mid-19th century, Columbia Heights (then Columbia Street) became one of the most fashionable strips in Brooklyn. A row of eight three-story, wooden, Greek Revival–style houses connected by a common colonnaded portico was erected in 1835 on the most prominent point on the Heights, between Cranberry and Middagh streets. Known as General Underhill's Colonnade Row, or simply **Underhill's Colonnade**, it was the area's most significant landmark until one cold December morning in 1853, when it was consumed in a spectacular conflagration. Occupying the east side of Columbia Heights between Pineapple and Clark streets from 1844 to 1904 was the sumptuous **Leavitt-Bowen Mansion**, with a monumental Corinthian portico facing the harbor. Another long-vanished landmark was **Dr. Charles H. Shephard's Turkish Bath**, which occupied a Greek Revival house on the corner of Cranberry Street from 1863 until 1913.

Turn left (east) at Clark Street to Willow Street.

The **former Towers Hotel**, on the northeast corner of Clark and Willow streets, was purchased by the Watchtower Bible and Tract Society to house staff members of its expanding world headquarters office. The Towers, a prominent feature of the Heights skyline since its opening in 1928, was one of Brooklyn's last luxury hotels. Designed by architects Starrett & Van Vleck, the building's four octagonal towers, illuminated at night, were a familiar landmark.

Continue east on Clark Street to Hicks Street and turn right (south).

Nos. 131 and 135 Hicks Street, on the east side, are rare examples of brownstones in the Gothic Revival style. No. 131 is by far the better preserved of the pair, with its elaborate cornice still intact, and without the abominable penthouse that surmounts its twin. It is referred to as the **Henry C. Bowen House**, after the original merchant-owner who had the house built around 1848. Bowen was a founder of the Plymouth Church as well as the abolitionist newspaper, *The Independent*, which Henry Ward Beecher edited. Both houses share Tudor Gothic arched doorways and ornately carved spandrels, square-topped windows with sash in imitation of casements, hood (or label) moldings over the windows, cast-iron railings with traceries, and the original iron fence. The cornice of No. 131 is set above a bead-and-reel molding, and only the missing cast-iron finials from the newel posts would complete this lovely house. (Perhaps the owner could make a deal with his neighbor in No. 135 to obtain his finials). The Gothic Revival style was in vogue in Brooklyn Heights between 1844 and 1865. Note the plaque.

Returning to Clark Street, the **Hotel St. George**, in a massing of several buildings of different styles and eras, occupies the entire block from Hicks to Henry, and Clark to Pineapple streets. Built in 1885 by William Tumbridge, a retired sea captain, from plans by August Hatfield, it then grew piecemeal until 1929, and became the largest hotel in the city. The original section is still visible a few steps east of Hicks Street, split into two wings, surmounted

The Congregational Church of the Pilgrims on Remsen and Henry streets still had its steeple in this ca. 1880 engraving. In 1934, the congregation moved to the Plymouth Church and the building now houses Our Lady of Lebanon Maronite Cathedral. (Long Island Historical Society)

Of these five unusual row houses on Clinton Street and Aitken Place, only two survive (Nos. 140 and 142). Most unusual are the cast-iron lintels, moldings and cornices. (Long Island Historical Society)

Hezekiah Beers Pierrepont's Anchor Gin Distillery in 1823, near the present site of Joralemon and Furman streets, in a painting by an unknown artist. The windmill and boats are reminiscent of a 17th-century Dutch landscape. (Brooklyn Collection. Brooklyn Public Library).

The Fulton Ferry slip in 1746, showing the step-gabled Dutch-style house of the ferrymaster, at right. (Author's collection)

Map showing the five
Dutch towns and the one
English town (Gravesend)
which during the 17th
century constituted Kings
County. The original
names of the Dutch towns
are in parentheses. (The
Williamsburgh Savings
Bank)

The first village map of Brooklyn showing the street patterns, which are virtually the
same today, and the estates of the landowners, many of whom were not averse to having
their names perpetuated in street designations. (Author's collection)

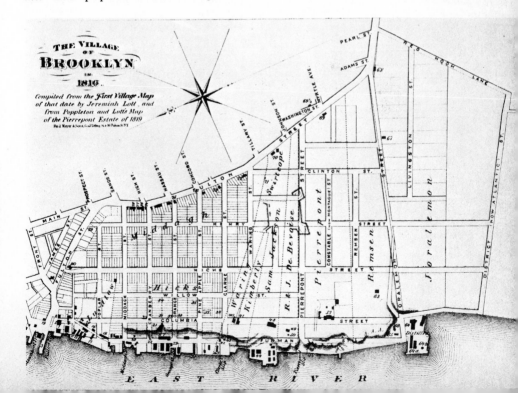

City dignitaries gathered to inspect the cables of the Brooklyn Bridge in 1873. Judging from engineer Roebling's warning sign, the terrifying hike on the Bridge's catwalk across the river must have been fairly commonplace. (Brooklyn Union Gas Company)

The Bridge Promenade has always been a popular attraction. In warm weather hundreds of commuters from Brooklyn Heights still use it daily. (Long Island Historical Society)

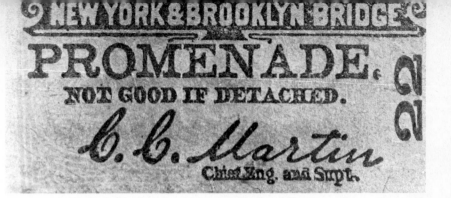

A two-cent ticket to walk across the Brooklyn Bridge after it was opened to the public in 1883. (*Brooklyn Union Gas Company*)

Traffic was already heavy on the Brooklyn Bridge in 1905. (*Long Island Historical Society*)

New-York and Brooklyn Ferry.

SUCH persons as are inclined to compound, agreeable to law, in the Steam Ferry-Boat, Barges, or common Horse Boats, will be pleased to apply to the subscribers, who are authorized to settle the same.

GEORGE HICKS, Brooklyn,
JOHN PINTARD, 52 Wall-st

Commutation for a single person not transferable, for 12 months, $10 00
    Do.   do.   8 months,   6 67

May 3, 1814.   6m.

The ferry from the tip of lower Manhattan entering its slip at the foot of Atlantic Avenue, Brooklyn, ca. 1830. (South Street Seaport Museum)

Brooklyn Union Gas Company emergency wagon leaving on a call for assistance, ca. 1900. (Brooklyn Union Gas Company)

Pierrepont Street is piled high in snowdrifts after a near-record blizzard on February 14, 1899. (Long Island Historical Society)

Brooklyn's Romanesque Revival–style General Post Office is a designated landmark. Completed in 1891, it represents an unusually high standard of government-sponsored architecture. The tree-lined plot to the right was the site of the Brooklyn Eagle. (*Brooklyn Union Gas Company*)

Opening day of the Brooklyn Elevated Railroad with its special trainload of city officials, May 13, 1888, from an engraving in Leslie's Illustrated Newspaper *of the following week.* (*Long Island Historical Society*)

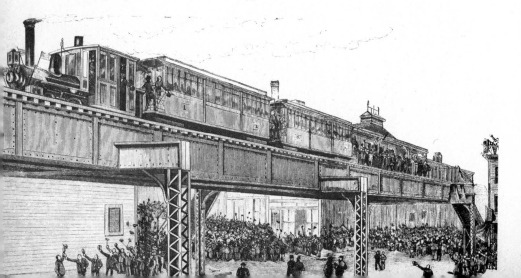

by a mansard roof and capped by a pediment inscribed with a rusting date, "188—". Few old-timers will forget the once-famous Grand Ballroom; and just about anyone who grew up in Brooklyn in the '30s remembers swimming in the enormous saltwater pool and watching his floating reflection in the room-length ceiling mirrors. It was also the favorite hotel of the old Brooklyn Dodgers. Those were the halcyon days of the St. George as a hotel.

By the mid-1970s the hotel had deteriorated so badly that it became a source of serious concern to the community. But with the skyrocketing real-estate values of a few years later, along came the developers, and within a brief period the property was divided into several parcels and major renovation projects begun. The "Tower" section facing Hicks Street was converted into a luxury rental unit. The rear wings on Pineapple Street were rebuilt as cooperative apartments, with the late-19th-century façades sympathetically restored. The west wing on Henry Street, however, remains as the only surviving member to stay as a hotel, catering primarily to senior citizens. At this writing, the center section on Clark Street, which once housed the main entrance, is still vacant, with its massive gates sealed. Still in litigation, it lies dark and deserted, the bronze doors sealed with plywood.

The famed ballroom, however, which once echoed to the strains of society music and the din of gala celebrations, now reverberates to the thumps and thuds of two levels of squash and racquetball courts. And the gargantuan, block-long tiled and mirrored swimming pool, destroyed through the intervening years

This charming residence, the Peck House, stood on the southwest corner of Clark and Willow streets until it was demolished ca. 1905. (Long Island Historical Society)

The lavish Bowen-Leavitt mansion was one of the area's most elegant. Razed over a half-century ago, it faced Columbia Heights at the northwest corner of Clark Street. (Long Island Historical Society)

by neglect and saltwater deterioration, has been divided into two spaces, one for a smaller and more manageable pool which incorporates some of the surviving mosaics, and one a cavernous area to be rebuilt as a gymnasium—all a worthy adaptive reuse by the St. George Health & Racquet Club, which has taken over a large section of the original hotel building at 43 Clark Street.

Take a quick walk around the hotel, then return to the corner of Clark and Willow streets, and proceed south on Willow Street.

Nos. 101 and 103 Willow Street are a pair of Greek Revival–style houses, both with an added fourth story. No. 101, built 1839, displays the characteristic (for Brooklyn Heights) pedestal blocks flanking the stairway with an ornate wrought-iron railing adorned with cast-iron rosettes rising to an elaborate swirl. On No. 103, dating from ca. 1848, look for the "Greek ears" at the corners of the entrance door enframement.

Across the street is the **Danish Seamen's Church,** 102 Willow Street, a reminder of earlier days when the busy Brooklyn waterfront was crowded with sailors from many nations, and Brooklyn Heights and adjacent Cobble Hill had a large Scandinavian population. Its neighbor, **No. 104,** was built ca. 1829. A frame house, it has a rather high basement laid in Flemish bond, and was the home of a baker.

The best example of the Queen Anne style in the Heights are the three houses **Nos. 108–112.** More a fashion than a revival, the basic characteristics of "Queen Anne" are the picturesque massing of different building materials (stone, brick, terra-cotta, shingles, and slate) in a harmonious potpourri of gables, chimneys, bay windows, dormers, towers, rectangular and arched windows and entrances, balconies, and porches—combining elements of the Romanesque, Gothic, and Renaissance styles. The major advocate of the so-called Queen Anne style was English architect Richard Norman Shaw. Its popularity in America became fairly widespread after its introduction at the British Pavilion during the Philadelphia Centennial Exposition in Philadelphia in 1876, and lasted for about 20 years. Actually, Queen Anne of England died in 1714; however, some of the Gothic and Renaissance elements popular during the reign of the last Stuart queen are evident in the design motifs. This group is considered the finest Queen Anne row in the city.

No. 151 Willow Street, set back from the street and occupying part of the site of a former house, is a nicely restored brick carriage house dating from the 1880s. The stars are the heads of tie rods, used to strengthen a brick bearing wall. (These may be decorative, however.) The adjacent pleasant garden has a brick path leading to a side entrance. Playwright Arthur Miller lived here in the 1950s until he left to marry Marilyn Monroe.

A charming trio of Federal-style houses are **Nos. 155, 157, and 159** (the latter having lost its dormers to a third-floor addition). All were built before 1829 and retain much of their original appearance. The articulated stone lintels above the windows and doorways are somewhat unusual. The trim buildings are laid in Flemish bond, have handsome entranceways framed by Ionic colonnettes and leaded-glass side lights and transom, and are topped by a peaked, or curb, roof with twin arched dormers set over a simple cornice. Note that the houses are not parallel to the street, as they were built in accordance with an earlier street pattern. (Love Lane [*see* map] formerly extended to Willow Street and emerged adjacent to No. 155.) A tunnel is supposed to lead from No. 159 to a former stable that was located at the site of No. 151. Look for the skylight imbedded in the pavement near the gate of No. 157.

Turn left (east) on Pierrepont Street.

Note: If you are taking only the First Tour, turn *right* on Pierrepont Street, and walk down to the Esplanade for a spectacular view of the Manhattan skyline. A description will be found in the Second Tour, page 383. After enjoying the view, follow the itinerary below.

Pierrepont Street, opened in 1832 and named for Hezekiah Beers Pierrepont, whose estate occupied the surrounding area, extends from Fulton Street to the Esplanade. Before the construction of the Brooklyn-Queens Expressway, the western end dipped down to the waterfront. The two oldest houses on the street are Nos. 27 (at the corner of Willow Street) and 58, farther down the block. **No. 27,** one of the oldest Greek Revival houses in Brooklyn Heights, has suffered many alterations, including a dropped entrance and an added mansard roof. **Nos. 24–30** is a fine row of ca. 1890 town houses, with uniform L-shaped entrance stairways.

At the southwest corner of Hicks Street, 36 Pierrepont Street, is the **George Hastings House,** an attractive Gothic Revival–style residence. Built ca. 1844, it features the typical hood molds over lancet arches, trefoil and quatrefoil motifs, traceries, a handsome wrought-iron side balcony replete with Gothic designs, and a fence to match.

No. 55, the **former Hotel Pierrepont,** was designed in 1928 by Herman I. Feldman and completed just before ornamentation on commercial buildings became passé. Look up at the griffin gargoyles and lion finials! The hotel ceased operations in 1975 and is now a senior citizens' residence.

Across the street, **No. 58** (previously mentioned) shares with No. 27 the distinction of being the oldest house on Pierrepont Street. Adjacent **No. 60** (ca. 1849) has a Greek Revival–style doorway with "Greek ears." Note the mansard roofs on the whole row.

No. 62 was built in 1911 as **The Woodhull,** a residential apartment house, from plans by George Fred Pelham, in a French Renaissance Eclectic style.

The Herman Behr House, at the southwest corner of Henry Street, is an exquisite Romanesque Revival mansion, designed in 1890 by architect Frank Freeman. This massive style was popularized by Boston architect Henry Hobson Richardson in the early 1880s, and is characterized by heavy masonry walls, usually of rough-faced sandstone; low-relief carvings; a fortresslike design; restrained terra-cotta ornamentation, usually in wide bands or courses; tan-colored upper brickwork; tile or slate roofs with gables and chimneys; arched openings; rounded bays; substantial stone entranceways; and an overall pleasantly asymmetrical composition. This "Richardsonian Romanesque" was applied not only to large residences, but to public buildings as well—banks, offices, city halls, courthouses, and even railroad stations. The style remained popular until the turn of the century. The Behr house was enlarged with a six-story addition in 1919 and became the Hotel Palm. Declining fortunes compromised its former elegance, and according to local legend, "the Behr *House* was no longer a *Home.*" As if to redeem it from its life of sin, the mansion was acquired by nearby St. Francis College as a residence for novitiates. It was sold in 1976 for conversion into apartments.

Diagonally opposite the Behr House, on the northeast corner, is **No. 161 Henry Street,** a delightfully exuberant brick and limestone trim Renaissance Eclectic apartment house. Designed in 1906 by Schneider & Herts, it has a large mansard roof with a huge pediment over the attic windows, plus a monumental Baroque entranceway.

Turn left (north) on Henry Street in Love Lane.

Love Lane was, as its name implies, a favorite path in Colonial times for young swains to promenade with their maidens fair. Earlier, it had been an Indian trail leading from a village to the water's edge. In 1822, the Brooklyn Collegiate Institute for Young Ladies was built on the site between Henry Street and the present **College Place.** The Institute later became a hotel called the *Mansion House,* and the former hotel stables on College Place now serve "horseless carriages." The neo-Federal D'Agostino supermarket at the entrance to Love Lane is a pleasant and appropriate reproduction.

Return to Pierrepont Street and turn left (east).

No. 104 Pierrepont Street, originally the Thomas Clark Residence, is a handsome four-story brownstone row mansion, built ca. 1857. The roof cornice is supported by ornate console brackets, with hoods similarly set on brackets over the windows and doorway. **No. 106** has an attractive bay window and entrance doors, both with art nouveau stained glass, and both surmounted by a decorative frieze.

Nos. 108 and **114** must be compared from across the street. The two were built as an identical pair around 1840 in Greek Revival style for Messrs. P. C. Cornell and George Cornell. Clay Lancaster, in *Old Brooklyn Heights,* calls the pair "the noblest residential building ever to grace Pierrepont Street." Today, only the right-hand half bears any resemblance to the original appearance, as No. 114 was completely remodeled in Romanesque Revival style around 1877 for Alfred C. Barnes. No. 108, the **P. C. Cornell House,** retains just one of its original Greek Revival elements, the pedimented entranceway with anthemion motif as an acroterium. In a 1907 remodeling, the neo-Colonial doorway and adjacent bay window were added. Its former look-alike twin, No. 114, is now sheathed with brownstone, brick, and terra-cotta, with typical Romanesque Revival features, including rounded bays, gables, a turret, and carved reliefs. In 1912, the George Cornell (or Alfred C. Barnes) House became the headquarters of the Brooklyn Women's Club.

Across Pierrepont Street is the **Church of the Saviour,** now the First Unitarian Church (Minard Lafever, 1844). The lovely Gothic Revival–style church is the home of the oldest Unitarian Society in Brooklyn, organized in 1833. The tall pinnacles and high central gable emphasize the verticality of the sandstone edifice, while a broad roof extends beyond the nave over the side aisles, with small skylights illuminating the interior. In 1890 a new set of windows was installed from the studios of Louis Comfort Tiffany. Lafever, a trained carpenter and skilled architect whose buildings were executed almost always in the Greek Revival style, used the *Gothic* Revival exclusively for his many churches. (Another of his fine churches will be seen shortly.) The church is on the approximate site of a British fort built here between 1780 and 1781.

On the northwest corner stands the **Appellate Division of the New York State Supreme Court,** designed by Slee & Bryson and built in 1938 in a simple Classic Revival–style.

Walk up Monroe Place to **No. 46,** on the right side of the street. Set on a paneled pedestal block is a lovely wrought-iron basket urn, once fairly prevalent throughout the Heights, and now reduced to this last survivor. (The matching mate disappeared recently.) The pineapple atop the urn was a traditional symbol of hospitality. Both No. 46 and its neighbor No. 44 are Greek Revival–style houses laid in Flemish bond, and like the trio of houses on Willow Place (Nos. 155–159), are built askew from the street line. The houses were originally aligned

There is now a parking lot where the Frank Freeman–designed Brooklyn Savings Bank stood at the northeast corner of Pierrepont and Clinton streets. A delightful Classic Eclectic building erected in 1893, it was taken down in 1962 when the bank built a modern structure around the corner on Montague Street. (The Brooklyn Savings Bank)

with Love Lane, which in the early 19th century extended through to Fulton Street.

Monroe Place is the widest street in Brooklyn Heights and, unlike others in the Heights, has the even-numbered houses on the *east* side. It also retains the original house-numbering system, which was abandoned on all other streets in 1871. The street is named for James Monroe, fifth president of the United States, who spent the last years of his retirement in New York City.

Continue east on Pierrepont Street to Clinton Street.

The handsome **Long Island Historical Society Building** is best viewed from the diagonally opposite corner. Built for the Society between 1878 and 1880 from plans by George B. Post (architect of the New York Stock Exchange), it is a pleasing combination of Richardsonian Romanesque and Classical styles, which properly should be called Eclectic. Since its organization in 1863, the Society has amassed one of the finest historical collections in the country. Although primarily concerned with the four counties that comprise Long Island, it has extensive source material on New York City and New York State. The library contains over 125,000 volumes plus a collection of manuscripts, periodicals, pamphlets, newspapers, maps, paintings, photographs, prints, and other Long Island memorabilia. The library is considered one of the three best in the nation in the field of genealogy. Many paintings by famous American artists are displayed in the hall and reference room, and so extensive and valuable are its historical holdings that it has earned the sobriquet "Long Island's strongbox." The building is open to the public Tuesday through Saturday, 9 A.M. to 5 P.M., and The Seated Indian, a gift shop inside, is open from 11 A.M. to 5 P.M. A visit is a "must" (be sure to pick up a membership application!). On exiting, note the high-relief sculptures of the Viking and Indian in the spandrels of the entrance arch, as well as the rich façade with busts of Columbus and Franklin, and its earthy tones of red and brown in the terra-cotta adornments and Philadelphia pressed brick. The Latin inscription on the Clinton Street side is from Cicero, and means "History is Witness of the Times."

On the northwest corner, **St. Ann's Episcopal School** occupies the building of the **former Crescent Club,** one of a number of private athletic clubs that prevailed around the turn of the century. Designed in 1906 by architect Frank Freeman (of the Behr Mansion and the Hotel Margaret), it was the club's second building. Find the little stone crescents set in the upper section of the façade. Across Clinton Street on the northeast corner stood another Frank Freeman building—the Brooklyn Savings Bank—a splendid Classic Eclectic edifice with an extravagant oval interior. Built in 1893, it was lost to the wrecker's ball in 1962, and the bank moved into more modern quarters on Montague near Court Street, and the site is now a parking lot. On the southeast corner, and extending to Montague Street, is the old **Brooklyn Trust Company Building,** now a branch of the Manufacturers Hanover Trust Company. Designed in 1915 by the noted architects York & Sawyer, the exterior is said to be patterned after the Palazzo della Gran Guardia in Verona, and the interior possibly after the Tepidarium of the Roman Baths of Caracalla. The impressive granite-and-limestone Renaissance Revival–style *palazzo* was the home office of the Brooklyn Trust Company until it was absorbed by the present bank in 1950. And when you get to Montague Street, don't miss the splendid bronze lamp standards in whose delicately sculptured bases are griffins and turtles.

Turn right on Clinton Street to Montague Street.

Back to back with the Long Island Historical Society is the **Diocesan Church of St. Ann and the Holy Trinity, formerly the Holy Trinity Protestant Episcopal Church,** and another fine example of architect Minard Lafever's ecclesiastical work. Completed in 1847 in his customary Gothic Revival style, it is reminiscent, in its dark-red color, of an old English church. Unfortunately, the porous brownstone has weathered very badly. The interior is constructed of cast and painted terra-cotta, a departure from the usual carved stone or plaster. The lovely windows were designed by William Jay Bolton, America's foremost stained-glass artist of the time. The reredos are by Frank Freeman, and a bust of John Howard Melish by sculptor William Zorach is mounted in the vestibule. The church's tall spire was dismantled early in the century when blasting for the new Montague Street tunnel of the BMT subway made it unsafe. St. Ann's Holy Trinity Church is now headquarters of the Episcopal Diocese of Brooklyn.

Cross the intersection of Clinton and Montague streets to the corner diagonally opposite the church.

The block of Montague Street between Clinton and Court streets is considered part of the downtown Brooklyn business section and is known as **"Bank Row."** From left to right across Montague Street are:

The just-mentioned Manufacturers Hanover Trust Company, No. 177, in the building of the old **Brooklyn Trust Company,** erected in 1915. The structure occupies the site of the George Taylor residence, the home of a mid-19th-century congressman. His house was sold to the Brooklyn Trust Company in 1873, and was enlarged and altered through the years until 1914, when it was razed to make way for the present building.

The Citibank branch, No. 181, is in the **former People's Trust Company building,** designed as a reproduction of a Roman temple, in 1904, by Mobray & Uffinger. It sports a large and impressive pediment complete with reclining classical figures, and rests on four huge Ionic fluted columns that frame what is known as an engaged tetra-style portico. The effect on the public must have been one of unquestioned security and solvency. An addition was designed in 1929 by Shreve, Lamb & Harmon, whose design for the Empire State Building was being carried out that same year.

The **National Title Guaranty Building,** No. 185, although no longer known by that name, is an imposing 15-story structure in a bold, three-dimensional Art Deco style, and was erected from plans by Helmle, Corbett & Harrison in 1929. The closely spaced stone piers rise dramatically in a group of rhythmic setbacks to create a strong sense of verticality. A mindless alteration in 1970 destroyed the entrance and lobby. The building has seen many banks as tenants through the years, and at present awaits a new one.

Adjacent to the right, and totally unrecognizable in its present "glassy box" disguise is the nine-story **former Real Estate Exchange,** No. 189–191, erected in 1891. Built originally in a Renaissance Eclectic style, it was remodeled in 1911 by Brooklyn's most famous architect, Frank Freeman. Then in 1916, 1953, and 1957, further modifications were made to the façade and interior; and finally in 1972, the present bronze glass "skin" was attached. The ultimate indignity came with the installation of a "Colonial" doorway by the present ground-floor occupant, the European-American Bank.

The final group of buildings includes the Brooklyn Union Gas Company, the Bankers Trust Company, and the Brooklyn Savings Bank (now merged with the Metropolitan Savings Bank), all built between 1959 and 1962. The Gas Company's headquarters occupies the **site of the Mercantile Library** (Peter B. Wight, 1864), a modified High Victorian Gothic–style building which later became the home of the Brooklyn Library, until it merged with the Brooklyn Public Library in 1903. It then became the library system's main office until its central building was erected near Prospect Park in 1941; the building was then reduced to the Montague Street Branch, and was demolished in 1960.

Cross to the north side of Montague Street.

The tall building halfway down the block on the south side is the **Lawyers Title Insurance Company,** No. 188–190 (Helmle, Huberty & Hudswell, 1904). Adjacent to the east stood another Frank Freeman building, the Title Guaranty & Trust Company, erected in 1905 in neoclassic style, and torn down in 1959. At the far end of the block, at the corner of Court Street, is one of Brooklyn's genuine skyscrapers, the **Montague-Court Building** (H. Craig Severance, 1927). Rising 35 stories in a series of setbacks (as required by the 1916 zoning resolution), it is an attractive addition to the Brooklyn skyline.

Before the financial institutions came to Montague Street, this block had another distinction. It was **the most important cultural center in all of Brooklyn.** In addition to the library on the north side, the south side was the site of two famous institutions, one of which was the **Brooklyn Art Association.** In 1872, architect J. Cleveland Cady was hired to design an appropriate building for the Association, whose primary purpose was the promotion of the fine arts to Brooklyn residents. The result was an impressive High Victorian Gothic structure with lively use of polychromatic stone and brick whose façade dominated the block. The Art Association merged with the Brooklyn Institute of Arts & Science in 1899 to form one of the nation's greatest cultural institutions, the **Brooklyn Museum.** With the completion of the museum's magnificent first building (designed by McKim, Mead & White) on Eastern Parkway near Prospect Park the same year, the Brooklyn Art Association abandoned its Montague Street home, and its name became only a memory. The building, however, survived until 1936, when all but a few interior walls were demolished.

The third cultural institution on the block was the **Brooklyn Academy of Music,** founded in 1859 as an outgrowth of the Brooklyn Philharmonic Society. Architect Leopold Eidlitz designed an enormous brick structure for the BAM, also in High Victorian style, at Nos. 176–190 Montague Street, just to the east of the site that would later be taken by the Brooklyn Art Association. Opening night was January 15, 1861, and Walt Whitman, writing in the *Brooklyn Standard,* described the building as "magnificent . . . on a scale commensurate with similar buildings, even in some of the largest and most polished capitals of Europe." The Academy remained as the center of all major cultural events in Brooklyn until it was destroyed in a fire in 1903. Five years later, a new Academy building arose a mile to the east [*see* Fort Greene, 14] and soon became one of New York City's major cultural centers. The mid-block Lawyers Title Insurance Company building now occupies the western end of the old Brooklyn Academy site.

Return to the corner of Clinton Street.

Completing the row of banks is the picturesque **Franklin Trust Company Building** on the southwest corner. With the invention of the elevator, the skyscraper came into its own, and this charming Romanesque Revival château, complete with moat, is an outstanding example of the style applied to commercial buildings. Built in 1891 (see date in the pediment) from plans by George L. Morse, the bank presents a striking façade of limestone arches on a granite base, brick and terra-cotta piers, columns topped by arches, and a charming Spanish tile roof with dormer windows.

End of First Tour. To return to Manhattan, the BMT Court Street station of the RR line is here at the intersection of Montague and Clinton streets. For the IRT Broadway-Seventh Avenue or Lexington Avenue lines, walk one block east on Montague Street to Borough Hall. For the IND, take either IRT line and change at Fulton Street.

SECOND TOUR

Continue west on Montague Street.

Montague Street is named for Lady Mary Wortley Montagu, née Pierrepont, the English author of wit and letters who died in 1762. (No one seems to know how Montague Street got its final "e".) It is the principal commercial thoroughfare of Brooklyn Heights and an appropriate place to stop for some refreshment. When the street was opened through to the river front around 1850, ferry service was begun to Wall Street in Manhattan.

In 1887 a cable car began operating the full length of Montague Street, providing a convenient transportation link for Manhattan commuters who arrived on the brand-new Fulton Street El at the Court Street station and were then whisked down to the Wall Street Ferry. In 1909 the trolley was electrified, remaining in service until 1924 when the BMT's four-year-old Montague Street Tunnel rendered it obsolete.

The street has a variety of shops, including interesting bookstores, boutiques, and ethnic restaurants. Along the south side, cast-iron stoops lead up to raised first-floor retail establishments whose wares are displayed in large triple-bay windows. There is a gay, relaxed, continental atmosphere which adds charm to the lively street.

At Henry Street, turn left (south) one block to Remsen Street.

Our Lady of Lebanon Maronite Cathedral, originally the Congregational Church of the Pilgrims, was a radical departure for architect Richard Upjohn, renowned for his Gothic Revival–style churches, particularly Trinity Church in Manhattan; and this early Romanesque Revival church, built in 1846, is thought to be the first building of that style in this country. When the church merged with the Plymouth Church on Orange Street in 1934, the fragment of Plymouth Rock imbedded in the tower was brought along. The new church acquired the building in 1944. It practices the Maronite Rite, serving a large and long-established Lebanese community, much of which is clustered along Atlantic Avenue in "Brooklyn's Middle East" [*see* Cobble Hill walking tour]. The interior of the church is surprisingly delicate, with widely spaced slender columns and semicircular arches supporting the ceiling. Unfortunately, the

The "Penny Bridge" over Montague Street, ca. 1922, when the street sloped downhill to the Wall Street Ferry. In the background are the side-by-side Low and White Mansions (Nos. 3 and 2 Pierrepont Place) and the now-demolished Pierrepont Mansion. (Long Island Historical Society)

steeple deteriorated and was removed. Newly installed windows detract from the overall effect. The west and south portals are made from metal panels rescued from the *Normandie,* which burned and capsized at its Hudson River pier in 1942, during World War II. Only a few of the circular door panels on the west side have anything to do with churchly matters; the rest are all landscapes or nautical scenes.

Return to Montague Street and turn left (west).

Nos. 111–115 Montague Street are an interesting pair of Queen Anne–style apartment houses, built in 1885, with a particularly engaging common façade. The *Berkeley* and *Grosvenor* display a combination of building materials: red brick, brownstone, and ornamental terra-cotta. The houses were designed by Parfitt Brothers, an important Brooklyn architectural firm of three English-born brothers. Both have been converted to co-ops.

No. 105 Montague Street, by the same architects and from the same period, is another good example of the style. Look up at the sculptured figure in the gable. Built in 1890, The Montague is now a condominium.

The Hotel Bossert, at the corner of Hicks Street, was built for lumber merchant Louis Bossert in 1909–12. Designed by architects Helmle & Huberty, the Bossert was a center of Brooklyn social life for many years; and its Marine Roof, decorated like a yacht, provided an unsurpassed view of the harbor. In spite of the demise of virtually all of its competitors, the Bossert steadfastly hangs on as the last first-class hotel in Brooklyn Heights, attempting to emulate the tradition of its predecessor hotel on the site, the elegant mid-19th-century Pierrepont House. Peek into the lobby, or what remains of it after its partitioning. The massive columns and coffered ceiling give some idea of what a luxurious space it once was. Alas, the Marine Roof and elegant ballroom are no more. Then cross to the diagonally opposite corner of Montague Street and examine briefly the Beaux Arts lower section of the hotel. On the Hicks Street side are no fewer than twelve tall arches running the full length of the building, each with a carved lion's head in the keystone console. Above the columned main entrance is a balcony with filigree ironwork that includes the hotel's initials as a central design.

The Heights Casino, 75 Montague Street, an exclusive tennis and squash club, was designed by Boring & Tilton and opened in 1905. In front of the site of the Casino stood the H. B. Pierrepont Mansion, "Four Chimneys," built before the American Revolution and used briefly by General Washington as headquarters before the retreat to Manhattan. The mansion was razed in the mid-19th century when Montague Street was extended to the water's edge. At about the site of No. 63, the street began its descent to the harbor. The street was elevated in the late 1940s when the Esplanade was built. The architects also designed the U.S. Immigration Station on Ellis Island.

No. 76 Montague Street, **Sirius House,** a two-and-a-half-story Federal build-ing with a turn-of-the-century storefront, is a ship broker's office. The firm takes its name from the paddle steamer *Sirius,* the first ship of its kind to cross the Atlantic in a westward direction, in 1838. A plaque illustrating the ship, which is named after the navigational star, is imbedded in the sidewalk; a 19th-century British Admiralty-type anchor, secured from a ship-breaker's yard in Staten Island, rests solidly in front. Brooklyn Heights was for many years the home of sea captains and shipping people, and the Sirius Brokers, Inc. found it appropriate to move here from Manhattan in 1981 and restore the oldest house on the block (1859) for their offices. (Those making the walking tour in the winter will appreciate that this building and the Brooklyn Union Gas Company's headquarters are the only two in the Heights to have heated sidewalks, this one by electricity, and the Gas Company's, obviously, by gas.)

Continue west on Montague Street to just opposite **No. 62,** an enormous red-brick apartment house of ca. 1885. Erected in a mixture of Queen Anne and what might be called "Edwardian" styles, it is an early example of the luxury multifamily residence, then called the French flat. The six-story oriel on the Montague Street side is overshadowed by the ten-story round tower that rises majestically, past nine levels of ornate iron fire escapes, to a pyramidal mansard roof.

From this point to the waterfront, Montague Street once dropped steeply to connect with the **Wall Street Ferry** (service discontinued in 1912). At this spot architect Minard Lafever built a charming but short-lived arch in 1855 that spanned Montague Street. And just ahead, where Pierrepont Place and Montague Terrace meet at street level, there was an iron footbridge over the then-depressed Montague Street, known as **The Penny Bridge,** which survived until 1946 when the land was filled in for the Brooklyn-Queens Connecting Highway. Some idea of the depth of the old street can be had by examining the wall and deep cellar of the last house on the left, just at the stop sign at Montague Terrace.

At the end of Montague Street, walk a few steps to the right into Pierrepont Place.

Facing the end of Montague Street are **Nos. 3 and 2 Pierrepont Place,** considered to be the most elegant brownstone dwelling houses in the city. Designed by noted architect Richard Upjohn [*see* page 412] and built in 1856–57, they form a splendid pair of Italianate mansions situated in an ideal location. A third house, No. 1, whose empty plot now serves as a playground, was built for Henry E. Pierrepont, and was demolished in 1946. The twin mini-*palazzi* were built for Abiel Abbott Low, a tea merchant (No. 3), and for Alexander M. White, a fur dealer (No. 2). A. A. Low's son, **Seth Low,** served as mayor of Brooklyn from 1882 to 1886, then as president of Columbia University, and in 1901 was elected mayor of the City of New York. He is remembered for his vigorous campaigns to reform the police, finance, and education departments, and for his donation of the Library to Columbia. No. 2 was later occupied by Alfred Tredway White, a wealthy businessman and philanthropist, and president of the Brooklyn Bureau of Charities. It was White who believed in "philanthropy plus 5%" when he built the Riverside Houses on Columbia Place (to be seen shortly) and the Tower and Home Apartments in the Cobble Hill section [*see* Cobble Hill, page 410]. Walk back around the south side of No. 3 to the Esplanade for a rear view of the lavish mansions and a 100-year-old gingko tree that stands in the southwest corner of the private garden. Before reaching the Esplanade, read the bronze tablet at the entrance that marks the **site of the mansion "Four Chimneys."** The film *No Way to Treat a Lady* was filmed here some years ago.

The Esplanade, called "The Promenade" by local residents, provides one of the most unforgettable harbor panoramas, which can be enjoyed while relaxing on one of the convenient benches. Considered by many to be New York City's most spectacular vantage point, its design is a commendable attempt at separation of vehicular and pedestrian traffic, and a tribute to the planning of our city fathers. Local civic groups such as the Brooklyn Heights Association cooperated with Parks Commissioner Robert Moses in the planning, and the resultant cantilevered Esplanade over the Brooklyn-Queens Connecting Highway, completed in 1950, gave sudden impetus to the redevelopment of Brooklyn Heights. A somewhat better design would have duplicated the almost total separation of roadway from pedestrian mall that was achieved with the East River Drive on the Upper East Side, where traffic noise and fumes were completely eliminated. Spend a few minutes enjoying the magnificent view of the unique Lower Manhattan skyline.

Turn right on the Esplanade, and after a few minutes of contemplation, take the next right, exiting just beyond the two mansions. Turn left into Columbia Heights for a brief detour. Walk to No. 210, then turn back.

Nos. 210–220 Columbia Heights, a splendid row of Italianate brownstones (some painted white), were erected between 1857 and 1860. The entrance to No. 210 is flanked by a pair of Corinthian columns, and the doorway is framed by masonry blocks with alternating vermiform ("wormlike") rustication. No. 214's entrance was once as grand as the others. Nos. 216 and 218 are (fortunately) unpainted and show their warm brownstone color. Both had mansard roofs added, probably in the 1870s when the Second Empire style became the rage. And look what was added to the roof of No. 220, giving it an Italian Renaissance *villa* appearance!

Continue south on Pierrepont Place (the extension of Columbia Heights), past Montague Street, where the street changes its name again to Montague Terrace.

Nos. 1–13 Montague Terrace, built ca. 1886, are a charming English-style "terrace row" in almost pristine condition. Author Thomas Wolfe, while living

The Brooklyn Heights Esplanade provides one of the finest views in the country. This photo was taken in the early 1960s before the construction of the huge boxlike office buildings which now obscure much of the traditional skyline. The Singer Tower, demolished in 1968, is visible to the left of the tree. (Brooklyn Union Gas Company)

at No. 5 in 1935, wrote *Of Time and the River.* Wolfe spent a number of years in the Heights and nearby Cobble Hill, and his novels are drawn from personal experiences. **No. 11** is the most authentic, having undergone the fewest alterations, and preserving its broad entrance stairway. The last house on the west side, No. 13, which appears to have no entrance, has its Remsen Street wall completely covered with ivy.

Turn left into Remsen Street.

Named for Henry Remsen, who lived nearby and opened the street in 1825, this shady, quiet thoroughfare is lined with interesting mid- and late-19th-century residences. The houses on the south side to Hicks Street date mostly from the pre–Civil War period, while those on the north were built in the 1880s and '90s.

Turn right (south) into Hicks Street.

Grace Court Alley, a charming little mews running eastward to a dead end, was formerly the stable alley for the patrician residents of Remsen Street. The stables and carriage houses, considered very chic, are luxurious duplexes. Note particularly the solidly built **Nos. 2, 4, 12,** and **14.**

Walk a few yards down **Grace Court** and look through the tall iron fence into the spacious backyards of the houses that face Remsen Street.

Grace (Protestant Episcopal) Church of Brooklyn Heights is another Richard Upjohn work, completed in 1847. In style it is typical Gothic Revival, much like an English parish church, but rather low, long, and narrow. The side entrance court offers a delightful spot of repose, tucked under a magnificent 85-foot-high elm. The boldly carved moldings, capitals, and brackets are highlighted against the textured wall surface with its pattern of varied tooled groovings. Inside, open wood-vaulted trusses support the roof, but matching wooden piers were replaced by stone during a 1909 restoration. At that time, the handsome J. Pierpont Morgan Memorial Doorway was installed. In the sanctuary are an alabaster altar and reredos surmounted by an artistic stained-glass window. The church boasts three Tiffany stained-glass windows in the nave and aisles.

Turn right (west) into Joralemon Street.

Joralemon Street is named for Teunis Joralemon, who purchased the Philip Livingston estate in 1803. You have doubtless noticed the sudden change in the atmosphere of the neighborhood. While still very attractive, it is apparent that Joralemon Street cannot compare in elegance to the streets just visited. This area was originally a district of small merchants, artisans, and tradesmen. There are no mansions or fancy town houses here, just straightforward Greek Revival–style row houses. The street was opened in the 1840s after the Remsen farm was subdivided. Note, too, the "cobblestoned" street (properly called Belgian blocks) and the old bluestone sidewalks.

Nos. 29–75 Joralemon Street are 24 modified Greek Revival–style houses, built from 1844 to 1848 in neatly descending pairs, each about 30 inches lower than the next, and most still retain their pilastered entranceways and original iron fences. **No. 58** was converted unobtrusively into a ventilation chamber and emergency exit for the IRT subway tunnel far below the street.

At the southwest corner of Columbia Place are the remarkable **Riverside Houses,** model tenements built for Alfred Tredway White in 1890 by William Field & Son. These multiple dwellings followed on the heels of his revolutionary Tower and Home Apartments in Cobble Hill [*see* page 410], the first such project in America and a rare example (in public housing, anyway) of enlightened self-interest. His motto "Philanthropy plus 5%" actually did bring him a profit. These houses were aptly named, but in the construction of the expressway, the "river side" was demolished, along with a superb view of the harbor. A remnant of the original central garden, which was a major part of the plan to provide as much light and air as possible for the 280 apartments, is still visible between the remaining building and the expressway.

Turn south into Columbia Place.

Across from Riverside Houses is a charming row of four clapboard frame houses, **Nos. 7–13 Columbia Place,** which were once part of the nine-unit "Cottage Row" built in the late 1840s.

Return to Joralemon Street, turn right one block into Willow Place.

Nos. 2–8 Willow Place are a most unusual row of Gothic Revival–style duplex houses, built about 1847. Among their interesting features are the coupled porches with clustered colonnettes, diamond-paned side lights and transoms in the entranceways, Tudor arches with trefoils in the spandrels, recessed panels connecting the second and third floors with wooden "chevron" moldings (forerunners of the spandrels used on tall modern buildings), hood labels over the third-floor windows, and an appropriate iron fence and stoop railings. Note the plaque on No. 6.

Farther down the street is the **former Willow Place Chapel,** built in 1876 (architect unknown) by the First Unitarian Church, and closed in 1945. The diminutive Gothic-style building now serves as a community center.

Buildings **Nos. 38–40, 44,** and **48,** erected in 1966, are an excellent example of the use of modern materials and techniques applied harmoniously in a more traditional environment. Designed by Joseph and Mary Merz, the arrangement of garage space and the use of special 8-by-8-inch cement blocks gives the houses a simple dignity and helps them blend well with their venerable neighbors.

Across the street is the **last surviving "Colonnade Row" in Brooklyn Heights, Nos. 43–49 Willow Place.** Designed ca. 1846 as a middle-class imitation of the elegant multicolumned row houses such as Underhill's Colonnade or the very sumptuous marble Colonnade Row on Manhattan's Lafayette Place, it is reminiscent of an antebellum Southern mansion. The two-story brick houses are revealed behind the twin-story porches whose square wooden columns support the entablature and cornice. Although the continuous portico is only a foot above ground level, the total effect is undiminished—even enhanced by the simple Greek Revival doorways flanked by pilasters. (Across Willow Street, almost hidden by its neighbors and partly obscured by a small but lush garden, its wooden columns overgrown with ivy, is lovely **No. 46,** painted a harmonious shade of green, and looking for all the world like a set from *Gone With the Wind.*) In *Bricks and Brownstone,* author Charles Lockwood refers to the dignified wooden porch of the Willow Place Colonnade Row as "an easily forgivable architectural fraud . . . [which] holds great appeal today because of its modest scale and the naïveté of its conception and execution."

Turn left (east) on State Street to Hicks Street, then left again.

Nos. 284–276 Hicks Street are a row of five former carriage houses. Note the round and elliptical arches, and the carved woman's head on the dormer of **No. 276,** formerly the studio of sculptor William Zorach. Adjacent is **Engine Company 224,** in a Beaux Arts–style fire house, designed in 1903 by Adams & Warren, and set in perfect scale with its neighbors.

Across the street, the exterior **cast-iron spiral staircase** on the former St. Charles Orthopaedic Clinic (281 Hicks Street) is an interesting addition to the streetscape. This is the approximate site of the Philip Livingston house, built ca. 1764. It was in the Livingston House that George Washington, on August 29, 1776, planned the strategic withdrawal of his Continental Army to Manhattan, following the Battle of Brooklyn.

Nos. 270–262, built in 1887, add to the variety of the street with their romantic Queen Anne–style grouping of picturesque details.

Turn right (east) on Joralemon Street to Garden Place.

Take a brief detour down **Garden Place,** laid out in 1842 and named for the garden that once graced the Philip Livingston estate. The back fence of the houses on the east side of the street from Nos. 29 to 41 incorporate part of the brownstone retaining wall that once separated the terraced garden from the orchard. (Livingston was one of the signers of the Declaration of Independence.) Note the Queen Anne style of **No. 26,** and the storybook converted carriage house at **No. 21;** note also the atmosphere created by the addition of trees, in this case the row of London planes, which since their planting in the early 1940s have grown to provide a charming umbrella for the street.

Continue east on Joralemon Street to Henry Street, and turn left (north) for a brief detour to Hunts Lane.

Hunts Lane is another former stable alley, whose brick carriage houses were converted to duplexes, and which, like nearby Grace Court Alley, served the affluent homeowners on Remsen Street whose backyards abutted the Lane.

Return to Joralemon Street and continue east.

No. 129 Joralemon Street, the former David Chauncey Mansion, was designed by C. P. H. Gilbert in 1891 in an odd combination of Romanesque Revival and Colonial Revival details. A massive stone and yellow brick mansion, it gives the impression, nonetheless, of being a "bungalow." It is now subdivided into apartments.

No. 135 always astonishes the visitor. Almost hidden between two overpowering neighbors, this decrepit but delightful gem of a house is reminiscent of No. 24 Middagh Street, its "cousin" seen at the beginning of the tour. Built ca. 1833, and known as the **John Haslet House** (after its first owner, a U.S. Navy surgeon), it is the sole survivor of a row of similar residences that once lined the street, and is a sadly deteriorating example of Federal-style architecture. The ornate cast-iron porch was added in the mid-19th century and the parlor-floor windows were lowered, but otherwise the house is in virtually pristine condition. Note the Flemish bond brickwork of the basement, the handsome entranceway with Ionic colonnettes (alas, the door has an unauthentic glass panel in it!), the neat clapboarding, simple cornice, twin dormers, and gambrel roof. Will someone *please* do something to save it!

Turn right into Sidney Place.

Sidney Place is even more varied than its neighbor Garden Place. It is named after Sir Philip Sidney, or Sydney (1554–1586), an English author, statesman, and soldier who was a distinguished figure in the court of Queen Elizabeth. Most of the houses on the west side date from the 1840s. **No. 2,** the corner house, built about 1848, has a peculiar appendage facing Sidney Place in the form of a wooden two-story-high vestibule, with—lo and behold!—a delicate Federal-style entryway. Twin Ionic colonnettes and wreathed side lights flank the door, with a transom and carved plaque above. It is said that the entranceway originally belonged to a house that was demolished to make way for the construction of the Towers Hotel. **No. 18,** a Greek Revival house of about 1838, has an attractive recessed doorway flanked by Doric columns. Some years later, three additional floors were added, making this doubtless the tallest Greek Revival house in the city.

Beyond Aitken Place, the row of houses on the east side is set back behind lush gardens and iron fences, adding to the charm of the shady street. **Nos. 31–49,** a continuous row of Greek Revival–style houses, were all built about 1845. Most have suffered modifications, but **No. 35** is closest to the original appearance.

Framing the entrance to Aitken Place are the **St. Charles Borromeo (Roman Catholic) Church** (1869), and across the street, the Rectory (1929) and adjacent parish school (1916). The church, designed by that prolific architect of so many Catholic churches in the 19th century, Patrick C. Keely, is a simple modified Gothic Revival–style structure in dark-red painted brick, but in scale with its surrounding neighbors. Inside, the supporting arches and trim are in a delicate "carpenter Gothic" style. The plain, light-colored walls contrast strongly with the dark-brown ceiling. Rev. Ambrose S. Aitken was a former pastor of the congregation, and the adjoining street is named for him.

Follow Aitken Place to Clinton Street.

Clinton Street is named for De Witt Clinton (1769–1828) who served ten annual terms as mayor of New York City and two terms as governor. He was the guiding spirit behind the construction of the Erie Canal, ran unsuccessfully for president, was an amateur naturalist, and for his entire career a dedicated public servant.

At the corner, look south down **Clinton Street.** Except for some modifications to the exteriors of the Greek Revival–style row houses, little has changed in the past 100 years. On the southeast corner is a row of four red brick houses, **Nos. 133–139 Clinton Street,** whose appearance is enhanced by the trio of gaslights. The corner house was once the home of the *Excelsiors,* an early Brooklyn baseball team and champions of the world in 1860. Read the plaque on No. 133 and learn who pitched the first curve ball, and how baseball is so closely tied to the history of Brooklyn.

The **former St. Ann's Episcopal Church** was closed in 1966 and merged with the Holy Trinity Church, three blocks north. In a move to cut costs and help maintain their parochial school, the Episcopal Diocese of Brooklyn sold the church to the nearby Packer Collegiate Institute, and moved its headquarters along with its congregation to Holy Trinity. Designed in 1869 by famed architect James Renwick, Jr. (who planned St. Patrick's Cathedral as well as Manhattan's Grace Church), this is the only example in Brooklyn of the Ruskinian or Venetian Gothic style. Where this style differs from the more conventional Gothic Revival is in the use of polychromy in the façade. The arch blocks (voussoirs) are in alternating white and dark brown, while horizontal bands of white stone run across the full width of the exterior.

Nos. 142 and **140,** across the street from the church, are survivors of a row of five similar houses, built ca. 1855. Most unusual are the bracketed gables and the highly ornate black-painted cast iron lintels set over the windows and entrances. [*See* photo, bottom of page 363.]

Walk north on Clinton Street to Joralemon Street.

The **Packer Collegiate Institute,** designed in the "Collegiate" Gothic Revival style by Minard Lafever in 1854, was built on the site of the Brooklyn Female Academy destroyed by fire two years earlier. These lovely "halls of ivy" were endowed by Mrs. William S. Packer to honor her late husband's interest in women's education. The delightful exterior was published by Lafever in his *Architectural Instructor* and reflected his belief that churches as well as schools should be constructed in the medieval Gothic tradition. The Gothic-style wing at the east end was added in 1886.

Continue one block to Remsen Street, and turn right (east).

The little Gothic Revival–style brownstone church at the corner is the **former Spencer Memorial Church,** built in 1850–53 (architect unknown) for the First Church (Presbyterian) of Brooklyn. The church was closed in the early 1970s and was later sold to a developer and converted into 11 cooperative apartments. An alley to the left is called "Spencer Mews" and has entrances to some professional apartments. Other tenants enter at what were once the various doorways to the church. On the alley wall is a memorial tablet saved from the interior, honoring the former church's first pastor, Ichabod Spencer.

Just beyond the glass-box main building of **St. Francis College** is the tall Classic Revival–style building that housed the **former headquarters of the Brooklyn Union Gas Company** until their most recent structure was erected in 1962 on Montague Street. The building was designed in 1914 by Frank Freeman, and has been converted to classroom and office use by St. Francis College. Interesting is the Classic colonnade on the upper stories.

Immediately to the left, in what resembles a Greek temple, is the gem of the block, the **original headquarters of the Brooklyn Gas Light Company,** erected in 1857. The firm became the Brooklyn Union Gas Company in 1895, and remained in this diminutive white marble building until architect Freeman's plans for its new offices next door were executed twenty years later. Like its neighbor, it too has been incorporated into the St. Francis campus, but as the McGarry Library.

Brooklyn's Civic Center at the turn of the century. To the left rear of Brooklyn's City Hall is the Court House (now the site of the Brooklyn Law School). Also gone are the trolley lines and the Brooklyn Rapid Transit Elevated on curving Fulton Street. The statue of Henry Ward Beecher in front of City Hall has been moved several hundred yards farther north. (Author's collection)

Continue to Court Street, turn right (south) one block to Joralemon Street, and cross to the opposite side of Court Street.

The tall commercial structure on the northwest corner, the **Temple Bar Building** (44 Court Street), was the tallest in Brooklyn when completed in 1901. Interesting are the ogee-shaped twin cupolas (the one on the right has lost its copper sheathing) and the Classic Eclectic details of the façade. Court Street between Livingston and Pierrepont streets is the major axis of the Brooklyn "Financial District," conveniently located opposite the Borough Hall (former City Hall), the Brooklyn Municipal Building, and the various city, state, and federal courthouses. Within just a few blocks are six colleges and universities, the main Brooklyn post office, the Transit Authority headquarters, the Brooklyn Heights branch of the Brooklyn Public Library, the New York City Board of Education, and Fulton Street, Brooklyn's major retail center.

End of Second Tour. At Borough Hall are the IRT Lexington and Broadway-Seventh Avenue lines, and at Montague Street the BMT RR line. For the IND A line, walk past Borough Hall to Fulton Street, then two blocks east to Jay Street.

A BRIEF LOOK AT BROOKLYN'S CIVIC CENTER

The Brooklyn Municipal Building, an immense and functional Indiana limestone structure, was designed in a modified Roman Eclectic style by McKenzie, Voorhees & Gmelin, and completed in 1926. The granite for the base came from Deer Island, Maine, and the interior marble was quarried in Vermont and Tennessee. The building houses most of the offices of borough government, including the files from the demolished Court House and Hall of Records, which stood just to the east.

Directly in front, and facing Cadman Plaza, is **Borough Hall, formerly the Brooklyn City Hall.** Said to be one of the most beautiful public buildings in the entire city, the old City Hall was built in 1836–49 in Greek Revival style, although its cupola is strictly Georgian, and was added in 1898. The Hall was originally planned to be a replica of Manhattan's City Hall, but instead the Greek Revival style was selected. The architect, Gamaliel King, was in fact a grocer and carpenter! An excellent view is from the Plaza where the splendid façade with its broad staircase gracefully ascending to the Ionic colonnade is seen to best advantage. Borough Hall houses the offices of the president of the borough of Brooklyn.

From the colonnade of Borough Hall there is a broad perspective of **Cadman Plaza.** Named for Rev. S. Parkes Cadman, an active community leader and America's first radio preacher [*see* Clinton Hill, 8], the Plaza was the result of major urban renewal in the 1950s, including the razing of the Fulton Street El, which came over the Brooklyn Bridge and darkened Fulton Street for miles,

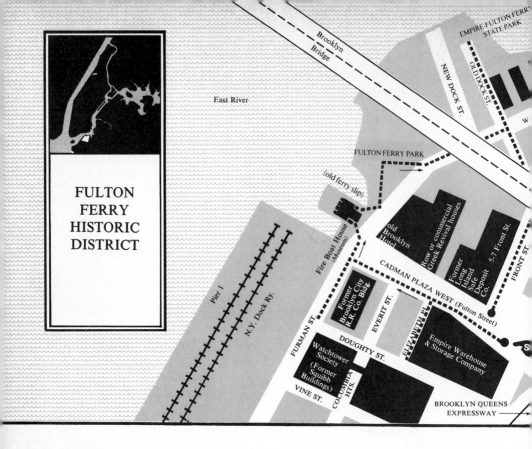

FULTON
FERRY
HISTORIC
DISTRICT

East River

Brooklyn
Bridge

EMPIRE-FULTON-FERRY
STATE PARK

NEW DOCK ST.

OLD DOCK ST.

W

FULTON FERRY PARK

(old ferry slip)

Row of commercial
Greek Revival houses

old
Brooklyn
Hotel

Former
Long
Island
Safe
Deposit
Co.

5-7 Front St.

FRONT ST.

Pier 1

N.Y. Dock Ry.

Fire Boat House
(Museum)

CADMAN PLAZA WEST (Fulton Street)

EVERIT ST.

ELIZABETH PL.

Former
Brooklyn City
R.R. Co. Bldg.

DOUGHTY ST.

Empire Warehouse
& Storage Company

S

FURMAN ST.

Watchtower
Society
(Former
Squibb
Buildings)

VINE ST.

COLUMBIA HTS.

BROOKLYN QUEENS
EXPRESSWAY

the removal of trolley tracks, and the rebuilding of major traffic arteries. A pleasant park resulted, which acts as a "buffer zone" between Brooklyn Heights and the rest of the borough.

To the right is the modern **New York State Supreme Court,** designed in 1957 by Shreve, Lamb & Harmon (architects of the Empire State Building). At its south end are **lamp standards from the old Hall of Records;** and to the east, the **Federal Building and Court House,** completed in 1961 from plans by Carson, Lundin & Shaw.

To the west, rising like a medieval château, is the **Brooklyn Central Office of the U.S. Post Office.** Designed in 1885 in Romanesque Revival style by Mifflin E. Bell, the work was later assumed by William A. Freret, supervising architect for the Treasury Department, and completed in 1891. A north section, in harmonious style, was created by James A. Wetmore in 1933. The post office, built of granite while Brooklyn was still an independent city, represents a high standard of government-sponsored architecture, and with the great advances in stone-cutting techniques achieved late in the 19th century, it was possible to produce masonry buildings of great beauty. To the south of the post office stood the Brooklyn Eagle Building, built in 1893 and demolished in the late 1950s as part of the civic center redevelopment plan.

Directly in front of Borough Hall is a **Memorial to John Cashmore,** former Brooklyn borough president under whose administration the Cadman Plaza project was realized. Near the entrance to the Supreme Court is a bronze plaque honoring **Washington Augustus Roebling** and his marvelous Brooklyn Bridge. When completed in 1883, it was the longest suspension bridge in the world. To the west is a **bust of Senator Robert F. Kennedy,** by Anneta Duveen. Farther to the north is a life-size marble statue of **Christopher Columbus,** by Emma Stebbins which she carved in Rome in 1867.

A half-block farther west is the best piece of sculpture in the plaza, and one of the finest in the city, the extraordinary bronze **statue of Henry Ward Beecher,** by John Quincy Adams Ward, unveiled in 1891, with a black granite pedestal designed by Richard Morris Hunt. When Beecher died on March 8, 1887, Ward received a telegram urgently requesting that he make a death mask within four hours. Complying, he then received the commission for the eight-foot-high statue. In the completed monument, an austere Beecher, in a simple knee-length Inverness cape, stands above three intimate figures of youngsters, a young black girl placing a palm frond in gratitude at the abolitionist's feet, and a young boy helping a girl climb the base to lay flowers at Beecher's feet— all three representing his love and devotion to children. The statue originally stood in front of Borough Hall, but was moved to its present site in 1959. The Metropolitan Museum of Art praised the Beecher Monument and called it "public statuary at its best."

End of tour. (The following tour may be made by either walking the short distance indicated below, or by taking the three-minute bus ride.)

THE FULTON FERRY HISTORIC DISTRICT

Walk down Cadman Plaza to the waterfront (about a third of a mile) or take the B-25 or B-41 bus to the end of the line at Furman Street. (Fulton Street to the river has been renamed Cadman Plaza West.)

The modern history of Brooklyn began at the waterfront hamlet of Fulton Ferry, which after the introduction of Robert Fulton's steam ferry in 1814 became the gateway not only to Brooklyn but to Long Island as well. (The first record of a ferry to Manhattan was Cornelis Dircksen's regular rowboat crossings in 1642. Crossings were later made with sailboats, and even with boats propelled by horses walking on treadmills.) Other ferries subsequently linked Manhattan with Brooklyn, and in 1872 as many as 1,200 daily crossings were recorded, but the Fulton Ferry was by far the most important. The little village grew rapidly and soon boasted several hotels, a newspaper (the Brooklyn *Daily Eagle*), a bank, law offices, and a stagecoach terminal. With the opening of the Brooklyn Bridge in 1883, the Fulton Ferry district began a gradual decline, becoming an almost forgotten backwater by the 20th century. The ferry hung on, however, until 1924, for 110 years of service. Plans are well underway to restore many of the old landmarks and to re-create much of the early 19th-century atmosphere of the Village of Fulton Ferry, and the area has been designated a Historic District.

The tour begins on Cadman Plaza West (Fulton Street) in front of the Empire Warehouse and Storage Company building.

The Eagle Warehouse and Storage Company of Brooklyn engaged architect Frank Freeman to design this massive red brick "fortress" in 1893. Completed a year later, it became a notable example of his Romanesque Revival style. The arched main entrance with the company's bold lettering is particularly impressive. A stylized horse's head is mounted on a gooseneck post at the entry gate, which separates the vehicular entrance from the former office. Very impressive is the symmetrical façade and the heavy iron grilles on the windows. Above is a row of round arches surmounted by corbels that resemble the machicolations of a medieval castle. On the parapet is a clock flanked by the name of the establishment.

Once a warehouse for the storage of household furnishings and silverware, the enormous structure was renovated in 1980 and adaptively reused as an apartment building. In the lobby (if you can persuade the doorman or a tenant to let you peek inside) is an atrium in which an old "birdcage" elevator has been "adaptively reused" as a garden trellis (a real birdcage wouldn't be a bad idea). The lobby also has a colorful mural of Cadman Plaza West looking

The Fulton Ferry terminal, built in 1871 in Victorian style, continued in operation until 1924. This 1891 view shows a steam train of the Brooklyn Elevated Railroad about to leave from the adjacent El station for its run on the Fulton Street line. (Long Island Historical Society)

Looking northeast on Fulton Street (now Cadman Plaza) in 1954, toward the old Brooklyn Eagle Building and the still-standing General Post Office Building. (Brooklyn Picture Collection. Brooklyn Public Library)

toward the river, and on the wall is an incongruous assortment of pieces of sculpture from demolished buildings.

Walk around to the rear, on Elizabeth Place, and see if you can discover the old three-story brick building, with segmental-arc window lintels, that has been incorporated into the warehouse. This is the last physical vestige of the *Brooklyn Eagle*'s first office, **its old pressroom.** Built in 1882 from a design by G. L. Morse, it functioned until 1893 when the newspaper erected its new building next to the Brooklyn post office. The name of the warehouse was appropriated from the newspaper, as two of its directors were executives of the *Eagle*.

At 8 Fulton Street (or Cadman Plaza West), the corner of Furman Street, is the **former headquarters of the Brooklyn City Railroad Company,** the horsecar enterprise that replaced the stages and built ribbons of track throughout most of the city of Brooklyn. (A track is still visible on the west side, in the rear.) The structure was designed in Italianate style and is constructed of brick with granite trim. Completed in 1861, it occupies the riverfront site of the former Judge William Furman residence. From 1910 until the mid-1970s, the building housed a toilet-seat factory, and in 1975 it was converted to an apartment house by architect David Morton.

Up the hill to the south rise the yellow-painted twin factory buildings that were once the **Squibb Pharmaceutical Company plant.** Connected by a "Bridge of Sighs" over Everit Street (whose name changes to Columbia Heights after one block), the once-busy drug manufacturing facility is now the printing plant of the Watchtower Bible & Tract Society, the Jehovah's Witnesses.

Across Fulton Street—which in the early 19th century was called Old Ferry Road—is a **row of commercial structures in Greek Revival style,** built between 1836 and 1839. The corner building once housed the Franklin House, the others comprised a variety of merchandising establishments. Observe the remains of the old sidewalk canopy in front of No. 15—a fairly common feature in the 19th century.

Notice the painted names of merchants and their wares fading from the façades of the row of buildings. These four-story houses retain much of their original appearance and are significant as one of the few surviving examples in the city of commercial Greek Revival architecture.

At the end of the commercial row, at the corner of Water Street, the **old Franklin House** was the most important dining saloon and hotel in the district during the 19th century. Its prime location at the Fulton Ferry made it a favored stop for commuters for over sixty years. It is now the Harbor View Restaurant, with rental apartments above.

Ahead, at the river's edge, the small wood-frame building with hipped roof and tower is the **former Marine Fire Boat Station.** Erected in 1930 on the site of the old Victorian-style Ferry Terminal, it served the harbor firefighting patrol until the station became obsolete in the late 1970s. (The tower was used to hang the fire hoses to dry.) The building was then acquired by the National Maritime Historical Society for the **Fulton Ferry Museum.** Inside are exhibits of sailing-ship memorabilia, including photographs of some of the Cape Horners and other multimasted schooners from the Great Age of Sail. The Museum still preserves the call board from the fireboat station, listing the locations of waterfront fire alarms. Admission is free, with hours from noon to 6 P.M. (knock if closed). The former fireboat pier occupies the site of the old Fulton Ferry slip, and is now a marina. Anchored to the left is **"Bargemusic,"** a former coffee barge refitted as a chamber music concert hall.

Just to the right and in the shadow of the Brooklyn Bridge is **Fulton Ferry Park.** Built by the city's Department of Ports & Terminals, it is a small but attractive patch of green with a nautical motif, and provides a delightful spot for river gazing. The iron railings along the water were salvaged from the "islands" on Manhattan's Park Avenue. In storage for five years, they were installed when the park was opened in 1976. The privately owned River Café, set on a barge, offers an unequaled but expensive panorama for evening dining.

On Water Street, directly under the bridge, is the Art Moderne concrete and brick **New York City Department of General Services Warehouse B-53,** formerly the Department of Purchase Storehouse, built in 1936. Interesting are the horizontal concrete bands that accentuate the wide steel-strip windows.

Follow Water Street to the first street on the left, New Dock Street. The old red brick structure that extends to the next corner was built in the early 1870s as the **Tobacco Inspection Warehouse.** It was used until well after the turn of the century for the storage of tobacco and as a customs inspection center for tobacco imports, since 90 percent of Brooklyn's tobacco trade was carried on here.

At the next corner, turn left into *New* Dock Street, and walk to the entrance to **Empire-Fulton Ferry State Park.** The park, still incomplete at this writing, has a pleasant boardwalk with benches along the East River, offering splendid vistas of the Lower Manhattan skyline, with an underbelly view of the Brooklyn Bridge and its graceful Gothic-style towers, the Manhattan Bridge, recently painted bright blue, and in the distance, the Williamsburg Bridge. One can relax and watch the passing parade of East River ship traffic, or turn around and enjoy the lush green lawn, designed to be walked on. To the right of the Manhattan Bridge, the tall building with the cupola and clocktower is one of the Gair (warehouse) Buildings (William Hugginson, 1914). At the end of the boardwalk is a cut-away wooden water tank, to be used as a shelter or for a concessionnaire. These ubiquitous water tanks that adorn so many of New York's buildings are made by the Rosenwach Water Tank Company of Long Island City, the last survivor of many such manufacturers.

The backdrop of the park, and its main feature, is the **Empire Stores,** a monumental row of seven connected brick warehouses with long rows of similar round-arched windows and doors. Erected in two stages, the first group to the west in 1870, and the westernmost section in 1885, by architect Thomas Stone, they share a unified façade. Loading hoists project from the flat roofs under corbelled roof cornices, and the doors and windows have heavy iron shutters that swing on pintle-type hinges. Metal tie-rod caps in the shape of stars reinforce the walls and add a decorative touch. In front of the Stores and leading to the water's edge were once railroad sidings to accommodate freight cars brought by car floats from the various railroad terminals around the city. The Empire Stores were used originally for the general storage of such raw materials as coffee beans, animal hides, grains, raw sugar and molasses, brought from points all over the world. They were just one of many such warehouses that lined the Brooklyn waterfront for miles, earning the borough the sobriquet "the walled city." No longer in use, they were acquired in 1963 by Con Edison, and are to be turned over to the city for a permanent home for the National Marine Historical Museum.

Turn left on Water Street and right on Dock Street to Front Street, and turn right again.

No. 5–7 Front Street is a small Greek Revival structure built in 1834 for the Long Island Insurance Company, and may be the earliest example of an office building which still survives in the entire city. The insurance company lasted until 1867, when the building was sold to the bank that erected its office at the corner to the left. Note the original iron hand-railings, ornamented with scrolls and acorns, which are preserved at the central doorway. The façade above the first floor is in Flemish-bond brickwork, with alternating long bricks (stretchers) and short bricks (headers), typical of better buildings erected during the Federal and Greek Revival periods. Stone windowsills and cap-molded lintels and a brick fascia below the roof cornice are typical of the style. The building is now occupied by the Under the Bridge Tavern. Peek in at the rolled sheet-tin ceilings, still in place and in good condition.

At the northeast corner of Fulton and Front streets is a highly ornate cast-iron-front building erected in 1869 for the **Long Island Safe Deposit Company.** Designed by William Mundell at a time when cast iron had come into vogue as a successful building medium, the highly decorative façade is modeled after a Venetian Renaissance palace. The company's safety-deposit vaults were once visible on the first floor of the bank, set in their own granite foundations. The bank closed in 1891 and the building has since served a wide variety of owners; and in 1981 it was converted into a two-level restaurant, called the Ferrybank. The new owners have retained the bank's old balcony for part of the dining area, and have managed exceedingly well to restore much of the ornate ironwork, both inside and out, in spite of the ravages of time and indifferent previous owners.

The cast-iron façade is unique in this area, and its delicate detailing is worth a few minutes' examination. The first-floor round-arched windows are protected by iron window guards with fleur-de-lis cresting, and are separated by pilasters with egg-and-dart capitals. The second-story windows are even more ornate and recall the style of the Venetian Renaissance *palazzi.* All details, both of the exterior as well as the interior, were rendered in cast iron, since it was its fireproofing qualities that attracted the original owners. The old bank is on the site of the 19th-century Abraham Remsen home and dry goods store which had replaced the original stone farmhouse of the Rapelje family.

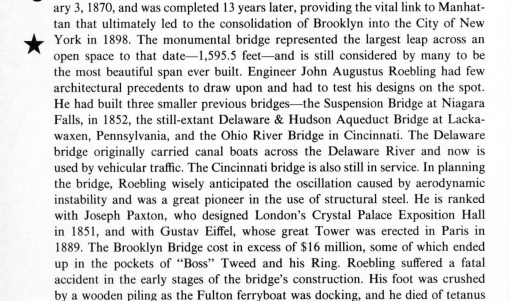

A BRIEF NOTE ABOUT THE BROOKLYN BRIDGE. Construction began on January 3, 1870, and was completed 13 years later, providing the vital link to Manhattan that ultimately led to the consolidation of Brooklyn into the City of New York in 1898. The monumental bridge represented the largest leap across an open space to that date—1,595.5 feet—and is still considered by many to be the most beautiful span ever built. Engineer John Augustus Roebling had few architectural precedents to draw upon and had to test his designs on the spot. He had built three smaller previous bridges—the Suspension Bridge at Niagara Falls, in 1852, the still-extant Delaware & Hudson Aqueduct Bridge at Lackawaxen, Pennsylvania, and the Ohio River Bridge in Cincinnati. The Delaware bridge originally carried canal boats across the Delaware River and now is used by vehicular traffic. The Cincinnati bridge is also still in service. In planning the bridge, Roebling wisely anticipated the oscillation caused by aerodynamic instability and was a great pioneer in the use of structural steel. He is ranked with Joseph Paxton, who designed London's Crystal Palace Exposition Hall in 1851, and with Gustav Eiffel, whose great Tower was erected in Paris in 1889. The Brooklyn Bridge cost in excess of $16 million, some of which ended up in the pockets of "Boss" Tweed and his Ring. Roebling suffered a fatal accident in the early stages of the bridge's construction. His foot was crushed by a wooden piling as the Fulton ferryboat was docking, and he died of tetanus a few weeks later. His son, Washington Augustus Roebling, carried on the project, and proved himself as capable an engineer as his father. He, too, was struck down by the bridge, suffering a disabling attack of caisson disease (the bends) from a too-rapid ascent from the underwater pressure chambers, and he directed the remaining work from the window of his sickroom, several blocks away. Little was known then of nitrogen narcosis, and the dangerous construction job took the lives of many workers. Opening day caused some furor among the Irish population of the city, as the date coincided with Queen Victoria's birthday. Shortly thereafter, a tragedy occurred that took the lives of a number of bridge pedestrians caught in an unexplained panic at the Manhattan end. Newspaper accounts attributed the crush to an organization of pickpockets who spread confusion to facilitate their criminal activities. To date 45 people have leaped from the bridge, of whom only 11 survived, including a Bowery saloonkeeper named Steve Brodie, whose claim of having survived the plunge may have been a publicity stunt. For many years the bridge carried cable cars, then the trains of the Brooklyn Elevated Railway, as well as trolley cars. The trolleys and trains were removed in the early 1940s and replaced by additional traffic lanes. More supporting cables were added later, but the strength and beauty of the bridge remains an enduring monument to the genius and skill of the Roeblings. A few years ago the twin Gothic-style stone piers were sand-blasted, and to everyone's surprise, the original color of the granite was revealed to be pink!

The view of the Manhattan skyline at dusk, framed in the dark arches and gossamerlike cables of the great span, is a never-to-be-forgotten experience. Thomas Wolfe, in *Of Time and the River,* extolled the beauty of the bridge "whose wing-like sweep" reached across to the "shining city, far-flung and blazing into tiers of jeweled light."

End of tour. To reach the IND A line, walk back along Fulton Street (Cadman Plaza West) two blocks past the expressway ramp. (Be very careful of oncoming traffic!) The station entrance is opposite Cranberry Street, adjacent to the Whitman Close town houses, where the first Brooklyn Heights tour began. Or take the B-25 or B-41 bus at its turnaround at the corner of Furman Street to Borough Hall for the IRT or BMT subways.

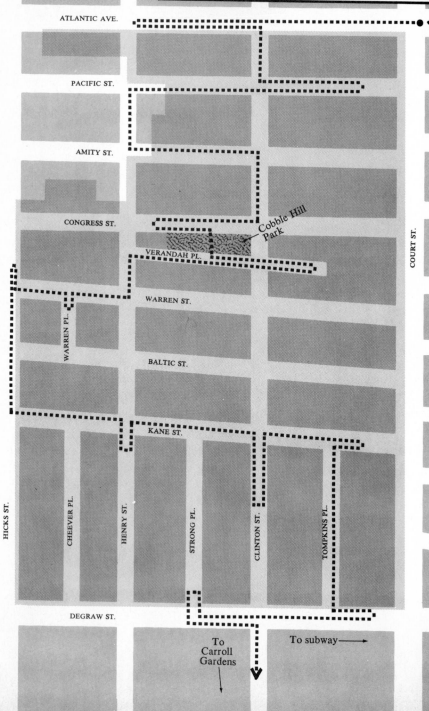

STATE ST.

COBBLE HILL

Shaded area indicates
boundaries of
Cobble Hill Historic District

ATLANTIC AVE.

start

PACIFIC ST.

AMITY ST.

CONGRESS ST.

Cobble Hill Park

VERANDAH PL.

WARREN ST.

WARREN PL.

BALTIC ST.

KANE ST.

HICKS ST.

CHEEVER PL.

HENRY ST.

STRONG PL.

CLINTON ST.

TOMPKINS PL.

DEGRAW ST.

To subway →

To
Carroll
Gardens

COURT ST.

BROOKLYN-QUEENS EXPRESSWAY

16. Cobble Hill and Carroll Gardens

[*IRT Lexington Avenue or Broadway-Seventh Avenue lines to Borough Hall, walk south on Court Street four blocks to Atlantic Avenue; IND F, GG lines to Bergen Street, walk back (north) three blocks to Atlantic Avenue and left (west) two blocks to Court Street*]

The history of Cobble Hill began in the mid-17th century when Dutch colonists were granted patents to farm the land between the Gowanus * valley and the East River shore. The hilly terrain was very fertile and the area remained a bucolic suburb for over 10 years.

At the outbreak of the Revolutionary War, Cobble Hill figured in the Battle of Long Island, when the garrison of a small fort built on a promontory known as "Cobbleshill" fired a prearranged two-gun signal to warn General Washington's Continental Army that the British had landed at Gravesend, down the bay. It was from this redoubt—one of several strong points along the heights of Brooklyn—that Washington and his generals on August 27, 1776, observed the massive forces of Lord Howe gradually overwhelm the patriot defenders and force them into a strategic withdrawal across the East River to Manhattan. The British Army subsequently destroyed the fort and painstakingly cut away the commanding high ground on which it was built.

During the War of 1812, another fortification was erected nearby, and named Fort Swift; however, no invading forces attacked New York, and the defending cannon remained silent.

In 1834 Cobble Hill was annexed by the newly incorporated City of Brooklyn, joining adjacent Brooklyn Heights, which earlier comprised most of the original Village of Brooklyn. Many of the old Dutch land holdings were broken up

---

* *Gowanus* derives from the name of the Indian sachem, Gouwane, who sold the first land to the Dutch in 1636.

into smaller lots for residential development, and with the opening two years later of the South Ferry connecting District Street (now Atlantic Avenue) with the southern tip of Manhattan, the area grew rapidly. The street pattern of Cobble Hill was laid out from Atlantic Avenue south to what is now Kane Street and Strong Place, and row-house construction began in earnest. By the mid-19th century, the district referred to as "South Brooklyn" had lost all of its rural character and become largely a residential suburb of mostly wealthy merchants and a completely self-contained community with its own shops, churches, school, and bank, and some light manufacturing. The growing population was swelled by an influx of immigrants, particularly from Germany and Italy; and with the opening in 1879 of Alfred T. White's famous "model tenements," other nationality groups—Irish, English, Swedes, and Norwegians—settled in Cobble Hill. After World War I, the neighborhood attracted large numbers of Syrians and Lebanese, and today Atlantic Avenue is known as Brooklyn's Middle East. In more recent times, new immigrants from Latin America have joined the proverbial "melting pot"; and young families of all backgrounds, in search of lower-cost housing, have been buying up row houses, carefully restoring them, and putting Cobble Hill into the front ranks of New York's "Brownstone Revolution." What was at the turn of the century merely a "workingman's district" has become a very desirable place to live. Cobble Hill has a unique quality of its own, with 19th-century moderate-income houses, much well-preserved ironwork, a uniform skyline punctuated only by occasional churches—many of them architectural gems—tree-lined streets, and a surprising small-town atmosphere. In 1969 22 blocks were designated by the New York City Landmarks Commission as the **Cobble Hill Historic District.**

The walking tour begins at Atlantic Avenue and Court Street.

In 1836 ferry service was inaugurated between **Atlantic Avenue** (then Atlantic Street) and the southern tip of Manhattan. The same year, the Brooklyn & Jamaica Railroad constructed a right of way along Atlantic Street, connecting the South Ferry with the town of Jamaica and the Long Island Rail Road, and the thoroughfare developed quickly as one of the major commercial arteries of Long Island. The grade up Atlantic Street proved to be too steep for the tiny wood-burning locomotives, and in 1844 construction was begun on a half-mile-long tunnel under the street, extending from Columbia Street almost to Boerum Place. Seven months later, New York's first underground railroad began operation, with trains preceded through the tunnel by a man on horseback. It remained in service for only 16 years, as a group of merchants and politicians pushed through legislation banning all steam railroad operations from the City of Brooklyn. The tunnel was closed, and the reorganized Brooklyn Central & Jamaica Railroad moved its terminal to Flatbush Avenue, where it was forced to use horsecars as far as the city line. The tunnel is still in existence under Atlantic Avenue and has been the subject of much speculation for many years. In 1911 the Brooklyn _Daily Eagle_ reported at length on a fruitless search for an entrance to the tunnel, as rumors were rampant on its use by counterfeiters, smugglers, bootleggers, and white slavers. Ultimately, access was obtained, but the search was called off prematurely because of the large river rats and an inadequate means of illuminating the tunnel. Stories still persist about the mysterious underground passage, and it is even claimed that a complete train with locomotive and string of wooden coaches lies hidden in the dark recesses under the avenue. One merchant swears that late at night he occasionally hears the muffled blast of a steam whistle beneath the streets (the Long Island *was* the first railroad to use the steam whistle).

The Long Island Rail Road tunnel under Atlantic Avenue, from an engraving, ca. 1844. The tunnel was used for only 16 years, before being forced to close by a City of Brooklyn ordinance against steam locomotives. (Long Island Historical Society)

At the turn of the century, Atlantic Avenue was heavily Swedish and was known locally as "Swedish Broadway." The Avenue is now famous for its variety of Middle Eastern establishments that line the street almost to the river. As you walk along the avenue, notice the restaurants and souvenir stores; but more importantly, the Syrian-Lebanese groceries and specialty food shops, stocked with their special hollow, flat bread, twisted cheese, halvah, baklava, pistachio nuts, stuffed grape leaves, yoghurt, and a thousand other taste-tempting delicacies. Take a pocketful of goodies with you, as there are few places of refreshment along the way.

The Independence Savings Bank, formerly the South Brooklyn Savings Bank, at the corner of Atlantic Avenue and Court Street, is reminiscent of a Florentine *palazzo*. Typical is the heavily rusticated façade and the highly ornamental door frame with sculpture above (on the Court Street side). The roof cornice is rather unusual with its row of carved stone eagles supporting it. The bank building was completed in 1922 from plans by McKenzie, Voorhees & Gmelin. An addition (No. 136 Court Street) was built in 1936, also in Italian Renaissance style. This was the site of "Cobbleshill," the conical-shaped hill on which the Revolutionary War fort was built. The little promontory was also called "Ponkiesbergh." Nearby, and roughly following the present route of Court Street, was the old Red Hook Lane, laid out in 1760. When the Cobble Hill street grid was laid out, the ancient road was demapped. Read the historical plaque on the Court Street side.

Walk west on the right (north) side of Atlantic Avenue.

No. 180 Atlantic Avenue is a commercial cast-iron-front building, erected in 1873. Except for the storefront, the structure is in pristine condition. Cast iron was a very popular medium of building-front construction during the period 1860–90 [for information on cast-iron building construction, *see* introduction to the SoHo Cast-Iron District walking tour]. The roof cornice has a typical Victorian design. Compare the window enframements of the upper two floors with those of the second story.

Although Nos. 164–168 would seem to have been built in 1859, according to the date set in the gable, the two houses were each built at a different time, but joined together with a common roof cornice. No. 166–168 was actually erected in 1860, and No. 164 in 1864. The house is somewhat representative of the Italianate style, especially in the bracketed cornice and the stone quoins. Sadly, the ground floor was "modernized" with no understanding of the architectural style of the whole, and mars the elegant appearance of the building.

The building at the southeast corner of Clinton Street was the original home of the South Brooklyn Savings Bank, built in 1871. Constructed of Tuckahoe marble and designed by E. L. Roberts, what is left of this once-magnificent Italian Renaissance–style structure is still impressive. The roof balustrade has been removed and the street level has also been "modernized" into incongruity. In its *Cobble Hill Historic District Designation Report,* the Landmarks Commission mentions that "the vault (of the old bank) was constructed of granite blocks mortised out to receive cannon balls between each pair, so that the stones could not be forced out of alignment without demolishing the entire wall." There was once "an imposing central doorway flanked by columns that supported the balcony of a pedimented window which was also enframed by columns."

On the northeast corner of Atlantic Avenue and Clinton Street stood the Atheneum, a public hall built in 1853, which became the home four years later of the Brooklyn Philharmonic Society. The orchestra soon found the space inadequate, and in its search for a "large lyric hall," the idea to erect a grand cultural center for Brooklyn was born. The result was the founding in 1859 of the Brooklyn Academy of Music on Montague Street [see page 379]. The Atheneum building survived until 1942.

Beyond Clinton Street is a **group of houses that still show traces of the Greek Revival period.** Most were erected during the years 1848–52. Many still retain their original roof cornices. Note the cap moldings above the second- and third-floor windows on Nos. 152 and 154, and the wood panels under the parlor windows of No. 140. Although all were residences, the first-floor stores are original.

No. 130, a much altered Italianate brownstone, was built in the 1850s as Brooklyn's branch office of the City Bank, later the National City Bank, and now Citibank. Observe the typically Italianate pedimented windows and the roof cornice with its dentils ("toothlike" blocks) and supporting brackets, but ignore the altered ground floor.

No. 124–128 was once the most important dry-goods emporium in the neighborhood, **the former Journeay & Burnham Store.** The firm began in 1851, at No. 126, now No. 124, and was so successful that new quarters were built in 1884, adding to an already large annex on Court Street built five years before.

Return to Clinton Street and turn right (south).

Nos. 197 and **199 Clinton Street,** on the east side near the corner of Pacific Street, are the only two surviving Italianate row houses of the group of four that still have any character left. Look for the following typical features: high stoops, round- and segmental-arc entranceways, floor-length parlor windows, and a bracketed roof cornice. The brownstone facing, a type of sandstone, was usually quarried in Connecticut or New Jersey.

The apartment houses across the street, **Nos. 214–220,** were erected in 1892 and reflect the style of multiple-dwelling house construction of the 1890s. Decorated with classical motifs and some Romanesque Revival influence, they are representative of the so-called "transitional period." The sheet-metal bay windows serve two purposes: to admit more light and air, and to add a decorative facet to the broad façade of the building. Note, too, the ornamental doorway with its round arch and carvings, surmounted by a pediment. The same type of entrance is repeated around the corner on Pacific Street.

Turn left (east) into Pacific Street.

The change in atmosphere from bustling Atlantic Avenue to quiet residential **Pacific Street** is immediately evident. The feeling of remoteness and tranquility increases with each block. The architecture of this block is varied, with fine examples of Victorian and Romanesque Revival styles. The diversity is due to the former role of Pacific Street (particularly the north side) as the stable row for the establishments on Atlantic Avenue.

No. 172 Pacific Street, built in an early Romanesque Revival style of the 1850s, was formerly a stable, and has been remodeled as a residence. A rather handsome building with its three arches and gable, it is an interesting counterpart to its neighbor across the street, **No. 173.** Built about ten years later, it is also an example of the Romanesque Revival–style stable converted to residential use. The center wagon entrance is now the garage door, and the old hayloft above embraces a picture window. Nowadays, a converted stable is often more desirable than an original house.

Old Public School No. 78, now the Louis Hirsch Memorial Jewish Education Center, was built in 1888–89 in the tradition of the small neighborhood public school and designed in early Victorian style. The roof line presents a dramatic profile with its elaborate cornice, gables, and central tower. A truncated slate roof crowns the projecting entrance tower.

A fine example of the Romanesque Revival style is **No. 162,** with its *rundbogenstil,* or round-arch windows and doors on each floor. A divided stoop climbs to a central landing in an eye-catching effect. Notice the elaborate cornice and the blind bull's-eyes on the stepped gables, which were added later, and the massiveness of the first floor with its piers and corbeled arches. Typical, too, is the extensive use of red brick. As you return to Clinton Street, observe the second-floor hoist on No. 169.

Return to Clinton Street, and continue west on Pacific Street.

The **south side of Pacific Street** reveals row houses built in groups of two or three, many in the Greek Revival style. Particularly attractive is the wrought ironwork of the stoops' handrailings, with their swirls in Greek motifs. **No. 122 is the oldest house in the neighborhood,** built before 1833. The mansard roof was added later, but the Greek Revival–style doorway with sidelights still remains. The doorways at **Nos. 126–130** and **116–120** are framed by stone pilasters supporting entablatures. Note the yard railings in front of **Nos. 118–120** with anthemion-motif finials.

Three Greek Revival–style houses on the north side of the block near Henry Street **(Nos. 117–119)** are quite simple in design, but the eye is drawn to the very ornate stoop and yard iron railings. The adjacent building, **Nos. 121–125,** was an extension of the Journeay & Burnham Dry-Goods Store on Atlantic Avenue. It was completed in 1881 and was designed by architect John A. Raymond in neo-Grec style. Note the typical incised floral motifs on the window lintels.

Turn left (south) on Henry Street.

The **Long Island College Hospital** occupies several blocks, and dates back to 1857, when it was organized by a group of German immigrants who fled persecution in Europe in 1848. None of the original buildings remain. Interestingly, according to hospital records, the original medical staff included a leecher and cupper. Across the street, the main building dates from 1905. At the southeast corner of Pacific and Henry streets stood the Hoagland Laboratory, the first private bacteriological laboratory in the country, built in 1888. The magnificent Flemish Revival building was destroyed by fire several years ago, and the hospital could not afford the exorbitant reconstruction costs. **The Nurses' Residence** (Beeston & Patterson, 1963) at the northeast corner of Amity Street is a modern addition to the campus. Diagonally across the street is the **Polhemus Clinic** (Marshall L. Emery, 1897), a good example of the Classical Eclectic style, representing the transition from the so-called Romantic Era to the more functional and less ornate modern style.

Turn left (east) on Amity Street.

The Dudley Memorial, 110 Amity Street (William C. Hough, 1903), was built in the style of a small French Renaissance château. The roof deck contains a small loggia with Doric columns, and the roof cornice, constructed of sheet metal, is painted to simulate stone and is set on very elaborate brackets. Named for the hospital's first council member, Dr. William H. Dudley, it was originally built as a nurses' residence, but now serves as a pediatric disabilities center.

Along the north side of Amity Street are several **rows of neo-Grec-style houses,** dating from the period of popularity of the style, 1875–81. Typical are **Nos. 129–133.**

No. 155 is a very late Queen Anne–style building, so late in fact (1903!) that it is almost an anachronism. The treatment of the windows is the interesting element—wooden two-story polygonal bays made of wood and supported on basket-shaped corbels, with a cartouche design.

Before turning the corner at Clinton Street, step back and admire the magnificent **Degraw Mansion** across the street at the southeast corner (actually **219 Clinton Street**). Built in 1844 and enlarged in 1891, it occupies a beautiful setting on ample grounds with lush plantings. The Landmarks Commission calls it "without a doubt the most imposing property in the Cobble Hill Historic District." The original house, in Greek Revival style, was built for Abraham J. S. Degraw, a Manhattan commission merchant. The major remodeling of the building was planned by the architects D'Oench and Simon for the second owners, Laura and Ralph Cutter. Mr. Cutter was a dry-goods merchant and treasurer of the nearby First Presbyterian Church on Henry Street. The Romanesque touches on the ground floor and the Flemish stepped gable roof stem from the 1891 reconstruction, as well as the lofty tower, which was equipped with the first private passenger elevator in Brooklyn! The sideways-facing brownstone stoop was also added, giving a feeling of elegance and dignity. The house was acquired in 1924 by its third owner, A. N. Saab, who has wisely made no exterior changes in this lovely mansion. It is indeed rare for such an old house to have been owned by only three families. The view of the harbor from the tower is probably reminiscent of the broad panoramas enjoyed by the early landholders whose large houses overlooked the Upper New York Bay in the early 19th century.

(Although not on the itinerary of the tour, No. 197 Amity Street, one block farther, near the corner of Court Street, is the **birthplace of Jennie Jerome** [January 9, 1854], mother of Winston Churchill. The house was built five years earlier in Greek Revival style, but except for some attractive ironwork on the stoop, little remains of the original, the façade having been "modernized" with a fake stone siding. Her father, Leonard Jerome, was a wealthy financier and race-horse fancier who built Jerome Avenue in the Bronx as a direct route to his race track. Jenny grew up to marry Lord Randolph Churchill in 1874. Incidentally, it was commonly believed that Jennie Jerome was born at 426 Henry Street, and a plaque on the house makes the claim; however, it is incorrect—she was indeed born here.)

At the southwest corner of Amity and Clinton streets stood the **Church of St. Mary the Virgin.** Built in 1922, it was planned as a much larger house of worship but was never completed, as the Syrian congregation acquired the former Congregational Church of the Pilgrims in Brooklyn Heights, now renamed Our Lady of Lebanon. The church was demolished in 1982.

Turn right (south) on Clinton Street to Congress Street.

Take a few steps down the block, then turn around and look back again at the DeGraw Mansion (219 Clinton Street) and its lofty tower. The need for its elevator is immediately apparent.

The rather large three-story house on the northeast corner (**No. 235**) was built in the 1840s. Originally a Greek Revival house, it was remodeled in the late 19th century with neo-Grec motifs (pedimented lintels); on the Congress Street side, it was given rectangular bay windows of stained glass, but the entrance stairway was removed. It is now the Convent of the Sisters of Charity of nearby St. Paul's Roman Catholic Church, on Court Street.

Turn right (west) on Congress Street, and walk on the park side.

Cobble Hill Park, a pleasant green plot, has become a very attractive open space since its construction in the early 1970s, with many benches for shady sitting and socializing. The original garish light pylons have been replaced with more appropriate older-style lampposts, rescued from the Parks Department's warehouse. The park was not part of a neighborhood plan, but resulted when the Second Unitarian Church was demolished. Built in 1857–58 from plans by J. Wrey Mould, it was fondly referred to as "The Church of the Holy Turtle" because the rather squat building's huge dome-shaped roof resembled the carapace of a Galapagos tortoise. Built by New Englanders, its first pastor was Samuel Longfellow, a brother of the famous poet and an active abolitionist. Until its removal, the Second Unitarian Church was considered an important center of cultural and community activity. When the church was abandoned in the early 1950s, a supermarket was planned for the site; however local community groups protested so vigorously that the park was substituted by the city.

Congress Street, opposite the park and almost to Henry Street, offers an interesting variety of Anglo-Italianate brownstones. (*Anglo-Italianate* refers to the English custom of having low stoops of only two or three steps.) Note the stairway balusters of **No. 173,** and the ornate door and window lintels on **No. 169. Nos. 159–163** are a trio of Anglo-Italianate houses which share a common double-bracketed cornice, complete with a rope molding and a gablelike pediment in the center.

Look across the street at its little cousin, **Nos. 166–170.** And next door, peek into the entrance of **No. 164,** whose inner doors still retain their etched glass panels. It shares a cast-iron fence with **No. 162,** with huge octagonal newel posts.

Back across the street again, **No. 155** is a *brick* Italianate house, with original entranceway and doors, a fairly elaborate roof cornice and individual window cornices, plus a neat cast-iron fence complete with fancy newels. Observe how the windows diminish in size at each floor, creating the illusion of greater height.

The red sheet-metal oriel on the house to the left (which faces Henry Street) is a curiously ornate appendage that was added long after the house was built.

The last house on the north side facing Congress Street, **No. 147,** is also the newest on the block, built around the turn of the century. It is another anachronistic Queen Anne building, but it is nonetheless quite charming. Note how the entry tower, like a medieval *donjon,* culminates in a high pyramidal roof. Note, too, the cast-iron newel posts and the ornate daisies on the handrails. The "brownstone" veneer, however, was added later.

Return to the park, and walk across it to Verandah Place.

Charming **Verandah Place,** which extends for only a block and a half, was probably built as an alley for carriage houses and stables, and dates from the 1840s and 1850s. The owners of the carriages and horses no doubt lived in the large row houses on Clinton, Henry, Congress, and Warren streets. Before the construction of the park, the little mews must have been much less inviting than it is today. **Thomas Wolfe,** who lived for a brief time at little **No. 40,** described his basement apartment in *No Door:*

> *The place is shaped like a Pullman car, except that it is not so long and has only one window at each end. There are bars over the window that your landlady has put there to keep the thugs in that sweet neighborhood from breaking in; in winter the place is cold and dark, and sweats with clammy water, in the summer you do all the sweating yourself.*

The diminutive "railroad flats" have been restored and are now much sought after, and the "sweet neighborhood" is much more peaceful than during Wolfe's Depression-years sojourn. He later moved a mile north to Brooklyn Heights where he finished *Of Time and the River.*

Explore Verandah Place (including the short cul-de-sac that extends on the other side of Clinton Street dating from 1876–78), noting how the new owners have used their imagination to convert their little two-and-a-half and three-story houses into handsome dwellings. The upstairs hayloft doors are now large windows, and some even retain the old iron hoists in the gable. At the Henry Street end, a former 19th-century corner store adds a nostalgic touch, with its ornate sheet-metal cornice and a three-story corner bay window.

Turn left (south) on Henry Street.

On the west side of Henry Street is the **Cobble Hill Nursing Home.** The nursing home, rebuilt in 1963, was formerly St. Peter's Hospital, erected in 1888 by William Schickel & Co., and later called the Congress Nursing Home. The original Romanesque Revival building lost all of its distinguishing features in the renovation.

Turn right (west) on Warren Street to Warren Place.

One of the most remarkable housing developments in the city, and probably the earliest, is the **Warren Place Workingmen's Cottages** and adjacent **Tower and Home Apartments.** The "cottages" and apartment houses were built in 1878–79 by businessman Alfred Tredway White, who believed in "Philanthropy plus 5%." White was also president of the Brooklyn Bureau of Charities, and after a visit to the slums of London, he returned convinced that "No European city suffers so much and so unnecessarily from the evils of overcrowding as does New York today." Deciding to help remedy the evil, he engaged the firm of William Field & Son to build the Cottages and Towers, to give the workingmen of the city "the chance to live decently, and to bring up their children to be decent men and women. . . ."

Of the 44 brick cottages, the 26 that face the pedestrian walkway are "triplexes" 24 feet high—precisely the width of the common garden. Only 11½ feet wide, they are small by modern standards, but in 1879 they were revolutionary. The flanking cottages at the Warren and Baltic Street ends of the walk are four stories high, neatly framing the garden and its twin row of charming row houses. In White's time, they rented for $18 per month. Each cottage cost $1,100 to build, but at today's prices the purchase price would be at least 70 times that amount (if one ever became available).

Walk around the Tower Apartments to Hicks Street. (For the best view, cross to the west side of the Brooklyn-Queens Expressway.)

Between Warren and Baltic streets are the **Tower Buildings,** and between Baltic and Kane streets, the **Home Buildings.** The architecture of these Victorian-inspired tenement houses is both innovative and attractive. White's aim of supplying each tenant with sunshine and air is admirably accomplished through the use of outside recessed balconies and three open stair towers, providing tenants with separate entrances and cheerful apartments. The buildings are U-shaped to allow for more light and ventilation. (Compare these buildings with the thousands of dismal "dumbbell" tenements built in the following 20 years throughout the city's poor neighborhoods, in which millions lived in squalor and misery.) The bold towers and decorative iron balconies create a dramatic effect. A central courtyard around which the six-story buildings are grouped was designed as a recreational area for the residents of the 226 apartment units. Shortly after opening, a four-room apartment could be rented for $1.93 per week, or $7.00 per month if paid for in advance. Three rooms rented for $1.48 per week, or $6.00 per month. And White still made his 5 percent profit!

Return to the corner of Warren and Hicks streets.

St. Paul's, St. Peter's, Our Lady of Pilar Roman Catholic Church (originally St. Peter's) was built in 1859–60 from plans by Patrick Charles Keely. Keely is noted for the number of Catholic churches he designed throughout Brooklyn, and the church, an interesting example of early Romanesque Revival style, has some unusual details. Note the crenelated effect of the round-arched window heads, and the little gables above the front side doors. Unfortunately, the tall octagonal spire has disappeared from the steeple. Beneath the louvered belfry are attractive brick corbels extending around the sides of the steeple. Because its congregation has dwindled, most of the church's activities have been moved to St. Paul's R. C. Church on Court Street, which now shares the same name. Only a Sunday mass is conducted in this building. The ubiquitous architect, Keely, is said to have designed some 700 church buildings in his lifetime. The adjacent **former St. Peter's Academy** (later School) was founded by the church's first pastor, Father Fransioli, in 1866. The architectural style, with its round-arched windows and crenelated doorway, is quite similar to the church. The building is now used by the nursing school of Long Island College Hospital.

Walk south on Hicks Street, past both the Tower and Home Buildings, and turn left (east) on Kane Street.

The street pattern between Kane Street and Degraw Street (one block south) is interrupted by an additional street between each of the major north-south thoroughfares: Cheever Place, Strong Place, and Tompkins Place [see map].

On the south side of Kane Street between Hicks Street and Cheever Place are an engaging **group of ca. 1850 town houses** that ascend in pairs to conform to the slope of the street. A corner store at each end enframes the row, but more interesting is the Greek fret design cast into the iron railings on the stoops of each house.

No. 139, across the street, also has attractive ironwork on the stoop and areaway. Star-shaped tie-rod caps strengthen the walls of Nos. 139 and 141. **Nos. 147–149** are a fine example of Greek Revival–style architecture, and have survived since their building date of 1845–46 in a relatively good state of preservation. Note particularly the doorway of No. 149 with its sidelights and fivepaned transom. It is believed that the ironwork gate and railing of No. 147 are original.

At the southwest corner of Henry Street, the house (actually No. 424 Henry Street) has a little attic room built in between the chimneys. On the Kane Street side is an **unusual two-story brick garage** (No. 140 Kane Street) which was erected in 1892 by owner-architect Owen McShane as a soda water factory, with space for horse stables. Above, the hayloft doors can still be distinguished.

Turn right to 426 Henry Street.

Although the plaque proclaims this as the birthplace of Winston Churchill's mother, Jennie Jerome, it is the incorrect location. As previously mentioned, the site is at 197 Amity Street. Before Jennie was born, however, her parents did stay briefly at this address with uncle Addison G. Jerome.

At the northeast corner of Kane and Henry streets is **Public School 29,** built in 1919 in the so-called Collegiate Gothic style of the period. The school blends well with the neighboring brick houses, and is a good example of a modern building complementing its more traditional surroundings.

Continue on Kane Street to Strong Place.

Standing alone at the southeast corner of Strong Place is **No. 176,** an imposing residence built in the late 1840s in largely Italianate style. It is believed that the house once served as the rectory for Christ Church at the corner of Clinton Street.

Christ Church and the Holy Family (Episcopal), formerly Christ Church, was the first religious organization in Cobble Hill, and was designed by architect Richard Upjohn, * and built in 1841–42. Its imposing tower rises 117 feet above the street, adding graceful punctuation to the Cobble Hill skyline. The church is built of varying color sandstone blocks that give the building a venerable and elegant appearance. Typical of the English Gothic style are the pointed windows on the main body of the church, on the chancel, and on the tower; the polygonal turrets above the crenelated tower, and the drip moldings above the windows. The tower itself is divided into several sections: the pointed-arch entrance with drip molding, a triple-pointed window, the clock faces, a belfry with louvered "windows" under pointed arches, and the four turrets. In 1917 the church acquired a number of furnishings designed by Louis Comfort Tiffany (son of the founder of Tiffany & Company, and himself a distinguished artist and noted stained-glass designer), including the altar, altar railings, pulpit, reredos, lectern, and chairs—all damaged in a 1939 fire, but meticulously restored.

---

* Richard Upjohn designed many beautiful Episcopal churches in New York City: Grace Church in Brooklyn Heights, Christ Church in the Riverdale section of the Bronx, St. Alban's Church in Staten Island, The Church of the Holy Communion and The Church of the Ascension in Manhattan, and many others. His most celebrated is Trinity Church, at Wall Street and Broadway. Upjohn's churches were virtually all built in the Gothic Revival style so popular in the 1840s.

Upjohn lived nearby in a house at 295 Clinton Street (near Baltic Street, one block north). Take a moment to visit the attractive interior.

The adjacent **rectory** (No. 326 Clinton Street) is in Greek Revival style. Its most notable feature, and one which is almost unique to the Cobble Hill section, is the splendid ironwork design in the form of a **swirl** at both top and bottom of the hand railings. Notice also the Gothic quatrefoil designs on **No. 328,** and on its twin, **No. 330,** with quatrefoil motifs at the pediments over the parlor windows and doorway, and a very ornate molding on the entrance. The pair of houses was built in the mid-1840s. Note, too, the circular iron coal-chute cover in the sidewalk.

No. 334, built ca. 1850, has a Queen Anne–style façade, added in 1888. The details in brick, stone, and terra-cotta were designed and assembled with great care, creating the impression of more building width than is there. One of the characteristics of the style is the quaintness caused by asymmetry, very evident in the relative positions of the entrance tower and bay window. The top floor is built into both the mansard roof and the tower, adding to the storybook effect. The remodeling was designed by architect James W. Naughton, who was Superintendent of Buildings of the Brooklyn Board of Education. It is hard to believe that its neighbor, **No. 336,** was an identical twin when built in the mid-19th century. How interesting it would have been to compare its original appearance with the remodeled Queen Anne house, but alas, a "Howard Johnson" doorway and an imitation stone façade deny us the pleasure.

No. 340, built in the early 1860s, is a one-family Victorian-style house. The widest in the Historic District, it has exceptionally high stories and an attic built into the mansard roof.

Cross Clinton Street and walk back toward Kane Street.

Nos. 301–311, reaching to the corner of Kane Street, represent an early example of community planning. The row is part of a group, some of which are immediately around the corner on Kane Street, and some one block farther on Tompkins Place. Built during the period 1849–54, they are interesting for their doorways, which are paired in projecting bays, and for their ironwork with Gothic trefoil motif.

Turn right (east) into Kane Street, and walk on the left (north) side.

Nos. 206–224 Kane Street are a continuation of the development just seen on Clinton Street. The group, built by Gerard W. Morris, a New York lawyer, consists of 18 Italianate row houses on three adjoining blocks. The effect of the paired projecting entranceways with their joined pediments gives an impression of spaciousness and charm, eliminating the monotony sometimes associated with row-house construction. Fortunately, the ironwork with its Gothic trefoil motifs is still intact on most of the houses.

The ironwork on this side is also worthy of mention. Almost all have ornate swirling stoop railings. Note, too, the Italianate ironwork on the balconies of

Nos. 219, 223, and 225—the latter two with palm-leaf motifs; and the railings on Nos. 231, 239, and 241.

Congregation Baith Israel Anshei Emes, at the corner of Tompkins Place, was organized in 1856, and is the oldest Jewish congregation in Brooklyn. The so-called "Mother Synagogue" acquired the building from the Trinity German Lutheran Church in 1905, which in turn had purchased it in 1887 from the original Middle Dutch Reformed Church. The early Romanesque Revival–style church building was erected in 1855. Originally trimmed with brownstone, it is now stuccoed. The main entrance is enframed by round arches supported by clustered columns, between which is a handsome triple doorway. On the Tompkins Place side, pointed buttresses alternate with the windows, and towers of different dimensions rise at the front corners. The changes in congregation through the years reflect the shifting population of the Cobble Hill area.

Turn into Tompkins Place.

Nos. 10 and **12** Tompkins Place belong to the same development as Nos. 206–224 Kane Street and 301–311 Clinton Street.

Tompkins Place is a particularly attractive street because of the narrow row-house arrangement as well as its outstanding and varied ironwork. Unusual, too, is the profusion of ornate window lintels over doorways and parlor-floor windows.

On the east side of the street are two rows of Greek Revival houses, **Nos. 13–25,** built in the 1840s. The splendid line of stoop railings with their ornamental vertical scrolls and paneled pedestals can best be appreciated by standing alongside the stairway of No. 13 and looking down the row at the diminishing perspective of the line of railings. This angle of view also enhances the three-dimensional effect of the façades, intended by builders of row houses.

Back across the street, a pleasant feature of these houses is the setback arrangement that allows for small gardens and extensive use of yard railings and gates. Note the elaborate curved lintels above the doorways and windows of **No. 42** and **Nos. 48–52,** built in the early 1850s by two owners who wisely decided to share the common design. A passing glance across the street reveals fake Colonial-style façades on Nos. 41–47, although they do have nicely landscaped front gardens. **Nos. 58–62** still retain their original Anglo-Italianate ironwork and low three-step stoops.

The visual effect of **Nos. 53–61** on the east side, in which alternate houses project and are crowned by a pediment, is very striking. Since small houses were very much in demand in this neighborhood, such an architectural procedure compensated for the 15-foot widths of each row house. **No. 61** is probably the best example of the style, with its low stoop and Italianate curved ironwork both on the railings and on the oversize newel posts. **Nos. 53** and **55** in the row have similar ironwork enclosing their front yards. It was not unusual for the builder to live in one of his row houses, and No. 55 was the home of Thomas Sullivan, after Nos. 53–61 were completed in the early 1850s.

A brief detour to the east on Degraw Street reveals three charming houses in the middle of the block. **No. 271** is a Gothic Revival–style house of unusual richness, built in 1850. Notice the characteristic pointed arches of the ironwork designs and the drip moldings over the windows, and don't miss the miniature pointed arches that support the roof cornice. Only 21½ feet wide, it has no room for a window in its angular bay. Above the entranceway, a molding ends in ornate impost blocks.

Nos. 273 and **275** display Romanesque Revival touches, particularly in their arcades supporting the dentiled brick roof cornice. Both have a paired entranceway flanked by masonry bays that climb to the full height of the houses, giving an appearance of more than their 42-foot combined width. These lovely forerunners of the Romanesque Revival period were constructed in 1847–48.

Now walk west on Degraw Street.

Degraw Street is named for Abraham J. S. Degraw, who in 1844 built the only remaining freestanding house with spacious grounds in Cobble Hill, at 219 Clinton Street (seen earlier on the tour). The Cobble Hill Historic District extends only to the north side of Degraw Street.

The brick church in the middle of the block, in a late Gothic Revival style (Theobald Engelhardt, 1905), was built for the Trinity German Lutheran Church, which had just sold its building to the synagogue at Kane Street and Tompkins Place. Much of the early German population has long since gone, and the building is now the house of worship of the **South Brooklyn Seventh Day Adventist Church.** Worthy of note is the ogee arch over the central doorway, the corniced pointed arches over the windows, and the church's high railing. Unfortunately, most of its stained glass is gone.

Continue on Degraw Street beyond Clinton Street to the church at the corner of Strong Place.

Formerly the **Strong Place Baptist Church,** this handsome Gothic Revival–style edifice since 1969 has been the St. Frances Cabrini Roman Catholic Chapel. Erected in 1851–52 from plans by famed architect Minard Lafever,* its massive corner tower dominates the site. At the west aisle, a small turret with lancet windows rises asymmetrically. The main section of the church is designed with a gabled façade and a triple-pointed arched window, while triple-arched belfry openings in the tower are flanked by high stepped buttresses. A solid iron railing with tall gateposts surrounds the church.

Adjoining the church, around the corner on Strong Place, is the Lafever-designed **chapel,** where the church held its first services in 1849. It then became

---

* Minard Lafever designed many churches and a number of private residences in the decade of the 1840s. Among his works are two churches in Brooklyn Heights, the Church of the Saviour and the Holy Trinity Protestant Episcopal Church; and in Manhattan, the Church of the Holy Apostles, St. James Roman Catholic Church, and the Mariners' Temple. He remodeled the Bartow-Pell Mansion in the Bronx, and is believed to be the architect of the Old Merchant's House on East 4th Street in Manhattan's East Village.

the church's Sunday school and is said to have been one of the most popular in Brooklyn. The chapel, now stuccoed, with its adjacent building (No. 56 Strong Place) is now the Strong Place Day Care Center. The Catholic church now caters mostly to the Italian community of Cobble Hill and the contiguous Carroll Gardens section.

Return to Clinton Street. End of tour.

Although the Cobble Hill walking tour ends at Clinton and Degraw streets, a short optional walking tour can be made into the Carroll Gardens section, ending conveniently close to subway transportation.

To return directly, walk east on Degraw Street two blocks to Smith Street, where the B-75 bus goes north to Fulton Street near the IRT subway Borough Hall station as well as the Jay Street–Borough Hall station of the IND A and F lines. Or turn south on Smith Street and walk four short blocks to the Carroll Street station of the IND F and GG lines.

A WALK THROUGH CARROLL GARDENS

Continue south on Clinton Street.

No. 363 Clinton Street was formerly a livery stable, where before the advent of the automobile, a horse and carriage could be rented or your own horse boarded. Those who could not afford the luxury of their own stable used such facilities. Before the turn of the century, livery stables were as common as today's public garages. The two-story sealed-up building was once a story higher, and traces of its third floor roof line can be seen to the right, where some of the original cornice shows through the brickwork.

Nos. 382A–386 are a handsome row of ca. 1850 Italianate brownstones, so narrow that they are only two bays wide and occupy only half a lot each. **No. 384** has the best preserved entranceway of the group, and its cast-iron banisters and balusters are in excellent condition.

Glance eastward down Union Street at the diminutive Gothic-style garage on the right side, that was once the stable of No. 393 Clinton Street.

No. 396 is the handsome **Carroll Park Branch of the Brooklyn Public Library.** Still an independent library system, the Brooklyn Public Library began lending books in 1897, antedating the New York Public Library by several years. The building, designed in a modified Classic Revival style, was opened in 1905.

Continue south on Clinton Street to Carroll Street.

At the northeast corner of Clinton and Carroll streets is **St. Paul's Episcopal Church of Brooklyn,** another Richard Upjohn church, this one designed together with son Richard W. Upjohn. Built in 1867–1884, it is a simple but rather heavy English Gothic Revival–style building. Enter the church and notice the unusual treatment of the interior. The transepts are extremely narrow because of the shape of the lot, and the supporting columns, instead of rising to the clerestory, terminate in capitals under large arches. The arrangement of the pulpit is said to be French in style, set halfway down the nave, together with a *banque* (a row of double pews directly in front of the pulpit to seat clergy and servers who would be too far back in the sanctuary to hear the sermon). The church is constructed of dark-brown sandstone and has no spire. St. Paul's adds "of Brooklyn" to its name to distinguish it from St. Paul's of Flatbush, as the two Episcopal houses of worship were originally in separate towns. The town of Flatbush was not annexed by the City of Brooklyn until 1894. Although it took 17 years to erect the building, the church was never completed. The base of the tower is quite massive, and had the steeple been added, it would have been one of the tallest in the city.

Although **Carroll Gardens** is a veritable "melting pot," the largest group are the Italians. Mainly from southern Italy and Sicily, they began arriving in the late 19th century, and their influence will be clearly visible in the names of many commercial establishments when we come to nearby Court Street.

No. 440 Clinton Street, on the southwest corner, is considered one of the finest masonry Greek Revival town houses in the city. Built ca. 1840 for well-to-do merchant John Rankin, it is in a superb state of preservation in its adaptive

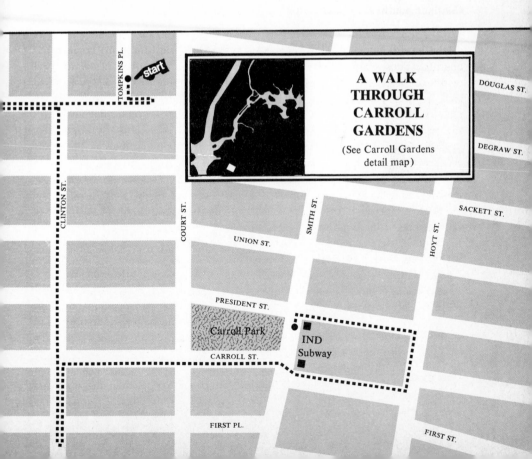

A WALK THROUGH CARROLL GARDENS

(See Carroll Gardens detail map)

reuse as the Guido Funeral Home. The salmon-colored brick façade is flanked by pilasters that rise to the full height of the house, and are crowned by granite capitals. The stoop, on a slightly projecting central section, is also made of granite, as are the cap-molded window lintels, the sills, newel posts, and basement facings. The Guido family, which lives in the house as well as using it as a funeral parlor, takes pride in maintaining the elegant mansion, and will on special occasions trot out an ornate horse-drawn hearse to re-create a dignified 19th-century funeral. When built, the house was surrounded by farmland and commanded an unobstructed view of the Upper Bay.

One block south, at the corner of Clinton Street and First Place, is the **Norwegian Seamen's Church,** built ca. 1865 for the Westminster Presbyterian Church. When the present congregation acquired the church in 1929, an imposing Norwegian-style wood pulpit was installed, and an old sailing-ship anchor placed on the lawn. Although most of this Scandinavian community has moved to the Bay Ridge section of Brooklyn, a substantial number of older members still come here to worship. Don't try to identify the style of this brownstone church—it is as eclectic as can be, with Gothic, Romanesque, and Renaissance Revival elements.

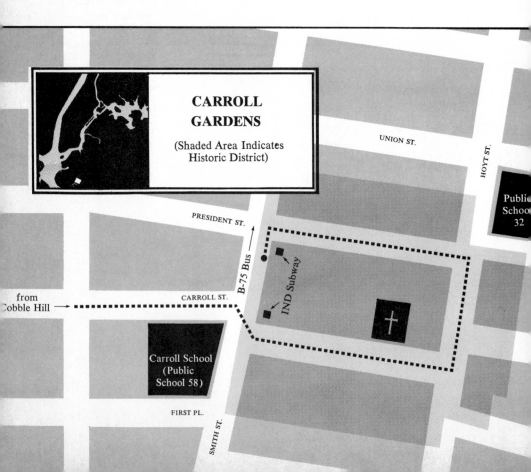

First Place looking west from Clinton Street, in 1896. Few changes have occurred through the years, giving Carroll Gardens a very special atmosphere not often found in a big city. (Long Island Historical Society)

Continue to First Place.

Here we enter the "real" Carroll Gardens (although not yet the Historic District). Look east (left) down **First Place,** then compare the view with the 1896 photograph above . . . virtually unchanged! The recessed row houses with gardens in front—the hallmark of the neighborhood—are a credit to an unsung hero of a land surveyor, Richard Butts, whose unusual and farsighted urban design of so-called deep blocks was first published in his 1846 survey map.

Turn east into First Place.

No. 70 First Place, although in need of maintenance, is rather well preserved. The stately entrance gates, iron fence, cast-iron balustrated stairway, the consoles framing the doorway, and the enframed windows all add up to a charming and stylistically accurate house.

Turn left (north) on Court Street to Carroll Street, then right, following the park, to Smith Street. Cross Smith Street and continue east on Carroll Street.

The park and street are named for Charles Carroll of Maryland, a signer of the Declaration of Independence. It was a Maryland regiment under General Stirling that during the Battle of Long Island fought a desperate delaying action at the "Old Stone House at Gowanus" * on August 27, 1776—an act of bravery by a small, outnumbered garrison that permitted General Washington to evacuate the entire Continental Army safely to Manhattan. The park was originally a private garden, but was acquired by the State of New York in 1850 and made into a public park 20 years later.

The Carroll Gardens Historic District [*see* map] is a small, quiet residential district, and very much a separate enclave within the city. Why the Historic District does not encompass the charming streets to the west (First and Second Place, for example) is a source of irritation to many residents who feel that the limited area of designation was the result of local political pressure.

Because of the peculiar street pattern, Carroll and President streets both appear to be dead-end streets, probably a contributory factor to the feeling of separateness of these two blocks. The pleasant appearance of the district is the fortunate result of foresighted 19th-century planning. Immediately evident is the row of set-back front yards, ranging from 25 to 39 feet. The uniform pattern

---

* The "Old Stone House at Gowanus," known now as the Vechte-Cortelyou House, was reconstructed in 1935 by the Department of Parks with the original stones. The 1699 Dutch farmhouse is located in the James J. Byrne Memorial Playground, at 3rd Street, west of Fifth Avenue, five blocks east and three blocks south. Cross the Gowanus Canal on the Third Street Bridge.

The Vechte-Cortelyou House, known familiarly as the Old Stone House at Gowanus, was built in 1699 and figured importantly in the Battle of Long Island. The house has been reconstructed with the original stones and can be seen in a playground at 3rd Street, west of Fifth Avenue in Brooklyn. (Long Island Historical Society)

of two- and three-story brick and brownstone houses built in long rows on shady, tree-lined streets, each with a well-tended garden, creates a sense of open space and architectural harmony. The houses date mostly from the late 1860s to the early 1880s, and represent a spirit of cooperation among the various builders. The row houses, built for middle-class merchants, were designed in two of the popular styles of the late 19th century: late Italianate and French neo-Grec. In spite of some building modifications, most of the neighborhood remains uniquely homogeneous.

Halfway down Carroll Street, approaching Hoyt Street, the houses on the south side become two-story brownstones; later, on President Street, the same pattern reappears, but on both sides of the street.

The group of new houses, Nos. 297–299 Carroll Street, erected in 1982, are on **the site of the Church of the South Brooklyn Christian Assembly.** The church began its life as the Carroll Park Methodist Episcopal Church in 1873; with the Scandinavian influx, it became the Norwegian M. E. Church in 1891; and in recent times, the Christian Assembly. In the late 1970s it fell victim to the arsonist's torch. Built in a flamboyant Victorian Gothic style, it was for years the dominant landmark in the district. Some idea of its ornate polychrome style can be had by examining **No. 295,** the original parsonage of the church, which survived the disastrous fire and is now a residence.

Space does not permit a detailed house-by-house description, but do make a circuit of the District by walking east on Carroll Street, north on Hoyt Street, and west on President Street [*see* map].

Although the tour ends at Smith and President streets, you might want to take a few minutes to walk one block west to Court Street, where on the northwest corner stands the architecturally significant **South Congregational Church** (more recently associated with the United Church of Christ). Erected in 1850 (architect unknown), it has a rather unusual façade with a series of stepped planes rising from the central window, much like a proscenium. Above are verdigris-colored copper finials which contrast well with the red-brick masonry. Walk around to the President Street side for a pleasant surprise. The two adjoining buildings, in different architectural styles, are the **Ladies' Parlor and Sunday School** (F. Carles Merry, 1889) and the **Parsonage** (Woodruff Leeming, 1893). Merry worked in the office of Henry Hobson Richardson, and the influence of the master is evident in the riot of terra-cotta adornment and other Richardsonian touches. The parsonage, a gem of Gothic Revival style, has typical design elements above, and on the entrance and ground-floor window lintels. The church building has been sold to a developer for conversion to cooperative apartments, while the congregation will retain the two rear buildings for religious purposes. The site for the church was selected personally by the Rev. Henry Ward Beecher.

End of tour. The IND F Line Carroll Street station is at the corner of Smith Street, with another entrance on President Street. For the A line, change at Jay Street–Borough Hall.

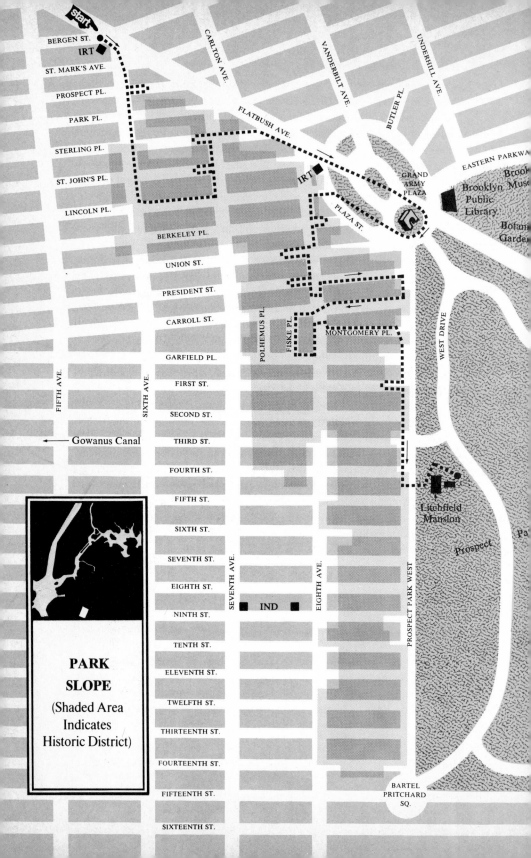

start

BERGEN ST.
IRT

ST. MARK'S AVE.

PROSPECT PL.

PARK PL.

STERLING PL.

ST. JOHN'S PL.

LINCOLN PL.

BERKELEY PL.

UNION ST.

PRESIDENT ST.

CARROLL ST.

GARFIELD PL.

FIRST ST.

SECOND ST.

THIRD ST.

FOURTH ST.

FIFTH ST.

SIXTH ST.

SEVENTH ST.

EIGHTH ST.

NINTH ST.

TENTH ST.

ELEVENTH ST.

TWELFTH ST.

THIRTEENTH ST.

FOURTEENTH ST.

FIFTEENTH ST.

SIXTEENTH ST.

CARLTON AVE.

FLATBUSH AVE.

VANDERBILT AVE.

UNDERHILL AVE.

BUTLER PL.

EASTERN PARKWAY

GRAND ARMY PLAZA

IRT

PLAZA ST.

Brooklyn Public Library

Brooklyn Mus

Botani Garde

POLHEMUS PL.

FISKE PL.

MONTGOMERY PL.

WEST DRIVE

FIFTH AVE.

SIXTH AVE.

← Gowanus Canal

SEVENTH AVE.

IND

EIGHTH AVE.

PROSPECT PARK WEST

Litchfield Mansion

Prospect   Pa

Pa

BARTEL PRITCHARD SQ.

PARK SLOPE

(Shaded Area Indicates Historic District)

17. Park Slope

[*IRT Broadway-Seventh Avenue No. 2 or No. 3 lines to Bergen Street; IRT Lexington Avenue Line to Nevins Street, change for No. 2 or No. 3 to Bergen Street*]

The "Slope" rises gradually eastward from the Gowanus Canal to Prospect Park in a several-square-mile sweep; however, the Park Slope neighborhood is usually defined as the area encompassed by Flatbush Avenue and Prospect Park on the east, St. Marks Place south to Fifteenth Street, and Fifth or Sixth Avenue on the west. The New York City Landmarks Preservation Commission designated a section of Park Slope as a Historic District in 1973 [*see* map]. From Dutch colonial times until the last quarter of the 19th century, the area remained largely rural in character—a hilly terrain of farms, fields, and pastures—bypassed by the developers of the nearby towns of Flatbush and Brooklyn. Flatbush, from the Dutch *Vlacke Bos* (Flat Woods), was not annexed by the City of Brooklyn until 1894.

At the outbreak of the Revolutionary War, the Park Slope area was the scene of the retreat of the Continental Army after the battle of Flatbush Pass. Outnumbered and overwhelmed by the combined British and Hessian forces that had made an amphibious landing on August 26, 1776, at Gravesend, the patriots pulled back along the Port Road, located approximately parallel to the present First Street. A brilliant delaying maneuver was executed by General William Alexander, Lord Stirling with a small Maryland regiment about a mile west at the "Old Stone House at Gowanus," at the present corner of Fifth Avenue and Third Street [*see* Cobble Hill, page 420]. Although his brave defending force was decimated and he himself was captured, Stirling's action permitted General Washington to withdraw safely across the East River to Manhattan.

Development came relatively late to Park Slope, in spite of the proximity of the heavily traveled Flatbush Road (now Avenue) and the opening of Prospect Park in the late 1860s. It was not until the mid-1880s that its potential was really discovered. While it is true that adjacent Prospect Park was a major influence in the growth of Park Slope, the completion in 1883 of the great Brooklyn Bridge was the catalyst. Within a decade, rows of brownstones, like

parades of caterpillars, inched their way up the gentle hill. In the blocks closest
to the park, wealthy merchants and professionals built lavish town houses and
opulent mansions. So many imposing residences were constructed that the section
came to be called the "Gold Coast." And so it remained for almost half a
century, rivaling Manhattan's Fifth Avenue in grandeur. The Park Slope neighborhood still retains much of its charm in the tree-lined streets, uniform row
houses, attractive churches, tranquil atmosphere, and the exciting variety of
architectural styles of its once-rich mansions. It remains a stable family community with a deep sense of civic pride, strongly dedicated to preserving the very
special quality of the neighborhood.

The tour begins at the corner of Flatbush Avenue and St. Marks Place.

Until late in the 19th century, **Flatbush Avenue** was the main thoroughfare
connecting the City of Brooklyn with the towns to the south (Flatbush, Gravesend, New Utrecht, and Flatlands). Stagecoaches gave way to horsecars, then
trolleys, and finally buses, while below the street came the subway in 1920—
built as the Interborough Rapid Transit and now part of the municipally owned
Metropolitan Transit Authority. Even before the mid-19th century, the Long
Island Rail Road had its Brooklyn terminal on Flatbush Avenue, one mile
north.

The opening in 1909 of the Manhattan Bridge with its direct connection
with Flatbush Avenue made it for a time the busiest thoroughfare in the entire
city. Until after World War II, it was a bustling and important commercial
street, but as population patterns shifted, it declined rapidly, yielding to the
effects of urban blight. Yet surprisingly, little of this very contagious decay
seems to have seeped across into the Park Slope neighborhood. Looking up
Flatbush Avenue, the Brooklyn skyline is dominated by the lofty **Williamsburgh
Savings Bank Building** with its 512-foot, gold-domed tower. Built the same
year as Manhattan's Chrysler and Empire State buildings (1929–30), it is Brooklyn's only real skyscraper. [*See* pages 462–463.]

Walk south on Flatbush Avenue and turn half-right into Sixth Avenue.

At the northwest corner of St. Marks Place is the **former Cathedral Club
of Brooklyn.** Built in 1890 as the Carlton Club, it was one of several exclusive
clubs for the wealthy. It later became the Monroe Club, followed by the Royal
Arcanum Club, ending in 1907 as a Roman Catholic fraternal club organized
by a young priest, George Mundelein, who ultimately became Cardinal of Chicago. The Club is now a Masonic Lodge, *Le Soleil,* whose members are from
the Haitian community, one of Park Slope's newest immigrant groups.

Turn left on Prospect Place.

On the left side of the street are three neo-Colonial-style houses completed
in 1971, **Nos. 77–85,** called the **"Cinderella of Prospect Place."** They were

Brooklyn Union Gas Company's "Cinderella of Prospect Place" project—a trio of decaying, abandoned stores before their conversion to town houses and the revitalization of the street in 1971. (Brooklyn Union Gas Company)

formerly one-story boarded-up and abandoned stores—an eyesore on the block and a symptom of the growing deterioration of the periphery of Park Slope [*see* photo, above]. The success of the transformation, using the original strong framework of the stores instead of demolishing them and starting from scratch, was the innovative plan of the Brooklyn Union Gas Company, and a joint endeavor with builders Asen Bros. and Brook. One of a growing number of Brooklyn Union Gas's "Cinderella" projects, they demonstrate the feasibility of restoring decrepit and abandoned buildings, and serve to encourage neighborhood improvement and revitalization. Before this project was undertaken, the row houses across the street were in little better condition than the deteriorated stores in the photograph. Observe the difference and how contagious this revitalization can be.

Return to Sixth Avenue and continue a short distance on Prospect Place.

Nos. 54–64 Prospect Place form an engaging group of Queen Anne–style houses, with an exuberant assemblage of bay windows, ornate gables, stained glass, and L-shaped stoops. The side wall of No. 64 is almost completely covered by English ivy.

Return to Sixth Avenue and turn right.

The rows of brownstones on both sides of **Sixth Avenue** are typical of middle-class row-house architecture of the late 1870s to mid-1880s. Most are built in the earlier Italianate or contemporary neo-Grec styles. Look for these character-istics of the *Italianate* style: high stoops with cast-iron railings, usually in the form of a baluster; round-arched doorways with double entrance doors; a pedi-mented entranceway supported by foliate brackets; segmental-arc lintels over windows; rusticated basements; and a roof cornice above foliate brackets. The original brownstone facing may be disguised with ill-conceived coats of paint. At first glance, the *neo-Grec* style may appear similar, but observe the curvilinear, incised ornamentation (carved by machine, rather than hand-carved as in the Italianate); triple vertical grooves on the brackets; door and window lintels with acroteria ("ears" that protrude at the ends)—all Greek elements introduced at the Ecole des Beaux Arts in Paris. The neo-Grec houses are also much more angular, having three-sided, full-height bays up to the roof, and rather massive newel posts (usually in cast iron, but occasionally in stone) at the tall stoops. It is apparent that many of the minority groups that have moved into this part of Park Slope take great pride in the appearance of their new brown-stones. Sometimes, however, enthusiasm for appearance has resulted in the instal-lation of aluminum siding, fake carriage lamps, or garish adornments.

St. Augustine's Roman Catholic Church, between Sterling and Park places, is considered one of Brooklyn's finest church buildings. Designed in 1888 by the three English-born Brooklyn architects, Parfitt Brothers, it was completed four years later. Built in Victorian Gothic style of a mottled sandstone, it rises dramatically above the uniform rows of houses. The interior is almost as elaborate as the exterior, with excellent stained glass and ornate sculpture work. The tall tower virtually overwhelms in its mass and detail. Spend a few minutes inside and examine the well-proportioned and majestic nave. Reflecting the shifting populations, masses are conducted in English, Spanish, and Creole.

Look east down **Sterling Place** at the large garage on the left side. Unless it has since been repainted, an 85-year-old sign is still visible above, reading "Fleetwood Stables." Before the advent of the automobile, livery stables were as common as public garages are today—the local "rent-a-horse" agency of the neighborhood. Horse owners could also board them at the livery stable, or rent an appropriate rig: a victoria, landau, brougham, or, in winter, a cutter. Sterling Place is named for Revolutionary War General William Alexander, Lord St*ir*ling, mentioned earlier. The garage is being converted into co-ops in another "Cinderella" project, and will be seen shortly at close hand.

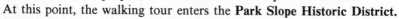

At this point, the walking tour enters the **Park Slope Historic District.**

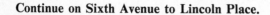

As you pass St. Johns Place, look to the left at the unbroken row of angular neo-Grec brownstone town houses whose symmetry is almost hypnotic.

Continue on Sixth Avenue to Lincoln Place.

The Sixth Avenue Baptist Church was designed in Victorian Gothic style by Lawrence B. Valk. Built in 1880, this picturesque church unfortunately lost its steeple in the hurricane of 1938. Unusual is the massive main tower, its attached polygonal turret, and the cupola over the transept. The horizontal stone band courses, which contrast with the red brick façade, are typical of the style, while the buttresses with stepped sandstone shoulders add another interesting touch. Look, too, at the ornamentation on the arches above the doors and on the corbels of the main gables.

Turn left on Lincoln Place.

Named for Abraham Lincoln in 1873, **Lincoln Place** is an extension of Degraw Street, an important street at the bottom of the "slope," in the Cobble Hill section.

Lincoln Place between Sixth and Seventh avenues has an interesting and varied collection of row houses. **Nos. 96–110** present an engaging combination of Queen Anne and Romanesque Revival styles, while **Nos. 99–113** show delicately incised neo-Grec detailing on the doors, cornices, and window lintels, including the characteristic "ears" on the lintels. The first two have French Second Empire mansard roofs. All have two-sided bays and are two stories high. The neo-Grec style is personified across the street in **Nos. 114, 116,** and **118.** Note their cast-iron balustrades and lovely newel posts, and the attractive yard railings with maple-leaf motif. Back on the north side is another row of handsome neo-Grec houses, **Nos. 127–135.**

No. 139, originally the John Condon residence, was built in 1881. Observe how the treatment of the bay with its pyramidal slate roof creates the impression of a tower, balanced at the right by a third-story mansard roof. Note, too, the sunflower designs in cut brick below the second-floor windows, and the entrance-door panels—both are typical Queen Anne features. Other little touches are the miniature Ionic capitals on the brackets below the mansard roof, the delicately designed stained-glass transom, and the lion's head corbel.

No. 153 is a massive Romanesque Revival town house with ample grounds. Now the Lincoln Plaza Hotel, it was built in 1886–87 by the architectural firm of Lamb & Rich as the residence of Frank L. Babbott. Typical of the Romanesque Revival style is the asymmetry of the façade. At the front, a three-sided bay at the corner, topped by a peaked roof, emphasizes the sweeping line of the whole roof. A large gable on the east side emphasizes the corner bay. The chimney rises high above a lion's head corbel at the second-story level. Note, too, the rough-cut lintel blocks above the first-floor windows, tied together below the chimney with lozenges; and the fret pattern beneath the eaves, combining brick, stone, and terra-cotta. Money went to money, as they say, for Babbott's wife was the daughter of Charles Pratt (discussed in the Clinton Hill walking tour) who made his fortune in kerosene, later merging with John D. Rockefeller's Standard Oil Company. In 1936 the former Babbott house became a rooming house, like so many in Park Slope. Nine years later it was acquired as a residence for the Presbyterian Home for the Aged, and in 1957 it was converted into a hotel.

Looking north on Seventh Avenue toward St. Johns Place in 1896. To the left rises the spire of Memorial Presbyterian Church, and across the Avenue, Grace Methodist Church. Both were built in 1882 in Gothic Revival style, but Grace Church lost its steeple in the Hurricane of 1944. (Long Island Historical Society)

Turn left on Seventh Avenue.

The corner mansion, once the William M. Brasher residence and now the **Brooklyn Conservatory of Music,** was erected in 1881 from plans by architect S. F. Evelette. Before becoming a music school in 1944, it had been the Park Slope Masonic Club for twenty years. The attractive Victorian Gothic–style house with some Queen Anne elements, built of brick and trimmed with brownstone and terra-cotta, is in an excellent state of preservation. Notice the decorative cast-iron crestings above the first floor of the projecting corner bay. An interesting roof line with gable, chimney, and dormer windows tops this fine mansion.

Across Seventh Avenue is the **only complete blockfront of French Second Empire houses** in Park Slope. The row was built in 1871–72.

At the intersection of St. Johns Place are two Victorian Gothic churches. **Memorial Presbyterian Church,** on the southwest corner, dominates the site with its octagonal spire rising from a square tower. Considered late Victorian Gothic (1882), it was designed by the firm of Pugin & Walter. The building is constructed entirely of rough Belleville (New Jersey) sandstone, with little of the polychromy so characteristic of most Victorian Gothic structures. Quatrefoils pierce the parapet above, adding a decorative element. The adjacent **Chapel** on St. Johns Place, designed by Marshall & Walter, was added in 1888. A charming decorative feature is the quatrefoil with a carving of three children being comforted by an angel. Only close inspection reveals that the Chapel and Church are separate entities, so well integrated are they architecturally. A number of the stained-glass windows in the chapel and church are from the Tiffany Studios.

Turn left on St. Johns Place.

Nos. **176** and **178 St. Johns Place** are two charming Queen Anne houses (R. L. Daus, 1888). Built for a pair of physicians, they present a fanciful array of gables, finials, dormer windows, Romanesque and Gothic arches, a conical roof, and even a tower. Although two separate buildings—No. 178 is wider—they blend together as a single unit. Note the caduceus in the ornate gable of No. 178, announcing to all that Edward Bunker, M.D., was in residence. Dr. William M. Thallon treated his patients in No. 176. A few minutes must be spent to take in all the delightful details of both houses' façades.

Across the street is the lovely **St. John's Protestant Episcopal Church**—the oldest in Park Slope, built in 1869 from plans by prominent architect Edward T. Potter in the style of an English country parish church. With its setback position on a grassy plot, it presents a harmonious grouping with its adjacent **Rectory** (No. 139), terminating the uniform line of row houses to the left. The church, originally called the Chapel of St. John's Episcopal Church, and rectory are fine examples of the Victorian Gothic style, and are built of rough-faced, random ashlar sandstone. The main gable includes seven narrow lancet windows, stepped over the pointed-arch doorway, and surmounted by a bell cote. The rectory has a Gothic cast-iron porch facing the yard, and an interesting colonnette set in a chamfered recess between paired windows on the southeast corner. St. Johns Place, formerly Douglass Street, was renamed in 1870 in honor of the church.

Return to Seventh Avenue.

The third member of the trio of Victorian Gothic churches is **Grace United Methodist Episcopal Church,** on the northeast corner, built from plans by the ubiquitous Parfitt Brothers in 1882. Constructed of a more varicolored stone than its neighbor diagonally across the street, the church presents a very picturesque addition to the cityscape. A rather large window and gable face Seventh Avenue, while a large tower dominates the corner. Its graceful brownstone spire, however, fell victim to the hurricane of 1944. Look for the ornate "diaper" pattern in terra-cotta around the nave's circular windows on the St. Johns Place side, and the foliate capitals on banded columns of the side windows.

To the left of the church, the **Parsonage and Sunday School** are an architectural transition to the row of town houses to the north. Completed five years after the church, also from Parfitt Brothers plans, it is a rough-faced building in a late Romanesque Revival style. Interesting is the two-story bay—curve ended—with transom bars and stone mullions at both levels. Notice the stained glass in the first-floor transoms. In harmony with the turret at the Ward Mansion farther up the block, the parsonage has a third-floor oriel on the south corner, providing visual balance to the blockfront.

The exceptionally fine row of four Romanesque Revival houses from the Parsonage to Sterling Place, **Nos. 21–27 Seventh Avenue,** were built in 1887 from designs by the architect of the Sixth Avenue Baptist Church, Lawrence

B. Valk. The row can best be appreciated by viewing it from the southeast corner of Sterling Place. **No. 21** was for a time the residence of opera singer Lillian Ward and, as the first house in the row, is the most handsome. Mounted on a second-floor corbel is an imposing projecting turret with a curvilinear peaked roof. Typical of the Romanesque Revival style are the contrasts in color, details, and materials, and although each house has its own particular details (as in the individual arched porches), the group gives an impression of unity. Note how the brick, brownstone, terra-cotta, and slate were employed, with even some ornate wrought-iron work. Try to find the Victorian "sunburst" motifs on some of the little dormer window gables. The entrance to No. 21 is on Sterling Place. Its handsome arched porch has dwarf columns protecting the original doorway, with wrought-iron work highlighting the transom and sidelights, and a bizarre cast-iron animal figure serves as the newel post for the entrance to the offset stoop. Look up at the Queen Anne–style ornamental band course just below the roof, and the profusion of gables and finials in the steep, hip-shaped slate roof.

A light covering of snow blanketed Grand Army Plaza when this picture was taken in 1898. The triumphal arch by John H. Duncan was still to be adorned by the monumental sculpture groupings by Frederick W. MacMonnies three years later. The Soldiers' and Sailors' Memorial was paid for by the citizens of Brooklyn and dedicated to the defenders of the Union in the Civil War. (Brooklyn Union Gas Company)

Turn left into Sterling Place.

The corner of Seventh Avenue and Sterling Place was the **site of a tragic plane crash,** when on the cold, misty morning of December 16, 1960, two commercial airliners collided over Brooklyn. One of the large planes fell on Staten Island; the other, in a vain attempt to reach the open ground of Prospect Park, careened into Sterling Place, the nose of the broken fuselage coming to rest against the doorstep of the Ward Mansion. A number of buildings were destroyed by the ensuing fire, including the prophetically named Pillar of Fire Church (which stood on the vacant lot on the north side of Sterling Place, just west of Seventh Avenue), the corner building (now a one-story funeral home), and the house that occupied the southwest corner—part of a row of 1873 residences. A large piece of the parapet of No. 116 Sterling Place was sheared off, and its replacement brick is of a noticeably different color. None of the passengers survived the crash, but astonishingly, there were no fatalities on the ground.

To the west of the lot which was the site of the burned-out church is a large garagelike building, and adjoining it is the red brick **former Fleetwood Stables** with a pair of two-story carriage houses of ca. 1885 attached. The trio of buildings were converted to co-ops in 1982, in another "Cinderella" project.

Return to Seventh Avenue and continue east on Sterling Place.

Just beyond the beautiful Lillian Ward Mansion is charming **No. 146,** a Queen Anne-style house designed by Lawrence B. Valk in 1887, and built at the same time as his handsome Romanesque Revival row around the corner on Seventh Avenue. On the west side are three lovely chimneys; while the main entrance has a pair of unusual wrought-iron hand railings mounted on wing-walls. The distinguishing feature of the house is its asymmetry. Adjoining the arched doorway is a wide-arched parlor-floor window, Romanesque Revival–style in character, divided in three sections. Above is a bay window, sheathed in sheet metal, with a predimented central arched window. A wide dormer rises on the third story, surmounted by a gable adorned with terra-cotta tile. A severe detraction are the white-painted mortar lines between the bricks.

The tour departs briefly from the Park Slope Historic District for a visit to Grand Army Plaza.

Continue ahead to Flatbush Avenue, turn right one block, walk through little gaslit Triangle Park, then cross to the mall of Grand Army Plaza.

GRAND ARMY PLAZA

The enormous oval plaza was designed by Frederick Law Olmsted and Calvert Vaux (the landscape architects of Central and Prospect parks) as a grandiose approach to Prospect Park. The plaza was designed in 1862, but the monumental arch and the accompanying groups of sculpture were not added until much later. At the time of the plan, the City of Brooklyn lay almost a mile to the north.

Enter from the north and, passing through a formal circle of sycamores, mount the terrace to see New York's only official **monument to President John F. Kennedy.** The latest addition to the plaza, the bust is the work of sculptor Neil Estern. The monument, with its unusually placed bust, was designed by Morris Ketchum, Jr., & Associates, and was installed in 1965. The original plan called for a marble cube with eternal flame, but was rejected as being too similar to the monument in Arlington National Cemetery.

The Bailey Fountain, built in 1932 and named for donor Frank Bailey, was designed by architect Edgerton Swarthwout with the central sculpture group by Eugene Savage. Male and female figures representing Wisdom and Felicity stand on the prow of a ship, while Neptune and his Tritons, together with a young boy grasping a cornucopia, present a humorous backdrop.

Ahead is one of the world's most magnificent triumphal arches, **the Soldiers' and Sailors' Memorial Arch,** erected in 1892. Its prizewinning design was done by John Hemingway Duncan (the architect five years later of Grant's Tomb) who planned it as an "armature" for patriotic sculpture dedicated to the Union forces of the Civil War. Several distinguished American sculptors designed the various groups that adorn the 80-foot-high granite arch. Topping the monument is a magnificent **triumphal quadriga** in bronze by Frederick MacMonnies, depicting a female figure carrying a banner and sword, flanked by two winged figures of Victory. The south pedestals display military **groupings representing the Army** (left) **and the Navy** (right)—both by sculptor MacMonnies. (Frederick MacMonnies was a pupil of Augustus Saint-Gaudens and a resident of Brooklyn.) The cornerstone of the arch, incidentally, was laid by General William Tecumseh Sherman in 1889. The **inner bas-reliefs of Lincoln and Grant** were executed by William R. O'Donovan, and their horses by Thomas Eakins (Eakins is best known as one of the great "realist" painters of the late 19th and early 20th centuries). The width of the arch is also 80 feet, and the aperture, 50 feet, with a span of 35 feet. Unfortunately, no sculpture was designed for the north pedestals, so the only view is from the park rather than from the approach. Framing the circular plot is a necklace of stanchions. The Soldiers' and Sailors' Memorial Arch is considered Brooklyn's most splendid monument, and is one of three triumphal arches in New York City. (The other two are the Washington Square Arch and the entrance arch to the Manhattan Bridge.)

Prospect Park is not within the purview of this walking tour, but should not be missed. At least a day is required for even a superficial visit. With the brief stop at the Litchfield Villa at the end of the tour, more details will be given,* including a suggested walk through the park.

---

* Information on Prospect Park, including a map and list of activities, can be obtained from the organization dedicated to its preservation and protection: the Greensward Foundation, Lenox Hill P.O. Box 610, New York, N.Y. 10021.

Return to the mall, then cross Grand Army Plaza (carefully!) to Plaza Street, on the west side.

An earth mound, or berm, along Plaza Street—part of Olmsted & Vaux's foresighted design for the plaza—shields the residential street from the noise and congestion of traffic. **Nos. 1–5 Plaza Street,** neoclassic-style limestone town houses built in 1901, may be considered the beginning of the **former "Gold Coast."** At the turn of the century, elegant mansions lined both sides of the Plaza; however, all but these four residences have been replaced by apartment houses. (The tour has now reentered the Park Slope Historic District.)

Turn right on Lincoln Place to Eighth Avenue.

The spectacular **Montauk Club** is one of Brooklyn's architectural treasures. One of the last of the many private clubs that abounded in Park Slope, the building's elegance is indicative of the affluent and influential membership. Completed in 1891 from plans by Francis H. Kimball,* it was inspired by the Cà d'Oro, a Venetian *palazzo* on the Grand Canal, whose glittering gold-painted

---

* Architect Kimball also designed the landmark Emmanuel Baptist Church in the Clinton Hill section of Brooklyn, the Trinity and U.S. Realty buildings on lower Broadway in Manhattan, and a number of other office buildings, theaters, and churches.

The house of Guido Plessner, designed by architect Frank Freeman, at the corner of Lincoln Place and Plaza Street ca. 1900. An apartment house now occupies the site. (Long Island Historical Society)

façade was symbolic of the glory of the Italian Renaissance. The best view of the building is from the end of Plaza Street at the head of Lincoln Place, where two of the elaborate façades can be studied. A warm golden color is produced through the careful blending of yellow and reddish brown bricks, brownstone, and matching terra-cotta. In its *Designation Report* for the Park Slope Historic District, the Landmarks Commission emphasizes "the contrast of solids and voids" in the design for the club. The groupings of traceried windows, the balconies and loggia, and the extravagant use of terra-cotta ornamentation engage the eye almost relentlessly. To the left of the elaborate main entrance is the separate ladies' entrance, as the Montauk Club was restricted exclusively to men. However, it was the first such club to extend the use of its facilities to women. This side entrance leads to the dining room floor, bypassing the main lobby. Above the main entrance is a band of carved Indian heads, while the spandrels between the arches depict American Indian motifs; look, too, for the little animals and birds. Above the second-floor round arch is a frieze representing the founders and builders laying the cornerstone. (The Montauk Club is named for the tribe of Indians that inhabited most of eastern Long Island.) Above the second-floor balcony on the Plaza Street side is a relief panel illustrating the inscription: "Wyandance, Sachame of Pamanack, His Wife and Son Wiankabone Giving a Deed to Lion Gardner of Saybrook, Easthampton, Long Island, July 14, 1659." Most striking, however, is the wide terra-cotta frieze that encircles the three principal façades of the Club, presenting a continuous history of the Montauk Indians.

Spend a few minutes and examine carefully the wide variety of detail in the imaginative façade. Let the eye drift slowly upward from the ornate cast-iron fence to the soaring chimneys above, as this is truly a unique edifice, which in its design successfully combines European tradition with American Indian themes.

Continue south on Eighth Avenue, observing the stately town houses on both sides.

The brownstone town house at **No. 20 Eighth Avenue** was the home of reform mayor William J. Gaynor, who took office in 1910. He regularly *walked* to his office at City Hall, via the Brooklyn Bridge, a distance of nearly four miles! On August 10th of that year, a discharged dock worker shot him, just as he was about to sail from Hoboken on a vacation trip to Europe. After an apparent recovery, he resumed his brisk walks to work; but by 1913 his health began to fail and the walks ended. At the Montauk Club, where he frequently dined, the waiters noticed that he hardly touched his food. Yet Gaynor sought and won nomination for a second term, and he set off for another trip to Europe. On September 12th, as the liner *Baltic* neared the coast of Ireland, the mayor was found dead in his deck chair.

Turn left on Berkeley Place.

Berkeley Place was renamed in 1881 for George Berkeley, an Episcopal minister and educator. It is said that many of his educational principles were adopted by King's College, later Columbia College. The original name, Sackett Street, is retained west of Fifth Avenue. The street is considered one of the finest in the "Slope."

No. 274–276, an exceptionally fine house, was built in 1890–91 by the architectural firm of Lamb & Rich for George P. Tangeman. The wealthy owner made his fortune through the Royal and Cleveland Baking Powder companies, and his handsome residence has been much admired for its transitional quality between the Romanesque Revival style and the newly awakening neoclassicism. At first glance the house seems to show all the characteristics of Romanesque motifs (massive rough-cut granite wall framing the open front terrace, the Roman-style brick at the second floor, the loggialike window with columns, a large central dormer window, and the tile roof whose windows have small lights in the upper half). The roof treatment is unusual, with a Dutch step-gable effect, meeting high paneled chimneys near the top. However, on closer observation, certain Classic elements can be seen: egg-and-dart molding enframing the entranceway, the Greek anthemion motif in the frieze, Ionic capitals and shell designs in the lintel blocks, and a delicate roof cornice. To the right of the entrance is a recessed, stained-glass window.

Return to Eighth Avenue and turn left (south).

No. 52–54 Eighth Avenue, at the corner of Berkeley Place, is another attractive mansion. Originally two separate town houses, they were built in 1886 and joined together after a fire in 1914. The building is now divided into apartments. Most interesting is the quality and variety of building materials: Euclid stone at the basement and parlor floor, red brick at the upper two stories, red Spanish tile at the roof, and terra-cotta for adornments. Note how the masonry is treated differently at each level. The Euclid stone is laid in rough-faced random ashlar; above the parlor floors, the stone is used to form a checkerboard design; and topping the next floor is a wide brick band of diagonal studding. At the corner of the building, the bay rises the full height of the building to a truncated, cone-shaped roof. On the Eighth Avenue side, the bay rises only two stories. Other noteworthy features are the huge chimney, the semicircular curved window, and the ornate wrought-iron work of the yard railing and the basement windows.

Nos. 64 and 66 are another pair of Parfitt Brothers houses, built in 1889 in a late Romanesque Revival style. Note how the proportions of the two houses mask the fact that No. 64 is four feet narrower than its neighbor. The stonework is excellent, providing an effective backdrop for the elaborate ornamentation. Polished granite columns at the top level support typical Romanesque Revival capitals. Both houses have L-shaped stoops with carved posts and street numbers hidden in the ornament above the doorways.

No. 70–72 is a massive Romanesque Revival mansion with some Queen Anne details, which balances the large house at the Berkeley Place end of the block. Built in 1887, it has several charming details: a Jacobean gable on the Union Street side with a brickwork design indicating the chimney flue, and a lovely corner turret with a wide band of studded brick whose design is repeated at the large gable in front of the house above the dormers. Terra-cotta ornamentation appears on the tower in sunflower panels and in the cresting of the roof ridges. Unfortunately, the wide-arched stone entrance has been filled in to accommodate a single entry door. In the early 1930s, the house was used by a bridge club and restaurant.

Make a short detour west on Union Street for a glance at the interesting rows of houses, **Nos. 905–913** and **889–903.** The latter dates from 1889, the former from 1895. Both display a riot of Romanesque Revival and Queen Anne details: oriels, arched windows, bull's-eye windows, crenelations, sheet-metal cornices with ball-topped spikes, dormers, gables, high pediments, and L-shaped stoops. Union Street's name reflects the national patriotic sentiment after the Civil War.

No. 860, across the street, was the carriage house for a mansion that stood at the southwest corner of Eighth Avenue until 1922. Few carriage houses exist in the neighborhood, and this small house, built originally in a Victorian Gothic style, was remodeled into a neo-Tudor residence in 1923. Its attractive leaded four-part window is typical.

Return to Eighth Avenue and turn right to President Street. Walk down the north side of President Street.

No. 873 President Street is one of the older houses in the neighborhood, completed in 1878. Designed as a "country villa," it has a "stick style" overhang at the front gable together with wooden supporting struts and elongated brackets. Sadly, a wood porch was removed some years ago from the east side. At the apex of the gable of this brick house is an ornate jigsaw grille. Wooden blinds once decorated the small windows under the projecting eaves. Note also the "toothed" brickwork at the parlor floor and second story.

No. 869, now the residence of the Missionary Servants of the Most Holy Trinity, was designed by architect Henry Ogden Avery for Stewart L. Woodford, ambassador to Spain and a prominent member of the Montauk Club. The rather individualistic house was completed in 1885 and is unusually wide (36 feet). Most striking are the twin oriels at the second floor, bracketed out from the masonry wall on struts. Unusual are the three wide arches above the entrance, the wrought-iron grille and glass entrance door with Art Deco–style peacocks, and a wooden roof cornice whose outlookers are carried on brick corbels. The façade is remarkable in its simplicity and is beautifully arranged; and, although somewhat Romanesque in style, its symmetry throughout is quite atypical.

Return to Eighth Avenue.

No. 101 Eighth Avenue, on the southeast corner of President Street, is a handsome neo-Georgian–style mansion built in 1909 for the president of a brewery. The stately building, set behind a wrought-iron fence with granite posts and approached by a low stoop, is a pleasant addition to elegant Eighth Avenue.

Take note of the Georgian elements which give such grace to the house: the fluted Doric columns flanking the entranceway, the well detailed roof entablature, the Flemish bond brickwork, the blind limestone arches with carved swags over the windows beside the entrance, and the balustrade above the roof cornice. The building is now the home of the Unity Club, which has occupied it for more than 30 years.

To its right, **No. 105** is a much more imposing mansion. Built in 1912 of marble in a neoclassic style, it was designed by architect Frank J. Helmle who designed the Tennis Pavilion and Boathouse on the Lullwater in Prospect Park, among many other public buildings in the city. A beautiful entablature is supported by four fluted Corinthian columns and is replete with motifs from ancient Greece, while the tall iron fence, main entrance with its bronze and glass doors, fanlight, and imposing central arch radiate elegance.

Adjacent **Nos. 109** and **111** are also worthy of note; the former, built in 1887, is in the Queen Anne style, and the latter is a Romanesque Revival house, completed in 1892.

The entire blockfront to Carroll Street remains intact and in pristine condition. The end mansion will be discussed shortly.

Return to President Street and turn right.

Nos. 902–906 are four pleasing Queen Anne houses built in the mid-1880s. The three-sided bays are complemented by triangular pediments in which Tritons' heads and scallop shells provide the embellishment. **Nos. 908–934** are a row of 14 town houses with L-shaped stoops, erected in 1899. The angularity of the façades is reflected in the shape of the roof cornices. According to the Landmarks Commission, No. 916 was the residence of novelist Laura Jean Libbey (Mrs. Van Mater Stilwell), author of some 80 books with such romantic titles as *The Price of a Kiss; Lover Then, But Stranger Now;* and *A Fatal Wooing.* Apparently quite popular in her day, her books sold millions of copies. She died in 1924 and is buried in Greenwood Cemetery.

Across the street, look for the unusual **cast-iron balustrades** atop the entrance cornices of **Nos. 923, 925, 931, 933, 935,** and **937.** And on the south side, **Nos. 944** and **946** are another pair of interesting Queen Anne houses, built in 1886. Note the terra-cotta gable shields with the date of construction. Noteworthy are the intricate terra-cotta panels between the parlor floor and the second story and the toothed brickwork. Battered brickwork flanks the parlor-floor windows and their stained glass, and at the left side of No. 946 is an impressive tall chimney. In the 1960s and '70s, the house was the Tollefson School of Music.

Turn right (south) on Prospect Park West.

Typical mansions of the "Gold Coast" are **Nos. 16 and 17 Prospect Park West.** Both were designed by Montrose W. Morris in 1899 and are representative of the "new wave" of Classical Eclecticism that began sweeping the country after its introduction at the 1893 Chicago Columbian Exposition. Architect Morris planned a number of imposing residences in Brooklyn, including Nos. 18, 19, and 22, and the soon-to-be-seen splendid mansion occupied by the Woodward School.

Prospect Park West was called Ninth Avenue before its "elevation to elegance."

Turn right on Carroll Street.

Carroll Street was named for Charles Carroll of Maryland, a signer of the Declaration of Independence.

The block between Prospect Park West and Eighth Avenue is one of the most interesting architecturally. The north and south sides of the street are quite different in style and arrangement, and it will be necessary to zigzag back and forth to study and compare the rather unusual aggregation of houses designed by some of the best-known architects in New York. (Odd-numbered houses are on the north side, even on the south.)

The house on the northwest corner (**No. 17 Prospect Park West**) has a handsome Ionic loggia on the third floor (Carroll Street side) above arched windows on the first floor. The pair of houses fronting Prospect Park West on the southwest corner (by Montrose W. Morris, 1898) were planned in neo-Italian Renaissance style. The corner residence marks the geographic high point in Park Slope with an appropriate pair of tall chimneys. A charming Palladian window emphasizes the first floor.

No. 863, with a full-height bay and unusual entablature frieze, was built in 1890 from plans by Napoleon LeBrun & Sons, architects of the Metropolitan Life Insurance Company Building and Tower on Manhattan's Madison Square, as well as many of the city's firehouses. Note the windows piercing the frieze and the lovely balustrade at the roof.

Nos. 888–880, built in 1894, are a row of late Romanesque Revival town houses. Look for the variety of window treatments: arched or flat, paired or triple. **No. 886** shows some of the Classic influence of the Columbian Exposition in its swags and dentils in the cornice; **Nos. 888, 882,** and **880** are perhaps the purest in late Romanesque Revival styling.

Adjacent **Nos. 878** and **876** were designed in 1911 by the Brooklyn firm of Chappell & Bosworth. Similar in plan except for their entrance porches and limestone bay on No. 876, they are reminiscent of the neo-Georgian style with their use of red brick and stone and their façade details. Pleasing is the modillioned roof cornice and the horizontal courses of stone at the second- and fourth-story windowsill levels.

Nos. 861–855 are a four-house row with alternate styling of each house. Built in 1892 and designed by Stanley M. Holden, they are basically Romanesque Revival with a proliferation of Italian Renaissance details. Note the polychrome effect achieved by the varying colors of the limestone, rough-cast brick, orange Roman brick, and copper and dark-red tile. The houses have alternating pyramidal and pseudo-hipped roofs, while a loggia effect is created by the columns supporting the lintels above the triple windows at the third floor on the second and fourth houses; but the dominant features are the ornamented copper oriels with tiled hip roofs at the second floor.

No. 853 is a very attractive Romanesque Revival–style house, built in 1888 by Harvey Murdoch, the developer of nearby Montgomery Place (to be discussed later). The massive structure is crowned by a peaked gable and flanked by pseudo-bartizans (small medieval castle-wall overhangs, added for defense).

No. 874, a neo-Georgian-style house built in 1904, has a pleasing Palladian window over the entranceway and a typical baluster over the roof cornice.

The five picturesque Queen Anne houses, Nos. 864–872, were designed in 1887 by architect William B. Tubby. Among other Tubby works in Brooklyn are the Charles Millard Pratt Residence and the Library of Pratt Institute [see Clinton Hill walking tour], as well as No. 53 Prospect Park West. The rambling quality of the roof line recalls the architectural innovations of English architect Richard Norman Shaw, who is generally credited with the so-called Queen Anne style. The fanciful profile is punctuated with gables, pseudo–hip roofs, and dormers. Note the "eyebrow" window of No. 870 and the Flemish gable of No. 872. A typical Queen Anne feature is the treatment of the windows and bays, in which the upper sash is divided into small lights (panes). A wide selection of building materials is used for contrast: brick, tile, wood, rough-cut brownstone, and sheet metal. Note, too, the "stepping" of the party walls between the individual houses, reminiscent of the Flemish Renaissance.

No. 860 is a satisfying blend of Queen Anne and Romanesque Revival styles, contemporary with its neighbors. The twin arched windows in the tall gable and the charming hooded dormers set in the roof are delightful touches.

Nos. 858 and 856 are a lovely pair of unified town houses that combine the Romanesque Revival with a neo-Colonial style. The rough-cut brownstone basement and stoop contrast in texture and color with the upper façade's smooth, orange-colored Roman brick. Note how the first floors are treated, with paired doors and wide windows unified by their arches. The fan design in the arched lunettes above both doors and windows is typical of the Georgian style. The stained glass, however, is more appropriate to the Romanesque Revival. A garlanded sheet-metal cornice is topped by a slate roof with tall, corbeled chimneys.

No. 848 is a very narrow four-story house, most of whose façade is taken up by the two-story central bay set on fluted columns in front of the entrance. Built in 1905, it reflects the turn-of-the-century popularity of red brick and limestone trim.

Adjacent No. 846 was completed in 1887 from plans by noted architect Charles P. H. Gilbert.* The house shows a transitional style from the late Romanesque Revival to the neo-Italian Renaissance. The stonework of the first floor—rough-hewn and light in color—and the large, arched doorway are associated with the Romanesque Revival style, as is the general asymmetry of the

---

* Charles P. H. Gilbert is best known for his designs for many of the finest residences in the city (the Warburg Mansion, now the Jewish Museum; the DeLamar Mansion, formerly the National Democratic Club, now the Polish Consulate General; the Burden House, now the Marymount School; plus most of the town houses on neighboring Montgomery Place).

façade; while the treatment of the upper windows and roof cornice foretells the awakening popularity of the Italian Renaissance style. Within a few years, such architectural firms as McKim, Mead & White would raise the style to its zenith. Note the unusual overhang at the roof cornice, with projecting rafters whose brackets end in carved animal heads.

Nos. **842** and **838** are by architect C. P. H. Gilbert, built in 1887. Both are in the late Romanesque Revival style and are particularly fine houses. The latter has an interesting V motif in the arch over the entranceway and a curved bay at the second story. More imposing is No. 838, built for James H. Remington, a president of the United States Law Association and a distinguished member of the Montauk Club. The two houses display the usual Romanesque Revival asymmetry, but the corner tower of 838 with its conical slate roof is its prime attraction. Notice the composition formed by the arched doorway and its adjacent window, surmounted by a three-sided bay, which is in turn topped by four arched windows, the whole being crowned by a triple-window dormer with a highly ornate peaked gable and finials. (There is no No. 840—it was skipped in the street numbering system.)

Across the street, **Nos. 817–831** are an eight-house row in Romanesque Revival style, built in 1896. Contrast the shallow two-story bays in the middle with the polygonal bays of the pairs at each end. Look, too, for the typical Romanesque Revival ornamentation on the stoops and parlor floors.

No. 813–803 is officially designated 115–119 Eighth Avenue, and is known as the **Thomas Adams, Jr., Residence.** Designed by the ubiquitous C. P. H. Gilbert in 1888, it is considered the finest example of Romanesque Revival–style residential architecture in the city! This grand double house was the home for a number of years of the Adams Chewing Gum king, whose huge white factory was a well-known and very visible landmark in Long Island City until its recent abandonment. Most striking is the overall use and variety of the masonry: sandstone, terra-cotta, and salmon-colored brick—the smooth brick contrasting in texture with the rough-cut brownstone base. Dominating the Carroll Street façade is a massive and deep entrance arch with a swirling leaf-pattern carving. Above the arch is a complementary trio of windows, enframed by the same foliate pattern, and supported on columns whose capitals have the Romanesque basket-weave design. Incidentally, note the clustered dwarf columns that support the elaborate entrance arch. The leaf design is again repeated in the peak of the gable. The huge corner tower, which is round at the first level, is polygonal above and rises to a tall, octagonal tile roof. Notice the quite beautiful stained glass in the first-floor transom bars and in the transoms above. Walking around the corner, the Eighth Avenue façade is also dominated by the corner tower, and is balanced by the two-story curved bay to the left, and the entrance arch is duplicated by a window arch to the right. Another member of the Adams family lived in this half of the house; later, relatives of the F. W. Woolworth family occupied the other. However, the day of the single-family mansion is past, a victim of the harsh realities of economics, and the Adams Residence has been subdivided into apartments.

Across Carroll Street, on the southeast corner of Eighth Avenue, **No. 123** is another Montrose W. Morris–designed residence. Built in a restrained neoclassical style, its soft, off-white appearance is extremely handsome. Brick, limestone, and terra-cotta, all of similar color, combine to create this monochromatic effect. The entrance is especially attractive with its arched tympanum above, displaying a variety of Renaissance motifs on composite columns. The anthemion designs on the long frieze below it are repeated around the building to the Carroll Street side. "Ears" can be seen on the corners of the attic story windows, while the roof cornice displays a lovely garland motif on its convex frieze.

Cross Eighth Avenue and continue west on Carroll Street.

In the distance, the 212-foot-high spire of the **Old First Reformed Church** punctuates the skyline. The Reformed Church is the descendant of the old Dutch Reformed Church, the first religious body in America. The church, located at the corner of Seventh Avenue, was designed in 1892 by George L. Morse.

Turn left into Fiske Place.

Charming little **Fiske Place** and its equally diminutive neighbor to the west, Polhemus Place, re-create much of the late 19th-century residential atmosphere of Brooklyn. Ignoring the apartment houses on the east side of the block (whose only merit is the pleasant view for its tenants), the small scale of the row houses across the street is quite appropriate for this short block.

Nos. 12–16 form a symmetrical group of late Romanesque Revival houses that date from the middle of the last decade of the 19th century. The second-floor bays of this trio resemble an exercise in geometry with their squared, semicircular, and triangular gables; otherwise their composition is basically unified. Back-to-back on Polhemus Place are a complementing trio of houses with identical façades.

Nos. 18–20, a dissimilar pair of town houses, were designed in 1889–90 by Parfitt Brothers. In common they share Romanesque Revival and neo-Italian Renaissance elements, but the differences in detail are clearly evident, and No. 20 is much more Renaissance in style.

The two neo-Grec-style apartment houses, **Nos. 22** and **24,** were built in 1888 and designed as "twins." Note their side-by-side arched doorways, three-sided bays rising full height, heavily bracketed roof cornices, and the still-intact cast-iron railings and newel posts.

Turn left into Garfield Place.

Originally called Macomb Street, the name was changed to honor the 20th president of the United States, James A. Garfield, two years after his assassination in 1881.

Nos. 248–256 Garfield Place are another attractive row of Romanesque Revival houses, each 20 feet wide, with alternating building designs (in a pattern "ABABA"). The "A" houses have full-height polygonal bays, while the "B"

The Charles L. Feltman Mansion, which stood on the southwest corner of Eighth Avenue and Carroll Street until 1950, when it gave way to an apartment house. Feltman is credited with having invented the "hot dog" at his popular beer garden in Coney Island. (Brooklyn Collection. Brooklyn Public Library)

houses have only two-story bays, above which is a third-floor balcony with Palladian window. Compare the treatment of the doors and windows of the two types.

Across the street, on the north side, are three **eight-family apartment houses,** typical of the kind erected in many sections of the city, including the Park Slope area, during the first decade of the 20th century. Built in 1903 in the then-popular neo-Italian Renaissance style, they bear rather fanciful and enigmatic names: *Serine, Lillian,* and *Ontrinue.* (*Ontrinue?* Could the builder have possibly meant *Entre Nous?*)

Congregation Beth Elohim ("House of God"), at the northeast corner of Garfield Place and Eighth Avenue, is an impressive eclectic structure with many Classic elements. Built in 1909–10, the synagogue was designed by Simon Eisendrath in association with B. Horwitz. Since the main entrance is at the corner of the building, the plan is pentagonal, possibly representative of the Five Books of Moses. A pair of enormous Ionic columns *in antis* flank the three-sided stairway, and are surmounted by an arched pediment with modillions, while a large dome with lantern on a polygonal drum is set above the entrance. On a pipe railing on both sides of the temple are seven-branched Menorah, or candelabrum, motifs. Across Garfield Place is the congregation's Temple House.

Turn left on Eighth Avenue.

The apartment house numbered **140,** on the west side of Eighth Avenue, has an Art Deco entrance located in a recessed central section. The adjacent building, **No. 130,** occupies the **site of the old Feltman Mansion.** Charles L. Feltman is credited with introducing the "hot dog" to the American scene at his famous beer garden in Coney Island. His opulent Romanesque Revival residence was designed by Montrose W. Morris, and dominated the corner lot until demolished to make way for the apartment house.

Turn right into Montgomery Place.

Montgomery Place, Park Slope's "Block Beautiful," is named for Revolutionary War general Richard Montgomery, who was killed in the abortive Battle of Quebec in 1775. The one-block street was developed as a single real-estate venture by Harvey Murdoch between 1887 and 1892. According to the *AIA Guide to New York City,* Murdoch wished "to create row houses that broke away from the traditional disciplined and repetitive approach." He commissioned

The northeast corner of Eighth Avenue and Carroll Street was the site of the J. H. Hannan House, designed ca. 1888 by C. P. H. Gilbert and built shortly before this heliotype was made. Another Gilbert-designed mansion, the Adams House, still stands across the street, while the fourth corner boasts an elegant house by Montrose W. Morris. (Long Island Historical Society)

C. P. H. Gilbert to design 20 of the 46 houses on the street, and the visitor may judge for himself how eminently successful the master plan was.

The following houses were designed by Gilbert: (north side) 11, 17, 19, 21, and 25; (south side) 14, 16, 18, 36, 38, 40, 42, 44, 46, 48, 50, 54, 56, 58, and 60. Harvey Murdoch himself resided at No. 11, the house with the impressive Dutch stepped gable. By now, the various architectural revival styles popular in Park Slope should be fairly familiar. Since space does not permit a building-by-building description, and the amount of time required to read it would render it impractical at this hour of the tour, the visitor should take a leisurely walk down this block, examining and comparing for himself each of the lovely houses, for nowhere else in the neighborhood is there such a picturesque assemblage of residential architecture so rich and so varied in detail and ornamentation. Don't miss a single oriel, arched window, step gable, bay window, L-shaped stoop, stained-glass transom, triangular pediment, corbel-sill, copper dormer, slate roof, or panel of ornamental brickwork!

Cross to the Prospect Park side of Prospect Park West.

The row of stately mansions along Prospect Park West can best be appreciated from across the street. **No. 22,** just north of the corner, was designed by Montrose

Millionaire industrialist Henry C. Hulbert commissioned this splendid house at 49 Prospect Park West by Montrose W. Morris in 1892. When built, it commanded an unobstructed view of the harbor. (Long Island Historical Society)

W. Morris in neoclassical style in 1899. Built of limestone with a bright-red, steep tile roof, it is an attractive, symmetrical building. **Nos. 24** and **25** also have red tile roofs, but share a façade of yellow Roman brick with limestone trim. Interesting is the frieze at the second-floor cornice of No. 24, with the typical Greek anthemion and palmette design, and the polygonal tower of No. 25, topped by a steep tile roof.

At the southwest corner of Montgomery Place stands a magnificent mansion, **No. 28,** built in 1901 and designed by Charles Brigham of Boston. Rising above smooth walls is a fanciful roof line with steep gables. Look for the fascinating sculpture work in the Indiana limestone walls: stone relief panels, bizarre human masks, grotesque animals, and finials in the shape of heraldic animals. The central gable is flanked by tall masonry chimneys as well as a pair of Flemish dormers. Note, too, the copper finial on the high dormer window to the left of the gable. Above the recessed doorway is a balcony with ornamental panels and rampant lions.

No. 32, designed in Romanesque Revival style by George W. Chappell in 1888, is approached by an imposing L-shaped stoop leading to a highly ornate entranceway. The color of the Belleville (New Jersey) rough-cut brownstone blends harmoniously with the brickwork on the upper floors. Observe how the coping, with its keystone motif, rises to form a finial, while the steep brick gable with its pair of arched windows and little slot window is highlighted by the upsweep of the stone coping.

Continue south to First Street (the old Port Road to Gowanus).

Montrose W. Morris's Park Slope masterpiece is the **Henry Carlton Hulbert Mansion** at 49–50 Prospect Park West. Built in 1892 for the millionaire industrialist, it is now the Woodward School, and one of the finest examples of residential architecture in the city. Hulbert was a paper-supply magnate and member of the board of a number of large corporations, including the Pullman Palace Car Company of Chicago and the New York Life Insurance & Trust Company. The massive fortresslike edifice is reminiscent of the work of architect Henry Hobson Richardson, one of the greatest exponents of the Romanesque Revival style. In its *Designation Report* for the Park Slope Historic District, the Landmarks Commission states that "one of the most dramatic features of the mansion is its picturesque castellated profile at the skyline created by the penetration of the roof line by bays, towers, gables, dormer windows, and tall chimneys arranged in vertical clusters representing the flues within." The freestanding, light-gray limestone mansion was originally two separate houses, the larger one at the corner the residence of Henry C. Hulbert, and the somewhat smaller one to the south built for his daughter and son-in-law (a practice not uncommon in those days). Although apparently equal in size, they are not quite, as "papa," of course, had to have the more imposing house. The tower on the north house is much more striking because of its polygonal shape on the upper floors. The south tower is designed in just the opposite manner, polygonal below, and round above! Unifying the pair, however, is a splendid entranceway with twin arches over the doors, "so beautifully joined by a single robust column," according to the *Designation Report,* "that they form a point of focus for the front." The houses also share a common entrance staircase and a third-floor loggia. Ornamentation is also used very effectively on the façade, combining Romanesque and Byzantine motifs to provide a pleasing contrast with the rugged walls. Lovely also are the rich carvings on the third-floor loggia enframement. To the rear, a second-floor porch was erected for a panoramic view of the harbor—a vista now totally obliterated by the adjacent houses. (When built, the mansion stood in "splendid isolation" at the crest of the "Slope.") The mansion was acquired in 1927 by the Brooklyn Ethical Culture School, which kept the building until 1977. After an interlude of ownership by another school, the mansion was taken over by the Woodward School a year later.

The adjacent mansion, **No. 53,** which now serves as the **Meeting House of the Brooklyn Ethical Culture Society,** was designed in 1900 by the noted architect William B. Tubby. The beautiful residence, whose broad entranceway is flanked by heraldic lions, was built for William H. Childs, founder of the Bon-Ami Cleansing Powder Company. The symmetrical red brick street façade is topped by a stepped, curved gable. Contrasting with the white limestone bay window enframements and gargoyles are the red tile roof and the bright red Flemish-bond brickwork wall. Pilasters flank the front door and arched window, adding to the symmetry of the house. Above is a wide bay window surmounted by a stone balustrade in front of handsome enframed windows on the third floor. Higher in the gable, these windows are connected to an upper window by a panel, carved medallion and a drip molding. To crown the composition, a finial adorns the top. Twin tall chimneys and a steep step gable dominate the south façade. A balustraded wing was added by the architect in 1907 to house a sunlit morning room with basement billiard room below. The spacious garden, which lends so much charm to the mansion's setting, is surrounded by an attractive wrought-iron railing set in brick piers. The Childs Mansion is a fine example of the rather scarce neo-Jacobean style in New York City.

No. 61, whose main entrance is on Second Street, was also designed by William B. Tubby. A brick house with a tile roof and striking projecting copper cornice, it presents quite a contrast with Tubby's Childs Mansion across the street. Built for Childs's married daughter, it is separated from "papa" (perhaps intentionally) by Second Street, and is also quite different in design. The architect employed the briefly popular North Italian provincial style, adding many interesting touches, such as the English crossband brick walls, the horizontal stone band courses and panels at the upper level, shallow bay windows, and the cornice brackets.

Between Fourth and Fifth streets, enter Prospect Park on the roadway leading to the Litchfield Villa.

Built almost a decade before the development of Prospect Park, this delightful Tuscan manor house and surrounding estate was the residence of lawyer and railroad magnate Edwin C. Litchfield. Designed in 1857 by Alexander Jackson Davis,* one of the greatest architects of the mid-19th century, it is the oldest mansion in Park Slope, and its survival (relatively) intact is a tribute to the aesthetic sensibilities of the municipal authorities of the old City of Brooklyn. Originally called "Ridgewood" and later "Grace Hill Mansion," the richly furnished villa was the center of social life of Brooklyn's high society shortly after the Civil War. The extensive grounds included virtually all of today's Park Slope neighborhood, from First to Ninth streets and all the land in between down to the Gowanus Canal. Not only did Litchfield make his fortune in Midwestern railroad development, but his Brooklyn Development Company undertook the draining of the swampland at the foot of the "Slope" and the construction of the Gowanus Canal. The canal is still one of the city's important commercial waterways. Litchfield lived in the villa until 1882, having sold part of his estate to the City of Brooklyn for the development of Prospect Park in 1869. It became the headquarters of the Brooklyn Parks Department in 1892

---

* Alexander Jackson Davis is noted chiefly for his Greek Revival–style buildings, some remarkable examples of which still survive: the old Custom House, now Federal Hall National Memorial (designed in cooperation with Ithiel Town) and Colonnade Row, on Lafayette Street; as well as the charming Nos. 3 and 4 Gramercy Park—all described in other walking tours. He also designed Jay Gould's palatial Lyndhurst, in Tarrytown—a magnificent mansion with all its furnishings in a charming rural setting, operated by the National Trust for Historic Preservation and open to the public.

Brooklyn south of Park Slope in the early 1860s was flat farmland with scarcely a house to be seen. Ten years later, Olmsted and Vaux's Prospect Park plan completely transformed the scene. (Brooklyn Union Gas Company)

The Battle Pass (now in Prospect Park) from a sketch made in 1791, where the Colonial Army failed to halt the advance of English and Hessian troops during the Battle of Long Island. (Long Island Historical Society)

and is still the Brooklyn office of the Department of Parks and Recreation. The Litchfield Mansion, or Villa, is considered the finest example of Alexander Jackson Davis's Italianate style. Time and Parks Department use have taken toll of some of the building's accouterments. Of the rich household furnishings, nothing whatever remains. Only the double stairway of cast iron, the central rotunda, and a few carved mantelpieces survive. The original stucco, simulating rough-cut stone, on the exterior walls has been removed, exposing the bare brickwork beneath. Unique decorative elements that have survived, however, are the corn and wheat motifs, instead of the traditional acanthus leaves, on the Corinthian capitals. The mansion also retains its lovely frieze and cornice, and displays a delightfully romantic aggregation of towers, turrets, balconies, bay windows, and porches.

To the rear of the villa, and attached by a colonnade, is the handsome **Annex,** designed in an architecturally harmonious style in 1911 by Helmle & Huberty, and completed two years later.

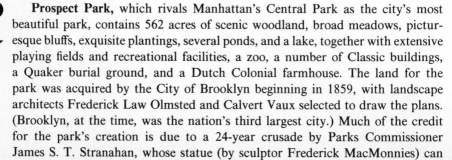

Prospect Park, which rivals Manhattan's Central Park as the city's most beautiful park, contains 562 acres of scenic woodland, broad meadows, picturesque bluffs, exquisite plantings, several ponds, and a lake, together with extensive playing fields and recreational facilities, a zoo, a number of Classic buildings, a Quaker burial ground, and a Dutch Colonial farmhouse. The land for the park was acquired by the City of Brooklyn beginning in 1859, with landscape architects Frederick Law Olmsted and Calvert Vaux selected to draw the plans. (Brooklyn, at the time, was the nation's third largest city.) Much of the credit for the park's creation is due to a 24-year crusade by Parks Commissioner James S. T. Stranahan, whose statue (by sculptor Frederick MacMonnies) can

be seen near the Grand Army Plaza entrance. An earlier design, known as
the Viele Plan, was rejected by Olmsted and Stranahan to avoid the bisecting
of the park by Flatbush Avenue; instead, land to the west was acquired for
the present layout. Much of the former land to the east was subsequently used
for the Brooklyn Botanic Garden, the landmark Brooklyn Museum, and the
main branch of the Brooklyn Public Library—all suitable companions to this
magnificent natural oasis. With the acceptance of the Olmsted & Vaux *Design
for Prospect Park* of 1866–67, the park project gradually took shape, culminating
with the monumental approach of the Grand Army Plaza in the 1890s.

**End of tour. To return to the IRT subway, walk back along Prospect Park
West to Grand Army Plaza, and bear left at the mall. The Grand Army Plaza
station is on the left side of Flatbush Avenue. If you wish to return to the
IRT via Prospect Park, walk back on Prospect Park West to the first park
entrance (between the panthers) and follow the West Drive to Grand Army
Plaza. The nearest IND subway, the F line, can be reached by turning left
on Prospect Park West to Ninth Street, then right to just beyond Eighth Avenue
for the Seventh Avenue station.**

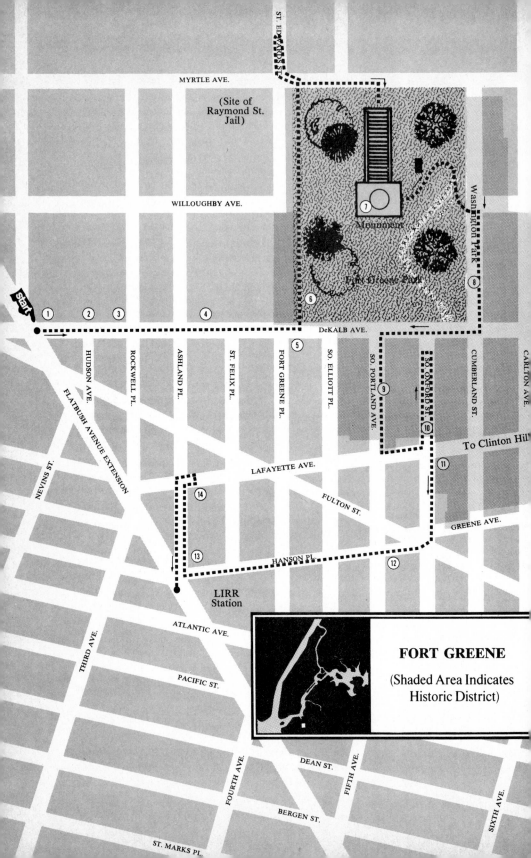

ST. EDWARDS ST.

MYRTLE AVE.

(Site of
Raymond St.
Jail)

WILLOUGHBY AVE.

Monument

7

Fort Greene Park

6

Washington Park

8

start

1   2   3   4   5

DeKALB AVE.

HUDSON AVE.

ROCKWELL PL.

ASHLAND PL.

ST. FELIX PL.

FORT GREENE PL.

SO. ELLIOTT PL.

SO. PORTLAND AVE.

SO. OXFORD ST.

CUMBERLAND ST.

CARLTON AVE.

9

10

To Clinton Hill

FLATBUSH AVENUE EXTENSION

NEVINS ST.

LAFAYETTE AVE.

FULTON ST.

11

GREENE AVE.

14

13

HANSON PL.

12

LIRR
Station

THIRD AVE.

ATLANTIC AVE.

PACIFIC ST.

FORT GREENE

(Shaded Area Indicates
Historic District)

FOURTH AVE.

DEAN ST.

FIFTH AVE.

BERGEN ST.

SIXTH AVE.

ST. MARKS PL.

18. Fort Greene

[IND B and D lines, BMT RR, N, M, and QB lines to DeKalb Avenue]

The tour begins at DeKalb Avenue and Flatbush Avenue Extension, northeast corner (in Brooklyn).

Flatbush Avenue Extension is a major connecting artery between Canal Street in Manhattan (via the Manhattan Bridge) and the downtown and central part of Brooklyn. Before the construction of the Brooklyn-Battery Tunnel and the network of expressways, Flatbush Avenue Extension was the busiest link between the two boroughs and one of the most heavily traveled streets in the world. Beneath the roadway is the DeKalb Avenue subway station, considered the busiest in the city transit system—particularly at rush hours—as so many lines to Manhattan converge at this station.

1. Long Island University's Main Building, at 385 Flatbush Avenue Extension, was originally the famous **Brooklyn Paramount Theater.** Built in 1928, it was one of the country's grandest movie palaces, and Brooklyn's No. 1 showplace for 34 years. When LIU saved it from demolition, the theater and office tower were converted to school use in two major steps. The tower, which housed the offices of many theatrical agents, was redesigned in 1950 for classrooms and administrative offices; and when the theater closed in 1962, the auditorium was rebuilt as a gymnasium and named Founders' Hall. The heavily ornate ceiling, balcony, and statuary are preserved intact, as are several thousand red-plush orchestra seats, which surround the new basketball court. The "mighty Wurlitzer"—second only in size and sound to the Radio City Music Hall organ—is still in use, restored to its original beauty and adding excitement to home basketball games.

When the neighborhood began to decline in the 1950s and '60s and threatened to become a seedy, decaying backwater, the city and local community leaders worked together on a plan for the **Central Brooklyn Urban Renewal Project.** Evidence of its success can be seen in the extensive building boom still in progress. To the southeast of the LIU campus a new commercial district has arisen from the urban blight of slums and abandoned factories, in many ways a tribute to the university's confidence in the neighborhood. Phoenix-like, the spanking new New York Telephone and Con Edison buildings have recently been completed, the latter on the site of Fabian's Fox Theater, another of the old vaudeville and movie palaces. Barton's Candy Company and other smaller firms, plus a new housing project, have emerged to bring jobs and vitality to this underdeveloped area.

Walk east on DeKalb Avenue one block to Hudson Avenue.

2. During the Revolutionary War this was the site of the **Oblong Redoubt,** one of a series of forts and entrenchments that extended across Brooklyn from Gowanus to nearby Fort Putnam (now Fort Greene Park). The Battle of Brooklyn, which took place in the last week of August 1776, not far from these battlements, was the first major engagement of the war. Outnumbered and outflanked by superior British and Hessian forces, General Washington's Continental Army was forced to withdraw across the East River to Manhattan from Brooklyn Heights, about a mile and a half to the west. Brooklyn was to remain in British hands until the end of the war.

3. On the corner of Rockwell Place is the turn-of-the-century **Goldner Building.** The "stars" on the walls are braces at the end of iron tie-rods, used to

The Terrace and former Prison Ship Martyrs' Monument in Fort Greene Park before its replacement in 1908 by Stanford White's marble shaft, a year and a half after the architect's death. The landscaping for the park was designed by Olmsted & Vaux, who also planned Central and Prospect parks. (Long Island Historical Society)

reinforce the walls and literally hold the building together. (In the Fulton Fish Market in lower Manhattan, one can even see tie-rod braces in the shape of star*fish.*) The **Benziger Brothers Building** on the diagonally opposite corner is a commercial structure of the 1880s, and is reminiscent of the architecture of San Francisco's Ghiradelli Square. Until its closing in the mid-1970s the firm manufactured Catholic religious articles. Typical of the period is the row of corbels below the cornice, imitating the machicolations of medieval castles.

At the corner of St. Felix Street, look to the right side of the street and note the former carriage houses at Nos. 8 and 10. The entire street is in an advanced state of decay, but despite its seedy appearance, traces of its former elegant rows of Italianate brownstones are still very much in evidence, and cry out for development.

At Ashland Place, Brooklyn's tallest skyscraper, the Williamsburgh Savings Bank Building (to be seen later) looms in the distance.

4. The Brooklyn Hospital, built in 1920 with additions and alterations in 1967, occupies the site of Brooklyn's first hospital. The original hospital was established through the efforts of Cyrus Smith, who, as mayor of Brooklyn, in 1839 started a vigorous campaign for a public hospital, only to receive a token $200 appropriation from the Board of Aldermen. He then contributed one of his own houses for the project, funding it himself. (Brooklyn was an independent city until 1898.)

5. Brooklyn Technical High School (1931), at the corner of Fort Greene Place, is one of the city's special schools, dedicated to pre-engineering training. Brooklyn Tech has always been considered one of the city's "better" schools. The antenna on the roof broadcasts the signal of the New York City Board of Education's radio station WNYE (95.5 khz). The antenna is the tallest *structure* in Brooklyn.

6. Fort Greene Park, with its commanding views of downtown Brooklyn and the Manhattan skyline, was the site of previously mentioned Fort Putnam during the Revolutionary War. When the War of 1812 brought the panic of another British invasion, the hill was fortified again and renamed Fort Greene (after Revolutionary War General Nathanael Greene). In 1847 it was named Washington Park; then in 1868 landscape architects Frederick Law Olmsted and Calvert Vaux combined their talents to convert the 30 acres of hill and old fort into an elegant park, which the City of Brooklyn renamed City Park. In the early 20th century the name was changed again to Fort Greene Park. (Olmsted & Vaux made their greatest contribution to the beauty of the city with their designs for Manhattan's Central Park and Brooklyn's Prospect Park.)

The Park is the focus of the **Fort Greene Historic District**—an area whose attractive brick and brownstone row houses display all the architectural features popular in the period 1850–70. It is also an integrated neighborhood "on the way up," with much civic pride and sense of history.

Enter the park and follow the path (which appears as an extension of Fort Greene Place) along the western perimeter, into St. Edward's Street, as far as Myrtle Avenue.

The fortresslike Raymond Street Jail, Brooklyn's own "Tombs," stood alongside Fort Greene Park until it was demolished in the early 1960s. When it neared completion in 1880, it was discovered that an entranceway had not been designed, and a consequent rapid revision of the building plan had to be made. (Long Island Historical Society)

At the crest of the hill, the distant twin spires of the **Church of St. Michael & St. Edward** can be seen among the 38 acres of towers of the Fort Greene Houses, the city's first postwar low-income housing project. Near the base of the hill, immediately to the left of the fence, is the **site of the former Raymond Street Jail,** built in 1880, a dismal gray fortress that was Brooklyn's answer to Manhattan's old "Tombs." (Raymond Street was the former name of Ashland Place.) Some of the *Prison—Keep Clear* signs are still visible on the wall under the fence. A bizarre sidelight to the history of the unlamented prison was the discovery when the building was partly completed in 1880 that there was no front entrance! This rather serious oversight was blamed on both the architect, William A. Mundell, and the Brooklyn Board of Supervisors.

On the site of the old jail, which was demolished in 1964, is the Dr. Edwin Post Maynard, Jr., Staff Residence of Brooklyn Hospital (Walker O. Cain & Associates, 1976), a much more appreciated replacement.

Cross Myrtle Avenue and follow St. Edward's Street to the church.

Rising like some French 17th-century Loire Valley château, the **Church of St. Michael and St. Edward** dominates the surrounding Raymond V. Ingersoll and Walt Whitman Houses. Ornate conical towers frame the angular front façade, which resembles the bow of a huge ship pointing appropriately toward the Brooklyn Navy Yard. Built in 1902 as the Church of St. Edward, it boasts a rather unusual recent addition, an altar and cross made from parts of the old Myrtle Avenue El and installed in 1972. (The El roared by the rear of the church until 1969.) By standing in front of the church, one can visualize the demapped Leo Place which formed the other altitude of a triangle with St. Edward's Street whose apex was at this point. Across the street is the diminutive Walt Whitman Branch of the Brooklyn Public Library. (Whitman, in addition to his other literary accomplishments, was editor of the *Brooklyn Eagle* for a time in the mid-19th century.)

Return to Myrtle Avenue, cross to the park side, and enter the park at the first entrance. Follow the path to the stairs, and climb to the top.

★ THE PRISON SHIP MARTYRS' MONUMENT

7. In 1780, at the height of the Revolutionary War, the British Navy anchored a flotilla of some 12 decrepit ex-men-of-war and hospital ships in Wallabout Bay (near the site of the present Navy Yard), and converted them into floating prisons for captured American seamen. They hoped that the unpleasant conditions aboard the crowded, filthy, and disease-ridden hulks would induce the captives to enlist in His Majesty's Navy. Few did, however, and the tale of privation and ultimate death of between 11,500 and 12,500 prisoners—no

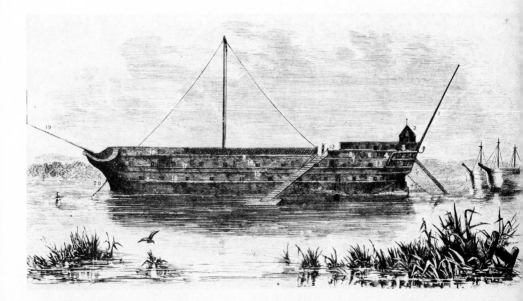

The British prison ship Jersey, *in an old engraving. About 12,000 American prisoners died of disease and maltreatment aboard this and 11 other prison ships anchored in Wallabout Bay. (Long Island Historical Society)*

The first Prison Ship-Martyrs' Monument, built in 1844 near Hudson Avenue. (Long Island Historical Society)

When the first Martyrs' Monument (left, below) fell into decay, its state of collapse was noted by an artist for a contemporary news magazine. In the rather grisly engraving above, coffins containing the heroes' skeletons, and labelled with the names of the 13 original states, are heaped in rows in the neglected tomb. The present, more permanent crypt was built in 1873. (Long Island Historical Society)

one will ever know for sure how many—is one of the most sorrowful events in American history. The worst of the prison ships was the H.M.S. *Jersey,* a decommissioned ship of the line, on which 1,100 men were jammed together between decks in unspeakable conditions. About a dozen died each night from a variety of causes—dysentery, typhoid, smallpox, yellow fever, food poisoning, starvation, and flogging. At the end of the war in 1783, there were from the whole prison fleet only 1,400 sick and emaciated survivors.

At the cry each morning of "Rebels, turn out your dead!" the bodies were hauled up on deck, lowered into boats, rowed ashore, and buried in shallow graves. There the bleaching bones remained until 1808 when as much of the remains as could be recovered were unearthed and reburied on the nearby John Jackson estate. The task was performed by the Columbian Order, a patriotic society that was later to become the political Tammany Society. As for the *Jersey,* it wallowed at anchor for several years, slowly rotting away until it disintegrated and slipped beneath the waters of the bay.

Thirty-six years later, a monument to these martyrs was erected; and in

EAGLE PHOTO

A heavy snowfall covers Fort Greene Park in this Brooklyn Eagle *photograph taken the morning of December 26, 1926. The new Martyrs' Monument rises solemnly at the top of the hill. (Brooklyn Collection. Brooklyn Public Library)*

1873, the remains were transferred to a crypt under the stairway of a new monument on the present site. (On June 17, 1973, a brief public ceremony was conducted by the city commemorating the 100th anniversary of this interment.)

On a cold, wet November 18, in 1908, President William Howard Taft dedicated the newest Prison Ship Martyrs' Monument. Designed by noted architect Stanford White, it stands on a 220-foot-square plaza at the top of the stairway, consisting of a simple granite shaft topped by a large brazier, or lantern. Measuring 148 feet 8 inches, it is the tallest Doric column in the world. The bronze brazier was executed by sculptor A. A. Weinman. The base of the fluted column consists of a double platform, or stylobate, with entrances on the north and south sides (now closed). The actual entrance to the crypt (also no longer open to visitors) is located two flights below, at the first landing. The entrance is so unobtrusive that it is usually unnoticed in ascending the stairs. A planned electric elevator for the monument was never installed, although for many years visitors were permitted to climb the interior stairway to the upper platform. In the original plans, a gas flame was to burn perpetually in the lantern. Granite standards at each corner of the plaza have disappeared, and the entire monument suffers from abuse and neglect . . . a parallel perhaps to the sufferings of the martyrs, but wholly inappropriate to their memory. Significantly, this was Stanford White's last commission. He was shot and killed a year and a half before the monument's dedication [*see* Madison Square, 11].

To the west of the monument is a shady terrace with a large plaque presented by King Juan Carlos of Spain in 1976 for the Bicentennial, commemorating the 126 Spanish volunteers who died in the prison ships.

Just to the east of the monument is a small white marble building designed by McKim, Mead & White as a public comfort station (also closed). The diminutive Doric "temple" has been referred to as "the most elegant outhouse in the world"!

Follow the path to the right of the comfort station down to the exit at Willoughby Avenue and Washington Park.

8. Washington Park was the most fashionable street in the Fort Greene section in the 1870s and '80s, when many of the affluent residents of nearby exclusive Clinton Hill found the newly created Olmsted & Vaux park very attractive. The row of old Italianate brownstone mansions is now but a shadow of its former opulence. All have been carved up into small apartments, and some are now rooming houses. But, here and there one does see evidence of pride of ownership in sympathetic restoration and repair, and many have become quite attractive again, as for example Nos. 192, 179–185, and 173–176.

Turn right on DeKalb Avenue, past South Oxford Street to South Portland Avenue.

9. The splendid rows of Anglo-Italianate brownstones along shady **South Portland Avenue** are typical of residential construction that became immensely popular throughout the city in the mid-19th century. Brooklyn by the 1870s had become the bastion of the brownstone row house in such neighborhoods as Brooklyn Heights, Cobble Hill, Bedford-Stuyvesant, Park Slope, Clinton Hill, and Fort Greene.

The characteristics of the style are evident in the tall stoop with cast-iron balustrades; elegant entranceway surmounted by a protruding arched pediment supported by consoles decorated with acanthus-leaf motifs; recessed portico with round-arch double entrance doors; stone-enframed windows, usually topped by curved lintels; and an elaborate cornice supported by console brackets with the familiar acanthus-leaf design. The houses were generally four stories high above a raised basement. The front masonry bearing wall was faced with chocolate-colored sandstone, quarried in Connecticut or New Jersey. The windows on the first, or parlor, floor were almost as high as the room itself and, like all the windows, were double-hung (plate glass had become much less expensive by mid-century). Most brownstones were owned by merchants or professionals. One of the early row-house builders was Walt Whitman.

The influence of fashionable London streets can be seen in the names of so many of Fort Greene's thoroughfares: Oxford, Adelphi, Carlton, Cumberland, and Waverly. South Portland Avenue was named for once-elegant Portland

Place. Other nearby avenues honor such Revolutionary War generals as Washington, Greene, DeKalb, Willoughby, Gates, and Lafayette.

With shifting populations in the 1940s and '50s, the Fort Greene neighborhood began to decline, succumbing rapidly to the effects of urban disintegration and decay. All seemed lost until the mid-1960s when a last-minute miracle occurred. A revolution broke out!—a "brownstone revolution"—which was to sweep not only Fort Greene, but virtually all the brownstone neighborhoods in Brooklyn and Manhattan as well. Armies of the middle class, beset by a growing shortage of family living space, began buying up the deteriorating row houses, which were available at bargain prices, and painstakingly renovating and restoring them to their former beauty. These new "brownstoners," banding together in brownstone-revival organizations, pooled their knowledge and experience, and set to work using every spare minute (and dollar) to restore the

The Lafayette Avenue Presbyterian Church, designed in 1860 by J. C. Wells, boasts one of the finest collections of Tiffany stained-glass windows. Pulitzer Prize–winning poet Marianne Moore was one of the church's most celebrated and devoted parishioners. The 200-foot steeple had to be dismantled when the IND subway construction threatened to topple it. (Long Island Historical Society)

once-elegant houses. Paradoxically, the recent quick decline of the neighborhood spared the row houses the effects of gradual "modernization" and great numbers of Fort Greene's brownstones survive in virtually pristine architectural condition. Explore the street, noting the harmonious, uniform cornice lines of the row houses, and the effect of depth created by the block-long repetition of balustrades, entranceways, and windows. The beauty of a brownstone row can best be appreciated when viewed at an angle, rather than *en face.*

Turn left at Lafayette Avenue, and left again at South Oxford Street.

10. Although lacking some of the quality of South Portland Avenue—mostly because of fewer trees—**South Oxford Street** presents a varied panorama of architectural styles used in row-house construction. It was not unusual for an owner to add a French Second Empire mansard roof, providing an extra attic bedroom or two. The sloping mansard roof, with its dormer windows and iron cresting, is not an unpleasant addition to the Anglo-Italianate brownstone.

The Roanoke (No. 69), built ca. 1893, was one of the city of Brooklyn's first luxury apartment houses. The addition above the cornice is a serious detraction, however.

11. The Lafayette Avenue Presbyterian Church was designed in 1860 in a modified Gothic Revival style by Joseph C. Wells (architect Wells was also responsible for the Church of the Pilgrims, in Brooklyn Heights, and the First Presbyterian Church, on Manhattan's Fifth Avenue). The sanctuary of the church boasts a magnificent set of Tiffany art-glass windows. All but one of the upper windows and half of the lower were made in the Tiffany Studios in 1890. In the Underwood Chapel, the large stained-glass window, installed in 1920, was the last to be produced by the firm. A towering 200-foot steeple had to be removed when blasting for the new IND subway line beneath Lafayette Avenue threatened to topple it.

One of the church's most celebrated and devoted parishioners in modern times was Pulitzer Prize–winning poet Marianne Moore (1887–1972), a longtime resident on nearby Cumberland Street.

At this point there are two alternatives:

(1) The walking tour of Fort Greene may be completed by following the remaining itinerary below, or

(2) the final portion of the Fort Greene tour may be skipped (or returned to later), and a tour made of neighboring **Clinton Hill,** by continuing east on Lafayette Avenue four blocks to the corner of Clermont Avenue [*see* map].

To complete the Fort Greene walking tour, continue south on South Oxford Street to Hanson Place and turn right (west).

Fulton Street is the borough's oldest thoroughfare. During the Colonial and Revolutionary periods it was known as the King's Highway (not to be

A helicopter view of Brooklyn's tallest skyscraper, the Williamsburgh Savings Bank Building, at 1 Hanson Place. Completed in 1929, the building's observatory commands a spectacular view of downtown Brooklyn and the Manhattan skyline. (Brooklyn Union Gas Company)

confused with the present Kings Highway in central Brooklyn), and later as the Old Ferry Road. Connecting with the first ferry to the island of Manhattan, its name was changed to honor Robert Fulton, whose steam ferry *Nassau* began regular service in 1814, opening the town of Brooklyn to an era of growth and development. The Fulton Street El, which rumbled overhead until it was dismantled in 1940, was built as the Kings County Elevated Railroad in 1887, and contributed to the rapid development of the city. Contrary to expectations, its removal did little to improve the neighborhood.

Turn right into Hanson Place.

12. The Hanson Place Seventh Day Adventist Church (No. 88) was built in 1857–60 as the Hanson Place Baptist Church. An exceptionally interesting combination of Greek Revival and Italianate decorative details, the imposing, gleaming white church building complements the surrounding neighborhood, which despite some urban blight still retains a good deal of its mid-19th-century atmosphere. The dominant features of the church building are the portico with its tall Corinthian columns and pilasters, a large pediment set on a cornice supported by carved modillions, typically Greek twin doorways and surmounting windows, and a similarly typical Italianate row of arcaded windows illuminating the nave. The church was acquired by the Seventh Day Adventists in 1963.

13. Brooklyn's tallest skyscraper, the **Williamsburgh Savings Bank Building,** called "The Tower of Strength," measures 512 feet to the top of its gold-domed tower. Completed in 1929 from plans by Halsey, McCormick & Helmer, this singularly conspicuous Byzantine-style landmark with its four illuminated tower clocks is clearly visible for miles around. The builders hoped in vain that its more central location on Brooklyn's Times Plaza (Brooklyn had its own *Times* for many years) would attract business away from the mile-distant civic center. Apparently the management of the Long Island Rail Road had the same opinion when they built the terminal across the street. A visit to the observatory for sweeping panoramas of Brooklyn and the Manhattan skyline is a "must." The tower is open weekdays 10 A.M. to 3 P.M. and on Saturday to 2 P.M.; closed holidays. Stop in and look at the impressive banking room on the ground floor.

The **Long Island Railroad Flatbush Avenue Terminal,** in Italianate style in red brick with limestone trim, marks the end of a branch (originally the main line) to Jamaica and Long Island points. In its heyday it saw an average of 133 trains a day enter the station. Now it is but a preserved relic. Go inside and see the square original waiting room with its arcaded balcony with balustrade, and old ticket windows, including one for parlor car seats.

Turn right (north) on Ashland Place to Lafayette Avenue, then right again.

14. The Brooklyn Academy of Music, which compares favorably in almost every respect with Carnegie Hall, was constructed in 1908 from plans by Herts & Tallant, and moved to this larger site from its original location on Montague Street in Brooklyn Heights. The BAM is the major cultural institution within

● the **Brooklyn Academy of Music Historic District**—a neighborhood comprising about three square blocks of residential streets, with row houses dating to the 1850s and '60s, unified by their scale and Italianate features. As Brooklyn's leading cultural center, founded in 1859, the Academy is noted for the variety and high quality of its musical programs, theater productions, lectures, and films. The main auditorium, or Opera House, with a seating capacity of 2,200, was inaugurated on November 14, 1908, with a production of *Faust,* sung by Geraldine Farrar and Enrico Caruso. Caruso opened the gala evening with a rendition of the "Star Spangled Banner."

A 1,400-seat Music Hall and a newly built flexible-seating Lepercq Space offer dance recitals and chamber music concerts. A Chelsea Theatre Centre on the fourth floor houses the Academy's resident professional drama company. The Brooklyn Philharmonia, conducted by musical director Lukas Foss, presents a concert series each season, and the resident Pennsylvania Ballet performs a wide spectrum of classical and modern dance. There are also regular series in chamber music, black theater, and films. Visiting groups from out of town and abroad are frequent, with recent performances by the Royal Shakespeare and Young Vic Companies. Some of the notables who have performed or given lectures at the Academy are: Sergei Rachmaninoff, Ignace Jan Paderewski, Ernestine Schumann-Heink, Fritz Kreisler, Jascha Heifetz, Pablo Casals, Carl Sandburg, Edna St. Vincent Millay, Sinclair Lewis, William Jennings Bryan, and Winston Churchill. It is unfortunate that the BAM's elegant cornice and roof balustrade were removed, as the ornate façade now appears "hatless." [For more background on the Academy, *see* Brooklyn Heights Tour, page 379.]

Return to the corner in front of the Long Island Rail Road Terminal.

The busy intersection just beyond is **Times Plaza,** the confluence of Flatbush, Atlantic, and Fourth avenues, plus a few side streets. On the center island is the **Atlantic Avenue Control House,** the **former IRT subway kiosk** (Heins and La Farge, 1908), now closed, but its "Atlantic Avenue" sign is still visible, half-hidden by a fast-food establishment. Many years ago, Brooklyn had its own *Times,* one of several dailies, and its publication office (now demolished) faced the plaza. While still a busy spot, the traffic is all motor vehicle. Less than a half-century ago, the streets were lined with trolley tracks whose cars came from all over the borough; the Fifth Avenue Culver Line El clattered overhead, and the streets were crowded with pedestrians streaming to and from the nearby downtown Brooklyn shopping district and such well-known emporiums as Frederick Loeser, Namm's, Oppenheim & Collins, and Abraham & Straus (only the last of which survives).

End of tour. The nearest subway station, Atlantic Avenue, adjacent to the Long Island Rail Road Terminal, is served by the IRT Lexington and Broadway-Seventh Avenue lines, the BMT RR, QJ and M lines, and the IND D and B lines.

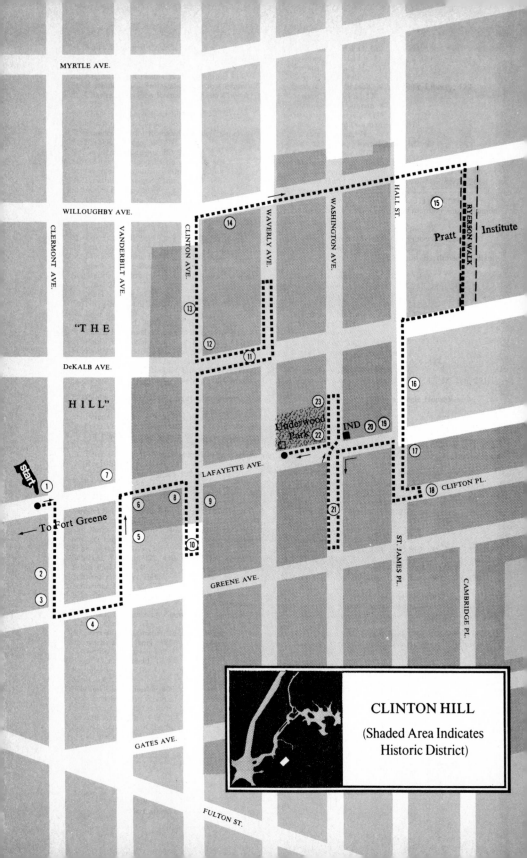

MYRTLE AVE.

WILLOUGHBY AVE.

CLERMONT AVE.

VANDERBILT AVE.

CLINTON AVE.

WAVERLY AVE.

WASHINGTON AVE.

HALL ST.

⑮ Pratt Institute

RYERSON WALK

"T H E

DeKALB AVE.

H I L L"

⑭

⑬

⑫ ⑪ ⑯

⑦

Start ①

To Fort Greene

② ⑥ ⑧ ⑨ ⑤ ⑩

GREENE AVE.

④ ③

⑮

Underwood Park ㉓ ㉒ IND ⑳ ⑲

⑰

⑱ CLIFTON PL.

LAFAYETTE AVE.

㉑

ST. JAMES PL.

CAMBRIDGE PL.

GATES AVE.

CLINTON HILL

(Shaded Area Indicates Historic District)

FULTON ST.

19. Clinton Hill

[*IND GG Line to Clinton-Washington. From lower Manhattan, take the IND A line to Hoyt-Schermerhorn and change for the GG; from upper Manhattan, take the E or F lines to Queens Plaza for the GG.*]

With Brooklyn's rapid growth of population in the mid-19th century, a boom in row-house construction began. Pushing east and west, new neighborhoods developed along the post roads that led to the suburban villages of Bushwick, Jamaica, Flatbush, New Utrecht, and Gravesend. As the Brooklyn Heights section became completely built up, prosperous merchants and professionals found the high ground to the east to be very much to their liking. By the 1840s, the "Hill" [*see* map] became second only to Brooklyn Heights in elegance. The majority of new residents worked in Manhattan, only a 20-minute ride by stagecoach or omnibus to the Fulton Ferry landing, enjoying a quiet suburban life within sight of the city. By the 1880s and '90s, Clinton Avenue became a "Millionaires' Row," lined with the mansions of the wealthy, and it remains in a remarkable state of preservation. Virtually all of Clinton Hill has survived the encroachments of rapid urban growth, and to this day presents a fascinating collection of architectural styles in its residences, churches, schools, and commercial buildings.

The tour begins at the corner of Clermont and Lafayette avenues.

1. The **Brooklyn Masonic Temple** was built in 1909 from plans by Lord & Hewlett, and it is indeed a temple! The stately Ionic columns and terra-cotta polychrome designs are reminiscent of ancient Greece of the fourth century B.C.

Turn right (south) on Clermont Avenue.

2. Bishop Loughlin High School, built in 1932, marks the **site of the proposed Brooklyn Cathedral,** whose cornerstone was laid in 1868. Planned to be the largest church in the city, construction was suddenly halted when the walls reached a height of 12 feet, and the entire project abandoned, with the money diverted to charitable purposes. The Roman Catholic Diocese of Brooklyn was founded in 1853, with John Loughlin appointed the first bishop.

3. The sole surviving part of the projected cathedral project is the **former Bishop of Brooklyn's Residence,** on the northwest corner of Clermont and Greene avenues, designed by architect Patrick Charles Keely in 1887. The mansard roof and smoothly grooved granite blocks of this Victorian building give it a somewhat forbidding appearance. The old incomplete cathedral walls were removed in 1931 to make way for the construction of the high school, and the former Episcopal Residence is now used by the school's teachers. Keely is believed to have designed some 700 churches across the country during his lifetime.

4. At 90 Greene Avenue, **The Clinton** was built ca. 1870 as a tenement house. Coinciding with the upgrading of the area at the end of the 19th century, the house was rebuilt in 1890 as a luxury "French flats," or apartment house for the affluent. "Tenement house" in those days did not have quite the negative connotation it does today—it was merely a multiple dwelling for the poorer classes.

Note how the old trolley tracks are again becoming visible through the macadam, at the intersection of Greene and Vanderbilt avenues. Brooklyn's trolley empire was one of the largest in the world by the turn of the century. The last line disappeared in 1955.

Turn left (east) on Greene Avenue to Vanderbilt Avenue.

5. The small residence at **375 Vanderbilt Avenue** was built originally as a stable in the mid-1880s.

6. The charming clapboard house at the southeast corner of Vanderbilt and Lafayette avenues presents something of an architectural mystery. Known officially as the **Joseph Steele House,** and locally as the Skinner House (after the family that has lived in it since 1900), its precise history is unclear. The two-story section that now serves as a wing was built in Federal style, probably in 1812 when the "Hill" area was a remote, rural farmland. In the 1840s the main section was added in Greek Revival style. The house, which was actually located about 150 yards farther east, was moved to the present site around 1853 to make way for the construction of the Clinton Avenue Congregational Church, and further alterations were made—this time in the *Italianate* style! The roof was raised and certain Renaissance features added: the elaborate cornice, a new entranceway, and pedimented lintels over the front windows. It is likely that the wooden cupola dates from this latest modification, but it could be earlier. In spite of the lack of architectural integrity, the Steele (or Skinner) House is a delightful addition to the cityscape.

7. The Catholic Church (and School) of Queen of All Saints, on the northwest corner, was designed by Gustave Steinbach in 1911. An impressive edifice, its splendid collection of stained-glass windows suggests the Sainte-Chapelle in

Paris, while the 36 excellent sculptures of saints are reminiscent of St. Peter's in Rome. The building of the church was commissioned by George Mundelein, pastor of St. John's parish, who went on to be named Cardinal of Chicago. Old-timers still refer to it as "Bishop Mundelein's Church." The bishop originally intended this to be the Cathedral Church for the projected Brooklyn Cathedral across the street. The interior, considered a fine example of Gothic-style architecture, has a narrow nave which sets off the magnificent windows, which contain no fewer than 22,882 pieces of stained glass in each complete mosaic window! The windows were manufactured by the Locke Decorative Company, in 1913.

Turn right on Lafayette Avenue to Clinton Avenue.

8. The Cadman Memorial Church is a relative newcomer to Clinton Hill. It was erected in 1923 to replace an earlier Gothic church built in 1853, which had been designed by noted architect James Renwick, Jr. Three beautiful Tiffany art-glass windows were saved from its predecessor, the Clinton Avenue Congregational Church, and incorporated into the design of the new building. In 1943 the congregation was merged with the Central Congregational Church and renamed in memory of the Central Church's former minister, Dr. S. Parkes Cadman. It was the Rev. Cadman who delivered the dedicatory invocation for the Prison Ship Martyrs' Monument in nearby Fort Greene Park [see Fort Greene, 7]. He was also the nation's first radio preacher, and was recognized by the City of New York for his activity in community affairs by the naming of downtown Brooklyn's Cadman Plaza.

9. The Clinton Hill Apartments, Section No. 2 of the Clinton Hill Development, were built in 1955 (Harrison & Abramovitz, Irwin Clavan) for families of naval personnel and workers in the nearby New York Naval Shipyard. Each entranceway has a different nautical motif.

10. Tree-lined **Clinton Avenue** still retains its 1880-period charm in the four-block stretch between Gates and Willoughby avenues. Turn right and walk a half-block, and return, observing the variety of styles of architecture.

At the turn of the century, Clinton Avenue was known as the "Fifth Avenue of Brooklyn," and nowhere is this more evident than in the next two blocks north, from Lafayette to DeKalb and Willoughby avenues. Walking on the left side of Clinton Avenue, look at **No. 324,** with a balustrade atop its mansard roof, drip mouldings over the windows, and a Classic-style portico. Across the street, **No. 321** (The Woodward School) is equally eclectic, with both Victorian and Italianate details. **Nos. 315** and **313** are a pair of fanciful Queen Anne–style houses.

Turn right (east) on DeKalb Avenue.

11. Two imposing groups of ca. 1890 town houses bracket DeKalb Avenue near the corner of Waverly Avenue: **Nos. 285–289** with a highly ornate terra-cotta frieze unifying the trio of brick and brownstone buildings, and **Nos. 284–288.** The houses are enormous, and when erected were designed for single-family occupancy. Today they are subdivided into small apartments. Nevertheless the effect is still that of an aristocratic old English street, with its pleasant mixture of Queen Anne and Romanesque Revival details.

Turn left (north) briefly on Waverly Avenue.

Although it is not within the purview of this guidebook to recommend restaurants, it is not unlikely that hunger has now replaced architecture and history as a primary concern. And inasmuch as there are no places of refreshment in the immediate vicinity (with but one exception), it is fortunate that **Joe's Place** offers good food at modest prices, in a converted carriage house at 264 Waverly Avenue. The interior garden is particularly pleasant in warm weather. Should Joe's be closed, all is not lost. The Pratt Coffee Shop, a so-so place just for basic survival, will be on the route in about 15–20 minutes.

Observe how narrow Waverly Avenue is, compared to Clinton and Washington avenues. Originally the stables and carriage houses of the wealthy residents were located on this street between the two "fashionable" streets.

Clinton Avenue between DeKalb and Willoughby avenues ca. 1895, showing three mansions built by petroleum industrialist Charles Pratt for his children. Clinton Avenue justly earned the reputation of being the "Fifth Avenue of Brooklyn." The scene is virtually the same today, only the homeowners are different. (Brooklyn Collection. Brooklyn Public Library)

Return to DeKalb Avenue, and turn right to Clinton Avenue, then right again.

12. No. 275 Clinton Avenue is a well-preserved triple-section luxury apartment building, built ca. 1895.

Across Clinton Avenue, **No. 282** is a stick and shingle–style Victorian house with some Gothic touches, built ca. 1875, and is appropriate in appearance to the bucolic atmosphere of the neighborhood at that time. Adjacent is the wildly eclectic **No. 278,** with a corner tower set at a 45-degree angle. **No. 266** is worthy of a passing glance.

13. The block between DeKalb and Willoughby avenues is a living memorial to the Pratt family, and unquestionably the most beautiful in Clinton Hill. No less than four family mansions survive, and in pristine condition. Although now in other hands, they are still lovingly preserved.

When Charles Pratt built his huge oil refinery at Kent Avenue and North 12th Street in the Greenpoint section of Brooklyn in 1867, he made his fortune with a successful coal-oil product called "Astral Oil." So widely used was this high-grade kerosene that it was said that "the holy lamps of Tibet are lit with 'Astral Oil.' " The kerosene's advantage and major selling point was its relative safety. It had a higher flash point than competing oils, and would not explode— a virtue that soon made Astral Oil a household term, and helped Pratt make a fortune. In 1874 Pratt became associated with John D. Rockefeller, and the firm was merged with the Standard Oil Company. He settled on Clinton Avenue and subsequently built homes for three of his sons in the same block, presenting each with a lovely mansion as a wedding present. And across the street is the magnificent trio of gifts:

No. 245, now occupied by a department of St. Joseph's College, was built by Pratt for son George DuPont Pratt in 1901. A large, stately mansion, it was designed by the architectural firm of Babb, Cook & Willard in a restrained Georgian style.

No. 241 was built for eldest son Charles Millard Pratt in 1893. Designed by William B. Tubby in Romanesque Revival style, it is probably the most elegant of all his wedding-gift houses. To the south of the building is a conservatory built in semicircular shape; and illuminating the spectacular arched porte-cochere is a decorative spherical bronze lamp (which probably burned "Astral Oil"). The mansion is now the residence of the Roman Catholic Bishop of Brooklyn.

No. 229, now the Caroline Ladd Pratt House, was built for son Frederick B. Pratt in 1898. The gray-and-white Georgian Revival–style house was designed by the same architects as No. 245, and presents a most unusual appearance, attached on its left and freestanding on the right. Atlantean figures and caryatids support a kind of pergola above a colonnaded entranceway.

No. 232, across the street, is the "daddy" of them all—the original Charles Pratt manor house, built ca. 1875. Designed in an Italianate style, the building and picturesque gardens are virtually unchanged—a credit to St. Joseph's College, the present owner. Pratt's fourth son, Harold I., chose instead to live on Manhattan's fashionable Park Avenue, building a mansion of his own in 1920, which still stands at the corner of East 68th Street.

The Main Building of Pratt Institute on Ryerson Street in 1910, designed in an "industrial Romanesque" style. Charles Pratt founded the institution in 1887 and ran it as his own private project. Adjacent to the right is South Hall, and at the extreme left is the original building of Pratt's Thrift Bank of Brooklyn, demolished in 1915 to make way for Memorial Hall. The school still maintains high standards in its major fields of science and art. (Brooklyn Collection. Brooklyn Public Library)

Across the avenue, Nos. 221–215 are an attractive row of town houses, originally designed for single-family occupancy.

Turn right (east) on Willoughby Avenue.

14. Nos. 112–122 Willoughby Avenue are an interesting row of middle-class town houses. Note the swags, or garlands, on the shallow bay windows, and the paired L-shaped entrance stairs.

Continue east on Willoughby Avenue past Hall Street (St. James Place) to the entrance to the Pratt Institute Campus.

15. Pratt Institute was the pet project of Charles Pratt himself. Founded in 1887 and dedicated to science and art, it was directed personally by the industrialist until his death in 1891. The school has an enviable reputation in the fields of art and design, fashion, architecture, engineering and science, and food science and management.

Entering the campus on Ryerson Walk (formerly Ryerson Street, and now demapped), the first building on the left is North Hall, followed by the neo-Byzantine–style **Memorial Hall,** designed in 1927 by John Mead Howells. Adjacent on the right is the original 1887 **Main Building,** designed by Lamb & Rich in an industrial Romanesque Revival style, with its wing, **South Hall.**

Between the Main and South buildings is an iron gate. Enter and walk through the courtyard, past the fountain, to the **East Building,** built at the same time as the Main Building, but designed by John Mead Howells. Originally the Machine Shop Building, it houses Pratt Institute's unofficial **Industrial Archaeology Museum.** Here on display to the public are the Ames Iron Works steam engines, installed in 1900 and still furnishing 120 volts of direct current to the campus. A number of other 19th-century artifacts are also exhibited: a steam whistle from the DeLavergne Refrigerating Company's ca. 1875 factory in the Bronx, chandeliers from the Singer Tower's board room, and the humorous "No Loafing" sign from the old Ruppert Brewery in Yorkville, plus other items from our early industrial era.

When Pratt Institute expanded its campus in the 1950s and '60s, a number of streets were closed and several unneeded buildings demolished, resulting in a five-square-block campus area in which the remaining school buildings stand in "splendid isolation."

The Pratt Institute **Library,** across the walk from South Hall, was built by the school's industrialist-benefactor as Brooklyn's first free public library. Completed in 1896 from plans by William B. Tubby (who designed the Charles Millard Pratt House), and altered in 1936 by John Mead Howells, it is a dramatic Romanesque Revival building with some Renaissance details. The heavy brick piers on the west façade (facing Hall Street) give the building a massive and overwhelming aspect. Interesting is the entrance portico with its diminishing arches. Since 1940 the library has served the needs of the student body only, and is no longer open to the public.

In the small quadrangle beyond the library is a mounted **bronze cannon.** Considered a notable example of bronze foundry work, the highly ornate piece was cast in Spain in 1721 and sent to Havana in 1859. During the Spanish-American War, it was acquired by the board of trustees for the Pratt Art Collection.

To the left of the walk, just before the exit gate, is a Beaux Arts–style red brick and limestone-trim building emblazoned with a beehive and **The Thrift** in the frieze. This was the Thrift Bank of Brooklyn (Shampan & Shampan, 1916), and served depositors until the early 1940s when the bank went out of business, with the building then taken over for Pratt's administrative offices. The Thrift was founded in 1889 by Charles Pratt as one of his investments, and its original building stood on the site of Memorial Hall.

Leave the campus through the DeKalb Avenue gate, and turn right to Hall Street. (If a "pit stop" is needed, the Pratt Coffee Shop is at the corner.) **Then cross DeKalb Avenue and continue south on St. James Place (the extension of Hall Street), past the University Terrace Apartments.**

16. An unusual feature of the **University Terrace Apartments** (Kelly & Gruzen, 1963) are the rows of *recessed* balconies, rather than the usual overhanging type.

Continue to the corner of Lafayette Avenue.

17. The enormous pair of brick buildings on the southeast corner, extending to Clifton Place, is **Higgins Hall** (of Pratt Institute). Built in 1887–88 for the now-defunct Adelphi Academy, the cornerstone was laid by the outspoken anti-slavery preacher, Henry Ward Beecher. The honors for the adjacent South Building's cornerstone were performed by Charles Pratt. The structures are a veritable exercise book in Romanesque Revival motifs, with their towering piers, corbel tables, and round arches.

Across the street, **Nos. 63–67** form an odd trio of narrow row houses (two bays wide), of ca. 1875, with huge arched doorways and a pretentious mansard roof.

18. Clifton Place, from St. James Place to Grand Avenue, is lined with middle-class row houses dating from the 1870s, set back from the street with pleasant front gardens. Standing at the corner, look down St. James Place at the unrelieved rows of brownstones that extend as far as the eye can see, in mute testimony to Brooklyn's uncontested reputation as the city with the greatest number of brownstone row houses.

Return to Lafayette Avenue and turn left (west).

19. The Emmanuel Baptist Church was built like a French 13th-century Gothic cathedral, and its massive square twin towers dominate the entire area. Architect Francis H. Kimball, who designed it in 1886, employed Ohio sandstone, which is by nature somewhat porous, thus creating an effect of aging. The plan of the interior is in startling contrast, with its radial seating plan spreading fanlike from the pulpit. The style is similar to that of the First Baptist Church on Broadway and West 79th Street in Manhattan [*see* West of Central Park, 15]. The church was cited in 1957 for its architectural distinction by the Municipal Art Society and the Society of Architectural Historians. The adjoining rectory (to the left) was erected in 1926, but its harmonious design and use of similar building materials render it almost indistinguishable from the style of the main structure.

20. The neighboring **Apostolic Faith Mission,** at the northeast corner of Lafayette and Washington avenues, was built in 1868 as the Orthodox Friends Meeting House. In restrained Northern Italian, or Lombardian Romanesque style, it has been "brightened" by coats of cream-colored paint by its congregation.

Turn left (south) on Washington Avenue, for a brief detour.

21. Washington Avenue, between Lafayette and Greene avenues, is a virtual encyclopedia of architectural styles, fads, and fancies. Note the following houses with their special features: **No. 353,** with added Classic-style porch and sawtooth ornamentation under the cornice; **Nos. 357** and **359,** a pair of dilapidated but charming Greek Revival–style wooden houses with lovely attic windows; **No. 361,** a tall red brick and brownstone Queen Anne–style house whose oversize bay window almost hides the delicate entranceway, plus Adam-style swags that ornament a Classic cornice below a mansard roof. Note, too, its square terra-cotta plaques and the pair of tiny circular plaques with a little animal (lion?) in each, and the stained glass in the round-arch windows on the parlor floor. **No. 363** has been remodeled into a neo-Georgian house. Across the street, **No. 364** is an especially engaging house, with its square porch colonnettes supporting a double-bracketed roof, the oriels on the south side, and segmental arc window lintels on the second floor, plus a *rundbogenstil* frieze. (Ignore the ugly protuberance on the roof.)

Walk beyond **No. 374** and look back—a Queen Anne–style house whose square tower with pyramidal roof and cast-iron finial are best appreciated at a distance. Just beyond the public library, **Nos. 388** and **390** are a fine pair of Italianate brownstones whose red brick side walls rise to a peaked roof and

The now defunct Adelphi Academy at St. James Place and Lafayette Avenue, photographed in 1896. The building is now part of Pratt Institute and was renamed Higgins Hall. The cornerstone was laid in 1887 by Henry Ward Beecher, and is almost a textbook example of the Romanesque Revival style. (Long Island Historical Society)

delicately carved cornice. Both houses are balanced with angular protruding bay windows and paired porticos.

The big "eyesore" of the block, however, is the former Hotel Mohawk, No. 379, a dismal ex–flop house that was once an elegant apartment building ("The Mohawk") when erected at the turn of the century, and is now owned by the city, sealed up, awaiting its fate. The absence of its former tenants has become a big plus for the block, and when the right developer comes along, the revitalization of the Renaissance Eclectic building will be another significant improvement. At this writing, the Pratt Area Community Council, an active force for housing renewal in the neighborhood, is planning a total renovation for the derelict hotel.

No. 402, at the southwest corner of Greene Avenue, has an imposing two-story-high oriel that dominates the entire corner. Diagonally across the intersection is a free-standing house, similar to No. 364, but with a Second Empire mansard roof.

Return to Lafayette Avenue.

22. Underwood Park, at the corner of Lafayette and Washington avenues, is named for typewriter king John T. Underwood, who donated the plot to the city. His family mansion, which formerly stood on the site, was a red brick

The Graham Home for Old Ladies at the corner of Washington and DeKalb Avenues was originally named The Brooklyn Society for the Relief of Respectable Aged Indigent Females. Erected in 1851, it is little changed from the outside. (Long Island Historical Society)

The dining room of the Graham Institution for Aged and Indigent Females in the mid-19th century. The building is now a hotel. (Long Island Historical Society)

and brownstone structure with a glass-enclosed greenhouse, and was demolished, according to his will, to make way for the park.

Turn right (north) on Washington Avenue.

23. One of the oldest structures of its kind in the city is the former **Graham Home for Old Ladies,** at 320 Washington Avenue. Built in 1851 on land donated by Underwood, it served for many years as a home for the aged, and was converted into a hotel in the early 1970s. The cornerstone was laid by founder, John B. Graham, and the institution named the Brooklyn Society for the Relief of Respectable Aged Indigent Females. According to its charter, it was designed "for the benefit of poor gentlewomen who had been unfitted by previous culture and refinement to accept willingly the public asylum provided by the State for the poor indiscriminately." One wonders what those "respectable poor gentlewomen" might think if they could see the recently changed name of the establishment, Bull Shippers Plaza Motor Inn—an indignity to the neighborhood and an unfortunate (and hopefully temporary) note on which to end the tour.

End of tour. The IND Subway station is at the corner of Lafayette and Washington avenues.

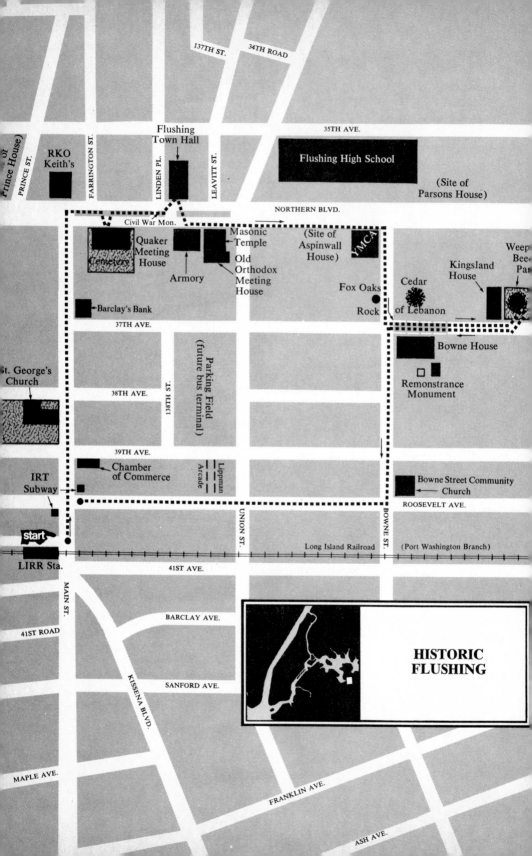

HISTORIC
FLUSHING

20. Historic Flushing

[*IRT #7 Flushing line to Main Street (travel time about 45 minutes); Long Island Railroad, Port Washington Branch, from Pennsylvania Station to Flushing–Main Street (travel time 17 minutes)*]

Among the earliest settlements in the Dutch colony of New Netherlands was the town of Vlissingen, now known as Flushing. In the charter granted by Governor William Kieft in 1645, six years after he purchased the land from the Matinecock Indians, the original 18 freeholders were assured of their freedom of religious worship. Although the town was named for its Dutch counterpart in Flanders, the settlers were all English. The tiny village on the north shore of Long Island soon figured in one of the great events in the cause of religious freedom in America. With the arrival in 1657 of a group of English Quakers, newly appointed Governor Peter Stuyvesant, ignoring the original charter, issued a proclamation banning all religious observance but the official Dutch Reformed.

In angry response, 30 townspeople signed a document of protest on December 27, 1657, known as the **"Flushing Remonstrance."** Stuyvesant's reaction was swift. A detachment of militia was dispatched to Flushing where all signers were arrested and fined. This did not put an end, however, to meetings by the Religious Society of Friends, as they gathered secretly in the house of a newly arrived Englishman, John Bowne, who invited them to worship in his kitchen. When news of this act of disobedience reached Governor Stuyvesant, he again took punitive action, imprisoning Bowne for a period of several months, then banishing him from the colony. Nevertheless, Bowne ultimately reached Amsterdam, where he successfully pleaded the cause of religious freedom before the Council of the Dutch West India Company. The Council then sent a strong letter to Peter Stuyvesant stating in no uncertain terms that all men could exercise freedom of conscience. The Quakers continued to meet in the Bowne House until a meeting house was built in 1694. Both buildings still remain and will be visited on the tour.

Flushing prospered for almost 200 years as one of several independent towns in what is now the borough of Queens, until 1900 when it was consolidated into the City of New York. With the opening of the Queensboro Bridge to Manhattan in 1909 and the Long Island Rail Road tunnel to Pennsylvania Station a year later, Flushing grew rapidly. In 1928 the subway arrived, opening the suburb for even more development. La Guardia Airport was built across Flushing Bay in 1939, the same year the New York World's Fair was inaugurated in nearby Flushing Meadow Park. In 1964–65 a second World's Fair was held at the same site, and with the accompanying construction of several major expressways, Flushing became another extension of the city's urban sprawl.

In recent years Flushing has become one of the most ethnically diverse neighborhoods in the country. The 1960s and early '70s witnessed the arrival of many Puerto Ricans and blacks, but by the end of the '70s and into the decade of the '80s, the area had become a mecca for a large-scale immigration of Asians. So many Koreans, Japanese, Chinese, Indians, and Southeast Asians have arrived that Flushing is often called **"Little Asia."** Add to this a number of Haitians and Latin Americans from many South American countries, and the mix is enormous. The variety of national and racial backgrounds is immediately apparent in the multilingual signs along Main Street and in the faces of the people who throng the streets.

Main Street, looking north toward Northern Boulevard from Thirty-seventh Avenue in 1914. Trolleys and horses were the major form of transportation in what still appears to be a typical small town. (Queens Borough Public Library)

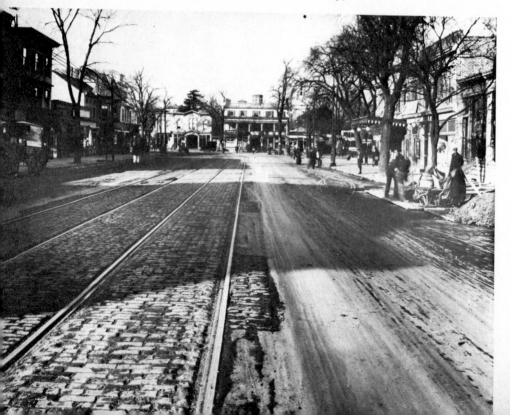

A supply of beer has just been delivered by horse and wagon to Edward McCormick's "Klondyke" at 115 Main Street, ca. 1910. (Wiener Collection. Queens Borough Public Library)

Part of the annual Farmers' Parade in front of the Fountain House, at the southeast corner of Main Street and Northern Boulevard, ca. 1898. The Fountain House was a small hotel and saloon, on the "other side of the tracks" from the elegant Flushing Hotel. (Queens Borough Public Library)

St. George's Episcopal Church is the third structure on the site. This view of the second building shows it on Lincoln Street (now 38th Avenue) in 1903. It was moved around the corner from Main Street in 1854, to make way for the new church, 33 years after it was built, and was used until 1930. The steeple of the present St. George's is visible at the left. (New-York Historical Society)

John Geddes's Paint Store, at 105 Main Street, ca. 1898. Note the hitching posts and stepping stone. (Wiener Collection, Queens Borough Public Library)

Battery-operated street car on Main Street, opposite the stately Flushing Hotel on Broadway (now Northern Boulevard), ca. 1900. The hotel was the center of Flushing social life during the latter 19th and early 20th centuries, and is now the site of the R.K.O. Keith's movie house. (David G. Oats, Flushing Tribune)

So many historic landmarks remain in a relatively small area that local historical societies have designated it as Flushing's "Freedom Mile." (*Note: The best day to visit is Saturday or Sunday when virtually all of the points of interest are open to the public.*)

The tour begins at the intersection of Main Street and Roosevelt Avenue.

Walk north on Main Street, the principal thoroughfare and commercial district of Flushing. The **Chamber of Commerce Building,** No. 39–01 Main Street, at the northeast corner of Thirty-ninth Avenue, is an interesting example of Art Deco style with polychrome tile spandrels and entranceway.

Diagonally across the street is **St. George's Episcopal Church,** occupying the entire block to Thirty-eighth Avenue. An earlier church on the site was built in 1746 and received its charter in 1761 from King George II of England. A subsequent house of worship replaced it in 1821, and the present structure dates from 1854. Built in Gothic Revival style from plans by Wills & Dudley, its graceful spire—alas, remodeled with wood shingles—is the tallest landmark in Flushing. Francis Lewis, signer of the Declaration of Independence from New York, served here as churchwarden and vestryman from 1769 to 1790. Peek over the iron fence at the early churchyard which contains the graves of many of the early residents.

The Prince House, located until the late 1950s at the intersection of Northern Boulevard and Prince Street. William Prince established the first tree nursery in the country in 1737. (David G. Oats, Flushing Tribune)

Little evidence remains of what Main Street looked like at the turn of the century when it became the main commercial thoroughfare of Flushing; however, a few vestiges can be found, disguised behind numerous remodelings and "modernizations." Directly across the street from St. George's Church, on the northeast corner of 38th Avenue, is **No. 38–01,** an aging house with a Second Empire mansard roof and dormers; and farther west on Main Street, just before Thirty-seventh Avenue, is a clapboard building whose wooden construction is quite visible.

On the northwest corner of Main Street and Thirty-seventh Avenue is Barclay's Bank of New York, designed in Art Deco style. Erected for the Flushing National Bank in 1929, its smooth limestone façade with low-relief "modernistic" sculpture and octagon-shaped clock are typical of the period. Just down Thirty-seventh Avenue, beyond the bank, is another surviving group of wooden houses, complete with a mansard roof and dormers, and a neat paint job. The clapboards, however, are aluminum siding.

At the head of Main Street, on Northern Boulevard, is the **RKO Keith's** movie house (Thomas Lamb, 1928). A popular vaudeville theater when it opened, its stage is said to have launched the careers of a number of Hollywood stars. The theater occupies the site of the old Flushing Hotel, a rambling wooden structure whose double tiers of broad porches and well appointed parlors made it the focal point in the 1880s and '90s of Flushing's social life.

After the theater was "triplexed" in 1976, the ornate Spanish Baroque–style interior decor could no longer be seen. At one time the theater boasted machinery that could create the illusion of clouds floating across a sky of twin-

The Flushing Quaker Meeting House on the south side of Northern Boulevard in the early 1930s. The building faces south, away from the winter's north winds. Built in 1694, it is New York's oldest house of worship. (Queens Borough Public Library)

In the Quaker Meeting House, a "ship's knee," removed from an old sailing vessel, helps support a 40-foot beam, hand-hewn in 1717 from a tall oak. (Office of the Borough President of Queens)

kling stars—an effect that was even extended to the ceiling of the lavish lobby; and a bubbling fountain that graced the entrance has given way to a popcorn machine. At this writing there is a plan underway to construct a $120 million shopping mall which would require demolition of the Keith's—a proposal that is being vigorously opposed by preservationists and many local merchants. The storekeepers fear that such a mall would have a very damaging effect on Main Street business. On the other hand, some feel that the mall would inject new life into the neighborhood. Since the theater is not a designated landmark, its future is uncertain.

To the left of the theater, from Prince Street down to Flushing Creek, was the world famous **Prince Nursery.** Established in 1737 by William Prince, it was the first tree nursery in the country. Known later as the Linnaean Botanic Garden, it provided thousands of tree specimens from all over the world. George Washington was a guest at the garden in 1789. Although it is now long since gone, the heritage of William Prince's old nursery lives on in the more than 200 species of trees growing throughout the country.

The "island" in the middle of Northern Boulevard marks the center of **Daniel Carter Beard Memorial Square.** "Dan" Beard, a naturalist and illustrator, and a native of Flushing, was one of the founders of the Boy Scouts of America,

A scene in the Flushing Town Hall's court room, ca. 1895. Flushing was an independent town until 1900, when it joined the City of New York. The Town Hall then became the Court House. (Wiener Collection, Queens Borough Public Library)

and served as National Scout Commissioner until his death in 1941 at the age of 91. (Walk right, east, along the center island.)

The flagpole is Flushing's **Spanish-American War Memorial,** erected in 1950. On the east side of the pedestal is a plaque cast from a piece of the battleship *Maine.* Just beyond is a group of five elm trees, the second (and tallest) of which is known as the **Washington Elm.** It was planted in 1932 by the American Legion to commemorate the first president's visit to Flushing on October 10, 1789.

To the right, opposite Linden Place, is the **Friends Meeting House,** the oldest house of worship in New York City and one of the earliest in the country. Built in 1694, with an addition in 1717, it provided a permanent place for religious observance for those who first met secretly in the home of John Bowne. Except for a period during the Revolutionary War when the occupying British forces used it as a prison, a hospital, and a storage place for hay, the Meeting House has been in continuous use for almost 300 years. The plain, rectangular building with a hiproof faces south—away from the winter winds—toward an interior burial ground. Two doorways on the open front porch originally served as separate entrances for men and women. Devoid of ornamentation, the simple meeting room with its plastered walls and unfinished wood benches reflects the Quaker spirit, which calls for undistracted devotion. Hand-hewn 40-foot oak beams, cut from a single tree, are still in place on the second story, and are as solid as the day they were installed. Timbers from a dismantled sailing ship were used in the 1717 section, and ships' "knees" can be seen supporting the ceiling beams. One of two early cast-iron heating stoves dating from 1760, and used until 1956, is on display in the Meeting House, while the original hand-wrought iron door hinges, latches, and locks are still in use. The church-yard, no longer used for interments, contains simple, low stones inscribed with the names of many prominent Long Islanders of the early 19th century. Head-stones placed before 1835 bear no inscriptions. The Friends Meeting House is the oldest house of worship in the New York area and is listed in the National Register of Historic Places. Visitors are welcome to visit the Meeting House and grounds, and to attend Sunday-morning worship meetings.

The **Civil War Monument** and surrounding mini-garden were erected in 1866 in memory of the young volunteers of the Flushing Battery who died in the tragic war to preserve the Union. The funds to build the monument were raised through public subscription. Enter through the iron gate and read the fading inscription on the east side of the pedestal.

Across Northern Boulevard, at the corner of Linden Street, is the **Flushing Municipal Court House,** formerly the Town Hall. Saved at the last minute from the wrecker's ball, it is now well protected as a designated New York City Landmark. Built in 1862 by Cornelius Howard, a local carpenter, in an early Romanesque Revival style, the Flushing Town Hall served the community until 1900 as a center of civic, cultural, and social life. In addition to its role as a town meeting house and seat of local government while the village was still independent, it hosted a variety of public events. The Hall witnessed celebra-tion balls, political meetings, community gatherings, and even operas and concerts. It was also the headquarters of the local Volunteer Artillery Unit. When it gave up its function as a municipal courthouse in the 1960s, it was slated for demolition. Faced with the loss of their oldest civic structure, concerned citizens and local historical societies raised a storm of protest, which ultimately convinced the city fathers of the need to preserve this picturesque and historic landmark. Until now, plans for its adaptive reuse have not been successful. A restaurant and community center project failed after a few years. At present a medical center is planning to take over and maintain the building. Note the tall, thin buttresses, paired arched windows with drip moldings, brick corbels under the cornice, and a charming porch, complete with its "Town Hall" sign.

Farther down the center mall is the **World War I Memorial Monument,** executed in pink-veined marble by famed sculptor Hermon MacNeil in 1925; it is best viewed from the north side of the Boulevard. Like the Civil War Monument, it was financed through public subscription.

Reminiscent of a medieval castle is the red brick **New York State National Guard Armory.** With its twin turrets, crenelations, machicolations, tower and ramparts, it resembles a medieval fortress. Built in 1905 in the typical "armory architectural style" popular in the late 19th and early 20th centuries, it still

The Samuel Bowne Parsons House stood on the site of Flushing High School's annex, on Broadway (now Northern Boulevard), opposite Bowne Street. Parsons maintained a tree nursery in the mid-19th century and many of his plantings are still to be seen throughout Flushing, particularly the weeping beech and cedar of Lebanon near the Bowne House. (Queens Borough Public Library)

A sketch of the Bowne House as it appeared ca. 1790. The "salt box" was built by John Bowne in 1661 and is considered a shrine to religious freedom in America. (Bowne House Historical Society)

conveys an impression of strength and security. On the site stood the house of Michael Milnor, where in 1657 the Flushing Remonstrance was signed, touching off the first struggle for religious freedom in America. The City of New York is using the Armory temporarily as sleeping quarters for homeless women.

To the left of the Armory, and attached to the rear of the adjacent Masonic Temple, is a two-story red brick structure which once served as the **meeting house for a breakaway group of Quakers.** Objecting to the liberal tendencies of preacher Elias Hicks, a schism developed, and the more orthodox group separated itself from the "Hicksites," erecting this building in 1827 as their own house of worship. The sect has long since disappeared. If the Armory's parking lot is open, tiptoe in, and examine the rear of the old meeting house, with its ancient brickwork and leaning chimneys.

Flushing High School, on the north side of the Boulevard, was built in 1915, in the then-popular Gothic Revival Public School style. The building replaced an earlier structure located a few blocks west, which received its first charter in 1875. Flushing High is the oldest free public high school in the City of New York. The newer east wing was completed in 1954 and is dedicated to those students who gave their lives in World War II.

Directly opposite Flushing High School, and to the right of the present Y.M.C.A. Building (1925), stood the **old Aspinwall House,** built in 1762. During the Revolutionary War it became the headquarters of the officer corps of the occupying British Army; and in the Civil War it was a station on the Underground Railroad, helping escaping slaves reach freedom. It is said that a secret tunnel connected the Aspinwall House with the nearby Bowne House, where these runaways were hidden and cared for while awaiting passage on a ship to New England. Unfortunately, the house was razed in the late 1950s.

Turn right at the Y.M.C.A. into Bowne Street.

About 150 yards down the street is a large gray boulder known as the **Fox Oaks Rock.** George Fox, who founded the Religious Society of Friends in England in 1645, came to America to preach in 1672. He intended to hold his meeting in the Bowne House, but the turnout was so great that he was forced to hold it outdoors under some tall oak trees opposite the house. The oaks have disappeared, but the site is marked with the inscription on the rock.

The **Bowne House,** across the street, is a landmark shrine to religious freedom and was built in 1661. Little did John Bowne anticipate when he arrived in Flushing in 1655 that he would be the central figure in a monumental struggle for freedom of religious observance—freedom for a sect to which he did not even belong at the time! That he would defy the law, be arrested, fined, imprisoned, and banished, later to return a hero, never entered his mind.

The Quakers had been holding clandestine worship meetings in nearby woods when Bowne built his home, embraced Quakerism, and invited the Friends to meet in his spacious kitchen. The rest is history. And the well-built house survives intact as a memorial to the accomplishments of this courageous, soft-spoken man. The House is now a museum maintained by the Bowne House Historical Society, which purchased it in 1945, and it is open to the public on Tuesdays, Saturdays, and Sundays, 2:30 to 4:30 P.M. (Adults $1.00, children 25¢.) The furnishings of the house are all original, with additions provided by each of the successive nine generations of Bowne descendants who lived in it until 1946. A number of periods are represented in the house's fine collection of antiques. Extensions were added to the house in 1680 and 1696—the latter a "salt box" section, with sloping roof. Additional living space was provided in 1830 when the roof on the main house was raised and an extra wing added. The kitchen is the focal point of the house, just as it was when John Bowne entertained George Fox and, later, William Penn.*

The kitchen has been restored to its original appearance and is the oldest part of the house. Not only was this the center of culinary activities, but it was the center of most of the family's domestic activities. The kitchen even housed overnight guests. Its enormous fireplace could easily roast an ox, and the "beehive" oven extends through the fireplace wall.

The wooden shed in the garden shelters a huge cast-iron cauldron formerly used for making soap. Across the garden is the **Remonstrance Monument** with

---

* It was William Penn, usually thought of only in connection with Pennsylvania, who in 1683 persuaded the Duke of York to grant permission to the towns of Long Island to establish their own Representative Assembly. This body then drafted its historic Charter of Liberties, almost 100 years before the Declaration of Independence!

The Kingsland House, on its former site at 155th Street near Roosevelt Avenue, is the only landmark that had to be relocated before it could be designated. The house was built in 1774 as a middle-class farm house, and has been moved twice. It is now a museum and stands adjacent to Weeping Beech Park. (Office of the Borough President of Queens)

a plaque containing the complete text and list of signers of the Flushing Remonstrance. To the rear of the house is a typical herb garden. The original Bowne property extended north for some distance and included much of the land up to where Flushing High School is now located.

After leaving the Bowne House, turn right on Bowne Street and enter the playground. Follow the path through to the cul-de-sac of Thirty-seventh Avenue.

Ahead to the left, the **Kingsland Homestead Museum** is New York City's only building that had to be relocated to maintain its landmark status. Built by Charles Doughty in 1774 as a typical middle-sized farmhouse, it was situated about one and a half miles east, at what is now the intersection of 155th Street and Northern Boulevard. "Kingsland" was named after Doughty's son-in-law, Joseph King, an English sea captain. In the early 19th century the house was acquired by William King Murray who moved the house to the site of 155th Street and Roosevelt Avenue. The Murray Hill section of Flushing is named for the family which occupied the house until 1932. An earlier relative, Robert Murray, owned a farm in the late 18th century on Manhattan's East River shore, and it is for him that the midtown Murray Hill neighborhood is named.

The great weeping beech, a city landmark, in 1926. The house to the left was demolished, and in its place stands the recently relocated Kingsland House. (Office of the Borough President of Queens)

In 1965 "Kingsland" was scheduled for demolition to make way for a shopping center. The Kingsland Preservation Committee was organized to save the house, and after four years of painstaking effort and negotiation, the 200-year-old house was moved on a flat-bed trailer to its present site in Weeping Beech Park. The operation required the cooperation of nine city departments, plus the New York Telephone Company and Con Edison. Six hundred feet of telephone and utility wire had to be removed from the city streets before the 38-foot-high house could make the journey.

The two-story house represents both Dutch and English Colonial architectural styles, particularly in the gambrel roof, central chimney, and round-headed and quadrant window in the gables. It is the second-oldest house in Flushing and the only surviving house from the 18th century. "Kingsland" is now owned by New York City's Department of Parks and Recreation, and serves as a museum of local history, architecture, and decorative arts, as well as a community center. It is staffed by volunteers, and is the headquarters of the Queens Historical Society. The landmark is listed in the National Register of Historic Places, and is open to the public at the same hours as the Bowne House (free).

At the rear of "Kingsland," in diminutive **Weeping Beech Park,** is one of the most extraordinary trees in the world. The weeping beech's enormous canopy of lush foliage presents an incredible vista of long, spreading branches reaching skyward, then arching gracefully to the ground, to create a charming, enclosed bower. The tree was planted by Samuel Parsons in 1847 from a small shoot brought by his son from Belgium. Parsons, who married into the Bowne family, established his nursery in 1838 on land obtained from his in-laws. Much of the nursery was located where the playground is today. Like the earlier Prince Nursery, Parsons grew many species of trees and specialized in exotic varieties that could adapt to the local environment. The lovely beech is one of his enduring successes. In the late 19th century the nurseries were moved to the Kissena Park district; however, a number of beautiful trees scattered throughout Flushing are reminders of the extensive horticultural industry. Flushing's involvement with trees is seen in the names of so many of its streets: Ash, Quince, Hawthorn, Laburnum, Maple, etc. The weeping beech is the oldest tree of its kind in

The cedar of Lebanon tree in mid-19th century stood alone in this uncultivated field. Today the tree, a little the worse for wear, is almost lost in the center of a playground on Bowne Street, surrounded by other trees and apartment houses. (Queens Borough Public Library)

America, and one of two official landmark trees in New York City (the other is a magnolia grandiflora, in Brooklyn, at 679 Lafayette Avenue).

Another example of the legacy of the Parsons Nursery is the **Golden Larch** on the lawn of the Kingsland House, facing Thirty-seventh Avenue, considered a very rare species by the Queens Botanical Garden.

On returning to Bowne Street by the path alongside the playground, notice the unusual **Cedar of Lebanon** in the middle of the playground; and at curbside on Bowne Street a mighty **Swamp Oak.** These trees are living evidence of Samuel Parsons's horticultural skill; his name is also immortalized by Parsons Boulevard, the next major thoroughfare to the east.

Turn left (south) on Bowne Street, past the Bowne House to the corner of Roosevelt Avenue.

On the northeast corner of Bowne Street and Roosevelt Avenue is the **Bowne Street Community Church.** Built in 1892 as the Protestant Reformed Church of Flushing, it is a descendant of the oldest denomination in New York, dating from 1628 when the Dutch Reformed Church was established in Nieuw Amsterdam. The church merged with the First Congregational Church of Flushing

Daniel Carter Beard's home at the northwest corner of Roosevelt Avenue and Bowne Street in a 1941 sketch. The site, coincidentally, is occupied by a "Dan's Supreme" supermarket. (Queens Borough Public Library)

after the latter's 114-year-old building on Bowne Street and Thirty-eighth Avenue was destroyed by fire at Christmas 1970. Four years later the Church was incorporated as the Bowne Street Community Church, preserving the tradition of religious freedom established by John Bowne. The Church is also associated with the United Church of Christ, and it makes its facilities available to the Korean Church of Flushing. The massive red brick structure is Romanesque Revival in style, but its huge tower is Bohemian in character. Note the elaborate detailing above the round-arched windows on the Roosevelt Avenue side.

On the northwest corner is the site of "Dan" Beard's home (coincidentally replaced by a "Dan's Supreme" supermarket).

A half-block to the south is the "cut" used by the Long Island Railroad Port Washington Branch. The ancestor of this line was the Flushing North Side Railroad, which reached Flushing in 1854.

Turn right (west) on Roosevelt Avenue to Main Street (the IRT and L.I.R.R. stations), and the end of the "Freedom Mile" tour.

A most interesting side trip can be made to the Hindu Temple of North America, located eight and a half blocks south, at 45–57 Bowne Street, beyond the railroad underpass. Walking south on Bowne Street after Forty-first Avenue, the cross streets begin their *alphabetica botanica* with Ash Avenue. (If you have the strength, take a brief detour left on Ash Avenue for one block as far as Parsons Boulevard, and enjoy the variety of residential architecture on this shady street, from Classic and Moorish to Shingle-Stick styles.)

As you continue along Bowne Street, notice how the scale of the houses is more suggestive of a small town. Were it not for the armies of aluminum-siding and Permastone salesmen that invaded the neighborhood after World War II, the effect would be even more pronounced. After Cherry Street there is a small Hindu temple on the right; however, the big surprise will appear on the left just after Forty-fifth Avenue.

The Hindu Temple of North America was erected over a period of several years in the late 1970s by artisans brought from India specifically for the task. The building is divided into three pavilions covered with intricate carvings of deities and other religious symbols, and surmounted by pyramidal roofs with gilt finials. Enter at the right-hand doorway, remove your shoes, and walk upstairs. (Visitors are welcome, but be respectful and unobtrusive.) The effect upon entering is so overwhelming that some time must be allowed to absorb it all. At the four corners of the marble-floor sanctuary are shrines to major deities, and dominating the center is the black Shrine of Lord Ganesha, the god with the elephant's trunk. On the walls are highly ornate sculptures of Vishnu, Siva, and many other deities of the Hindu pantheon; and scattered about the temple at different shrines are groups of monks and congregants chanting prayers, while in the background, bells are chimed and the air is perfumed with the aroma of exotic incense. (A small contribution would be appreciated.)

You can return quickly to the starting point of the tour by walking ahead to Holly Avenue, where the Q-27 bus takes five minutes to reach Main Street and Roosevelt Avenue. (Turn right at the corner to the first yellow-painted curb for the bus stop.) Or, if you wish to walk back, retrace your steps on Bowne Street to Cherry Street, turn left to Kissena Boulevard, then right. Kissena Boulevard will join Main Street six blocks farther. Passing Sanford Avenue, note the neoclassic-style **Free Synagogue of Flushing,** built in 1926.

There are a number of Indian, Korean, and Japanese restaurants and supermarkets on Main Street, just to the left.

The Long Island Rail Road station is just beyond the viaduct; turn left on 40th Avenue. The IRT Main Street station is one block farther at the corner of Roosevelt Avenue.

Recommended Reading: New York City Architecture and History

ALBION, ROBERT GREENHALGH. *The Rise of New York Port (1815–1860)*. New York: Charles Scribner's Sons, 1967.

ANDREWS, WAYNE. *Architecture in New York*. New York: Atheneum, 1969. Reprint, New York: Harper & Row Icon Books, 1973.

———. *Architecture, Ambition and Americans*. New York: The Free Press, 1964.

ASBURY, HERBERT. *All Around the Town*. New York: Knopf, 1929.

———. *The Gangs of New York*. Garden City, N.Y.: Garden City Publishing Co., 1927.

BALDWIN, CHARLES C. *Stanford White*. New York, 1931. Reprint with introduction by Paul Goldberger. New York: DaCapo Press, 1976.

BARAL, ROBERT. *Turn West on 23rd*. New York: Fleet Press, 1965.

BARLOW, ELIZABETH. *Frederick Law Olmsted's New York*. With an illustrative portfolio by William Alex. In association with the Whitney Museum of American Art. New York: Praeger, 1972.

———, with Vernon Gray, Roger Pasquier, and Lewis Sharp. *The Central Park Book*. New York: The Central Park Task Force, 1977.

BATTERBERRY, MICHAEL and ARIANE BATTERBERRY. *On the Town in New York, from 1776 to the Present*. New York: Charles Scribner's Sons, 1973.

BERGER, MEYER. *Meyer Berger's New York*. New York: Random House, 1960.

BETTMAN, OTTO L. *The Good Old Days—They Were Terrible!* New York: Random House, 1974.

BIXBY, WILLIAM. *South Street, New York's Seaport Museum*. New York: David McKay, 1972.

BLACK, MARY, ed. *Old New York in Early Photographs*. From the collection of the New-York Historical Society. New York: Dover, 1973.

BLIVEN, BRUCE, JR. *The Battle for Manhattan.* Baltimore: Penguin Books, 1965.

————. *Under the Guns—New York: 1775–1776.* New York: Harper & Row, 1972.

BLUMENSON, JOHN J.-G. *Identifying American Architecture: A Pictorial Guide to Styles and Terms, 1600–1945.* 2nd ed. New York: Norton, 1981.

BOTKIN, B. A., ed. *New York City Folklore.* New York: Random House, 1956.

BROWN, HENRY COLLINS, ed. *Valentine's Manual of the City of New York, 1916–1928.* (New Series) 12 vols. published annually. New York: The Valentine Co., 1916–1928.

BROWN, JOSHUA, and DAVID MENT. *Factories, Foundries, and Refineries.* "A History of Five Brooklyn Industries." Brooklyn: Brooklyn Rediscovery, Brooklyn Educational & Cultural Alliance, 1980.

BURNHAM, ALAN, ed. *New York Landmarks.* Middletown, Conn.: Wesleyan University Press, 1963.

CALLAS, MAY and WALLACE RANDOLPH. *Inside 42nd Street.* An Exhibition of Architecture and Decoration on 42nd Street. New York, 1978.

CHRISTMAN, HENRY M., ed. *Walt Whitman's New York.* New York: Macmillan, 1963.

CONDIT, CARL W. *American Building.* Chicago: University of Chicago Press, 1968.

————. *The Port of New York,* Vol. 1: *A History of the Rail and Terminal System from the Beginnings to Pennsylvania Station,* Vol. 2: *A History of the Rail and Terminal System from the Grand Central Electrification to the Present.* Chicago: University of Chicago Press, 1980, 1981.

CONDON, THOMAS J. *New York Beginnings. The Commercial Origins of New Netherland.* New York: New York University Press, 1968.

CORDASCO, FRANCESCO, ed. *Jacob Riis Revisited—Poverty and the Slums in Another Era.* Garden City, N.Y.: Doubleday Anchor Books, 1968.

CUDAHY, BRIAN. *Under the Sidewalks of New York. The Story of the Greatest Subway System in the World.* Brattleboro, Vt.: The Stephen Greene Press, 1979.

DELANEY, EDMUND T. *New York's Greenwich Village.* Barre, Mass.: Barre Publishers, 1965.

DICKENS, CHARLES. *American Notes.* Philadelphia: Lippincott, 1885.

DUNSHEE, KENNETH HOLCOMB. *As You Pass By. Old Manhattan Through the Fire Laddies' Eyes.* New York: Hastings House, 1962.

EDMISTON, SUSAN and LINDA D. CIRINO. *Literary New York—A History and Guide.* Boston: Houghton Mifflin, 1976.

The 1866 Guide to New York City. A facsimile edition of J. Miller's *New York as it is.* New York: Schocken, 1975.

ELLIS, EDWARD ROBB. *The Epic of New York City.* New York: Coward-McCann, 1966.

FABOS, JULIUS GY, GORDON T. MILDE, and V. MICHAEL WEINMAYR. *Frederick Law Olmsted, Sr.* Amherst, Mass.: University of Massachusetts Press, 1968.

FINNEY, JACK. *Time and Again.* New York: Simon & Schuster, 1970, 1978.

FISCHLER, STAN. *Uptown, Downtown. A Trip Through Time on New York's Subways.* New York: Hawthorn Books, 1976.

FLEMING, JOHN, HUGH HONOUR, and NIKOLAUS PEVSNER, eds. *The Penguin Dictionary of Architecture.* Baltimore: Penguin Books, 1966.

FRIED, FREDERICK and EDMUND V. GILLON, photographer. *New York Civic Sculpture— A Pictorial Guide.* New York: Dover, 1976.

GAYLE, MARGOT, ed. and EDMUND V. GILLON, JR., photographer. *Cast-Iron Architecture in New York.* New York: Dover, 1974.

GIFFORD, DON, ed. *The Literature of Architecture. Evolution of Architectural Theory and Practice in Nineteenth Century America.* New York: Dutton, 1966.

GOLDBERGER, PAUL. *The City Observed: New York. A Guide to the Architecture of Manhattan.* New York: Vintage Books, 1979.

————. *The Skyscraper*. New York: Knopf, 1981.

GOLDSTONE, HARMON and MARTHA DALRYMPLE. *History Preserved. A Guide to New York City Landmarks and Historic Districts*. New York: Simon & Schuster, 1974.

HAMLIN, TALBOT. *Greek Revival Architecture in America*. New York: Oxford University Press, 1944. Reprint, New York: Dover, 1964.

HAPGOOD, HUTCHINS. *The Spirit of the Ghetto*. New York, 1902. Reprint, New York: Schocken, 1966.

HEADLEY, JOEL TYLER. *The Great Riots of New York, 1712–1873*. A facsimile of the 1873 edition. New York: Dover, 1971.

HENDRICKSON, ROBERT. *The Grand Emporiums. The Illustrated History of America's Great Department Stores*. New York: Stein & Day, 1979.

HUXTABLE, ADA LOUISE. *Classic New York: Georgian Gentility to Greek Elegance*. Garden City, N.Y.: Doubleday Anchor Books, 1964.

IRVING, WASHINGTON. *Knickerbocker's History of New York*. New York, 1809.

JANVIER, THOMAS A. *In Old New York*. New York: Harper & Brothers, 1894.

JENKINS, STEPHEN. *The Greatest Street in the World: Broadway*. New York: G. P. Putnam's Sons, 1911.

JOHNSON, HARRY and FREDERICK S. LIGHTFOOT. *Maritime New York in Nineteenth-Century Photographs*. New York: Dover, 1980.

KAHN, ALAN PAUL. *The Tracks of New York, 1907: The Metropolitan Street Railway*. New York: Electric Railroaders' Association, 1973.

KAUFMANN, EDGAR, JR., ed. *Rise of an American Architecture, The*. Henry-Russell Hitchcock, Albert Fein, Winston Weisman, Vincent Scully, contributors. In association with The Metropolitan Museum of Art. New York: Praeger, 1970.

KIDDER SMITH, E. G. *Architecture of the United States*. 3 vols. Garden City, N.Y.: Doubleday Anchor Books, 1981.

KIDNEY, WALTER C. *The Architecture of Choice: Eclecticism in America, 1880–1930*. New York: George Braziller, 1974.

KING, MOSES, ed. *King's Handbook of New York City*. A facsimile of the 1896 edition. New York: Arno Press, 1974.

————, ed. *King's Views of New York 1896–1915, and Brooklyn 1905*. A facsimile of editions published between 1896 and 1915. Introduction by A. E. Santaniello. New York: Benjamin Blom, 1974.

KOCH, ROBERT. *Louis C. Tiffany, Rebel in Glass*. New York: Crown Publishers, 1964.

KOUWENHOVEN, JOHN A. *The Columbia Historical Portrait of New York*. New York: Doubleday, 1953. Reprint, New York: Harper & Row Icon Books, 1972.

LAAS, WILLIAM. *Crossroads of the World—The Story of Times Square*. New York: Popular Library, 1963.

LAMB, MRS. MARTHA J. *History of the City of New York*. 2 vols. New York: A. S. Barnes, 1877.

LANCASTER, CLAY. *Old Brooklyn Heights*. Rutland, Vt.: Charles E. Tuttle, 1961. Reprint, New York: Dover, 1979.

Landmarks Preservation Commission. *Greenwich Village Historic District*. Designation Report. 2 vols. New York: The City Record, 1969.

LEDERER, JOSEPH and ARLEY BONDARIN, photographer. *All Around the Town: A Walking Guide to Outdoor Sculpture in New York City*. New York: Charles Scribner's Sons, 1975.

LOCKWOOD, CHARLES. *Bricks and Brownstones. The Row House, 1783–1929. An Architectural and Social History*. New York: McGraw-Hill, 1972.

————. *Manhattan Moves Uptown: An Illustrated History*. Boston: Houghton Mifflin, 1976.

LOPEZ, MANUEL D., ed. *New York: A Guide to Information and Reference Sources.* Metuchen, N.J.: Scarecrow Press, 1980.

LYMAN, SUSAN. *The Story of New York. An Informal History of the City from the First Settlement to the Present Day.* New York: Crown Publishers, 1964; revised 1975.

———— and ANDREAS FEININGER, photographer. *The Face of New York. The City as it was and as it is.* New York: Crown Publishers, 1954.

MACOY, ROBERT, ed. *The Centennial Guide to New York City and Environs.* A facsimile of the 1876 edition. New York: Nathan Cohen Books, 1975.

MARCUSE, MAXWELL F. *This Was New York! A Nostalgic Picture of Gotham in the Gaslit Era.* New York: LIM Press, 1969.

MAYER, GRACE M. *Once Upon a City.* New York: Macmillan, 1958.

McCABE, JAMES D., JR. *Lights and Shadows of New York Life, or The Sights and Sensations of the Great City.* A facsimile of the 1872 edition. New York: Farrar, Straus & Giroux, 1970.

McCAUSLAND, ELIZABETH, ed. *New York in the Thirties as Photographed by Berenice Abbott.* Formerly titled *Changing New York,* New York, 1939. New York: Dover, 1963.

McCULLOUGH, DAVID. *The Great Bridge. The Epic Story of the Building of the Brooklyn Bridge.* New York: Simon & Schuster, 1972. Reprint, New York: Avon, 1976.

MENT, DAVID, with ANTHONY ROBINS and DAVID FRAMBERGER. *Building Blocks of Brooklyn.* "A Study of Urban Growth." Brooklyn: Brooklyn Rediscovery, Brooklyn Educational & Cultural Alliance, 1979.

A Monograph of the Works of McKim, Mead & White, 1879–1915. Introduction by Leland Roth. First published in 1915. New York: Benjamin Blom, 1973. Reprint, New York: Arno Press, 1977. Student's Edition, with introduction by Allan Greenberg and Michael George, New York: Architectural Publishing Co., 1981.

MORRIS, LLOYD. *Incredible New York.* New York: Random House, 1951.

MOSCOW, HENRY. *The Street Book. An Encyclopedia of Manhattan's Street Names and Their Origins.* New York: Hagstrom, 1978.

NEVINS, ALLAN, ed. *The Diary of George Templeton Strong, 1835–1875.* New York: Macmillan, 1952.

————. *The Diary of Philip Hone, 1828–1851.* 2 vols. New York: Dodd, Mead, 1936.

New York City Guide. Guilds' Committee for Federal Writers' Publications, Works Progress Administration. New York: Random House, 1939.

The New York Community Trust. *The Heritage of New York.* Introduction by Whitney North Seymour. New York: Fordham University Press, 1970.

New York, N.Y. New York: American Heritage, 1968.

New York Then and Now. 83 Manhattan Sites Photographed in Past and Present. Edward B. Watson, captions, and contemporary photographs by Edmund V. Gillon, Jr. New York: Dover, 1976.

PATTERSON, JERRY E. *The City of New York. A History Illustrated from the Collections of the Museum of the City of New York.* New York: Harry N. Abrams, 1978.

POPPELIERS, JOHN, S. ALLEN CHAMBERS, and NANCY B. SCHWARTZ. *What Style is It?* Articles reprinted from *Historic Preservation,* 1976–77. Washington: The Preservation Press of the National Trust for Historic Preservation, (undated).

———— and Sophia Duckworth. *Central Park. A History and Guide.* New York: Clarkson N. Potter, 1972.

REED, HENRY HOPE. *The Golden City.* New York: Norton, 1971.

REED, ROBERT C. *The New York Elevated.* Cranbury, N.J.: A. S. Barnes & Co., 1978.

REIER, SHARON. *The Bridges of New York.* New York: Quadrant Press, 1977.

RIFKIND, CAROLE. *A Field Guide to American Architecture. The Periods, the Styles, the Form and Function of Historical Buildings from Colonial Times to Today.* New York: New American Library Plume Books, 1980.

RIIS, JACOB. *How the Other Half Lives—Studies Among the Tenements of New York.* New York: Charles Scribner's Sons, 1890. Reprint, New York: Dover, 1971.

RISCHIN, MOSES. *The Promised City—New York's Jews, 1870–1914.* Cambridge: Harvard University Press, 1967.

ROBERTO, JOSEPH J. and BAYRD STILL, eds. *Greenwich Village. A Brief Architectural and Pictorial Guide.* New York: New York University, 1981.

ROBINSON, CERVIN, and ROSEMARY HAAG BLETTER. *Skyscraper Style: Art Deco New York.* New York: Oxford University Press, 1975.

ROSEBROCK, ELLEN FLETCHER. *Walking Around in South Street. Discoveries in New York's Old Shipping District.* New York: South Street Seaport Museum, 1974.

SANDERS, RONALD. *The Downtown Jews—Portraits of an Immigrant Generation.* New York: Harper & Row, 1969.

————— and EDMUND V. GILLON, JR., photographer. *The Lower East Side—A Guide to Its Jewish Past in 99 New Photographs.* New York: Dover, 1979.

SHARP, LEWIS I. and DAVID W. KIEHL, eds. *New York Public Sculpture by 19th Century American Artists.* New York: Metropolitan Museum of Art, 1974.

SHOPSIN, WILLIAM C. and MOSETTE BRODERICK. *The Villard Houses: Life Story of a Landmark.* Foreword by Henry-Russell Hitchcock, introduction by Brendan Gill, prologue by Sarah Bradford Landau. In cooperation with the Municipal Art Society of New York. New York: Viking Press, 1980.

SILVER, NATHAN. *Lost New York.* Boston: Houghton Mifflin, 1967. (Reprint 1971, Schocken)

SMALL, VERNA. *Nineteenth Century Dwelling Houses of Greenwich Village.* New York: Landmarks Committee, Association of Village Homeowners, 1968.

SMITH, THOMAS E. V. *The City of New York in the Year of Washington's Inauguration, 1879.* A reprint of the 1889 Trow's edition. Introduction by Joseph Veach Noble. In cooperation with the U.S. Department of the Interior, National Park Service. Riverside, Conn.: Chatham Press, 1972.

STEIN, LEON. *The Triangle Fire.* Philadelphia: Lippincott, 1962.

STILES, HENRY R., ed. *History of the County of Kings and the City of Brooklyn, N.Y., 1683–1884.* 3 vols. Brooklyn, 1884.

STILL, BAYRD. *Mirror for Gotham.* New York: New York University Press, 1956.

STOKES, ISAAC NEWTON PHELPS. *The Iconography of Manhattan Island, 1498–1909.* 6 vols. New York: Robert H. Dodd, 1915. Reprint, New York: Arno Press, 1971.

STURGES, WALTER KNIGHT, ed. *Origins of Cast Iron Architecture in America.* Daniel D. Badger's "Illustrations of Iron Architecture" (1865), and James Bogardus's "Cast Iron Buildings, Their Construction and Advantages" (1856). A facsimile edition. New York: DaCapo Press, 1970.

TAURANAC, JOHN. *Essential New York. A Guide to the History and Architecture of Manhattan's Important Buildings, Parks, and Bridges.* New York: Holt, Rinehart, Winston, 1979.

TRENT, GEORGE D., ed. *The Gentle Art of Walking.* A compilation from the *New York Times.* New York: Arno Press/Random House, 1971.

VLACK, DON. *Art Deco Architecture in New York, 1920–1940.* New York: Harper & Row, 1974.

WAITE, JOHN G., ed. *Iron Architecture in New York City.* The Edgar Laing Stores and the Cooper Union. Albany: New York State Historic Trust in conjunction with the Society for Industrial Archeology, 1972.

WHARTON, EDITH. *The Age of Innocence.* New York: D. Appleton & Co., 1921.

WHIFFEN, MARCUS. *American Architecture Since 1780: A Guide to the Styles.* Cambridge: M. I. T. Press, 1969.

WHITE, NORVAL and ELLIOTT WILLENSKY. *The AIA Guide to New York City.* New York: Collier-Macmillan, 1978.

WHITEHOUSE, ROGER. *New York Sunshine and Shadow. A Photographic Record of the City and Its People from 1850–1915.* New York: Harper & Row, 1974.

WOLFE, GERARD R. *The House of Appleton. The History of a Publishing House and Its Relationship to the Cultural, Social, and Political Events that Helped Shape the Destiny of New York City.* Metuchen, N.J.: Scarecrow Press, 1981.

——— and JO RENÉE FINE, photographer. *The Synagogues of New York's Lower East Side.* New York: New York University Press, 1978.

Index